THE CAMBRIDGE EDITION
JONATHAN

General Editors

Claude Rawson   *Yale University*
Ian Higgins   *Australian National University*
Ian Gadd   *Bath Spa University*
Valerie Rumbold   *University of Birmingham*
Abigail Williams   *University of Oxford*
James McLaverty   *Keele University*

Advisory Editors

Paddy Bullard   *University of Reading*
Adam Rounce   *University of Nottingham*

Advisory Board

John Brewer
Andrew Carpenter
Sean Connolly
Seamus Deane
Denis Donoghue
Mark Goldie
Phillip Harth
James E. May
Ronald Paulson
J. G. A. Pocock
Pat Rogers
G. Thomas Tanselle
David L. Vander Meulen

Founding General Editors

Claude Rawson, Ian Higgins, David Womersley

THE CAMBRIDGE EDITION OF THE WORKS OF
JONATHAN SWIFT

1. A Tale of a Tub and Other Works
2. Parodies, Hoaxes, Mock Treatises: Polite Conversation, Directions to Servants and Other Works

3.–6. Poems

7. English Political Writings 1701–1711: The Examiner and Other Works
8. English Political Writings 1711–1714: The Conduct of the Allies and Other Works
9. Journal to Stella: Letters to Esther Johnson and Rebecca Dingley 1710–1713
10. The History of the Four Last Years and Other Works
11. Writings on Religion and the Church to 1714: An Argument against Abolishing Christianity and Other Works
12. Writings on Religion and the Church after 1714: Sermons and Other Works
13. Irish Political Writings to 1725: Drapier's Letters and Other Works
14. Irish Political Writings after 1725: A Modest Proposal and Other Works
15. Gulliver's Travels
16. Personal and Miscellaneous Writings, Fragments and Marginalia
17. Index Volume

JONATHAN SWIFT

Irish Political Writings after 1725
A Modest Proposal and Other Works

Edited by
D. W. HAYTON AND ADAM ROUNCE

CAMBRIDGE
UNIVERSITY PRESS

University Printing House, Cambridge CB2 8BS, United Kingdom

One Liberty Plaza, 20th Floor, New York, NY 10006, USA

477 Williamstown Road, Port Melbourne, VIC 3207, Australia

314-321, 3rd Floor, Plot 3, Splendor Forum, Jasola District Centre, New Delhi - 110025, India

103 Penang Road, #05-06/07, Visioncrest Commercial, Singapore 238467

Cambridge University Press is part of the University of Cambridge.

It furthers the University's mission by disseminating knowledge in the pursuit of education, learning and research at the highest international levels of excellence.

www.cambridge.org
Information on this title: www.cambridge.org/9781009160391
DOI: 10.1017/9781139046060

© Cambridge University Press 2018

This publication is in copyright. Subject to statutory exception and to the provisions of relevant collective licensing agreements, no reproduction of any part may take place without the written permission of Cambridge University Press.

First published 2018
First paperback edition 2022

A catalogue record for this publication is available from the British Library

ISBN 978-0-521-83385-1 Hardback
ISBN 978-1-009-16039-1 Paperback

Cambridge University Press has no responsibility for the persistence or accuracy of URLs for external or third-party internet websites referred to in this publication, and does not guarantee that any content on such websites is, or will remain, accurate or appropriate.

CONTENTS

List of Illustrations   *page* viii
General Editors' Preface   ix
Acknowledgements   x
Chronology   xi
Abbreviations   xx
Introduction   xxiii

Upon Giving Badges to the Poor	1
Considerations About Maintaining the Poor	5
A Short View of the State of Ireland	13
An Answer to a Paper, Called A Memorial of the Poor Inhabitants, Tradesmen and Labourers of the Kingdom of Ireland	27
Intelligencer, No. 1	42
Intelligencer, No. 3	47
Intelligencer, No. 5	57
Intelligencer, No. 7	64
Intelligencer, No. 9	73
Intelligencer, No. 19	86
A Letter to the Archbishop of Dublin, Concerning the Weavers	98
An Answer to Several Letters from Unknown Persons	108
An Answer to Several Letters Sent Me from Unknown Hands	119
A Letter on M'culla's Project about Halfpence, and a New One Proposed	128

A Modest Proposal for Preventing the Children of Poor People from Being a Burthen to their Parents, or Country; and for Making Them Beneficial to the Publick	143
A Proposal that All the Ladies and Women of Ireland Should Appear Constantly in Irish Manufactures	160
Maxims Controlled In Ireland	171
Advertisement by Dr Swift, in His Defence Against Joshua, Lord Allen	181
The Substance of what was Said by the Dean of St Patrick's to the Lord Mayor and Some of the Aldermen, When His Lordship Came to Present the Said Dean with His Freedom in a Gold-Box	184
A Vindication of His Excellency the Lord Carteret, from the Charge Of Favouring None but Toryes, High-Churchmen and Jacobites	191
The Answer to the Craftsman	218
A Proposal for an Act of Parliament, to Pay Off the Debt of the Nation, Without Taxing the Subject	228
An Examination of Certain Abuses, Corruptions, and Enormities in the City of Dublin	240
The Humble Petition of the Footmen in and About the City of Dublin	264
Some Considerations Humbly Offered to the Right Honourable the Lord-Mayor, the Court of Aldermen, and Common Council of the Honourable City of Dublin, in the Choice of a Recorder	269
Prefatory Letter to Mary Barber, Poems on Several Occasions	274
Advice to the Free-Men of the City of Dublin in the Choice of a Member to Represent Them in Parliament	279
Observations Occasioned by Reading a Paper, Entitled, The Case of the Woollen Manufacturers of Dublin, &c.	288
A Letter on the Fishery	293

The Rev. Dean Swift's Reasons Against Lowering the Gold and Silver Coin 301

A Proposal for Giving Badges to the Beggars in all the Parishes of Dublin 305

ASSOCIATED MATERIALS 321
I   Hints for *Intelligencer* Papers, and *Maxims Examined* 321
II Letter to the Printer of *Thoughts on the Tillage of Ireland* 328

APPENDICES 330
A The Memorial of the Poor Inhabitants, Tradesmen, and Labourers of the Kingdom of Ireland 330
B The Craftsman's First Letter of Advice, Saturday 7 November 1730 333
C The Case of the Woollen Manufacturers 344
D To The Author of those Intelligencers Printed at Dublin 349
E From *The Dublin Weekly Journal*, Saturday, June 7th. 1729 365

GENERAL TEXTUAL INTRODUCTION AND TEXTUAL ACCOUNTS OF INDIVIDUAL WORKS 375
General Textual Introduction 376
Textual Accounts of Individual Works 388

Bibliography 494
Index 531

ILLUSTRATIONS

1. Jonathan Swift, *Upon Giving Badges to the Poor*, first page of Forster manuscript. V & A, Forster MS 518, F.48.G6/2 item 6. Reproduced by kind permission of the National Art Library, Victoria and Albert Museum.   *page* cviii
2. Jonathan Swift, *A Short View of the State of Ireland*, 1728. Title. Reproduced by kind permission of the Syndics of Cambridge University Library, Williams 349.   12
3. Jonathan Swift, *A Modest Proposal*, 1729. Title. Reproduced by kind permission of the Syndics of Cambridge University Library, Williams 327.   145
4. Jonathan Swift, *A Vindication of His Excellency the Lord Carteret*, 1730. Title. Reproduced by kind permission of the Syndics of Cambridge University Library, Williams 410.   193
5. Jonathan Swift, *An Examination of Certain Abuses*, 1732. Title. Reproduced by kind permission of the Syndics of Cambridge University Library, Williams 308.   239
6. Jonathan Swift, *A Proposal for Giving Badges to the Beggars*, 1737. Title. Reproduced by kind permission of the Syndics of Cambridge University Library, Williams 339.   307

1712 May: Swift, *Proposal for Correcting the English Tongue*. August: Swift, *Some Remarks on the Barrier Treaty*. Formation of the 'Scriblerus Club' with Pope, Gay, Parnell and Arbuthnot.

1713 January: Swift, *Mr. C[olli]ns's Discourse of Free-Thinking, put into Plain English*. May: public acrimony between Swift and Steele. June: Swift installed as Dean of St Patrick's Cathedral, Dublin. October: Swift, *Importance of the Guardian Considered*; composes 'Cadenus and Vanessa'.

1714 February: Swift, *Public Spirit of the Whigs* declared 'seditious and scandalous libel' by Lords; Swift Governor of Bethlehem Hospital ('Bedlam'). March: Swift helps draft Queen's speech. June: Swift leaves London for Letcombe Basset, Berkshire; Swift writes *Some Free Thoughts*. August: sails for Dublin, beginning of six-year break from publication.

1719 March 13: Swift writes birthday verses for Stella.

1720 Swift, *Proposal for the Universal Use of Irish Manufacture*; at subsequent trial of its printer, Edward Waters, Chief Justice Whitshed refuses to accept 'not guilty' verdict from jury.

1721 April: earliest references to writing of *Gulliver's Travels*, in a letter to Charles Ford. Swift travels over 400 miles on his 'Summer Rambles' in Ireland.

Essay on Criticism; Steele, *Tatler* final number, January; Addison and Steele, *Spectator* (1 March 1711 – 6 December 1712); Shaftesbury, *Characteristicks*.

July: St John created Viscount Bolingbroke. October: Oxford and Bolingbroke clash in Cabinet. Pope, *Rape of the Lock* (2-canto version); Arbuthnot, *Proposal for an Art of Political Lying*.

March: peace and commerce treaties signed by Britain and France at Utrecht. August: Bolingbroke's bid to control ministry defeated by Harley; general election, another Tory victory. December: Queen Anne seriously ill. Pope, *Windsor-Forest*; Gay, *Rural Sports*; Parnell, *Essay on the Different Styles of Poetry*; Addison, *Cato*; Steele, *Guardian, Englishman*.

January: Steele, *Crisis*. July: Oxford dismissed by Queen Anne. August: death of Queen Anne; accession of George I. Beginning of Whig supremacy.

1715 June: Pope, *Iliad*, books I–IV.

1717 January: Pope, Gay and Arbuthnot, *Three Hours After Marriage*. Pope, *Works*.

1718 Death of Parnell.

June: death of Addison.

March: Declaratory Act (that the British Parliament may make laws binding on Ireland). August: collapse of the 'South Sea Bubble'. November: Trenchard and Gordon begin publishing *Cato's Letters*.

Emergence of Robert Walpole as *de facto* Prime Minister. September: death of Prior. December: Parnell, *Poems on Several Occasions*, with Pope's 'Epistle to Oxford' as preface.

1722 July: patent to strike copper coins for Ireland granted to William Wood. August: Atterbury implicated in Jacobite 'Layer's Plot'.

1723 June: Death of Vanessa; Swift begins four-month tour of southern Ireland.

1724 January: Swift finishes book four of *Gulliver's Travels*, and begins book three. March: *Letter to the Shopkeepers of Ireland* (first *Drapier's Letter*). August: *Letter to Harding* (second *DL*). September: *Some Observations* (third *DL*). October: *Letter to Whole People of Ireland* (fourth *DL*). December: *Letter to Molesworth* (fifth *DL*).

May: death of Oxford; Carteret appointed lord lieutenant of Ireland. October: £300 reward offered for naming of the author of fourth *Drapier's Letter*. Gilbert Burnet, *History of his Own Time*.

1725 April: Swift created freeman of City of Dublin. April–October: Swift and Stella at Quilca with Sheridan family; completion of *Gulliver's Travels*.

April: Bolingbroke returns from exile in France. September: Cancellation of Wood's patent. Pope's edition of Shakespeare and translation of Homer's *Odyssey* (to 1726).

1726 March: Swift travels to London. April: audience with Princess of Wales. Meetings with patriot members of opposition, and with Walpole. May: at Pope's Twickenham villa with Gay and Martha Blount; visits Cobham at Stowe; Stella seriously ill. August: returns to Dublin amid public acclamation. 28 October: first edn of *Gulliver's Travels*.

March: Theobald, *Shakespeare Restored*. December: Pulteney and Bolingbroke launch opposition periodical *The Craftsman*.

1727 January: Swift attempts to correct early editions of *Gulliver*. April: travels to London for his last English visit. June: Pope/Swift *Miscellanies*, vols. I and II. August: returns to Ireland, writing 'Holyhead Journal' during a week of delays before crossing.

June: death of George I, accession of George II. Autumn: floods, crop failures and rural poverty in Ireland. Gay, *Fables*. Death of Newton.

1728 January: death of Stella. Swift, 'On the Death of Mrs Johnson'. March: 'last' volume of Pope/Swift *Miscellanies*; Swift, *A Short View of the State of Ireland*. May: Swift and Sheridan begin *The Intelligencer*, runs until May 1729.

January: Gay's *Beggar's Opera* begins triumphant run at Lincoln's Inn Fields. May: Pope, *Dunciad*; numerous printed attacks on Pope.

1729 October: Swift, *A Modest Proposal*. December: Swift meets Laetitia Pilkington, author of *Memoirs* (1748–54) concerning Swift, and her husband Matthew.

April: Pope, *Dunciad Variorum*.

1730 February: Swift tells Pope of his friendship with a 'triumfeminate' of Dublin literary Bluestockings (Mary Barber, Constantia Grierson, Mrs Sican).

Townshend resigns as Secretary of State. Trial of Francis Charteris. Colley Cibber made Poet Laureate.

1731 Swift works on *Verses on the Death of Dr Swift* (published 1739) and the scatological poems published in 1734.

1732 April: Swift, *Life and Character of Dr Swift*. June: Swift, *The Lady's Dressing Room*. October: Pope/Swift *Miscellanies*, 'third' vol.; Swift has met his future biographer, the Earl of Orrery.

1734 A letter of commendation from Swift appears as preface to Mary Barber's *Poems on Several Occasions*. November: George Faulkner begins to publish Swift's *Works* in Dublin. December: Swift, 'A Beautiful Young Nymph Going to Bed' published with 'Strephon and Chloe' and 'Cassinus and Peter'.

1735 Death of Swift's faithful housekeeper, Mrs Brent.

1736 December: Swift tells Pope that 'I now neither read, nor write; nor remember, nor converse. All I have left is to walk, and ride'. June: *A Character of the Legion Club*.

1737 August: Swift created freeman of the City of Cork.

1738 Spring: Swift, *Genteel and Ingenious Conversation*; fifth and sixth volumes of the Faulkner *Works*.

1739 January: Swift, *Verses on the Death of Dr Swift*, edited by Pope and William King, followed by Dublin edn in February.

1740 May: Swift makes his last will, on the brink of his final decline; bequests to Rebecca Dingley (Stella's companion), Martha Whiteway (guardian during his final years) and others; land purchased for St Patrick's Hospital.

1742 November: Swift's understanding 'quite gone'.

1745 19 October: death of Swift.

December: Pope, *Epistle to Burlington*. First issue of *Gentleman's Magazine*. Death of Defoe.

December: Death of John Gay. Hogarth, *Harlot's Progress*.

1733 January: Pope, *Epistle to Bathurst*. February: Pope, first *Imitation of Horace*; *An Essay on Man*. Excise Crisis.

January: Pope, *Epistle to Cobham*. Hogarth, *Rake's Progress* (engravings published 1735).

January: Pope, *Epistle to Arbuthnot*. February: death of Arbuthnot. Bolingbroke returns to France.

Porteous Riots; repeal of Test and Corporation Acts defeated. Butler, *Analogy of Religion*.

May: Pope's edn of his letters. Prince of Wales expelled from court; death of Queen Caroline.

October: death of Thomas Sheridan. Pope visited by Bolingbroke. Last report of Society for Reformation of Manners.

October: War of Jenkins' Ear.

War of Austrian Succession.

March: Pope, *The New Dunciad* (i.e. book IV).

1744 May: death of Pope.

Death of Walpole. Jacobite rebellion.

ABBREVIATIONS

Add.MS(S)	Additional Manuscript(s)
BL	British Library
Bodl.	Bodleian Library
Boulter Letters	*Letters Written by his Excellency Hugh Boulter . . .*, 2 vols., Dublin, 1770
C.J.Ire.	*The Journals of the House of Commons of the Kingdom of Ireland*, 2nd edn
Cal. Anc. Recs Dublin	*Calendar of the Ancient Records of Dublin*, ed. J. T. Gilbert and R. M. Gilbert, 17 vols., Dublin: Joseph Dollard, 1889–1921
Coghill Letters	*Letters of Marmaduke Coghill, 1722–1738*, ed. D. W. Hayton, Dublin: Irish Manuscripts Commission, 2005
CUL	Cambridge University Library
CWJS	*The Cambridge Edition of the Works of Jonathan Swift*, ed. Claude Rawson, Ian Higgins, James McLaverty, *et al.*, Cambridge: Cambridge University Press, 2008–
Davis	*The Prose Writings of Jonathan Swift*, ed. Herbert Davis *et al.*, 16 vols., Oxford: Basil Blackwell, 1939–74
del.	deleted
DIB	*Dictionary of Irish Biography*, ed. James McGuire and James Quinn, 9 vols., Cambridge: Cambridge University Press, 2009
Dobbs, *Essay*	Arthur Dobbs, *An Essay on the Trade and Improvement of Ireland*, Dublin, 1729
Dobbs, *Essay*, pt 2	Arthur Dobbs, *An Essay on the Trade and Improvement of Ireland. Part II*, Dublin, 1731
ECI	*Eighteenth-Century Ireland*
ECS	*Eighteenth-Century Studies*
Econ. Hist. Ire.	George O'Brien, *The Economic History of Ireland in the Eighteenth Century*, Dublin, 1918
Ehrenpreis	Irvin Ehrenpreis, *Swift: The Man, His Works, and the Age*, 3 vols., London: Methuen, 1962–83
Ferguson	Oliver W. Ferguson, *Jonathan Swift and Ireland*, Urbana: University of Illinois Press, 1962

Hist. Ir. Parl.	Edith Mary Johnston-Liik, *History of the Irish Parliament 1692–1800*, 6 vols., Belfast: Ulster Historical Foundation, 2002
HLQ	*Huntington Library Quarterly*
HMC	Historical Manuscripts Commission (printed reports)
HP 1690–1715	*The History of Parliament. The House of Commons 1690–1715*, ed. Eveline Cruickshanks, Stuart Handley and D. W. Hayton, 5 vols., Cambridge: Cambridge University Press, 2002
HP 1715–54	*The History of Parliament. The House of Commons 1715–1754*, ed. Romney Sedgwick, 2 vols., London: HMSO, 1970
ins.	inserted
Landa	Louis A. Landa, *Swift and the Church of Ireland*, Oxford: Clarendon Press, 1954
Library and Reading, I	Dirk F. Passmann and H. J. Vienken, *The Library and Reading of Jonathan Swift: A Bio-bibliographical Handbook. Part I, Swift's Library in Four Volumes*, 4 vols., Frankfurt am Main: Peter Lang, 2004
MLQ	*Modern Language Quarterly*
Münster (date)	*Proceedings of the First Münster Symposium on Jonathan Swift*, ed. Hermann J. Real and Heinz J. Vienken, Munich: Wilhelm Fink Verlag, 1985. *Reading Swift: Papers from the [Second, Third, Fourth] Münster Symposium*, ed. Hermann J. Real *et al.*, 1993, 1998, 2003
NLI	National Library of Ireland
ODEP	*The Oxford Dictionary of English Proverbs*, ed. F. P. Wilson, 3rd edn, Oxford: Clarendon Press, 1970
ODNB	*The Oxford Dictionary of National Biography*, ed. H. C. G. Matthew and Brian Harrison, 60 vols., Oxford, 2004
OED	*Oxford English Dictionary Online*
Orrery	John Boyle, Earl of Orrery, *Remarks on the Life and Writings of Dr. Jonathan Swift*, ed. João Frées, London, 1752; repr. Newark: University of Delaware Press, 2000
PBA	*Proceedings of the British Academy*
Poems	*The Poems of Jonathan Swift*, ed. Harold Williams, 2nd edn, 3 vols., Oxford: Clarendon Press, 1958
Prior, *Absentees*	Thomas Prior, *A List of the Absentees of Ireland, and the Yearly Value of their Estates and Incomes Spent Abroad*, Dublin, 1729
PRONI	Public Record Office of Northern Ireland
RIA	Royal Irish Academy, Dublin
Spectator	*The Spectator*, ed. Donald F. Bond, 5 vols., Oxford: Clarendon Press, 1965
SStud	*Swift Studies*

Steele, *Tracts*	*The Tracts and Pamphlets of Richard Steele*, ed. Rae Blanchard, Baltimore: Johns Hopkins University Press, 1944
SwJ	Alexander Lindsay, 'Jonathan Swift 1667–1745', in *Index of English Literary Manuscripts, Vol. III, Part 4*, London: Mansell, 1997
Tatler	*The Tatler*, ed. Donald F. Bond, 3 vols., Oxford: Clarendon Press, 1987
TCC	Trinity College, Cambridge
TCD	Trinity College Dublin
TNA	The National Archives [of the UK], Public Record Office
TS	H. Teerink, *A Bibliography of the Writings of Jonathan Swift*, 2nd edn, revised and corrected by Arthur H. Scouten, Philadelphia: University of Pennsylvania Press, 1963
V & A	Victoria and Albert Museum
Woolley, *Corr.*	*The Correspondence of Jonathan Swift, D.D.*, ed. David Woolley, 5 vols., Frankfurt am Main: Peter Lang, 1999–2014
Woolley, *Intelligencer*	Jonathan Swift and Thomas Sheridan, *The Intelligencer*, ed. James Woolley, Oxford: Clarendon Press, 1992

INTRODUCTION

The appearance of the *Drapier's Letters* in 1724 had transformed Swift's standing as a public figure in Ireland, and restored his reputation as a political commentator to the vertiginous heights previously reached by *The Conduct of the Allies*, written for Robert Harley's Tory administration in England in November 1711. Nothing he published after the *Drapier's Letters* had the same political impact. This judgement applies even to the *Modest Proposal*, which in retrospect was recognised as by some distance the most important of his writings on public affairs after 1725, but which received a relatively muted reception in Ireland when it first appeared. Indeed, in many of the works included in this volume (which excludes publications on purely ecclesiastical subjects), Swift was in effect re-treading old ground. His observations on the state of the Irish economy reiterated the pessimistic assessment which he had consistently articulated in the years following his exile to the deanery of St Patrick's in 1713, and which had been given a particularly sharp edge in the arguments of the Drapier. He saw Ireland's problems – the backwardness of agriculture, the decline in manufacture and trade, the scarcity of money, even the moral inadequacies of the people – as deriving ultimately from the kingdom's constitutional inferiority, and the way in which this had been, and was still being, exploited by ministers and Parliaments at Westminster to protect English interests and disadvantage the inhabitants of Ireland. But after the withdrawal of 'Wood's Halfpence' in 1725 the debate in Ireland over political economy moved on, and took a more constructive turn. A succession of poor harvests from 1727 to 1728 triggered subsistence crises, resulting in the impoverishment and near starvation of small farmers and labourers in the countryside, hosts of beggars on the streets of Dublin, and renewed (and overwhelmingly Protestant) emigration from Ulster to north America. In response, other commentators revisited the fundamental causes of Ireland's woes, and offered variations on Swift's themes. Pamphleteers and parliamentarians discussed ways in which Ireland might be 'improved', and in 1731 these would-be 'improvers' founded the Dublin Society, a forum for the exchange of ideas and information, with the intention that it should become an engine of economic development.

The discourse of 'improvement', or so it has been argued, represented a new departure in Irish political thinking, superseding the emphasis in Swift's writings on constitutional inequality. The progenitors of the Dublin Society hoped that former differences over religious and political principle might be set aside, to create a new form of civil society on the basis of a shared commitment to natural philosophy and economic development. It was an approach more likely to emphasise pragmatism than confrontation in Anglo-Irish politics: the benefits of working within existing constitutional frameworks, and co-operating with, rather than confronting, English government. Indeed, one of the most prominent ideologues of 'improvement', Arthur Dobbs (1689–1765), a County Antrim landowner and a future governor of North Carolina, was a friend, and to some extent a protégé, of the Prime Minister Sir Robert Walpole.[1] Soon this became the prevailing mentality in the Dublin administration, whose officials sought to exploit existing constitutional arrangements to improve Ireland's trading opportunities.[2] The Dublin Society included in its ranks a number of such men, advocates of a more realistic and constructive brand of Irish patriotism, who were impatient with the kind of language and arguments to be found in the writings of Swift and some other unreconstructed Anglophobes, which risked provoking resentment at Westminster and sabotaging possible concessions to Irish interests.[3]

This shift in the ideological consensus did not render all Swift's economic arguments passé. The emerging generation shared his concern at the detrimental impact on local industry of the fashion for imported luxury goods, and the haemorrhage of bullion from Ireland to absentee landlords and placemen. Nevertheless, the broad current of economic thought was now running in a new direction, and in consequence Swift came into conflict with writers who in his view exaggerated the potential of Irish agriculture and industry, overestimated the volume of Irish trade, or persisted in the delusion that Ireland's surplus population was a valuable national resource rather than a drain on the wealth of the nation.

The crisis that gripped Ireland in the late 1720s, and to which Swift responded in different ways in the works gathered in this volume, was not just a matter of food shortages and perceived economic stagnation. The very existence of the Protestant establishment seemed to be endangered. Besides

---

1 Dobbs to Alexander MacAulay, 2 June 1732 (PRONI, Dobbs papers, D/162/26).
2 D. W. Hayton, *The Anglo-Irish Experience, 1680–1730: Religion, Identity and Patriotism*, Woodbridge: Boydell Press, 2012, pp. 132–44.
3 See, for example, Marmaduke Coghill to Lord Perceval, 14 Apr. 1731 (*Coghill Letters*, p. 112).

mass emigration from Ulster, which reduced the size of the Protestant population (albeit in the main the Presbyterian element), other evidence pointed towards a revival of the Catholic interest. The broader European context was ominous: the Walpole ministry had failed to deal firmly with the diplomatic and commercial threats posed by the Catholic powers of France and Spain, while stories continued to appear in the newspaper press of the persecution of Protestants in the Habsburg lands. In Ireland itself the general election of 1727 was followed by complaints of the intrigues of Catholic or crypto-Catholic factions in constituencies across the country. The subsequent appearance of French army officers in County Cork, recruiting for the Irish brigades, created further alarm, despite (or perhaps because of) the fact that these agents had been licensed by government. Prompted by a rising apprehension that the popery laws of the 1690s and 1700s had failed to dent the Catholic allegiance of the majority of the population, the Irish House of Lords commissioned an enquiry in 1731 into 'the state of popery' in the kingdom, which revealed large numbers of unlicensed priests and a network of illegal schools. The response was a further batch of 'popery' bills, some of which reached the statute book, and in 1734 a renewed campaign to convert Catholics by educating their children, through the charter given to the Incorporated Society in Dublin for Promoting English Protestant Schools in Ireland.

Anti-Catholic alarmism did not, however, necessarily result in a reaction in favour of the Church of Ireland. Instead, to Swift's consternation, the rapid decline after 1714 of the Irish Tory party, the self-styled guardians of the 'Church interest', was followed by the adoption among many in the propertied classes of an openly critical attitude towards the ecclesiastical establishment. Although this did not extend to acquiescing in measures to relieve Protestant Dissenters from legal disabilities, the financial interests of the church came under sustained attack, including the cherished privilege of collecting tithe, a vital source of income for parish clergy. Many country squires, especially advocates of economic 'improvement', began to see tithe as a national rather than a sectional grievance: a significant obstacle to Ireland's progress. The issue came to a head in 1736 with a public debate over the right of the clergy to claim a tithe on pasturage, the so-called 'tithe of agistment', which was eventually condemned in a resolution of the Irish House of Commons, provoking Swift to one of his harshest satires, the verses directed against MPs as the 'Legion Club'.

Not surprisingly, perhaps, given the drift of public events and public discourse in Ireland in the late 1720s and 1730s, and given his own increasing age, ill health and deafness, many of Swift's writings in this period exhibit a nostalgic quality. The focus of economic debate was moving away from the kind of trenchant rhetoric he had deployed in the *Drapier's Letters*, while the appearance of what he interpreted as a vicious strain of anticlericalism among Protestant landlords in Ireland, and their parliamentary representatives, emphasised a new configuration of politics in an era of Whig consensus. At the same time, his Tory friends in England – men like Pope and Bolingbroke – remained politically impotent and could do no more than rail at the corruption of Walpole's rule, the so-called 'Robinocracy'. Little wonder, then, that in the tracts, essays and fragments presented here, Swift harked back to former glories, basking in the popularity he enjoyed with ordinary Dubliners in the character of 'the Drapier', and sometimes looking even further back into his past, to recall the four last years of Queen Anne's reign, when the 'Church party' controlled government in both Westminster and Dublin.

1   The World of the Drapier

Following the British government's withdrawal of the patent for Wood's Halfpence, which marked the final success of the long-drawn-out campaign of the 'Drapier', Swift took himself to England in March 1726, bringing with him the completed manuscript of *Gulliver's Travels*. He rented lodgings in London, staying five months, during which time he visited Pope in Twickenham, Bolingbroke in Uxbridge, and other acquaintances farther afield. Surprisingly, he was also afforded an audience with Walpole. In consequence, rumours circulated in Ireland that he might at last receive some additional preferment, but these were soon dispelled. The disappointment in fact added to his public reputation in Ireland, being interpreted there as further proof of his honesty, and of his deep attachment to principle. When he returned to Dublin in August he was greeted as a conqueror. His friend Knightley Chetwode observed that 'Illuminations, bonfires and ringing of bells to welcome him, will perhaps make him a mark of envy, with the great ones, whom he has not gratified and complied with in England.'[4] According to one witness, 'several heads of different corporations' (presumably the guilds) in Dublin hired boats to go out into the bay to meet the packet before it docked, and Swift was 'brought to his landing place in a kind of triumph... amid repeated acclamations of "Long live the Drapier"'.[5] The

---

4   Knightley Chetwode to ——, 27 Aug. 1726 (NLI, Mahon papers, MS 47,891/1).
5   Quoted in Ehrenpreis, vol. III, pp. 495–6. See also *An Account of the Journey-men Weavers Grateful Congratulation of the Rev. Dr. Swift Dean of St. Patrick's Safe Arrival, with His Kind Answer, and Bounty to Their Corporation, Sep. the 5th 1726*, [Dublin,] 1726.

English Tory news-writer, Nathaniel Mist, proclaimed that 'so grateful a sense do the people preserve of the merits of the Drapier's books against Wood's brass coin, that there's scarce a street in town without a representation of him for a sign'.[6]

By his writings against Wood's Halfpence Swift had created an image for himself as a popular hero that was not only iconic but seemingly imperishable.[7] Invocation of the Drapier's name was common practice among all political groupings in Dublin, and while his endorsement would be trumpeted as a guarantee of popularity, the disclosure in 1729 that a candidate in the parliamentary by-election for the city, Alderman James Somerville, had five years earlier argued for the prosecution of Swift and his printer proved sufficiently alarming for Somerville's supporters to publish a printed denial under the Drapier's name.[8] In 1731 a 'weekly writer' proposed the erection of a statue in Dublin to 'the Drapier'; in April 1733, when news of the defeat of Walpole's excise bill reached Ireland, a group of 'young men' set up bonfires near the deanery, and dispensed ale to passers-by, to drink to 'that worthy patriot the Drapier, who saved our nation from ruin'; and when Swift's birthday was publicly celebrated in 1736, with 'bonfires and illuminations', the healths drunk included 'long life to the Drapier'.[9] Swift's publishers kept the character alive, through reprinting the *Drapier's Letters* – an edition of 1729 being entitled *The Hibernian Patriot*[10] – or in appending the *nom de plume* to other works: a collection published in 1733 by James Hoey, which included several pieces by Swift alongside effusions of other authors, was given the title *The Drapier's Miscellany*, presumably in the hope of boosting sales.[11] Swift's rivals also cashed in: three pamphlets appearing in Dublin in 1729 appropriated the Drapier's name to enhance their appeal, including a disquisition on 'the inconveniences which the people of Ireland

6 *Mist's Weekly Journal*, 3 Sept. 1726, quoted in Ehrenpreis, vol. III, p. 496.
7 Clive Probyn, 'Jonathan Swift at the Sign of the Drapier', in *Münster* (1998), pp. 225–37.
8 *Dublin Intelligence*, 30 Sept., 11, 14 Oct. 1729.
9 *A Letter to the Right Honourable Sir Ralph Gore, Bart. Speaker of the Honourable House of Commons...*, [Dublin, 1732], p. 11; *St James's Evening Post*, 28 Apr. – 1 May 1733; *London Daily Post*, 11 Dec. 1736; Orrery, pp. 74–5. See also the crudely satirical *Letter from Dermott Mac-Poverty to the Author of the Intelligencer*, Dublin, 1728, p. 7: 'I shall spake no more or [*sic. recte* of] de stori but shomting pon de statures of the Draper, dat shall be shet up, and I tink if I wash to advise upon dem, dere shall be wans in evry markets-town in Irlands, de shall be made of de shilver or golds, caush he keeps the braush from us.'
10 *The Hibernian Patriot: Being a Collection of the Drapier's Letters to the People of Ireland...*, Dublin, 1729, repr. London, 1730. George Faulkner had previously used this title when reprinting the *Drapier's Letters* as *Fraud Detected, or The Hibernian Patriot...*, Dublin, 1725.
11 *The Drapier's Miscellany, in Verse and Prose...*, Dublin, 1733.

labour under for the want of small change', prepared by a writer who had himself crossed swords with Swift, John Browne (d. 1761).[12]

The city in which Swift now enjoyed such an elevated reputation possessed a vibrant political and print culture. Dublin itself was growing rapidly, and the 'constitutional revolution' that had established the Irish Parliament as the principal theatre of Irish political life had created a ravenous appetite for news, opinion and gossip, which the burgeoning book trade both serviced and encouraged. It has been estimated that the number of printers in the city quadrupled in the first three decades of the eighteenth century.[13] No longer did Dublin presses merely reprint the work of London publishers. Their output was as much a product of the local scene: newspapers originated their own stories, pamphleteers debated specifically Irish issues, squibs and ballads satirised local institutions and personalities, with a strong focus on the life of the capital itself. Dublin also had its own literary periodicals, in emulation of English publications of which the *Spectator* had been the prototype: the *Dublin Weekly Intelligence* established by the printer James Carson in 1725, whose contributors were Whiggish writers such as James Arbuckle; and *The Intelligencer*, which Swift and his friend Thomas Sheridan produced in 1728–9. The greater physical durability of the pamphlet, sermon and tract has induced historians to emphasise these more substantial literary products, but such ephemeral single-sheet or half-sheet publications as have survived hint at a treasure of now vanished riches: for example, a 'vindication' in 1733 of the conduct of the popular Dublin Lord Mayor Humphrey French noted that several 'papers', now lost, had been circulating in the city concerning a report that French had behaved badly towards a chandler called Williams, an incident which in political terms seems trivial, or at best parochial, but which evidently provoked a significant skirmish in the press.[14]

---

12 John Browne, *The Drapier Reviv'd: or, Considerations on the Inconveniences Which the People of Ireland Labour Under for the Want of Small Change*, [Dublin, 1729]; 2nd edn, Dublin, 1731; *A Letter, to M. B. Drapier, Occasionally Writ, on the Late Oppressive Villainy of the Br[ewer]s, in Raising the Price of their Malt-liquors*, Dublin, 1729; *A Letter to the People of Ireland. By M. B. Draper*, Dublin, 1729. For Browne, see *DIB*, and below, pp. xlii–xliii.

13 Robert Munter, *The History of the Irish Newspaper 1685–1760*, Cambridge: Cambridge University Press, 1967; Mary Pollard, *Dublin's Trade in Books 1550–1800*, Oxford: Oxford University Press, 1989, chs. 3–5; James Kelly, 'Political Publishing, 1700–1800', in Raymond Gillespie and Andrew Hadfield (eds.), *The Oxford History of the Irish Book*, vol. III: *The Irish Book in English 1550–1800*, Oxford: Oxford University Press, 2006, pp. 215–21. See also, in general, T. C. Barnard, '"Grand Metropolis" or "the Anus of the World"? The Cultural Life of Eighteenth-Century Dublin', in Peter Clark and Raymond Gillespie (eds.), *Two Capitals: London and Dublin 1500–1840* (*PBA* 107 (2001)), pp. 185–210.

14 *A Full Vindication of Humphrey French, Late Lord Mayor of the City of Dublin*, Dublin, 1733.

As a capital city, Dublin was expanding and maturing rapidly.[15] 'The metropolis is exceeding large', wrote the contemporary author of *A Humourous Description of the Manners and Fashions of the Inhabitants of the City of Dublin*; 'the people, pleasures and customs, almost infinite'.[16] Swift's Dublin occupied the same position in relation to the rest of Ireland as London occupied in England, that is to say it was by a very long way the largest conurbation in the country, the centre of government, commerce, the law, education and the church. It was also a 'leisure town', the centre of fashionable society, where members of the propertied elite would lodge for the winter season, or purchase town houses, in order to avail themselves of the delights on offer – balls at the castle, evenings of music or theatre, promenades in pleasure-gardens, or the daily round of coffee-house conversation. In a comparative context, Dublin thus combined the facilities and functions of the cities of London and Westminster, and in so doing brought together men of trade and men of fashion, government officials, members of Parliament, clergymen, scholars and writers.

The rapidly developing city exhibited two very different faces. On the one hand, the social life of the elite was buoyant. The coffee-houses and the numerous taverns that Swift enumerated in *An Examination of Certain Abuses, Corruptions, and Enormities in the City of Dublin*, formed the backdrop to what modern historians would recognise as a genuine 'public sphere'.[17] The theatre and music rooms enabled performances of plays and entertainments that had recently graced the London stage, such as *The Beggar's Opera*, the occasion of one of Swift's essays in *The Intelligencer*, while 'assemblees', card-schools and other fashionable gatherings provided ample opportunities for pleasant sociability (or what Swift deplored as occasions of wasteful feminine self-indulgence). Extensive construction work in the city suggested confidence, and not only the speculative developments of town residences for gentlemen, of which Swift was suspicious (remembering English speculators a generation before), but great public buildings. In 1729 the foundation stone was laid for an impressive new parliament house in College Green, to an innovative design by the young architect Edward Lovett

---

15 For the condition and development of Dublin in this period, see David Dickson, *Dublin: The Making of a Capital City*, London: Profile Books, 2014, ch. 3.
16 *A Humourous Description of the Manners and Fashions of the Inhabitants of the City of Dublin, in a Letter from a Gentleman to his Friend in ... Drogheda*, Dublin, 1734, p. [3].
17 For a discussion of this phenomenon in early eighteenth-century England, see Brian Cowan, *The Social Life of Coffee: The Emergence of the British Coffeehouse*, New Haven & London: Yale University Press, 2005.

Pearce.[18] Yet, at the same time, economic depression increased the numbers of the destitute. An influx of 'strollers' (as Swift called them) from the countryside served as a highly visible daily reminder of the distress of the lower orders. Beggars filled the streets, and crime spiralled. Prostitution seems to have been a particular problem, to judge by the emphasis placed by the city authorities on closing brothels and arresting street-walkers.[19] It also seems to have been a particular concern of Swift's, whose references to female vagrants, and even the female hawkers whose street cries are described in the *Examination of Certain Abuses* . . . , repeatedly suggest that these women were of low morals, and in reality no more than whores.

The topography of Dublin, and especially Swift's corner of it, meant that the worlds of rich and poor came into direct contact. The cathedral and deanery of St Patrick's, though within walking distance of the castle, the new parliament house, Trinity College, and the haunts of the *beau monde*, were also surrounded by the slums of the Archbishop's and Earl of Meath's Liberties. Here were the weavers and street gangs for whom 'the Drapier' was a patriotic hero, and here also were crowds of beggars, alarming creatures whose presence on the streets made travelling short distances seem hazardous. The visible contrast of wealth and poverty, and a sense of physical insecurity, gave Dublin its essential character. A former lord mayor argued in 1733 that it was a far livelier, and more disorderly, city even than London:

> The Court is in the heart of our City, our Nobility and Gentry are intermixed Inhabitants . . . besides we have a College with about four Hundred Students. It is for the Accommodation of these that Coaches and Chairs ply almost all Nights, Taverns, Publick-houses and Coffee-houses are kept open most part of the Nights, and a continual Noise, and Quarrels often ensue; Numbers passing and repassing the whole Nights long, lewd Women tempted to strole about to meet with those disorder'd by Drinking, etc.[20]

For much of the year, the tumult of Dublin (and especially the area around St Patrick's cathedral) constituted Swift's personal landscape. But for all the adulation he claimed to receive from the populace, and the pleasure he derived from the company of friends, it was not a landscape in which he was content. 'Going to England is a very good thing', he wrote in a letter in 1726, 'if it were not with an ugly circumstance of returning to

---

18 Edward McParland, 'Building the Parliament House in Dublin', *Parliamentary History* 21 (2002), 131–40.
19 See below, p. xcvii.
20 Sir William Fownes, *A Letter to the Right Honourable Humphrey French, Esq., Present Lord Mayor of the City of Dublin*, Dublin, 1733, pp. 4–5.

Ireland'.[21] He journeyed across the water for the last time in 1727, before being called back by news of what turned out to be the fatal illness of Esther Johnson ('Stella'). His peregrinations within Ireland were also more tightly circumscribed than they had once been. In the first decade of his return to Ireland he had established a wide-ranging itinerary: there were visits to the Rochforts in County Westmeath, to Bishop Stearne in Clogher in County Tyrone, to Bishop Bolton in County Galway, and in 1723 a journey to the wilds of west Cork.[22] This extensive travelling, as well as the time he had spent attending to his parish duties at Kilroot in County Antrim (at the outset of his clerical career) and then at Laracor, near Trim in County Meath, has encouraged scholars to emphasise Swift's familiarity with the country, its resources and its problems.[23] But this was not the case after 1725, when not only had life become much harder for tenants and labourers because of persistent bad weather and poor harvests, but significant underlying changes were happening to the Irish economy. In the period covered by this volume, Swift travelled much less. Aside from a lengthy visit in 1728 to his friends the Achesons at Markethill in County Armagh (where he again confessed 'I hate Dublin and love the retirement here'[24]) and another, briefer stay in the autumn of 1735 with Thomas Sheridan at Quilca in County Cavan, his country visits were now confined to the hinterland of the city: to Belcamp, Grange and Howth, just north of Dublin, to Powerscourt in County Wicklow, and to his first cousin once removed, Deane Swift, at Castlerickard near Trim.

Increasingly, Swift's vision of Ireland was seen through the lens of the capital city. Brief sojourns in comfortable villas in County Dublin, amid the prosperous pastureland of the Pale, afforded only a limited insight into conditions in the countryside; and while travel in south Ulster, to Markethill and Quilca, offered a different perspective, this was in its way equally unrepresentative. Avoiding Munster meant that Swift did not see for himself how Ireland's principal wool-producing region was responding to the challenges of restrictive English legislation, and how graziers and merchants in Cork were exploiting opportunities to trade with Britain's transatlantic plantations. At the same time, the fact that he went no farther north than Counties Armagh or Cavan left him reliant on second-hand information

---

21 Swift to Pope and Gay, 17 Nov. 1726 (Woolley, *Corr.*, vol. III, p. 35).
22 Ehrenpreis, vol. III, pp. 426–30.
23 Joseph McMinn, *Jonathan's Travels: Swift and Ireland*, Belfast: Appletree Press, 1994, provides a full picture.
24 Swift to Sheridan, 2 Aug. 1728 (Woolley, *Corr.*, vol. III, p. 192).

about the state of Presbyterian communities in Ulster, the reality behind emigration to America, and the transformative potential of the new linen manufacture.

Moreover, even on these visits to northern friends, he seems to have been insulated from the realities of life in the Irish countryside. Markethill, for example, was situated in an area notorious for rural banditry, and for the brutalities of the local 'rapparee-hunter', John Johnston, on whose largely unofficial policing activities depended the maintenance of public order.[25] Swift, ensconced behind the walls of the Achesons' Gosford Park estate, would appear not to have fully appreciated the violent reputation of the neighbourhood. Indeed, he was either ignorant of the details of recent local history, or perhaps sufficiently confident in Johnston's abilities to contemplate purchasing a property there for himself.[26]

The world Swift inhabited was circumscribed not just by his own travelling habits, but also by the scope of his social contacts. The death of Esther Johnson in 1728 put an end to his most intimate relationship, but he retained a coterie of friends in Ireland: representatives of the next generation, like the Achesons, Patrick Delany or Thomas Sheridan (his collaborator on *The Intelligencer*); slightly older men like Charles Ford or Knightley Chetwode; and apprentice poets like Mary Barber and Laetitia Pilkington. In essence, this was a community of inferiors: cronies, admirers and protégé(e)s. Beyond the shores of Ireland, of course, older and grander friendships continued, with Lords Bolingbroke and Orrery, Alexander Pope and John Gay, and with the family of his former patron Robert Harley, but after 1727 these relationships were maintained on an epistolary rather than a personal basis.

One obvious feature of Swift's social circle was its strongly literary character; another was an enduring strain of Tory sympathies, allegiances and prejudices, which informed not just the poetry of Pope and the political journalism of Bolingbroke, but, on a lesser scale, the High Churchmanship of Dr Delany and the rustic Tory 'patriotism' of Sir Arthur Acheson.[27] A

---

25 T. G. F. Paterson, 'The Black Bank and Fews Barracks', *Ulster Journal of Archaeology* 1 (1938), 108–12; L. M. Cullen, *The Emergence of Modern Ireland 1600–1900*, London: Batsford, 1981, p. 207; Neal Garnham, *The Courts, Crime and the Criminal Law in Ireland 1692–1760*, Blackrock, Co. Dublin: Irish Academic Press, 1996, pp. 44–5.

26 J. G. Simms, 'Dean Swift and County Armagh', *Seanchas Ardmhacha* 6 (1971), 131–40. It is worth noting, however, that in a poem in which he explained his reasons 'for not Building at Drapier's Hill', he made reference to the situation of the place: 'How could I form so wild a vision, / To seek, in deserts, Fields Elysian? / To live in fear, suspicion, variance, / With Thieves, Fanatics, and Barbarians' (*Poems*, vol. III, p. 899).

27 For Delany, see *DIB*; *ODNB*; for Acheson, John Bayly to George Dodington, 31 July 1736 (NLI, MS 16,139, p. 29); *Hist. Ir. Parl.*, vol. III, pp. 52–3.

less obvious feature, perhaps, in the list of Swift's closest acquaintances is the absence of figures of influence at the centre of politics. Swift remained at some distance from the key men in Dublin Castle or in the Irish Parliament; and after the death of Archbishop King of Dublin in May 1729, he had few contacts within the higher reaches of the established church. Among Irish politicians, he had little to do with the pro-government party headed first by Speaker William Conolly (*d.* 1729) and then by Sir Ralph Gore (*d.* 1733), aside from an amiable acquaintance with the Prime Serjeant Henry Singleton, himself a former Tory. And his only connection with the rival Whig faction, headed first by the Brodricks and then after 1728 by Henry Boyle, was the maverick patriot Eaton Stannard, whose candidacy for municipal office in Dublin in 1729 Swift advocated in *Some Considerations Humbly Offered to the... Lord-Mayor, the Court of Aldermen, and Common Council... in the Choice of a Recorder.*[28] Otherwise, Swift's Irish friends were minor players on the public stage. As for his English correspondents – with the exception of William Pulteney, Walpole's principal parliamentary antagonist, with whom in any case he was not close – they were, in political terms, internal exiles. Bolingbroke, whom Swift first encountered at the heart of English political life in Queen Anne's reign, was now an archetypal outsider, his influence resting entirely on his writings.

With one exception, Swift's relationships with successive viceroys were also distant. The exception was John, Lord Carteret, lord lieutenant from 1724 to 1730. Carteret was another ex-Tory, and an old London acquaintance, who welcomed Swift into Dublin Castle and into his private apartments, did what he could to protect him from prosecution over the *Drapier's Letters*, and at first accepted his recommendations for the advancement of clerical friends. But Carteret regarded Swift as a source of entertaining company rather than serious counsel. He took his political advice from other sources (notably Conolly and Gore). There was no bishopric for Swift himself, despite the wholly unrealistic expectations of his supporters,[29] and the preferments provided for those whom the dean recommended were very small beer. The dukes of Dorset and Devonshire, the lords lieutenant who followed Carteret, showed Swift no more than the formal courtesy due to a man of his position and reputation.

The relatively narrow compass of Swift's social life from the late 1720s onwards had two main consequences for his writings. In the first place,

---

28 For more on Swift's relationships during the period, see A. C. Elias, '*Senatus Consultum*: Revising Verse in Swift's Dublin Circle, 1729–1735', in *Münster* (1998), pp. 249–67.
29 Knightley Chetwode to ——, 5 July 1726 (NLI, MS 47,891/1).

his contributions to political debate in Ireland possessed a strongly self-referential quality. He wrote about his own experiences, cited and justified his own previously published work, and endlessly pursued quarrels with other writers. Even his *Vindication* of Carteret in 1730 from the charge of favouring Tories was constructed around a narrative of the patronage the viceroy had doled out to Swift's friends. Moreover, the individual Irish politicians whom Swift attacked most vehemently and most often, Viscount Allen, Richard Tighe and Richard Bettesworth, were singled out by personal vendetta. Admittedly, each was a prominent parliamentarian, but, with the possible exception of Allen, they were not figures of the front rank. They were notorious because Swift's satires made them so. His practice of coining abusive nicknames for personal enemies based on physical infirmities or doubtful ancestry – 'Traulus' (the stammerer) for Allen, 'Dick Fitzbaker' for Tighe (referring to Tighe's supposed descent from a supplier of bread to the Cromwellian army) – and re-using these without explanation suggests that his satire was operating in an artificial political environment of his own creation: a kind of micro-system with himself at the centre, rather than the greater world of Irish parliamentary politics as contemporaries understood it.

It was also a political environment with the strong flavour of a bygone era. Swift's emphasis on party identity and party hostility, in a Whig and Tory sense, was inappropriate to the Ireland of the late 1720s and 1730s, when such distinctions, though they had left traces in men's thoughts and writings, seem to have been largely absent from the political scene.[30] His presentation of pro-government interests (for example, in *An Examination of Certain Abuses, Corruptions, and Enormities in the City of Dublin*) as obsessed with a fear of the Jacobite Pretender, and determined at all costs to smear their critics as Jacobites, may have had some resonances at a local level, especially on the streets of Dublin, where Catholic mobs adopted Jacobite emblems and catch-cries.[31] But it does not reflect the tenor of Irish parliamentary debates, as reported in the surviving sources. As Swift himself acknowledged, many of those who had been active in the Tory party in Ireland in the period before 1715 had now reconciled themselves to the Whig ascendancy, to the extent of holding high office themselves in the Dublin government.

Swift's depiction of Whig paranoia was in fact more appropriate to the political situation in Walpole's England, where party distinctions were still important, both in terms of practical politics and in the rhetoric of

---

30 See below, pp. xlviii–liii.
31 Patrick Fagan, 'The Dublin Catholic Mob (1700–1750)', *ECI* 4 (1989), 139.

parliamentary and extra-parliamentary debate.³² He was interpreting Irish politics in English terms, rather than reflecting the very different circumstances that now obtained in the Dublin Parliament. He was also viewing contemporary events through the prism of his own past. In several of the works included in this volume we can see Swift harking back to what were for him the great days of Queen Anne's reign. His *Letter on the Fishery* in 1734, for example, included attacks on the Dutch (never too far beneath the surface of his thought) and gratuitous references to the 'great ministry' of Robert Harley, Earl of Oxford, which had dished the Whigs, protected the established churches in England and Ireland, and made peace with France in spite of the machinations of selfish allies abroad and warmongering financiers at home. Even the literary expression of his continuing attachment to his friend Francis Atterbury, the High Church bishop of Rochester deprived and banished in 1723 after accusations of Jacobite conspiracy, was rooted in the past. In one of his *Intelligencers*, Swift appears to contrast Atterbury's sufferings with the worldly success and material comforts of unworthy Whig clergymen (though disguising the identification of Atterbury by depicting his fate as rustic obscurity rather than continental exile). The story he tells, however, focuses on the education and early career of the protagonists before the Hanoverian succession. The recollection of such distant days, which were not only a golden age for the 'Church interest' but also a time of great success for Swift personally, was of a piece with his continued emphasis on the triumphs of the Drapier long after Wood's Halfpence had been abandoned and new issues had arisen. The nature of public debate in Ireland was changing, but Swift was not changing with it.

2 Irish Economic Writings 1727–1731: Problems and Solutions

The condition of the Irish economy in the early eighteenth century attracted an inordinate amount of interest from contemporary commentators. By English standards Ireland was poor and underdeveloped, lagging behind its more prosperous neighbour not only in manufactures, trade and commerce, but in agriculture, the principal economic activity of the majority

---

32 Linda Colley, *In Defiance of Oligarchy: The Tory Party 1714–60*, Cambridge: Cambridge University Press, 1982, chs. 7–8; Nicholas Rogers, *Whigs and Cities: Popular Politics in the Age of Walpole and Pitt*, Oxford: Clarendon Press, 1989, ch. 1. Cf. William Speck, 'Whigs and Tories Dim Their Glories', in John Cannon (ed.), *The Whig Ascendancy: Colloquies on Hanoverian England*, London: Edward Arnold, 1981, pp. 51–70.

of the population. The Irish countryside did not appear to have recovered from the damaging effects of the 'war of the two kings' and the widespread reorganisation of tenurial agreements arising from the post-war land settlement. Harvest failures produced periodic crises, which were exacerbated by the scarcity of coin. It was easy to recognise major structural weaknesses in the Irish economy. Irish agriculture was perceived to concentrate on pastoral rather than arable farming, and thus to be dependent on imports of basic foodstuffs. The only significant manufacture, woollens, had received a serious blow from the English Woollen Act of 1699, which prevented the export of yarn and cloth to England or its plantations. From the mid-1720s, the balance of trade ran against Ireland, a situation that seemed to be exacerbated by excessive imports of luxury goods that could not be offset by exports. Worse still, from the perspective of the mercantilist beliefs that still underpinned much contemporary economic theory, the country's stock of bullion seemed to be draining away: remitted to absentee landowners and officials, and exported by opportunistic bankers who took advantage of the differences in the relative values of gold and silver in Ireland and England. With no facility to mint coin in Ireland and a chaotic variety of foreign moneys in circulation, the currency was chronically weak. And, indeed, the financial sector in general was relatively primitive. There were no public banks, and the small Irish finance houses were in constant danger of collapse (as indeed happened in 1733, when Benjamin Burton's bank closed, owing over £90,000 to between 8,000 and 9,000 creditors), thus preventing the level of capital formation necessary for investment in commercial or industrial enterprises. Public finance was equally fragile: persistent shortfalls in tax revenue after 1714 had created a 'national debt', which stood at £300,000 in *c.* 1730. Although, of course, minuscule by English standards (where the national debt was at least 100 times as large), this represented a substantial sum for the Irish treasury, whose annual expenditure in this period ranged from £400,000 to £600,000, and was therefore a source of considerable public concern.[33]

Such was the perception. The reality, as modern scholars have shown, was much less gloomy, at least in relation to the potential for development.

---

33 Charles Ivar McGrath, 'Money, Politics and Power: The Financial Legislation of the Irish Parliament', in D. W. Hayton, James Kelly and John Bergin (eds.), *The Eighteenth-century Composite State: Representative Institutions in Ireland and Europe, 1689–1800*, Basingstoke: Palgrave Macmillan, 2010, pp. 27–32; McGrath, *Ireland and Empire, 1692–1770*, London: Pickering & Chatto, 2012, pp. 171, 183–9. The national debt and its management are central themes of Sean D. Moore, *Swift, the Book, and the Irish Financial Revolution: Satire and Sovereignty in Colonial Ireland*, Baltimore: Johns Hopkins University Press, 2010.

Economic historians have identified the 1740s as the decade in which the Irish economy finally 'took off'.[34] What remained of the legal trade between Ireland and the north American plantations, in particular the provisions trade in beef and butter from Munster, was promoting a healthy expansion in cattle-grazing, and enhancing the prosperity of Cork and its subsidiary ports.[35] At the same time, large-scale clandestine exports of contraband goods to France and Spain, especially woollen yarn and cloth, was compensating in no small measure for the legislative restrictions imposed on trade to Britain and her dominions: indeed, in some parts of the south-west of Ireland smuggling was so well organised, and maintained on such a large scale, as to occupy a central place in the structure of the local economy.[36] Elsewhere, especially in north-east Ulster, patient nurturing of the infant linen manufacture was beginning to show beneficial results.[37] With the benefit of hindsight, we can see that Ireland's economy was by no means as stagnant, nor its future as hopeless, as contemporaries believed. But, of course, this was less apparent to contemporaries. With some notable exceptions – economic writers like John Browne and David Bindon (*c.* 1690–1761), with whose opinions Swift profoundly and bitterly disagreed – they could see little further than the depressing commercial statistics available to Parliament, the newspaper reports of bankruptcies, and the evidence of their own eyes in relation to poverty and starvation in town and countryside.[38]

Swift's analysis of Ireland's economic problems was set forth clearly in his *Short View of the State of Ireland*, published in 1728.[39] Here he established a

---

34 David Dickson, *New Foundations: Ireland 1660–1800*, 2nd edn, Dublin: Irish Academic Press, 2000, ch. 4, esp. p. 116.
35 David Dickson, *Old World Colony: Cork and South Munster 1630–1830*, Cork: Cork University Press, 2005, chs. 4, 7.
36 L. M. Cullen, 'Five Letters Relating to Galway Smuggling in 1737', *Journal of the Galway Historical and Archaeological Society* 27 (1959), 10–25; Cullen, *Anglo-Irish Trade 1660–1800*, Manchester: Manchester University Press, 1968, pp. 5, 26; Cullen, *An Economic History of Ireland since 1660*, London: Batsford, 1972, pp. 39–42; Dickson, *Old World Colony*, pp. 124–35.
37 See Conrad Gill, *The Rise of the Irish Linen Industry*, Oxford: Oxford University Press, 1923, chs. 2–4.
38 See, for example, *Dublin Intelligence*, 28 Dec. 1728, 8 Feb. 1729; Lord Midleton to Thomas Brodrick, 9 July 1727, 30 Apr., 2, 18 May 1728 (Surrey History Centre, Brodrick papers, 1248/7/77–8, 231–4, 235–6, 243–4); Henry Crofton to William Smyth, 18 Aug., 19 Sept. 1729 (NLI, Smythe of Barbavilla papers, MS 41,586/3); Bishop Robert Howard to Hugh Howard, 2, 27 Nov. 1728, 9 Apr. 1729 (NLI, Wicklow papers, MS 38,598/4, 38,598/5); Hugh Howard to Bishop Robert Howard, 20 Mar. 1728[/9] (NLI, Wicklow papers, MS 38,598/4); and, in general, James Kelly, 'Harvests and Hardship: Famine and Scarcity in Ireland in the Late 1720s', *Studia Hibernica* 26 (1991–2), 65–85.
39 See below, pp. 13–26.

series of requirements for prosperity, and showed how the condition of Ireland failed to meet them. His later writings recapitulated the same points. In essence, however, this was a political explanation. In Swift's view, the nature of Anglo-Irish governance, in which Ireland's administration and legislature were subordinated to England's, inevitably resulted in the sacrificing of Irish economic interests. The government at Westminster ruled Ireland in England's interests: they would not permit the Irish to mint their own coins, gave jobs and pensions in Ireland to Englishmen, and interfered with the legislation prepared by the Irish Parliament, which under Poynings' Law required the approval of the English (after 1707, British) privy council. And the Westminster Parliament went further, passing laws that undermined the capacity of Irish agriculturalists and manufacturers by refusing them the right to export their products: not only the hated Woollen Act but the various Navigation Acts that controlled transatlantic commerce. At the same time, the proclaimed constitutional inferiority of Ireland, and the experience of living under laws which they themselves had no part in making, infused into the minds of Irish men and women the mentality of slavery, reducing the 'vulgar' to a brutish state in which they were unable to help themselves, and creating among the wealthy a vain aspiration to live in the manner of their counterparts across the water. In consequence, absentee landlords extorted unreasonably high rents from their tenants in order to draw away the wealth of the country to support conspicuous consumption in London or Bath, while the gentlemen, and especially the ladies, who did remain in Dublin were keen to ape English fashions and import luxury goods at the expense of native manufactures.

Constitutional patriotism of this kind had a well-established pedigree. In particular, there had been a sustained chorus of protest from Protestants in Ireland at the turn of the century over repeated English parliamentary interference in Irish affairs: the Woollen Act in 1699, the enforced resumption of Irish forfeited estates in 1699–1700, and attempts by the English House of Lords in 1697–1703 to assert their appellate jurisdiction over Irish litigation. Some had returned to the historical claim of the Irish Parliament to parity with Westminster, and thus in effect a legislative autonomy, most notably William Molyneux, in *The Case of Ireland's Being Bound by Acts of Parliament in England, Stated* (1698), a work which acquired a brief notoriety in England and a lasting fame in Ireland.[40] Similar sentiments had also

---

40 J. G. Simms, *William Molyneux of Dublin: 1656–1698*, ed. P. H. Kelly, Dublin: Irish Academic Press, 1982; D. W. Hayton, *Ruling Ireland, 1685–1742: Politics, Politicians and Parties*, Woodbridge: Boydell Press, 2004, pp. 66–84; Patrick Kelly, 'Conquest versus

been aroused two decades later by the passage at Westminster in 1720 of the Declaratory Act, which confirmed unilaterally and finally the right of the British House of Lords to act as a last court of appeal for lawsuits begun in Ireland, and also the right of the British Parliament to legislate directly for Ireland.[41] Swift's calculation of the deleterious effects of the denial of Irish constitutional rights stood directly in this tradition: indeed, the controversy over the Declaratory Act had formed the background to his incendiary pamphlet *A Proposal for the Universal Use of Irish Manufacture . . . Utterly Rejecting and Renouncing Everything Wearable that Comes from England* (1720). His point of departure was indignation at English discriminatory legislation over wool, and the iniquity of binding a people with laws to which they had not given their consent, arguments to which he would return. Moreover, in developing his case he made several other points which were to be found in the *Short View* – for example, lamenting the export of bullion to England and condemning landlords who 'racked' their tenants with exorbitant rents, instead of discharging their proper social responsibilities (a point he returned to in *Maxims Controlled in Ireland* in lamenting the decline of the traditional dispensation of hospitality in aristocratic houses).[42]

Those who thought and wrote in the same vein as Swift were not necessarily in the majority. Even at the height of the outrage against the English Forfeitures Resumption Act of 1700, which generated a national campaign of addresses to the king, any suggestion that the protesters were aiming at independence was quickly denied.[43] Later, during the prolonged jurisdictional dispute over the case of *Annesley* v. *Sherlock*, which was the immediate occasion for the introduction of the Declaratory Bill, there were inflammatory speeches in the Irish House of Lords about 'certain men's being slaves who are to be bound by laws where they have no representatives', but once the bill passed, the public response in Ireland was strangely muted.[44] This

---

Consent as the Basis of the English Title to Ireland in William Molyneux's *Case of Ireland . . . Stated* (1698)', in Ciaran Brady and J. H. Ohlmeyer (eds.), *British Interventions in Early Modern Ireland*, Cambridge: Cambridge University Press, 2005, pp. 334–56.

41 Isolde Victory, 'The Making of the Declaratory Act of 1720', in Gerard O'Brien (ed.), *Parliament, Politics and People: Essays in Eighteenth-century Irish History*, Blackrock, Co. Dublin: Irish Academic Press, 1989, pp. 9–29; D. W. Hayton, 'The Stanhope/Sunderland Ministry and the Repudiation of Irish Parliamentary Independence', *English Historical Review* 113 (1998), 610–36.

42 See below, pp. 171–80.

43 Patrick Walsh, *The Making of the Irish Protestant Ascendancy: The Life of William Conolly, 1662–1729*, Woodbridge: Boydell Press, 2010, pp. 56–9; Hayton, *Ruling Ireland*, pp. 79–80.

44 Hayton, 'Stanhope/Sunderland Ministry and Repudiation of Irish Parliamentary Independence', pp. 618, 635–6.

was not simply a matter of political timidity among people whose memories of their 'deliverance' from the Catholic government of James II in 1690 were still vivid. There was always another style of political discourse in Ireland, less strident and more pragmatic, whose proponents sought to persuade the English government and Parliament that it was in their own interest to accommodate Irish manufacturers and merchants in their extensive commercial networks. Examples include Sir Francis Brewster (*d.* 1705), whose published writings recommended the adoption of a generous imperial policy based on the colonial practices of the ancient Romans, and Henry Maxwell (1669–1730), who in 1704 presented the argument for an Anglo-Irish union, instead of, or in addition to, the proposed English treaty with Scotland.[45] And there were writers – including Maxwell again – who continued the tradition of urging Irish Protestants to help themselves through a process of social and economic reform, to be achieved either by educating the 'native Irish' and converting them to Protestantism and English civility, or by a renewed policy of inviting over Protestant settlers.

These less confrontational approaches gained significant ground after 1715. The proposal for a national bank in 1721 stimulated a pamphlet debate which explored the ways in which the Irish economy could be kick-started without any revisions of the system of governance;[46] and in 1723 Robert, Viscount Molesworth, published his *Considerations for the Promoting of Agriculture*, which offered a range of practical schemes that could be adopted within Ireland, without reference to the English, including the granting of longer leases to tenants, the foundation of local agricultural schools, 'praemiums' awarded for excellence in husbandry, and (something Swift would not have welcomed) a rational reform of the system of ecclesiastical taxation through tithes.[47] By the late 1720s, a new generation of

---

45 Sir Francis Brewster, *Essays on Trade and Navigation...*, London, 1695; Brewster, *A Discourse Concerning Ireland and the Different Interests Thereof...*, London, 1698; Brewster, *New Essay's on Trade...*, London, 1702; Henry Maxwell, *An Essay upon an Union of Ireland with England...*, Dublin, 1704; Maxwell, *Reasons Offer'd for Erecting a Bank in Ireland; in a Letter to Hercules Rowley, Esq.*, Dublin, 1721; Maxwell, *Mr Maxwell's Second Letter to Mr Rowley; Wherein the Objections Against the Bank are Answer'd*, Dublin, 1721; D. W. Hayton, 'Henry Maxwell, Author of *An Essay Towards an Union of Ireland with England* (1703)', *ECI* 22 (2007), 28–63.

46 Michael Ryder, 'The Bank of Ireland, 1721: Land, Credit and Dependency', *Historical Journal* 25 (1982), 557–82. See also Patrick Kelly, 'Industry and Virtue versus Luxury and Corruption: Berkeley, Walpole and the South Sea Bubble Crisis', *ECI* 7 (1992), 57–74.

47 Molesworth, *Some Considerations for the Promoting of Agriculture, and Employing the Poor*, Dublin, 1723.

economic writers had emerged, most notably David Bindon, John Browne, Arthur Dobbs, William Maple (d. 1762) and Thomas Prior (1681–1751), who based their work on detailed analyses of trading patterns and prospects.[48] Together, they developed a new and persuasive ideology of the 'improvement' of Ireland through the modernisation of agriculture and the promotion of new industrial enterprises.[49] This was a significant departure from demands for constitutional equality.[50] Swift was not entirely isolated in his continuing rage against English legislative discrimination,[51] but his arguments were being superseded by a different line of thought, one that by contrast emphasised the advantages offered by the connection with Britain. The new literature of political economy in Ireland took its cue from the work of established English authorities on trade, like Charles Davenant (1656–1714), and more recent authors such as the London-based transatlantic merchant Joshua Gee (1667–1730), himself the son of an Irishman, whose most important publication, *The Trade and Navigation of Great Britain Consider'd*, appeared in 1729, and dealt with a range of very specific problems in a highly practical way. This style of writing also adopted the statistical emphasis

---

48 For Bindon, see *DIB*. For Dobbs, see Desmond Clarke, *Arthur Dobbs, Esquire, 1689–1765*, Chapel Hill: University of North Carolina Press, 1957; Helen Rankin and Charles Nelson (eds.), *Curious in Everything: The Career of Arthur Dobbs of Carrickfergus, 1689–1765*, Carrickfergus: Carrickfergus and District Historical Society in association with Society for the History of Natural History, 1990; *ODNB*; *DIB*. For Maple, see *DIB*. For Prior, see Desmond Clarke, *Thomas Prior, 1681–1751, Founder of the Royal Dublin Society*, Dublin: Royal Dublin Society, 1951; Teddy Fennelly, *Thomas Prior: His Life, Times, and Legacy*, Port Laoise: Arderin Publishing, 2001; *ODNB*; *DIB*.
49 Patrick Kelly, 'The Politics of Political Economy in Mid-Eighteenth-Century Ireland', in S. J. Connolly (ed.), *Political Ideas in Eighteenth-Century Ireland*, Dublin: Four Courts Press, 2000, pp. 106–9; James Livesey, 'The Dublin Society in Eighteenth-Century Irish Political Thought', *Historical Journal* 47 (2004), 615–40. See also Livesey, *Civil Society and Empire: Ireland and Scotland in the Eighteenth-Century Atlantic World*, New Haven & London: Yale University Press, 2009, ch. 2, esp. pp. 57–62.
50 Even if, as James Kelly has argued, this ideology could not have been developed without the foundations laid by Swift's critique of Irish economic conditions in *A Short View* and other writings: 'Jonathan Swift and the Irish Economy in the 1720s', *ECI* 6 (1991), 7–36; see also Patrick Kelly, '"Conclusions by No Means Calculated for the Circumstances and Condition of Ireland": Swift, Berkeley, and the Solution to Ireland's Economic Problems', in Aileen Douglas *et al.* (eds.), *Locating Swift: Essays from Dublin on the 250th Anniversary of the Death of Jonathan Swift, 1667–1745*, Dublin: Four Courts Press, 1998, p. 55.
51 See, for example, [?Sir Richard Cox,] *Some Observations on the Present State of Ireland, Particularly with Relation to the Woollen Manufacture*, Dublin, 1731, and the reaction to this pamphlet in Lord Perceval to Marmaduke Coghill, 8 Apr. 1731 (BL, Egmont papers, Add. MS 47033, fo. 70).

of the nascent science of 'political arithmetic', which dated back to the work of Sir William Petty in the Restoration period.[52]

Swift's *Short View* offered superficial concessions to political arithmetic. It began in a theoretical style, with an enumeration of 'the true causes of any country's flourishing and growing rich', which included 'the conveniency of safe ports and havens' and 'the privilege of free trade'. But it was not long before Swift was rehearsing familiar grievances, through recording the many inadequacies of the Irish case: denied the opportunity to export their manufactures; denied the basic freedom to coin their own money; denied a resident monarch to provide a focus around which the social elite might cluster instead of always looking to England; even denied access to places in the Irish administration which their own taxes paid for. The conclusion turned the tables neatly on the arithmeticians: 'if Ireland be a rich and flourishing kingdom, its wealth and prosperity must be owing to certain causes, that are yet concealed from the whole race of mankind'.

In composing the *Short View*, Swift was taking as his principal antagonist John Browne, a scion of a Catholic landed family in County Mayo now suffering under reduced circumstances, who had conformed to the established church in 1722 and was attempting to make his way in the world as a writer and 'projector'. Having previously given evidence before the privy council in Whitehall in support of the patent for Wood's Halfpence, Browne had made Swift his enemy, a state of affairs he was anxious to put right. Unfortunately for him, the pamphlet with which he hoped to recover Swift's good opinion, *Seasonable Remarks on Trade, with Some Reflections on the Advantages that Might Accrue to Great Britain, by a Proper Regulation of the Trade of Ireland*, published in 1728, only antagonised the dean further, since it presented a highly optimistic view of the prospects for the development of Irish commerce, which in Swift's view was entirely counter-intuitive, given the food shortages in the summer of 1727, the destitution of the Dublin population, and the ongoing emigration from Ulster.[53] Of particular concern to Swift was Browne's endorsement of a popular saying which he himself regarded as a dangerous fallacy and which he denounced in, among other works, *Maxims Controlled in Ireland*, namely that 'people are the riches of a nation'. In Swift's view, Ireland's overpopulation, far from being a potential source

---

52 George Wittkowsky, 'Swift's *Modest Proposal*: The Biography of an Early Georgian Pamphlet', *Journal of the History of Ideas* 4 (1943), esp. pp. 81–3; G. A. Rees, 'Pamphlets, Pamphleteers and the Problems of Irish Society, c. 1727–1749', Ph.D. thesis, Queen's University Belfast, 2011, pp. 65–8.
53 Kelly, 'Swift and the Irish Economy', pp. 20–31.

of prosperity, was in fact a dead weight on the country's economy, since one consequence of the flood of paupers that was inundating Dublin and other urban centres was that money would be spent on poor relief rather than invested in agriculture or manufacturing. It was a theme to which he would return in the *A Modest Proposal*, which at last found a practical use for the children of beggars by treating them as livestock: in that pamphlet, his readers were asked to accept the horrifying prospect of cannibalism as the only way in which, in Ireland, human beings could conceivably constitute a source of wealth.

Browne's simple remedy for Ireland's ills was founded on the therapeutic power of trade, and the primary purpose of this work and another pamphlet, *An Essay on Trade*, which he published shortly afterwards, was relatively innocent: to persuade the English government to open up imperial commerce.[54] But for Swift this was tantamount to addressing the symptom rather than the disease. Worse still, Swift feared that such fallacious nostrums might convince politicians and members of Parliament in Westminster and Dublin, and divert their minds from attending to the real, deep-rooted, problem of Anglo-Irish governance. He therefore maintained a particular antipathy to Browne, responding acidly to his *Memorial of the Poor Inhabitants, Tradesmen and Labourers of the Kingdom of Ireland*, and casting further sneers in Browne's direction in his own *Answer to Several Letters from Unknown Persons*, and even, by implication, in *A Modest Proposal*, in a sidelong reference to one of Browne's recognised pen-names.[55]

More formidable writers than Browne, however, soon appeared on the scene. In 1729 Arthur Dobbs, who had been elected to a seat in the Irish House of Commons two years earlier, published the first part of his *Essay on the Trade and Improvement of Ireland* (the second appeared in 1731). At over 250 pages, bolstered by detailed statistical tables, the *Essay* was an even more solid contribution than Browne's *Seasonable Remarks* (against which Dobbs also launched significant criticisms). It was founded on a formidable grasp of the data available from governmental and parliamentary sources relating to trade and population, which compared favourably with Swift's sometimes cavalier way with figures. In his later writings, Swift occasionally disagreed with Dobbs's statistics, providing alternative numbers of his own without any acknowledged basis, but, unlike in his treatment of Browne, he

---

54 John Browne, *Seasonable Remarks on Trade with Some Reflections on the Advantages that Might Accrue to Great Britain by a Proper Regulation of the Trade of Ireland*, Dublin, 1728; Browne, *An Essay on Trade in General; and, on that of Ireland in Particular*, Dublin, 1728.
55 See below, pp. 22–39, 116, 152–3.

did not engage directly in dispute with the younger man.[56] Then Thomas Prior, a well-connected and unusually intellectual Irish estate agent, who had worked for the Rawdon family in Ulster and was now managing George Berkeley's properties during Berkeley's absence in America, published a *List of the Absentees of Ireland*, which brought statistical rigour to the issue of absenteeism. Prior quickly followed this success with a second pamphlet, the *Observations on Coin* in 1730, which took another issue of concern to Swift and subjected it to a similar exercise in political arithmetic. Again, Swift steered clear of direct conflict with Prior. Browne had been a relatively weak opponent, but Dobbs and Prior were made of different stuff, bringing to the debate on the Irish economy a statistical precision that Swift could only parody. Moreover, each had an entrée into official circles, which afforded them privileged access to information derived from revenue returns, while another contemporary, the Dublin merchant David Bindon, author of *A Scheme for... the Better Providing for the Poor of Ireland* (1729) and *Some Thoughts on the Woollen Manufactures* (1731), had a personal experience of the realities of commerce that was on a higher level altogether than the knowledge Swift derived from his conversations with the weavers of the Liberties.[57]

The rash of publications on the Irish economy in 1727–9, to which Swift contributed, was clearly owing to the sense of doom enveloping Ireland, as one failed harvest followed another. But the fact that pamphlets clustered at particular times, in 1727–8 and again in 1729–30, was owing to the nature of their intended audience. We know relatively little of the economics of publishing in this period, the size of print-runs, the profits to be made, and where the money went. But it has been suggested that, even by the middle of the century, the readership of pamphlets did not extend much below freehold voters in counties.[58] None of the major productions of the period, including Swift's, was provided with a price on its title page, which may indicate that they were not intended primarily to make money for the authors or printers. Instead, they were intended to be read by government ministers, and especially the parliamentarians in Dublin – the men who could make decisions. The Irish Parliament was in session from November 1727 to May 1728, and

---

56 See below, pp. 103, 135, 169, 235.
57 It should be noted, however, that John Perceval, the son of the first Lord Egmont, found on a visit to Dublin in May 1731 that Bindon 'has a very bad character here, and is very little esteemed' (John Perceval to his father, 5 May 1731 (BL, Add. MS 47033, fo. 98)).
58 James Kelly, 'Political Publishing, 1700–1800', in Raymond Gillespie and Andrew Hadfield (eds.), *The Oxford History of the Irish Book*, vol. III: *The Irish Book in English 1550–1800*, Oxford: Oxford University Press, 2006, p. 227.

again from September 1729 to April 1730, and in both sessions discussed a raft of measures designed to tackle both short-term and long-term economic problems. Pamphlets like Prior's exposure of the extent of absenteeism, or his discussion of the problem of the coinage, were clearly intended to recommend specific forms of legislative action. Swift's contributions were not focused in quite the same way. The *Modest Proposal*, the most famous of these works (which will be discussed at length later in this introduction), did of course advocate a particular scheme, to wit, the breeding of Irish children for the butchery trade but only on the assumption that the other remedies being proposed would never be implemented, and in any case Swift could hardly expect the Parliament to take this recommendation seriously.

Dobbs, Prior and Bindon also played an important part in the promotion of schemes for the improvement of Ireland's economic base through their involvement in the establishment of the Dublin Society in 1731. That the country required 'improvement' was an incontestable assumption among politicians and pamphleteers, and a variety of initiatives were undertaken during the 1720s for this purpose: tracts, like Molesworth's, recommending particular schemes for the employment of the poor, or the modernisation of agriculture, or the systematic exploitation of resources like the fisheries; parliamentary legislation to promote new industrial enterprises, or to enhance infrastructure by building roads and repairing bridges and harbours; and the establishment of charity schools to educate the children of the poor in basic literacy and numeracy and in useful skills such as spinning and weaving. These various strategies had come together in the widespread effort to encourage the production of linen as an alternative to the hamstrung woollen manufacture, a national enterprise which was backed by parliamentary funds, administered by the Linen Board, and was a central feature of the curriculum of many charity schools. In response to the agricultural crisis of the 1720s, the Irish Parliament adopted a similarly co-ordinated strategy over the issue of promoting tillage when it erected a Navigation Board, on the same lines as the Linen Board, to fund schemes for the reclamation of bog land and the construction of canals.

It was in this atmosphere, in which enthusiasm for 'improvement' dominated Irish public life, that Prior and his friends came together in June 1731 to form the Dublin Society, as a forum for the sharing of ideas and practical experience of industrial and agricultural enterprises. Among the members attending the inaugural meeting were Prior, Dobbs, Maple, and the clergyman and *littérateur* Samuel Madden, who had already submitted to Trinity College a plan for the encouragement of useful learning through the awarding of financial 'premiums', and who in 1738 was to publish his own attack on economic absenteeism, *Reflections and Resolutions Proper for the Gentlemen of Ireland, as to their Conduct for the Service of their Country*.[59] The society grew rapidly, admitting a range of men who were active in Irish public life, including a number of practising politicians, judges and, eventually, in 1732, the then viceroy, the Duke of Dorset, who was elected president. The clergy were particularly well represented, with archbishops, bishops, deans and archdeacons, some of them firmly establishment figures like Primate Boulter, but others of a High Church kidney.[60] The name of the dean of St Patrick's, however, was absent.

By the time the Dublin Society was inaugurated, the tenor of public debate in Ireland had shifted away from the abrasive 'patriotism' that had characterised Swift's successful resistance to Wood's Halfpence. Within the Irish administration, politicians whom Swift decried as 'paltry underlings of state' – self-interested and mealy-mouthed apologists for English misrule – were negotiating to modify the harsh legislative regime under which Irish commerce laboured, through a constructive engagement with Walpole's ministry, and with the support of the 'Irish lobby' at Westminster headed by John, Viscount Perceval (later first Earl of Egmont).[61] It was a strategy endorsed even by opposition Whigs.[62] Sharp assertions of Ireland's 'rights', in the style in which Swift specialised, could only undermine negotiations. Occasionally, other pamphleteers overstepped the mark – Prior in particular[63] – and in the Irish House of Commons back-benchers might become over-excited, but in general the public discussion in Ireland on economic questions tended to stay safely within accepted limits.

3 The Political Context: Lord Carteret's Administration 1724–1730

Lord Carteret's appointment as lord lieutenant of Ireland in 1724 had been contrived by Sir Robert Walpole with malice aforethought. Carteret was not

---

59 For Madden, see Mairead Dunlevy, 'Samuel Madden and the Scheme for the Encouragement of Useful Manufactures', in Agnes Bernelle (ed.), *Decantations: A Tribute to Maurice Craig*, Dublin: Lilliput Press, 1992, pp. 21–8; *ODNB*; *DIB*.
60 Dublin Society Register, 1731 (Royal Dublin Society, minute book 1).
61 F. G. James, 'The Irish Lobby in the Early Eighteenth Century', *English Historical Review* 81 (1966), 543–57; James, *Ireland in the Empire, 1688–1770: A History of Ireland from the Williamite Wars to the Eve of the American Revolution*, Cambridge, MA: Harvard University Press, 1973, pp. 154–7.
62 Andrew Crotty to [Henry Boyle], 31 Dec. 1730 (NLI, Shannon papers, MS 13,297/31).
63 Coghill to Lord Perceval, 14 Apr. 1731 (*Coghill Letters*, p. 112); Lord Perceval's diary, 24 Feb. 1731 (HMC, *Egmont Diary*, vol. I, p. 148).

only a rival, but was suspected of intriguing with one of the major players on the Dublin political scene, the Irish lord chancellor, Alan Brodrick, Viscount Midleton, whose family's behaviour over Wood's Halfpence had been equivocal. While Midleton had been ostensibly loyal to government during the viceroyalty of Carteret's predecessor, the Duke of Grafton, his eldest son, St John Brodrick, had in effect acted as the leader of the opposition in the Irish House of Commons. Whichever strategy Carteret adopted in his new office, he stood to lose: either he would seek a compromise over the halfpence and be seen to fail in his viceregal responsibility, so forfeiting the confidence of the king, or he would decide to enforce the wishes of the English Cabinet at all costs and thus sacrifice the trust of his Irish friends, which would inevitably make his management of the Irish Parliament more difficult.

No viceroy had enjoyed an easy passage in Ireland since the Hanoverian succession. The fact that the Irish general election of 1715 had returned a huge Whig majority, far from smoothing out parliamentary opposition, had created a new set of problems. It proved impossible to satisfy all the powerful individuals or family connections among the Irish Whigs, and, from the first, those left out of government had made common cause with Tories in a 'country' or 'patriot' alliance. Most serious was the competition for power between the two most important and successful Whig politicians in Ireland, Lord Midleton and the Speaker of the Commons, William Conolly. The conflict between Conolly's followers and the faction headed in the Commons by St John Brodrick had caused difficulties for the Duke of Bolton in 1717–19 – among other things, wrecking his plans for a repeal of the sacramental test – and had rendered Grafton's position as lord lieutenant untenable. In 1720, the Stanhope–Sunderland ministry had determined to dismiss Midleton but had lost its nerve. To continue for any length of time with both factions in government was not sustainable. At some point, an English viceroy would have to take decisive action and restore clarity to management. As Walpole put it, the choice facing Carteret in Ireland was obvious: he would have to 'take his party, between the two great men there'.

Carteret arrived in Dublin in October 1724, well in advance of the time at which he would have to call a parliament, and set about trying to cool the rage against Wood's Halfpence. Outwardly, he acted to maintain the royal prerogative, persuading the Irish privy council to prosecute the printer of the fourth *Drapier's Letter*, but privately was more conciliatory, warning Swift against admitting authorship of the pamphlet, and urging the Cabinet in Whitehall to withdraw Wood's patent. He was equally cautious in tackling the question of political management. Unwilling to risk the wrong choice between Speaker and lord chancellor, he made no decisive move at all, attempting instead to keep himself and his administration above the squabbles of local politicians, and behaving towards the two rivals with equal friendliness, and with equal distance. The consequence was that, for a time, matters seemed so uncertain that he dare not recall the Irish Parliament, given the likelihood of continued factional infighting, spiced by popular outrage against the halfpence. Although this was a perilous course, it eventually paid off, and in retrospect might well be described as masterly inactivity. In the summer of 1725, both his problems were solved for him. One Gordian knot was severed when Midleton resigned the seals, taking his faction into open opposition; then, even more important, Walpole finally bowed to the inevitable, and agreed to recall Wood's patent.[64]

Carteret was thus able to summon an Irish Parliament in the winter of 1725–6, with some hope of success. The removal of the halfpence had secured his personal popularity, while Midleton's resignation, followed by the summary rejection by the viceroy of an offer from St John Brodrick to take over responsibility for parliamentary management, removed any ambiguity over which Irish political grouping enjoyed viceregal favour.[65] Conolly was now firmly established as the leader of the Castle interest in the Commons, the 'undertaker' for government business, with a key role in the Irish administration as one of the triumvirate of lords justices which substituted for the viceroy in the intervals between parliamentary sessions. Like some of his predecessors, Carteret took an active part himself in the business of parliamentary management, even to the extent of lobbying individual MPs, but he did this in support of the Speaker rather than in an attempt to create a separate 'Castle interest'. His famously gregarious and charming personality attracted a personal devotion that more than once proved crucial in important divisions.[66]

Although William Conolly's personal political history had been staunchly Whiggish, he had been able since 1715 to recruit former Tories, men like the Prime Serjeant Henry Singleton, revenue commissioner Marmaduke Coghill, and the future accountant-general Agmondisham Vesey (son of the archbishop of Tuam who had served as a lord justice in the controversial

---

64 Patrick McNally, 'Wood's Halfpence, Carteret, and the Government of Ireland, 1723–56', *Irish Historical Studies* 30 (1996–7), 354–76.

65 R. E. Burns, *Irish Parliamentary Politics in the Eighteenth Century*, 2 vols., Washington, DC: Catholic University of America Press, 1989–90, vol. I, p. 203.

66 McNally, 'Wood's Halfpence'. According to Bishop Robert Howard, Carteret had a 'rattle wit and humour to a great degree' (Robert to Hugh Howard, 25 Apr. 1730 (NLI, MS 38,598/6)).

Tory ministry of 1711–13).⁶⁷ The relatively broad-based nature of his 'Castle party' reflected a more general political process in Ireland after the Hanoverian succession, as 'party' divisions became blurred. The establishment of a Whig ascendancy in government, and the tarring of Tories with the Jacobite brush following the abortive rebellion of 1715–16, had resulted in a collapse of support for the Tory interest, as the more 'moderate' and more ambitious Irish Tories enlisted in government and became indistinguishable from Whig placemen. The remaining Tories were obliged to make common cause with discontented Whigs, which they could only do by focusing attention on issues of common concern: economic and constitutional grievances and alleged corruption in government, the staples of any 'country' or 'patriot' opposition.

The old Tory interest was not yet defunct, however, and seems still to have been identifiable in Parliament and the constituencies until 1727. Although operating in collaboration with discontented Whigs, these diehards constituted a separate group in George I's Parliament, with their own leaders. For a time, even the more accommodating Tories on the government side seem to have retained a residual sense of their historic identity.⁶⁸ In the localities, Tory loyalties and connections survived into the 1720s, even if they now adopted different factional labels.⁶⁹ In some borough corporations, there was even a revival: in Clonmel in County Tipperary, for example, where an intruding Whig faction was successfully resisted in 1722;⁷⁰ in the city of Limerick, whose governor, Major-General Thomas Pearce, himself a former Tory MP in England, made a bid for power in 1723–6, supported by Tory 'minions and favourites';⁷¹ and in Youghal in County Cork, where the 'town party' – that is to say, the Tories – succeeded in overturning Whig hegemony.⁷² Even in Galway Corporation, whose Tories had once been identified as crypto-Jacobite, even crypto-Catholic, and had been forcibly

---

67 *Hist. Ir. Parl.*, vol. III, pp. 442–5; vol. VI, pp. 276–7, 468–9.
68 Arthur Hill to Henry Boyle, 15 Apr. 1729 (PRONI, Shannon papers, D/2707/A/1/2/39).
69 D. W. Hayton, 'Voters, Patrons and Parties: Parliamentary Elections in Ireland, c. 1692–1727', in Clyve Jones, Philip Salmon and R. W. Davis (eds.), *Partisan Politics, Principle and Reform in Parliament and the Constituencies, 1689–1880: Essays in Memory of John A. Phillips*, Edinburgh: Edinburgh University Press, 2005, pp. 66–7.
70 W. P. Burke, *History of Clonmel*, Clonmel: Neil Harvey, 1907, pp. 116–17; *The Munster Combat, or The Invasion of the Moors...*, [Dublin, 1722].
71 D. A. Fleming, *Politics and Provincial People: Sligo and Limerick, 1691–1761*, Manchester: Manchester University Press, 2010, pp. 72–7.
72 T. C. Barnard, 'Considering the Inconsiderable: Electors, Patrons and Irish Elections 1659–1761', in D. W. Hayton (ed.), *The Irish Parliament in the Eighteenth Century: The Long Apprenticeship*, Edinburgh: Edinburgh University Press, 2001, pp. 118–19.

excluded from power by a specific Act of Parliament (4 Geo. I c. 15 [Ire.]), the leading families from the previous era, the Blakeneys, Eyres and Stauntons, gradually re-established themselves and by 1725 recovered control of the corporation.[73]

What is interesting about this rehabilitation is the extent to which Carteret's Irish administration was involved in promoting erstwhile Tory interests. In Limerick, Youghal and Galway, the Irish privy council intervened in 1725–6 to support local Tory factions, in the same way that the Tory ministry of 1711 had used its powers under the 'new rules' of 1672 to approve or disapprove the election of chief magistrates in borough corporations according to party complexion. At least some of the responsibility for this shift in the 1720s must lie with Speaker Conolly.[74] In Galway, he was himself admitted a freeman in 1722, alongside one of the Stauntons.[75] But a significant contribution was also made by Carteret, under whose aegis these decisions were taken, and who was, for example, responsible for appointing General Pearce to the governorship of Limerick.

Carteret's family background, on both sides, was staunchly Cavalier and High Church, and when he had made his appearance on the political stage, in the 'four last years' of Queen Anne's reign, his party allegiance had been unequivocally Tory, although he had been situated on the 'Hanoverian' wing of the party. After 1714, he moved across to support successive Whig administrations, but did not shake off the effects of his upbringing, and those in Ireland who still possessed Tory sympathies, or at least retained a visceral aversion to politicians parading their Whiggish credentials, welcomed his appointment as likely to bring better times. As we have seen, Swift himself was on warm personal terms with Carteret, frequented Dublin Castle, and sought to use whatever influence he possessed with the lord lieutenant to assist his own clerical friends. Two did receive preferment soon after Carteret's arrival: Thomas Sheridan was made a viceregal chaplain, and given a benefice at Rincurran in County Cork;[76] and the young James

73 Galway Corporation Archives, minute book E (National University of Ireland, Galway, Hardiman Lib.), pp. 75–155.
74 Barnard, 'Considering the Inconsiderable', p. 118.
75 Galway Corporation Archives, minute book E (National University of Ireland, Galway, Hardiman Lib.), p. 88; John Staunton to Anne Donnellan, 15 Feb. 1731[/2] (BL, Wentworth papers, Add. MS 22228, fo. 349).
76 Rincurran was scarcely a plum. The parish church had been demolished in 1690 and the stones used to repair the Charles Fort at Kinsale. Not long before Sheridan's appointment, an appeal had been made to government for financial assistance with restoration, on the grounds that the congregation consisted only of 'poor fishermen' (William Bolton to Archbishop King, [c. 1723] (TCD, Lyons collection, MS 1995–2008/2045)).

Stopford, Knightley Chetwode's brother-in-law and himself the nephew of a former Tory MP, became vicar of Finglas, north of Dublin.[77] This was part of what had seemed at first to be a broader change in the direction of ecclesiastical patronage, manifested most strikingly in the promotion of a pair of once-notorious High Churchmen: William Perceval, prolocutor of the lower house of the Irish convocation in 1713, who received the lucrative Dublin rectory of St Michan's to hold alongside his much less valuable deanery of Emly; and the firebrand preacher Francis Higgins, sometime associate of Dr Sacheverell, who in the twilight of his career was made archdeacon of Cashel.[78]

This was, however, a false dawn for the High Church party. Wild rumours that high-flying Tory lawyers like Richard Nutley would be given places on the Irish bench and privy council came to nothing,[79] while episcopal promotions were still confined to Whiggish clergy, often sent over from England. Such lingering Tory sympathies as Carteret may have entertained were insufficient to counter the recommendations of the primate (archbishop of Armagh), Hugh Boulter – himself an English import – or Speaker Conolly, not to mention the powerful influence exerted in England by 'Walpole's pope', Bishop Edmund Gibson of London. Furthermore, Sheridan's appointment demonstrated the danger of indulging men with strong Tory prejudices and limited self-restraint. When Sheridan tactlessly preached a High Church sermon in Cork in August 1725, on the anniversary of George I's accession, Carteret faced a chorus of complaint, and was obliged to remove him from the list of chaplains and banish him from the viceregal court.[80] It is therefore unlikely that Carteret had a hand in the election of another of Swift's friends, Patrick Delany, as chancellor of Christ Church, Dublin, by the cathedral chapter in 1728. In any case, this was not a straightforward matter, since there were advantages to government in getting such a 'rank Tory' away from the undergraduates at Trinity, where Delany was considered by Primate Boulter to be a bad influence.[81]

---

77 Technically, the vicarage at Finglas was in the nomination of the Archbishop of Dublin. One of Stopford's predecessors in the incumbency was the poet Thomas Parnell (1679–1718), preferred by Archbishop King in 1716, also on Swift's recommendation (*DIB*).
78 Archbishop Boulter to Duke of Newcastle, 12 Oct. 1725 (*Boulter Letters*, vol. I, pp. 39–40).
79 Knightley Chetwode to ——, 17 May 1726 (NLI, MS 47,891/1); Boulter to Carteret, 14 May, 16 June 1726 (*Boulter Letters*, vol. I, pp. 57–8, 67).
80 Ehrenpreis, vol. III, pp. 362–3.
81 Boulter to Archbishop Wake, 8 Dec. 1725 (*Boulter Letters*, vol. I, pp. 47–8).

Swift's personal relationship with Carteret does not seem to have been seriously damaged by the way in which the viceroy rowed back on his early patronage of High Churchmen, although trust may have been compromised to some extent. When Delany appealed for advancement to the lord lieutenant in a published poem in December 1729, Swift responded quickly with his own verse *Epistle upon an Epistle*, which chided Delany for vainly presuming as an Irishman to apply for favour to an English governor. The satire was ambiguous, to say the least: Lord Chancellor Wyndham, for one, found it impossible to decide whether the piece was intended as a 'compliment' or a 'libel' on the lord lieutenant.[82] A few months afterwards appeared Swift's prose *Vindication* of Carteret, 'from the charge of favouring none but Tories, High-Churchmen and Jacobites'.[83] The tone was ironical, since by this time the accusation could not have been taken seriously. Swift's primary objective, however, was neither to defend the lord lieutenant against the supposed outrage of Whig critics, nor to criticise him for failing in the duties of friendship, but to illustrate the fatuity of outdated sloganising by self-proclaimed Whigs, whose accusations of Tory conspiracies were shown to be not only baseless but absurd.[84]

The 1727 general election was the last flourish of Irish Toryism. After George I's death, Lord Anglesey was reported to have addressed a gathering of Tories in Dublin as to their future political strategy, and in the ensuing election Tory interests were active in several counties, but the Tories did not put up a candidate for the Speakership in November, when Conolly was returned unopposed.[85] The issues that divided the members of the new Parliament arose from 'patriotic' rather than party concerns: government interference with the process of legislation; the management of the Irish public revenue and national debt; and, increasingly, the state of the Irish economy. The political 'structure' of the Irish House of Commons also became more fluid, especially with the dissolution of the Brodrick faction in 1728 following the deaths, in quick succession, of St John Brodrick and his father Lord Midleton.[86] There was a 'Castle party', presided over by

---

82 Ehrenpreis, vol. III, pp. 646–50; Wyndham to Philip Yorke, 7 Feb. 1729[/30] (BL, Hardwicke papers, Add. MS 35585, fos. 110–11).
83 Below, pp. 191–217.
84 Davis, vol. XII, p. xxvii; J. S. Malek, 'Swift's "Vindication of Lord Carteret": Authorial Intention and Historical Context', *Rocky Mountain Review of Language and Literature* 29 (1975), 10–23.
85 Hayton, *Ruling Ireland*, p. 122; Edward Maurice to Bishop Sir Thomas Vesey of Ossory, 20 Sept. 1727 (NLI, De Vesci papers, MS 38,869/2).
86 Burns, *Irish Parliamentary Politics*, vol. I, p. 258.

Conolly and his lieutenants, which was said to be composed of various 'clans', and on the other side shifting groups of 'patriots' which included family-based 'connections' as well as professional lawyer-politicians out of office and country gentlemen of substantial means and independent opinions. It was even possible for the new members in 1727, young men with high ideals, or at least high self-esteem, to band together in a group nicknamed 'toopees' after the new style of hairpiece that was the height of fashion.[87] The wig had replaced Whiggism as a distinguishing mark of political allegiance.

This political environment proved surprisingly comfortable for Carteret and his parliamentary undertakers, despite the sudden loss of William Conolly, the government's principal parliamentary 'undertaker', who died shortly after the beginning of the 1729–30 parliamentary session. Conolly's successor in the Speakership, and in the leadership of the government forces in the Commons, was his former principal lieutenant, Sir Ralph Gore, who, with the assistance of close allies like Coghill, and the backing of the lord lieutenant, was able to mobilise the old Castle party with remarkable success. Gore was even able to secure a substantial majority to pass a money bill that the British privy council had altered, normally the reddest of red rags to Irish MPs. Carteret had been furious at this conciliar intervention and had told the British secretary of state, the Duke of Newcastle, that he could not guarantee 'to bring [the Commons] to temper again'. But in fact the bill was passed by a two-to-one majority.[88] Carteret and Gore were also able to take advantage of some hints of optimism in the popular mood concerning the Irish economy, following a much improved harvest. They succeeded in defusing the 'patriotic' enthusiasm that characterised the early stages of the session[89] by accepting a back-bench initiative to tax the remuneration paid to absentee office-holders and pensioners, and by giving strong government support to a portmanteau bill for the improvement of river navigation, the expansion of tillage and the draining of bogs.[90]

This was not simply a matter of making concessions in order to pacify vociferous back-benchers. Gore himself, and a number of other leading figures in the Castle party, could boast a long-standing interest in the

---

87 Edward Cooke to [Sir Richard Cox], 22 Feb. 1727[/8] (NLI, Fownes papers, MS 8,802/11).
88 Burns, *Irish Parliamentary Politics*, vol. I, pp. 256–7.
89 Boulter to Newcastle, 23 Oct. 1729 (*Boulter Letters*, vol. I, pp. 264–5); Marmaduke Coghill to Edward Southwell, 23 Oct. 1729 (*Coghill Letters*, pp. 74–5).
90 Burns, *Irish Parliamentary Politics*, vol. I, pp. 253–6; Coghill to Southwell, 3 Jan. 1729[/30] (*Coghill Letters*, pp. 83–4); Carteret to same, 8, 28 Jan. 1729/30 (BL, Southwell papers, Add. MS 38016, fos. 19, 21).

'improvement' of Ireland, and a record of having drafted and advocated legislative initiatives to this end.[91] When Speaker Conolly had fallen ill in 1728 and his retirement from active politics seemed inevitable, there had been concern among his colleagues that whoever should replace him – as 'undertaker' and lord justice – would have to be just as fervently committed as he had been to advancing Irish national interests.[92] At Conolly's funeral in 1729, his widow ordered that 700 Irish linen scarves should be distributed among the mourners, in order to demonstrate publicly the deceased Speaker's support for Irish manufacture.[93] Gore proved equally conscientious in defending his country's interests, thwarting plans by fellow lords justices for a reform of the coinage that he felt was inappropriate and would rightly be unpopular. This brought him into difficulties with English colleagues on the commission who, as his friend Marmaduke Coghill observed, neither knew nor cared for Ireland as much as he did.[94] A few years earlier, Swift had satirised this particular variety of patriotism in the Drapier's *Letter to the Whole People of Ireland*, when he parodied the arguments that Castle politicians would use to convince Irish MPs to accept Wood's Halfpence. Among other suggestions, 'It might, perhaps, have been hinted... that Gentlemen ought to consider, whether it were prudent or safe to disgust England: They would be desired to think of some good Bills for encouraging of Trade, and setting the Poor to work.'[95] By 1730, the observation was still accurate, but the satire had lost some of its edge.

4   The Survival and Revival of 'Popery'

Historians have long debated whether the 'penal laws' enacted between 1695 and 1709 (or to give them their contemporary title, the 'popery laws') were seriously intended to extirpate Roman Catholicism from Ireland, or were directed merely towards the reinforcement of the Protestant monopoly of

---

91 D. W. Hayton, '"Paltry Underlings of State"? The Character and Aspirations of the "Castle" Party, 1715–32', in Claude Rawson (ed.), *Politics and Literature in England and Ireland in the Age of Swift*, Cambridge: Cambridge University Press, 2010, pp. 234–8.
92 Coghill to Edward Southwell, 13 June 1728 (*Coghill Letters*, p. 53); same to Edward Southwell, jr, 22 Feb. 1732[/3] (ibid., p. 120).
93 Francis Burton to Jane Bonnell, 19 Nov. 1729 (NLI, Smythe of Barbavilla papers, MS 41,579/9); Walsh, *Making of the Irish Protestant Ascendancy*, pp. 194–5.
94 Coghill to Edward Southwell, jr, 31 Mar. 1733 (*Coghill Letters*, p. 124).
95 Davis, vol. X, p. 60. See also the *Humble Address to Both Houses of Parliament*, with its reference to 'certain bold UNDERTAKERS of weak Judgment, and strong Ambition; who think to find their Accounts in the Ruin of the Nation, by securing or advancing themselves' (ibid., p. 120) and its further condemnation of corrupt office-holders (ibid., pp. 120–1).

property and office. Whatever the intention, there can be little doubt that, had these laws been put fully into operation, the surviving Catholic landowning, professional and commercial classes would have been drastically attenuated and the numbers of Catholic priests and religious in Ireland would have declined almost to the point of extinction. Neither eventuality had come to pass. True, the incentives to apostasy for the propertied were considerable: if they conformed to the established church, Catholics could maintain through primogeniture the integrity of landed estates which otherwise would have to be divided among all the father's children; they could purchase freehold land; could qualify for crown and municipal office; and could practise the profession of the law.[96] Such potential advantages produced a substantial and increasing flow of converts: by 1710, 117 names were entered on the so-called 'convert rolls'; by 1720, a further 150; and between 1721 and 1730, another 365.[97] But there were other ways to protect estates – principally by the collusion of friendly Protestants – and in any case the simple evidence of the convert rolls was not particularly comforting to those anxious members of the Ascendancy class who doubted the sincerity of convenient conversions, seeing this as yet another ruse by Catholic landed families to preserve their estates. In 1731, an Irish bill 'for the more effectual obliging converts and guardians to educate children in the Protestant religion' only failed because of scruples in the British privy council, and two years later another, 'to prevent persons converted from the popish to the Protestant religion and married to popish wives, from acting as justices of the peace', did reach the statute book (as 7 Geo. II c. 6).

By lumping together these 'new converts' with the surviving Catholic landed proprietors and merchants, Protestant commentators alarmed themselves with the nightmare of a resurgent Catholic interest. This anxiety was particularly obvious at general elections. By the Popery Act of 1704 (2 Anne c. 6 [Ire.]), voters at parliamentary elections in Ireland could be required to take an oath abjuring the Jacobite Pretender, which of course no self-respecting Catholic would do. But whether or not the oath was applied depended on the returning officer, and there were many instances of Catholics being reported as voting, especially in counties where Protestant freeholders were thin on the ground and candidates were desperate

---

96 Charles Ivar McGrath, 'The Provisions for Conversion in the Penal Laws, 1695–1750', in Michael Brown *et al.* (eds.), *Converts and Conversion in Ireland, 1650–1850*, Dublin: Four Courts Press, 2005, pp. 35–59.

97 T. P. Power, 'Converts', in Power and Kevin Whelan (eds.), *Endurance and Emergence: Catholics in Ireland in the Eighteenth Century*, Blackrock, Co. Dublin: Irish Academic Press, 1990, p. 102.

to muster support wherever they could. In 1715, the Irish Parliament had tried to tighten up the law by requiring the abjuration to be taken at least six months beforehand. But this does not seem to have worked. Election petitions commonly complained that 'papist' votes had been allowed, contrary to law, or that a crypto-Catholic interest, consisting predominantly of 'new converts', had played a sinister part in the defeat of staunch Protestant candidates. The chorus of protest reached a climax after the 1727 general election when a further bill was passed specifically disfranchising Catholics.[98]

The persistence of a Catholic or crypto-Catholic electoral interest was, however, only one among many causes of Protestant anxiety. According to Archbishop Boulter of Armagh, the legal profession in Ireland was dominated by new converts, and in many cases, he reported, there would be a Catholic wife at home 'who has mass said in the family and the children are brought up papists'.[99] This was undoubtedly an exaggeration, but recent research has uncovered a network of Irish Catholic lawyers active in England who seem to have had strong connections in Ireland;[100] and, in any case, popular belief was as important as, if not more important than, the reality. There were also enough surviving Catholic landowners to band together in 1727, under the leadership of Lord Delvin, to make an address of loyalty to King George II, in the hope of establishing the grounds for being relieved of some of their legal disabilities.[101] The prospect of any such weakening of the penal laws naturally frightened Protestant landowners: witness the panicky reaction in 1735 to reports that the Catholic heir to the earldom of Clancarty intended to petition the Westminster Parliament for the restitution of family property forfeited after the Jacobite war, on the grounds that the forfeiting earl had only been tenant for life.[102]

Equally important was the growing perception among Protestants that the penal laws had failed to weaken, let alone destroy, the organisation of the Catholic church in Ireland. Theoretically, the combined effects of the legislation passed between 1697 and 1709 should have been sufficient

---

98 J. G. Simms, 'Historical Revision: X. Irish Catholics and the Parliamentary Franchise, 1692–1728', *Irish Historical Studies* 12 (1960–1), 35–6.
99 Boulter to Newcastle, 7 Mar. 1727[/8] (*Boulter Letters*, vol. I, p. 182).
100 John Bergin, 'The Irish Catholic Interest at the London Inns of Court, 1674–1800', *ECI* 24 (2009), 36–61.
101 Ian McBride, 'Catholic Politics in the Penal Era: Father Sylvester Lloyd and the Delvin Address of 1727', in John Bergin *et al.* (eds.), *New Perspectives on the Penal Laws*, *ECI* special issue, 1 (2011), pp. 115–48.
102 Coghill to Edward Southwell, jr, 2, 18 Dec. 1735 (*Coghill Letters*, pp. 178, 179).

to limit the numbers of Catholic clergy to the 1,100 secular (or parochial) priests who had been prepared to register under the terms of the 1704 Popery Act and had given securities for their 'good behaviour', and should also have prevented further recruitment of resident priests. With bishops banished and Catholics who had been educated abroad prevented by law from returning to Ireland, there should have been no newly ordained priests in the country. Yet, twenty years later, Catholic priests were still highly visible, especially in towns, and not just those who were registered, such as the Dubliner Cornelius Nary, who gave himself a public profile through published works that brought him into direct conflict with Church of Ireland bishops.[103] The heyday of 'priest-hunting' was long past, when bishops and regulars had been exposed by informers and brought before magistrates, and the general pattern was one of a peaceful, if generally clandestine, existence. Swift's friend, Archbishop King of Dublin, was deeply alarmed at what he described as 'the swarm of vermin of popish priests that overspread the kingdom'.[104] He was convinced that there were more Catholic than Protestant bishops in Ireland 'and twice (at least) as many priests', and ascribed this state of affairs to the unwillingness of magistrates to put the laws into effect, either because as individuals they were intimidated by fear of violent reprisals, or because they were in general discouraged by a government unwilling to offend its Catholic allies in Europe.[105] His fellow bishops were sufficiently concerned to prompt the Irish House of Lords in 1731 to order an inquiry into the state of 'popery' that revealed the presence of 1,445 secular priests and 254 friars (the latter figure almost certainly a substantial understatement).[106]

Churchmen had also to admit that their own attempts at proselytising had largely failed. Certainly, there were instances of Catholics being persuaded to convert, as distinct from those who were induced to conform, and these were usually given considerable publicity, but they were relatively few. The principal initiatives designed to encourage conversions through education had not been successful. A scheme to print translations into the Irish language of the New Testament, the Book of Common Prayer and an Anglican

---

103 Patrick Fagan, *Dublin's Turbulent Priest: Cornelius Nary, 1658–1738*, Dublin: Royal Irish Academy, 1991.
104 King to Mr Radcliff, 30 Sept. 1725 (TCD, King letterbooks, MS 750/8, p. 29).
105 King to Carteret, 22 June 1727 (ibid., p. 213); to Archbishop Wake of Canterbury, 12 July 1727 (ibid., pp. 231–3).
106 Gerard O'Brien (ed.), *Catholic Ireland in the Eighteenth Century: Collected Essays of Maureen Wall*, Dublin: Geography Publications, 1989, pp. 35–50; S. J. Connolly, *Religion, Law and Power: The Making of Protestant Ireland 1660–1760*, Oxford: Clarendon Press, 1992, pp. 150–1.

catechism, as an aid to proselytising in schools or parishes, had foundered on the general unavailability of Irish-speaking clergy, and what was in essence factional opposition within the Irish convocation.[107] Archbishop King evidently supported the proposal, which was enough to determine those whose ecclesiastical politics were the reverse of King's Low Churchmanship to damn the project along with its patron.[108] The High Churchmen favoured an alternative, the establishment of schools, usually with private financial endowments, to teach Catholic children the Protestant faith through the medium of English. Swift's own position in this debate is unclear. He may have followed Archbishop King in arguing for attempts to proselytise the natives in their own tongue, for he had friends, like the clergyman and fellow of Trinity, Anthony Raymond, who were interested in the Irish language (though Swift's own attitude to the language was at best ambivalent).[109] He may also have shared some of King's scepticism of lay enthusiasts though he subsequently gave charity schools his 'qualified support', provided that they had 'good Foundation and rents to support them'.[110] In any case, despite a substantial degree of philanthropic investment from pious churchmen and women, the charity schools established between c. 1695 and c. 1725 were ultimately unsuccessful. One problem lay in the fact that they were not directed at the conversion of Catholics so much as the recovery of backsliding Protestants; another weakness was the lack of firm direction. Even though these schools were gathered under the umbrella of a 'Society for Promoting Christian Knowledge in Ireland by the Method of Charity Schools', connected with the Society for Promoting Christian Knowledge

---

107 T. C. Barnard, 'Protestants and the Irish Language, c. 1675–1725', *Journal of Ecclesiastical History* 44 (1993), 261–5.

108 Sir Charles S. King, *A Great Archbishop of Dublin William King D.D...*, London: Longmans, Green and Co., 1906, pp. 291–8; S. J. Connolly, 'Reformers and Highflyers: The Post-Revolution Church', in Alan Ford, James McGuire and Kenneth Milne (eds.), *As by Law Established: The Church of Ireland since the Reformation*, Dublin: Lilliput Press, 1995, pp. 163–4; D. W. Hayton, 'The High Church Party in the Irish Convocation, 1703–13', *Münster* (1998), p. 132.

109 Andrew Carpenter and Alan Harrison, 'Swift's "O'Rourke's Feast" and Sheridan's "Letter": Early Transcripts by Anthony Raymond', *Münster* (1985), pp. 27–46; Alan Harrison, *The Dean's Friend: Anthony Raymond (1675–1726), Jonathan Swift and the Irish Language*, Dublin: Éamonn de Burca, 1999; D. W. Hayton, 'Did Protestantism Fail in Early Eighteenth-Century Ireland? Charity Schools and the Enterprise of Religious and Social Reformation, c. 1690–1730', in Ford et al. (eds.), *As by Law Established*, pp. 171, 182. See also below, p. 125.

110 *Causes of the Wretched Condition of Ireland* (Davis, vol. IX, pp. 202–5); Claude Rawson, *Order from Confusion Sprung: Studies in Eighteenth-Century Literature from Swift to Cowper*, London: George Allen & Unwin, 1985, pp. 122–3.

(SPCK) in England, they were still very much local and personal initiatives. And by the late 1720s not only were individual foundations withering, but the central organisation, such as it was, had ceased to function.[111]

It is no surprise, therefore, to find that by c. 1730 Irish Protestants were displaying an uneasy interest in relative demography (a point picked up in *A Modest Proposal*).[112] In 1732, a pamphlet was published in Dublin under the title *Scheme of the Proportions which the Protestants of Ireland may probably bear to the Papists; Humbly Offer'd to the Public*. Tellingly, the preamble began with the words, 'As popery is of late become the subject of most conversations'. The author sought to bring up to date Sir William Petty's calculations from 1672, using evidence from a variety of sources, and concluded that Catholics still comprised roughly 70 per cent of the inhabitants of Ireland. Elsewhere, unsystematic estimates put the proportion at between 80 and 90 per cent.[113] But there was also more positive news. In 1732, the collectors of the hearth tax were required to state the number of Catholic and Protestant families in their districts. The results were printed and analysed in a pamphlet published four years later by David Bindon, who used them (together with the bills of mortality) to argue that Ireland was now a much more Protestant country than it had been in Petty's time, the proportion of Catholics to Protestants having sunk below three to one. Indeed, in Ulster, and in some towns, especially Dublin, Protestants were now, he stated, in a solid majority. Ostensibly, Bindon wrote 'for the satisfaction of those who are curious in political arithmetic', but he also intended to reassure pessimists about Ireland's capacity for economic development.[114]

Obsessive concern over the size of the Catholic population was symptomatic of a more visceral emotion than the anxiety of Protestant proprietors over the retention of their lands. Reactions to reports of popular violence, whether the actions of the Dublin mob (represented in the newspaper press, rightly or wrongly, as predominantly Catholic),[115] or the rural brigandage of 'rapparees', called to mind images of the ancient savagery of the native Irish, which, encouraged by the 'atrocity' literature surrounding the 1641

---

111 Hayton, 'Did Protestantism Fail?', pp. 166–86.
112 See below, p. 154.
113 Boulter to Archbishop Wake, 13 Feb. 1727[/8] (*Boulter Letters*, vol. I, p. 169); to Newcastle, c. 4 Dec. 1731 (vol. II, p. 57); Archbishop King to Wake, 12 July 1727 (TCD, King letterbooks, MS 750/8).
114 David Bindon, *An Abstract of the Number of Protestant and Popish Families in the Several Counties and Provinces of Ireland, Taken from the Returns made by the Hearthmoney Collectors...*, Dublin, 1736.
115 Fagan, 'Dublin Catholic Mob', 133–42.

rebellion, formed a persistent feature of the mental landscape of the Irish Protestant ascendancy.

Atavistic fears of the violent hostility of the 'native Irish' helped preserve a belief in the potential danger from Jacobitism despite all evidence to the contrary. The Pretender and his advisers did not exhibit any interest in Ireland after 1714, and there were no stirrings of rebellion in 1715 or 1719 when Jacobites in Scotland rose. But Irish Protestants were easily aroused by reports of Jacobite activity or interest in Ireland. The decision by the Walpole administration to permit the French to recruit soldiers in Ireland in 1730 touched a raw nerve, especially in the Blackwater valley in Counties Cork and Waterford, where the agents went to work. Swift himself intervened in the public debate on this issue, in the *Answer to the Craftsman*, though with characteristic irony, arguing that this was one more example of the draining away of Ireland's natural resources, and taking the episode as a point of departure for yet another discussion of the fundamental issue of Anglo-Irish trading relations. The response of his fellow Irish Protestants was, however, more straightforward and predictable. There was much speculation about the real intentions of the recruiters and the connections that were being established between the local Catholic population and the exiled Stuart court. The fact that the French officers involved were all of Irish extraction did not help, and after considerable local agitation the licence was revoked.[116] But the furore did not die down. There were further reports in 1732 and 1734 of Catholics being enlisted in the south-west, in Counties Kerry and Clare, and of the arrest of recruiting officers. As Under-Secretary Thomas Tickell wrote, this offence was perceived to be 'so very dangerous to the liberty of the subject, and fills the Protestants with so reasonable a terror of being forced out of their country'.[117]

The resurgence of anti-popery can be seen in the way in which the attention of the Irish Parliament became once again focused on the Catholic issue, producing a flurry of new bills.[118] In the session of 1727–8, besides

116 L. M. Cullen, 'The Blackwater Catholics and County Cork Society and Politics in the Eighteenth Century', in Patrick Flanagan and C. G. Buttimer (eds.), *Cork: History and Society*, Dublin: Geography Publications, 1993, pp. 560–1; Éamonn Ó Ciardha, *Ireland and the Jacobite Cause, 1685–1766: A Fatal Attachment*, Dublin: Four Courts Press, 2002, pp. 255–60; Dickson, *Old World Colony*, pp. 266–7.
117 Thomas Tickell to Walter Cary, 25 Nov. 1732 (PRONI, Wilmot papers, T/3019/107); lords justices to Duke of Dorset, 20 Dec. 1732 (ibid., T/3019/110), Duke of Newcastle to same, 17 May 1734 (ibid., T/3019/143).
118 James Kelly, 'Sustaining a Confessional State: The Irish Parliament and Catholicism', in Hayton *et al.* (eds.), *Eighteenth-Century Composite State*, pp. 59–61. For an attempt to explain the phenomenon, see Lord Chancellor Wyndham to Philip Yorke, 5 Jan. 1731[/2] (BL, Add. MS 35585, fos.147–8).

the Elections Act, a bill was passed to prevent Catholics acting as solicitors (1 Geo. II c. 20); another, 'to prevent Protestants intermarrying with papists', was rejected by the Irish privy council; and leave was given for heads of a bill 'to more effectually provide for the guardianship of Popish minors, and to prevent their being bred papists', which in the event was not introduced. In 1729, amidst a plethora of legislative initiatives concerned to deal with the effects of the economic crisis, Bishop Lambert of Meath failed in an attempt to secure a bill 'for better securing the Protestant religion and interest of this kingdom, against the further attempts of the papists', and in 1731/2 there were unsuccessful proposals to tighten up the statutes for the registration of priests, the banishment of regulars, the disarming of Catholics, and the exclusion of Catholics from the legal profession, and to enforce the obligation on converts to bring up their children as Protestants. The solicitors' bill was successfully reintroduced in the following session (7 Geo. II c. 5), and a further act was passed to prevent any convert who kept a popish wife, or educated his children as Catholics, from acting as a justice of the peace (7 Geo. II c. 6).

The same anxieties lay behind a revival of interest in schemes for the conversion of the native Irish by means of education, with the grant in 1733 of a royal charter for an 'incorporated society in Dublin for promoting English Protestant schools in Ireland'. These 'charter schools' grew out of the charity school movement, but their primary purpose was to proselytise; indeed, it was agreed that the new society should begin by establishing a school in each province in a 'very popish and extended parish'.[119] In order to attract investment, the charter schools, like their predecessors, emphasised training in useful skills such as spinning and weaving, and in this way they have been linked to the contemporary campaign for economic improvement, and in particular to the Dublin Society, several of whose members were involved in the early work of the 'incorporated society'. But the original impulse had come from the clergy, from Archbishop Boulter of Armagh and Bishop Maule of Cloyne, and the original stimulus had been the church's insecurity in the face of a resilient Catholicism.

5 The Enemy Inside the Gates: Protestant Dissent

For men of Swift's cast of mind, Protestant Dissent offered an equal – if not a greater – threat to the maintenance of the established church in the decades following the Williamite settlement. Although there were substantial

---

119 Kenneth Milne, *The Irish Charter Schools 1730–1830*, Dublin: Four Courts Press, 1997, p. 24.

Dissenting communities (Independents, Baptists and Quakers) in Dublin and other major port towns in the south, attention focused on Ulster, where the Presbyterian community was reinforced by extensive immigration from Scotland during the 1690s. However unrealistic it may seem to modern eyes, Churchmen in Ireland genuinely imagined the possibility of a Presbyterian coup similar to the Scottish ecclesiastical revolution of 1689, which had abolished episcopacy and purged the parochial ministry. 'High Church' controversialists inveighed against the religious and social practices of Presbyterians, who were accused of entrenching on the corporate privileges of the church, and conspiring to expand their influence beyond Ulster. In the absence of a legal toleration, church authorities exerted their legal powers to curb Dissent, summoning Presbyterians to ecclesiastical courts on various charges, including fornication if they had been married by their own minister and not in the parish church. Then, in 1704, an Irish statute imposed a sacramental test on holders of crown and municipal office, designed to exclude Dissenters by obliging them to take communion in the established church. Ulster Presbyterians, unlike their English counterparts, refused to compromise by conforming 'occasionally', and in consequence Presbyterian strongholds like the corporations of Belfast and Derry fell to Anglican domination. The test then became a focus of political debate, as Presbyterians concentrated their energies on arguing for repeal, going over the heads of Irish MPs to sympathetic Whig politicians in London.

By the mid-1720s, the anxiety that had once seized Irish churchmen over the expanding ambitions of the Presbyterians in the north was diminishing. To all intents and purposes, the General Synod of Ulster had dropped its campaign for repeal of the test after the failure of an attempt in 1719, engineered by the then lord lieutenant, the Duke of Bolton, at the behest of the Whig ministry in England. Bolton had consulted his parliamentary advisers and been convinced of the likelihood of overwhelming opposition in the Irish House of Commons.[120] The broader context was also more encouraging. Not only had the inrush of Presbyterian immigrants from the west of Scotland in the 1690s proved a temporary phenomenon, but in the late 1710s the demographic balance had tilted in the opposite direction, as distress propelled the first wave of emigration from Ulster to north America, a process that would be repeated in 1728–9. More insidiously, the class of Presbyterian landlords which had once provided political leadership was thinning out, through a gradual and apparently inexorable process of

---

120 Hayton, *Ruling Ireland*, pp. 224–6.

induced conformity to the established church. The doctrinal divisions which increasingly plagued Presbyterianism also made Protestant Dissent as a whole seem less coherent and formidable. In particular, the controversy over the question of ministerial subscription to the Westminster Confession gave rise to prolonged debates in the General Synod and in the press, and eventually resulted in some congregations of non-subscribers splintering off to form the semi-independent Presbytery of Antrim.

There were, however, still reasons why churchmen should have remained on the watch. Although the subject of the test was not even raised for over a decade after 1719, pressure was maintained for statutory relief in relation to other supposed injustices. In 1719, the Irish Parliament passed a Toleration Act to enable Dissenters to qualify themselves for exemption from the penalties prescribed by the Elizabethan Act of Uniformity for non-attendance at a parish church, and to enable their ministers to avoid prosecution for celebrating the Lord's Supper.[121] Then, in the Irish parliamentary session of 1723–4, an unsuccessful attempt was made to settle the vexed question of the validity of marriages contracted outside the established church.[122] The resumption of Presbyterian emigration to north America prompted a government inquiry into this and other similar grievances, which were cited by spokesmen for the Dissenters themselves as reasons for the general exodus of their brethren from Egyptian captivity at home.[123] It was not obvious to Swift and his contemporaries that Presbyterian political influence had waned sharply: there was a tendency to exaggerate the influence of Dissenting electoral interests, among freeholders in counties like Antrim and Monaghan, and in some corporations outside Ulster (notably in Dublin). With more justification, those who were anxious about the security of the test continued to suspect the worst of English Whig ministers. There was thus no expression of surprise in Ireland when Walpole relaunched the forlorn hope of the repeal of the test in 1731. The prime minister's intention was probably to convince English Dissenting deputies of his sincerity in their cause, but he may have had the subsidiary objective of embarrassing a political enemy, the Duke of Dorset, whom he had sent over to Dublin as viceroy.[124] As in 1719, Dorset was advised by parliamentary managers that the Irish Parliament would not accept repeal and abandoned the idea. Two years later, he was asked to try

---

121 J. C. Beckett, *Protestant Dissent in Ireland 1687–1780*, London: Faber & Faber, 1948, ch. 7; Connolly, *Religion, Law and Power*, pp. 165–6.
122 Beckett, *Protestant Dissent*, p. 121.
123 Ibid., p. 122.
124 Hayton, *Ruling Ireland*, pp. 189–90, 223–4, 258–63.

again, and again drew back in the face of opposition.[125] In the meantime, another 'paper war' had broken out in Dublin over the issue, with Swift taking a prominent part. The urgency of this public debate demonstrates the extent of continuing fear for the maintenance of Anglican privilege, despite the evident decline in the political strength of the Dissenting community, and the repeated reassurance of parliamentary backing for the status quo.

6 An Uncertain Marriage: Church and State; Parson and Squire

The nature of the 'confessional state' in eighteenth-century Ireland presumed an identity of interest between the Protestant landlord class and the established church. However, the involvement of the clergy in the economy and governance of the kingdom always created the potential for friction. As a major proprietor, the church could influence the pattern of land use and the working of the land market through the detail of sales and leases. Financial exactions — not only tithes on agricultural produce but the rates collected by the parish vestry and the 'small dues' or 'book money' required by the parish incumbent for the performance of baptisms, marriages and burials — also bore heavily on tenants and reduced their capacity to pay rent. In terms of government and politics, the clergy were active as justices of the peace and as voters in parliamentary elections, while the bishops were a significant force in the House of Lords and in government, the primate (archbishop of Armagh) customarily serving on the commission of lords justices. When the exertion of clerical influence, either locally or nationally, proved controversial, this could easily result in resentment at the pretensions of the clergy and suspicion of their motives.

Swift (and he was not alone) tended to regard criticism of ecclesiastical privilege or jurisdiction as a manifestation of anticlerical prejudice. But this was an over-reaction. Only a few Irish writers condemned 'priestcraft' in the manner of contemporary English radicals. Certainly, the overfed parson was an easy target for humour in popular literature, and in some Irish political salons mockery of the clergy may have been commonplace: at Speaker Conolly's house parties, for example, one aspiring politician sought to ingratiate himself by telling 'ill stories of bishops and clergymen'.[126] But the notion of a conflict of interests between secular and clerical estates should not be

---

125 Ibid., pp. 190–1, 258–62.
126 Mary Jones to Jane Bonnell, 13 Jan. [?1727] (NLI, Smythe of Barbavilla papers, MS 41,577/1).

over-emphasised. These were not discrete social groups. Most clergymen – at least those of Irish parentage and education – shared the social background and attitudes of the gentry. The parson was on a social level with the squire, and in remote parts of the country his presence was considered essential to agreeable social intercourse (a point Swift himself made at various times in his own work).[127] Nor, despite the existence of a few clerical dynasties (such as the Synges or Veseys) did the clergy form a separate caste.[128] As Swift informed Carteret in 1725: 'There is hardly a gentleman in the nation, who hath not a near alliance with some of that body [the clergy]; and most of them [that] have sons, usually breed one to the church.'[129] The alienation of ecclesiastical property into lay hands – 'impropriation' – which affected advowsons (the right of appointment to a cure of souls), glebe land and tithes, also created a class of proprietors who stood to lose income and patronage if the position of the established church were to be altered.

During the 'age of party' in Ireland – roughly speaking, the reign of Queen Anne – the clergy derived obvious political benefits from the public attachment of the Tories to the interests of the Church of Ireland. After 1714, however, not only did the Tory party decline, but the church itself became attached to unpopular causes. The intrusion of bishops from England, like Hugh Boulter of Armagh, with the express purpose of defending the interests of imperial government in council and Parliament, identified the hierarchy with ministerial rather than national interests. Nor was the survival of a vocal 'Irish' party in the episcopate of much help, since gossip focused on the injustices done to these 'patriots' in every round of episcopal promotions. Even more worrying was the emergence in the late 1720s and early 1730s of a strain of opinion critical of the influence of the church in Irish society. Boulter reported in 1736 that 'there was a rage stirred up against the clergy, that ... equalled anything ... seen against the popish priests, in the most dangerous times'.[130] There is a temptation to connect this negativity with the simultaneous growth of anticlericalism at Westminster, as expressed

---

127 *Considerations upon Two Bills Sent Down from the R[ight] H[onourable] the H[ouse] of L[ords] to the H[onoura]ble H[ouse] of C[ommons] Relating to the Clergy of I[relan]d*, London, 1732, pp. 14–17. See also *An Apology for the Clergy of Ireland in Respect of their Civil Rights, Especially as to Agistment for Dry and Barren Cattle*, Dublin, 1737/8, p. 7; *An Argument against Abolishing Christianity* (Davis, vol. II, p. 30); and the dedication to Lord Somers in *A Tale of a Tub* (*CWJS*, vol. I, p. 16).
128 T. C. Barnard, *A New Anatomy of Ireland: The Irish Protestants, 1649–1770*, New Haven & London: Yale University Press, 2003, ch. 4.
129 Swift to Carteret, 3 July 1725 (Woolley, *Corr.*, vol. II, pp. 566–8).
130 Boulter to Earl of Anglesey, 8 Jan. 1736[/7] (*Boulter Letters*, vol. II, pp. 150–2).

in a clutch of bills in the mid-1730s to reform ecclesiastical courts (1733, 1734), exempt Quakers from tithe (1736) and curtail charitable bequests of property (mortmain) (1736).[131] The same issues were raised in Ireland: in 1737, a measure was brought into the Irish House of Commons to regulate church courts, while the Lords debated a version of the English mortmain bill. Criticism of tithe was even more virulent. English influence cannot thus be entirely discounted, but in Ireland the mainsprings were different. The anticlericalism of radical Whigs in England was a reflection of their ideological inheritance, bound up with an ambition to dismantle the confessional state, whereas their Irish counterparts had little sympathy for Dissenters, and derived their principles from another source.

Impatience with ecclesiastical pretensions in Ireland was stimulated by a growing perception that the established church was hindering economic development. The two principal complaints were the restrictive terms on which bishops could make leases, and the effects of tithe. An Irish statute of 1635 limited to 21 years the length of time for which ecclesiastical land could be set, in order to prevent bishops from raising money through high fines while binding their successors to long leases at fixed rent.[132] But short leases denied the stability which would encourage tenants to invest. Although for some clergy the 1635 act was 'the great Magna Carta of our church revenues',[133] economic 'improvers' thought otherwise, and made several attempts to repeal it. The first, in 1723, produced a heated debate in the press and Parliament, in which the clergy were condemned for their aggrandisement of wealth and power.[134] Twelve years later, the cause was revived, again unsuccessfully, by one of Swift's *bêtes noires*, Richard Bettesworth.[135] At the

131 T. F. J. Kendrick, 'Sir Robert Walpole, the Old Whigs and the Bishops, 1733–1736: A Study in Eighteenth-Century Parliamentary Politics', *Historical Journal* 11 (1968), 421–35; Stephen Taylor, 'Sir Robert Walpole, the Church of England, and the Quakers' Tithe Bill of 1736', *Historical Journal* 28 (1985), 51–77; Taylor, 'Whigs, Tories and Anticlericalism: Ecclesiastical Courts Legislation in 1733', *Parliamentary History* 19 (2000), 329–56. The connection was made explicitly in 'Late Proceedings in Ireland, in Opposition to the Clergy's Demand of Tithe Herbage . . .' [1736] (BL, Egmont papers, Add. MS 47089, fo. 5; further copies in BL, Add. MS 21132, fos. 49–53, 54–9, 60–4).
132 Landa, pp. 96–111; A. P. W. Malcomson, *Archbishop Charles Agar: Churchmanship and Politics in Ireland, 1760–1810*, Dublin: Four Courts Press, 2002, pp. 399–401.
133 Bishop John Evans to Archbishop Wake, 5 Dec. 1723 (Christ Church, Oxford, Wake papers, Arch Epist. W. xiv).
134 Philip Perceval to Viscount Perceval, 30 Jan. 1723/4 (BL, Egmont papers, Add. MS 47030, fos. 57–8); Landa, pp. 97–111. The bill was described by one angry clergyman as 'downright plunder by law': James Smyth to William Smyth, 11 Nov. 1723 (NLI, Smythe of Barbavilla papers, MS 41,582/4).
135 *C.J.Ire.*, vol. VI, 570.

same time, a second front was opened on the vexed question of tithe. Bitterly resented, and frequently unpaid, tithes were a major popular grievance, adduced by Presbyterian ministers as a principal reason for emigration.[136] By the 1730s, a connection with economic stagnation had been established in the press. Dobbs, in his first *Essay on the Trade and Improvement of Ireland*, denounced tithes as responsible for the impoverishment of the country, and recommended various reforms, including a proposal that part of the yield be devoted to the setting up and maintenance of poorhouses.[137] Often stress was laid on the protection of the linen industry, as a key to Ireland's prosperity. In 1738 Samuel Madden recommended that anyone sowing 10 acres of flax be excused payment of tithe.[138] Dobbs himself introduced a parliamentary bill in 1735 'to ascertain the tithes of hemp and flax'. The fact that his bill was followed in the same session by another, sponsored by Hercules Rowley, the author of the leases bill of 1723, indicates how intimately those two issues were connected.[139] Neither Madden nor Dobbs could be described as anticlerical; indeed, Madden was himself a clergyman. Their opinions were symptomatic of a general movement among parliamentarians and political economists, as discontented Anglicans who had once seen the church as an instrument for economic transformation now took quite the opposite view.

The first major conflagration over tithe began in the Irish House of Commons in 1735, sparked by clerical insistence on the need for a levy on pasturage – the so-called tithe of herbage or 'agistment'.[140] A number of clergymen, led by Bishop Synge of Ferns, began cases in the law courts to secure their dues, provoking protests from tithe-payers across Ireland and a resolution of the Commons declaring the exaction illegal.[141] Synge then

---

136 Boulter to Carteret, 8 Mar. 1728[/9] (*Boulter Letters*, vol. I, p. 229); to Newcastle, 13 Mar. 1728[/9] (vol. I, pp. 229–35); Coghill to Edward Southwell, 23 Oct. 1729 (*Coghill Letters*, pp. 74–5).
137 Dobbs, *Essay*, pp. 54, 87–8, 92–5.
138 Samuel Madden, *Reflections and Resolutions Proper for the Gentlemen of Ireland, as to their Conduct for the Service of their Country*, Dublin, 1738, p. 134.
139 A previous Commons bill in 1733 to encourage the hempen and flaxen manufactures had included a clause to limit the tithe on 'flax and hemp' and had been opposed in the House of Lords by all the bishops (Coghill to Edward Southwell, 29 Dec. 1733 (*Coghill Letters*, p. 151)).
140 Landa, pp. 135–50; T. C. Barnard, '"Almoners of Providence": The Clergy, 1647 to *c*. 1780', in T. C. Barnard and W. G. Neely (eds.), *The Clergy of the Church of Ireland, 1000–2000: Messengers, Watchmen, and Stewards*, Dublin, Four Courts Press, 2006, p. 85.
141 Boulter to Anglesey, 8 Jan. 1736[/7] (*Boulter Letters*, vol. II, pp. 150–2); to Sir Robert Walpole, 9 Aug. 1737 (vol. II, pp. 181–4); 'Some Considerations upon the Late Proceedings in Ireland...' [1736] (BL, Add. MS 47089, fos. 1, 3–4); *An Apology for the Clergy...*, p. 7.

published a vindication of his actions, complete with documentary evidence, setting in motion what became a lengthy and acrimonious controversy.[142] The Commons' vote was memorialised in Swift's satire 'The Legion Club', which dismissed the opponents of the tithe as enemies of the church, and thus as knaves or fools.[143] It also opened up a frank public debate on the issue of tithe in general. A pamphlet entitled *Prescription Sacred* (1736), responding directly to Synge's self-justification, contained a prolonged attack on 'the new demand of herbage', and in turn gave rise to blasts and counter-blasts.[144] Critics argued that the clergy were amply provided for despite the poverty of the country and condemned the extortions of tithe-farmers, and 'tithe-jobbers'. It was no wonder that clergymen in general took a dim view of the legislature: Archdeacon Crofton of Cork, discussing the business prospects of one of the MPs for Cork city in 1737, described him as 'a very honest man, *though a Member of Parliament*',[145] while the author of *An Apology for the Clergy of Ireland* (1737/8) complained that the Commons vote had initiated 'an inquisition into their [the clergy's] lives and manners ... as if they were a body of men, who had distressed the nation to the last degree', and warned that 'to break any gap into the lawful enclosure for one sort of tithes, is to open a way to invade the clergy's rights in every other'.[146]

7 Poverty and Vagrancy

Ireland, as one historian has observed, was unique among European countries in having no systematic nationwide provision for the relief of poverty until the nineteenth century.[147] This does not mean there was no provision at all; but what was available was an assortment of parochial, municipal and private philanthropy. In general terms, the Church of Ireland seems to have accepted an institutional responsibility for the provision of charity to the poor. Parish vestries levied money and appointed overseers to organise the distribution. But this had no statutory basis. It was merely a

---

142 Edward Synge, *Two Affidavits in Relation to the Demands of Tythe-agistment in the Diocese of Leighlin; with an Introduction*, Dublin, 1736.
143 *Poems*, vol. III, pp. 827–39.
144 *Prescription Sacred: or, Reasons for Opposing the New Demand of Herbage in Ireland*, [Dublin?], 1736; Alexander MacAulay, *Property Inviolable: or, Some Remarks upon a Pamphlet Entituled, Prescription Sacred*, Dublin, 1736.
145 Crofton to William Smyth, 30 Jan. 1737 (NLI, Smythe of Barbavilla papers, MS 41,586/23). Emphasis added.
146 *An Apology for the Clergy ...*, pp. 3–4.
147 Paul Slack, *The English Poor Law 1531–1782*, Basingstoke: Palgrave Macmillan, 1990, p. 159.

custom, albeit based on the precedent set in an Act of Parliament of 1666 relating to the Dublin parish of St Andrew's, which specifically required the collection of money for the poor.[148] Distribution was also restricted to members of the established church, and although other religious denominations (notably the Presbyterians) collected and dispensed money to the distressed among their own congregations,[149] such relief could not touch the majority of the population, especially in the towns, and most particularly the rapidly increasing numbers of destitute in the capital. Efforts were made in 1695 and 1697 to pass legislation that would enable every parish in the kingdom to assess inhabitants for this purpose, but neither bill made any headway.

In his principal contribution to the public debate on the question of provision for the poor, the *Proposal for Giving Badges to the Beggars* (1737), Swift assumed that in Ireland, as in England, 'every Parish is bound to maintain its own Poor', but this was not the case.[150] What had been taken over from England was only the settlement legislation which formed an important prop of the Tudor and Stuart poor law. The Henrician vagrancy acts, which the Irish Parliament re-enacted, empowered justices of the peace to register the 'impotent poor', who were entitled to beg within the particular town or rural parish where they were 'settled', and were provided with identification seals (later with badges) for the purpose, but liable to penalties if they wandered. At the same time, the able-bodied poor – 'sturdy beggars' – were liable to confinement in the stocks. The distinction between the impotent and the able-bodied lay at the heart of attitudes to the poor throughout the early modern period. While the former were to be assisted, the latter were subjected to punishment, and in the 1630s the Irish Parliament strengthened the statutes against vagrancy by adopting a further English innovation, the house of correction, or bridewell.[151] This approach was further refined in England through the development of the workhouse, which combined punishment with education, in obliging the poor to work and thus (it was hoped)

---

148 Rowena Dudley, 'The Dublin Parishes and the Poor, 1660–1740', *Archivium Hibernicum* 53 (1999), 81–8; *The Vestry Records of the Parishes of St Catherine and St James, Dublin, 1657–1692*, ed. Raymond Gillespie, Dublin: Four Courts Press, 2002, p. 13.
149 Robert Whan, *The Presbyterians of Ulster, 1680–1730*, Woodbridge: Boydell Press, 2013, pp. 171–7.
150 Below, pp. 305–19.
151 David Dickson, 'In Search of the Old Irish Poor Law', in Rosalind Mitchison and Peter Roebuck (eds.), *Economy and Society in Scotland and Ireland 1500–1939*, Edinburgh: John Donald, 1988, p. 149. For the problem of poverty in Dublin, and the means taken to deal with it, see in general Dickson, *Dublin*, pp. 117–20.

inculcating in them the 'habits of industry'. By 1700, the educational element had become more pronounced, with the foundation of 'corporations of the poor' in London, Bristol and other major cities, the purpose of which was to find useful work for 'sturdy beggars'. Accustoming the children of the poor to work and training them in basic industrial skills was central to the ethos of charity schools and the SPCK. There was also a powerful moral imperative: indeed, the benefactors who founded schools or workhouses were also likely to be involved in the coercive campaign of social reform spearheaded by 'societies for the reformation of manners'.[152]

The idea of managing poverty and vagrancy by setting the poor to work – if necessary with an element of constraint – was soon adopted in Ireland. It was seen most obviously in the charity schools, and their successors the charter schools, but in general, from the 1690s onwards, pamphleteers were emphasising the necessity of finding suitable work for the poor, and bills were brought into the Dublin Parliament designed to assist in 'the better employment of the poor'.[153] Early legislation for the promotion of the linen industry in 1695 and 1697 envisaged setting up what would have been in effect corporations for the poor in various counties to employ children in manufacture, and eventually, in 1704, the first workhouse was established in Dublin, under an Act of Parliament.[154] Although this was to some degree a municipal enterprise, funded through a local tax administered by the city corporation, the governing body included leading office-holders in central government, the Church of Ireland archbishops of Dublin and Armagh, and the deans of the two Dublin cathedrals. The workhouse was also patronised by philanthropists of an evangelical disposition, including clergymen – precisely the kind of individuals who were also involved in the work of charity schools. Among the most prominent were Lord Lanesborough and his pious wife, the niece of Bishop Compton of London, and the evidence of

152 See, for example, the proposal sent in 1728 by an unnamed Member of Parliament (possibly from Ulster) to the bishop of Cloyne, Henry Maule (who had been heavily involved in the charity school movement and was connected with the SPCK in London), advocating the establishment of a national system of workhouses: Marsh's Lib., MS Z. 3.1.1 (142).
153 A charity sermon preached in Dublin in March 1730 (after the publication of *A Modest Proposal*) by the bishop of Elphin, declared that it was 'no part of charity to provide for those who can be usefully employed for themselves or the public'. Indeed, those who 'withdraw their labour from the common stock' were to be regarded as 'traitors to society'; 'they must submit to the common lot of labour, and ought not, as indeed they cannot, eat unless they work': Robert Clayton, *A Sermon Preach'd in the Parish Church of St. Mary, Dublin: March the 22d. 1729[/30]. At the General Meeting of the Children Educated in the Charity-Schools in Dublin*, Dublin, 1730, p. 19.
154 Dickson, 'In Search of the Old Irish Poor Law', p. 150.

Lanesborough's papers shows that they were looking for inspiration to an English example, the corporation of the poor in Bristol.[155] Although in due course the Dublin workhouse came to specialise in catering for the 'deserving poor' (and especially orphans), its first impact was on the beggars, or, as Swift and others put it, the 'strollers', who were flooding into the expanding city from the depressed countryside. Over 120 vagrants were forced into the new building when it was opened in 1706, before local churchwardens could bring in their own parish dependants.[156] The harsher side of the 'moral reform' movement was also visible in unsuccessful parliamentary attempts to reinforce the vagrancy laws. In 1711, Sir William Fownes, a Tory alderman of Dublin, brought in a bill (which got no further than its committee stage) to bring up to date the Henrician act. Fownes was a friend of Swift's and subsequently the author of a work published in 1725 under the title of *Methods Proposed for Regulating the Poor, Supporting of Some and Employing Others*.[157] Six years later, Abel Ram, another Tory and a Dublin banker who was an enthusiast for charity schools, sponsored a bill 'for better regulating the poor in this kingdom, and for punishing idle persons, vagrants and vagabonds', which suffered the same fate.[158]

By 1725 it was clear that the accommodation provided in the Dublin workhouse was entirely inadequate to cope with the number of beggars being referred to it. The population of the workhouse in 1726 numbered 222 in all, of which nearly half (110) were children, 30 were 'superannuated', and almost none appear to have been able-bodied.[159]

The situation was plain enough for the Irish House of Commons to establish a committee of inquiry, after which draft legislation was prepared, only to be amended in the British privy council and dropped on its return to Dublin. In the following parliamentary session, in 1727–8, another committee of inquiry reported at length on inefficiency and corruption in the workhouse, and this time the resultant bill passed into law (1 Geo. II c. 27), reorganising the governing board, broadening the membership and putting the institution's finances on a sounder footing (based on a local tax on those involved in transport services). Although 'sturdy beggars' were still to be committed by the board of governors, emphasis was placed on the

---

155 'Abstract of the Account from the Corporation of the Poor at Bristol for the Use of the Irish Corporation for the Poor in Dublin . . .' (NLI, Lane papers, MS 8,645/1).
156 Dickson, 'In Search of the Old Irish Poor Law', pp. 150–1.
157 *C.J.Ire.*, vol. II, pp. 831, 869. For Fownes, see *Hist. Ir. Parl.*, vol. IV, pp. 232–3; and for his friendship with Swift, Ehrenpreis, vol. III, pp. 346, 435, 818.
158 *C.J.Ire.*, vol. IV, pp. 324, 392; *DIB*.
159 See Marsh's Lib., MS Z. 3.1.1 (146).

provision that was also to be made for foundling children, who were to be accommodated and given a basic education. A further act of 1732 (5 Geo. II c. 14 [Ire.]) did no more than tighten up financial arrangements, but the description of the workhouse given in this act had significantly changed. Its purpose now was not just to provide work for the poor and punishment for 'vagabonds', but to look after foundlings and lunatics, an indication of the direction which would increasingly be taken, as the workhouse metamorphosed into a hospital. But at this stage the problem of vagrancy in the capital was still a sufficiently important issue for the bill to permit the governors to transfer inmates to the bridewell, since 'by the great number of idle vagabonds and strolling beggars that are from time to time committed to the workhouse... great disorders are committed therein'.[160] Although we have no direct evidence of the nature of the regime operating in the workhouse at this time, it is worth noting that in 1729 a Dublin newspaper reported that one woman who had just been committed tried to recover her freedom by jumping out of a window so high that she broke both legs in the attempt.[161]

Advocacy of harsh treatment of the able-bodied poor, especially those who resorted to begging (whether aggressively or not), was common among the propertied elite. Those working for the economic and moral regeneration of Irish society were particularly susceptible. One noted 'improver', Bishop Francis Hutchinson of Down, in the course of a pamphlet in which he proposed a constructive solution to the problem of poverty, found time to recommend condign punishment for 'idle beggars', while one of Swift's local political heroes, the almost unbearably upright lord mayor of Dublin Humphrey French, took a personal interest in the commitment of 'vagabonds', 'beggars' and 'shoe-boys' to the workhouse and houses of correction.[162] It therefore became essential to distinguish between the licensed, impotent poor and idle and sturdy vagrants. And in Dublin in particular, the problem of vagrancy was widely assumed to be an importation from outside – as indeed, given the nature of the Irish economy, and the extent of internal migration, it almost certainly was. Elsewhere in Ireland – and the evidence is especially strong in Ulster – we can see local initiatives to import the English practice

---

160 Cf. *Cal. Anc. Recs. Dublin*, vol. VII, pp. 440–1, for the building of a new bridewell in 1728 near the gate of the Dublin workhouse.
161 *Dublin Weekly Journal*, 12 July 1729.
162 Francis Hutchinson, *A Letter to a Member of Parliament, Concerning the Imploying and Providing for the Poor*, Dublin, 1723, p. 18; *Pue's Occurrences*, 5–9, 25–28 Nov. 1732.

of providing badges for licensed beggars, so that the unlicensed might be more easily identified, then committed, or sent away.[163]

The issuing of badges to licensed beggars by parish vestries was far from unknown in Ireland in the late seventeenth century. Examples can be found in Dublin parishes (St Mark's and St Ann's), in Waterford, and especially in the north-east of the country, where badges survive from five parishes in Counties Antrim, Down and Armagh between 1695 and 1709.[164] Indeed, it is possible that Swift's time at Kilroot accustomed him to badging as common practice. Such fragmentary evidence as survives also suggests a revival in the 1720s: in Cork in 1721 and 1728;[165] and in Dublin, where in 1724 St Catherine's parish required eighty-six badges for its poor; and two years later badges were provided for the indigenous poor in St Werburgh's.[166]

Sir William Fownes's *Methods Proposed for Regulating the Poor*, in 1725, had recommended the introduction of badging into Dublin city on a systematic basis, and in 1726 Swift had tried unsuccessfully to do the same throughout the diocese of Dublin by means of his own influence with Archbishop King (towards which end, presumably, he began to draft the commentary *Upon Giving Badges to the Poor*).[167] It is not surprising, then, that the dean should have returned to this theme in 1737, and that his preferred solution to the problems caused by the beggars who infested the capital, and especially the streets surrounding his own deanery, was to imprison them or drive them back to their home parishes and thus restore the proper social order to the city and to the countryside. In his view, these wandering 'strollers' constituted a social problem which outside interests – the irresponsible gentry of rural Ireland, and even the calculating English – had dumped on Dublin. Such people should be disqualified from benefiting from the produce of local

---

163 Dickson, 'In Search of the Old Irish Poor Law', p. 151; Dudley, 'Dublin Parishes and the Poor', p. 89. On the English practice, see Steve Hindle, 'Dependency, Shame and Belonging: Badging the Deserving Poor, c. 1550–1750', *Cultural and Social History* 1 (2004), 6–35.
164 W. A. Seaby and T. G. F. Paterson, 'Ulster Beggars' Badges', *Ulster Journal of Archaeology*, 3rd ser., 3 (1970), 96, 99, 102–4.
165 Ibid., p. 99; Rowena Dudley, 'The Dublin Parish, 1660–1730', in Elizabeth FitzPatrick and Raymond Gillespie (eds.), *The Parish in Medieval and Early Modern Ireland: Community, Territory and Building*, Dublin: Four Courts Press, 2006, p. 293.
166 Barnard, *New Anatomy of Ireland*, p. 287; S. C. Hughes, *The Church of S. Werburgh, Dublin*, Dublin: Hodges Figgis, 1889, p. 44.
167 See below, p. 2. Fownes noted in his pamphlet that 'It is reported, other Cities and Towns, as also many Country Parishes, have begun to Badge their Poor' (Preface, A3r).

taxation, which took money from the pockets of honest workmen. Instead, the poor rate should be used to provide relief for the resident poor of the city's parishes, and the limited number of unfortunates – increasingly orphans and lunatics – whom the workhouse was able to help.

8 *A Modest Proposal*

Since the mid nineteenth century, Swift's *A Modest Proposal for Preventing the Children of Poor People from Being a Burden to their Parents or Country; and for Making Them Beneficial to the Publick* has been regarded as one of his most important works, its irony touching depths not to be found in other contemporary satire.[168] Throughout its long literary afterlife, *A Modest Proposal* has inspired the production of masterpieces of macabre humour and satiric aesthetics, and its presence can be detected in work by writers as diverse as Thomas De Quincey, H. G. Wells, Bram Stoker and Evelyn Waugh.[169] The notion that over-population might be rectified by treating the children of the Irish poor as livestock for the butchery trade is in itself gruesome enough, even to modern sensibilities, but in following through with brutal clarity the practical details of his scheme Swift presented a vision that still has the power to shock. Modern sensibilities are uneasy with the black humour of the piece, and few readers are likely to appreciate it as a sardonic joke; rather, it comes across as Swift's most powerful meditation on the inhumanity of mankind and the particular hopelessness of the Irish condition, the most savage example of his savage indignation. Yet there is no agreement as to its primary intention. Critics and biographers have cited it as proof of Swift's essential pessimism about the human condition, and also of his loathing for English misgovernment of Ireland, his sympathy for the poor in general and for the native Irish in particular. For a relatively short pamphlet (only fourteen pages of text in the original Dublin edition), it has spawned a variety of differing interpretations: was Swift's principal aim to satirise 'projectors' and 'proposers' of practical schemes for improving the Irish economy and occupying the poor; to condemn English government for reducing all of Irish society to the level of primitive savagery which was the heritage of the natives; to shock his audience into revising their facile preconceptions of the 'wild Irish'; even to suggest a comparison between cannibalism and

---

168 Wittkowsky, 'Swift's *Modest Proposal*', p. 75.
169 Ian Higgins, 'The Afterlife of *A Modest Proposal*', in *Dean Swift's Modest Proposal at 280: A Symposium on Swift and Ireland*, Dublin: Deanery of St Patrick's Cathedral, 2009, available at http://hdl.handle.net/1885/50380.

the consumption of Ireland's resources, and to imply that absentee landlords and unscrupulous financial interests were already 'devouring' the country? The complexity of the arguments in *A Modest Proposal*, the elusiveness of the authorial voice, and the multiplicity of allusions, both to contemporary Irish society and politics, and to literary precedents, allows for a range of interpretations, yet for all its timeless fascination this is a work which needs to be tied closely to its context.

The form which Swift adopted in the pamphlet – a 'proposal' – was indeed typical of many publications designed to suggest solutions to Ireland's economic and social ills that were laid before the Irish reading public, and the political classes in particular, in the early decades of the eighteenth century. He was himself to use it again soon afterwards in the *Proposal that all the Ladies and Women of Ireland Should Appear Constantly in Irish Manufactures*. That he chose this mode of address has naturally prompted the idea that he was aiming his satire at his fellow authors – earnest 'virtuosi' and political arithmeticians – making *A Modest Proposal* echo his ridicule of the professors whose pointless experiments were described in *Gulliver's Travels*. But this may well be to confuse form with purpose. As Oliver Ferguson observed, the fact that Swift showed contempt for useless learning did not mean that he despised those who offered serious and practical schemes for advancing the common good. He was on amicable terms with Arthur Dobbs, for example, and in private spoke well of Thomas Prior.[170] Nor should we place too much weight on the occasions when he crossed swords with individual 'projectors'. As we have seen, the main reason for his dismissal of John Browne's 'scheme[s] for improving the trade of this kingdom' was that they ignored the basic fact of Ireland's constitutional subordination, which vitiated any simple importation of ideas and practices from other states. In a rather different way, his rejection of James Maculla's idea for the circulation of promissory notes printed on copper as an alternative to the coinage Ireland so desperately needed (in *A Letter on Maculla's Project about Halfpence*), was partly based on the view that it was impractical, and partly on a visceral suspicion of any project that could turn out to be a money-making enterprise for the projector. Such enterprises reeked of the financial quackery of an earlier generation whom he had encountered in England: individuals like the speculative builder Nicholas Barbon, whose activities Swift recalled in *Maxims Controlled in Ireland*, gloating that Barbon, in common with others of his ilk, had 'died bankrupt'.[171]

170 Ferguson, pp. 165–6.
171 Below, p. 178.

Furthermore, there is little reason to suppose that Swift was hostile towards those who put forward constructive ideas for the relief and re-education of the poor, who at first glance might appear to have been his prime target. Charitable initiatives intended to assist the poor, such as schools or workhouses, were generally associated with those of an evangelical cast of mind, devoted members of the established church who were not easily made objects of derision. Indeed, the most recent offering along these lines, which some have suggested was in Swift's mind when he wrote *A Modest Proposal*, was in fact written by his old friend, the Tory MP and former lord mayor of Dublin, Sir William Fownes, whose attitudes towards poverty and vagrancy were not much different from Swift's own.[172] Moreover, the dean was not himself so well disposed to the poor as to disdain coercive measures, whether the establishment of workhouses or the expulsion of unlicensed beggars from the urban parishes to which, in desperation, they had resorted.

This is not to say that Swift was incapable of satirising views which were akin to his own, or at least of presenting them in a distorted and wildly exaggerated form. It may be, as David Womersley has suggested, that he was intent on showing the world the depths of the moral degeneration that would inevitably follow the slavish condition in which he and other Irishmen found themselves, so that during the course of the work the proposer grew into 'a terrible imaginative projection of what Swift could be driven to become'.[173] Alternatively, it may simply be counted as an additional complexity, in an already complex work, that he presented in an extreme and satirical form a calculating and authoritarian attitude to the poor which was commonplace among contemporaries, and to an extent even understandable in the context of the prevailing instability, real and perceived, in Irish social relations and public order. Published analyses of the problem of poverty in Ireland viewed the children of the poor as a potential national resource (even if, in their current state, they were a drain on the economy) and a fit subject for social engineering.[174] This was the ethos of the charity-school movement, which took in children in order to make them 'useful' and docile. If schooled in this

---

172 Sir William Fownes, *Methods Proposed for Regulating the Poor. Supporting of Some, and Employing Others: According to Their Several Capacities*, Dublin, 1723–4; repr. 1725; Fownes to Swift, 9 Sept. 1732 (Woolley, *Corr.*, vol. III, pp. 535–9); Ehrenpreis, vol. III, p. 818. Fownes, like Swift, was a keen supporter of the mayoral government of Humphrey French (Fownes, *Letter to ... Humphrey French*).
173 *CWJS*, vol. XVI, p. c.
174 For example, Hutchinson, *Letter to a Member of Parliament, Concerning the ... Poor*, p. 8, asserted that the beggar 'eats your Meat, and drinks your Milk, and pays you nothing for it', while the vagrant 'both eats and steals, and spoils your inclosures, and fills you with Children'.

way, they would be a benefit to the country; if not, they offered a real threat to social order. It is of course conceivable that Swift had reservations about the severity of the regimes under which the destitute laboured in workhouses and the children of the poor were put to manual labour in schools, or that he took private exception to the contemptuous and inhumane tone in which other writers discussed the poor (though he was fully capable of expressing similar sentiments in his own writings). But his principal objection to pamphlets of this kind was that the answers they proposed to the great question of poverty would ultimately prove futile. Putting the unemployed poor to work served no purpose while the Irish economy languished, which was an inevitable consequence of Ireland's crippled constitution.

This point is underlined by the precise wording of the title of *A Modest Proposal*. While the literary device of a 'proposal' was commonplace in 1729, to add the adjective 'modest' in front of it was not. According to the *English Short Title Catalogue*, the words 'modest proposal' had been used in this way only once before, in the title of an obscure English pamphlet from the early years of William III's reign, which it would have been pointless for Swift to have referred to.[175] Nor was the phrase popular in printed works, though it had appeared the previous year in the Whig journalist James Ralph's priggish denunciation of fashionable theatrical taste, *The Touch-Stone*, and, since Ralph had recently criticised Pope, Swift would at least have been aware of him.[176] As Claude Rawson has pointed out, it also harks back to Bernard Mandeville's *A Modest Defence of Public Stews* (1724), which, in advocating state-controlled prostitution, performed a similar satirical exercise to Swift, advocating a scheme that outraged public decency by challenging accepted moral values in order to achieve a material good, or set of goods.[177]

Leaving aside echoes of other writers, Swift's use of the phrase may simply have been intended to enhance the ferocity of the irony: 'modest' in the sense of morally decent or respectable.[178] But it may also have held a political meaning: 'modest' in the sense of limited and (in this fantastic scenario) practicable. His was not a scheme which required parliamentary legislation,

---

175 *An Essay, or, Modest Proposal, of a Way to Encrease the Number of People, and Consequently the Strength of this Kingdom*..., [?London, 1693].
176 James Ralph, *The Touch-Stone: or, Historical, Critical, Political, Philosophical, and Theological Essays on the Reigning Diversions of the Town*, London, 1728, p. 193. For Ralph, see *ODNB*.
177 Rawson, 'Mandeville and Swift', in *Swift and Others*, Cambridge: Cambridge University Press, 2015, pp. 51–69. One of the benefits envisaged by Mandeville was a reduction in instances of infanticide, which constitutes a further link with the *Modest Proposal*.
178 As, for example, in Richard Allestree, *The Government of the Tongue*, Oxford, 1702, p. 203.

interventionist government regulation or the establishment of new institutions (whether poor-houses or Molesworth's agricultural colleges). Above all, it was something the Irish could do for themselves. Since this particular commodity by its very nature could not be exported, the English government and Parliament would have no cause to intervene.

In disparaging 'the several schemes of other projectors', Swift was making two points: first, contrary to accepted wisdom, the 'prodigious number' of the children of the poor constituted a dead weight on the economy and not, in normal circumstances, a potential source of economic growth; second, and more important, that Ireland's problems were so intractable that nothing but the most brutally radical solution could put them right. In a lengthy passage towards the end of the pamphlet he listed other options, including not only a tax on absentees, but also a boycott of foreign goods, sumptuary laws, even the development of a spirit of patriotism, only to conclude: 'let no Man talk to me of these and the like Expedients, till he hath at least some glimpse of hope, that there will ever be some hearty and sincere Attempt to put them in Practice.'[179] In other words, Swift's intention was not to ridicule practitioners of political economy as such, but, as Ferguson observed, to show 'their foolishness in trying to help an indifferent Ireland',[180] or, indeed, the unreality of proposing remedies that either required the consent of the British ministers or could be undone by legislative action at Westminster. The fundamental problem remained a political one: Ireland's status as a 'dependent kingdom', which Irish parliamentary patriots seemingly had neither the will nor the capacity to challenge. Ultimately, the exploitation by British government and Parliament of its power over the Irish economy was what would keep the country poor. In one of the several sidelong comments with which *A Modest Proposal* was peppered, Swift made a characteristic allusion to English rapacity. Referring to the possibility of curing the flesh of Irish children, he conceded that it was too tender to 'admit a long continuance in Salt' but added sharply, '*I could name a Country, which would be glad to Eat up our whole Nation without it.*'[181]

At the same time, the conceit that lies at the heart of *A Modest Proposal*, the scheme to breed and sell the children of the natives for meat, enabled Swift to weave a web of ironic meanings which, taken together, exposed the complex nature of Ireland's predicament: not only its powerlessness against malign English government, but the decadence of the Protestant elite, reduced by slavery to a moral condition no better than the indigenous

179 Below, p. 157.
180 Ferguson, p. 175.
181 Below, p. 158.

inhabitants of the country whom it was their religious and moral duty to bring to civility. The association of cannibalism with the native Irish, through their supposed Scythian ancestry, was well established in literary tradition, dating back to Herodotus, who recorded how the Scythians drank blood to seal and sanctify an agreement, and the geographer Strabo, who described both the Scythians and the ancient inhabitants of Ireland as anthropophagous. It had been taken up by Edmund Spenser, who devoted a lengthy passage of his *A View of the Present State of Ireland* to a detailed comparison of the 'evil' customs of the native Irish with those of their Scythian and Gaulish forebears, and included a reference to drinking the blood of defeated enemies.[182] Both Spenser and his fellow Elizabethan Fynes Moryson described how, in the famine conditions of the 1590s, the starving Irish had been reduced to eating the bodies of the recently deceased. One particularly horrible story of Moryson's, of the orphan children of a widow consuming in desperation the carcass of their dead mother, had been related by Sheridan in *The Intelligencer* a year earlier.[183] In *A Modest Proposal*, Swift also refers to well-known examples of cannibalism among the native peoples of the Americas, especially the Tupi or Tupinamba of coastal Brazil, in order to underscore the supposedly innate barbarism of the Irish. Cannibalism, either in the way the Scythians and the Tupi disposed of the bodies of defeated enemies, or in the supposed practice of the Incas, in raising children as gastronomic delicacies[184] – a precedent that was closer to the proposer's intention – was made to seem a characteristic of 'savage' peoples wherever they might be found.

182 Herodotus, *History*, IV, 70. Strabo, *Geography*, VII, iii, 7; IV, v, 4. *The Works of Edmund Spenser*, ed. Edwin Greenlaw *et al.*, 11 vols., Baltimore: The Johns Hopkins Press, 1943–57, vol. IX, p. 112. That the idea was current in Swift's generation can be illustrated by a passage in a typically condescending work of English travel-writing, *A Brief Character of Ireland, with Some Observations on the Customs &c. of the Meaner Inhabitants of That Kingdom*, London, 1692, whose author writes, of the 'native Irish' (pp. 46–7): 'Were it not for the industrious English and strangers among them, I am persuaded in process of time they would let it [the country] all run into its original wilderness, and live either like cannibals upon one another, or like the native wolves... upon the next prey they light on, tho' of the nearest blood, rather than take the least honest pains to provide better for themselves, or their wretched progeny'. It is, of course, possible that such views also formed an object of Swift's satire.
183 Woolley, *Intelligencer*, p. 198. Fynes Moryson, *An Itinerary... Concerning His Ten Yeeres Travel through the Twelve Dominions of Germany... Scotland and Ireland*, London, 1617, p. 271. For a summation of these influences on the pamphlet, see Claude Rawson, *God, Gulliver and Genocide: Barbarism and the European Imagination, 1492–1945*, Oxford: Oxford University Press, 2001, pp. 70–91.
184 Ian Campbell Ross, '"A Very Knowing American": The Inca Garcilaso de la Vega and Swift's *A Modest Proposal*', *MLQ* 68 (2007), 493–516.

The assumption that lay behind *A Modest Proposal* was presumably that Irish 'savages', long accustomed to the idea of eating human flesh, would take no exception to such an outlandish idea; indeed, they would embrace it with alacrity. Yet *A Modest Proposal* was not simply a further statement of the barbarism of the Irish Yahoos. For while the indigent natives were to raise this new source of food, it was the propertied classes, people like Swift and his readers, the English in Ireland, who would consume the product. Moreover, as Swift was quick to point out, the English in England would happily consume everything, and everyone, in Ireland if they could. The nature of the Irish condition had therefore reduced the settlers, and their English exploiters, to the same level of barbarism as the natives.

Although the thrust of Swift's satire is against the consumers of this ghastly trade, the enslaving English and enslaved Irish Protestants who are responsible for the degradation of the country to such a pitch that organised cannibalism offers the only solution to its difficulties, the attitude towards the native Irish embodied in *A Modest Proposal* remains problematic. For some commentators the author's intentions are clear: Swift is identifying with the oppressed. In 1882, Leslie Stephen (at that time an influential representative of popular literary culture) described the pamphlet as 'the most complete expression of burning indignation against intolerable wrongs', reflecting a belief in the uncomplicated nature of the authorial voice, and Swift's ironic distance from the subject; eating people is wrong, and Swift is obviously repudiating the mad theory of the proposer.[185] This view survives in modern scholarship, and has been extended to claim for Swift an honoured place in the gallery of writers against colonial exploitation. According to Carole Fabricant,

> *A Modest Proposal* is governed by a central metaphor that for Swift automatically conveyed a definite political and economic – specifically anticolonialist – statement: one that assumed the existence of close ties between Ireland's self-destructive tendencies and England's brutal oppressions. As Swift saw it, England's lawless seizure of Ireland's earthly produce, like Eve's wilful plunder of the forbidden fruit, generated a fundamentally anarchic and predatory world founded upon a grotesque Chain of Devouring.[186]

This straightforward interpretation has been challenged, however, by readings which point up the contrast with the derisive and dismissive attitude

---

185 Leslie Stephen, *Swift*, London: Macmillan, 1882, p. 163.
186 Carole Fabricant, *Swift's Landscape*, Baltimore: Johns Hopkins University Press, 1982, p. 79.

towards the native Irish expressed in Swift's other writings. The idea that *A Modest Proposal* was written in defence of the native Irish peasantry flies in the face of this other evidence. In the words of Claude Rawson, 'to suggest that... [Swift's] attitude on certain central questions (poverty, beggars, the care of children) was "humane" or "liberal" in a sense which a modern reader would understand or assent to, is misleading'.[187] Swift's satire targeted Anglo-Irish settlers, but did not defend the poor, who were almost beneath consideration.

Swift's attitude to the native Irish was complex. To understand it, we have first to consider his perception of his own national identity. Here, residence and ethnicity were in conflict. In common with other Irish Protestants in this period, he was able to consider himself as English and as Irish at different times and in different circumstances.[188] Put simply, when their interests were threatened by the actions of the English/British government, members of the Protestant elite in Ireland defined themselves as 'Irish'; when they faced the danger of rebellion, and the expropriation of their property by Catholics, they were 'the English interest' in Ireland and their enemies were 'the native Irish' or 'the Irish' *tout court*. This at least was the situation at the Glorious Revolution; in the succeeding generations, a sense of 'Irishness' gradually took over, but suspicion and the historical sense of alienation from the native Irish Catholics did not disappear entirely, and in consequence neither did the Protestant's residual ethnic, religious and political identification with England. As has often been observed, Swift's outrage at the English Parliament's interference in Irish affairs was grounded on the belief that Protestants in Ireland were being deprived of their liberties as Englishmen.

The idea that the Anglo-Irish Ascendancy was a self-consciously 'colonial' caste currently finds little favour with historians, however attractive it has proved to be to literary and cultural critics wishing to draw modern Ireland into the maw of 'subaltern studies'. For a time it was fashionable to equate eighteenth-century Protestant Irish 'patriotism' with the 'colonial nationalism' that emerged in the white dominions of the British empire in

---

187 'A Reading of *A Modest Proposal*', in *Order from Confusion Sprung: Studies in Eighteenth-Century Literature from Swift to Cowper*, London: Allen & Unwin, 1985, p. 121.
188 D. W. Hayton, 'Anglo-Irish Attitudes: Changing Perceptions of National Identity among the Protestant Ascendancy in Ireland, ca. 1690–1750', *Studies in Eighteenth-century Culture* 17 (1987), 145–57 (repr. and expanded in Hayton, *Anglo-Irish Experience*, pp. 25–48); Jim Smyth, '"Like Amphibious Animals": Irish Protestants, Ancient Britons, 1691–1707', *Historical Journal* 36 (1993), 785–97.

the late 1800s.[189] The idea that Protestant Ireland was in essence a 'colony' – or even a 'garrison' – has of course been central to the nationalist narrative of Ireland's past, and has given rise to debates among historians as to whether the Ascendancy is still best described objectively as a colony, or whether its colonial features – the equation of political rights with landownership and the sectarian exclusiveness of the ruling class – were in fact typical of the states of 'ancien régime' Europe.[190] It is clear, however, that Irish Protestants did not see their position as equivalent to that of the colonial planters of north America or the Caribbean. They did not use the term 'colony' of Ireland, nor did they concede that Ireland's Parliament was a mere colonial assembly.[191] Nonetheless, the history of English settlement in Ireland and the nature of the relationship between landed Protestants and landless Catholics could not but impart some element of the colonial into Irish Protestants' self-image. After all, for Swift, Catholics were 'the native Irish', whom it had been the mission of the English in Ireland to civilise.[192]

The statements of sympathy for the Irish Catholic population that are to be found in Swift's writings are few and far between. As Rawson has put it, his 'bitterness about the oppression of the Irish natives... is sparsely expressed, and usually mixed with gruff contempt for their laziness and ignorance, and the squalor of their mode of life'.[193] Where Swift shows concern for the plight of the poor in general, as in his sermon on the *Causes of the Wretched Condition of Ireland*, the principal subjects of his pity are 'the lower Sort of Tradesmen, Labourers and Artificers' of Dublin, 'not able to find Cloaths and Food for their Families' – in other words, the industrious Protestant artisans and tradesmen who have been brought low by the English discriminatory legislation which has destroyed their

---

189 J. G. Simms, *Colonial Nationalism, 1698–1776: Molyneux's 'The Case of Ireland... Stated'*, Cork: Mercier Press, 1976; T. W. Moody and W. E. Vaughan (eds.), *A New History of Ireland*, vol. IV: *Eighteenth-century Ireland 1691–1800*, Oxford: Clarendon Press, 1986, pp. 104–22, 196–235; Patrick Kelly, 'Archbishop William King (1650–1729) and Colonial Nationalism', in Ciaran Brady (ed.), *Worsted in the Game: Losers in Irish History*, Dublin: Lilliput Press, 1989, pp. 85–94.
190 S. J. Connolly, 'Eighteenth-century Ireland: Colony or Ancien Régime', in D. G. Boyce and Alan O'Day (eds.), *The Making of Modern Irish History: Revisionism and the Revisionist Controversy*, London: Routledge, 1996, pp. 15–33; Ian McBride, *Eighteenth-century Ireland: The Isle of Slaves*, Dublin: Gill & Macmillan, 2009, pp. 100–3.
191 D. G. Boyce, *Nationalism in Ireland*, Dublin: Gill & Macmillan, 1982, pp. 106–8; Connolly, *Religion, Law and Power*, pp. 105–6.
192 See also *A Proposal for Giving Badges to the Beggars* (below, pp. 312, 314), where Swift uses the term 'colonies' to refer to the impoverished tenantry and labourers on country estates in Ireland, whom the landlords have 'sent up' to beg on the streets of Dublin.
193 Rawson, *God, Gulliver and Genocide*, p. 81.

livelihoods.[194] Where we can detect glimmers of sympathy for the 'poor Popish natives', these are an instrumental part of his critique of the selfish behaviour of landlords, and though Swift does at one point refer to the expropriation of Catholic lands in moralistic terms, the phrasing is still not entirely straightforward: the rural poor have been oppressed and degraded by landlords 'who stripped them of all of their substance', but the more serious charge against land-grabbers is not that they took estates away (which would be justified by their civilising mission), but that they have since failed to discharge the social responsibility that the acquisition of property entailed.[195]

Where Swift was quite uncompromising was in his observations on the mendicant poor, and in particular the children of beggars, in both town and country, whom he presented as pathologically vicious. In this respect he was at one with other contemporary commentators, who wrote about the children of the poor in a highly pejorative manner. Even Sir William Fownes, whose intentions were essentially benevolent, could lose his self-control on this subject:

> there are numbers of these straggling about, running into evil Courses, sculking about Gentlemens Stables and Houses; and are privately supported by Servants, and some by Servants to whom they are related, and this by stealing from their Masters and Mistresses; others pretend to live by selling News-Papers, blacking of Shoes, and running often on pimping Errands from Taverns; tho' these kinds make a sorry Shift to get Bread; yet they are notoriously wicked, and ought to be confined to Work-houses.[196]

Even more violent language was to be found in Viscount Molesworth's *Considerations for the Promoting of Agriculture, and Employing the Poor* (1723), where fear gave way to loathing. He described the poor Irish in the countryside who

> live under Hedges, in Ditches and Hutts, worse than Hog-sties; from whence you shall often see creeping out like Vermin, whole swarms of Bastards; the Produce of Adultery and Incest, and whereof, there are more in the Neighbourhood of *Dublin*, than any other part of the World; a Race of People like Gypsies, which no Priest takes any care of; yet are the Seminaries of all rebellions, dangerous in Plague Times, revengeful at all times, in burning Barns and Houses of such as are not kind to them, and Harbourers of Robbers.[197]

194 Davis, vol. IX, p. 199.
195 Ibid., p. 209.
196 Fownes, *Methods for Regulating the Poor* (1725), p. 9.
197 Molesworth, *Considerations for the Promoting of Agriculture*..., pp. 40–1.

Swift wrote in the same vein, of 'the Tribe of wicked Boys, wherewith most Corners of the Town are pestered', many of them immigrants from the city's rural hinterland, where they had been 'bred up from the Dunghill in Idleness, Ignorance, Lying and Thievery', 'from their Infancy so given up to Idleness and Sloth, that they often chuse to beg or steal, rather than Support themselves with their own Labour'.[198]

This belief in pathological criminality, combined with what appears to have been an obsessive concern with the prevalence of prostitution in Dublin, produced in Swift a revulsion against female vagrants in particular, whom he described in one telling passage as 'profligate abandoned Women, who croud our Streets with their borrowed or spurious issue'. In this mindset, the children themselves appeared, at best, as the badge of a squalid and habitual immorality; and, at worst, as the product of a base calculation, as these 'strolling women' deliberately surrounded themselves with bands of 'naked children', as much the appurtenances of their trade of begging as the rags in which all were clothed.[199] In consequence, there would be a bitter logic in the proposal that such women should be enabled to contribute positively to the Irish economy by selling their offspring for butcher's meat, their reproductive capacity for once harnessed to a profitable end.

Thus, *A Modest Proposal* is far from being a simple repudiation of the inequities and inhumanity of dominant social systems and economic relations. Rawson has pointed out that this popular misconception of the pamphlet obscured both the workings of 'an irony a good deal less simple than is normally thought', and Swift's 'complicated interplay of compassion and contempt', where 'feelings oscillate starkly among extreme positions'. These positions do not include sympathy in any simple way. The Modest Proposer 'is not mainly parodying other pamphleteers, so much as giving vent to a certain side of Swift himself'.[200] This side is not easily sympathetic to the modern reader, is implicated in Swift's own satire (on weakness, and the intractable ways in which human clay cannot be remoulded, which is the larger vista beyond the local ironies of the *A Modest Proposal*), and reflects Swift's sense of being (and not being) English and Irish, amongst other contradictions.

Despite its status as a classic exemplar of Swift's fierce irony, and the treatment it often receives as a timeless satire on the inhumanity of man,

---

198 *Causes of the Wretched Condition of Ireland* (Davis, vol. IX, pp. 201–2).
199 Ibid. In the *Proposal for Giving Badges to Beggars*, Swift noted that rags were 'Part of their Tools with which they work' (below, p. 319).
200 Rawson, 'A Reading of *A Modest Proposal*', in *Order from Confusion Sprung*, pp. 121, 128.

A Modest Proposal is also a piece of writing that reflects its chronological context. Although the issue that the pamphlet addressed directly was the acute economic hardship visible on the streets of the capital, it was also an indirect response to what was perceived as a general crisis threatening Irish Protestant society. Demographically, the principal cause for concern was the renewed emigration from Ulster to north America, at a time when fear of 'popery' was resurgent. A scheme to engineer a comparable reduction in the Catholic population would have obvious resonances. But Swift himself was ambivalent about the events in Ulster. The migrant ships departing from Derry and other northern ports undoubtedly represented a weakening of the Protestant interest, but he was contemptuous of the way in which Presbyterian ministers and controversialists opportunistically cited emigration to make a case for the redress of grievances. In common with other clergymen, he could not accept the argument that these emigrants had been driven away by any form of religious discrimination, observing that they had 'chosen rather to leave their Country, than stay at home, and pay Tythes against their Conscience, to an *Episcopal Curate*'.[201] The embattled position of the established church, having to defend its privileges against increasing criticism, also weighed on Swift's mind. We can also see it expressed, more obliquely, in his repeated denunciations of Irish landlords, which reflects resentment at what he saw as the gathering anticlericalism of the propertied elite.

A Modest Proposal needs also to be understood as Swift's particular contribution to the chorus of printed advice being prepared for the members of the Irish Parliament who were to meet in session over the winter of 1729–30. In this respect, it enjoyed only a limited success in Ireland. The appearance of the pamphlet created ripples in the political waters there, but no great splash. It attracted considerably more attention in London, where the reading public were more likely to be intrigued and amused by fantasies of Irish depravity. The rather nondescript Dublin edition was soon reprinted by two different London booksellers, both of whom advertised it in November 1729; one of these, Weaver Bickerton, had offered three editions by the end of 1730 (albeit possibly the same edition with new title pages), and combined it with two other Irish pamphlets, in a portmanteau publication entitled *A View of the Present State of Affairs in Ireland* (perhaps a nod towards Swift's *Short View*). It was referenced in November 1730 in the issue of *The Craftsman* to which Swift penned a

---

201 Below, p. 154. The introduction, before 'Episcopal', of the adjective 'idolatrous' into the 1735 edition (whether by Swift or someone else) effectively parodied the rhetoric of a bigoted Ulster Presbyterian minister.

response,[202] and was translated into French by the Piedmontese Count Adalberti Radicati di Passerana in 1736.[203] But of the immediate impact in Ireland we know very little. James Arbuckle's collection of essays, *The Tribune*, published a month or so later, offered proposals for curing Ireland's ills, and in particular for social engineering among the debased peasantry, in reasonable and relatively humane terms, which might have been read as an implicit response to *A Modest Proposal*.[204] But for direct contemporary comment, all that survives is a short comment from the Irish revenue commissioner, Marmaduke Coghill, who in November 1729 sent a publication to his friend Edward Southwell in London with the laconic explanation, 'the enclosed is a book of Swift's'.[205] This was presumably *A Modest Proposal*. By comparison, Coghill's comments on the publication of Thomas Prior's *A List of the Absentees of Ireland*, published a few weeks in advance of Swift's masterpiece, were almost animated: 'We have a bitter book published against absentees, [which] though it has some truths in it, has many faults and [is] liable to many objections.'[206]

Prior's book (which at over eighty pages was more than four times as long as *A Modest Proposal*) did indeed create a minor sensation in Dublin, so much so that 'patriot' MPs were encouraged to prepare a bill for the forthcoming session of the Irish Parliament that would have imposed a tax on the incomes of absentee landlords, placemen and pensioners.[207] The *List* also went through three editions in its first year: two in Dublin and the third printed in London, again by Weaver Bickerton, who bundled it, together with a rejoinder on behalf of the absentees, and *A Modest Proposal*, in his *View of the Present State of Affairs in Ireland*. Interestingly, he placed Prior's tract, and the reply, ahead of Swift in the running order. It looks very much as though Prior had scooped the dean. Bishop Robert Howard of Killala thought that the *List of Absentees* 'had some strokes of Jonathan', and there are hints that Swift himself may have been piqued by its success. He had, after all, already played this card himself. He wrote to

202 *The Answer to the Craftsman* (below, pp. 218–27).
203 Flavio Gregori, 'The Italian Reception of Swift', in Hermann J. Real (ed.), *The Reception of Jonathan Swift in Europe*, London: Thoemmes Continuum, 2005, p. 26.
204 [James Arbuckle,] *The Tribune*, London, 1729, pp. 125, 129–30; Richard Holmes, 'James Arbuckle and Dean Swift: Cultural Politics in the Irish Confessional State', *Irish Studies Review* 16 (2008), 437–8.
205 Marmaduke Coghill to Edward Southwell, 13 Nov. 1729 (*Coghill Letters*, p. 78).
206 Same to same, 14 Oct. 1729 (ibid., p. 74).
207 Carteret to Edward Southwell, 30 Nov. 1729 (BL, Add. MS 38016, fos. 9–10); James Smyth to William Smyth, 23 Dec. 1729 (NLI, Smythe of Barbavilla papers, MS 42,582/7).

Pope on 31 October 1729, 'we return thrice as much to our absentees as we get by trade, and so are all inevitably undone; which I have been telling them in print these ten years, to as little purpose as if it came from the pulpit'.[208] In *A Modest Proposal*, he included the proposed tax on absentees as one of the various 'other expedients' to which his own scheme was an alternative.

We know nothing of the genesis of *A Modest Proposal*, nor of the circumstances of its composition, so it would be rank speculation to suggest that Swift may have been seeking to overbid Prior by the 'shock value' of his own work. But although he fully endorsed the case against absenteeism, he would not have been happy at an analysis which ascribed all the blame for Ireland's economic woes to the irresponsibility of Irish landowners, while to all intents and purposes ignoring the essentially iniquitous nature of Ireland's constitutional dependency. Prior's pamphlet also shared the assumption of other writers of whom Swift very much disapproved, like John Browne, that the Irish economy might be improved without the necessity for fundamental constitutional change. *A Modest Proposal* maintains Swift's frequently expressed disdain for Browne's optimistic view of Irish prospects, based as it was on an ingenuous belief in the potential of the country's economic resources; indeed, the foundation of his argument is to satirise the idea that population density was a resource to be exploited. But it might also be seen as a riposte to Prior, and it would therefore have been doubly galling for Swift to find that (if only in the short term) Prior's pamphlet had made an even greater impact than his own.

9 Dublin Politics

In June 1725, at the height of the excitement about Wood's Halfpence, some fervent 'patriots' tried in vain to secure for Swift the freedom of Dublin. On that occasion, the ruling oligarchy in the city – primarily the aldermen – resisted what would undoubtedly have been a serious affront to government.[209] When the aldermen reversed their position in January 1730, and a general assembly of the corporation (comprising aldermen and 'commons' or common council) voted to offer the dean his freedom in a gold box,[210] Swift's political enemies were disgusted. The Whig politician Lord Allen, formerly a friend of Swift's but now seeking to curry favour with

---

208 Swift to Pope, 31 Oct. 1729 (Woolley, *Corr.*, vol. III, pp. 262–3).
209 Ehrenpreis, vol. III, p. 298.
210 *Cal. Anc. Recs. Dublin*, vol. VII, p. 476; Ehrenpreis, vol. III, p. 650.

the administration, vented his spleen at a meeting of the Irish privy council, to which the lord mayor and sheriffs had been summoned to account for their failure to suppress rioting in the city. At their pleas of poverty, he 'took them up very roundly, and wondered how they should complain of poverty, when they were so lavish as to give a gold box to a man who neither feared God nor honoured the king, who had wrote a libel on the king, queen and government'.[211] These words were reported to the deanery, and Swift naturally took deep offence. When they were repeated in the Irish House of Lords Allen found himself the subject of a series of stinging satires, in verse and prose.

Allen was not the only Castle politician to be nauseated by the assembly's vote. The revenue commissioner Marmaduke Coghill, remembering how the civic authorities had resisted 'patriotic' pressure in 1725, wrote to an Irish correspondent in London: 'You very justly observe how our angels of aldermen are turned from those of light to those of darkness, for once nothing was too good for them, so now nothing is bad enough for them, and they are the most despicable set of men in the kingdom.'[212] From a government point of view, worse was to come. In February 1733, Swift's friend, the 'patriot' MP Eaton Stannard, was elected to the vacant position of recorder of the corporation, after Swift had listed his virtues in an appeal to the public spirit of the aldermen and common council.[213] And, later that year, a hard-fought parliamentary by-election for the city ended with the return of another 'patriot' candidate, the outgoing lord mayor Humphrey French, who had also been strongly endorsed by Swift in his *Advice to the Free-men of the City of Dublin in The Choice of a Member to Represent Them In Parliament.*[214]

The background to the changing political climate in the corporation is obscure. Histories of eighteenth-century Dublin have tended to slide over this period, and to pick up the narrative with the rise of a 'patriot' element among the citizenry in the 1740s, and the radical challenge of the apothecary Charles Lucas to the oligarchic rule of the aldermen. As yet, we have insufficient evidence of the ideological sympathies and factional allegiances of aldermen and common councilmen to enable events to be

---

211 Coghill to Edward Southwell, 21 Feb. 1729[/30] (*Coghill Letters*, pp. 91–2).
212 Same to same, 3 Jan. 1729[/30] (ibid., p. 83).
213 Below, pp. 240–3. For Stannard, see *Hist. Ir. Parl.*, vol. VI, pp. 319–21; and for his friendship with Swift, Ehrenpreis, vol. II, pp. 819, 842.
214 Below, pp. 247–54. On French's 'patriot' credentials, see also *Astræa's Congratulation: an Ode upon Alderman Humphrey French being Elected Representative for the City of Dublin*, [Dublin], 1733.

explained with confidence: little or no correspondence survives between the principals, and the existing printed sources – pamphlets, broadsheets and newspaper reports – are fragmentary. Nevertheless, the bare record of the city corporation's 'Monday books' and assembly rolls, stating decisions made by the aldermen and common council, suggests that there had been significant tremors since at least 1728. Elections at all levels proved unusually difficult. In July 1728, the choice of a new alderman – at which the lord mayor customarily proposed a panel of three candidates from which the rest of the aldermen selected one – required six attempts before a successful nomination was made; another aldermanic election the following year saw seven mayoral nominations rejected; and in February and April 1730, and again in January 1731, there were contested votes in elections for aldermen and for the city coroner.[215] Although Humphrey French was recorded as having been chosen lord mayor in 1732 unanimously at the first attempt, only half the aldermen were present on that occasion, which might well indicate a division of opinion. The following year it took two attempts to secure the appointment of Stannard as recorder.[216] This level of seismic activity in municipal elections was unusual, and was accompanied by hard-fought contests over parliamentary seats, in a constituency whose combined freeman and freeholder franchise made it the largest urban electorate in the country, with between 2,000 and 3,000 voters.[217] The 1727 general election cost one successful candidate over £1,000, which in Ireland was an unheard-of, and potentially ruinous, expense.[218] An unusually high level of mortality among the city's representatives then produced by-elections in 1728, 1729, and again in 1733, when French was returned. Each gave rise to frenetic activity, including elaborate entertainments for voters, and the frequent resort to printed broadsheets or ballads to assert a candidate's virtue or to denounce opponents.

The nature of corporate governance in Dublin suggests that an explanation should first be sought in the personalities and rivalries of the twenty-four aldermen, in whose hands power was concentrated, and who usually provided the rival candidates in parliamentary as well as municipal elections. A

---

215 Dublin Corporation 'Monday book', 22 July 1728, 16 May 1729, 7 Feb. 1729[/30], 9 Apr. 1730, 19 Jan. 1730[/1] (Dublin City Archives, G/102/05, pp. 90–1, 95–6, 107, 108, 116).
216 'Monday book', 21 Apr. 1732 (ibid., p. 128); *Pue's Occurrences*, 13–17 Feb. 1733; *Daily Courant*, 1 Mar. 1733; *Daily Journal*, 1 Mar. 1733.
217 *Hist. Ir. Parl*, vol. II, p. 229; Sean Murphy, 'Charles Lucas and the Dublin Election of 1748–1749', *Parliamentary History* 2 (1983), 95.
218 Hugh Howard to Bishop Robert Howard, 27 Feb. 1727/8 (NLI, MS 38,598/3).

classic self-perpetuating oligarchy, they served for life, and themselves chose new members to fill vacant places. They were also responsible for electing the lord mayor, and other officers, and the members of the common council, the body from which recruits to the aldermanic dignity were drawn. The easiest explanation for divisions within this narrowly circumscribed community would be conflicts of personality, tending by a natural process to produce factional conflicts. But the political history of early eighteenth-century Ireland suggests that issues could also figure. Twenty years earlier, in Queen Anne's reign, the city had been riven by the conflict of Whigs and Tories. True, the long-running dispute which brought corporate government to a standstill in 1711–14 had been in essence a quarrel between aldermen, a handful of Tories exploiting the powers of the Irish privy council in order to frustrate the wish of the Whig majority for a lord mayor of their own persuasion.[219] On the other hand, Whig and Tory loyalties clearly extended far below the level of the aldermanic court, and the parliamentary election for the city in 1713 had given rise to mob violence, with fatalities when troops were called out to protect municipal officials.[220]

Underlying the antagonism between these parties, at every level, was tension between Churchmen and Dissenters, arising from the existence of a substantial minority of Protestant Nonconformists, mainly Presbyterians, in the city's population. By the late 1720s, 'party', in the Whig and Tory sense, was no longer acknowledged as a significant factor in Dublin politics, despite the survival of some Tory aldermen like Sir William Fownes who were veterans of the battles of Queen Anne's reign. There was, however, still a Nonconformist presence in the corporation, for southern Presbyterians, unlike their Ulster brethren, were happy to conform 'occasionally' (that is to say, to serve a turn), and thus circumvent the requirements of the sacramental test. This may well have exacerbated other differences between aldermen. The belated election of the Nonconformist clothier Alderman Joseph Kane as lord mayor in 1725–6 seems to have marked a recovery in the Dissenting interest in city politics.[221] Dissenters were particularly active in parliamentary elections, where ordinary freemen could be mobilised by

---

219 C. M. Flanagan, '"A Merely Local Dispute?" Partisan Politics and the Dublin Mayoral Dispute of 1709–1715' (Ph.D. thesis, University of Notre Dame, 1983); Jacqueline Hill, *From Patriots to Unionists: Dublin Civic Politics and Irish Protestant Patriotism, 1660–1840*, Oxford: Clarendon Press, 1997, ch. 2.
220 J. G. Simms, 'The Irish Parliament of 1713', in G. A. Hayes-McCoy (ed.), *Historical Studies, IV*, London: Bowes & Bowes, 1963, pp. 85–6.
221 J. R. Hill, 'Dublin Corporation, Protestant Dissent, and Politics, 1660–1800', in Kevin Herlihy (ed.), *The Politics of Irish Dissent 1650–1800*, Dublin: Four Courts Press, 1997, pp. 32–3.

their ministers.[222] In the 1727 general election, one of the three candidates, William Howard (who was in fact a younger brother of the bishop of Killala), was said to have relied on Nonconformist voters in his successful campaign against Swift's friend, Alderman John Stoyte; and the following year, at a by-election to replace Howard, who had barely lived long enough to take his seat in the Commons, Stoyte was again opposed, this time unsuccessfully, by a Dissenting lobby, on this occasion supporting John Forbes, a young lawyer and the son of an alderman.[223] When Stoyte died, within a year of his election, the contest for the vacancy was between two aldermen, James Somerville and Peter Verdoen, and although there are no contemporary reports of the involvement of Dissenters on Somerville's side, Verdoen, like Stoyte before him, was presented as a stalwart of the established church, and was said to have enjoyed the backing of staunch churchmen within the city.[224] It may also be significant that Swift was accused by Howard's friends of supporting Stoyte in 1727 – reasonably enough, given their friendship, but also to be expected in the sectarian atmosphere in which the election was fought – and that in 1729 the dean's name was also made use of to discredit Somerville.[225] When Forbes appeared in 1733 as an aspirant for the recordership, in a contest with Eaton Stannard, Swift once more weighed in against him, though on this occasion religious allegiance does not seem to have been a factor. Instead, Forbes was the candidate of the aldermen against the popular vote.[226]

It was not just in parliamentary elections that 'ordinary' Dubliners could exercise their prejudices. Politics in the corporation was not entirely a closed shop, even in relation to municipal government, and the aldermen were not insulated from the concerns and opinions of the population at large. Within the corporation itself, there was a role – albeit a restricted one – for the 'commons'. While routine business was undertaken by the lord mayor and aldermen at weekly meetings, it was at the quarterly 'assemblies' of aldermen and 'commons' together that by-laws were made, funds awarded, and municipal elections ratified. What is more, motions in the assembly

---

222 *A Letter to the Freemen and Freeholders of the City of Dublin, who are Protestants of the Church of England as by Law Established*, [Dublin, 1727].
223 T. C. Barnard, 'The Government and Irish Dissent, 1704–1780', in Herlihy (ed.), *Politics of Irish Dissent*, pp. 24–5; Marmaduke Coghill to Edward Southwell, 12 Jan. 1727[/8] (*Coghill Letters*, p. 46).
224 *An Elegy on the Much Lamented Death of Alderman John Stoyte . . .* , Dublin, 1728; *Dublin Intelligence*, 11 Oct. 1729.
225 *The Last Speech and Dying Words of the Election of the City of Dublin, Ended November the 1st, 1727*, [Dublin, 1727]; see above, p. xxvii.
226 *Daily Courant*, 20 Feb. 1733; *Daily Journal*, 1 Mar. 1733; Swift to Stannard, 12 Dec. 1733, 12 Mar. 1734 (Woolley, *Corr.*, vol. III, pp. 713, 726–7).

frequently originated in petitions from the 'commons', agreed beforehand at separate meetings. In normal circumstances, the aldermen need not have feared displays of independence, for the size of the common council made it an unwieldy instrument of resistance – it comprised 48 'sheriffs' peers' and 92 'numbers' (representatives of the various trade guilds) – and the members were hand-picked, the 'sheriffs' peers' chosen by a committee of aldermen, the 'numbers' selected by the aldermen from a slate put forward by each guild master.[227] (The role of the guilds was a further complicating factor, with some aldermen serving as guild brothers.) Nevertheless, even this carefully selected group was capable of flashes of independence. The offer of the freedom of the city to Swift in January 1730 may have been one such episode. As mentioned above, the election of Stannard in February 1733 was another act of defiance, the aldermen having first favoured one of their own number, John Forbes, whom the 'commons' rejected by a vote of 70 to 37 before Stannard was nominated and accepted.[228]

If, as seems likely, the 'commons' were becoming more restive from the late 1720s, and more sceptical of their civic leaders, it is likely that the aldermen's own failings were at least a contributory factor. Among the wider urban public, the Dublin corporation was a byword for incompetence and dishonesty. Even the financial distress of individual aldermen became fodder for satirists, one 'scandalous paper' being circulated in July 1729 at the expense of the hapless Alderman Henry Burrows, a bankrupt who had been obliged to appeal to his colleagues for money to provide for himself and his family.[229] But the most serious revelations came as a consequence of parliamentary inquiries in the autumn of 1729 into law and order in the capital, which exposed systematic corruption in the administration of justice in the city, centring on the dubious figure of John Hawkins, the keeper of Newgate gaol. The first reaction of the aldermen was to ignore the evidence against Hawkins, which only had the effect of tarring themselves with the same brush, before they were embarrassed into backtracking and removing him from office.[230] Worse still, the Irish House of Commons

---

227 Sean Murphy, 'The Corporation of Dublin, 1660–1760', *Dublin Historical Record* 38 (1984), 22–35; Hill, *From Patriots to Unionists*, pp. 43–4.
228 *Daily Courant*, 1 Mar. 1733; *Pue's Occurrences*, 13–17 Feb. 1733; *Cal. Anc. Recs. Dublin*, vol. VIII, p. 92.
229 *Dublin Intelligence*, 12 July 1729, 14 Apr. 1730; *Dublin Weekly Journal*, 30 Aug. 1729; *Cal. Anc. Recs. Dublin*, vol. VII, pp. 461, 465, 488–9; vol. VIII, pp. 61–3.
230 *C.J.Ire.*, vol. V, pp. 668, 708; *Cal. Anc. Recs. Dublin*, vol. VII, pp. 467, 472, 477; T. D. Watt, 'The Corruption of the Law and Popular Violence: The Crisis of Order in Dublin, 1729', *Irish Historical Studies* 39 (2014–15), 8–19.

discovered that two aldermen and the city coroner, Sir Nathaniel Whitwell, had solicited bribes to drop prosecutions, and took them into custody.[231]

The collapse of public trust in the civic elite was exacerbated by the economic crisis which gripped Ireland in the late 1720s, and which affected Dublin perhaps even more seriously than the countryside. Shortages in the supply of basic foodstuffs coincided with a slump in trade, which for the ordinary inhabitants of the city – and especially the journeymen weavers and their families in the neighbourhood of St Patrick's – meant that incomes fell while the cost of living rose: a deadly combination.[232] The consequences were dire. Not only did working families drop into poverty: as we have seen, there was also a very visible increase in the numbers of beggars and 'disorderly persons' on the streets. The city became an even more violent place: riots were commonplace, with groups of weavers frequently involved, and marauding gangs – notably the 'Kevan Bail', whose home ground was the area around St Kevan (or Kevin) Street – fighting running battles with each other and with the watchmen and constables. All of this took place close enough to the seat of government, and to the town houses of the wealthy, to make Irish politicians fearful for their own safety. On one occasion, an affray took place in St Stephen's Green, where the well-to-do would promenade; there were confrontations between the populace and students from Trinity College; and the Kevan Bail also transgressed barriers of social status by attacking 'gentlemen'.[233] In June 1729, the lords justices and privy council issued a proclamation against the 'riots and tumults' that were a daily occurrence in the city,[234] but were unable to restore calm, and in the following autumn the Irish Parliament began its inquiries into the activities of Dublin magistrates and their officials. Little wonder that Lord Allen should have been so furious at a corporation which not only seemed incapable of preserving public order but was – in his view – guilty of offering encouragement to political and social insubordination by lionising the Drapier.

Whether or not a specific connection could be made between the excitements of the populace and Swift's particular brand of 'patriot' rhetoric, it is clear that the street violence of Dublin was far from being devoid of political content. The more obsessive Whigs were inclined to suspect Jacobite

---

231 *C.J.Ire.*, vol. V, pp. 733–5.
232 For the sufferings of the weavers, see *Dublin Intelligence*, 14 Jan. 1729. A thousand of them signed a petition to the Commons (Carteret to Edward Southwell, 9 Dec. 1729 (BL, Add. MS 38016, fos. 11–16)).
233 *Dublin Intelligence*, 12, 16 Apr. 1729, 16 Mar. 1730/1.
234 Ibid., 10 June 1729.

ambitions in the mob, though there is little to bear this out. A proclamation by the lord mayor in 1729 banning the wearing of white roses and other 'distinguishing marks of disloyalty' on the Pretender's birthday, 10 June, could be dismissed as hysterical, and seems to have been ridiculed by Swift on just this basis, in his *Vindication of... Carteret* (1730), and possibly again in the *Examination of Certain Abuses, Corruptions, and Enormities in the City of Dublin* (1732).[235] If genuine, the practice was as likely to have been sectarian as Jacobite, or (to adapt the argument of one scholar on the character of protest in early eighteenth-century England) simply a ready means of expressing a generalised opposition to authority.[236] Other instances of crowd behaviour show a clearer motivation, with grievances and objectives that were local in nature and economic in motivation. Protests against high food prices were often directed against the engrossers, the supposed 'monsters in retailing', who were exploiting bread shortages to raise their prices, a complaint taken up in the Irish House of Commons in November 1729 by the Dublin city recorder, Sir John Rogerson, when he was given leave to introduce heads of a bill 'against forestallers, regratters, and engrossers, [and] for... regulating the price and assize of bread'.[237] There were also tensions between journeymen and their masters, in various trades, including hosiery, when the journeymen found themselves obliged to pay so much for the materials supplied to them that they could not make enough on their work. In 1731, a Dublin newspaper reported instances of ritualised violence – 'colting' – against rivals prepared to work at a cheaper rate, and a proclamation was issued against 'assemblies of journeymen'.[238] This must have been an ongoing concern, for in 1730 the Irish Parliament had passed an act (3 Geo. II. c. 14 [Ire.]) 'to prevent unlawful combinations of workmen, artificers, and labourers, employed in the several trades and manufactures of this kingdom'.[239]

---

235 *Faulkner's Dublin Journal*, 7–10 June 1729; below, pp. 217, 240–63.
236 Nicholas Rogers, 'Riot and Popular Jacobitism in Early Hanoverian England', in Eveline Cruickshanks (ed.), *Ideology and Conspiracy: Aspects of Jacobitism, 1689–1759*, Edinburgh: John Donald, 1982, pp. 70–88. For a different view, see P. K. Monod, *Jacobitism and the English People, 1688–1788*, Cambridge: Cambridge University Press, 1989; and for Jacobitism in Ireland, Ó Ciardha, *Ireland and the Jacobite Cause*.
237 *C.J.Ire.*, vol. V, p. 709; see also *A Poem Occasion'd by the Lord Mayor's Reducing the Price of Coals &c.*, Dublin, 1729.
238 *Dublin Intelligence*, 14, 28 July 1731; *The Poor Man's Case Consider'd; or a Pill for Colts and Cure for the Publick: Being the Address of All and Singular the Journeymen of the City of Dublin*, Dublin, 1732.
239 See Mel Doyle, 'The Dublin Guilds and Journeymen's Clubs', *Saothar: Journal of the Irish Labour History Society* 3 (1977), 6–14.

How did Swift negotiate his way through this strained and often conflicted environment? At the most basic level he could rely on his iconic status as 'the Drapier' to protect him from the daily perils of his violent neighbourhood, as well as his reputation for acts of personal charity to the poor of the Liberties. When he returned to Dublin after a prolonged rustication in 1729, the Kevan Bail lit bonfires to celebrate his safe arrival back in his deanery.[240] 'I walk the streets in peace', he boasted to Alexander Pope in 1733, 'without being justled, nor ever without a thousand blessings from my friends the Vulgar'.[241] There is some evidence that he associated himself with the artisan class, groups like the 'poor inhabitants, tradesmen and labourers' whose memorial he answered in 1728.[242] When he spoke of meeting and talking with representatives of the 'several societies of handicrafts-men... in this city', it is likely that these were associations of journeymen rather than the trade guilds, which represented the masters and were headed by wealthy businessmen, and even city aldermen.[243] These journeymen societies were evidently 'friendly societies', which had been established 'for the improvement of trade and the relief of indigent and decayed workmen': in Dublin they numbered over 1,500 members, and they included 'the Loyal and Charitable Society of Broadcloth Weavers', 'the Society of Journeymen, Shearers and Dyers', the 'Society of Journeymen Tailors' and 'the Loyal and Charitable Society of Stocking-Frame Knitters'.[244] Thus, 'the corporation of weavers in woollen and silk', with whom Swift claimed to have had personal dealings, is more likely to have been some such organisation as the 'loyal and charitable society of woollen broad-cloth weavers' who published their welcoming address on his return from England in 1727, or the 'Society of Journeymen Tailors' whose annual meeting was recorded in a Dublin newspaper in 1731,[245] rather than the principal weavers' guild, the Guild of the Blessed Virgin Mary, represented in the city 'commons', in whose minutes for this period

---

240 *Faulkner's Dublin Journal*, 7–11 Oct. 1729.
241 Swift to Pope, 8 July 1733 (Woolley, *Corr.*, vol. III, p. 663).
242 Below, pp. 27–41.
243 For these journeymen societies, see Patrick Walsh, 'Club Life in Late Seventeenth- and Early Eighteenth-Century Ireland: in Search of an Associational World, *c.* 1680–*c.* 1730', in James Kelly and Martyn Powell (eds.), *Clubs and Societies in Eighteenth-Century Ireland*, Dublin: Four Courts Press, 2010, pp. 44–8.
244 Marsh's Lib., MS Z.3.1.1. (136–7, 164); William O'Brien, *An Epick Poem on... William Leigh*, Dublin, 1727; *A Congratulatory Speech of the Loyal and Charitable Society of Woollen Broad-Cloath-Weavers, in Honour to the Reverend Doctor Jonathan Swift*, [Dublin, 1727]; *Dublin Intelligence*, 28 July 1731.
245 *A Congratulatory Speech of the Loyal and Charitable Society of Woollen Broad-Cloath Weavers*; *Dublin Intelligence*, 28 July 1731.

Swift's name does not appear, although a number of other public figures were admitted as members, headed by the lord lieutenant and including MPs and the economic writer David Bindon.[246] Swift's constituency was emphatically not the civic elite, even if he did have friends among some leading men in the corporation, including Sir William Fownes, not only an alderman but a prominent member of the weavers' guild.[247] Instead, he appealed to the ordinary citizen – specifically to the freemen in his published advice on the 1733 parliamentary election[248] – and it was the 'commons' rather than the aldermen who responded to him, who voted to offer him the freedom of Dublin in 1730, and who elected Eaton Stannard into the recordership and Humphrey French into Parliament in 1733.

There was, however, a limit to Swift's advocacy of the interests of the common man. He did not choose to comment in print on the scandals breaking in Dublin in 1729–30 over the administration of justice, and only once did he allude to the frequent communal violence in the city, despite the geographical proximity of the deanery to the epicentre of the disturbances. In the poem 'The Yahoo's Overthrow' (1734), directed at his old enemy Richard Bettesworth, he made reference both to the 'Kevan Bayl' and to the practice of 'colting' in a surprisingly jocular fashion, contemplating how Bettesworth might be punished for the crime of insulting the dean, by the 'jolly boys of St Kevans'.[249] Swift's contributions to the debate over the depressed condition of trade and manufacture ignored the grievances of journeymen against masters, and of consumers against profiteers, in favour of a rehearsal of the main themes of his economic and social discourse, the iniquity of English policy, which by discriminating against Irish trade and restricting economic opportunities had reduced the population of Ireland to the status of slaves, and the blind refusal of the fashionable – especially the female of the species – to support their country by purchasing garments of Irish manufacture.

These omissions suggest that, whatever the public response to his work, Swift himself identified not with the interests of the 'vulgar' urban population as a whole, but with those who had – or in a properly governed society ought

---

246 Guild of the Blessed Virgin Mary, Dublin, 'book of brothers', 1693–1722, 1722–43 (Royal Society of Antiquaries of Ireland, SAI/BV/WRVS, 005, 009). Bindon was admitted in 1733, alongside the 'patriot' MPs Warden Flood and Anthony Malone.
247 Fownes had been admitted into the Weavers' Guild by 1715 (Guild of the Blessed Virgin Mary, 'book of brothers', 1693–1722 (Royal Society of Antiquaries of Ireland, SAI/BV/WRVS, 005, unfol.).
248 Below, pp. 279–87.
249 *Poems*, vol. III, pp. 814–17.

to have had – the means for self-sufficiency: small manufacturers and traders like the Drapier who were bearing the brunt of English economic oppression. In the corporation these were the freemen, and ordinary guild members – at a pinch, the city 'commons'. Their interests were distinct not only from those of the wealthier merchants above them in the civic hierarchy, but also from the desperate anxieties preoccupying the mass of poor Dubliners below them, and especially the begging and criminal classes.

In promoting the popular parliamentary candidature of Humphrey French, Swift was throwing his weight behind a municipal figure whose 'patriotic' virtue, proven by a record of public service and a deserved reputation for philanthropy, was combined with a tough approach on issues of law and order. French almost perfectly represented the concerns of small manufacturers and traders, who responded by offering him tributes that were not given to other lord mayors, the corporation of shoemakers making him a present of plate, and the city's common council paying for his portrait to be painted.[250] In Parliament, French sponsored a bill to rescue Dublin's woollen manufacture by prohibiting the importation of silks and other luxury fabrics.[251] As lord mayor he intervened directly to alleviate bread shortages by confiscating 'unmerchantable provisions' from bakers and distributing them among the poor, spent his own money in releasing unfortunates from imprisonment for debt in the Marshalsea, sought to correct abuses in the city government, and organised a rescue package agreed by leading merchants and members of the corporation to guarantee the capital of investors when the banks threatened to fail.[252] At the same time, he personally led the reformed city constabulary in putting down disturbances, in raiding brothels, and in campaigns dedicated to the arrest and committal of large numbers of destitute vagrants, with whom he filled the workhouse and the new bridewell.[253] These two sides of his mayoralty were complementary, and indeed there is no reason to suppose that his most prominent clerical supporter felt the slightest qualm about a policy which in asserting public morality and securing public safety, to the benefit of honest tradesmen,

---

250 *Daily Journal*, 3 July 1733; *St James's Evening Post*, 27 Oct. 1733; *Address of the Society of Yellows, to Alderman Humphry French, Late Lord Mayor of the City of Dublin*, [Dublin], 1733.
251 *C.J.Ire.*, vol. VI, pp. 562, 565.
252 *Pue's Occurrences*, 31 Oct. – 4 Nov. 1732, 23–27 Jan., 14–18 Aug., 22–25, 25–29 Sept. 1733. See also *The Lamentation of the Poor of the City of Dublin; After the Late Lord Mayor...*, [Dublin], 1733; *A Full Vindication of Humphrey French, Late Lord Mayor of the City of Dublin...*, [Dublin,] 1733.
253 *Pue's Occurrences*, 14–18 Nov. 1732.

also produced brutal outcomes for those at the very bottom of the social scale.

Swift's contributions to the political debates fermenting within the city in 1728–33 were not, however, related to any of these issues, but instead reproduced in a local context more general 'patriotic' concerns. He did not, unlike some contemporaries, ridicule aldermen who were financially embarrassed, or condemn the corporate oligarchy as a whole for corruption and misgovernment. There was no radical civic agenda, but an entirely orthodox 'patriotic' political opposition, and in this sense he seems detached from much of the contemporary discourse in the Dublin press on the challenges facing the capital. Thus, his advocacy of Eaton Stannard as Dublin's recorder was based on an appreciation of Stannard's already well-established reputation as a parliamentarian, not on what he might achieve for the corporation. Similarly, preference for Humphrey French in the parliamentary election of 1733 was founded on French's credentials as a 'patriot' rather than his exemplary record as a reforming lord mayor. French's personal qualities, his integrity and philanthropy, were translated from a municipal to a national context. He was distinguished from his original opponent John Macarell by a presumed independence from government and by his principled appeal to the electorate, disdaining to acquire votes by bribery or treating.[254] Macarell had been the first to declare, and although he subsequently withdrew, leaving French to contest the poll against the current lord mayor, Thomas Howe, he was still a candidate when Swift intervened. Macarell had only recently been elected an alderman, but what Swift emphasised was the fact that he also held a government office, as register of the barracks, and therefore as a placeman could not be trusted to serve the country's interests.[255]

10 *The Changing Character of Irish Politics, 1730–1737*

The replacement of Lord Carteret as lord lieutenant by the Duke of Dorset in 1730 had little immediate effect on the political scene in Dublin. Dorset made no changes to the commission of lords justices – Lord Chancellor Wyndham, Archbishop Boulter and the Speaker, Sir Ralph Gore – and when he came to Dublin in 1731 to preside over his first session of Parliament, he retained in their offices the parliamentary 'undertakers' he

---

254 *Astræa's Congratulation....*; *A Full Vindication of Humphrey French...*; *Advice to the Freemen and Freeholders of the City of Dublin; in Their Choice of a Representative in the Ensuing Election*, Dublin, 1733.
255 Below, pp. 279–87.

had inherited, Gore and the other remnants of Speaker Conolly's party. But, unlike Carteret, he sought to keep himself above the parliamentary fray, leaving the routine work of management to others, with the intention that, by remaining aloof from the factional struggles of Irish politicians, he might attract support from a broader spectrum of opinion, including the independent, back-bench country gentlemen who were vociferous in defending Ireland's interests and promoting measures to improve the kingdom's economic prospects. This, at least, was the theory. In practice, he had his favourites and particular advisers, although they were not men of the first flight. Colonel William Flower, a wealthy Kilkenny squire, was one; and, unfortunately for Swift, Lord Allen – 'Traulus' – was another, which seems to have set the seal on Swift's exclusion from the new viceregal court.[256]

Dorset's first parliamentary session, in the winter of 1731–2, was neither an outstanding success nor a dismal failure. More by luck than judgement, and probably owing a great deal more than he was willing to admit to the skill and loyalty of Gore and his friends, Dorset avoided humiliation and secured a short-term grant of supply. He was, however, obliged by Sir Robert Walpole to attempt a repeal of the sacramental test, and in that respect succeeded only in provoking a storm of outrage from members of the established church, both clerical and lay. The idea was for a repeal clause to be tacked by the British privy council to a further popery bill sent from Ireland, but when Dorset grasped the extent of the likely opposition in the Irish House of Commons he persuaded Cabinet colleagues that the scheme should be dropped, at least for the time being. But the issue did not go away. The implications for English politics were too important for Walpole simply to forget about it, and in any case the prime minister's difficult relationship with Dorset, which only worsened during the Excise Crisis of 1733, made the prospect of causing embarrassment for the viceroy a very tempting one. And in the Irish context the damage had already been done: the proposed repeal had reanimated an issue that had previously seemed settled, and had focused political debate once more on the relationship of church and state. Parliament's response had been discouraging for the Presbyterians, but as far as Swift and his fellow clergymen were concerned prospects were still clouded. Besides the evident determination of the English ministry to see something done, there were worrying doubts

---

256 Henry Boyle to Earl of Burlington, 17 Aug. 1731 (PRONI, Chatsworth papers, T/3158/13); Henry Rose to Sir Maurice Crosbie, 21 Sept. 1731 (NLI, Talbot-Crosbie papers, P.C. 188).

about the reliability of Irish MPs, and when this was combined with what Swift regarded as the intrinsic corruption of the political system on both sides of the Irish Sea, nothing could be taken for granted.

Further complications arose before the next parliamentary session in Dublin, which was to take place in the winter of 1733–4. The death of Sir Ralph Gore in February 1733 not only created a vacancy in the Speakership of the Commons, but promised a major alteration in the Irish administration. There was no obvious successor from within the old 'Castle' party, and the individuals in whom Dorset had confided on his first visit to Dublin had proved that they lacked sufficient personal influence in the Commons. The answer, which Dorset eventually realised, was to turn to the leader of the quondam Brodrick faction, the County Cork squire Henry Boyle, whose personal following, based around the Brodricks' supporters and his own extended family, gave him enough votes to be able to 'undertake' for a supply. Boyle was elected as Speaker in October 1733, and after initial difficulties, caused by Dorset's unwillingness to give the new 'undertaker' his full support, settled into the position that Conolly and Gore had occupied before him, managing the passage of government business through the Commons, and joining the primate and lord chancellor on the commission of lords justices during the long recess.

In some respects, Swift could rest easy with this changeover, in so far as Boyle's appointment did not carry with it any particular threat to the church. Indeed, on the issue of the sacramental test, Boyle's elevation actually constituted an encouragement to opponents of repeal. Throughout the period 1716–19, when successive British administrations had sought to force the issue, the Brodricks had appeared strongly in defence of the test, and in opposition in the 1720s they had cultivated an alliance with the Tories. That Boyle was Lord Midleton's political heir in this respect, as in much else, was shown by the way in which he successfully argued Dorset out of a second attempt at removing the test in the 1733–4 session. But there were other aspects of the ministerial reconstruction in Dublin that were less welcome: Swift's particular enemies in the old regime, Lord Allen and Richard Tighe, retained their places, and were joined on the government side by others against whom he had developed a particular animus, notably Richard Bettesworth, the 'booby' who had long been a stalwart of the Brodrick faction and had slipped smoothly into Henry Boyle's slipstream after Midleton's death.[257]

---

257 See Andrew Crotty to Henry Boyle, 13 July 1727 (PRONI, D/2707/A/1/2/17A); [Thomas Carter] to Henry Boyle, 8 Aug. 1727 (ibid., D/2707/A/1/2/21).

In fact, apart from the Speaker and his immediate cronies, the new Castle party looked very much like the old. Although Boyle had come in on his own terms, he had not insisted on a purge of his previous political opponents. Key figures in the Conolly faction, such as Marmaduke Coghill, Henry Singleton and Agmondisham Vesey, held on to their offices, and Boyle's system of management, like his predecessors', involved knitting together a coalition of placemen and the major 'connections': the Wynnes and their followers in Counties Sligo, Roscommon and Galway, the Ponsonbys in County Kilkenny, and the much-ramified family of the Gores. As before, the advocacy of the 'patriot' cause in Parliament was left to independent country gentlemen and vociferous individuals like Eaton Stannard and his protégé, the young lawyer Anthony Malone.

Realisation that the change of Speaker had merely been a change in personnel did not produce a massive effect on Irish public opinion comparable to the disillusionment manifest in England after the fall of Walpole in 1742 and the coming to power of the Earl of Bath and other erstwhile 'patriots'. By contrast, relatively little had been expected of Boyle and his friends. Even though Boyle had appealed to back-bench squires for their votes on the basis that he was a country gentleman like them and also a patriot,[258] his opposition to Conolly and Gore was recognised, and accepted, by many as having been opportunist and factional. He himself was no orator, and had created few hostages to fortune through flights of parliamentary rhetoric while in opposition. He does seem to have suffered some difficulties with former allies in County Cork, who were anxious to press their concerns over the government's management of economic issues, but these difficulties derived from the regional nature of his power-base, and not from any perception that he had reneged on promises.

For Swift, on the other hand, hostility to the governing forces in Irish politics now overflowed. His most famous expression of bile against the denizens of the new and very grand Irish parliament house (opened in 1731), 'A Character, Panegyric and Description of the Legion Club', was written in March–April 1736, and swung the sword of satire in several directions, though with some particular thrusts reserved for old enemies. The immediate context was the opposition in the House of Commons to the assertion by representatives of the Church of Ireland clergy of their right to the 'tithe of agistment'. This attack on clerical privilege was not, however, associated with a particular faction, nor indeed exclusively with the

---

258 Boyle to John King, 18 Mar. 1732/3 (NLI, MS 8,645/3).

pro-government side in the house.[259] Swift's universal condemnation of MPs – which extended to all major groupings, whether supporters of the new Speaker or adherents of other major factions – reflected the confused and fluid structure of 'parties' within the House of Commons. Contemporary commentators divided Parliament into the 'court' and 'country' parties – as Sir Richard Cox put it, 'the courtiers' on the one hand and 'the gentlemen of the country' on the other.[260] But the government's 'patriot' critics lacked the coherence of the Brodrick faction in the 1720s. Indeed, apart from a few loquacious lawyers, like Stannard or Malone, who might be assumed to have ambitions for office, these 'patriots' seemed to resemble closely the 'independent country gentlemen' who were such a feature of the English political scene in the 1740s and 1750s.

The real conflict in the Commons, sometimes hidden and sometimes out in the open, was actually within the Court party: between, on the one hand, Speaker Boyle and his followers, and, on the other, the faction headed by one of Conolly's former lieutenants, Brabazon Ponsonby, now Earl of Bessborough. Dorset's replacement as lord lieutenant in 1737 by the Duke of Devonshire was followed by the aggrandisement of the Ponsonby family. Brabazon Ponsonby cultivated a close friendship with the new viceroy and eventually married his eldest son to one of Devonshire's daughters. He was now prepared to challenge Boyle's predominance within the government party. The Ponsonby grouping was partly based on family and friends, partly on the remnants of the old Conolly connection, and partly on those who saw Bessborough as the rising star of Irish politics. However, this crucial subtext of Irish parliamentary history in the years after 1735 was unrepresented in Swift's own writings. Old, ill and deaf, he seems now to have become entirely alienated from Irish political life, very much the outside observer of a drama to whose essential plot-line he was indifferent.

11   An Improving Economy?

In May 1731, the young John Perceval, who was eventually to succeed his father as second Earl of Egmont, paid a visit to Dublin. A young man possessed by a zealous Irish patriotism, he immediately sought an audience with the dean of St Patrick's. There, he reported proudly to his father, he was 'received... as I am told with unusual complaisance'. During their

---

259 D. W. Hayton and Stephen Karian, 'Select Document: The Division in the Irish House of Commons on the "Tithe of Agistment", 18 Mar. 1736, and Swift's "Character... of the Legion Club"', *Irish Historical Studies* 38 (2012–13), 304–21.
260 Sir Richard Cox, 'Irish Politics Displayed' (1737) (PRONI, Armagh diocesan registry papers, DIO/4/5/8).

interview, Swift 'lamented the miserable condition of Ireland, and said that he had pretty much left off writing in a political way, because he found there was no stemming the torrent, and that the evil in time would remedy itself'. He added that 'the two great misfortunes of the country were poverty and oppression'. And, although he expressed some hope for the future, envisaging a sudden end to absenteeism, this was wishful thinking and based on no rational analysis: 'the gentlemen of Ireland will soon be obliged to return, which will enrich the kingdom and make it so powerful that it will be dangerous to oppress it'.[261]

By this time, Swift's diagnosis of Ireland's condition was as unusual as his identification of the likely source of her recovery. Among writers like Prior, Dobbs and Bindon, and Castle politicians like Sir Ralph Gore and Marmaduke Coghill, political economy had replaced constitutional reform as the key to national progress. In public debates on the condition of the Irish economy, Swift's rhetoric seemed increasingly out of place.[262] However, despite what he had said to Perceval, he did make further short contributions on three specific issues: the continued difficulties of the woollen trade; public interest in encouraging the development of the inland and maritime fishing industries; and the implications of any attempt to regulate the coinage. In each case, he seems to have been working outside the parameters of the current public discourse, reiterating arguments he had made before.

Just as in England and Scotland, enthusiasts for the improvement of Ireland had fastened on the potential of the fishing industry there, both inland and maritime. Molesworth's *Considerations for the Promoting of Agriculture* (1723) had noted 'how many natural advantages' Ireland enjoyed 'beyond any part of Europe, proper for this great and most beneficial trade'. Bishop Francis Hutchinson had devoted a pamphlet to the subject in 1729, and another writer, John Knightley, had petitioned the Irish Parliament in 1733 to support his own scheme for the development of these valuable natural resources.[263] Then an apparent drop in the yields of the existing fisheries

---

261 John Perceval to Lord Perceval, 4 May 1731 (BL, Add. MS 47033, fo. 93).
262 A point made by Patrick Kelly in 'Swift on Money and Economics', in Christopher Fox (ed.), *The Cambridge Companion to Jonathan Swift*, Cambridge: Cambridge University Press, 2003, p. 140.
263 Molesworth, *Considerations for the Promoting of Agriculture* . . . , p. 42; [Francis Hutchinson], *A Second Letter to a Member of Parliament, Recommending the Improvement of the Irish-Fishery*, Dublin, 1729; John Knightley, *To the Honourable the Lords Spiritual, Temporal and Commons in Parliament Assembled . . . this Essay toward Proving the Advantages which may Arise from Improvements on Salt Works, and in the Fishing Trade of Ireland*, Dublin, 1733. See, in general, Andrew Sneddon, 'Legislating for Economic Development: Irish Fisheries as a Case Study in the Limitations of "Improvement"', in Hayton *et al.* (eds.), *Eighteenth-century Composite State*, pp. 136–59.

focused minds, and produced, first, a parliamentary inquiry, and second a bill, introduced into the Irish House of Commons in December 1737 and managed by Richard Bettesworth, 'for the further improvement and encouragement of the fishery of this kingdom'. Despite opposition from fishing interests in England, this eventually passed into law in 1738 as 11 Geo. II c. 14 [Ire.].[264] Swift's single contribution to the public debate on fishing was a short response to Francis Grant, a Scottish businessman based in London, who had written to him in 1734, soliciting Swift's support for a pamphlet of his own, *The British Fishery Recommended to Parliament*. Swift welcomed the potential of any project to expand Irish fisheries but considered 'the vulgar folks of Ireland' to be 'too lazy and knavish' to carry it out successfully: 'oppressed beggars are always knaves, and, I believe, there are hardly any other among us; they had rather gain a shilling by knavery, than five pounds by honest dealing'. Cured fish from Ireland would be the same as Irish cloth: 'abominable' in quality and thus unable to find a market even if allowed.[265]

The one issue on which Swift could still strike a chord with his audience was the availability and value of money. The lack of hard currency remained a problem in Ireland throughout Swift's life, and was generally identified as one of the fundamental causes of the country's failure to progress. In particular, the amount of silver in circulation was perceived to be declining steadily. Some commentators emphasised as underlying causes the imbalance of Irish trade, and the remittances to absentees, but the Irish privy council focused on a more immediate and specific issue, the relative value of gold and silver coins in Ireland, and in the spring of 1736, before Dorset left Ireland as viceroy, decided on a radical solution.[266] Dorset brought with him to England an application for a proclamation to reduce the value of gold coins in Ireland to the same level as in England. A guinea in Ireland was worth 21s 3d in English silver coins, whereas what was being proposed was a modest reduction to 21s. The higher relative value of gold in Ireland (including foreign coins like the Portuguese moidore, which circulated in Ireland because of the unavailability of Irish coins) meant that Irish merchants were paying their debts in England in silver, and that gold was being brought into the country from England instead of silver in order to pay for goods. It seemed a sensible proposal, but immediately ran into difficulties.

Swift was not the only opponent of the reduction in the value of gold. The issue was fully debated in the press, though much of the discussion was

---

264 Edward Walpole to Devonshire, 26 Jan. 1737/8; Wilmington to Devonshire, 6 Mar. 1737/8 (PRONI, Chatsworth papers, T/3158/44, 49).
265 Below, pp. 293–300.
266 For what follows, see Ehrenpreis, vol. III, pp. 840ff.

on points of practical detail rather than principle, in all probability because, as Eoin Magennis has suggested, it was widely accepted that something had to be done to alleviate the chronic shortage of coin.[267] Other, more progressive economic thinkers were experimenting with notions of paper credit, but Swift still adhered to the older, Lockeian, definition of money in terms of gold and silver bullion.[268] But there was also a powerful vein of concern among the merchants and financiers in Dublin, who had found ways to profit from the differing exchange rates, and feared the loss of gold bullion as well as silver across the water. Swift's own objections were based on his atavistic suspicion of office-holders, absentees and other profiteers, who would ruin Ireland for their own advantage.

He was given an early opportunity to express these views, even before Dorset had embarked for England, when his friend Richard Grattan, then lord mayor of Dublin, invited him to address a meeting of the aldermen and common council on 19 April 1736, called to discuss the proposal to revalue gold, news of which had got abroad. Swift attended a meeting of merchants called to discuss the same problem at the Guildhall that Saturday, 24 April, and spoke. The speech was printed as *The Rev. Dean Swift's Reasons against Lowering the Gold and Silver Coin*.[269] In it he denounced government officials, bishops and absentee landlords, and declared that those who favoured lowering the value of gold were 'no friends to this poor kingdom'. Indeed, the absentees were its 'greatest enemies'. He concluded, 'Can there be a greater folly than to pave a bridge of gold at your own expense, to support them in their luxury and vanity abroad, while hundreds of thousands are starving at home, for want of employment?' The upshot was a formal protest, which Swift signed alongside the aldermen and common councilmen, and the presentation of a petition to the lord lieutenant and privy council, with Swift accompanying the lord mayor, the sheriffs of Dublin, and the city's two MPs to deliver it.

Despite these representations, Dorset's application was granted, and the following year Devonshire, his successor, transmitted a proclamation to that effect.[270] In the meantime, there had been a further provocation, in the form of a new coinage of halfpence, which arrived in Dublin in March 1737 and

---

267 Eoin Magennis, 'Whither the Irish Financial Revolution? Money, Banks, and Politics in Ireland in the 1730s', in Charles Ivar McGrath and C. J. Fauske (eds.), *Money, Power and Print: Interdisciplinary Studies on the Financial Revolution in the British Isles*, Newark: University of Delaware Press, 2008, pp. 200–2.
268 Kelly, '"Conclusions by No Means Calculated"', p. 57.
269 Below, pp. 301–4.
270 Order in council, 21 July 1737 (BL, Hardwicke papers, Add. MS 35586, fos. 125–6); proclamation of lords justices [Ire.], 29 Aug. 1737 (ibid., fos. 33–5).

was declared legal tender in a proclamation in May. Swift called a meeting of the inhabitants of the Archbishop's Liberty in which he publicly denounced the new copper coin as likely to meet the same fate as Wood's, a speech which was reported in the press and, Swift thought, might have led to his arrest. But this was nothing in comparison to his reaction in September, when the proclamation about the value of gold was finally issued. On that occasion, Swift published nothing, but instead 'had a great black flag on the top of St Patrick's steeple and wrote in gold letters "O poor Ireland", and the bells and clappers done round with black and tolled a most melancholy sound'.[271] In terms of exciting the populace, this stunt was at least as effective as anything he had ever written.[272] The capital – and, some said, the whole country – was 'in a ferment'. One minor official reported that 'all our merchants and trading people are exasperated to a great degree and a certain eminent writer is inflaming the people as if Hannibal was at our gates'.[273] There were riots in Dublin, and Archbishop Boulter, who had been one of the chief architects of the new policy, feared for his life.[274] The worst that happened to the archbishop, however, was to find himself seated near Swift at the lord mayor's feast on 29 September. Boulter allegedly 'taxed the doctor before the company for endeavouring to raise the mob, and to begin a rebellion on account of the lessening the value of gold'. Needless to say, he received a bitter reply.[275]

This affair was the last kick of the Drapier *redivivus*, and briefly recalled the great days of Wood's Halfpence in the way that Swift became once more the hero of the populace, single-handedly defending Ireland's interests against a corrupt government. But, in fact, it was very different from the great events of the previous decade. His attacks on the new copper halfpence in the spring of 1737 proved a damp squib;[276] and even the ferment against the lowering of the value of gold, in which he had more support from Dublin's commercial oligarchy, did not last long. Moreover, this time the Irish Parliament declined to follow his lead. Despite the general strength of the 'patriot'

---

271 Mrs Jones to Mrs Bonnell, 16 Sept. [1737] (NLI, Smythe of Barbavilla papers, MS 41,577/3); Devonshire to Duke of Newcastle, 10 Sept. 1737 (BL, Newcastle papers, Add. MS 32690, fo. 354). See also *Ireland's Mourning Flagg*, Dublin, 1737 (a single-sheet ballad).
272 Boulter referred to it as an insult against government: Boulter to Bishop Gibson, 10 Feb. 1737[/8] (*Boulter Letters*, vol. II, pp. 191–2).
273 John Bayly to George Dodington, 6 Sept. 1737 (NLI, MS 16,139, p. 59).
274 It was reported that the Dublin mob had burned the primate in effigy (Mrs Jones to Mrs Bonnell, 16 Sept. [?1737] (NLI, Smythe of Barbavilla papers, MS 41,577/3)).
275 Ehrenpreis, vol. III, pp. 861–2. See also *Poems*, vol. III, pp. 842–3.
276 Boulter to Cary, 26 Mar. 1737 (*Boulter Letters*, vol. II, p. 162).

party in this session, the ministers secured a massive majority in a vote on the proclamation.[277] The nature of the discussion in the public prints about the issue of the coinage also showed the extent to which things had moved on from 1724–5, since no one took up Swift's intemperate denunciations of ministers and absentees, the focus instead being on practicalities. A comment by the painter Hugh Howard, writing from London to his brother, the bishop of Elphin, encapsulates this sense of Swift being left behind. Howard had been told 'odd stories' of Swift's opposition to the alterations in the coinage, and was sorry to hear them: 'I believe he means well', he observed of the Drapier, but quite simply, in the matter of the coinage, 'he does not understand it'.[278]

[277] Devonshire to Newcastle, 13 Sept., 5, 26 Oct. 1737 (BL, Add. MS 32690, fos. 356–7, 388, 398); Bayly to Dodington, 25 Oct. 1737 (NLI, MS 16,139, p. 60).
[278] Hugh Howard to Bishop Robert Howard, 29 Sept. 1737 (NLI, MS 38,958/14).

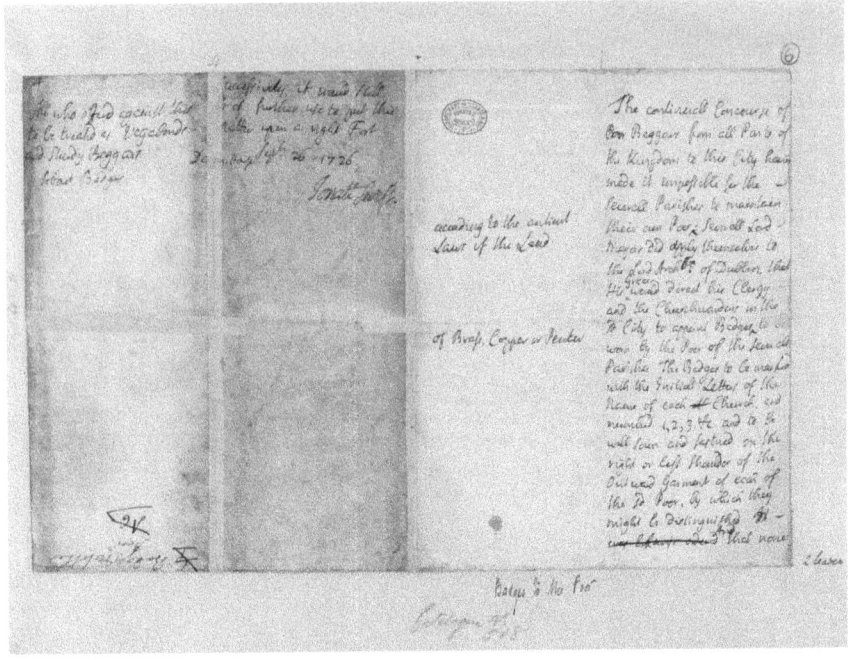

Figure 1. Jonathan Swift, *Upon Giving Badges to the Poor*, first page of Forster manuscript.

UPON GIVING BADGES TO THE POOR

Headnote

Composed September 1726; published posthumously, 1765; copy text SwJ 479 (see Textual Account).

This fragment is dated September 1726, and was written in the aftermath of the *Drapier's Letters*. The giving of badges to licensed beggars was not uncommon in contemporary Ireland, and this was Swift's first attempt at a subject which was discussed in Sir William Fownes's *Methods Proposed for Regulating the Poor*, in 1725. It joined considerable contemporary writing concerned with poverty and vagrancy, particularly with regard to the distress in the countryside and how such problems moved into Dublin (see Introduction, above, pp. xxx, lxxii). The practice of badging resident beggars was already borrowed from England, where the Poor Law intended to admit the aged and infirm, but not sturdy beggars. The Irish never enacted this, but seemed to adopt the idea of returning beggars to their own parish (a process already operative in the north of Ireland and some Dublin parishes). Swift himself was seeking to interest Archbishop King in his proposal, both as a friend and because of King's interest in poverty: King's papers in Marsh's Library (Z.3.11) contain a number of writings relating to the Dublin workhouse and to the problem of poverty more generally.

As well as its relation to the context of Swift's other pamphlets on the social effects of Irish economic problems from 1728 (most famously *A Modest Proposal*), Swift would return to the abiding question of controlling vagrancy in 1737, in his more extensive *Proposal for Giving Badges to the Beggars* (see below, pp. 305–19). *Upon Giving Badges* was first published posthumously in 1765, though the present copy text – the manuscript from the Forster Collection of the Victoria and Albert Museum – has not been published before.

UPON GIVING BADGES TO THE POOR

The continuall Concourse of Beggars from all Parts of the Kingdom to this City having made it impossible for the severall Parishes to maintain their own Poor, according to the antient Laws of the Land.[1] Severall Lord Mayors did apply themselves to the Lord Arch^{bp} of Dublin,[2] that His Grace would direct his Clergy and the Churchwardens in the sd City, to appoint Badges of Brass, Copper or Pewter to be worn by the Poor of the severall Parishes.[3] The Badges to be marked with the Initiall Letters of the Name of each Church, and numbred 1, 2, 3, & c. and to be well sewn and fastned on the right and left shoulder of the Outward Garment of each of the sd Poor, by which they might be distinguished. And that none of the sd Poor should go out of their own Parish to beg Alms; whereof the Beadles[4] were to take Care.

His Grace the Lord Archbishop, did accordingly give his Directions to the Clergy, which however have proved wholly ineffectual, by the Fraud, Perverseness, or Pride of the sd Poor, several of them openly protesting they will never submit to wear the sd Badges, and of those who received them, almost every one, either keep them in their Pockets, or hang them on a String about their Necks, or fasten them onely with a Pin, or wear them under their Coats, not to be seen; by which means the whole design is eluded, so that a Man may walk from one end of the Town to the other, without seeing one Beggar regularly badged, and in such great Numbers,

---

1 *the antient Laws of the Land*: in fact, Ireland differed from England in that until the statute of 1665, parish vestries were not legally permitted to raise money from the inhabitants in order to relieve the poor, earlier Irish acts having only provided for the licensing of beggars: Rowena Dudley, 'The Dublin Parishes and the Poor: 1660–1740', *Archivium Hibernicum* 53 (1999), 81.

2 *Lord Arch^{bp} of Dublin*: William King (1650–1729), bishop of Derry 1691–1703, archbishop of Dublin 1703–29, for whom see *ODNB*; *DIB*; Philip O'Regan, *Archbishop William King... and the Constitution in Church and State*, Dublin, Four Courts Press, 2000; Christopher Fauske, *A Political Biography of William King*, London: Pickering & Chatto, 2011.

3 *to appoint Badges... of the severall Parishes*: in order to distinguish those licensed to beg, according to the major Irish poor law statutes, of 1537 (33 Hen. VIII c. 15) and 1634–5 (10 & 11 Car. I c. 4) which for this purpose required the registration of the impotent poor in every parish. On the practice of badging beggars, see above, pp. lxxii–lxxiii.

4 *the Beadles*: inferior parish officers, whose duties included the maintenance of order and the punishment of petty offenders.

that they are a mighty Nuisance to the Publick, most of them being Foreigners.[5]

It is therefore proposed, that his Grace the Ld Arch. Bp would please to call the Clergy of the City together, and renew his Directions and Exhortations to them, to put this Affair of Badges effectually in practice, by such Methods as his Grace and they shall agree upon. And I think it would be highly necessary that some Paper should be pasted up in severall proper Parts of the City signifying this Order, and exhorting all People to give no Alms except to those Poor who are regularly badged, and onely while they are within the Precincts of their own Parishes, and if something like this were delivered by the Ministers in the reading desk two or three Lords days successively, it would still be of further use to put this Matter upon a right Foot.

All who offend against this to be treated as Vagabonds and Sturdy Beggars[6]

Deanry. House.
Sept. 26 1726.
                              Jonath Swift.

---

5 *Foreigners*: not belonging to the parish.
6 *Vagabonds and Sturdy Beggars*: the Irish Acts of 1537 and 1634–5 also provided for the punishment of able-bodied beggars, denoted in the former as 'vagabonds and mighty strong beggars' and in the latter as 'rogues, vagabonds, [and] sturdy beggars'.

CONSIDERATIONS ABOUT MAINTAINING THE POOR

Headnote

Probably composed September 1726; published posthumously, 1765; copy text *1765a* (see Textual Account); the footnote that forms part of this text was provided by the editor, Deane Swift.

A fragment printed alongside *Upon Giving Badges to the Poor* in 1765, and generally thought to be from the same period of composition (*c.* 1726), *Considerations* revisits the same issues of poverty and vagrancy, reflecting the deteriorating situation in Dublin from 1726 onwards, which marked the beginning of continuing bad harvests for three years. It was becoming increasingly clear that the Dublin workhouse could not cope with the increased numbers of indigent coming to the city from the countryside, and there was therefore much discussion of amelioration.

Near the end of the fragment, Swift refers to a complaint against the workhouse under its former governors (see below, pp. 308–9). This might indicate (if the reference is specific, rather than general) that the draft was written after the restructuring of its governing body after an Act of Parliament in 1728, and not at the same time as *Upon Giving Badges*, as is usually assumed.

CONSIDERATIONS ABOUT MAINTAINING THE POOR.

We have been amused, for at least thirty years past, with numberless schemes in writing and discourse, both in and out of parliament, for maintaining the poor, and setting them to work, especially in this city;[1] most of which were idle,[2] indigested, or visionary,[3] and all of them ineffectual, as it hath plainly appeared by the consequences. Many of those projectors were so stupid, that they drew a parallel from Holland and England, to be settled in Ireland;[4] that is to say, from two countries with full freedom and encouragement for trade, to a third where all kind of trade is cramped, and the most beneficial parts are entirely taken away. But the perpetual infelicity of false and foolish reasoning, as well as proceeding and acting upon it, seems to be fatal to this country.

For my own part, who have much conversed with those folks who call themselves Merchants,[5] I do not remember to have met with a more ignorant and wrong thinking race of people in the very first rudiments of trade; which, however, was not so much owing to their want of capacity, as to the crazy constitution of this kingdom, where pedlars are better qualified to thrive than the wisest merchants. I could fill a volume with only setting down a list of the public absurdities, by which this kingdom hath suffered within the compass of my own memory, such as could not be believed of any nation, among whom folly was not established as a law. I cannot forbear instancing a few of these, because it may be of some use to those who shall have it in their power to be more cautious for the future.

---

1 *We have been amused... especially in this city*: bills had been introduced in the Irish Parliament for the relief of the poor in 1695, 1697, 1698, 1703, 1709, 1711, 1717, 1723 and, most recently, in 1725. With the exception of the Dublin Workhouse Bill of 1703, none had been enacted. There had been something of a rush of printed proposals in the mid-1720s: Edward Gosnell, *Irelands Redress, from Popular Greivances Attempted; a Scheme for Employing the Poor...*, Dublin, 1723; Francis Hutchinson, *A Letter to a Member of Parliament, Concerning the Imploying and Providing for the Poor*, Dublin, 1723; Robert, Viscount Molesworth, *Some Considerations for the Promoting of Agriculture, and Employing the Poor*, Dublin, 1723; Sir William Fownes, *Methods Proposed for Regulating the Poor. Supporting of Some, and Employing Others: According to Their Several Capacities*, Dublin, 1723–4; repr. 1725; *Enquiries into the Principal Causes of the General Poverty of the Common People of Ireland. With Remedies Propos'd for Removing of Them*, Dublin, 1725.
2 *idle*: worthless, ineffectual (*OED*).
3 *visionary*: incapable of being carried out.
4 *Many of those projectors... settled in Ireland*: see above, pp. xl–xliii.
5 *Merchants*: wholesale traders, especially those involved in overseas trade.

The first was the building of the barracks,[6] whereof I have seen above one half, and have heard enough of the rest, to affirm that the public hath been cheated of at least two thirds of the money raised for that use by the plain fraud of the undertakers.

Another was the management of the money raised for the Palatines;[7] when, instead of employing that great sum in purchasing lands in some remote and cheap part of the kingdom, and there planting those people as a colony, the whole end was utterly defeated.

A third is the insurance-office against fire,[8] by which several thousand pounds are yearly remitted to England (a trifle it seems we can easily spare), and will gradually encrease until it comes to a good national tax. For the society-marks upon our houses (under which might properly be written, *The Lord have mercy upon us*) spread faster and farther than the* colony of

---

* This similitude, which is certainly the finest that could possibly have been used upon this occasion, seems to require a short explication. About the beginning of this current century, Doctor Gwythers, a physician and Fellow of the University of Dublin, brought over with him a parcel of frogs from England to Ireland, in order to propagate the species in that kingdom; and threw them into the ditches of the University-park; but they all perished. Whereupon he sent to England for some bottles of the frog-spawn, which he threw into those ditches, by which means the species of frogs was propagated in that kingdom. However, their number was so small in the year 1720, that a frog was no where to be seen in Ireland, except in the neighbourhood of the University-park: But, within six or seven years after, they spread thirty, forty, and fifty miles over the country; and so at last, by degrees, over the whole nation.

6 *the building of the barracks*: for the activities of the Barrack Board, the body established by Act of the Irish Parliament in 1701 to oversee the building of army barracks across the kingdom in accordance with a scheme approved in 1696, see Edward McParland, *Public Architecture in Ireland, 1680–1760*, New Haven & London: Yale University Press, 2001, ch. 5; Charles Ivar McGrath, *Ireland and Empire, 1692–1770*, London: Pickering & Chatto, 2012, ch. 4. In the Irish parliamentary session of 1717, concern had been expressed at serious overspending on the annual barrack fund, a situation which persisted into the 1730s and beyond, despite adverse comment in the House of Commons and the persistent scrutiny of the accounts committee. In 1724, the Commons had carried out an inquiry into the management of the barracks, to which Lord Carteret had responded in such a way as to prompt a vote of thanks for the 'rules' he had 'prescribed . . . for their future regulation' (McGrath, *Ireland and Empire*, p. 92).

7 *the management of the money raised for the Palatines*: money to support the settlement in Ireland in 1709 of refugees from the Rhineland – 'the poor Palatines' – had been raised by public collection, and administered by commissioners. By 1711, two-thirds of the Palatines who had come to Dublin from London had returned to England. See Vivien Hick, 'The Palatine Settlement in Ireland: The Early Years', *ECI* 4 (1989), 120–4.

8 *the insurance-office against fire*: following a failed attempt to establish a fire insurance company in Ireland in 1720, two English companies, the Royal Exchange Assurance Company and the London Assurance Company, had set up in business in Dublin in 1722: see F. B. Relton, *An Account of the Fire Insurance Companies . . . and Schemes Established and Projected in Great Britain and Ireland During the 17th and 18th Centuries*, London, 1893,

frogs.[9] I have, for above twenty years past, given warning several thousand times, to many substantial people, and to such who are acquainted with Lords and Squires, and the like great folks, (to any of whom I have not the honour to be known:) I mentioned my daily fears, lest our watchful friends in England might take this business out of our hands; and how easy it would be to prevent that evil, by erecting a society of persons who had good estates, such, for instance, as that noble knot[10] of bankers under the style of Swift and Company.[11] But now we are become tributary to England,[12] not only for materials to light our own fires; but for engines to put them out; to which, if hearth-money be added, (repealed in England as a grievance)[13] we have the honour to pay three taxes for fire.

p. 198; Rowena Dudley, 'Fire Insurance in Dublin, 1750–1850', *Irish Economic and Social History* 30 (2003), 24–5.
9 *the colony of frogs:* in June 1706 Swift wrote from Dublin to John Temple that 'about seven Years ago, Frogs were imported here, and thrive very well' (Woolley, *Corr.*, vol. I, p. 161). The story of their introduction was told in the *Tatler* 236 (12 Oct. 1710), (*Tatler*, vol. III, pp. 218–19), where it was dated to about 1692:

> ... an ingenious physician, to the honour as well as improvement of his native country, performed what the English had been so long attempting in vain. This learned man, with the hazard of his life, made a voyage to Liverpool, when he filled several barrels with the choicest spawn of frogs that could be found in those parts. This cargo he brought over very carefully and afterwards disposed of it in several warm beds that he thought most capable of bringing it to life. The doctor was a very ingenious physician, and a very good Protestant; for which reason, to show his zeal against popery, he placed some of the most promising spawn in the very fountain that is dedicated to the saint, and known by the name of St Patrick's Well, where these animals had the impudence to make their first appearance. They have since that time very much increased and multiplied in all the neighbourhood of this city.

The physician concerned was Charles Gwithers (?1664–1700), MD, fellow of TCD, for whom see T. W. Belcher, *Memoir of Sir Patrick Dun (Knt.)...*, 2nd edn, Dublin, 1866, pp. 37–8; J. B. Leslie, *History of Kilsaran Union of Parishes in the County of Louth*, Dundalk: William Tempest, 1908, pp. 289–91.
10 *noble knot*: from Shakespeare, *Coriolanus*, Act IV, Scene ii, ll. 40–2: 'I would he had continued to his country as he began, and not unknit himself the noble knot he made.'
11 *that noble knot of bankers... Swift and Company*: James Swift (d. 1749) maintained a private bank in Dublin: *Econ. Hist. Ire.*, p. 135; J. T. Gilbert, *A History of the City of Dublin*, 3 vols., Dublin, 1854–9, vol. I, p. 26.
12 *tributary to England*: paying monetary tribute to England, in the manner of a conquered people.
13 *hearth-money... as a grievance*: the hearth duty (of 2s p.a. on every fire, hearth or stove), had first been imposed by the Irish Parliament in 1662, as a compensation to the crown for the abolition of the court of wards (T. J. Kiernan, *History of the Financial Administration of Ireland to 1817*, London: T. S. King, 1930, pp. 82–3, 85). In England, this unpopular tax had been abolished in 1689 as a 'badge of slavery' (John Brewer, *The Sinews of Power: War, Money and the English State, 1688–1783*, London: Routledge, 1989, p. 95) but it remained operative in Ireland.

A fourth was the knavery of those merchants, or linen-manufacturers, or both; when, upon occasion of the plague at Marseilles,[14] we had a fair opportunity of getting into our hands the whole linen-trade with Spain;[15] but the commodity was so bad, and held at so high a rate, that almost the whole cargo was returned, and the small remainder sold below the prime cost.

So many other particulars of the same nature crowd into my thoughts, that I am forced to stop, and the rather because they are not very proper for my subject, to which I shall now return.

Among all the schemes for maintaining the poor of the city, and setting them to work, the least weight hath been laid upon that single point which is of greatest importance; I mean that of keeping foreign beggars from swarming hither out of every part of the country; for, until this be brought to pass effectually, all our wise reasonings and proceedings upon them will be vain and ridiculous.

The prodigious number of beggars throughout this kingdom, in proportion to so small a number of people, is owing to many reasons: To the laziness of the natives; the want of work to employ them; the enormous rents paid by cottagers for their miserable cabbins and potatoe-plots; their early marriages, without the least prospect of establishment;[16] the ruin of agriculture, whereby such vast numbers are hindred from providing their own bread, and have no money to purchase it; the mortal damp upon all

14 *plague at Marseilles*: bubonic plague had broken out in Marseilles in the summer of 1720. A detailed history was given in *A Brief Journal of What Passed in the City of Marseilles, While It Was Afflicted with the Plague, in the Year 1720...*, London, [1721].
15 *the whole linen-trade with Spain*: the impact of the plague on trade between France and Spain was considerable. The port of Marseilles was shut and the city itself isolated. The Spanish also closed border crossings from France, erecting a *cordon sanitaire* to prevent infection: Peter Sahlins, *Boundaries: The Making of France and Spain in the Pyrenees*, Berkeley: University of California Press, 1989, pp. 75–6. There was a further problem with exports of French linen, since clothing was seen as a principal agent of the spread of plague, and the importation of contaminated cloth into Marseilles had been a contributory factor in the outbreak (G. C. Kohn, *Encyclopaedia of Plague and Pestilence: from Ancient Times to the Present*, New York: Infobase Publishing, 2008, p. 254). Although the main centres of linen production in France were in the north, there was a growing manufacture in Provence, centred on Toulon.
16 *their early marriages... prospect of establishment*: Hutchinson's *A Letter to a Member of Parliament* had specifically argued against early marriage, which in his view inevitably multiplied the number of the poor. A strict execution of the law, by confining the 'honest poor' to their parishes, and punishing vagrants, 'will discourage young people from Marrying till they have a House to live in, and some probable way for an honest livelyhood' (p. 14).

kinds of trade, and many other circumstances too tedious or invidious to mention.

And to the same causes we owe the perpetual concourse of foreign beggars[17] to this town, the country landlords giving all assistance, except money and victuals, to drive from their estates those miserable creatures they have undone.

It was a general complaint against the poor-house, under its former governors,[18] that the number of poor in this city did not lessen by taking three hundred into the house, and all of them recommended under the minister and church-wardens hands of the several parishes; and this complaint must still continue, although the poor-house should be enlarged to maintain three thousand, or even double that number.

The revenues of the poor-house, as it is now established, amount to about two thousand pounds a year;[19] whereof, two hundred allowed for officers, and one hundred for repairs, the remaining seventeen hundred, at four pounds a head, will support four hundred and twenty-five persons. This is a favourable allowance, considering that I subtract nothing for the diet of those officers, and for wear and tare of furniture; and, if every one of these collegiates should be set to work, it is agreed they will not be able to gain by their labour above one fourth part of their maintenance.

At the same time the oratorial part of these gentlemen[20] seldom vouchsafe to mention fewer than fifteen hundred, or two thousand people, to be maintained in this hospital, without troubling their heads about the fund,

* *
* *

---

17 *foreign beggars*: from outside the parish.
18 *its former governors*: the governors who held office when the workhouse was first established by Act of Parliament in 1704 (2 Anne c. 19 [Ire.]) were replaced in the Act in 1728 (1 Geo. II c. 27 [Ire.], introduced 21 December 1727, received royal assent 6 May), which revised the regulations under which the workhouse operated.
19 *The revenues of the poor-house... two thousand pounds a year*: see above, pp. lxx–lxxi.
20 *the oratorial part of these gentlemen*: those proponents of schemes for poor relief who made speeches in Parliament.

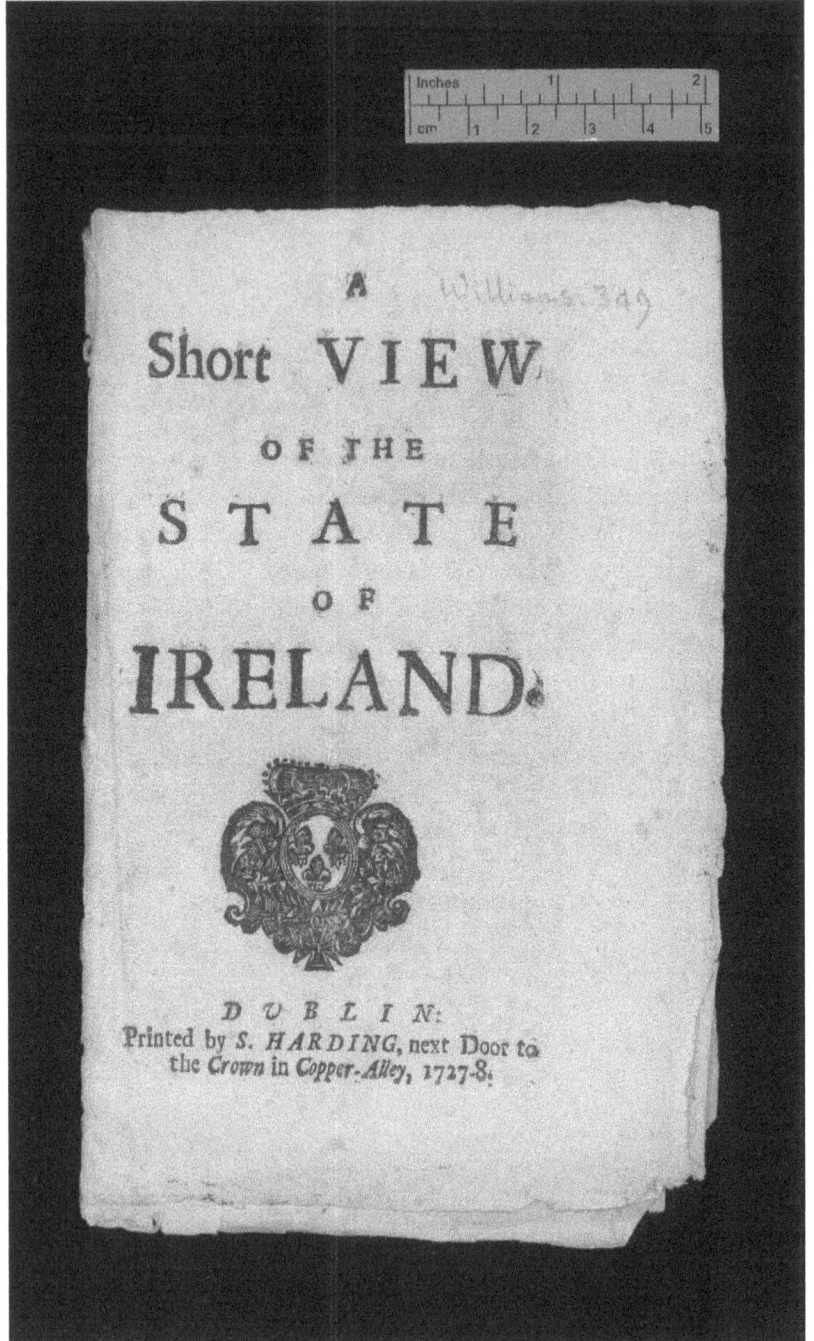

Figure 2. Jonathan Swift, *A Short View of the State of Ireland*, 1728. Title. Williams 349.

A SHORT VIEW OF THE STATE OF IRELAND

Headnote

Probably composed March 1728; published 19 March 1728; copy text *1728a* (see Textual Account).

A Short View was published in Dublin during the parliamentary session of November 1727 to May 1728. Swift was one of several writers who responded to what was perceived, by 1728, as a crisis in the Irish economy caused by bad harvests, the consequent increase in numbers of the poor, and a rapid decline in basic industries such as woollen and cloth manufacture, resulting in a deterioration in Ireland's balance of trade. Swift felt that the various suggestions and proposals of a constructive nature that were being made by contemporary economic writers did not deal with the root causes of the crisis, which were in his view political. *A Short View* is usually thought to be a specific response to the two contemporaneous Dublin pamphlets of John Browne, *Seasonable Remarks on Trade* and *An Essay Upon Trade* (published in the same week as Swift's work), and by implication others like Browne, who argued for the potential improvement of Ireland predicated upon her natural resources. Swift sets out basic obstacles to Irish economic reform which he would reiterate in the following years: the absence of free trade deriving from the constitutional subordination of the Irish Parliament to Westminster; the monopoly of Irish offices by the English; the absenteeism of Irish landowners; and the importation of foreign luxuries at the expense of native industries.

A Short View was reprinted in 1728 as number 15 of *The Intelligencer*, with an introduction by Sheridan, and was thereafter included (in its original form) in all collected editions of Swift's prose writings.

A SHORT VIEW, &c.

I am assured that it hath for some time been practised as a method of making Men's Court, when they are asked about the Rate of Lands, the Abilities of Tenants, the State of Trade and Manufacture in this Kingdom, and how their Rents are payed; to Answer, That in their Neighbourhood all things are in a flourishing Condition, the Rent and Purchase of Land every Day encreasing. And if a Gentleman happens to be a little more sincere in his Representations, besides being looked on as not well affected, he is sure to have a Dozen Contradictors at his Elbow. I think it is no manner of Secret why these Questions are so cordially asked, or so obligingly Answered.

But since with Regard to the Affairs of this Kingdom, I have been using all Endeavours to subdue my Indignation, to which indeed I am not provoked by any Personal Interest,[1] being not the Owner of one Spot of Ground in the whole *Island*, I shall only enumerate by Rules generally known, and never Contradicted, what are the true Causes of any Countries flourishing and growing Rich, and then examine what Effects arise from those Causes in the Kingdom of *Ireland*.

The first Cause of a Kingdom's thriving is the Fruitfulness of the Soyl, to produce the Necessaries and Conveniencies of Life, not only sufficient for the Inhabitants, but for Exportation into other Countries.

The Second, is the Industry of the People in Working up all their Native Commodities to the last degree of Manufacture.

The Third, is the Conveniency of safe Ports and Havens, to Carry out their own Goods, as much manufactured, and bring in those of others, as little manufactured as the Nature of mutual Commerce will allow.

The Fourth, is, That the Natives should as much as possible, Export and Import their Goods in Vessels of their own Timber, made in their own Country.

The Fifth, is the Liberty of a free Trade in all Foreign Countries, which will permit them, except to those who are in War with their own Prince or State.

---

1 *any Personal Interest*: had Swift been writing under his own name, this would have been disingenuous, since his income as a clergyman, through rents and tithes, depended on land values and agricultural returns. However, the phrase also serves the function of suggesting a character akin to the honest tradesman, which distances the writer from landlords who squeeze money from their tenants and send it out of the country.

The Sixth, is, by being Governed only by Laws made with their own Consent, for otherwise they are not a free People.[2] And therefore all Appeals for Justice, or Applications, for Favour or Preferment to another Country,[3] are so many grievous Impoverishments.

The Seventh, is, by Improvement of Land, encouragement of Agriculture, and thereby encreasing the Number of their People, without which any Country, however Blessed by Nature, must continue Poor.[4]

The Eighth, is the Residence of the Princes, or Chief Administrators of the Civil Power.

The Ninth, is the Concourse of Foreigners for Education, Curiosity or Pleasure, or as to a general Mart of Trade.

The Tenth, is by disposing all Offices of Honour, Profit or Trust, only to the Natives, or at least with very few Exceptions, where Strangers have long Inhabited the Country, and are supposed to Understand, and regard the Interest of it as their own.

The Eleventh is, when the Rents of Lands, and Profits of Employments, are spent in the Country which produced them, and not in another, the former of which will certainly happen, where the Love of our Native Country prevails.

The Twelfth, is by the publick Revenues being all Spent and Employed at Home, except on the Occasions of a Foreign War.

The Thirteenth, is, where People are not obliged, unless they find it for their own Interest, or Conveniency, to receive any Monies, except of their own Coynage by a publick Mint, after the manner of all Civilized Nations.

The Fourteenth, is a Disposition of a People of a Country to wear their own Manufactures, and Import as few Incitements to Luxury, either in

---

2 *being Governed only by Laws made with their own Consent... free People*: a doctrine derived from the second of Locke's *Two Treatises of Government*, ch. 14, 'Of Slavery' (ed. Ian Shapiro, New Haven & London: Yale University Press, 2003, pp. 109–10); and William Molyneux, *The Case of Ireland's Being Bound by Acts of Parliament in England, Stated*, Dublin, 1698, pp. 18, 23, 25, 48, 113, 150, 152, 166, 169; and previously asserted by Swift in his *Letter to... Viscount Molesworth* (1724) (Davis, vol. X, pp. 86–7).
3 *Appeals for Justice... to another Country*: the British Declaratory Act of 1720 (6 Geo. I c. 5) had asserted the right of the British House of Lords to act as a final court of appeal for legal cases begun in Ireland.
4 *must continue Poor*: on the idea that tillage fostered a large population, see C. D. Lein, 'Jonathan Swift and the Population of Ireland', *Eighteenth-Century Studies* 8 (1975), 445–6.

Cloaths, Furniture, Food or Drink, as they possibly can live conveniently without.

There are many other Causes of a Nation's thriving, which I cannot at present recollect, but without Advantage from at least some of these; after turning my Thoughts a long time, I am not able to discover from whence our Wealth proceeds, and therefore would gladly be better informed. In the mean time, I will here examine what share falls to *Ireland* of these Causes, or of the Effects and Consequences.

It is not my Intention to complain, but barely to relate Facts, and the matter is not of small Importance. For it is allowed, that a Man who lives in a Solitary House far from help, is not Wise in endeavouring to acquire in the Neighbourhood, the Reputation of being Rich, because those who come for Gold, will go off with Pewter and Brass,[5] rather than return empty; and in the common Practice of the World, those who possess most Wealth, make the least Parade, which they leave to others, who have nothing else to bear them out, in shewing their Faces on the *Exchange*.[6]

As to the first Cause of a Nation's Riches, being the Fertility of the Soyl, as well as Temperature of Clymate, we have no Reason to complain;[7] for although the Quantity of unprofitable Land in this Kingdom, reckoning Bog, and Rock, and barren Mountain, be double in Proportion to what it is in *England*, yet the Native Productions which both Kingdoms deal in, are very near on equality in point of Goodness, and might with the same Encouragement be as well manufactured, I except Mines and Minerals, in some of which however we are only defective in point of Skill and Industry.

In the Second, which is the Industry of the People, our misfortune is not altogether owing to our own Fault, but to a million of Discouragements.

---

5 *because... Pewter and Brass*: in *Upon Giving Badges to the Poor* (see above, p. 2), beggars' badges are made of brass, copper or pewter.

6 *on the Exchange*: a generic reference to the public arena of commerce, rather than a specific allusion, either to the Royal Exchange in London or to the Exchange in Dublin, which at this time (before the building of the Royal Exchange) occupied rooms in the Tholsel (*A Description of the City of Dublin in Ireland, wherein, Besides taking Notice of Every Thing Remarkable in the City, and the Grandeur of the Court, is Represented the Happy Situation of Ireland for Commerce...*, London, 1732, p. 27).

7 *As to the first Cause... we have no Reason to complain*: according to John Lyon, who cared for Swift in his old age, the Dean 'loved Ireld & often spoke with pleasure of its excellent Soil, fine Climate Harbours & many other natural Advantages': Forster MS 579, Victoria and Albert Museum, National Art Library; John Hawkesworth, *The Life of the Revd. Jonathan Swift, D.D.*, Dublin: Cotter, 1755, Lyon's annotations to preliminary leaves.

The conveniency of Ports and Havens which Nature bestowed us so liberally is of no more use to us, than a beautiful Prospect to a Man shut up in a Dungeon.

As to Shipping of it's own, this Kingdom is so utterly unprovided, that of all the excellent Timber cut down within these fifty or sixty Years, it can hardly be said that the Nation hath received the Benefit of one valuable House to dwell in, or one Ship to Trade with.

Ireland is the only Kingdom I ever heard or read of, either in ancient or modern Story, which was denied the Liberty of exporting their native Commodities and Manufactures wherever they pleased,[8] except to Countries at War with their own Prince or State, yet this by the Superiority of meer Power is refused us in the most momentous parts of Commerce, besides an Act of Navigation[9] to which we never consented, pinned down upon us, and rigorously executed, and a thousand other unexampled Circumstances as grievous as they are invidious to mention. To go unto the Rest.

It is too well known that we are forced to obey some Laws we never consented to, which is a Condition I must not call by it's true uncontroverted Name[10] for fear of my *L– C– J– W–*'s Ghost[11] with his *LIBERTAS*

---

8 *denyed the Liberty... wherever they pleased*: by the English Parliament, through the various Navigation Acts, the Cattle Act of 1666 (18 Chas II c. 2), which prevented the exporting of livestock from Ireland to England, and the Woollen Act of 1699 (10 & 11 Will. III c. 10), which prohibited the exporting of woollen cloth from Ireland, and allowed exports of yarn and raw wool only to England.

9 *an Act of Navigation*: the English Navigation Act of 1663 (15 Chas II c. 7) required that goods imported into England's transatlantic colonies be carried in English-built vessels and loaded at English ports, and goods brought from the colonies be imported only at English ports. Ireland's exclusion from the colonial trade was specifically confirmed in two further explanatory Acts passed at Westminster (22 & 23 Chas II c. 26, and 7 & 8 Will. III c. 22). Swift's view directly contradicts the roseate view of Ireland's commercial potential under the English colonial system presented in John Browne, *Seasonable Remarks on Trade with Some Reflections on the Advantages that Might Accrue to Great Britain by a Proper Regulation of the Trade of Ireland*, Dublin, 1728, pp. 6–7.

10 *uncontroverted Name*: slavery.

11 *L[ord] C[hief] J[ustice] W[hitshed]'s Ghost*: William Whitshed (1679–1727), of Mary Street, Dublin, and Killincarrig, Co. Wicklow, chief justice of king's bench [Ire.] 1714–27, common pleas [Ire.], 1727–d. Whitshed had presided over the trial of Edward Waters in 1720 for publishing Swift's *Proposal for the Universal Use of Irish Manufacture*, and in 1724 had attempted unsuccessfully to persuade the Dublin grand jury to indict John Harding for publishing the *Seasonable Advice*. See F. E. Ball, *The Judges in Ireland, 1221–1921*, 2 vols., London: John Murray, 1926, vol. II, pp. 189–90; *Hist. Ir. Parl.*, vol. VI, pp. 538–40; Sabine

ET NATALE SOLUM,[12] written as a Motto on his Coach, as it stood at the Door of the Court, while he was Perjuring himself to betray both. Thus, we are in the Condition of Patients who have Physick sent them by Doctors at a Distance, Strangers to their Constitution, and the nature of their Disease: And thus, we are forced to pay five hundred *per Cent* to divide our Properties,[13] in all which we have likewise the Honour to be distinguished from the whole Race of Mankind.

As to improvement of Land, those few who attempt that or Planting, through Covetousness or want of Skill, generally leave things worse than they were, neither succeeding in Trees nor Hedges, and by running into the fancy of Grazing[14] after the manner of the *Scythians*,[15] are every Day depopulating the Country.

Baltes, '"The Grandson of that Ass Quin": Swift and Chief Justice Whitshed', *SStud* 23 (2008), 126–46.
12 *LIBERTAS ET NATALE SOLUM*: 'Liberty and my native soil' (translated by Faulkner as 'Liberty and my native Country' in the 1735 edition). In the Drapier's *Letter to the Lord Chancellor Middleton*, Swift recalled seeing, 'and I shall never forget upon what occasion [the trial of Edward Waters in 1720], the device upon his coach to be *Libertas & natale solum*; at the very point of time when he was sitting in his court, and perjuring himself to betray both' (Davis, vol. X, pp. 100–1). He dwelt on the irony in a poem of 1724: 'Fine Words; I wonder where you stole 'um' (*Poems*, vol. I, p. 348). To set against Swift's opinion, however, we should note the panegyric written by Archbishop King (King to Lord Carteret, 12 Sept. 1727 (TCD, King letterbooks, MS 750/9, p. 20)) to the effect that Whitshed was 'loved and admired by the whole kingdom'.
13 *five hundred per Cent… Properties*: Swift may have been alluding to the cost of passing a private Act of Parliament in England (for example, in order to break an entail), or of taking an appeal to the British House of Lords, which the Declaratory Act (6 Geo. I c. 5) passed at Westminster in 1720 had confirmed as the final court of appeal for all legal cases originating in Ireland.
14 *by running into the fancy of Grazing*: L. M. Cullen, *An Economic History of Ireland since 1660*, London: Batsford, 1972, pp. 47–8, has suggested that the concern shown by Swift and others over the decline in tillage in the 1720s was misplaced, and that the recent expansion of cattle grazing in Ireland largely 'consisted of substituting cattle for sheep on existing grazing land'.
15 *after the manner of the Scythians*: it was a commonplace of chronicles and histories, going back to Gerald of Wales (*Topographia Hibernia*, III, 87), that the native Irish were descended from Scythian invaders, and English commentaries on Irish society from Edmund Spenser's *View of the Present State of Ireland* (written *c.* 1596) onwards had traced Irish agricultural backwardness to this source. Despite being rebutted by Sir William Petty (*Sir William Petty's Political Survey of Ireland…*, London, 1719, p. 101), the notion of a Scythian descent persisted in early eighteenth-century published histories (e.g. Sir James Ware, *Inquiries Concerning Ireland, and its Antiquities*, Dublin, 1703, pp. 2–4, 26; Geoffrey Keating, *The General History of Ireland*, Westminster, 1726, p. 16), and was repeated by Swift (in *An Answer to a Paper, Called a Memorial*, below, p. 29, and *An Answer to The Craftsman*, below, p. 200) and by Berkeley in *The Querist* (Joseph Johnston, *Bishop*

We are so far from having a King to reside among us, that even the Viceroy is generally absent four Fifths of his time[16] in the Government. No Strangers from other Countries make this a part of their Travels, where they can expect to see nothing but Scenes of Misery and Desolation. Those who have the Misfortune to be born here, have the least Title to any considerable Employment, to which they are seldom preferred, but upon a Political[17] Consideration. One third part of the Rents of *Ireland* is spent in *England*,[18] which with the Profit of Employments, Pensions, Appeals, Journeys of Pleasure or Health, Education at the *Inns* of Court,[19] and both Universities, Remittances at Pleasure, the Pay of all Superior Officers in the Army and other Incidents,[20] will amount to a full half of the Income of the whole Kingdom, all clear profit to *England*.

Berkeley's Querist in Historical Perspective, Dundalk: Dundalgan Press, 1970, p. 168). As a nomadic people, the Scythians grazed their livestock until pasture was exhausted, before moving on and leaving the land desolate.
16 *generally absent four Fifths of his time*: it was an established convention that the lord lieutenant only came to Ireland every other year to preside over a parliamentary session.
17 *Political*: Politic.
18 *One third part of the Rents of Ireland is spent in England*: in the Drapier's *Humble Address to Both Houses of Parliament* (1724) (Davis, vol. X, p. 128), Swift estimated the annual rents in Ireland at £2 million, 'whereof one third Part, at least, is directly transmitted to those, who are perpetual absent in *England*', although in a private letter to Lord Peterborough on 28 April 1726 (Woolley, *Corr.*, vol. II, p. 644), he computed them at 'about a million and a half, whereof one half million at least is spent by lords and gentlemen residing in *England*, and by some other articles too long to mention'. In 1728 John Browne estimated Irish rents at £2,025,000 p.a. (*An Essay on Trade in General; and, on That of Ireland in Particular*, Dublin, 1728, p. 37) and noted that the money remitted annually to 'Out-Lyers [absentees]... has lately been estimated at £600,000' (ibid., p. 38), though he did not commit himself to this figure. A year later, however, in *A Scheme of the Money-matters of Ireland...* (Dublin, 1729, p. 50), Browne was happy to assert that the English 'draw annually from us, upwards of £600,000 per Annum, or close upon one third of our whole Rental in ready Money'. Thomas Prior estimated that £40,000 p.a. of Irish rental income was spent by landowners resident for all or part of the year in England, and that overall more than £600,000 p.a. was remitted from Ireland to England (Prior, *Absentees*, pp. 9, 15). Among modern calculations, L. M. Cullen has suggested that in the 1720s the amount was 'probably in excess of £300,000, although in years of economic difficulty the amount actually remitted could decline sharply' (Cullen, *Economic History of Ireland*, p. 45). On the complexities involved in any general assessment of absentee proprietorship, see A. P. W. Malcomson, 'Absenteeism in Eighteenth Century Ireland', *Irish Economic and Social History* 1 (1974), 15–35.
19 *Inns of Court*: lawyers practising in Irish courts were required by the Irish Act of 1542 (33 Hen. VIII, sess. 2, c. 3) to have spent at least six terms in one of the English inns of court.
20 *Incidents*: incidental expenses.

We are denyed the Liberty of Coining Gold, Silver, or even Copper.[21] In the Isle of *Man*, they Coin their own Silver,[22] every petty Prince, Vassal to the *Emperor*[23] can Coin what Money he pleaseth. And in this as in most of the Articles already mentioned, we are an exception to all other States or Monarchies that were ever known in the World.

As to the last, or Fourteenth Article, we take special Care to Act diametrically contrary to it in the whole Course of our Lives. Both Sexes, but especially the Women despise and abhor to wear any of their own Manufactures, even those which are better made than in other Countries, particularly a sort of Silk Plad, through which the Workmen are forced to run a sort of Gold-thread that it may pass for *Indian*.[24] Even Ale and Potatoes in great quantity are Imported from *England* as well as Corn, and our foreign Trade is little more than Importation of *French* Wine, for which I am told we pay ready Money.

Now if all this be true, upon which I could easily enlarge, I would be glad to know by what secret method it is that we grow a Rich and Flourishing People, without Liberty, Trade, Manufactures, Inhabitants, Money, or the privilege of Coining; without Industry, Labour or Improvement of Lands, and with more than half of the Rent and Profits of the whole *Kingdom*, Annually exported, for which we receive not a single Farthing: And to make up all this, nothing worth mentioning, except the Linnen of the *North* a Trade casual corrupted and at Mercy, and some Butter from *Cork*. If we do flourish, it must be against every Law of Nature and Reason, like the Thorn at *Glassenbury*,[25] that blossoms in the midst of Winter.

---

21 Swift had complained in the Drapier's *Letter to Mr Harding*... that Ireland lacked its own mint (Davis, vol. X, p. 16), and James Maculla had raised the issue in *Proposals for a Publick Coinage of Copper Half-Pence and Farthings in the Kingdom of Ireland* (Dublin, 1727) and *The Lamentable Cry of the People of Ireland to Parliament*... (Dublin, 1728).
22 *they Coin their own Silver*: the first government issue of coins minted on the Isle of Man had taken place in 1709.
23 *the Emperor*: the Holy Roman Emperor.
24 *it may pass for Indian*: poplin, of which Swift had given presents to Mrs Howard and the Princess of Wales in the autumn of 1726 (Swift to Mrs Howard, [Oct. 1726] (Woolley, *Corr.*, vol. III, p. 41)). The small but not insignificant silk industry in Ireland was concentrated in Dublin: *Econ. Hist. Ire.*, pp. 208–9.
25 *the Thorn at Glassenbury*: the supposedly miraculous hawthorn, which according to folklore had been brought to Glastonbury in Somerset by Joseph of Arimathea, and which bloomed twice a year, once in spring and once in midwinter.

Let the worthy C———rs[26] who come from *England* ride round the Kingdom, and observe the face of Nature, or the faces of the Natives, the Improvement of the Land, the thriving numerous Plantations, the noble Woods, the abundance and vicinity of Country-Seats, the commodious Farmers-Houses and Barns, the Towns and Villages, where every body is busy and thriving with all kind of Manufactures, the Shops full of Goods wrought to Perfection, and filled with Customers, the comfortable Dyet and Dress, and Dwellings of the People, the vast Numbers of Ships in our Harbours and Docks, and Shipwrights in our Seaport-Towns. The Roads crouded with Carryers laden with rich Manufactures, the perpetual Concourse to and fro of pompous Equipages.

With what Envy and Admiration would these Gentlemen return from so delightful a Progress? What glorious Reports would they make when they went back to *England*?

But my Heart is too heavy to continue this Irony longer, for it is manifest that whatever Stranger took such a Journey, would be apt to think himself travelling in *Lapland*[27] or *Ysland*,[28] rather than in a Country so favoured by Nature as Ours, both in Fruitfulness of Soyl, and Temperature of Climate. The miserable Dress, and Dyet, and Dwelling of the People. The general Desolation in most parts of the Kingdom. The old Seats of the Nobility

---

26 *the worthy C[ommissioner]s*: Englishmen appointed to the Irish revenue commission. The seven commissioners at the time Swift was writing were William Conolly (the Speaker of the Irish House of Commons), Thomas Wylde, William Harrison, Sir Thomas Frankland, Edward Thompson, Anthony Lowther and Robert Sawyer Herbert. Although Harrison may have been English-born, he was a well-established Cork landowner with a seat in the Irish Parliament (*Hist. Ir. Parl.*, vol. IV, p. 373). But apart from Conolly the remainder were English. In December 1728 Marmaduke Coghill, one of Conolly's principal lieutenants in the Irish Commons, wrote of the 'differences and disputes' that had recently taken place between the revenue commissioners, some of which were 'thought [to have been] raised rather to lay imputations on Mr Conolly, than on any other account... the inference made from this is, that means must be found out, to suffer no man of this country to be at that board, and therefore all the load must be laid on him, being the only one of this country there...' (Coghill to Edward Southwell, 14 Dec. 1728 (*Coghill Letters*, p. 59)).
27 *Lapland*: an English translation of *Lapponia* (1673), the account of Lapland by the German Johannes Schefferus, had appeared in 1704, entitled *The history of Lapland*. See P. O. Clark, 'Lapponia, Lapland and Laputa', *MLQ* 19 (1958), 342–51. In *A Modest Proposal* and elsewhere, Swift uses Lapland and its inhabitants as an archetype of a primitive and undeveloped society. See below, pp. 156, 298.
28 *Ysland*: Iceland.

and Gentry all in Ruins,[29] and no new Ones in their stead. The Families of Farmers who pay great Rents, living in Filth and Nastiness upon Buttermilk and Potatoes, without a Shoe or Stocking to their Feet, or a House so convenient as an *English* Hog-sty to receive them. These indeed may be comfortable sights to an *English* Spectator, who comes for a short time only *to learn the Language*,[30] and returns back to his own Country, whither he finds all our Wealth transmitted.

Nostrâ miseriâ magnus es.[31]

There is not one Argument used to prove the Riches of *Ireland*, which is not a logical Demonstration of it's Poverty. The Rise of our Rents is squeesed out of the very Blood and Vitals, and Cloaths, and Dwellings of the Tenants who live worse than *English* Beggars. The lowness of Interest in all other Countries a sign of Wealth is in us a proof of misery,[32] there being no Trade to employ any Borrower. Hence alone comes the Dearness

29 *The old Seats... all in Ruins*: in the Drapier's *Address to Both Houses of Parliament*, Swift had lamented the depopulation of the kingdom and 'the Ruin of so many Country-Seats and Plantations' (Davis, vol. X, p. 130).
30 *an English Spectator, who comes for a short time only to learn the Language*: English travel-writers habitually derided the manner of speaking of the native Irish, whether in Gaelic or English: see, for example, *The Comical Pilgrim; or, Travels of a Cynick Philosopher...*, London, 1722, pp. 95–6. One of the principal authors of the *Spectator*, Joseph Addison, had spent time in Dublin as chief secretary to Lord Wharton in 1709 and 1710, though he is not known to have commented in print on the spoken language. Cf. the Drapier's *Letter to the Whole People of Ireland* (Davis, vol. X, p. 61), in which Swift refers to English appointees to Irish office as 'those who, in the common phrase, do not come hither to learn the language'.
31 *Nostrâ miseriâ magnus es*: Cicero, *Att.* 2. 19.3, 'nostra miseria tu es magnus' (you are great by our misery), said to have been spoken by the actor Diphilus while staring at Pompey the Great.
32 *lowness of Interest... proof of misery*: Swift makes the same assertion in *Maxims Controlled in Ireland* (see below, pp. 154–5). L. M. Cullen, *Anglo-Irish Trade 1660–1800*, Manchester: Manchester University Press, 1969, p. 20, suggests that the going rate in Ireland was 7 per cent from 1722, reduced to 6 per cent in 1731. This was slightly higher than in contemporary England, for which see Sidney Homer and Richard Sylla, *A History of Interest Rates*, 3rd edn, New Brunswick: Rutgers University Press, 1991, p. 165. However, there is a suggestion of a recent decline in Irish interest rates in that the publication *Tables of Interest at Six, Seven, and Eight, Per cent* (Dublin 1727) appends, apparently as an afterthought, 'Tables of Interest at Five per Cent'. Swift's own account books record 'Debts and mortgages due to me' in 1732–6, on which the interest varies between 6 and 5 per cent (Paul V. Thompson and Dorothy Jay Thompson (eds.), *The Account Books of Jonathan Swift*, London: Scolar Press, 1984, pp. 310, 312).

of Land,[33] since the Savers have no other way to lay out their Money. Hence the Dearness of Necessaries for Life, because the Tenants cannot afford to pay such extravagant Rates for Land (which they must take, or go a begging) without raising the Price of Cattle, and of Corn, although they should live upon Chaff. Hence our encrease of Buildings in this City,[34] because Workmen have nothing to do but employ one another, and one half of them are infallibly undone. Hence the daily encrease of *Bankers*,[35] who may be a necessary Evil in a Trading-Country, but so ruinous in Ours, who for their private Advantage have sent away all our Silver, and one third of our Gold, so that within three Years past, the running Cash of the Nation, which was about Five hundred thousand Pounds, is now less than two,[36] and must daily diminish unless we have Liberty to Coin, as

33 *Dearness of Land*: cf. the Drapier's *Humble Address to Both Houses of Parliament* (1724) (Davis, vol. X, p. 128), which asserted that rents in Ireland had been 'enormously raised, and screwed up'. Modern historians have noted a sharp rise in rents in the 1710s and 1720s but from a low base, and by no means uniform across the country, or even across different regions (Cullen, *Economic History of Ireland*, pp. 44–5).

34 *our encrease of Buildings in this City*: on the expansion of the built environment in Dublin in this period, see Edel Sheridan, 'Designing the Capital City: Dublin, c. 1660–1810', in Joseph Brady and Anngret Simms (eds.), *Dublin through Space and Time*, Dublin: Four Courts Press, 2001, pp. 68–9, 81–93; Christine Casey, *The Buildings of Ireland: Dublin: The City within the Grand and Royal Canals and the Circular Road with the Phoenix Park*, New Haven & London: Yale University Press, 2005, pp. 43–5; Brendan Twomey, *Smithfield and the Parish of St. Paul, Dublin, 1698–1750*, Maynooth Studies in Local History, 63, Dublin: Four Courts Press, 2005, pp. 14–25; Twomey, 'Financing Speculative Property Development in Early Eighteenth-century Dublin', in Christine Casey (ed.), *The Eighteenth-century Dublin Townhouse: Form, Function and Finance*, Dublin: Four Courts Press, 2010, pp. 29–45; and, in general, Nuala Burke, 'Dublin 1600–1800: A Study in Urban Morphogenesis', Ph.D. thesis, TCD, 1972, and Dickson, *Dublin*, pp. 139–42.

35 *the daily encrease of Bankers*: for the rapid increase in banking in Ireland in the 1720s, see L. M. Cullen, 'Landlords, Bankers and Merchants: The Early Irish Banking World 1700–1820', *Hermathena* 135 (1983), 31–2, 35–6. Swift's animus against bankers, and to paper credit, was expressed in his poems 'The Run upon the Bankers' (*Poems*, vol. I, pp. 238–41), and 'The Bank Thrown Down' (I, pp. 286–8), the latter celebrating the defeat in 1721 of the project to establish a national bank. It reflected the hostility to the 'moneyed interest' that had been such a feature of Tory polemic against the Junto Whig administration in England in the reign of Anne. On the survival of similar attitudes in Ireland during the debates on the bank project, see Michael Ryder, 'The Bank of Ireland, 1721: Land, Credit and Dependency', *Historical Journal* 25 (1982), 557–82.

36 *less than two*: in the Drapier's *Letter to the Lord Chancellor Middleton* (Davis, vol. X, p. 112), Swift had estimated 'the current money' in Ireland at under £500,000, and, in the *Humble Address to Both Houses of Parliament* (1724) (Davis, vol. X, pp. 125, 135), had also complained of the shortage of gold and silver coin in circulation. In his *Scheme of the Money-matters of Ireland...*, p. 17, John Browne postulated a total of not more than £500,000 in gold coin circulating in Ireland, with about £10,000 in silver and £4,000 in

well as that important Kingdom the Isle of *Man*, and the meanest Prince in the *German Empire*, as I before observed.

I have sometimes thought, that this Paradox of the Kingdom growing Rich, is chiefly owing to those worthy Gentlemen the BANKERS, who, except some Custom-house Officers,[37] Birds of Passage, oppressive thrifty 'Squires, and a few others that shall be Nameless, are the only thriving People among us: And I have often wished that a Law were enacted to hang up half a Dozen *Bankers* every Year, and thereby interpose at least some short Delay, to the further Ruin of *Ireland*.

Ye are idle, ye are idle, answered *Pharoah* to the *Israelites*, when they complained to his M A J E S T Y, that they were forced to make Bricks without Straw.[38]

England enjoys every one of these Advantages for enriching a Nation, which I have above enumerated, and into the Bargain, a good Million returned to them every Year without Labour or Hazard, or one Farthing value received on our side.[39] But how long we shall be able to continue the payment, I am not under the least Concern. One thing I know, that *when the Hen is starved to Death, there will be no more Golden Eggs.*[40]

I think it a little unhospitable, and others may call it a subtil piece of Malice, that, because there may be a Dozen Families in this Town, able to entertain their *English* Friends in a generous manner at their Tables,

---

copper, while Thomas Prior, in *Observations on Coin in General. With Some Proposals for Regulating the Value of Coin in Ireland...*, Dublin, 1729, p. 44, supposed a total of £400,000 cash in circulation, £40,000 of it in silver.

37 *Custom-house Officers*: officials of the customs and excise in Ireland, more especially the customs and excise commissioners (generally referred to as the revenue commissioners) who administered the service, and were based in the Dublin Custom House on Essex Quay.

38 *forced to make Bricks without Straw*: Exodus, 5: 15–17: 'Then the officers of the children of Israel came and cried unto Pharaoh, saying, Wherefore dealest thou thus with thy servants? There is no straw given unto thy servants, and they say to us, Make brick: and, behold, thy servants are beaten; but the fault is in thine own people. But he said, Ye are idle, ye are idle: therefore ye say, Let us go and do sacrifice to the Lord.'

39 *on our side*: all remittances from Ireland, not merely the rents to absentee landlords. In the Drapier's *Humble Address to Both Houses of Parliament* (1724), Swift had estimated that in total two-thirds of the annual revenues of Ireland were remitted into England, which he calculated on the basis of about £700,000 in rents, plus a further £700,000 in various other forms, but including the adverse balance of trade (Davis, vol. X, pp. 128–9). Thomas Prior, on the other hand estimated the total of remittances at a little over £621,499 (Prior, *Absentees*, p. 14).

40 *no more Golden Eggs*: an allusion to Aesop's fable of the goose that laid the golden eggs and was killed by her owners in the mistaken belief that she must herself be made of gold.

their Guests upon their Return to *England*, shall report that we wallow in Riches and Luxury.

Yet I confess I have known an Hospital,[41] where all the Houshold-Officers grew Rich, while the Poor for whose sake it was built, were almost starving for want of Food and Raiment.

To Conclude. If *Ireland* be a rich and flourishing Kingdom, it's Wealth and Prosperity must be owing to certain Causes, that are yet concealed from the whole Race of Mankind, and the Effects are equally Invisible. We need not wonder at Strangers when they deliver such Paradoxes, but a Native and Inhabitant of this Kingdom, who gives the same Verdict,[42] must be either ignorant to Stupidity, or a Man-pleaser[43] at the Expence of all Honour, Conscience and Truth.

FINIS

---

41 *an Hospital*: the Dublin workhouse.
42 *a Native... same Verdict*: John Browne.
43 *Man-pleaser*: cf. Gal. 1:10; Eph. 6:6; Col. 3:22; and Richard Baxter, *A Christian Directory*, ch. 4, pt 4, 'Directions against Inordinate Man-pleasing', in his *Practical Works* (London, 1707), vol. I, pp. 173–82.

AN ANSWER TO A PAPER, CALLED A MEMORIAL OF THE POOR INHABITANTS, TRADESMEN AND LABOURERS OF THE KINGDOM OF IRELAND.

BY THE AUTHOR OF THE SHORT VIEW OF THE STATE OF IRELAND.

Headnote

Composed March 1728 (dated 25 March); published March 1728; copy text *1728* (see Textual Account).

This is a product of the reaction to *A Short View of the State of Ireland*; after its publication in March 1728, Swift received a short pamphlet, *To the R—d Dr. J—n S—t, The Memorial of the Poor Inhabitants, Tradesmen, and Labourers of the Kingdom of Ireland* (see Appendix A, below), usually attributed to John Browne. The *Answer to a Paper*, Swift's refutation of the pamphlet's assertions, is dated less than a week after the publication of *A Short View*, and it was published quickly, appearing in Dublin only a few days later (see Ferguson, pp. 151–2).

The related rising price of corn after two bad harvests, complaints of monopolies and profiteering, and the issue of whether Ireland could feed itself, led to Swift recommending (as other writers were to do, and Parliament was to pick up on during the following session) the need to increase the amount of land in Ireland under tillage.

In the parliamentary session of 1727–8, two bills were brought forward to promote tillage: the first was rejected by the British privy council; the second eventually received the royal assent as I Geo. II c. 10 in May 1728. The tillage bill was part of a broader concern with regulating the market in corn. A separate Act was passed for regulating the assize of bread, enacted 1728 (I Geo. II c. 16). The tillage bill was much solicited by Archbishop Boulter (see his letter to Newcastle, 24 Feb. 1727[/8] *Boulter Letters*, vol. I, p. 177)). Swift also comments on the monopolising of land by graziers to the detriment of the ordinary cottier and labourer. The context of this particular agricultural problem begins with the passage by the Irish Parliament in 1704 of an Act (II Anne c. 15) to prevent butchers becoming graziers, in an attempt to halt the process by which land in certain parts of Ireland was increasingly being let to large-scale graziers. Popular anger at the expansion of grazing had erupted in 1711–12 with a campaign of houghing (hamstringing) of livestock in the midlands and west of Ireland, a sustained popular protest directed against landlords and middlemen who were evicting tenants and consolidating their landholdings into large expanses of pasturage (see S. J. Connolly, 'Law, Order and Popular Protest in Early Eighteenth-century Ireland: the Case of the Houghers', in P. J. Corish (ed.), *Radicals, Rebels and Establishments*, Belfast: Appletree Press, 1985, pp. 51–68; and 'The Houghers: Agrarian Protest in Early Eighteenth-century Connacht', in C. H. E. Philpin (ed.), *Nationalism and Popular Protest in Ireland*, Cambridge: Cambridge University Press, 1986, pp. 139–62). For

Swift as a clergyman, there was a further complication in that the legal right of the clergy to claim a tithe on lands given over to pasture was hotly disputed, a struggle that climaxed in 1736 in a vote in the Irish House of Commons declaring the tithe on pasture (the 'tithe of agistment') to be unlawful (see Landa, pp. 135–50; D. W. Hayton and Stephen Karian, 'Select Document: The Division in the Irish House of Commons on the "Tithe of Agistment", 18 Mar. 1736, and Swift's "Character... of the Legion Club"', *Irish Historical Studies* 38 (2012–13), 304–21).

An Answer was usually reprinted in Swift's prose alongside *A Short View* from the 1735 Faulkner edition of Swift's *Works* onwards.

AN ANSWER TO A PAPER, &c.

I Received a *Paper* from you wherever you are, Printed without any Name of Author or Printer,[1] and sent, I suppose to me among others, without any particular Distinction. It contains a Complaint of the Dearness of Corn, and such Schemes of making it Cheaper which I cannot approve of.

But pray permit me before I go further, to give you a short History of the Steps, by which we arrived at this hopeful Situation.

It was indeed the shameful practice of too many *Irish* Farmers, to wear out their Ground with Plowing, while either through Poverty, Laziness or Ignorance, they neither took Care to Manure it as they ought; nor gave time to any part of the Land to recover it self: And when their Leases were near expiring, being assured that their Landlords would not renew, they Plowed even the Medows, and made such a Havock, that many Landlords were considerable sufferers by it.

This gave Birth to that abominable Race of Graziers,[2] who upon Expiration of the Farmers Leases, are ready to engross great Quantities of Land, and the Gentlemen having been before, often ill payed, and their Land worn out of Heart, are too easily Tempted, when a Rich Grazier made him an offer to take all his Land,[3] and give him Security for payment. Thus a vast Tract of Land where twenty or thirty Farmers lived together, with their Cottagers, and Labourers in their several Cabbins, became all Desolate, and easily managed, by one or two Herdsmen and their Boys, whereby the Master Grazier with little Trouble, seized to himself the Livelyhood of a Hundred People.

It must be confessed, that the Farmers were justly punished for their Knavery, Brutality and Folly. But neither are the 'Squires and Landlords to be excused; For to them is owing the Depopulating of the Country, the

---

1 *Printed without any Name of Author or Printer*: [John Browne,] *To the R[everen]d Dr. J[onathan] S[wif]t; the Memorial of the Poor Inhabitants, Tradesmen and Labourers of the Kingdom of Ireland* ([Dublin,] 1728).
2 *that abominable Race of Graziers*: Swift's aversion to graziers was shared by some, but not all, commentators on the Irish economy. For a different view, see Dobbs, *Essay*, p. 144.
3 *all his Land*: in *A Proposal for Universal Use of Irish Manufacture*, Swift had commented that 'the politick Gentlemen of Ireland have depopulated Vast Tracts of the best Land, for the feeding of Sheep' (Davis, vol. IX, p. 15). See also the Drapier's *Humble Address to Both Houses of Parliament* (1724) (Davis, vol. X, p. 135). On the expansion of grazing in Munster, see David Dickson, *Old World Colony: Cork and South Munster 1630–1830*, Cork: Cork University Press, 2005, ch. 7.

vast Number of Beggars, and the Ruin of those few sorry Improvements we had.

That Farmers should be limited in Plowing, is very reasonable, and practised in *England*,[4] and might have easily been done here, by penal Clauses in their Leases: But to deprive them in a manner altogether from Tilling their Lands, was a most stupid want of thinking.

Had the Farmers been confin'd to plow a certain Quantity of Land, with a Penalty of ten pounds an Acre, for whatever they exceeded, and farther limited for the three or four last Years of their Leases, all this Evil had been prevented; The Nation would have saved a Million of Money, and been more populous by above two Hundred Thousand Souls.

For a People denyed the Benefit of Trade, to manage their Lands in such a manner, as to produce nothing but what they are forbidden to Trade with, or only such things as they can neither export, nor manufacture to advantage, is an Absurdity, that a Wild *Indian* would be asham'd of, especially when we add, that we are content to purchase this hopeful Commerce, by sending to Foreign Markets for our Daily Bread.

The Graziers Employment is to feed great Flocks of Sheep, or Black-Cattle,[5] or both. With regard to Sheep, as folly is usually accompanied with perverness, so it is here. There is something so monstrous to deal in a Commodity, (further than for our own use) which we are not allowed to export manufactured, nor even Un-manufactured but to one certain Country,[6] and only to some few Ports in that Country,[7] there is, I say, something so Sottish that it wants a Name in our Language to express it

---

4 *That Farmers... practised in England*: there was no statutory limitation on tillage in England, but most farmers would have been subject to a clause in their leases relating to the husbandry they were to practise, which in turn meant how much they could plough in a single year. (This applied only to freehold leases, not usually to copyhold or customaryhold.) Any landowner wishing to ensure the long-term fertility of the soil would seek to prevent a farmer from ruining the land, usually by underploughing, or ploughing land that should have been in fallow. We are grateful to Professor John V. Beckett for explaining this point.
5 *Black-Cattle*: Welsh black cattle, a native British breed, used for both beef and dairy production.
6 *we are not allowed... one certain Country*: by the terms of the English Woollen Act of 1699 (10 & 11 Will. III c. 10), Irish woollen cloth could not be exported at all, while yarn and raw wool could only be exported to England.
7 *only to some few Ports in that Country*: by the English Woollen Act, wool and yarn exported to England could only be embarked from Cork, Drogheda, Dublin, Kinsale, Waterford or Youghal, and landed at the ports of Barnstaple, Bideford, Bridgwater, Bristol, Chester, Milford Haven, Minehead or Liverpool.

by, and the good of it is, that the more Sheep we have, the fewer humane Creatures are left to wear the Wooll, or eat the Flesh.[8] *Ajax* was Mad when he mistook a Flock of Sheep for his Enemies:[9] But we shall never be sober till we have the same way of thinking.

The other part of the Graziers Business is, what we call Black-Cattle, producing Hydes, Tallow and Beef for Exportation. All which are good and useful Commodities if rightly managed. But it seems the greatest part of the Hydes are sent out Raw, for want of Bark to Tann it,[10] and that want will Daily grow stronger, for, I doubt, the new project of Tanning without it,[11] is at an End. Our Beef, I am afraid, still continues scandalous in Foreign Markets for the old Reasons.[12] But our Tallow, for any thing I

---

8 *the more Sheep we have... eat the Flesh*: echoing the observation of Thomas More in *Utopia*, bk 1, that the spread of pastoral farming had destroyed men's livelihoods and depopulated the countryside, so that, as More put it, sheep, 'which are naturally mild, and easily kept in order, may now be said to devour men'. Swift owned a copy of the 1631 edition (*Library and Reading, I*, vol. III, pp. 1833–4). He expressed his admiration for More in *Concerning that Universal Hatred Which Prevails against the Clergy* (1736) (Davis, vol. XIII, p. 123).
9 *mistook a Flock of Sheep for his Enemies*: Sophocles' eponymous tragedy tells how Ajax, enraged at the award of Achilles' armour to Odysseus rather than himself, swore vengeance against the Greeks, but, having been tricked by the goddess Athena into believing that the sheep and cattle taken in plunder by the Achaeans were his enemies, tortured and killed them.
10 *want of Bark to Tann it*: the use of various forms of tree bark in the tanning process dated back to ancient Egypt. Oak was the type of bark most commonly used in Britain and Ireland.
11 *the new project of Tanning without it*: in March 1728, the Dublin chemist William Maple, later a founder-member of the Dublin Society, was paid a bounty of £200 by order of the Irish Parliament for his 'discovery of a new method of tanning leather with a vegetable of the growth of Ireland' (*C.J.Ire.*, vol. V, p. 681), details of which he published in *A Method of Tanning without Bark*, Dublin, 1729. In the *Proposal for the Universal Use of Irish Manufactures* (1720), Swift observed how 'Mr. Shuttleworth and others on the Cheshire Coasts sell us bark to tan our own hydes into leather' (Davis, vol. IX, p. 18).
12 *for the old Reasons*: throughout the seventeenth century, Irish cattle were 'commonly considered to be scrawny, their meat tough, their butter inferior, and their hides lank and thin' (Carolyn A. Edie, 'The Irish Cattle Bills: a Study in Restoration Politics', *Transactions of the American Philosophical Society*, new ser., 60 (1970), 5). Donald Woodward, 'The Anglo-Irish Livestock Trade in the Seventeenth Century', *Irish Historical Studies* 18 (1972–3), 491, has argued, however, that this view was not universal and was in any case incorrect. English anxiety in the first half of the seventeenth century at the volume of imported Irish cattle, which culminated in the passage at Westminster of the Cattle Act of 1667, was based instead on the fact that the volume of imported lean cattle for fattening was depressing the price of English beef (Joan Thirsk (ed.), *The Agrarian History of England and Wales*, vol. V: *1640–1750*, Cambridge: Cambridge University Press, 1985, pt 2, pp. 309, 326, 346–53).

know, may be good. However to bestow the whole Kingdom on Beef and Mutton, and thereby drive out half the People who should eat their share, and force the rest, to send sometimes as far as *Egypt*, for Bread to eat with it,[13] is a most peculiar and distinguished piece of publick Oeconomy, of which I have no Comprehension.

I know very well that our Ancestors the *Scythians*,[14] and their Posterity our Kinsmen the *Tartars*, liv'd upon the Blood and Milk, and raw Flesh of their Cattle, without one Grain of Corn,[15] but I confess my self so degenerate, that I am not easy without Bread to my Victuals.

What amazed me for a Week or two was to see in this prodigious plenty of Cattle, and Dearth of Humane Creatures, and want of Bread as well as Money to buy it, that all kind of Flesh-meat should be monstrously Dear, beyond what was ever known in this Kingdom. I thought it a Defect in the Laws; That there was not some Regulation in the price of Flesh, as well as Bread: But I imagine my self to have guessed out the Reason. In short I am apt to think, that the whole Kingdom is overstocked with Cattle, both Black and White:[16] And as it is observed, that the poor *Irish* have a Vanity, to be rather Owners of two lean Cows, than one Fat, although with double the Charge of Grazing, and but half the Quantity of Milk; so I conceive it much more difficult at present to find a fat Bullock, or Weather,[17] than it would be, if half of both were fairly knocked on the Head, for I am assured, that the District in the several Markets, called *Carrion-Row*,[18] is as Reasonable, as the Poor can desire, only the Circumstance of Money to purchase it, and of Trade, or Labour to purchase that Money, are indeed wholly wanting.

Now Sir, to return more particular to you, and your Memorial.

13 *to send... for Bread to eat with it*: a reference to the biblical story of Joseph, who sent to his father 'ten asses laden with the good things of Egypt, and ten she-asses laden with corn and bread and meat' (Gen., 45: 23).
14 *our Ancestors the Scythians*: the supposed racial ancestors of the native Irish. For the belief that they drank a mixture of the milk and blood of their livestock, see below, pp. 226–7.
15 *without one Grain of Corn*: a contemporary account of the Tartars and their customs was available in English in *A General History of the Turks, Moguls, and Tatars, Vulgarly called Tartars, together with a Description of the Countries they Inhabit*, 2 vols., London, 1729, esp. vol. II, p. 403.
16 *both Black and White*: the British white was a breed of cattle originating in Lancashire.
17 *Weather*: wether: a castrated male sheep, the ovine equivalent of a bullock.
18 *Carrion-Row*: in 1776 there was a 'Carrion Row' off Meath Street in the Liberties, near other food markets (*Wilson's Dublin Directory, for the Year 1776...*, Dublin, [1776], p. vi).

A Hundred thousand Barrels of Wheat, you say, should be imported hither, and Ten thousand pounds premium to the Importers.[19] Have you looked into the Purse of the Nation? I am no Commissioner of the Treasury,[20] but am well assured that the whole running Cash would not supply you with a Summ to purchase so much Corn, which only, at twenty Shillings a Barrel, will be a hundred thousand pounds, and ten Thousand more for the Premiums. But you will Traffick for your Corn with other Goods: And where are those Goods? If you had them, they are all engaged to pay the Rents of Absentees, and other occasions in *London*, besides a huge Ballance of Trade this Year against us.[21] Will Foreigners take our Bankers paper? I suppose they will value it at little more than so much a Quire. Where are these rich Farmers and Ingrossers of Corn in so bad a Year, and so little sowing?

You are in pain of two Shillings premium, and forget the twenty Shillings for the Price, find me out the latter and I will engage for the former.

Your Scheme for a Tax for raising such a Summ is all Visionary[22] and owing to a great want of Knowlege in the miserable State of this Nation. Tea, Coffee, Sugar, Spices, Wine, and foreign Cloaths, are the particulars you mention, upon which this Tax should be raised.[23] I will allow the two first, because they are unwholsome; and the last because I should be glad if they were all burned, but I beg you will leave us our Wine to make us a while forget our Misery,[24] or give your Tenants leave to plow for Barly.[25] But I will tell you a Secret, which I learned many years ago

19 *premium to the Importers*: Browne (*Memorial*, p. 6) had argued that a premium of 2s per barrel of wheat would encourage sufficient imports from the plantations and other neighbouring countries, at a total cost, he suggested, of no more than £10,000, a figure Swift ridiculed.
20 *Commissioner of the Treasury*: an office in the British administration, but not existing as such in Ireland, where the Treasury was not in commission.
21 *a huge Ballance of Trade this Year against us*: Browne had himself admitted a steady shift in the balance of trade to Ireland's detriment, in John Browne, *Seasonable Remarks on Trade with Some Reflections on the Advantages that Might Accrue to Great Britain by a Proper Regulation of the Trade of Ireland*, Dublin, 1728, p. 143, and *A Scheme of the Money-matters of Ireland...*, Dublin, 1729, p. 45.
22 *Visionary*: incapable of being carried out.
23 *the particulars you mention... Tax should be raised*: Browne, *Memorial*, pp. 7–8.
24 *our Misery*: cf. his comment in *A Proposal that All the Ladies and Women of Ireland Should Appear Constantly in Irish Manufactures* that 'there is no nation yet known... where the people of all conditions are more in want of some cordial, to keep up their spirits' (below, p. 146).
25 *Barly*: for brewing beer.

from the Commissioners of the Customs in *London.* They said, when any Comodity appeared to be taxed above a moderate Rate, the Consequence was to lessen that Branch of the Revenue by one half, and one of those Gentlemen pleasently told me, that the mistake of Parliaments on such occasions was owing to an Errour of computing two and two to make Four. Whereas in the Business of laying heavy Impositions, two and two never made more than One, which happend by lessening the Import, and the Strong Temptation of Running[26] such Goods as payed high Duties. And at least in this Kingdom, although the Women are as vain and extravagant as their Lovers or their Husband can deserve, and the Men are fond enough of Wine, yet the number of Both who can afford such Expences is so few, that the major part must refuse gratifying themselves, and the Duties will rather be lessen'd than encreased. But allowing no force in this Argument, yet so prœternatural Sum[27] as one hundred and Ten thousand pounds, raised all on a sudden (for there is no dallying with Hunger) is just in proportion with raising a Million and half in *England,* which, as things now Stand, would probably bring even that opulent Kingdom under some Difficulties.

You are concerned how strange and surprising it would be in foreign parts to hear that the Poor were starving in a *RICH*-Country &c. Are you in earnest? Is *Ireland* the Rich Country you mean? Or are you insulting our Poverty? Were you ever out of *Ireland?* Or were you ever in it till of late? You may probably have a good Employment and are saving all you can to purchase a good Estate in *England.* But by talking so familarly of one hundred and ten thousand Pounds by a Tax upon a few Comodities it is plain you are either naturally or affectedly ignorant of our present condition, or else you would know and allow that such a Sum is not to be raised here, without a general excise,[28] since in proportion to our Wealth

---

26 *Running*: smuggling.
27 *so prœternatural Sum*: abnormally large.
28 *a general excise*: in theory, a tax levied on all saleable goods within the kingdom (as opposed to the customs duties levied on imported goods), but understood by contemporaries as a tax on all foodstuffs. Besides its unpopular historical association with the Parliamentarian administrations during the English Civil War, a 'general excise' was detested because of its destructive effects on the poor. It was a particular bugbear of oppositionists in England, who repeatedly alleged in 1732–3 that Walpole's excise scheme was in effect the bringing in of a 'general excise' (Paul Langford, *The Excise Crisis: Society and Politics in the Age of Walpole*, Oxford: Clarendon Press, 1975, pp. 159–62). In *The Conduct of the Allies* (1711),

we pay already in Taxes more than *England* ever did in the Heighth of the War.[29] And when you have brought over your Corn who will be the Buyers; Most certanly not the poor who will not be able to purchase the twentieth part of it.

Sir, upon the whole your paper is a very crude piece lyable to more objections than there are lines but I think, your meaning is good and so far you are pardonable.

If you will propose a general contribution in supporting the Poor in Potatoes and Butter-milk till the new Corn comes in, perhaps you may succeed better, because the thing at least is possible, and I think if our Bretheren in *England* would contribute upon this Emergency out of the Million they gain from us every year, they would do a piece of Justice as well as Charity. In the Mean time go and preach to your own Tenants to fall to the Plow as fast as they can, and prevail with your Neighbouring Squires to do the same with theirs, or else dye with the Guilt of having driven away half the Inhabitants, and starving the Rest. For as to your Scheme of raising one hundred and ten thousand Pounds it is as vain as that of *Rabelaies*,[30] which was to squeeze out wind from the Posteriors of a dead Ass.[31]

But why all this concern for the Poor? We want them not, as the Country is now Managed; they may follow thousand of their leaders and seek their Bread abroad.[32] Where the Plow has no work, one family can do the Business of fifty and you may send away the other forty nine. An admireable piece of Husbandry never known or practised by the wisest nations, who erroniously thought People to be the Riches of a Country.

If so wretched a state of things would allow it, methinks I would have a Malicious pleasure, after all the warning I have in vain given the publick, at my own peril for several years past, to see the consequences and Events answering in every particular. I pretend to no Sagacity. What I writ was

---

Swift alleged that a general excise would have been the inevitable consequence of the Whig ministry's war policy (*CWJS*, vol. VIII, p. 90).

29 *the War*: the War of the Spanish Succession, 1702–13.
30 *Rabelaies*: François Rabelais (1494–1553) was one of Swift's favourite writers (*Library and Reading*, I, vol. III, pp. 1559–60).
31 *to squeeze out wind from the Posteriors of a dead Ass*: *Gargantua and Pantagruel*, v, 22: 'I saw a spodizator, who very artificially got farts out of a dead ass, and sold 'em for fivepence an ell.' Swift reworked the same idea in his satire on projectors in *Gulliver's Travels*, part III, ch. v (*CWJS*, vol. XVI, pp. 263–4).
32 *seek their Bread abroad*: Irish Catholic soldiers who held commissions in the armies of European powers.

little more than what I had discoursed to several persons, who were generally of my Opinion, and it was obvious to every common Understanding that such Effects must needs follow from such Causes. A fair Issue of things, begun upon party Rage, while some Sacrificed the publick to Fury, and others to Ambition: While a Spirit of Faction and Oppression reigned in every part of the Country, where Gentlemen, instead of consulting the Ease of their Tenants or cultivating their Lands, were worrying one another upon points of *Whig and Tory*, of *high Church and low Church*, which no more concerned them, than the long and famous controversy of Strops for Razors.[33] While Agriculture was wholly discouraged and consequently half the Farmers, and Labourers and poorer Tradesmen forced to Beggary or Banishment, *Wisdom cryeth in the Streets, because I have called on ye, I have streatched out my hand, and no Man regarded. But ye have set at nought all my Counsels and would none of my Reproof. I also will laugh at your Calamity, and mock when your fear cometh.*[34]

I have now done with your Memorial, and freely excuse your mistakes, since you appear to write as a Stranger, and as of a Country which is left at liberty to enjoy the Benefits of Nature, and to make the best of those Advantages which God hath given it in Soyl, Climate and Situation.

But having sent out a paper some days ago entitled, *A Short View of the State of Ireland*, and hearing of an Objection, that some people think I have treated the Memory of a departed J———ge,[35] with an appearance of Severity. Since I may not probably have another opportuinity of explaining my self in that particular, I chuse to do it here. Laying it therefore down for a Postulatum,[36] which I suppose will be universally granted. That no

---

33 *the long and famous controversy of Strops for Razors*: the rivalry between inventors and retailers of razor-strops, as manifested in the London press, c. 1703–10, had been the subject of comment by Steele in *The Spectator* (*Spectator*, vol. III, p. 5), and by Addison in the *Tatler* (*Tatler*, vol. III, p. 167); and had been noted by Swift in *Journal to Stella*, 13 Jan. 1711 (*CWJS*, vol. IX, p. 119).

34 *and mock when your fear cometh*: Proverbs 1:20–6: 'Wisdom crieth without; she uttereth her voice in the streets: She crieth in the chief place of concourse, in the openings of the gates: in the city she uttereth her words, saying, How long, ye simple ones, will ye love simplicity? and the scorners delight in their scorning, and fools hate knowledge? Turn you at my reproof: behold, I will pour out my spirit unto you, I will make known my words unto you. Because I have called, and ye refused; I have stretched out my hand, and no man regarded; But ye have set at nought all my counsel, and would none of my reproof: I also will laugh at your calamity; I will mock when your fear cometh'.

35 *departed J[ud]ge*: William Whitshed, chief justice of Common Pleas in Ireland, died on 19 Aug. 1727.

36 *a Postulatum*: a statement which can be taken as true.

little Creature of so mean a Birth[37] and Genius had ever the Honour to be a greater Enemy to his Country, and to all kinds of Virtue than He. I answer thus, whether there be two different Goddesses called Fame, as some Authors Contend, or only one Goddess, sounding two different Trumpets.[38] It is certain that People distinguished for their Villiany have as good a Title for a Blast from the proper Trumpet, as those who are most renowned for their Virtues, and have equal reason to complain if it be refused them, and accordingly the Names of the most Celebrated Profligates, have been faithfully Transmitted down to Posterity. And although the Person here understood, Acted his part in an obscure Corner of the World, yet his Talents might have shone with Lustre enough in the Noblest Scene.

As to my Nameing a Person Dead, the plain honest Reason is the best. He was Armed with Power, Guilt, and Will to do Mischief, even where he was not provoked, as appeared by his Prosecuting two *Printers*, one to Death, and both to Ruin,[39] who had neither offended God, nor the King, nor Him, nor the Publick.

What an Encouragement to Vice is this? If an ill Man be Alive and in Power, we dare not Attack him, and if he be weary of the World, or of his own Villianies, he has nothing to do but Dye, and then his Reputation is

---

37 *of so mean a Birth*: Whitshed was descended on both sides from Dublin merchants, though his father Thomas was a barrister and had sat as an MP in the Irish House of Commons. On his mother's side, the recent family history was disreputable. His maternal grandfather, Mark Quin, lord mayor of Dublin in 1667, had committed suicide, allegedly as a result of marital difficulties, while Whitshed's uncle on his mother's side was a bigamist, whose own son, the renowned actor James Quin, was thus illegitimate: see Baltes, '"The Grandson of that Ass Quin'", 138–9.

38 *two different Goddesses . . . only one Goddess, sounding two different Trumpets*: for differing literary representations of the Roman goddess Fama, as a single deity, with one trumpet, or as twin deities, one positive and one negative (*bona fama* and *mala fama*), each with her own trumpet (as depicted, for example, in the frontispiece to Sir Walter Raleigh, *The Historie of the World In Fiue Books . . .*, London, 1628), see Philip Hardie, *Rumour and Renown: Representations of Fama in Western Literature*, Cambridge: Cambridge University Press, 2012. In Chaucer, *House of Fame*, bk III, the goddess Fama summons Aeolus, the god of wind, who has two trumpets, praise and slander. This was rendered as a single trumpet in Pope's version of the poem, *The Temple of Fame* (*The Twickenham Edition of the Poems of Alexander Pope*, ed. John Butt *et al.*, 3rd edn, 11 vols., London: Methuen, 1962–9, vol. II, pp. 278–89), which was to be found in Swift's copy of the 1717 edition of Pope's works (*Library and Reading, I*, vol. II, p. 1490).

39 *Prosecuting two Printers, one to Death, and both to Ruin*: Swift blamed Whitshed for the prosecution of his printers Edward Waters (in 1720) and John Harding (in 1724). Harding had died within a year of the failed prosecution against him, in April 1725.

safe. For these excellent Casuists, know just *Latin* enough to have heard a most foolish precept, that *De mortuis nil nisi bonum*,[40] so that if *Socrates* and *Anytus* his accuser[41] had happened to Dye together, the Charity of Survivers must either have obliged them to hold their peace, or to fix the same Character on both. The only crime of charging the Dead, is when the least Doubt remains whether the Accusation be true, but when Men are openly abandoned and lost to all shame they have no reason to think it hard, if their Memory be reproached. Whoever reports or otherwise publisheth any thing which it is possible may be false, that Man is a Slanderer. *Hic niger est, hunc tu Romane cavetto.*[42] Even the least Mis-representation or Agravation of Facts, deserves the same Censure in some digree: But in this case I am quite deceived if my Error hath not been on the side of Extenuation.

I have now present before me the Idea of some persons (I know not in what part of the World) who spend every moment of their Lives and every turn of their Thoughts while they are awake (and probably of their Dreams while they sleep) in the most detestable Actions and Designs, who delight in Mischief, Scandal and Obloquy, with the Hatred and contempt of all Mankind against them, but chiefly of those among their own party and their own family, such whose odious Qualities Rival each other for perfection: Avarice, Brutality, Faction, Pride, Malice, Treachery, Noise, Impudence, Dullness, Ignorance, Vanity and Revenge contending every moment for Superiority in their Breasts. Such Creatures are not to be reformed, neither is it prudence or safety to attempt a Reformation. Yet although their memories will Rot, there may be some Benefit for their Survivers to smell it while it is rotting.

I am Sir,
Your humble Servt.
A.B.

Dublin,
March 25th, 1728,

FINIS

40 *De mortuis nil nisi bonum*: 'Let nothing be said of the dead but what is good.'
41 *Anytus his accuser*: Anytus, a wealthy politician whose son had been one of Socrates' pupils, played a prominent part in his trial.
42 *Hic niger est, hunc tu Romane cavetto*: Horace, *Satires*, 1, 4, 85: 'This is a black [soul]; O Roman, beware of him'.

THE INTELLIGENCER

Headnote

The Intelligencer, the journal jointly written by Swift and Thomas Sheridan, consisted of twenty papers published in 1728–9 in Dublin. Swift made seven prose contributions, one of which (No. 15) was a reprint of *A Short View of the State of Ireland*, with an introduction by Sheridan. (In this volume, Sheridan's introduction is provided in the textual apparatus, pp. 357–9.)

The Intelligencer was not the first periodical in Ireland: it followed the *Dublin Journal* in importing from England the format of the *Spectator*, *Tatler* and *Examiner* (which Swift had edited from 1710 to 1711, and contributed to thereafter). The rationale for *The Intelligencer* is explained by Swift in the first number: topics were to be miscellaneous, but able to include observations on contemporary political and cultural issues as well as arguments concerning education, agriculture, economics and emigration.

The Dublin printings by Sarah Harding published each number as a separate pamphlet. There were collected London editions in 1729 and 1730; numbers 5, 7 and 9 were included in the so-called 'Third' volume of the Pope–Swift *Miscellanies* of 1732; and all Swift's papers, save the first, in Faulkner's 1735 *Works*. For plans of potential *Intelligencer* papers, see Associated Materials I, pp. 283–6, 'Hints for *Intelligencer* Papers'.

THE INTELLIGENCER, NUMB. I.
SATURDAY, MAY 11.
TO BE CONTINUED WEEKLY.

Headnote

Published 11 May 1728; copy text *1728* (see Textual Account).

In the opening number, Swift follows the introductory form for a journal, established by Steele, Addison and others, and familiar from Swift's years of political journalism in England. The paper offers a rationale of the journal's ambitions and approach, a description of its intended readership, and a general encouragement to contributors, while stressing its consistent promotion of virtue and appropriate moral considerations.

THE INTELLIGENCER.

It may be said, without offence to other *Cities*, of much greater consequence in the World, that our Town of *Dublin* doth not want it's due proportion of *Folly*, and Vice, both Native and Imported; And as to those Imported, we have the advantage to receive them last, and consequently after our happy manner to improve, and refine upon them.

But, because there are many Effects of *Folly* and *Vice* among us, whereof some are *general*, others confined to smaller Numbers, and others again, perhaps to a few *individuals*; There is a *Society* lately established, who at great expence, have Erected an *Office of Intelligence*, from which they are to receive Weekly Information of all *Important Events* and *Singularities*, which this famous *Metropolis* can furnish. Strict injunctions are given to have the truest Information: In order to which, certain qualified Persons are employed to attend upon Duty in their several Posts; some at the *Play-house*, others in *Churches*, some at *Balls, Assemblees*,[1] *Coffee-houses*, and *meetings* for *Quadrille*;[2] some at the several *Courts of Justice*, both *Spiritual* and *Temporal*, some at the *College*,[3] some upon my *Lord Mayor* and *Aldermen* in their publick Affairs; lastly, some to converse with *favourite Chamber-maids*, and to frequent those *Ale-houses*, and *Brandy-Shops*, where the *Footmen* of great Families meet in a Morning;[4] only the *Barracks*[5] and *Parliament-house* are excepted; because we have yet found no *enfans perdus*[6]

---

1 *Assemblees*: elegant social gatherings.
2 *Quadrille*: a card game for four hands, played with forty cards (the tens, nines and eights having been removed): a craze among fashionable ladies in both England and Ireland and the subject of *The Intelligencer* 4 (1 June 1728), by Sheridan. A Dublin half-sheet of 1728 referred to Dawson Street as 'Quadrill-Row' (Woolley, *Intelligencer*, p. 70). Swift would describe the game in *Polite Conversation* as bearing 'some Resemblance to a State of Nature, which, we are told, is a State of War, wherein every Woman is against every Woman' (*CWJS*, vol. II, p. 289), and satirised feminine devotion to the game in 'The Journal of a Modern Lady' (*Poems*, vol. II, pp. 443–53).
3 *College*: Trinity College.
4 *meet in a Morning*: in *Directions to Servants*, Swift alluded to the tendency of footmen to trade the secrets of each other's families (*CWJS*, vol. II, p. 483).
5 *Barracks*: the Royal Barracks at Oxmantown.
6 *enfans perdus*: the French term for the 'forlorn hope', troops deployed in a leading role in any military operation where the risk of casualties was high. A contemporary explanation can be found in 'J. W.', *A Military Dictionary, Explaining All Difficult Terms in Martial Discipline, Fortification, and Gunnery*..., 4th edn, London, 1730: 'Men... appointed to give the first Onset in Battle... so call'd because of the imminent Danger they are expos'd to. In *English* they are commonly call'd, *The Forlorn*.'

bold enough to venture their Persons at either. Out of these and some other *Store-houses*, we hope to gather Materials enough to *Inform*, or *Divert*, or *Correct*, or *Vex* the Town.

But as *Facts*, *Passages*,[7] and *Adventures*[8] of all kinds, are like to have the greatest share in our *Paper*, whereof we cannot always Answer for the Truth; due Care shall be taken to have them applyed to feigned Names,[9] whereby all just Offence will be removed; for if none be guilty, none will have cause to Blush or be Angry; if otherwise, then the guilty Person is safe for the future upon his *present* Amendment, and safe for the *present*, from all but his *own Conscience*.

There is another Resolution taken among us, which I fear will give a greater and more general discontent, and is of so singular a Nature, that I have hardly confidence enough to mention it, although it be absolutely Necessary by way of Apology, for *so bold and unpopular an Attempt*. But so it is, that we have taken a desperate Counsel to produce into the World every distinguished Action, either of *Justice, Prudence, Generosity, Charity, Friendship*, or *publick Spirit*, which comes well attested to us. And although we shall neither here be so daring as to Assign Names, yet we shall hardly forbear to give some hints, that perhaps to the great displeasure of such deserving Persons may endanger a Discovery. For we think that even *Virtue it self*, should submit to such a *Mortification*, as by it's *visibility* and *example*, will render it more useful to the World. But however, the *Readers* of these *Papers*, need not be in pain of being over-charged, with so dull and ungrateful a Subject. And yet who knows, but such an occasion may be offered to us, once in a Year or two, after we shall have settled a Correspondence round the *Kingdom*.

But after all our boasts of *Materials*, sent us by our several *Emissaries*, we may probably soon fall short, if the Town will not be pleased to lend

---

7 *Passages*: Incidents or transactions.
8 *Adventures*: chance occurrences.
9 *feigned Names*: an established, if commonly violated, ideal of satire was to avoid naming names: see Martial, *Epigrams*, X, xxxiii, ll. 9–10; Ben Jonson, *Works*, ed. C. H. Herford and Percy Simpson, 11 vols., Oxford: Clarendon Press, 1925, vol. IV, pp. 319–20; Dryden, 'Discourse Concerning the Original and Progress of Satire' (1693), in *The Works of John Dryden*, ed. Edward Niles Hooker, H. T. Swedenberg, jr, Vincent A. Dearing *et al.*, 20 vols., Berkeley, CA: University of California Press, 1956–2000, vol. IV, pp. 60–3, 81; Addison in *Spectator*, vol. I, p. 148; and Swift himself, in 'Verses on the Death of Dr. Swift', in *Poems*, vol. II, p. 571, ll. 459–60: 'Yet, Malice never was his Aim; / He lash'd the Vice but spar'd the Name'.

us further Assistance towards entertaining it self. The *World* best knows it's own *Faults* and *Virtues*, and whatever is sent shall be faithfully returned back, only a little Embellished according to the Custom of AUTHORS. We do therefore *Demand* and *Expect* continual *Advertisements* in great Numbers, to be sent to the *PRINTER* of this *Paper*, who hath employed a *Judicious Secretary* to Collect such as may be most useful for the *Publick*.[10]

And although we do not intend to expose our own Persons by mentioning Names, yet we are so far from requiring the same Caution in our *Correspondents*, that on the contrary, we expressly *Charge* and *Command* them, in all the Facts they send us, to set down the Names, Titles, and Places of Abode at length; together with a very particular Description of the *Persons*, *Dresses*, and *Dispositions* of the several *Lords, Ladies, Squires, Madams, Lawyers, Gamesters, Toupees*,[11] *Sots, Wits, Rakes,* and *Informers*,[12] whom they shall have occasion to mention; otherwise it will not be possible for us to adjust our Style to the different Qualities, and Capacities of the Persons concerned, and Treat them with the *Respect* or *Familiarity*, that may be due to their *Stations* and *Characters*, which we are Determined to observe with the utmost strictness, that none may have cause to Complain.

---

10 *Publick*: Swift wrote to Pope on 12 June 1732: 'If we could have got some ingenious young man to have been the manager, who should have published all that might be sent to him, it [*The Intelligencer*] might have continued longer, for there were hints enough' (Woolley, *Corr.*, vol. III, p. 489).
11 *Toupees*: the toupee (deriving from the French toupet, a hair tuft) was a type of short wig in which the front hair was combed up over a pad into a top-knot (*OED*). It was in fashion in London by 1727 (*Miscellanies, the Last Volume*, London, 1727, p. 45) and was associated with young men-about-town, so much so that it became synonymous with foppery and gallantry, and was used to denote a social type: see, for example, Caleb D'anvers, *The Twickenham Hotch-Potch...*, London, 1728, p. 36; *An Essay upon the Taste and Writings of the Present Times...*, London, [1728], p. 26; *Universal Spectator and Weekly Journal* (25 Oct., 15 Nov. 1729); Mrs Aldcroft to Mrs Macro, 29 Jan. 1729/30 (BL, Macro papers, Add. MS 32556, fo. 174). To some commentators, its French origin made it politically suspect – Defoe, for one, considered its adoption in place of the traditional full English wig to be a symptom of the creeping effeminacy that was weakening English manhood: Daniel Defoe, *Augusta Triumphans*, London, 1728, p. 51. Swift's Dublin contemporary, John Browne, made repeated references to the toupee in *The Lucubrations of Sallmanazor Histrum, esq....*, Dublin, 1730, pp. 84, 86, 95, 96.
12 *Informers*: Swift's contempt for informers led him to preach an entire sermon against them (*On False Witness...* (Davis, vol. IX, pp. 180–9)). In the *Letter to... Mr Pope* (1721), he called informers 'the most accursed, and prostitute, and abandoned race, that God ever permitted to plague mankind' (ibid., pp. 32–3). In Lilliput, Gulliver finds that informing is a capital offence (*Gulliver's Travels*, pt III, ch. vi (*CWJS*, vol. XVI, p. 281; see also ibid., pp. 298, 417)).

THE INTELLIGENCER, NUMB. III.

Ipse per Omnes ibit Personas,
Et turbam reddet in uno.[1]

---

1 *Ipse per Omnes... reddet in uno*: Manilius, *Astronomica*, v, 480–1: 'Solusque per omnis / ibit personas et turbam reddit in uno' ([of an actor] He will go through all the roles, one man representing a multitude of characters). Swift could have found the motto in his copy of Michel Mattaire, *Opera et Fragmenta Veterum Poetarum Latinorum Profanorum & Ecclesiasticorum*, London, 1713, vol. I, p. 784 (*Library and Reading*, I, vol. II, p. 1166). Swift had cited Manilius in *Mr Collins's Discourse of Free-Thinking* (1713); see Davis, vol. IV, p. 45.

Headnote

Published *c*. 25 May 1728; copy text *1728* (see Textual Account).

Swift's next contribution to the journal was a brief account of his friend John Gay's *Beggar's Opera*, which had, since the success of its London premiere in January, been received equally enthusiastically in Dublin, when it opened there in March. This provides Swift with opportunities for observations on the distinction between wit and humour, and on the nature of satire.

THE INTELLIGENCER.

The *Players* having now almost done with the Comedy, called The *Beggar's Opera*[2] for this Season, it may be no unpleasant Speculation, to reflect a little upon this *Dramatick Piece*, so singular in the Subject, and the manner, so much an Original, and which hath frequently given so very agreeable an Entertainment.

Although an evil *Tast* be very apt to prevail, both here, and in *London*, yet there is a point which whoever can rightly Touch, will never fail of pleasing a very great Majority; so great, that the Dislikers, out of Dulness or Affectation will be silent, and forced to fall in with the Herd; the point I mean, is what we call *Humour*, which in its Perfection is allowed to be much preferable to *Wit*, if it be not rather the most useful, and agreeable Species of it.[3]

I agree with Sir *William Temple*, that the Word is peculiar to our *English Tongue*, but I differ from him in the Opinion, that the thing it self is peculiar to the *English Nation*,[4] because the contrary may be found in many *Spanish*, *Italian*, and *French* Productions, and particularly, whoever hath a *Tast* for *True Humour*, will find a Hundred Instances of it in those

---

2 *The Beggars Opera*: Swift wrote to Pope on 10 May 1728 that 'Mr Gay's opera hath been acted here twenty times, and my Lord Lieutenant tells me it is very well perform'd; he hath seen it often and approves it much' (Woolley, *Corr.*, vol. III, p. 180). The first performance took place on *c.* 14 March, and the second on Saturday the 16th (*Dublin Intelligence*, 19 Mar. 1728). A week later, the theatre was reportedly sold out for two weeks in advance (ibid., 3 Mar. 1728). By October, the opera had been performed nearly forty times in Dublin and had enjoyed a provincial tour (ibid., 3 Oct. 1728). See W. E. Schultz, *Gay's Beggar's Opera: Its Content, History and Influence*, New Haven: Yale University Press, 1923, pp. 38–42; T. J. Walsh, *Opera in Dublin 1705–1797: The Social Scene*, Dublin: Allen Figgis, 1973, pp. 34–5.
3 *agreeable Species of it*: in the poem 'To Mr. Delany' (1718), Swift distinguishes between wit and humour: 'by Wit is only meant / Applying what we first Invent', while 'Humour is odd, grotesque and wild. / Onely by Affectation spoild, / Tis never by Invention got, / Men have it when they know it not' (*Poems*, vol. I, pp. 215–16). On contemporary discussions of the relationship of humour to wit, see S. M. Tave, *The Amiable Humorist: A Study of the Comic Theory and Criticism of the Eighteenth and Early Nineteenth Centuries*, Chicago: University of Chicago Press, 1960, pp. 91–120.
4 *peculiar to our English Tongue... English Nation*: in his essay 'Upon Poetry' (Temple, *Miscellanea. The Second Part*, London, 1705, pp. 355–7).

Volumes Printed in *France*, under the Name of *Le Theatre Italien*,[5] to say nothing of *Rabelais*,[6] *Cervantes*,[7] and many others.

Now I take the *Comedy* or *Farce*, (or whatever Name the *Criticks* will allow it)[8] called the *Beggars Opera*; to excel in this Article of *Humour*. And, upon that Merit, to have met with such prodigious success both here, and in *England*.[9]

As to *Poetry*, *Eloquence*, and *Musick*, which are said to have most Power over the minds of Men,[10] it is certain that very few have a *Tast* or *Judgment* of the Excellencies of the two former, and if a Man succeeds in either, it is upon the Authority of those *few Judges*, that lend their *Taste* to the bulk of Readers, who have none of their own. I am told there are as few good Judges in *Musick*, and that among those who Crowd the Operas, Nine in Ten go thither meerly out of *Curiosity*, *Fashion*, or *Affectation*.

But a Taste for *Humour* is in some manner fixed to the very Nature of Man, and generally Obvious to the Vulgar, except upon Subjects too refined, and Superior to their Understanding.

And as this *Taste* of *Humour* is purely Natural,[11] so is *Humour* it self, neither is it a *Talent* confined to Men of *Wit*, or *Learning*; for we observe

---

5 *Le Theatre Italien*: Evaristo Gherardi, *Le Théatre Italien: ou, Le Recueil de toutes les Scenes Françoises, qui ont esté Joüées sur le Theatre Italien de l'hostel de Bourgogn*, Paris, 1694, was a compilation of the plays and scenes comprising the *commedia dell'arte*.
6 *Rabelais*: François Rabelais (*c.* 1494–1553).
7 *Cervantes*: Miguel de Cervantes Saavedra (1547–1616). Pope had informed Swift in October 1727 that his poem *The Dunciad* would associate Swift with both Rabelais and Cervantes (Pope and Gay to Swift, 22 Oct. 1727 (Woolley, *Corr.*, vol. III, p. 136)).
8 *allow it*: for the controversy that Swift is avoiding here, see Leo Hughes, 'Attitudes of Some Restoration Dramatists toward Farce', *Philological Quarterly* 19 (1940), 268–87.
9 *England*: Swift had heard from Gay of the great success of the play in England (Gay to Swift, 15 Feb. 1727/8, 20 Mar. 1727/8 (Woolley, *Corr.*, vol. III, pp. 159–60, 165–6)). For its rapturous reception in Dublin, see *Dublin Intelligence*, 23 Mar. 1727/8.
10 *Poetry, Eloquence, and Musick . . . minds of Men*: Temple, in his essay 'Upon Poetry', had written: 'Nor is it any great wonder that such force should be found in poetry, since in it are assembled all the powers of eloquence, of music and of picture, which are all allowed to make so strong impressions upon humane minds' (*Miscellanea. Second Part*, p. 311).
11 *purely Natural*: In the 'Apology' (1710) prefixed to *A Tale of a Tub*, Swift had written, 'as Wit is the noblest and most useful Gift of humane Nature, so Humor is the most agreeable, and where these two enter far into the Composition of any Work, they will render it always acceptable to the World. Now, the great Part of those who have no Share or Tast of either, but by their Pride, Pedantry and Ill Manners, lay themselves bare to the Lashes of Both, think the Blow is weak, because they are insensible, and where Wit hath any mixture of Raillery; 'Tis but calling it *Banter*, and the work is done' (*CWJS*, vol. I, pp. 13–14). The suggestion that some people have no taste for humour stands in contradiction to the statement made here.

it sometimes among common Servants, and the meanest of the People, while the very Owners are often Ignorant of the Gift they possess.

I know very well, that this happy *Talent* is contemptibly Treated by *Criticks*, under the Name of *low Humour*, or *low Comedy*;[12] but I know likewise, that the *Spaniards* and *Italians*, who are allowed to have the most Wit of any *Nation* in *Europe*, do most excell in it, and do most esteem it.

By what Disposition of the mind, what Influence of the Stars, or what Situation of the *Clymate* this endowment is bestowed upon Mankind,[13] may be a Question fit for *Philosophers* to Discuss. It is certainly the best Ingredient towards that kind of Satyr, which is most useful, and gives the least Offence; which instead of lashing, Laughs Men out of their Follies, and Vices, and is the Character which gives *Horace* the Preference to *Juvenal*.[14]

And although some things are too Serious, Solemn, or Sacred to be turned into Ridicule, yet the Abuses of them are certainly not, since it is allowed that Corruption in *Religion*, *Politicks*, and *Law*, may be proper *Topicks* for this kind of Satyr.[15]

There are two ends that Men propose in Writing Satyr, one of them less Noble than the other, as regarding nothing further than personal Satisfaction, and pleasure of the Writer; but without any View towards *Personal Malice*; The other is a *Publick Spirit*, prompting Men of *Genius* and Virtue, to mend the World as far as they are able. And as both these ends are innocent, so the latter is highly commendable. With Regard to the former, I demand whether I have not as good a Title to Laugh, as

---

12 *low Comedy*: Dryden opposed low comedy in his preface to *An Evening's Love* (1671). John Dennis, however, maintained that 'Humour is more the business of Comedy than Wit: And... Humour is more to be found in low Characters, than among Persons of a higher Rank' (*The Critical Works of John Dennis*, ed. E. N. Hooker, 2 vols., Baltimore: The Johns Hopkins University Press, 1939–43, vol. I, p. 281).
13 *this endowment is bestowed upon Mankind*: Temple had speculated that the English propensity to humour might be ascribed to 'the native plenty of our soil, the unequalness of our climate, as well as the ease of our government, and the liberty of expressing opinions and factions, which perhaps our neighbours may have about them, but are obliged to disguise' (p. 357).
14 *gives Horace the Preference to Juvenal*: Dryden had endeavoured a similar (and more extended) comparison between Horace and Juvenal in his 'Discourse Concerning... Satire' (1693), though ultimately his preference was for the latter (*Works*, vol. IV, pp. 49–76).
15 *proper Topicks for this kind of Satyr*: Swift may be alluding to his justification for satirising the corruptions of religion in *A Tale of a Tub*, in the 'Apology' prefaced to the *Tale* (*CWJS*, vol. I, pp. 6–7).

Men have to be Ridiculous, and to expose Vice, as another hath to be Vicious. If I Ridicule the Follies and Corruptions of a *Court*, a *Ministry*, or a *Senate*; are they not amply payed by *Pensions*, *Titles*, and *Power*, while I expect and desire no other Reward, than that of Laughing with a few Friends in a Corner. Yet, if those, who take Offence, think me in the Wrong, I am ready to Change the Scene with them, whenever they please.

But if my Design be to make Mankind better, then I think it is my Duty, at least I am sure it is the Interest of those very *Courts* and *Ministers*, whose Follies or Vices I Ridicule, to reward me for my good Intentions; For, if it be reckoned an high point of Wisdom to get the Laughers on our side, it is much more easy, as well as Wise to get those on our side, who can make Millions Laugh when they please.

My Reason for mentioning *Courts*, and *Ministers*, (whom I never think on, but with the most profound Veneration) is because an Opinion obtains, that in the *Beggars Opera* there appears to be some Reflections upon *Courtiers* and *States-Men*, whereof I am by no means a Judge.

It is true indeed that Mr. *GAY*, the Author of this Piece, hath been somewhat singular in the Course of his Fortunes, for it hath happened, that after Fourteen Years attending the *Court*,[16] with a large Stock of real Merit, a Modest, and Agreeable Conversation, a *Hundred Promises*, and five *Hundred Friends*, he hath failed of Preferment, and upon a very Weighty Reason. He lay under the Suspicion of having Written a Libel, or Lampoon against a great M———[17] It is true that great M——— was demonstratively convinced, and publickly owned his Conviction, that Mr. *Gay* was not the Author;[18] but having lain under the Suspicion, it seemed very just, that he should suffer the Punishment; because in this

---

16 *after Fourteen Years attending the Court*: Gay had sought to ingratiate himself with the Hanoverians in the spring of 1714, when he had travelled to Hanover as secretary to the Earl of Clarendon. After the accession of George I, he had published the 'Letter to a lady' in a desperate effort to secure preferment, and continued to pay court to the Prince and Princess of Wales (the future George II and Queen Caroline). See *ODNB*.
17 *a great M[inister]*: Sir Robert Walpole.
18 *Author*: a reference to a dinner held at Walpole's Chelsea house during the time Swift was in England in March or April 1726, to which he had been invited with 'some of my friends', and at which Walpole made this admission: Swift to Lady Elizabeth Germain, [8] Jan. 1732/3 (Woolley, *Corr.*, vol. III, pp. 574–5). By 'publickly', Swift simply means in front of witnesses.

most reformed Age, the Virtues of a great M—— are no more to be suspected, than the Chastity of *Caesar*'s Wife.[19]

It must be allowed, That the *Beggars-Opera* is not the first of Mr. *Gay*'s Works, wherein he hath been faulty, with regard to *Courtiers* and *States-Men*. For, to omit his other Pieces, even in his Fables, published within two Years past, and Dedicated to the *D. of Cumberland*, for which he was PROMISED a Reward;[20] he hath been thought somewhat too bold upon *Courtiers*. And although it is highly probable, he meant only the *Courtiers* of former times, yet he acted unwarily, by not considering, that the Malignity of some people[21] might misinterpret what he said to the disadvantage of present *Persons*, and Affairs.

But I have now done with Mr. *Gay* as a Politician, and shall consider him henceforward only as Author of the *Beggars Opera*, wherein he hath by a turn of *Humor*, entirely New, placed Vices of all Kinds in the strongest and most odious Light; and thereby done eminent Service, both to *Religion* and *Morality*. This appears from the unparallel'd Success he hath met with. All *Ranks*, *Parties* and *Denominations* of Men, either crowding to see his *Opera*, or reading it with delight in their Closets, even *Ministers* of State, whom he is thought to have most offended (next to those whom the Actors more immediately represent) appearing frequently at the *Theatre*,[22] from a consciousness of their own Innocence, and to convince the World how

---

19 *the Chastity of Caesar's Wife*: in 62 BC, Caesar's wife Pompeia was presiding over the festivities of Bona Dea, attendance at which was forbidden to men, when a young patrician, Publius Clodius Pulcher, was discovered there, in female attire. It was assumed that his intention had been to seduce Pompeia, and even though there was no evidence of her complicity, Caesar had divorced her, declaring that his wife ought to be above suspicion. The story was told in Plutarch's *Lives* of Caesar and Cicero: *Caesar*, X; *Cicero*, XXVIII.

20 *for which he was PROMISED a Reward*: John Gay, *Fables, Invented for the Amusement of his Highness William, Duke of Cumberland*, London, 1727; repr. Dublin, 1727. Prince William Augustus, Duke of Cumberland, George II's second surviving son, was six years old in 1727. Swift certainly believed that, shortly after George II's accession, Queen Caroline had promised to assist Gay towards preferment, and in October he was offered a place as gentleman usher to the infant Princess Louisa, which he declined as demeaning (a decision of which Swift approved; see Gay and Pope to Swift, 22 Oct. 1727 (Woolley, *Corr.*, vol. III, pp. 135–6); Swift to Lady Elizabeth Germain, [8] Jan. 1732/3 (ibid., pp. 574–5); J. H. Plumb, *Sir Robert Walpole: The King's Minister*, London: Cresset Press, 1960, p. 175; *ODNB* (Gay, John)).

21 *the Malignity of some people*: presumably Walpole.

22 *Theatre*: at one performance in London, '2 great Ministers were in a Box together, and all the world staring at them': Swift to Gay, 28 Mar. 1728 (Woolley, *Corr.*, vol. III, p. 170). In Dublin, the lord lieutenant, Carteret, was among the audience (Walsh, *Opera in Dublin*, p. 34).

unjust a Parallel, *Malice, Envy,* and *Disaffection to the Government have made.*

I am assured that several worthy *Clergy-Men* in this *City*, went privately to see the *Beggars-Opera* represented; and that the *fleering*[23] *Coxcombs* in the *Pit,* amused themselves with making Discoveries, and spreading the Names of those Gentlemen round the Audience.

I shall not pretend to vindicate a *Clergy-Man,* who would appear openly in his Habit at a *Theatre,* among such a vicious Crew, as would probably stand round him, and at such lewd *Comedies,* and prophane *Tragedies* as are often represented. Besides I know very well, that Persons of their Function are bound to avoid the appearance of Evil, or of giving cause of Offence.[24] But when the *Lords Chancellors,* who are Keepers of the King's Conscience,[25] when the *Judges* of the Land, whose Title is *Reverend,*[26] when *Ladies,* who are bound by the Rules of their Sex, to the strictest Decency, appear in the *Theatre* without Censure, I cannot understand, why a young Clergy-man who goes concealed out of Curiosity to see an innocent and moral Play, should be so highly condemned; nor do I much approve the Rigor of a great P—te who said, *he hoped none of his Clergy were there.*[27] I am glad to hear there are no weightier Objections against that Reverend Body, planted in this City, and I wish there never may. But I should be very sorry that any of them should be so weak, as to imitate a COURT-CHAPLAIN in *England,* who preached against the *Beggars-Opera,*[28] which will probably do more good than a thousand Sermons of so stupid, so injudicious, and so prostitute a Divine.

23 *fleering*: smirking or laughing derisively.
24 *Offence*: in 'The Form and Manner of Ordaining Priests' in the Book of Common Prayer, the bishop exhorts those about to be ordained 'to beware, that neither you offend, nor be occasion that others offend'. Swift is also alluding to the passage in 1 Thess., 5: 22: 'Abstain from all appearance of evil.'
25 *Keepers of the King's Conscience*: medieval lord chancellors, who were invariably priests, served as spiritual advisers to the sovereign. The title 'Keeper of the King's Conscience' survived into the eighteenth century, but in practice the lord chancellor's responsibility in religious affairs was confined to the management of the crown's ecclesiastical patronage, and the visitation of hospitals and colleges of royal foundation.
26 *whose Title is Reverend*: an archaic form of address for members of the judiciary, still occasionally used.
27 *a great P[relat]e . . . none of his Clergy were there*: it is unclear which Church of England bishop Swift is aiming at, but an obvious candidate would be the bishop of London, Edmund Gibson (1669–1748).
28 *who preached against the Beggars-Opera*: Thomas Herring (1693–1757), chaplain to George II and future archbishop of Canterbury, had brought himself into the public eye through attacking the *Beggar's Opera* as immoral. See *ODNB*.

In this happy Performance of Mr. *Gay*, all the Characters are just, and none of them carried beyond Nature, or hardly beyond Practice. It discovers the whole System of that Common-Wealth, or that *Imperium in Imperio*[29] of Iniquity, established among us, by which neither our Lives, nor our Properties are secure, either in the High-ways, or in publick Assemblies, or even in our own Houses. It shews the miserable Lives, and the constant Fate of those abandoned Wretches; for how little they sell their Lives and Souls; betrayed by their *Whores*; their *Comrades*; and the *Receivers* and *Purchasers* of these Thefts and Robberies. This *Comedy* contains likewise a *Satyr*, which, although it doth by no means affect the present Age, yet might have been useful in the former and may possibly be so in Ages to come.[30] I mean where the Author takes occasion of comparing those *common Robbers to Robbers of the Publick*; and their several Stratagems of betraying, undermining, and hanging each other, to the several Arts of *Politicians* in times of Corruption.

This *Comedy* likewise exposeth with great Justice, that unnatural Taste for *Italian* Musick among us, which is wholly unsuitable to our Northern *Climat*, and the *genius* of the People, whereby we are over-run with *Italian Effeminacy*, and *Italian*-Nonsense.[31] An old Gentleman said to me, that many Years ago, when the practice of an unnatural Vice grew so frequent in *London*, that many were Prosecuted for it,[32] he was sure it would be

---

29 *Imperium in Imperio*: 'Empire within an empire', a group or organisation working against the interests of the greater community or institution of which it forms a part.
30 *Ages to come*: a principle to which allusion had previously been made in the preface to *The Battle of the Books* (*CWJS*, vol. I, p. 142). In a letter to Charles Wogan in 1732, responding to Wogan's expressed disapproval of *The Beggar's Opera* as an encouragement to vice, Swift wrote that, on the contrary, 'we think of it as a very severe Satyr upon the most pernicious Villanies of Mankind': Swift to Wogan, [July–] 2 Aug. [1732] (Woolley, *Corr.*, vol. III, p. 516).
31 *Italian Effeminacy, and Italian Nonsence*: contemporary suspicion of Italian opera, and its link with effeminacy and 'unnatural' sexual practices, were articulated most forcefully in John Dennis, *An Essay on the Operas after the Italian Manner, Which Are About to Be Establish'd on the English Stage: with Some Reflections on the Damage Which They May Bring to the Public*, London, 1706, esp. p. 14. Dennis had repeated his denunciations in *The Stage Defended, from Scripture, Reason, Experience, and the Common Sense of Mankind, for Two Thousand Years...*, London, 1726, dedication, pp. v, x, while the following year the genre was devastatingly satirised in Thomas D'Urfey, *The English Stage Italianiz'd, in a New Dramatic Entertainment, Called Dido and Æneas...*, London, 1727.
32 *many were Prosecuted for it*: prosecutions for homosexuality in England seem to have peaked in the late 1690s (as part of the campaign for the 'reformation of manners') and in the mid-1720s: Alan Bray, *Homosexuality in Renaissance England*, London: Gay Men's Press, 1982, pp. 90–103, 132–9; Randolph Trumbach, 'Sodomitical Assaults, Gender Role, and Sexual Development in 18th-Century London', *Journal of Homosexuality* 16 (1988), 409.

a Fore-runner of *Italian-Opera*'s, and Singers; and then we should want nothing but Stabbing[33] or Poysoning, to make us perfect *Italians*.

Upon the Whole, I deliver my Judgment, That nothing but servile Attachment to a Party, affectation of Singularity, lamentable Dullness, mistaken Zeal, or studied Hypocrisy, can have the least reasonable Objection against this excellent Moral-performance of the CELEBRATED MR. GAY.

33 *nothing but Stabbing*: John Chamberlayne's *Magnae Britanniae Notitia* in 1728 noted that 'Stabbing in England is much more seldom than in Italy' (Woolley, *Intelligencer*, p. 69).

THE INTELLIGENCER, NUMB. V.

Describ'd it's thus: Defin'd would you it have?
Then the World's honest Man's an errant Knave.[1]

Ben. Johnson

---

[1] *Describ'd it's thus... an errant Knave*: the concluding couplet of Epigram 115, 'On the Townes Honest Man', in Jonson's folio *Workes* (1640), of which Swift owned a copy (*Library and Reading, I*, vol. II, pp. 980–2).

Headnote

Composed *c.* 8 June 1728; published; copy text *1728* (see Textual Account).

Published in June 1728, this introduces the general contrast between the calculating uses of discretion and prudence in the making of a career, and the worldly failure of the more ingenuous and principled, and was continued and exemplified in the two character studies in *The Intelligencer*, no. 7, with which it was later combined as 'An Essay on the Fates of Clergymen', when reprinted in the Pope/Swift *Miscellanies* of 1732.

The idea that discretion in public life is more of a veil for ambition and a form of self-interest appears frequently in Swift's writings, albeit in slightly different ways. The general premise that the discreetly ambitious are prepared to make great sacrifices (even of their self-respect) in order to advance is phrased in *Thoughts on Various Subjects*: 'AMBITION often puts Men upon doing the meanest Offices; so climbing is performed in the same Posture with Creeping' (Davis, vol. I, p. 245). Gulliver is advised by the Emperor of Lilliput to 'acquire, by my Patience and discreet Behaviour, the good Opinion of himself and his subjects'. Conversely, the King of Brobdingnag remarks that, in Gulliver's milieu, it seems unlikely 'that Men are ennobled on Account of their Virtue', or 'that Priests are advanced for their Piety or Learning' (*CWJS*, vol. XVI, pp. 49, 189). And in 'On Poetry: A Rhapsody', the prospective poet, upon publication, is advised not to attempt to influence public opinion directly, but rather 'Be silent as a Politician' (*Poems*, vol. II, p. 644). Such examples could be multiplied, given Swift's suspicion of the ostensible means of advancement in public life.

THE INTELLIGENCER.

There is no *Talent* so useful towards rising in the World, or which puts Men more out of the reach of Fortune, than that Quality generally possessed by the Dullest sort of People, and is in common Speech, called *Discretion*,[2] a species of lower Prudence, by the assistance of which, People of the meanest Intellectuals, without any other Qualification, pass through the World in great Tranquility, and with Universal good Treatment, neither giving nor taking Offence. *Courts* are seldom unprovided of Persons under this Character, on whom, if they happen to be of great Quality, most Employments, even the greatest naturally fall, when Competitors will not agree; and in such Promotions, no Body rejoyces or grieves. The Truth of this I could prove by several Instances, within my own Memory (for I say nothing of present Times.)

And indeed as Regularity and Forms are of great use in carrying on the Business of the World, so it is very convenient, that Persons endued with this kind of Discretion, should have that share which is proper to their Talents in the Conduct of Affairs, but by no means to meddle in matters which require *Genius, Learning, strong Comprehension, quickness of Conception, Magnanimity, Generosity, Sagacity,* or other superior Gift of Human minds. Because this sort of *Discretion*, is usually attended with a strong desire of Money, and few Scruples about the way of obtaining it, with servile Flattery and Submission, with a Want of all publick Spirit or Principle, with a perpetual wrong Judgment when the Owners come into Power, and High Place, how to dispose of Favour and Preferment, having no measure for Merit, and Virtue in others, but those very Steps by which themselves ascended; Nor the least Intention of doing Good or Hurt to the Publick, further than Either one or t'other, is likely to be subservient to their own Security or Interest. Thus being void of all Friendship and Enmity, they never complain nor find Fault with the Times, and indeed never have reason to do so.

Men of eminent Parts and Abilities as well as Virtues do sometimes rise in the *Courts*, sometimes in the *Law*, and sometimes even in the *Church*.

---

2 *Discretion*: Addison devoted no. 225 of *The Spectator* (17 Nov. 1711) to the praise of discretion, of which, he wrote, 'There are many more shining Qualities in the Mind of Man, but there is none so useful' (*Spectator*, vol. II, pp. 375–8).

Such were the Lord *Bacon*,³ the Earl of *Strafford*,⁴ Arch-bishop *Laud*⁵ in the Reign of King *Charles* I. and others in our own times whom I shall not Name: But these and many more under different Princes, and in different Kingdoms, were *Disgraced* or *Banished*, or *suffered Death*, meerely in Envy to their Virtues and Superior *Genius*,⁶ which emboldned them in great Exigencies and distresses of State (wanting a reasonable Infusion of this Aldermanly Discretion)⁷ to attempt the Service of their Prince and Country out of the common Forms.⁸

This evil Fortune, which generally attends extraordinary Men in the Management of great Affairs, hath been imputed to divers Causes, that need not be here set down, when so obvious a One occurs. For, if what a certain Writer observes, be true, *when a great Genius appears in the World, the Dunces are all in Confederacy against him*:⁹ And thus although he imploys his *Talents* wholly in his Closet, without interfaring with any Man's Ambition or Avarice; what must he expect when he ventures out to seek for Preferment in a Court, but Universal Opposition, when he is mounting the Ladder, and every hand ready to turn him off, when he is at the Top? And in this point Fortune generally Acts directly contrary to Nature, For

---

3 *Lord Bacon*: Francis Bacon (1561–1626), 1st Viscount St Alban, lord chancellor of England 1618–21.
4 *the Earl of Strafford*: Thomas Wentworth (1593–1641), 1st Earl of Strafford, lord deputy of Ireland, 1632–41. In *An Enquiry into the Behaviour of the Queen's Last Ministry* (Davis, vol. VIII, p. 138), Swift included Strafford (along with Themistocles, Aristides, Scipio, Sir Walter Raleigh and Edward Hyde, Earl of Clarendon) in a list of men of 'exalted abilities', who, when 'called to public Affairs', were 'drawn into Inconveniencies and Misfortunes, which others of Ordinary Talents avoid'.
5 *Archbishop Laud*: William Laud (1573–1645), bishop of London 1628–33, archbishop of Canterbury 1633–45. All three named here had been impeached by Parliament. See also Swift to Bolingbroke, 19 Dec. 1719 (Woolley, *Corr.*, vol. II, p. 316): 'Think upon Lord Bacon, Williams, Strafford, Laud, Clarendon, Shaftesbury, the last Duke of Buckingham; and of my own acquaintance, the earl of Oxford and yourself: all great geniuses in their several ways, and if they had not been so great, would have been less unfortunate.'
6 *Superior Genius*: in a note to the 1762 edition, Faulkner makes reference to the case of Swift's friend Francis Atterbury (1663–1732), bishop of Rochester, exiled in 1723 after the passage of an act of pains and penalties, for alleged involvement in Jacobite conspiracy.
7 *a reasonable Infusion of this Aldermanly Discretion*: see *An Enquiry into the Behaviour of the Queen's Last Ministry*: 'A small infusion of the alderman [is] necessary to those who are employed in publick affairs' (Davis, vol. VIII, p. 139).
8 *out of the common Forms*: see *An Enquiry into the Behaviour of the Queen's Last Ministry*: 'I take the infelicity of such extraordinary men to have been caused by their neglect of common forms' (ibid., pp. 138–9).
9 *are all in Confederacy against him*: Swift is quoting from *Thoughts on Various Subjects, Moral and Diverting* (1706): Davis, vol. I, p. 242.

in Nature we find, that Bodies full of Life and Spirit mount easily, and are hard to fall, whereas heavy Bodies are hard to rise,[10] and come down with greater Velocity, in Proportion to their weight.[11] But we find Fortune every Day Acting just the reverse of this.

This Talent of *Discretion*, as I have described it in it's several Adjuncts and Circumstances, is no where so serviceable as to the *Clergy*, to whose Preferment, nothing is so fatal as the Character of Wit, Politeness in Reading, or Manners, or that kind of Behaviour which we contract, by having too much Conversed with Persons of high Stations and Eminency, these Qualifications being reckoned by the *Vulgar* of *all Ranks* to be marks of *Levity*, which is the last Crime the World will pardon in *a Clergy-Man*. To this I may add a free manner of speaking in mixt Company, and too frequent an Appearance in places of much resort, which are equally Noxious to Spiritual Promotions.

I have known indeed a few Exceptions to some parts of these Regulations. I have seen some of the Dullest Men alive aiming at Witt, and others with as little Pretensions, affecting Politeness in Manners and Discourse, but never being able to persuade the World of their Guilt, they grew into considerable Stations, upon the firm Assurance which all People had of their *Discretion*, because they were a Size too low to deceive the World to their own Disadvantage. But this I confess is a Tryal too dangerous often to engage in.

There is a known Story of a *Clergy-Man*, who was recommended for a Preferment by some great Man at Court, to *A.B.C.T.*[12] His Grace said, he had heard that the *Clergy-Man* used to play at Whisk and Swobbers,[13] that as to playing now and then a Sober Game at Whisk for pastime, it

---

10 *heavy Bodies are hard to rise*: an idea found in classical writers – for example, Aristotle, *De caelo*, book iv.
11 *in Proportion to their weight*: Lucretius, *De rerum natura*, ii, 231, asserted that velocity was proportional to weight.
12 *A.B.C.T.*: A[rch]b[ishop] C[anterbury] T[enison] — Thomas Tenison (1636–1715), archbishop of Canterbury 1695–1715.
13 *Whisk and Swobbers*: played in both Britain and Ireland, these were early forms of what was later systematised as the game of whist. Swift records losses at 'whisk' when in London in 1709–13: Paul V. Thompson and Dorothy Jay Thompson (eds.), *The Account Books of Jonathan Swift*, London: Scolar Press, 1984, pp. 97, 116, 142. He concluded his poem 'To Charles Ford Esqr. On his Birth-day...' (31 Jan. 1722/3) with the lines, 'So — let us now for Whisk prepare; / Twelvepence a Corner, if you dare' (*Poems*, vol. I, p. 315).

might be pardoned, but he could not digest those wicked Swobbers,[14] and it was with some pains that my Lord S———rs[15] could undeceive him. I ask, by what Talents we may suppose that great Pr———[16] ascended so high, or what sort of Qualifications he would expect in those whom he took into his Patronage, or would probably recommend to Court for the government of *Distant Churches*.[17]

Two *Clergy-Men* in my Memory stood Candidates for a small *Free-School*[18] in ———*Shire*, where a Gentleman of Quality and Interest in the Country, who happened to have a better understanding than his Neighbours, procured the place for him who was the better Schollar, and more Gentlemanly Person of the two, very much to the Regret of all the Parish; The other being disappointed, came up to *London*, where he became the greatest Pattern of this lower *Discretion*, that I have known and possessed with as heavy Intellectuals, which together with the coldness of his Temper, and gravity of his Deportment, carried him safe through many Difficulties, and he lived and dyed in a great Station, while his Competitor is too obscure for Fame to tell us what became of him.[19]

---

14 *Swobbers*: four privileged cards used for betting. While Whisk by itself seems not to have attracted moralistic criticism, Swobbers (or Whisk and Swobbers) became synonymous with the dangers of gaming (see, for example, *Hesperi-Neso-Graphia: or, A Description of the Western Isle in Eight Cantos...*, London, 1716, p. 18), and was for that reason condemned by Archbishop Tenison, himself a noted supporter of the societies for the reformation of manners (*ODNB*), and an opponent of gaming (Leo Damrosch, *Jonathan Swift: His Life and His World*, New Haven & London: Yale University Press, 2013, p. 160). The author of *Hannibal Not at Our Gates...*, London, 1714, p. 40, noted that 'Plain simple Whisk, according to the A[rch]B[ishop] of C[anterbu]ry is tolerable, but Whisk and Swobbers is the vengeance.'
15 *Lord S[ome]rs:* John Somers (1651–1716), 1st Lord Somers, lord keeper 1693–7, lord chancellor 1697–1700, lord president of the council 1708–10.
16 *Pr———*: in the 1732 reprinting this is extended to 'Prelate', though as archbishop of Canterbury Tenison was also the primate of England.
17 *would probably recommend... Distant Churches*: Swift is presumably alluding to the Church of Ireland. Tenison was still archbishop of Canterbury at the time when Swift, disappointed in his ambition of a bishopric, was himself appointed to St Patrick's.
18 *Free-School*: a school charging no fees, intended for the children of the poor, and established through benefaction, often by an individual.
19 *to tell us what became of him*: Faulkner's editions identify the county as Yorkshire, which has led one commentator (Woolley, *Intelligencer*, pp. 82–3) to identify the disappointed clergyman as John Sharp (1645–1714), later archbishop of York, who as a young man had applied unsuccessfully for the incumbency of Wibsey chapel, near Bradford in his home county, a place in the gift of Richard Richardson of Byerley Hall, who instead appointed one Samuel Crowther. See A. Tindal Hart, *The Life and Times of John Sharp Archbishop of York*, London: SPCK, 1949, pp. 52–3.

This Species of *Discretion* which I so much celebrate, and do most heartily recommend, hath one Advantage not yet mentioned, that it will carry a Man safe through all the Malice and Variety of Parties, so far, that whatever Faction happen to be uppermost, his Claim is usually allowed for a share of what is going. And the thing seems to be highly reasonable. For in all great Changes, the prevailing side is usually so Tempestuous, that it wants the balast of those whom the World calls moderate Men and I call *Men of Discretion*, whom People in Power may with little Ceremony load as heavy as they please, drive them through the hardest and deepest Roads without danger of Foundring,[20] or breaking their Backs, and will be sure to find them neither Resty[21] nor Vicious.[22]

In some following Paper, I will give the Reader a short History of two *Clergy-Men* in *England*, the Characters of each, and the Progress of their Fortunes in the World.[23] By which the force of worldly Discretion and the bad Consequences from the want of that Virtue will strongly appear.

---

20 *Foundring*: becoming lame: founder was an inflammatory condition of the foot in horses. Swift complained to Pope in 1729 of 'grooms who foundered all my horses' (Woolley, *Corr.*, vol. III, p. 284).
21 *Resty*: a variant of 'restive', meaning, in an equine context, refractory, refusing to go forward (*OED*).
22 *Vicious*: of a horse, prone to bite or kick. Cf. Swift's 'Directions to the Coachman', in *Directions to Servants* (*CWJS*, vol. II, p. 498).
23 *and the Progress of their Fortunes in the World*: in *The Intelligencer*, no. 7.

THE INTELLIGENCER, NUMB. VII.

———Probitas laudatur & alget.[1]

---

1 *Probitas laudatur & alget[i]*: Juvenal, *Satires*, i, 74: 'Honesty is praised and left to shiver.'

Headnote

Published c. 22–5 June; copy text *1728* (see Textual Account).

A continuation of the discussion of the meanings of so-called 'discretion' in *The Intelligencer*, no. 5, this paper offers the parabolic cases of the self-serving Corusodes, and his inevitable advancement, with the failures of Eugenio, a talented but uncalculating student who becomes trapped in the life of genteel poverty of a provincial clergyman. Although the paper is meant to represent the sombre universal theme of the triumph of calculation and the insincere, Swift's story has more immediate relevance: the depiction of the snivelling and time-serving can be seen as Low Church characteristics. Equally, the talented and scholarly (but over-looked) clergyman would have had strong political resonance in the ecclesiastical preferment of Whig clergymen after 1714 and the corresponding reduced circumstances of High Churchmen like Swift and his friend Francis Atterbury.

THE INTELLIGENCER.

CORUSODES[2] an *Oxford* Student, and a Farmer's Son,[3] was never absent from Prayers, or Lecture, nor once out of his *College* after *Tom* had tolld.[4] He spent every Day ten hours in his Closet, in Reading his Courses, Dozing, clipping[5] Papers, or darning his Stockings, which last he performed to Admiration. He could be soberly Drunk at the expence of others, with *College* Ale,[6] and at those Seasons was always most Devout. He wore the same Gown five Years, without dagling[7] or tearing. He never once looked into a Play-book or a Poem. He read *Virgil* and *Ramus*[8] in the same Cadence, but with a very different Taste. He never understood a Jest, or had the least Conception of Wit.

For one saying he stands in Renown to this Day. Being with some other Students over a Pot of Ale; one of the Company said so many pleasant

---

2 *CORUSODES*: a sniveller; from the Greek *koryzodes* (suffering from catarrh): J. G. Gilbert, *Jonathan Swift: Romantic and Cynical Moralist*, Austin: University of Texas Press, 1966, p. 36. Woolley, *Intelligencer*, pp. 93–4, suggests that Swift's model for Corusodes may have been the Low Churchman White Kennett (1660–1728), bishop of Peterborough 1718–28 (for whom, see G. V. Bennett, *White Kennett*, London: SPCK, 1957, and *ODNB*), but the details of Corusodes's career do not correspond consistently with Kennett's, and a case might equally well be made for William Wake (1657–1737), archbishop of Canterbury 1715–37 (for whom, see Norman Sykes, *William Wake, Archbishop of Canterbury, 1657–1737*, 2 vols., Cambridge: Cambridge University Press, 1957, and *ODNB*). More likely, Corusodes is a composite character, since neither Kennett nor Wake is a perfect fit. Both Kennett and Wake had crossed swords with Swift's friend, the High Churchman Francis Atterbury (1663–1732), in the so-called 'Convocation controversy', 1697–1703, and, in narrating the respective biographies of Corusodes and Eugenio, Swift may have intended to contrast the worldly success of Whig Low Churchmen with the dismal fate of Atterbury, then in exile in France or indeed his own disappointments. For Atterbury, see *ODNB* and G. V. Bennett, *The Tory Crisis in Church and State, 1688–1730: The Career of Francis Atterbury, Bishop of Rochester*, Oxford: Clarendon Press, 1975.
3 *a Farmer's Son*: true of neither Kennett nor Wake.
4 *after Tom had tolld*: Great Tom, the largest bell of Christ Church, tolled the curfew for Oxford colleges at nine o'clock. Wake was an undergraduate at Christ Church, as was Hugh Boulter (1672–1742), archbishop of Armagh, 1724–42, another Low Churchman whom Swift detested; Kennett was not.
5 *clipping*: used in the sense of reducing; thus sorting or editing papers.
6 *College Ale*: Swift returned to this image in 'To Doctor D–l—y, on the libels writ against him' (1730), where he wrote, 'So Academick dull Ale-drinkers / Pronounce all Men of Wit, Free-thinkers' (*Poems*, p. 503).
7 *dagling*: to daggle is to soil a garment by dragging it through mud (*OED*).
8 *Ramus*: Pierre de la Ramée or Peter Ramus (1515–72), French humanist and philosopher; depicted by Aristotle during the 'Voyage to Laputa' as a great dunce: *Gulliver's Travels*, part III, ch. viii (*CWJS*, vol. XVI, p. 295).

things, that the rest were much diverted, only *Corusodes* was silent and unmoved. When they parted, he called this merry Companion aside, and said; Sir, *I perceived by your often speaking, and our Friends laughing, that you spoke many jests, and you could not but observe my Silence. But Sir this is my humour, I never make a jest myself, nor ever laugh at another Man's.*

Corusodes thus endowed, and got into Holy Orders, having by the most extreme Parsimoney, saved thirty four Pounds out of a very Beggarly Fellowship[9] went up to *London*, where his Sister was Waiting-woman to a Lady, and so good a Sollicitor, that by her means he was admitted to Read Prayers in the Family twice a Day, at fourteen shillings a Month. He had now acquired a low Obsequious awkward Bow, and a talent of gross flattery both in and out of season; he would shake the Butler by the Hand; He taught the Page his *Catechism*, and was sometimes admitted to Dine at the Stewards Table. In short he got the good Word of the whole Family, and was Recommended by my Lady for Chaplain to some other Noble House,[10] by which his Revenue (beside Vales)[11] amounted to about 30 *l.* a Year. His Sister procured him a Scarf[12] from my Lord (who had a small design of Gallantry upon her) And by his Lordships Sollicitation he got a Lectureship in Town[13] of 60 *l.* a Year; where he Preached constantly in Person, in a grave manner, with an Audible Voice, a Style Ecclesiastick, and the matter (such as it was) well suited to the intellectuals of his Hearers. Some time after, a Country Living fell in my Lord's Disposal, and his Lordship who had now some encouragement given him of Success in his Amour, bestowed the Living on *Corusodes*, who still kept his Lectureship and Residence in Town,[14] where he was a constant Attendant at all

---

9 *a very Beggarly Fellowship*: Wake had been a student (i.e. lecturer) at Christ Church while taking his BA and MA.
10 *Chaplain to some other Noble House*: Wake had served between 1682 and 1685 as chaplain to Richard Graham, 1st Viscount Preston (1648–95).
11 *Vales*: vails, gratuities given to servants.
12 *a Scarf*: vestment worn by a household chaplain; thus a chaplain's position.
13 *a Lectureship in Town*: a position short of a legal benefice, and requiring only preaching duties. Wake was appointed as lecturer at St Anne's, Soho, in 1686, probably through Viscount Preston's influence: *Survey of London*, 47 vols., London: Athlone Press, 1900–2012, vol. XXXIII, p. 260. Holding a London lectureship was one way for an ambitious young clergyman to get himself noticed: the future Bishop Atterbury, for example, while still an Oxford don, had been appointed to the lectureship of St Bride's, Fleet Street, in 1691. Kennett had been a lecturer at St Martin's in Oxford 1691-4.
14 *bestowed the Living... Residence in Town*: here the biography of Corusodes departs from that of Wake, whose first benefice was the rectory of St James's, Westminster, in 1695.

Meetings relating to Charity, without ever contributing further than his frequent Pious Exhortations. If any Woman of better fashion in the Parish happened to be absent from Church, they were sure of a Visit from him in a Day or two, to Chide and to Dine with them.

He had a select number of Poor constantly attending at the Street Door of his Lodgings, for whom he was a common Sollicitor to his former Patroness, dropping in his own Half Crown among the Collections and taking it out when he disposed the money. At a Person of Qualities House, he would never sit down till he was thrice bid, and then upon the corner of the most distant chair. His whole demeanor was formal and Starched which adhered so close, that he could never shake it off in his highest Promotion.

His Lord was now in high Employment at Court, and attended by him with the most abject Assiduity, and his Sister being gone off with Child to a private Lodging, my Lord continued his Graces to *Corusodes*, got him to be a Chaplain in ordinary,[15] and in due time a Parish in Town, and a *Dignity in the Church*.[16]

He paid his *Curates* punctually, at the lowest Sallery, and partly out of the communion money,[17] but gave them good advice in abundance. He Marryed a Citizens Widow,[18] who taught him to put out small sums at *ten*

Kennett, on the other hand, had been preferred in 1685 to the vicarage of Ambrosden in Oxfordshire by his patron Sir William Glynne, 2nd Bt (1663–1721), and after a spell back in Oxford as vice-principal of St Edmund Hall, and as a lecturer at the church of St Martin, Carfax, was given the rectory of Shottesbrooke, Berkshire, by another patron, the nonjuror Francis Cherry (1667–1713), holding the two livings simultaneously.

15 *a Chaplain in ordinary*: the monarch had forty-eight chaplains in ordinary, each required to preach once a year. Both Wake and Boulter were royal chaplains (to William III and George I respectively); Kennett was not.

16 *a Parish in Town, and a Dignity in the Church*: Wake became curate of St James's, then dean of Exeter in 1701, bishop of Lincoln in 1705, and archbishop of Canterbury in 1715; Kennett became curate of St Botolph, Aldgate in 1700, then rector of St Mary Aldermary and St Thomas the Apostle, also in London, dean of Peterborough in 1708, and finally bishop of Peterborough in 1718. Hugh Boulter's career followed a similar trajectory: rector of St Olave, Southwark, archdeacon of Surrey, and in 1719 bishop of Bristol, before his translation to Armagh.

17 *the communion money*: money collected from parishioners at Holy Communion, intended to be given for alms.

18 *He married a Citizens Widow*: strictly true of Boulter, whose father-in-law was a London merchant. Kennett's second wife was the daughter of a London physician, while Wake married into a family of Norfolk gentry.

per cent,[19] and brought him acquainted with Jobbers in *Change-Alley*.[20] By her dexterity he sold the Clarkship of his Parish, when it became vacant. He kept a miserable house, but the Blame was layed wholly upon *Madam*; For the good Doctor[21] was always at his *Books*, or visiting the Sick, or doing other Offices of Charity and piety in his Parish. He treated all his inferiors of the Clergy with a most sanctifyed pride; was rigorously and universally, censorious upon all his brethren of the Gown, on their first appearance in the world, or while they continued meanly preferred; But gave large allowance to the Layity of high rank, or great riches, using neither Eyes nor Ears for their faults. He was never sensible of the least corruption in *Courts*, *Parliaments*, or *Ministries*, but made the most favourable constructions of all publick proceedings; and Power, in whatever Hands, or whatever Party, was always secure of his most charitable opinion. He had many wholsome maxims ready to excuse all miscarriages of State. *Men are but Men.*[22] *Erunt vitia donec homines*;[23] and *quod Supra nos nihil ad nos*.[24] with several others of equal weight.

It would lengthen my paper beyond measure to trace out the whole System of his conduct; His dreadfull apprehensions of Popery; his great moderation towards Dissenters of all Denominations; with hearty wishes that by yielding somewhat on both sides, there might be a general Union among Protestants; his short inoffensive Sermons in his turns at Court,[25] and the matter exactly suited to the present juncture of prevailing Opinions. The arts he used to obtain a Mitre, by writing against Episcopacy,[26] and

---

19 *cent*: an extortionate rate: 6 per cent was the highest legal rate of interest in England before 1714 (Homer and Sylla, *History of Interest Rates*, p. 165).
20 *Jobbers in Change-Alley*: Exchange or 'Change Alley, near the Royal Exchange in the City of London, connected Lombard Street with Cornhill and Birchin Lane. The coffee-houses there, especially Jonathan's and Garraway's, were a frequent resort of stock-jobbers (those who traded in stock on their own account).
21 *the good Doctor*: Wake, Kennett and Boulter all held the degree of Doctor of Divinity.
22 *Men are but Men*: 'The best of men are but men at best' (*ODEP*, p. 48).
23 *Erunt vitia donec homines*: 'Vitia erunt, donec homines' (Tacitus, *Histories*, iv, 74): 'There will be vices so long as there are men.'
24 *Quod Supra nos nihil ad nos*: a Latin proverb whose origin is attributed to Socrates (e.g. in Minucius Felix, *Octavius*, xiii, 1): 'That which is above us does not concern us.'
25 *his short inoffensive Sermons in his turns at Court*: as a chaplain in ordinary: see above, n. 15.
26 *writing against Episcopacy*: in writings on the constitutional position of Convocation, in response to Atterbury, both Wake and Kennett had emphasised the authority of the king over the church and its bishops. In addition, in 1712 Kennett had defended lay baptism against the insistence of High Churchmen that baptism could only be undertaken by a minister who had been episcopally ordained (Bennett, *Kennett*, 122).

the proofs he gave of his loyalty by palliating or defending the murder of a martyred Prince.[27]

Endowed with all these accomplishments we leave him in the full Carrier of Success, mounting fast towards the top of the Ladder Ecclesiastical, which he hath a fair probability to reach, without the merit of one single Virtue, moderately stocked with the least valuable parts of Erudition, utterly devoyd of all *Taste, Judgment* or *Genius*; and in his grandeur naturally chusing to hawl up others after him, whose accomplishments most resemble his own, except his beloved Sons, Nephews, or other kindred be not in competition, or lastly except his inclinations be diverted by those who have power to mortify or further advance him.

Eugenio[28] set out from the same University, and about the same time with *Corusodes*;[29] He had the reputation of an arch Lad at School, and was unfortunately possessed with a *Talent* for *Poetry*,[30] on which account he received many chiding Letters from his Father,[31] and grave advice from his Tutor. He did not neglect his College Learning, but his chief Study was the Authors of Antiquity, with a perfect knowledge in the *Greek* and *Roman Tongues*; He could never Procure himself to be chosen Fellow;[32] for it was

---

27 *the murder of a martyred Prince*: Kennett had preached a controversial sermon on 31 January 1704, the anniversary of the execution of Charles I, which blamed Queen Henrietta Maria and the 'French interest and alliance', for bringing about the Civil War (*A Compassionate Enquiry into the Causes of the Civil War. In a Sermon Preached in the Church of St. Botolph Aldgate, on January XXXI, 1703/4...*, London, 1704, pp. 6–10). The *Compleat History of England* (1706) – published anonymously but known to be Kennett's work – was also seen by Tories as purveying a derogatory view of Charles I and his queen (Bennett, *Kennett*, p. 91). Wake's published sermons on the commemoration of the death of the royal martyr, while careful to condemn the regicide, also drew attention to the abuses committed under Charles I's 'personal rule' (1629–40), when 'the prerogative had been strained to an exorbitant height, and the subject too much provoked to complain, if not of the King himself, then of those about him', including his queen (*A Sermon Preach'd before the House of Lords, at the Abbey-Church in Westminster, on Friday, Jan. XXX. MDCCVII...*, London, 1708, pp. 13–14; *A Sermon Preached before the King in St. James's Chapel, upon the Thirtieth of January, 1715...*, London, 1715, pp. 12–15, 19, 26).
28 *Eugenio*: from the classical Greek *eygeyes*, meaning well-born, noble-minded or generous.
29 *set out... Corusodes*: Francis Atterbury attended Christ Church, Oxford, and took his degree in 1687 (Wake took his in 1679, Kennett his in 1685).
30 *a Talent for Poetry*: when Princess Anne visited Oxford in 1688, Atterbury composed the Latin and Greek verses recited in her honour.
31 *many chiding Letters from his Father*: for an example of the correspondence between Atterbury and his father, see *The Epistolary Correspondence... of the Right Reverend Francis Atterbury, D.D. Lord Bishop of Rochester...* 3 vols., London, 1783–4, vol. I, pp. 9–13.
32 *could never Procure himself to be chosen Fellow*: Atterbury did become a student (fellow) of Christ Church.

objected against him that he had written Verses, and particularly some
wherein he glanced at a certain Reverend Doctor, famous for Dullness:[33]
That he had been seen bowing to Ladies, as he met them in the Streets;
And it was proved that once he had been found dancing in a private family
with half a dozen of both Sexes.

He was the younger Son to a Gentleman of a good birth, but small
fortune,[34] and his Father Dying[35] he was driven to *London*, to seek his
fortune: he got into Orders, and became Reader in a Parish Church[36] at
twenty Pounds a Year; was carryed by an *Oxford* friend to *Wills Coffee-
house*,[37] frequented in those Days by the Men of Wit; where in some time
he had the bad luck to be distinguished. His Scanty Sallery compelled
him to run deep in debt for a new Gown and Cassock, and now and then
forced him to Write some Paper of Wit or humour, or Preach a Sermon
for Ten shillings, to supply his Necessities. He was a thousand times
recommended by his Poetical Friends to great Persons, as a young man
of excellent parts, who deserved encouragement and received a thousand
Promises; But his modesty, and a generous spirit which disdained the
Slavery of continual application, and attendance, always disappointed him,
making room for Vigilant Dunces, who were sure to be never out of
sight.

---

33 *a certain Reverend Doctor, famous for Dullness*: Swift may well have had in mind Richard
Bentley (1662–1742), the classical scholar and keeper of the royal libraries (and himself a
chaplain-in-ordinary to William III), whose *Dissertation on the Epistles of Phalaris* (1697)
had, with profound and heavy learning, demolished the arguments for authorship of this
text advanced by Sir William Temple and Charles Boyle (later 4th Earl of Orrery), but in
turn had been attacked as ill-mannered by Francis Atterbury and a circle of Oxford wits,
intervening on Boyle's behalf, in *Dr. Bentley's Dissertations on the Epistles of Phalaris . . .
Examin'd* (1698). The episode had formed the subject of Swift's *Battle of the Books* (1704).
34 *the younger Son . . . but small fortune*: Atterbury was the younger son of Lewis Atterbury, a
country parson of modest means, who was himself the grandson of a Northamptonshire
country gentleman (*ODNB*).
35 *his Father Dying*: Lewis Atterbury died in 1693.
36 *Reader in a Parish Church*: Francis Atterbury was elected to a lectureship at St Bride's, Fleet
Street, in 1691.
37 *Wills Coffee-house*: at the corner of Russell Street and Bow Street, Covent Garden: a resort
of 'wits' since the reign of Charles II; although in decline by the latter years of Queen
Anne's reign, it was still capable of attracting the custom of men of letters such as Addison
(Bryant Lillywhite, *London Coffeehouses*, London: George Allen & Unwin, 1963,
pp. 655–8; Markman Ellis, *The Coffee-house: A Cultural History*, London: Weidenfeld &
Nicolson, 2004, pp. 150–5; Brian Cowan, *The Social Life of Coffee: The Emergence of the
British Coffeehouse*, New Haven & London: Yale University Press, 2005; Peter Smithers,
The Life of Joseph Addison, Oxford: Clarendon Press, 1968, pp. 92, 242–3).

He had an excellent faculty in preaching,[38] if he were not sometimes a little too refined, and apt to trust too much to his own way of thinking, and reasoning.

When upon the vacancy of Preferment he was hardly drawn to attend upon some promising Lord he received the usual Answer, that he came too late for it had been given to another the very day before. And he had onely this comfort left, that every body said, it was a thousand pities some thing could not be done for Poor Mr. *Eugenio*.

The Remainder of his Story will be dispatched in a few Words.[39] Wearied with weak hopes, and weaker pursuits he accepted a Curacy in *Darby-Shire*,[40] of thirty Pounds a Year, and when he was five and forty, had the great felicity to be preferred by a friend of his Father to a Vicaridge worth annually 60 pound, in the most desert parts of *Lincoln-shire*, where his spirit quite sunk with those reflections, that solitude and disappointments bring, he married a Farmers widow, and is still alive, utterly undistinguished and forgotten, onely some of the Neighbours have accidentally heard *that he had been a notable man in his Youth*.[41]

---

38 *an excellent faculty in preaching*: for Atterbury's talents as a preacher, see Bennett, *Tory Crisis*, p. 36.
39 *The Remainder of his Story . . . a few Words*: henceforth the narrative of Eugenio's life departs radically from Atterbury's.
40 *a Curacy in Darby-shire*: in his Introduction to *A Treatise on Polite Conversation* (1738), Swift, in the persona of 'Simon Wagstaff', explained that, by his characterisation of the provincial squire Sir John Linger, 'I intended not the least Reflection upon Derby-shire, the Place of my Nativity. But, my Intention was only to shew the Misfortune of those Persons, who have the Disadvantage to be bred out of the Circle of Politeness, whereof I take the present Limits, to extend no further than London, and ten Miles round' (*CWJS*, vol. II, p. 290).
41 *in the most desert parts of Lincoln-shire . . . a notable man in his Youth*: possibly a reference to the High Church clergyman and minor poet Samuel Wesley (1662–1735), rector of Epworth in Lincolnshire (*ODNB*). In March and April 1730, Oxford, Pope and Bolingbroke had recommended Wesley's commentary on Job to Swift as the work of a 'poor' man and 'an old Tory' (Oxford to Swift, 4 Mar. 1729/30, Pope and Bolingbroke to Swift, [*c*. 9 Apr. 1730] (Woolley, *Corr.*, vol. III, pp. 289–90, 300), but Swift held Wesley's poetical efforts in contempt (Ehrenpreis, vol. I, p. 194) and had made this plain in *The Battle of the Books*, in which 'Homer slew Wesley with a kick of his Horse's heel' (*CWJS*, vol. I, p. 157); he therefore replied to Oxford, 'The author's name is utterly unknown here except some who read verses and have chanced to read somewhere he is distinguished as an unfortunate meddler in poetry' (28 Apr. 1730; Woolley, *Corr.*, vol. III, p. 305).

THE INTELLIGENCER, NUMB. IX.

Headnote

Published *c*. 6–9 July; copy text *1728* (see Textual Account).

This examination of modern ideas of education, and the false sense of refinement and effete foreign manners inculcated into the sons of gentlemen, also reflects, in passing, on the qualities of some of the statesmen who have passed over the public stage since 1660. It is possible that this essay was composed at the same time as the fragmentary 'Hints of the Education of Ladies', a work sometimes dated earlier (see *CWJS*, vol. II, pp. 212–17). Both works are concerned with the ways in which the superficial and artificial have led to the denigration of intellectual attainment in children's education amongst the children of the gentry and nobility, with damaging consequences. Both also show the influence of Locke's *Some Thoughts Concerning Education* (1693), the most influential modern work on education, in terms of challenging the ramshackle methods of learning described by Swift.

The essay was later given the title 'An Essay on Modern Education', when reprinted in the Pope/Swift *Miscellanies* of 1732.

THE INTELLIGENCER.

From frequently reflecting upon the Course and Method of Educating Youth in this and a Neighbouring Kingdom,[1] with the general Success and consequence thereof; I am come to this Determination, That Education is always the worse in Proportion to the Wealth and Grandeur of the Parents. Nor do I doubt in the least, that if the whole World were now under the Dominion of one Monarch (provided I might be allowed to chuse where he should fix the Seat of his Empire) the only Son and Heir of that Monarch, would be the worst Educated Mortal, that ever was born since the Creation: And, I doubt the same Proportion will hold through all Degrees and Titles, from an Emperor downwards, to the common Gentry. I do not say that this hath been always the case: for in better times it was directly otherwise; and a Scholar may fill half his *Greek* and *Roman* Shelves with Authors of the Noblest Birth, as well as highest Virtue. Nor, do I tax all Nations at present with this defect, for I know there are some to be excepted, and particularly *Scotland*, under all the Disadvantages of it's Clymate and Soyle, if that happiness be not rather owing even to those very dis-advantages. What is then to be done, if this Reflection must fix on two Countries,[2] which will be most ready to take Offence, and which of all others it will be least prudent or safe to offend?

But there is one Circumstance yet more Dangerous and Lamentable. For if, according to the Postulatum[3] already laid down, the higher Quality any Youth is of, he is in greater likelyhood to be worse Educated, it behooves me to dread, and keep far from the Verge of *Scandalum Magnatum*.[4]

Retracting therefore that hazardous Postulatum, I shall venture no further at present than to say, that perhaps some Additional Care in Educating the Sons of Nobility, and principal Gentry, might not be ill employed.[5] If this be not delivered with softness enough, I must for the future be Silent.

---

1 *a Neighbouring Kingdom*: England is meant, though technically, since the Anglo-Scottish Union, the 'neighbouring kingdom' was Great Britain.
2 *two Countries*: England and Ireland.
3 *Postulatum*: a statement which can be taken as true.
4 *Scandalum Magnatum*: 'scandal of magnates': in law, the utterance or publication of a malicious report against any person holding a position of dignity.
5 *employed*: in *Gulliver's Travels*, part IV, ch. vi, Swift embarked on a prolonged denunciation of the English aristocracy, following his observation that Gulliver's 'plain, honest Parents' had been 'just able to give me a tolerable Education' (at Emmanuel College, Cambridge). By contrast, 'our young *Noblemen* are bred from their Childhood in Idleness and Luxury' (*CWJS*, vol. XVI, pp. 385–6).

In the mean time, let me ask only two Questions, which relate to a Neighbouring Kingdom, from whence the Chief among us are descended,[6] and whose manners we most affect to follow. I ask first, how it comes about, that for above 60 Years past, the Chief Conduct of Affairs in that Kingdom hath been generally placed in the Hands of *New-men*, with very few Exceptions. The Noblest Blood of *England* having been shed in the grand Rebellion, many great Families became extinct,[7] or supported only by Minors: when the King was Restored, very few of those Lords remained, who began, or at least had improved their Education, under the happy Reign of King *James*, or King *Charles* I, of which Lords the two principal were the Marquiss of *Ormonde*,[8] and the Earl of *Southampton*.[9] The Minors had, during the Rebellion and Usurpation, either received too much Tincture of bad Principles from those Fanatick Times, or coming to Age at the Restoration, fell into the Vices of that dissolute Reign.

I Date from this Æra, the Corrupt Method of Education among us, and the consequence thereof, in the Necessity the Crown lay under of Introducing *New-men* into the chief Conduct of publick Affairs, or to the Office of what we now call Prime Ministers, Men of Art, Knowledge, Application and Insinuation, meerly for want of a supply among the Nobility. They were generally (though not always) of good Birth, sometimes Younger Brothers, at other times, such who although inheriting good Estates, yet happened to be well Educated, and provided with Learning; such under that King, were *Hyde*,[10] *Bridgman*,[11] *Clifford*,[12] *Coventry*,[13] *Osborn*,[14]

---

6 *a Neighbouring Kingdom... descended*: England.
7 *extinct*: in fact, most members of the English House of Lords in 1640 survived until 1660, and of the titles that became extinct in that period, the vast majority were of recent creation.
8 *Marquiss of Ormonde*: James Butler (1610–88), 12th Earl, 1st Marquess and 1st Duke of Ormond, Charles I's lord lieutenant of Ireland from 1644.
9 *Earl of Southampton*: Thomas Wriothesley (1608–67), a leading Royalist during the First Civil War.
10 *Hyde*: either Edward Hyde (1609–74), 1st Earl of Clarendon, lord chancellor 1658–67; or one of his sons, Henry (1638–1709), 2nd Earl, lord chamberlain 1665–8, treasurer- and receiver-general 1680–6, and Laurence (1642–1711), later 1st Earl of Rochester, first lord of the treasury 1679–84.
11 *Bridgman*: Sir Orlando Bridgeman, 1st Bt (1606–74), lord keeper 1667–72.
12 *Clifford*: Thomas Clifford (1630–73), 1st Baron Clifford, lord treasurer 1672–3.
13 *Coventry*: either Hon. Henry Coventry (1618–86), secretary of state 1672–80, or his brother, Hon. William (1627–86), lord of the treasury 1667–9.
14 *Osborn*: Sir Thomas Osborne, 2nd Bt (1632–1712), 1st Earl of Danby and later Duke of Leeds, lord treasurer 1673–9.

Godolphin,[15] *Ashley-Cooper*,[16] Few or none under the short Reign of King *James* II. Under King *William*; *Summers*,[17] *Montague*,[18] *Churchil*,[19] *Vernon*,[20] *Harry Boyle*,[21] and many others: Under the Queen;[22] *Harley*,[23] *St. John*,[24] *Harcourt*,[25] *Trevers*,[26] who indeed were Persons of the best private Families, but unadorn'd with Titles.[27] So in the last Reign,[28] Mr. *Robert Walpole*, was understood for many Years, to be Prime Minister,[29] in which Post he still happily continues; His Brother *Horace* is Ambassador Extraordinary to *France*.[30] Mr. *Addison*,[31] and

15 *Godolphin*: Sidney Godolphin (1645–1712), 1st Baron Godolphin and later 1st Earl, lord of the treasury 1679–84.
16 *Ashley-Cooper*: Sir Anthony Ashley Cooper, 2nd Bt (1612–83), 1st Earl of Shaftesbury, chancellor of the exchequer 1661–72, lord chancellor 1672–4, lord president 1679.
17 *Summers:* John Somers (1651–1716), 1st Lord Somers, lord keeper 1693–7, lord chancellor 1697–1700, lord president of the council, 1708–10.
18 *Montague*: Charles Montagu (1661–1715), 1st Earl of Halifax, chancellor of the exchequer 1694–9.
19 *Churchil*: John Churchill (1650–1722), 1st Earl and 1st Duke of Marlborough, captain-general 1702–11, 1715–22.
20 *Vernon*: James Vernon (1646–1727), secretary of state 1697–1702.
21 *Harry Boyle*: Hon. Henry Boyle (1669–1725), later 1st Baron Carleton, chancellor of the exchequer 1701–8, secretary of state 1708–10.
22 *the Queen*: Queen Anne.
23 *Harley*: Robert Harley (1661–1724), 1st Earl of Oxford, secretary of state 1704–8, chancellor of the exchequer 1710–11, lord treasurer 1711–14.
24 *St. John*: Henry St John (1678–1752), 1st Viscount Bolingbroke, secretary at war 1704–8, secretary of state 1710–14.
25 *Harcourt*: Simon Harcourt (1661–1727), 1st Baron and later 1st Viscount Harcourt, solicitor-general 1702–7, attorney-general 1707–8, 1710, lord keeper 1710–13, lord chancellor 1713–14.
26 *Trevers*: Sir Thomas Trevor (1658–1730), solicitor-general 1692–5, attorney-general 1695–1701, lord chief justice of common pleas 1701–14.
27 *but unadorn'd with Titles*: while this applied to the Tories listed as having served under Queen Anne, it did not apply to all the ministers named as having served King William: Montagu and Boyle both came from families with existing peerage titles.
28 *in the last Reign*: that of King George I.
29 *Mr. Robert Walpole . . . Prime Minister*: (Sir) Robert Walpole (1676–1745), later 1st earl of Orford, secretary at war 1708–10, first lord of the treasury and chancellor of the exchequer 1715–17, 1721–42.
30 *His Brother Horace . . . Ambassador Extraordinary to France*: Horatio ('old Horace') Walpole (1678–1757), Sir Robert's younger brother, was ambassador extraordinary to Paris 1727–30. He was later ambassador to The Hague, 1734–7 and was ennobled in 1756 as 1st Baron Walpole.
31 *Mr. Addison*: Joseph Addison (1672–1719), the essayist, had been lord of trade 1715–17 and secretary of state 1717–18. His background was one of genteel poverty as the son of the dean of Lichfield.

Mr. *Craiggs*,[32] without the least Allyance to support them, have been Secretaries of State.

If the Facts have been thus for above 60 years past (whereof I could with a little further Recollection produce many more Instances) I would ask again, how it hath happened, that in a Nation plentifully abounding with Nobility, so great share in the most important parts of publick management, hath been for so long a Period chiefly entrusted to Commonners; unless some Omissions, or Defects of the highest Import, may be charged upon those to whom the care of Educating our Noble Youth hath been committed.[33] For, if there be any difference between human Creatures in the point of natural Parts, as we usually call them, it should seem, that the Advantage lyes on the side of Children born from Noble and Wealthy Parents; the same Traditional Sloth and Luxury which render their Body Weak and Effeminate, perhaps refining and giving a freer motion to the Spirits, beyond what can be expected from the gross robust Issue of meaner Mortals. Add to this, the peculiar Advantages, which all young Noblemen possess, by the Priviledges of their Birth; Such as a free access to Courts, and a universal Deference pay'd to their Persons.

But as my Lord *Bacon* chargeth it for a fault on Princes, that they are impatient to compass Ends without giving themselves the trouble of consulting or executing the means.[34] So perhaps it may be the disposition of young Nobles, either from the Indulgence of Parents, Tutors and Governors, or their own Inactivity, that they expect the accomplishments of a good Education without the least expence of Time or Study, to acquire them.

What I said last, I am ready to retract; For the case is infinitely worse; and the very Maxims set up to direct modern Education, are enough to destroy all the Seeds of Knowledge, Honour, Wisdom, and Virtue among

---

32 *Mr. Craiggs*: James Craggs (1657–1727), secretary at war 1717–18 and secretary of state 1718–21, was the son of the postmaster-general James Craggs and thus benefited from his father's wealth and influence. Swift may be confusing the generations, however, for Craggs *père* was a self-made man of 'mean extraction' (*HP 1690–1715*, vol. III, p. 776).

33 *the care of Educating our Noble Youth hath been committed*: Swift deprecated the education of the children of the nobility in *A Proposal for Correcting, Improving and Ascertaining the English Tongue* (*CWJS*, vol. II, p. 138).

34 *as my Lord Bacon chargeth it... executing the means*: in 'Of Empire' in his *Essays or Counsells, Civill and Morall* (1625), Bacon had written 'For it is the solecism of power, to think to command the end, and yet not to endure the mean.' Swift owned several editions of Bacon's works (*Library and Reading, I*, vol. I, pp. 125–9).

us. The current Opinion prevails that the study of *Greek* and *Latin* is loss of Time; that publick Schools by mingling the Sons of Noblemen, with those of the Vulgar, engage the former in bad Company;[35] That whipping breaks the Spirits of Lads well Born; That Universities make young Men Pedants. That, to Dance, Fence, speak *French*, and know how to behave your self among great Persons of both Sexes, comprehends *the whole duty of a Gentleman*.[36]

I cannot but think this wise System of Education, hath been much cultivated among us by those Worthies of the Army, who during the last War[37] returning from *Flanders* at the close of each Campaign, became the Dictators of Behaviour, Dress and Politeness to all those Youngsters, who frequent Chocolate-Coffee-Gaming-Houses, Drawing-Rooms, Opera's, Levees, and Assemblies;[38] where a Colonel by his Pay, Perquisites, and Plunder, was qualifyed to outshine many Peers of the Realm; and by the influence of an *exotick* Habit and Demeanor, added to other foreign Accomplishments, gave the Law to the whole Town, and were copied as the Standard-Patterns of whatever was refined in Dress, Equipage, Conversation, or Diversions.

I remember in those Times, an Admired Original of that Vocation, sitting in a Coffee-house near two Gentlemen, whereof one was of the Clergy, who were engaged in some discourse that savoured of Learning; This Officer thought fit to interpose, and professing to deliver the Sentiments of his Fraternity as well as his own (and probably did so of too many among them) turning to the Clergyman, spoke in the following manner. *D—n me, Doctor, say what you will, the Army is the only School for Gentlemen. Do you think my Lord* Marlborough *beat the* French, *with* Greek *and* Latin. *D—n me, a Scholar when he comes into good Company; what is he but an Ass? D—n me, I would be glad by G—d to see any of your Schollars*

---

35 Locke had warned of the deleterious effects of exposing children to the company of the vulgar, whether servants or schoolfellows, in *Some Thoughts on Education* (1693), §§ 68–70, ed. John W. Yolton and Jean S. Yolton (Oxford: Clarendon Press, 1989), pp. 126–8.
36 *the whole duty of a Gentleman*: an allusion to the popular devotional work *The Whole Duty of Man* (probably composed by Richard Allestree and originally published in 1658). In his posthumously published essay *On Good-Manners and Good-Breeding*, Swift had more harsh words for 'pedantry' in education, at the expense of 'good sense' (*CWJS*, vol. II, pp. 185–8). He also included 'dancing, fighting . . . and speaking French' among the characteristics of 'good breeding' (ibid., p. 190).
37 *the last War*: the War of the Spanish Succession (1702–13).
38 *Assemblies*: elegant social gatherings.

with his Nouns, and his Verbs, and his Philosophy, and Trigonometry, what a figure he would make at a Siege or Blockado or recountring — *D*—*n me* &c.[39] After which he proceeded with a Volley of Military Terms, less significant, sounding worse, and harder to be understood than any that were ever Coyned by the Commentators upon *Aristotle*. I would not here be thought to charge the Soldiery with Ignorance and contempt of Learning, without allowing Exceptions, of which I have known many, and some even in this Kingdom,[40] but however, the worse example, especially in a great Majority will certainly prevail.

I have heard that the late Earl of *Oxford* in the time of his Ministry,[41] never past by *White*'s *Chocolate-house*[42] (the common Rendezvous of infamous Sharpers,[43] and noble Cullies)[44] without bestowing a Curse upon that famous Accademy, as the Bane of half the *English* Nobility. I have been likewise told another passage concerning that great Minister; which because it gives a humorous Idea of one principal Ingredient in modern Education, take as followeth. *Le-Sac* the Famous *French* Dancing-master[45] in great Admiration asked a friend, whether it were true that Mr. *Harley*

---

39 *D*—*n me, Doctor . . . D*—*n me &c*: Swift's poem 'The Grand Question debated . . .' (1729), ll. 153–64, puts similar sentiments into the mouth of an army officer.
40 *in this Kingdom*: Swift's correspondent Charles Wogan (*c*. 1685–1754) was an obvious exception. A Jacobite soldier and diplomat, operating in Spain, Wogan sent Swift in 1732 various literary works, which sufficiently impressed the dean for him to reply that he and his friends had assumed the writer to be 'a Scholar, a Man of Genius, and of Honour. We guessed him to have been born in this Country from some Passages, but not from the Style, which we wondered to find so correct in an Exile, a Soldier, and a Native of Ireland.' Swift had little expected to receive 'a History, a Dedication, a poetical Translation of the Penitential Psalms, Latin Poems, and the like, and all from a Soldier. In these Kingdoms you would be a most unfashionable military Man, among Troops where the least Pretension to Learning or Piety, or common Morals, would endanger the Owner to be cashiered.' Those 'Gentlemen of Ireland' distinguishing themselves in Europe 'ought to make the English ashamed of the Reproaches they cast on the Ignorance, the Dulness, and the Want of Courage in the Irish natives' (Swift to Wogan, [July –] 2 Aug. 1732 (Woolley, *Corr.*, vol. III, pp. 514–15)).
41 *in the time of his Ministry*: between September 1710 and July 1714.
42 *White's Chocolate-house*: on St James's Street: notorious for the gaming that took place there. See *The History of White's*, London, 1892.
43 *Sharpers*: those who make their living by cheating others, usually at cards.
44 *Cullies*: dupes.
45 *Le-Sac the famous French Dancing-master*: a 'L'Sac' was active as a theatrical dancer in London in the early 1700s, though it is possible Swift may have mistaken this name for that of the well-known dancing master Edward Isaac (fl. 1675–1717) (*ODNB*).

was made an Earl, and Lord Treasurer: And finding it confirmed, said; *Well, I wonder what the Devil the Queen could see in him; for I attended him two Years, and he was the greatest Dunce that ever I taught.*[46]

Another hindrance to good Education, and I think, the greatest of any, is that pernicious custom in Rich and Noble Families, of entertaining *French* Tutors in their Houses. These wretched *Pædagogues*[47] are enjoyned by the Father, to take special care, that the Boy shall be perfect in his *French*; By the Mother, that *Master* must not walk till he is hot, nor be suffered to play with other Boys, nor be wet in his Feet, nor daub his Cloaths, and to see that the Dancing-master attends constantly, and does his Duty: she further insists that the Child be not kept too long poring on his Book, because he is subject to sore Eyes,[48] and of a weakly Constitution.

By these methods the young Gentleman is in every Article as fully accomplished at 8 Years old as at eight and twenty (Age adding only to the growth of his Person and his Vice) so that if you should look at him in his Boyhood through the magnifying end of a Perspective,[49] and in his Manhood through the other, it would be impossible to spy any difference: The same Airs, the same Strutt, the same Cock of his Hat, and posture of his Sword (as far as the change of fashions will allow) the same understanding, the same compass of knowlidge, with the very same Absurdity, Impudence, and Impertinence of Tongue.

He is taught from the Nursary that he must inherit a great Estate, and hath no need to mind his Book, which is a Lesson he never forgets to the end of his life. His chief Solace is to steal down and play at Span-farthing[50] with the Page, or young Black-a-moor, or little favorite Foot-boy, one of which is his principal Confident, and Bosom-friend.

---

46 *greatest Dunce that ever I taught*: as a young man Harley was certainly taught dancing – as he may well have confided to Swift – but the name of his tutor has not survived.
47 *Pædagogues*: tutors to young boys.
48 *because he is subject to sore Eyes*: in *Directions to Servants*, Swift instructs the 'Tutoress, or Governess' to 'Say the Children have sore Eyes; Miss *Betty* won't take to her Book' (*CWJS*, vol. II, p. 524).
49 *Perspective*: a telescope.
50 *Span-farthing*: or 'span counter': a child's game in which one player threw a coin or counter and his opponent tried to throw another to land within the span of one hand from the first.

There is one young Lord[51] in this Town, who by an unexampled piece of good Fortune, was miraculously snatched out of the Gulph of Ignorance, confined to a publick School for a due Term of Years, well Whipped when he deserved it; clad no better than his Comrades, and always their Playfellow on the same foot, had no Precedence in the School, but what was given him by his Merit, and lost it whenever he was Negligent. It is well known how many Mutinies were bred at this unpresidented Treatment, what complaints among his *Relations*, and other *Great ones* of both Sexes; that his Stockings with silver Clocks[52] were ravished from him, that he wore his own Hair, that his dress was undistinguished; that he was not fit to appear at a Ball or Assembly, nor suffered to go to either. And it was with the utmost difficulty that he became qualifyed for his present removal, where he may probably be farther Persecuted, and possibly with Success, if the firmness of a very Worthy Governor,[53] and his own good Dispositions will not preserve him. I confess, I cannot but wish he may go on in the way he began, because I have a curiosity to know by so singular an Experiment, whether Truth, Honour, Justice, Temperance, Courage and good Sense acquired by a *School* and *College* Education, may not produce a very tolerable Lad, although he should happen to fail in one or two of those accomplishments, which in the general Vogue, are held so important to the finishing of a Gentleman.

It is true, I have known an Accademical Education to have been exploded[54] in publick Assemblies; and have heard more than one or two

51 *one young Lord*: Edward Davys (1711–36), 3rd Viscount Mountcashel, to whom Thomas Sheridan, his former schoolmaster, addressed a poem at his entrance into Trinity College Dublin, in December 1727: *To the Right Honourable the Lord Viscount Mont-Cassel: This Fable is Most Humbly Dedicated by a Person Who Had Some Share in His Education*, Dublin, 1727.
52 *silver Clocks*: a 'clock' was a piece of material, often wedge-shaped, worked into a stocking at the ankle to provide a better fit, and protruding some way up the calf. Usually embroidered, it was found only in more expensive stockings, and was seen as a 'mark of great elegance in dress' (Katherine Morris Lester and Bess Viola Oerke, *Accessories of Dress*, Peoria, IL: Manual Arts Press, 1940, p. 296; Shaun Cole, *The Story of Men's Underwear*, New York: Parkstone, 2007, pp. 158–9). Clocks worked in gold and silver thread were particularly valued: the 'Silver-clock'd Stocking' had been identified as a high-fashion item in the *Spectator* as early as 1712 (*Spectator*, vol. III, p. 163).
53 *a very Worthy Governor*: Mountcashel's tutor at Trinity was 'Mr Clark', probably Henry Clarke (d. 1777), elected a fellow in 1724, who was to rise to the position of vice-provost of the college (Woolley, *Intelligencer*, p. 128).
54 *exploded*: discredited, exposed as hollow (*OED*).

Persons of high Rank, declare they could learn nothing more at *Oxford* and *Cambridge*, than to drink Ale and smoke Tobacco; wherein I firmly believ'd them, and could have added some hundred Examples from my own observation in one of those Universities,[55] but they all were of young Heirs sent thither, only for form, either from Schools where they were not suffered by their careful Parents, to stay above three Months in the Year, or from under the management of *French* Family-Tutors, who yet often attended them to their *College*, to prevent all possibility of their Improvement. But, I never yet knew any one Person of Quality, who followed his Studies at the University, and carryed away his just Proportion of Learning, that was not ready upon all occasions to celebrate and defend that course of Education, and to prove a Patron of Learned Men.

There is one circumstance in a learned Education, which ought to have much weight, even with those who have no Learning at all. The Books read at *Schools* and *Colleges*, are full of Incitements to Virtue, and Discouragements from Vice, drawn from the wisest Reasons, the strongest Motives, and the most influencing Examples. Thus, young Minds are filled early with an inclination to Good, and an abhorrence of Evil, both which encrease in them, according to the advances they make in Literature: And, although they may be, and too often are drawn by the Temptations of Youth, and the Opportunities of a large Fortune, into some Irregularities, when they come forward into the great World, it is ever with Reluctance and Compunction of Mind, because their Byas to Virtue still continues. They may stray sometimes out of Infirmity or Complyance, but they will soon return to the right Rode, and keep it always in view. I speak only of those Excesses, which are too much the Attendants of Youth and warmer Blood; for, as to the Points of Honour, Truth, Justice, and other noble Gifts of the Mind, wherein the temperature[56] of the Body hath no concern, they are seldom or never known to be misled.

I have engaged my self very unwarily in too copious a Subject for so short a Paper. The present Scope I would aim at is to prove, that some Proportion of human Knowledge appears requisite to those, who by their

---

55 *from my own observation in one of those Universities*: Swift had visited Oxford in December 1691 and was briefly a member of Hart Hall in 1692, when he took his MA. In 1714, he visited Oxford twice (Ehrenpreis, vol. I, p. 108; vol. II, pp. 733, 754).

56 *temperature*: 'The combination of "humours" in the body' (*OED*).

Birth or Fortune, are called to the making of Laws, and in a subordinate way to the execution of them; and that such Knowledge is not to be obtained without a Miracle under the frequent, corrupt, and sottish Methods, of educating those who are born to Wealth or Titles. For, I would have it remembred, that I do by no means confine these Remarks to young Persons of Noble Birth; the same Errors running through all Families, where there is Wealth enough to afford, that their Sons (at least the Eldest) may be good for nothing. Why should my Son be a Scholar, when it is not intended that he should live by his Learning? By this Rule, if what is commonly said be true, that Money answereth all Things,[57] why should my Son be honest, temperate, just, or charitable, since he hath no intention to depend upon any of these Qualities for a Maintenance.

When all is done, perhaps upon the whole, the matter is not so bad as I would make it; and, God, who worketh good out of evil, acting only by the ordinary cause and rule of Nature, permits this continual Circulation of human things,[58] for his own unsearchable Ends. The Father grows rich by Avarice, Injustice, Oppression; he is a Tyrant in the Neighbourhood, over Slaves and Beggars, whom he calls his Tenants. Why should he desire to have qualities infused into his Son, which himself never possessed, or knew, or found the want of in the acquisition of his Wealth? The Son bred in Sloth and Idleness, becomes a Spendthrift, a Cully, a Profligate, and goes out of the World a Beggar, as his Father came in: Thus, the former is punished for his own Sins, as well as for those of the latter.[59] The Dunghil having raised a huge Mushroom of short duration, is now spread to enrich other Mens Lands. It is indeed of worse consequence, where noble Families are gone to decay; because their Titles and Priviledges out-live their Estates: And, Politicians tell us, that nothing is more dangerous to the Publick, than a numerous Nobility without Merit or Fortune.[60] But even

---

57 *Money answereth all Things*: from Ecclesiastes, x, 19.
58 *human things*: *res humanae*: all the business of human life.
59 *the former is punished... those of the latter*: an allusion to Exodus, 20: 5: 'visiting the iniquity of the fathers upon the children'.
60 *Fortune*: most recently in the extensive pamphlet debate over the Peerage Bill that had been introduced into the Westminster Parliament in 1719, for which see Clyve Jones, '"Venice Preserv'd; or A Plot Discovered": The Political and Social Context of the Peerage Bill of 1719', in Clyve Jones (ed.), *A Pillar of the Constitution: The House of Lords in British Politics, 1640–1784*, London & Ronceverte: Hambledon Press, 1989, pp. 79–112.

here, God hath likewise prescribed some Remedy in the order of Nature; so many great Families coming to an end by the Sloth, Luxury, and abandoned Lusts, which enervated their Breed thorough[61] every Succession, producing gradually a more effeminate Race, wholly unfit for Propagation.[62]

---

61 *thorough*: through.
62 *Propagation*: cf. Swift's comments in *An Argument Against Abolishing Christianity* (Davis, vol. II, p. 30), questioning 'what would become of the Race of Men in the next Age, if we had nothing to trust to, besides the scrophulous consumptive Productions furnished by our Men of Wit and Pleasure', who had 'squandered away their Vigour, Health, and Estates'; also Gulliver's denunciation of the English nobility as degenerating through a devotion to 'Idleness and Luxury' (*Gulliver's Travels*, part IV, ch. vi; *CWJS*, vol. XVI, pp. 385–6). That this was Swift's personal opinion is clear from the fact of its being repeated in his letter to Charles Ford, 8 Dec. 1719 (Woolley, *Corr.*, vol. II, pp. 310–11).

THE INTELLIGENCER, NUMB. XIX.

Headnote

Published *c*. 3–7 Dec.; copy text *1728* (see Textual Account).

Like *An Answer to Several Letters from Unknown Persons* (see below, pp. 94–103), this paper is constructed as a response to two correspondents with Swift on Irish economic affairs, the pseudonymous 'Andrew Dealer and Patrick Pennyless' of the title, who had written to the *Intelligencer* (their letter has not survived; see Ferguson, p. 161).

Their letter and Swift's response arise from the continuing economic crisis in Ireland, following three bad harvests beginning in 1726. The effects of these were particularly felt in Ulster, hence Swift's pseudonym, 'A. North', a landowner and MP from County Down who explains the reasons for Ireland's financial woes, reiterating ideas Swift had previously put forward in *A Short View* and *An Answer to The Memorial*. Particular reference is made to the lack of a mint in Ireland, a point to which Swift would return in discussing the weakness of the currency.

The paper stimulated one of the earliest responses to Swift's work from America, *To The Author of those Intelligencers Printed at Dublin*, an anonymous pamphlet published in New York in 1733 (see below, Appendix D, pp. 349–65).

THE INTELLIGENCER, &c

Having on the 12th *of* October *last, receiv'd a* LETTER *Sign'd* Andrew Dealer, *and* Patrick Pennyless;[1] *I believe the following* PAPER, *just come to my Hands, will be a sufficient Answer to it.*
Sic vos non vobis vellera fertis oves.[2]
Virg.

SIR,

I am a Country Gentleman, and a Member of *Parliament*, with an Estate of about 1400 *l.* a Year, which as a *Northern* Landlord, I receive from above two Hundred Tenants, and my Lands having been Let, near twenty Years ago, the Rents, till very lately, were esteemed to be not above half Value;[3] yet by the intolerable Scarcity of *Silver*, I lye under the greatest Difficulties in receiving them, as well as in paying my Labourers, or buying any thing necessary for my Family from *Tradesmen*, who are not able to be long out of their *Money*. But the sufferings of me, and those of my Rank, are Trifles in Comparison, of what the meaner sort undergo; such as the *Buyers* and *Sellers*, at *Fairs*, and *Markets*; The *Shop-keepers* in every *Town*, the *Farmers* in general. All those who Travel with *Fish, Poultry, Pedlary-Ware*, and other Conveniencies to sell: But more especially *Handy-crafts-men*, who Work for us by the Day, and common Labourers, whom I have already

---

1 *Andrew Dealer, and Patrick Pennyless*: Oliver Ferguson has suggested that Swift was replying to an actual letter, sent under these pseudonyms, and that the same author or authors wrote again in April or May 1729, as 'Andrew Trueman and Patrick Layfield', to which Swift replied in *An Answer to Several Letters from Unknown Persons* (see Appendix E, below, pp. 365–74; Ferguson, pp. 161–2, 191–5).
2 *Sic vos non vobis vellera fertis oves*: a common epigraph to contemporary editions of Virgil, deriving from the life of the poet said to be written by Tiberius Claudius Donatus: 'Thus you sheep bear fleeces but not for yourselves.'
3 *half Value*: Here and elsewhere, Swift postulates a recent doubling in land values. The large-scale re-leasing of land in the immediate aftermath of the Williamite war meant that a large number of tenants had renewed in the 1710s. At that time, leases were customarily set for the relatively short term of 21 years. At this time, Ulster was still reckoned the poorest of the four provinces, and rents remained low until at least 1715: W. H. Crawford, 'Landlord–Tenant Relations in Ulster 1609–1820', *Irish Economic and Social History* 2 (1975), 9–10. In County Armagh, however, where Swift occasionally stayed with the Achesons at Markethill, the economy was undergoing significant improvement: R. G. Gillespie (ed.), *Settlement and Survival on an Ulster Estate: The Brownlow Leasebook 1667–1711*, Belfast: PRONI, 1988, pp. lix–lxiv.

mentioned. Both these kinds of People, I am forced to employ, till their Wages amount to a *Double Pistole*, or a *Moydore*,[4] (for we hardly have any *Gold* of lower Value left among us) to divide it among themselves as they can; and this is generally done at an *Ale-house* or *Brandy-shop*; where, besides the cost of getting *Drunk*, (which is usually the Case) they must pay *ten Pence* or a *Shilling*, for changing their *Piece* into *Silver*, to some *Huckstering-fellow*,[5] who follows that *Trade*. But what is infinitely worse, those Poor Men for want of due Payment, are forced to take up their *Oat-meal*, and other Necessaries of Life, at almost double Value, and consequently are not able, to discharge half their score,[6] especially under the scarceness of *Corn*, for two Years past, and the Melancholy disappointment of the present *Crop*.[7]

The Causes of this, and a thousand other Evils, are clear and manifest to you and all other Thinking Men, though hidden from the Vulgar: These indeed complain of hard Times, the Dearth of Corn, the want of Money, the badness of Seasons; that their Goods bear no Price, and the poor cannot find Work; but their weak reasonings never carry them to the Hatred, and Contempt, born us by our Neighbours, and Brethren,[8] without the least grounds of Provocation, who rejoice at our Sufferings, although sometimes to their own Disadvantage;[9] of the dead Weight upon every beneficial Branch of our Trade; of half our Revenues sent annually to *England*,[10] and many other Grievances peculiar to this unhappy Kingdom,[11] excepted for our Sins, which keeps us from enjoying the common Benefits of Mankind,

---

4   *a Double Pistole, or a Moydore*: the double pistole was a French or Spanish gold coin, worth £1. 17 s. Irish; the moidore, a Portuguese gold coin worth £1. 10s. Irish.
5   *Huckstering-fellow*: a pedlar or hawker.
6   *to discharge half their score*: to pay half of what they owe.
7   *Crop*: for the harvest failures of 1727–8, see James Kelly, 'Harvests and Hardship: Famine and Scarcity in Ireland in the Late 1720s', *Studia Hibernica* 26 (1991-2), 78–85.
8   *Neighbours, and Brethren*: The English.
9   *Disadvantage*: Here Swift appears to be accepting one of the arguments advanced by John Browne in *Seasonable Remarks on Trade with Some Reflections on the Advantages that Might Accrue to Great Britain by a Proper Regulation of the Trade of Ireland*, Dublin, 1728, a work whose economic analysis he otherwise disparaged, namely that Ireland's prosperity would be to the advantage of England (*Seasonable Remarks*, p. 53).
10 *England*: see above, p. 25.
11 *peculiar to this unhappy Kingdom*: Swift repeats the argument from *A Short View of the State of Ireland* (above, pp. 17–21) that the condition of the Irish economy is singular, and does not conform to the maxims of mercantilist economics.

as you and some other Lovers of their Country, have so often observed,[12] with such good Inclinations, and so little Effect.

It is true indeed, that under our Circumstances in general, this Complaint for the want of *Silver*, may appear as Ridiculous, as for a Man to be impatient about a *Cut Finger*, when he is struck with the *Plague*; and yet a poor Fellow going to the *Gallows*, may be allow'd to feel the smart of *Wasps*, while he is upon *Tyburn*[13] Road. This misfortune is too urging, and vexatious in every kind of small Traffick, and so hourly pressing upon all Persons in the Country whatsoever, that a hundred inconveniences, of perhaps greater Moment in themselves, have been timely submitted to, with far less disquietude and murmurs. And the Case seems yet the harder, if it be true, what many skilfull Men assert, that nothing is more easy, than a Remedy; and, that the Want of *Silver*, in proportion to the little *Gold* remaining among us, is altogether as unnecessary, as it is inconvenient. A Person of Distinction assured me very lately, that, in discoursing with the *Lord Lieutenant*, before his last Return to *England*, His *Excellency* said, *He had pressed the matter often, in proper Time and Place, and to proper Persons; and could not see any difficulty of the least Moment, that could prevent us from being easy upon that Article.*[14]

Whoever carrys to *England*, twenty seven *English* Shillings, and brings back one *Moydore*, of full Weight, is a gainer of nine pence *Irish*;[15] In a *Guinea*, the Advantage is three pence, and two pence in a *Pistole*. The BANKERS, who are generally Masters of all our *Gold*, and *Silver*, with this Advantage, have sent over as much of the latter, as came into their Hands. The Value of one thousand *Moydores* in *Silver*, would thus amount in clear profit, to 37 *l*. 10 *s*.[16] The *Shop-keepers*, and other *Traders*, who go

---

12 *observed*: according to Faulkner's headnote, this letter is addressed to the Drapier, but, as James Woolley observes, 'it could more probably be' supposed to be addressed to Mr Intelligencer, referring to numbers 6, 15, 16, 17, and 18 (*Intelligencer*, p. 214).
13 *Tyburn*: the place of execution for Middlesex, near what is now Marble Arch in London.
14 *his Excellency said... upon that Article*: Carteret sailed from Dublin in mid-May 1728. For Carteret's efforts to secure a revaluation of the coinage during his sojourn in Ireland in 1727–8, see Woolley, *Intelligencer*, p. 214.
15 *Irish*: Archishop Boulter informed Sir Robert Walpole on 25 May 1736 that 'A moidore, which is worth about 27*s*. in *England*, passes here for 30*s*. *Irish*, or 27*s*. *English*, and 9*d*.' (*Boulter Letters*, vol. II, p. 122). In an earlier letter, of 2 May 1730, he had told the Duke of Newcastle that 'the lowest price for changing a moidore' was '8*d*. and often 1*s*. or more' (vol. II, p. 8).
16 *10 s*: in Irish money.

to *London* to buy Goods, followed the same Practice, by which we have been driven into this insupportable Distress.

To a common Thinker, it should seem, that nothing would be more easy, than for the *Government* to Redress this Evil, at any time they shall please. When the value of *Guineas* was lowred in *England*, from 21 *s.* 6 *d.* to only 21 *s.*[17] the Consequences to this Kingdom, were obvious, and manifest to us all; and a sober Man, may be allowed at least to wonder, though he dare not complain, why a new Regulation of *Coin* among us, was not then made; much more, why it hath never been since. It would surely require no very profound skill in *Algebra*, to reduce the difference of *nine Pence* to *thirty Shillings*, or *three Pence* in a *Guinea*, to less than a *Farthing*; And so small a Fraction could be no Temptation, either to *Bankers*, to hazard their *Silver* at Sea, or Tradesmen to load themselves with it, in their Journeys to *England*. In my humble Opinion, it would be no unseasonable Condescension, if the *Government* would Graciously please, to signify to the *poor loyal Protestant Subjects* of *Ireland*, either that this miserable want of *Silver*, is not possible to be remedy'd in any degree, by the nicest skill in *Arithmetick*; or else, that it doth not stand with the good pleasure of *England*, to suffer any *Silver* at all among us. In the former Case, it would be madness, to expect Impossibilities: And in the other, we must submit: For, Lives, and Fortunes are, always at the Mercy of the CONQUEROR.[18]

The Question hath been often put in *printed Papers*, by the *DRAPIER*, and others, or perhaps by the same *WRITER*, under different Styles, why this Kingdom should not be permitted to have a *Mint* of its own, for the *Coinage* of *Gold*, *Silver*, and *Copper*, which is a Power exercised by many *Bishops*, and every petty *Prince* in *Germany*. But this Question hath never been answered, nor the least Application that I have heard of, made to the *Crown* from hence, for the grant of a *Publick Mint*, although it stands

---

17 *21 s*: on 22 Dec. 1717. In 1718, the Irish privy council unsuccessfully requested the lord lieutenant to proclaim a reduction in the guinea from £1 3s Irish to £1 2s 9d (Woolley, *Intelligencer*, p. 214 n.71).

18 *For, Lives, and Fortunes... Mercy of the CONQUEROR*: in other words, England has conquered Ireland, and can do as she pleases. But cf. John Locke, *Second Treatise of Civil Government*, ch. XVI, sect. 178: 'let us see... what power a lawful conqueror has over the subdued: and that I say is purely despotical. He has an absolute power over the lives of those who by an unjust war have forfeited them; but not over the lives or fortunes of those who engaged not in the war, nor over the possessions even of those who were actually engaged in it.'

upon Record, that several Cities, and Corporations here, had the Liberty of *Coining Silver*.[19] I can see no Reasons, why we alone of all Nations, are thus restrained, but such as I dare not mention;[20] only thus far, I may venture, that *Ireland* is the first Imperial Kingdom, since *Nimrod*,[21] which ever wanted Power, to *Coin* their own *Money*.

I know very well, that in *England* it is lawful for any Subject, to Petition either the *Prince*, or the *Parliament*, provided it be done in a dutiful, and regular Manner;[22] But what is lawful for a Subject of *Ireland*, I profess I cannot determine;[23] nor will undertake, that your *Printer* shall not be prosecuted,[24] in a *Court of Justice*, for publishing my *Wishes*, that a poor Shop-keeper might be able to change a *Guinea*, or a *Moydore*, when a Customer comes for a *Crown's* worth[25] of Goods. I have known less Crimes punished with the utmost Severity, under the Title of *Disaffection*: And, I cannot but approve the Wisdom of the *Antients*, who, after *Astrea*[26] had fled from the Earth, at least took care to provide *three upright Judges for Hell*.[27] Men's Ears among us, are indeed grown so nice, that whoever happens to think out of Fashion, in what relates to the Welfare of this Kingdom, dare not so much as complain of the *Tooth-ach*, lest our weak and busy Dablers in politick[28] should be ready to swear against him for *Disaffection*.

---

19 *Coining Silver*: in private correspondence, however, Swift only referred to copper coins having been produced in Waterford, Dublin and Drogheda: Swift to the Earl of Oxford, 26 Oct. 1725, 11 May 1728 (Woolley, *Corr.*, vol. II, p. 617; vol. III, p. 182).
20 *dare not mention*: because of the oppressive and partial nature of English government, against which the Irish Parliament had failed to exert itself.
21 *Nimrod*: the founder of Nineveh (Gen., 10: 8–10). On Swift's view of him as 'an archetype of tyrannical monarchy', see Daniel Eilon, 'Swift's Burning the Library of Babel', *MLR* 80 (1985), 269–82.
22 *it is lawful . . . dutiful, and regular Manner*: the right of the subject to petition the king was guaranteed in the English Bill of Rights (1689).
23 *determine*: there had been no Irish bill of rights: W. N. Osborough, 'The Failure to Enact an Irish Bill of Rights: A Gap in Irish Constitutional History', *Irish Jurist* 33 (1998), 392–415.
24 *your Printer shall not be prosecuted*: Edward Waters (d. 1751) had been tried in 1720 for publishing Swift's *Proposal for the Universal Use of Irish Manufacture*.
25 *a Crown's worth*: 5s 5d Irish.
26 *Astrea*: the personification of justice. According to Ovid, she was the last of the immortals to leave the earth, fleeing from the wickedness of humankind: *Metamorphoses*, i, 150.
27 *three upright Judges for Hell*: Minos, Rhadamanthus and Aeacus, the sons of Jupiter: ibid., xiii, 25–6.
28 *politick*: policy, or politics.

There was a Method practiced by Sir *Ambrose Crowley*, the great Dealer in *Iron-works*,[29] which I wonder the Gentlemen of our Country, under this great Exigence, have not thought fit to imitate. In the several Towns, and Villages, where he dealt, and many Miles round, he gave *Notes*, instead of *Money*, from *two Pence*, to *twenty Shillings*, which passed currant in all Shops, and Markets, as well as in Houses, where Meat, or Drink was Sold. I see no Reason, why the like Practice, may not be introduced among us,[30] with some degree of Success, or at least may not serve, as a poor Expedient, in this, our *blessed age of Paper*,[31] which, as it Dischargeth all our greatest Payments, may be equally useful in the Smaller, and may just keep us alive, till an *English Act of Parliament shall forbid it*.[32]

I have been told, that among some of our poorest *American* Colonies, upon the Continent, the People enjoy the Liberty of cutting the little *Money*, among them into halves, and quarters, for the conveniences of small Traffick.[33] How happy should we be in Comparison of our present Condition, if the like Priviledge, were granted to us, of employing the

29 *Sir Ambrose Crowley, the great Dealer in Iron-works*: Sir Ambrose Crowley (1658–1713), the great English ironmaster, had issued bills of exchange redeemable at his company's offices: M. W. Flinn, *Men of Iron: The Crowleys in the Early Iron Industry*, Edinburgh: Edinburgh University Press, 1962, pp. 55, 180–2.
30 *I see no Reason . . . may not be introduced among us*: as James Maculla was to propose in *A New Scheme Proposed, to the People of Ireland; for Increasing the Cash, of this Kingdom; by Making Promissary Notes of Copper, to Bear an Intrinsick Value to the British-half-pence . . .* , Dublin, 1728. For Swift's response, see below, pp. 128–42.
31 *blessed age of Paper*: Ovid, *Metamorphoses*, i, 89–150, to which Swift has already made reference in this essay, traced the decline of the world from the age of gold to the age of silver, and ultimately to the age of bronze, after which came flood and destruction. In relation to the development of paper currency, Thomas Prior commented in *Observations on Coin in General*, Dublin, 1729, p. 45, that 'were it not for bankers' notes which we have been passing in good plenty, it would be impossible to manage our domestic trade half so well as we do' (quoted in L. M. Cullen, 'Landlords, Bankers and Merchants: The Early Irish Banking World', *Hermathena* 135 (1983), 28–9). John Browne, in *A Scheme of the Money-matters of Ireland . . .* , Dublin, 1729, p. 17, assumed a circulation in Ireland of about £514,000 in specie and £400,000 in bankers' notes, while Berkeley's *Querist* asked in 1733 (query no. 33) 'Whether current bank-notes may not be deemed money? And whether they are not actually the greater part of the money of this kingdom?' (Joseph Johnston, *Bishop Berkeley's Querist in Historical Perspective*, Dundalk: Dundalgan Press, 1970, p. 127).
32 *forbid it*: the Declaratory Act passed at Westminster in 1720 (6 Geo. I c. 5) asserted the right of the British Parliament to pass laws binding Ireland.
33 *I have been told . . . for the conveniences of small Traffick*: colonial statutes or proclamations in Virginia (1683), Massachusetts (1707) and Maryland (1708) had set rates of exchange for foreign coins that included equivalents for halves and quarters: *Executive Journals of the Council of Colonial Virginia*, ed. H. R. McIlwaine, 4 vols., Richmond: Virginia State

Sheers, for want of a *Mint*, upon our *foreign Gold*; by clipping it into *half Crowns*, and *shillings*, and even lower Denominations; For Beggars must be content to live upon scraps; And it would be our Felicity, that these scraps would never be exported to other Countries, while any thing better was left.

If neither of these Projects will avail, I see nothing left us, but to truck and barter our Goods, like the *wild Indians*, with each other, or with our too powerful Neighbours; only with this disadvantage on our side, that the *Indians* enjoy the Product of their own Land, whereas the better half of ours is sent away without so much as a recompence in *Bugles*,[34] or *Glass*, in return.[35]

It must needs be a very comfortable Circumstance, in the present juncture, that some thousand Families are gone, or going, or preparing to go, from hence, and settle themselves in *America*.[36] The poorer Sort, for want of Work, the Farmers whose beneficial Bargains, are now become a Rackrent,[37] too hard to be born. And those who have any *ready Money*, or can purchase any, by the Sale of their Goods, or Leases; because they find their Fortunes hourly decaying; that their Goods will bear no Price, and that few or none, have any *Money* to buy the very necessaries of Life, are hastening to follow their departed Neighbours. It is true, *Corn* among us, carries a very high price; but it is for the same reason, that *Rats*, and *Cats*, and *Dead Horses*, have been often bought for *Gold*, in a Town besieged.[38]

There is a Person of Quality in my Neighbourhood, who twenty Years ago; when he was just come to age, being unexperienced, and of a generous

---

Library, 1925–78, vol. I, 35–8; *The Charters and General Laws of the Colony and Province of Massachusetts Bay*, Boston, 1814, pp. 383–5; *A Compleat Collection of the Laws of Maryland*, Annapolis, 1727, pp. 54–5.

34 *Bugles*: tube-shaped glass beads, usually black, used as ornamentation for clothing (*OED*).
35 *in return*: the produce of Ireland is taken away, without the inhabitants being given even the worthless trinkets which the native Americans receive in exchange for their resources.
36 *some thousand Families... settle themselves in America*: Archbishop Boulter wrote in November 1728 that 'it is certain that above 4,200 men, women, and children have been shipped off from hence for the West Indies within three years, and of these above 3,100 this last summer': Boulter to Archbishop Wake, 9 Nov. 1728 (*Boulter Letters*, vol. I, p. 210).
37 *a Rack-rent*: a high or extortionate rent. For similar criticisms of Irish landlords racking their tenants, see *A Proposal for the Universal Use of Irish Manufacture* (1720) (Davis, vol. IX, p. 21).
38 *Rats, and Cats, and Dead Horses... in a Town besieged*: all three items appear on the price list for food in the besieged city of Derry in July 1689, printed in *A True Account of the Siege of London-Derry by the Reverend Mr. George Walker...*, London, 1689, p. 39.

Temper, let his Lands, even as times went then, at a low Rate, to able Tenants, and consequently by the rise of Land, since that time, looked upon his Estate, to be set at half value.[39] But Numbers of these Tenants, or their Descendants are now Offering to sell their Leases by Cant,[40] even those which were for Lives,[41] some of them renewable for ever, and some Fee-farms,[42] which the Landlord himself, hath bought in, at half the Price, they would have yielded seven Years ago. And some Leases Let at the same time, for Lives, have been given up to him, without any Consideration at all.

This is the most favourable face of things at present among us, I say, among us of the *North*, who are esteemed the onely thriving people of the Kingdom: And how far, and how soon, this Misery, and Desolation may spread, is easy to foresee.

The vast Sums of *Money* daily carryed off, by our numerous Adventurers to *America*, have deprived us of our *Gold* in these Parts, almost as much as of our *Silver*.

And the good Wives who come to our Houses, offer us their Pieces of Linnen, upon which their whole Dependence lyes, for so little profit, that it can neither half pay their Rents, nor half support their Families.

It is remarkable, that this Enthusiasm spread among our *Northern* People, of sheltring them selves in the Continent of *America*,[43] hath no other foundation, than their present insupportable Condition at home. I have made all possible inquiries, to learn what Encouragement our People have met with, by any Intelligence from those Plantations, sufficient to make them undertake, so tedious, and hazardous a Voyage, in all seasons of the Year; and so ill accommodated in their Ships, that many of them have Dyed miserably in their Passage; But, could never get one satisfactory Answer.

---

39 *set at half value*: Swift assumes that land values have doubled since the lease was made.
40 *Cant*: auction.
41 *for Lives*: leases for the lifetimes of the persons named in the lease, and ending with the death of the last survivor. Leases for three lives were the most common.
42 *Fee-farms*: landholdings in fee simple subject to a fixed annual rent.
43 *sheltring them selves in the Continent of America*: the standard account of the transatlantic migration of Ulster Presbyterians is R. J. Dickson, *Ulster Emigration to Colonial America, 1718–1775*, London: Routledge and Kegan Paul, 1966. See also J. G. Leyburn, *The Scotch-Irish: A Social History*, Chapel Hill, NC: University of North Carolina Press, 1962, ch. 12; Patrick Griffin, *The People with No Name: Ireland's Ulster Scots, America's Scots Irish, and the Creation of a British Atlantic World*, Princeton: Princeton University Press, 2001, ch. 3.

Some body, they know not who, had Written a Letter to his Friend, or Cousin, from thence, inviting him by all means, to come over; that it was a fine fruitfull Country, and to be held for ever, at a *Penny* an Acre. But the Truth of the Fact is this, The *English* established in those Colonies, are in great want of Men to inhabit that Tract of Ground, which lyes between them, and the *Wild Indians*, who are not reduced under their Dominion. We Read of some barbarous People, whom the *Romans* placed in their Armies, for no other service, than to blunt their Enemies Swords, and afterwards to fill up Trenches with their dead Bodies.[44] And thus our People who Transport themselves, are settled in those interjacent Tracts, as a screen against the Insults[45] of the *Savages*[46] and may have as much Land, as they can clear from the Woods, at a very reasonable Rate, if they can afford to pay, about a *hundred* years Purchase by their Labour. Now besides the *Fox*'s reasons,[47] which inclines all those, who have already ventured thither, to represent every thing, in a false light, as well for justifying their own Conduct, as for getting Companions, in their misery; so, the Governing People in those Plantations, have Wisely provided, that no Letters shall be suffered to pass from thence hither, without being first viewed by the Council, by which our People here, are wholly deceived in the Opinions, they have of the happy condition of their Friends, gone before them. This was accidentally discovered some months ago, by an honest Man who having transported himself, and family thither, and finding all things directly contrary to his hope, had the luck to convey a private Note, by a faithful hand, to his Relation here, entreating him, not to think of such a Voyage, and to discourage all his friends from attempting it. Yet this, although it be a Truth well known, hath produced very little effects; which is no manner of wonder; For as it is natural to a Man in a *Fever* to turn often, although without any hope of Ease, or when he is pursued to leap down a Precipice, to avoid an Enemey just at his back; so, Men in the extremest degree of

---

44 *some barbarous People... with their dead Bodies*: Agricola was said to have used his Batavian and Tungrian auxiliaries in just such a way in the battle of Mons Graupius (Tacitus, *Agricola*, xxxv). Evidently 'the concept of saving Roman lives was a commonplace' of battle tactics (Tacitus, *Agricola*, ed. R. M. Ogilvie and Sir Ian Richmond, Oxford: Clarendon Press, 1967, p. 272). See below, *The Answer to The Craftsman*, pp. 197–8.
45 *Insults*: assaults.
46 *Savages*: in this case, native Americans, but Swift often applied the term to the native Irish.
47 *the Fox's reasons*: from Aesop's fable of the fox who had lost his tail and tried to convince the other foxes to cut off theirs.

Misery, and Want, will naturally fly to the first apperance of Relief, let it be ever so vain, or visionary.[48]

You may observe, that I have very superficially touched the subject I began with, and with the utmost Caution: For I know how Criminal the least Complaint hath been thought, however seasonable or just, or honestly intended, which hath forced me to offer up my Daily Prayers, that it may never, at least in my time, be Interpreted by innuendo's[49] as a false, scandalous, seditious, and disaffected action, for a Man to roar under an acute fit of the *Gout*, which beside the loss, and the danger, would be very inconvenient to one of my Age, so severely Afflicted with that Distemper.

I wish you good success, but I can promise you little, in an ungrateful Office you have taken up, without the least view, either to Reputation, or Profit. Perhaps your Comfort is, that none but *Villians*, and *Betrayers* of their Country, can be your *Enemies*. Upon which, I have little to say, having not the honour, to be acquainted with many of that sort, and therefore, as you easily may believe, am compelled to lead a very retired Life.

> I am Sir,
> Your most Obidient,
> Humble Servant,
> A. *NORTH*.

County of *Down*.
Dec. 2*d*. 1728.}

---

48 *visionary*: incapable of being carried out.
49 *innuendo's*: in a libel suit, a plaintiff's interpretation of what constitutes libellous or slanderous material.

A LETTER TO THE ARCHBISHOP OF DUBLIN, CONCERNING THE WEAVERS

Headnote

Composed spring 1729; published posthumously, 1765; copy text SwJ 436 (see Textual Account).

One of four pieces (along with the *Answers* to *Unknown Persons* and *Unknown Hands*, and the *Letter on M'culla*) written in the spring of 1729 concerning Irish economic and agricultural problems, and not published in Swift's lifetime, the *Letter to the Archbishop* can be dated reasonably accurately, being a response to an appeal from a spokesman for the Irish weavers, asking Swift to 'publish a recommendation that the Irish people should wear cloth made in their own country' made in the *Dublin Intelligence*, 29 April 1729. The intended recipient of Swift's piece, Archbishop William King, died on 8 May. This suggests a composition around the end of April or early May. King, like Swift, was the recipient of petitions and memorials from various associations of Dublin tradesmen.

Although resentment at the 1699 English Woollen Act was ongoing, and Swift's arguments about the unfairness and deleterious consequences of the Act had been elaborated in earlier writings from the *Proposal for Irish Manufacture* (1720) onwards, the economic difficulties of the late 1720s prompted several authors to discuss ways in which restrictions on Irish woollen exports might be ameliorated or modified, and make his argument particularly relevant. Smuggling of Irish woollen yarn to the continent, which benefited wool producers in Munster, was circumventing part of the restrictions of the Act. However, for the Dublin weavers with whom Swift was concerned, this was of no advantage, because their concern was to export manufactured cloth. Shortly afterwards, in 1731, the British administration sought a settlement by which the Irish Parliament would suppress the smuggling trade, in return for concessions in the English market (F. G. James, *Ireland in the Empire, 1688–1770*, p. 157; D. W. Hayton, 'Accounts of Debates in the House of Commons, March–April 1731, Supplementary to the Diary of the First Earl of Egmont', *Electronic British Library Journal* (2013)). This was unsuccessful.

A LETTER TO THE ARCHBISHOP OF DUBLIN,[1] CONCERNING THE WEAVERS.

My Lord,

The Corporation of Weavers in the wollen Manufacture,[2] who have so often attended your Grace and called upon me with their schemes and proposalls were with me on thursday last, when he who spoke for the rest and in the name of his absent brethren said it was the opinion of the whole body, that if somewhat were written at this time by an able hand to persuade the People of the Kingdom to wear their own woollen Manufactures it might be of good use to the Nation in generall, and preserve many hundreds of their Trade from starving. To which I answered that it was hard for any man of common Spirit to turn his thoughts to such Speculations, without discovering a Resentment which people are too delicate to bear. For, I will not deny to your Grace, that I cannot reflect on the singular condition of this Country different from all others upon the face of the Earth, without some Emotion, and without often examining as I pass the streets whether those animals which come in my way with two legs and human faces clad, and erect be of the same Species with what I have seen very like them in England,[3] as to the outward Shape, but differing in their notions, natures, and intellectualls more than any two kinds of Brutes in a forest, which any man of common prudence would immediately discover by persuading them

---

1 *ARCHBISHOP OF DUBLIN*: William King (1650–1729), bishop of Derry 1691–1703 and archbishop of Dublin 1703–29.
2 *The Corporation of Weavers in the wollen Manufacture*: unlikely to have been the Weavers' Guild (for which, see W. C. Stubbs, 'The Weavers Guild, the Guild of the Blessed Virgin Mary, Dublin, 1446–1840', *Journal of the Royal Society of Antiquaries of Ireland* 49 (1919), 60–88), which included MPs and city aldermen and would not have needed to apply to the archbishop or the dean to represent its interests. More likely, this refers to a charitable society of journeymen in Dublin, of which there were many (see above, p. xcv). However, it is worth noting that the 'Corporation of Weavers' at whose request Bishop Edward Synge published his sermon *Universal Beneficence. A Sermon Preached in the Parish-Church of St. Luke, Dublin. On Sunday the Nineteenth Day of March, 1720/21* . . . , Dublin, 1721, could well have been the guild, since it was responsible for building the Tailors' Hall in St Luke's parish in the Coombe in 1745.
3 *in England*: cf. Gulliver's revulsion from humanity after his return from the land of the Houyhnhnms: 'I . . . return to enjoy my own Speculations in my little Garden . . . to apply those excellent Lessons of Virtue which I learned among the Houyhnhnms; to instruct the Yahoos of my own Family as far as I shall find them docible Animals; to behold my Figure often in a Glass, and thus if possible habituate my self by Time to tolerate the sight of a human Creature' (*Gulliver's Travels*, part IV, ch. xii (*CWJS*, vol. XVI, p. 443)).

to define what they mean by Law, Liberty, Property, Courage, Reason, Loyalty or Religion.

One thing, my Lord, I am very confident of; that if God Almighty, for our sins would most justly send us a Pestilence, whoever should dare to discover his grief in publick for such a visitation would certainly be censured for disaffection to the Governmt. For I solemnly profess, that I do not know one calamity we have undergone this many year, whereof any man whose opinions were not in fashion dared to lament without being openly charged with that imputation; And this is the harder, because although a Mother when she hath corrected her child may sometimes force it to kiss the rod,[4] yet she will never give that power to the foot-boy or the Scullion.

My Lord, there are two things for the People of this Kingdom to consider. First their present evil Condition; and Secondly what can be done in some degree to remedy it.

I shall not enter into a particular Description of our present Misery, It hath been already done in severall Papers, and very fully in one, entitled A Short view of the State of Ireld. It will be enough to mention the entire want of Trad, the Navigation Act[5] executed with utmost rigor. The remission of a Million every year to England. The ruinous Importations of forein Luxury and vanity. The oppression of Landlords, and discouragemt of Agriculture.

Now all these evils are without the possibility of a Cure except that of Importations, and to fence against ruinous folly will be always in our power in Spight of the Discouragements, mortifications, contempt, hatred & oppression we can ly under. But our Trade will never mend, the Navigation act never be softened, our Absentees never return, our endless forein Payments never be lessened, our own Landlords never be less exacting.

All other Scheams for preserving this Kingdom from utter ruin are idle and Visionary,[6] consequences drawn from wrong reasoning and from generall Topicks which for the same Causes that they may be true in all Nations are certainly false in ours; as I have told the publick often

---

4 *to kiss the rod*: a common phrase for the humble submission to authority.
5 *Navigation Act*: the English Navigation Acts of 1663 (15 Chas II c. 7), 1670 (22 & 23 Chas II c. 26) and 1696 (7 & 8 Will. III c. 22), which effectively excluded Ireland from the English colonial trade.
6 *idle and Visionary*: worthless and incapable of being carried out.

enough, but with as little effect as what I shall say at present is likely to produce.

I am weary of so many abortive Projects for the advance^mt of Trade, of so many crude Proposals in letters sent me from unknown hands,[7] of so many contradictory Speculations about the raising or sinking the value of gold and Silver. I am not in the least sorry to hear of the great Numbers going to America,[8] though very much so for the Causes that drive them from us, Since the uncontrolled[9] Maxim that People are the Riches of a Nation[10] is no Maxim here under our Circumstances. We have neither manufactures to employ them about, nor food to support them.

If a private Gentleman's income be sunk irretrievably for ever from a hundred Pounds to fifty, and that he hath no other method to supply the Deficiency, I desire to know my Lord, whether such a Person hath any other course to take than to sink half his expences in every article of Oeconomy, to save himself from Ruin and the Jayl. Is not this more than doubly the case of Ireland, where the want of money the irrevocable ruin of Trade, with the other evils above mentioned, and many more too well known and felt, and too numerous or invidious to relate, have been gradually sinking us for above a dozen years past to a degree that we are at least by two thirds in a worse condition than was ever known since the Revolution. Therefore instead of Dreams and projects for advancing of Trade, we have nothing left but to find out some expedient whereby we may reduce our expences to our Incomes.

Yet this procedure allowed so necessary in all private familys and in its own nature so easy to be put into practice may meet with strong opposition by the cowardly slavish indulgence of the men to the intolerable pride,

---

7 *letters sent me from unknown hands*: see below, pp. 119–27.
8 *the great Numbers going to America*: see above, p. 95.
9 *uncontrolled*: undisputed. In his *Letter to... Viscount Molesworth* (1724), Swift had written, 'I ever thought it the most uncontrolled and universally agreed maxim' that the definition of freedom was that a people should be governed by laws to which they had given their consent (Davis, vol. X, pp. 86–7).
10 *Maxim that People are the Riches of a Nation*: an accepted dictum of mercantilist economics (for which, see L. A. Landa, '"A Modest Proposal" and Populousness', *Modern Philology* 40 (1942), 162–5) which had already been challenged by Sheridan in *The Intelligencer*, no. 6 (Woolley, *Intelligencer*, p. 89) and was to be included by Swift in *Maxims Controlled in Ireland* (below, pp. 156–7). By an irony, it had also been rebutted by Swift's former adversaries Arthur Maynwaring and John Oldmixon in the *Medley*, no. 19 (F. H. Ellis (ed.), *Swift vs. Mainwaring: The Examiner and The Medley*, Oxford: Clarendon Press, 1985, p. 225).

arrogance vanity and Luxury of the Women who strictly adhering to the rules of modern education seem to employ their whole Stock of Invention in contriving new arts of profusion faster than the most parsimonious husband can afford, and to compass this work the more effectually, their universal maxim is to despise and detest every theory of the growth and manufacture of their own Country,[11] and most to value whatever comes from the very remotest parts of the globe. And I am convinced, that if the Virtuosi[12] could once find out a world in the Moon[13] with a passage to it, our women would wear nothing but what came directly from thence.

The prime cost of Wine yearly imported to Ireld is valued at 30000^{ll}, and the Tea (including Coffee & Chocolate) at five times that Sum.[14] The Lace, Silk, Callicoes and all other unnecessary ornamen^{ts} for women including English Cloaths and Stuffs, added to the former Articles make up (to compute grossly,) about 400000^{ll}.

Now, if we should allow the thirty thousand Pounds for wine, wherein the women have their Share, and which is all we have to comfort us, and deduct 70000^{l}. more for over reckoning, there would still remain 300000^{ll}. annually spent for unwholesom drugs,[15] and unnecessary finery,

---

11 *every theory of the growth and manufacture of their own Country*: the phrase is ambiguous: the more likely meaning is that fashionable women despise every theory that has been grown or manufactured in Ireland, just as they despise Irish woollens and other native manufactures. It could also mean that they despise all theories about the produce of Irish industry, although the use of the word theory in relation to trade and manufacture was unusual. Swift may have had in mind the work of the pioneering political economist Isaac Gervaise, *The System or Theory of the Trade of the World*..., London, 1720.

12 *Virtuosi*: scholars, and especially natural philosophers; a term which, since Thomas Shadwell's comedy *The Virtuoso* (1676), had been applied specifically to Fellows of the Royal Society. The 'Voyage to Laputa' in *Gulliver's Travels* was only the most sustained of Swift's many satirical attacks on the Royal Society and its virtuosi.

13 *a world in the Moon*: in 1638, the theologian and natural philosopher John Wilkins (1614–72), one of the founding members of the Royal Society, had published *The Discovery of a World in the Moone. Or, A Discourse Tending, to Prove, That 'Tis Probable There May Be Another Habitable World in That Planet*, London, 1638, a serious, if speculative, scientific work, which had been followed shortly afterwards by the posthumous publication of the utopian fantasy *The Man in the Moone: or A Discourse of a Voyage Thither by Domingo Gonsales the Speedy Messenger*, London, 1638, by Francis Godwin (1562–1633), bishop of Hereford, and brother to Swift's great-grandmother (see Ehrenpreis, vol. I, pp. 5–6). Wilkins's earnest scientific writings were picked out for comic effect in *Gulliver's Travels* (part III, chs. ii, v; *CWJS*, vol. XVI, pp. 233, 273).

14 *prime cost of Wine . . . at five times that Sum*: cf. Dobbs, *Essay*, pp. 37–9, which estimated the average value of wine imported into Ireland (from France, Spain, Portugal and the Rhineland), at well over £100,000 p.a. and tea at between £18,000 and £19,000.

15 *unwholesom drugs*: chocolate, coffee and tea.

which prodigious sum would be wholly saved, and many thousands of our miserable Shopkeepers and manufacturers comfortably supported.

Let speculative people busy their Brains as much as they please, there is no other way to prevent this Kingdom from Sinking for ever than by utterly renouncing all forein dress and Luxury.

It is absolutely so in fact that every husband of any fortune in the kingdom is nourishing a devouring Serpent in his Bosom[16] with all the mischief but with none of it's wisdom.

If all the women were clad with the growth of their own Country they might still vye with each other in the course of Foppery, and still have room left to vye with each other, and equally show their wit and Judgment in deciding upon the variety of Irish Stuffs; And if they could be contented with their native wholsom slops for breakfast, we should hear no more of their Spleen, Hystericks, Cholicks Palpitations and Asthmas. They might still be allowed to ruin each other and their husbands at play, because the money lost would onely circulate among our selves.

My Lord; I freely own it a wild Imagination that any words will cure the sottishness of men, or the vanity of women, but the Kingdom is in a fair way of producing the most effective remedy, when there will not be money left for the common course of buying and selling the very necessaryes of life in our markets, unless we absolutely change the whole method of our Proceedings.

This Corporation of Weavers in woollen and silk, who have so frequently offered Proposalls both to Your Grace and to me, are the hottest and coldest generation of Men that I have known. About a Month ago they attended Your Grace when I had the honor to be with you, and design[ed] me then the same favor. They desired you would recommend to Your Clergy to wear Gowns of Irish Stuffs, which might probably spread the Example among all their Brethren in the Kingdom, and perhaps among the Lawyers and Gentlemen of the university and among the Citizens of those Corporations who appear in Gowns on solemn occasions. I then mentioned a Kind of Stuff, not above eight pence a Yard, which I heard had been contrived by some of the Trade and was very convenient. I desired they would prepare

---

16 *nourishing a devouring Serpent in his Bosom*: a reference to Aesop's fable of the countryman who found a serpent that was to all intents and purposes dead, and carried it home in his bosom. Placed by the hearth, it revived and was about to strike one of his children when the farmer killed it.

some of that or any sort of black stuff on a certain day when your Grace would appoint as many Clergy men as could redyly be found, to meet at your Palace,[17] and there give your Opinions; and that your Graces Visitations approaching[18] you could then have the best opportunity of seeing what could be done in a matter of such consequence as they seemed to think to the woollen Manufacture. But instead of attending, as was expected; They came to me a fortnight after, with a new Proposal; that something should be writ by an acceptable and able hand to promote in generall the wearing of home Manufacture, and their civilityes would seem to fix that work upon me. I asked whether they had prepared the Stuffs, as they had promised, and Your Grace expected; but they had not made the least step in the matter, nor as it appears thought of it more.

I did some years ago propose to the Masters and Principall Dealers in the home Manufactures of silk and wool, that they should meet together, and after mature Consideration, publish Advertisements to the following Purpose. That in order to encourage the wearing of Irish Manufactures in silk and woollen they gave notice to the Nobility and Gentry of the Kingdom, that they the undersigned, would enter into Bonds for themselves and for each other, to sell the severall sorts of Stuffs, Cloths and Silks, made to the best perfection they were able, for certain fixed prices, and in such a manner that if a Child were sent to any of their shops, the buyer might be secure of the value and goodness, and measure of the Ware, and lest this might be thought to look like a Monopoly any other member of the Trade might be admitted upon such conditions as should be agreed on. And if any Person whatsoever should complain that he was ill used in the value or goodness of what he bought, The matter should be examined, the Person injured be fully satisfied, by the whole corporation without delay, and the Dishonest seller be struck out of the Society, unless it appeared evidently that the failure proceeded onely from Mistake.

The mortal danger is, that if these Dealers could prevail by the goodness and cheapness of their Cloths and Stuffs to give a Turn to the principal People of Ireld in favor of their goods, they would relapse into the knavish

---

17 *at your Palace*: St Sepulchre's, in what was then St Kevin Street (now Kevin Street). King had been confined to his chambers in the winter of 1728–9, on doctor's orders (O'Regan, *King*, p. 331).
18 *Visitations approaching*: King's health rallied in March 1729 and he began to make plans to hold his triennial episcopal visitation (ibid.).

practice peculiar to this Kingdom, which is apt to run through all Trades even so low as a common Ale-seller, who as soon as he gets a vogue for his Liquer, and out sells his Neighbors, thinks his Credit will put off the worst he can buy; till his Customers will come no more. Thus I have known at London in a generall mourning,[19] the Drapiers dye black all their old Damaged goods, and sell them at double rates, and then complain and petition the Court, that they are ready to starve by the continuance of the mourning.

Therefore I say, those principal weavers who would enter in such a compact as I have mentioned, must give sufficient Security against all such practices; for, if once the Women can persuade their Husbands that forein goods besides the finery will be as cheap, and do more Service, our last state will be worse than the first.

I do not here pretend to digest perfectly the method by which These principall Shop-keepers shall proceed in such a Proposal; but my meaning is clear enough; and cannot reasonably be objected against.

We have seen what a destructive Loss the Kingdom received by the detestable fraud of the Merch^{ts}, or Northern Weavers or both, notwithstanding all the care of Governors at that Board;[20] the whole trade with Spain for our Linnen, when we had an offer of commerce with the Spaniards[21] to the value as I am told of 300000^{ll}. a year. But while we deal like Pedlars, we shall practice like Pedlars; and sacrifice all honesty to the present urging advantage.

What I have said may serve as an answer to the desire made me by the Corporation of Weavers, that I would offer my notions to the publick. As to any thing further, let them apply themselves to the Parlmt in their next Session.[22] Let them prevail in the H. of Commons to grant one

19 *a generall mourning*: a period of mourning, declared by royal order, usually for the death of a sovereign or sovereign's consort, in which all persons were required to dress in black, according to specific directions issued by the lord chamberlain.
20 *the Governors at that Board*: the Linen Board, which had been established by Act of Parliament in 1711 for the promotion of the linen manufacture (see *Precedents and Abstracts from the Journals of the Trustees of the Linen and Hempen Manufactures of Ireland*, Dublin, 1784).
21 *an offer of commerce with the Spaniards*: a reference to the opportunity presented for Irish linens to be imported exclusively into Spain at the time of the plague at Marseilles in 1720 (for which, see above, p. 10).
22 *let them apply themselves to the Parlmnt in their next Session*: the Weavers' Guild had presented petitions to the Irish House of Commons in 1715 and 1723 (*C.J.Ire*. (4th edn.), vol. III, pp. 51, 349), but did not do so in the session of 1729–30.

very reasonable request: and I shall think there is still some spirit left in the Nation, when I read a vote to this Purpose; Resolved *nemine contradicente*.[23] That this House will for the future wear no cloaths but such as are made of Irish growth or of Irish manufacture, nor will permit their Wives or Children to wear any other: and that they will to the utmost endeavor to prevayl with their Friends, Relations, Dependents and Tenants to follow their Example. And if at the same time they could banish Tea & Coffee and China ware out of their Familyes, and force their wives to chat their Scandal over an Infusion of sage or other wholesom Domestick vegetables, we might possibly be able to subsist, and pay our Absentees, Pensioners, Generalls, civil officers, Appeals,[24] Colliers,[25] temporary Travellers, Students, Schoolboys, spleentick Visitors of Bath Tunbridge and Epsom,[26] with all other smaller Drayns, by sending our crude unwrought goods to England, and receiving from thence and all other Countryes nothing but what is fully manufactured, and keep a few Potatoes and Oatmeal for our own subsistence.

I have been for a dozen years past wisely prognosticating the present condition of this Kingdom which every human creature of common sense could fortell with as little sagacity as my self. My meaning is that a Consumptive body must needs dye which hath spent all its spirits and received no nourishment; yet I am often tempted to pity when I hear the poor farmer and Cottager lamenting the hardness of the times, and imputing them either to one or two ill Seasons, which better Clymats than ours are more exposed to or to the scarcity of Silver which to a Nation of Liberty would be onely a sleight and temporary inconveniency to be removed at a months warning.

---

23 *nemine contradicente*: 'with nobody contradicting'; used in the parliamentary record for an unopposed decision.
24 *Appeals*: the cost of appeals in legal cases taken to the House of Lords at Westminster, whose appellate jurisdiction had been confirmed by the British Declaratory Act of 1720 (6 Geo. I c. 5).
25 *Colliers*: dealers in coal. According to Thomas Prior, because coal was imported into Ireland from north-west England and the south-west of Scotland, Irish consumers were at the mercy of traders who were able to push up the price, which resulted in the drainage of silver from the kingdom (Prior, *Absentees*, pp. 74–5).
26 *Bath Tunbridge and Epsom*: three of the most notable spa towns in England.

AN ANSWER TO SEVERAL LETTERS FROM UNKNOWN PERSONS

Headnote

Composed April–May 1729; published 1765; copy text SwJ 390 (see Textual Account).

One of the four unpublished pieces on contemporary Irish problems composed in the spring of 1729, *An Answer to Several Letters from Unknown Persons* was apparently written in April or May 1729 in response to a letter on the Irish economy from 'Andrew Trueman' and 'Patrick Layfield' (published in the *Dublin Weekly Journal* for 7 June 1729, sometime after it was sent to Swift; see below, Appendix E, pp. 365–74). *Intelligencer*, no. 19 is an earlier response to another letter, not extant, but presumed to be from the same source (see above, p. 74).

The *Answer to Several Letters from Unknown Persons* is chiefly concerned with the factors holding Ireland back from free participation in a modern economy: these include restrictions on trade, and limited access to preferments, jobs or careers for even the most talented, enlightened and ambitious of its inhabitants. Swift also bemoans that so much of Ireland's possible revenue money is sent overseas, in the form of remittances to absentee landlords and office-holders. In passing, he also criticises Presbyterians, and defends the church and the (perennially unpopular) institution of tithes. Underlying his arguments is a wider refutation of those who make projections for the improvement of Ireland based on the wealth of its natural resources, as this ignores the constitutional limitations which burden the state, and prevent the possibility of amelioration.

ANSWER TO SEVERAL LETTERS FROM UNKNOWN PERSONS

Gentlemen,

I am inclined to think that I received a Letter from you two last Summer, directed to Dublin, while I was in the Country,[1] whither it was sent me, and I ordered an answ[er] to it to be printed, but it seems [it] had little effect, and I suppose this will have not much more. But, the heart of this People is waxed gross, and their Ears are dull of hearing, and their eyes they have closed.[2] And, Gentlemen, I am to tell you another thing: that the world is so regardless of what we write for the publick good, that after we have delivered our thoughts, without any prospect of advantage, or of Reputation, which latter is not to be had but by subscribing our nam[es] we cannot prevayl upon a Printer to be at the charge of sending it into the World unless we will be at all or half the expence; And although we are willing enough to bestow our labors, we think it unreasonable to be out of pocket; because it probably may not consist with the Scituation of o[ur] Affairs.

I do very much approve your good intentions, and in a great measure your manner of declaring them, and I do imagine you intended that the world should not onely know your Sentiments, but my Answer, which I shall impartially give.

That great Prelate[3] in whose cover you directed your Letter sent it to me this morning, and I begin my answer to night, not knowing what Interruption I may meet with.

I have orderd your Letter to be printed as it ought to be, along with my answer,[4] because I conceive it will be more acceptable and informing to the Kingdom.

---

1 *while I was in the Country*: Swift stayed at the house of Sir Arthur Acheson at Markethill, Co. Armagh, between June 1728 and February 1729.
2 *and their eyes they have closed*: Matthew, 13: 15: 'For this people's heart is waxed gross, and their ears are dull of hearing, and their eyes they have closed'. This is in turn a reference back to Isaiah, 6: 10: 'Make the heart of this people fat, and make their ears heavy, and shut their eyes.'
3 *That great Prelate*: Archbishop King of Dublin, who would die on 8 May 1729.
4 *I have orderd... along with my answer*: *A Letter from a Gentleman in the North of Ireland, to a Person in an Eminent Post under His Majesty, Concerning the Transportation of Great Numbers from that Part of the Kingdom to America*, Dublin, 1729.

I shall therefore now go on to answer your Letter in all manner of Sincerity.

Although your letter be directed to me, yet I take my self to be onely an imaginary[5] Person; for although I conjecture I had formerly one from you, yet I never answered it otherwise than in print; Neither was I at a loss to know the Reasons why so many People of this Kingdom were transporting themselves to America. And, if this Encouragement were owing to a Pamphlet written, giving an account of the Country of Pensilvania, to tempt People to go thither,[6] I do declare that those who were tempted by such a Narrative to such a Journey, were fools, and the Author a most impudent Knave; at least, if it be the same Pamphlet I saw when it first came out, which is above 25 years ago, dedicated to Will Pen[7] (whom by a mistake you call Sr Willm Pen) and styling him by authority of the Scripture, Most noble Governor.[8] For, I was very wel acquainted with Pen, and did some years after talk with him upon that Pamphlet,[9] and the Impudence of the Author, who spoke so many things in Praise of the Soyl and Clymat, which Pen himself did absolutely contradict. For he did assure me that his Country wanted the shelter of mountains, which left it open to the Northern winds from Hudson's bay and the frozen sea,[10] which destroyed all Plantations of Trees, and was even pernicious to all common Vegetables. But indeed, New York, Virginia, and other parts less Northward; or more defended by Mountains, are described as excellent Countryes but, upon what Conditions of advantage, Foreigners go thither, I am yet to seek.

What Evils do our People avoyd by running from hence, is easyer to be determined. They conceive themselves to live under the Tyranny of

---

5 *imaginary*: representative.
6 *a Pamphlet... to tempt People to go thither*: Gabriel Thomas, *An Historical and Geographical Account of the Province and Country of Pensilvania; and of the West-New-Jersey in America*, London, 1698.
7 *Will Pen*: William Penn (1644–1718), the Quaker leader: founder, proprietor and first governor of Pennsylvania.
8 *by authority of the Scripture, Most noble Governor*: in his dedication, Thomas had addressed Penn as 'Most Noble and Excellent Governor', which Swift relates to the mode of address adopted by the tribune Claudius Lysias, commander of the garrison at Jerusalem, to Felix, the procurator at Caesarea, in Acts 23: 26.
9 *talk with him upon that Pamphlet*: see *Journal to Stella*, 7 Oct. 1710 (*CWJS*, vol. IX, p. 30), for an account of a two-hour discussion between Swift and Penn, which does not, however, include any details of the subjects discussed.
10 *the frozen sea*: the Arctic Ocean.

most cruel exacting Landlords, who have no view further than encreasing their rent rolls. Secondly, you complain of the want of Trade whereof you seem not to know the reason:[11] Thirdly, you lament most justly the money spent by absentees in England. Fourthly, you complain that your Linnen Manufacture declines; Fifthly, that your Tyth-collectors[12] oppress you. Sixthly, that your Children have no hopes of Preferment in the Church, the Revenue, or the Army to which You might have added the Law, and all civill Employmts whatsoever.[13] Seventhly, you are undone for Silver, and want all other money.

I could easily add some other motives, which to men of Spirit who desire and expect and think they deserve the common Privileges of human nature, would be of more force than any you have yet named, to drive them out of this Kingdom; but as these Speculations may probably not much affect the Brains of your people, I shall chuse to let them pass unmentioned. Yet I cannot but observe, that my very good and virtuous friend his Excellency Burnet[14] (O fili nec tali indigne parente)[15] hath not hitherto been able to persuade his Vassals by his oratory in the style of a command, to settle a Revenue on his Vice-royal Person.[16] I have been likewise assured that in one of those Colonyes on the Continent which Nature hath so far favored as by the Industry of the Inhabitants to produce a great quantity of excellent Rice, the Stubbornness of the People, who having been told that the world is wide, took it into their heads that they might sell their own Rice at

11 *whereof you seem not to know the reason*: for Swift, the self-evident cause is English discriminatory legislation.
12 *Tyth-collectors*: local officials responsible for the collection of tithe, the annual levy paid to the established church for the support of the parish incumbent, equivalent to a tenth part of agricultural produce. Tithes were taken in kind, or commuted to a cash payment. Not all tithes in Ireland were paid the clergy; some (impropriate tithes) had been alienated to lay proprietors.
13 *the Law, and all civill Employmts whatsoever*: a gross exaggeration in respect of Irish Protestants generally, but nearer the mark for Ulster Presbyterians. See Patrick McNally, *Parties, Patriots and Undertakers: Parliamentary Politics in Early Hanoverian Ireland*, Dublin: Four Courts Press, 1997, ch. 5; Whan, *Presbyterians of Ulster*, pp. 125–36.
14 *his Excellency Burnet*: William Burnet (1688–1729), son of Bishop Burnet of Salisbury; governor of New York and New Jersey 1720–7, Massachusetts and New Hampshire 1727–9. See *ODNB*.
15 *fili nec tali indigne parente*: 'O son, not unworthy of such a parent!'
16 *to settle a Revenue on his Vice-royal Person*: in the year following his appointment as governor, Burnet called his first assembly in Massachusetts but encountered opposition when the assembly refused to commit itself to paying him a fixed salary. Rather than compromise, Burnet refused to accept any salary, living off the charity of friends.

whatever forein markets they pleased,[17] and seem by their practice very unwilling to quit that Opinion.

But to return to my Subject, I must confess to you both, that if one reason of your Peoples deserting us be the Despair of things growing better in their own Country, I have not one Syllable to answer because that would be to hope for what is impossible, and so I have been telling the publick these ten years. For there are three events which must precede any such blessing; First, a liberty of Trade, Secondly a Share of Preferments in all kinds to the British Natives,[18] and thirdly a return of those absentees, who take away almost one half of the Kingdoms Revenues.[19] As to the first, there is nothing left us but despair, and for the third it will never happen till the Kingdom hath no money to send them; for which in my own particular, I should not be sorry.

The exaction of Landlords hath indeed been a grievance of above twenty years standing. But as to what you object about the severe Clauses relating to Improvement,[20] the fault lyes wholly on the other side: For the

---

17 *might sell their own Rice at whatever forein markets they pleased*: rice production, on which the economy of Carolina was becoming increasingly dependent in the early eighteenth century, was inhibited by the Navigation Acts, which meant that two-thirds of the crop was exported to Britain, and the vast bulk of this re-exported, having paid English duty. From 1714, the colonial assembly of what is now South Carolina petitioned government in Whitehall to permit direct shipment to continental Europe with duty paid in the colony. Permission was eventually forthcoming by an Act of the Westminster Parliament in 1730. See J. M. Price, 'The Imperial Economy, 1700–1776', in P. J. Marshall (ed.), *The Oxford History of the British Empire*, vol. II: *The Eighteenth Century*, Oxford: Oxford University Press, 1998, p. 85.

18 *British Natives*: the use of the term 'British' for the Protestant interest in Ireland was still relatively unusual, especially for someone of Swift's ethnic background and political persuasion. It is being used here specifically to comprehend Ulster Scots as well as 'new English' since, for all Swift's detestation of Presbyterian Ulster Scots, it is their emigration that he is seeking to attribute to the inequities of English rule. See D. W. Hayton, 'Anglo-Irish Attitudes: Changing Perceptions of National Identity among the Protestant Ascendancy in Ireland, ca. 1690–1750', *Studies in Eighteenth-Century Culture* 17 (1987), 151–2; Colin Kidd, *British Identities before Nationalism: Ethnicity and Nationhood in the Atlantic World 1600–1800*, Cambridge: Cambridge University Press, 1999, pp. 250–9.

19 *absentees . . . one half of the Kingdoms Revenues*: Thomas Prior calculated that £621,499 was remitted out of the kingdom every year to absentee landowners, office-holders, pensioners, etc., though he conceded that others might raise his estimate by as much as £200,000 (*Absentees*, pp. 14, 17). He also observed that "tis reasonable to suppose, that the quantity of species, required to carry on the trade of Ireland with ease and advantage, cannot be less than a million' (pp. 18–19).

20 *the severe Clauses relating to Improvement*: the rise in popularity of the 'improvements lease' in the early eighteenth century is discussed in David Dickson, *Old World Colony: Cork and South Munster 1630–1830*, Cork: Cork University Press, 2005, pp. 182–7.

Landlords either by their Ignorance, or greedyness, of making large rent-rolls, have performed this matter so ill, as we see by experience, that there is not one Tenant in five hundred who hath made any improvement worth mentioning. For which I appeal to any Man who rides through the Kingdom where little is to be found among the Tenants but Beggary and Desolation; the Cabbins of the Scotch themselves in Ulster being as dirty and miserable as those of the wildest Irish. Whereas, good firm penal Clauses for Improvement, with a tolerable easy rent, and a reasonable Period of time would in twenty years have encreased the Rents of Ireland at least a third part in the intrinsick value.

I am glad to hear you speak with some decency of the Clergy, and to impute the exactions you lament, to the Managers or Farmers of the Tythes.[21] But you entirely mistake the Fact; for I defy the wickedest and most powerful Clergy men in the kingdom to oppress the meanest Farmer in the Parish. and I likewise defy the same Clergyman to prevent himself from being cheated by the same Farmer, whenever that Farmer shall he disposed to be knavish or peevish.[22] For although the Ulster tithing-table[23] is more advantageous to the Clergy, than any other in the Kingdom, yet the

---

21 *the Managers or Farmers of the Tythes*: tithe-farmers (also known as tithe-jobbers) purchased from the owner the right of collection, and in consequence pressed harder on payers in order to make a profit on their transactions. For complaints against tithe-farmers, especially in Ulster, see Archbishop Boulter to Bishop Gibson, 13 Mar. 1729 (*Boulter Letters*, vol. I, pp. 231–5). On tithe in Ireland in general, see Maurice Bric, 'The Tithe System in Eighteenth-Century Ireland', *Proceedings of the Royal Irish Academy* 86 (1986), sect. C, 271–88. Among Swift's contemporaries, the Whig 'patriot' Robert, Viscount Molesworth, had denounced the 'tithe-jobber' as 'commonly a litigious, worthless, wrangling fellow, a papist and a stranger' (*Some Considerations for the Promoting of Agriculture, and Employing the Poor*, Dublin, 1723, pp. 23–4).

22 *I likewise defy... knavish or peevish*: for an example of an Irish clergyman at the mercy of recalcitrant parishioners, one of whom told him to his face that 'it was no sin to cheat the parson', see William Preston (rector of Tullow, Co. Carlow) to Edward Southwell, 3 Oct. 1740, quoted in D. W. Hayton, 'Parliament and the Established Church: Reform and Reaction', in D. W. Hayton, James Kelly and John Bergin (eds.), *The Eighteenth-century Composite State: Representative Institutions in Ireland and Europe, 1689–1800*, Basingstoke: Palgrave Macmillan, 2010, p. 79.

23 *Ulster tithing-table*: in 1629, a table of monetary equivalents (or *modi*) had been established for tithes levied in Ulster. This had been confirmed in 1695. See T. C. Barnard, *Cromwellian Ireland: English Government and Reform in Ireland, 1649–1660*, Oxford: Oxford University Press, 1975, p. 154; Bric, 'Tithe System', p. 273. Although, in the long run, monetary inflation would mean that the fixed nature of the Ulster 'tithing table' worked against the interests of the clergy, this development was not yet apparent. In his pamphlet *The Nature and Tendency of Popular Phrases in General*, Dublin [?1715], p. 26, Swift's friend William Tisdall, the High Church vicar of Belfast, had cited among other

Minister can demand no more than his tenth, and where the Corn much exceeds the small Tyths, as except in some Districts, I am told, it always doth, he is at the mercy of every Stubborn Farmer, especially of those whose sect as well as interest incline them to opposition.[24] However, I take it, that your People bent for America do not shew the best part of their prudence, in making this one part of their Complaint;[25] yet, they are so far wise as not to make the Payment of Tythes a Scruple of Conscience, which is too gross for any protestant Dissenter except a Quaker[26] to pretend. But, do your people indeed think, that if Tythes were abolished, or delivered into the hands of the Landlord after the blessed increase in the Scotch spiritual Oeconomy,[27] that the Tenant would sit easyer in his Rent under the same Person who must be Lord of the Soyl and of the Tyth together.

I am ready enough to grant, that the oppression of Landlords, the utter ruin of Trade, with its necessary consequence the want of money, half the revenues of the Kingdom spent abroad, the continued Dearth of three years, and the strong delusion in your People by false allurement from America may be the chief motives of their eagerness after such an Expedition.

But, I was surprised to find, that those Calamityes whereof we are innocent have been sufficient to drive many familyes out of their country who had no reason to complain of oppressing landlords; For while I was last year in the Northern parts,[28] A Person of Quality whose Estate was let above 20 years ago, and then at a very reasonable rent, some for Leases of Lives, and some perpetuityes, did in a few months purchase eleven of those Leases at a very inconsiderable price, although they were two years

---

evil machinations of Presbyterians and their allies, 'the dangerous attempt in parliament against the tithing table of Ulster, which must have ruined the northern clergy at once'.
24 *whose sect as well as interest incline them to opposition*: Presbyterians would be opposed on principle, as well as from self-interest, to the obligation to pay tithes to support the ministry of the established church.
25 *their Complaint*: in the person of the 'modest proposer', Swift was to assert that the only motive for Presbyterians' determination to emigrate was the requirement that they pay tithes 'against their Conscience, to an *Episcopal Curate*' (below, p. 154).
26 *except a Quaker*: an allusion to the Quakers' scruple of conscience in refusing to take oaths.
27 *Scotch spiritual Oeconomy*: under Scottish law, teinds (the Scottish equivalent of tithes) had been converted to a fixed burden on land, which could be redeemed or purchased by the landowner. Already before the Reformation, the process had begun by which teinds had been alienated to the laity. After the Reformation, those remaining in the hands of the church, or of bishops, were confiscated, and many granted out to laymen. The Teinds Act passed by the Scottish Parliament in 1690 gave power to commissioners to establish a stipend for a minister from the teinds appertaining to his parish.
28 *while I was last year in the Northern parts*: at Markethill, Co. Armagh (see above, p. 110).

ago reckoned to pay but half value. From whence it is manifest, that our present miserable condition and the dismal prospect of worse, with other reasons above assigned are sufficient to put men upon trying this desperate experiment of changing the scene they are in although Landlords should by a miracle become less inhuman.

There is hardly a Scheme proposed for improving the trade of this Kingdom, which doth not manifestly shew the Stupidity and ignorance of the Proposer, and I laugh with contempt at those weak wise heads, who proceed upon general Maxims, or advise us to follow the Examples of Holland and England.[29] These Empiricks talk by rote, without understanding the Constitution of the Kingdom; as if a Physician knowing that Exercise contributed much to health should prescribe to his Patient under a severe fit of the gout, to walk ten miles every morning. The Directions for Ireland are very short and plain, to encourage agriculture and home-consumption, and utterly discard all Importations which are not absolutely necessary for health or Life. And how few necessityes, conveniencyes or even comforts of Life are denyed us by Nature, or not to be attaind by Labor and Industry; Are those detestable Extravagancies of Flanders Lace, English Cloth of our own wooll,[30] and other Goods, Italian or Indian Silks, Tea, Coffee, Chocolate, China-ware and that profusion of Wines, by the Knavery of Merchants[31] growing dearer every Season, with a hundred unnecessary Fopperyes better know^n to others than me; Are these I say fit for us, any more than for the beggar who could not eat his Veal with out Oranges.[32]

---

29 *those weak wise heads... the Examples of Holland and England*: for example, John Browne, *Seasonable Remarks on Trade with Some Reflections on the Advantages that Might Accrue to Great Britain by a Proper Regulation of the Trade of Ireland*, Dublin, 1728, pp. 3–6, 16–17, 23, 27–36, 63; Browne, *An Essay on Trade in General; and, on That of Ireland in Particular*, Dublin, 1728, pp. 89–90ff.; David Bindon, *A Scheme for Supplying Industrious Men with Money to Carry on their Trades, and for Better Providing for the Poor of Ireland*, Dublin, [1729], pp. 6–9, 11–12, 20–1.

30 *English Cloth of our own wooll*: one effect of the English Woollen Act of 1699 was to confine exports of Irish wool to the English market, to serve as the raw material for English cloth manufacture.

31 *Merchants*: wholesale traders, especially those involved in overseas trade.

32 *the beggar who could not eat his Veal with out Oranges*: cf. Swift's 'Verses made for Women who cry Apples, &c', imitating a Dublin street-seller's cry: 'Come, buy my fine oranges, sauce for your veal' (*Poems*, vol. III, p. 953). Swift himself had a fondness for oranges (Paul V. Thompson and Dorothy Jay Thompson (eds.), *The Account Books of Jonathan Swift*, London: Scolar Press, 1984, p. lxxxii), and Lord Orrery complimented him on the preserved oranges served at the deanery table (Orrery to Swift, [Mar. 1740]: Woolley, *Corr.*, vol. IV, p. 610).

Is it not the highest Indignity to human nature that men should be such poltrons as to suffer the Kingdom and themselves to be undone, by the Vanity, the Folly; the Pride, and Wantonness of their Wives, who under their present Corruptions seem to be a kind of animal suffered for our sins to be sent into the world for the Destruction of Familyes, Societyes and Kingdoms, and whose whole study seems directed to be as expensive as they possibly can in every useless article of living, who by long practice can reconcile the most pernicious forein Drugs to their health and pleasure, provided they are but expensive; as Starlings grow fat with henbane,[33] who contract a Robustness by meer practice of Sloth and Luxury: Who can play deep severall hours after midnight, sleep beyond noon, revel upon Indian poisons,[34] and spend the revenue of a moderate family to adorn a nauseous unwholesom living Carcase. Let those few who are not concerned in any part of this accusation, suppose it unsaid; let the rest take it among them. Gracious God in his mercy look down upon a Nation so shamefully besotted.

If I am possessed of an hundred pounds a year, and by some misfortune it sinks to fifty, without a possibility of ever being retrieved; Does it remain a question in such an exigency, what I am to do; Must not I retrench one half in every article of expence? or retire to some cheap distant part of the Country where necessaryes are at half value?

Is there any mortal who can shew me under the Circumstances we stand with our neighbors, under their Inclinations towards us, under Laws never to be repealed, under the Desolation caused by absentees, under many other circumstances not to be mentioned, that this Kingdom can ever be a Nation of Trade, or subsist by any other method than that of a reduced family by the utmost parsimony; in the manner I have already prescribed.

I am tired with Letters from many unreasonable well-meaning People, who are daily pressing me to deliver my Thoughts in this deplorable

---

33 *as Starlings grow fat with henbane*: Richard Mead, A *Mechanical Account of Poisons in Several Essays*, 3rd edn, Dublin, 1729, p. 60, noted that 'noxious plants do vary their Effects in different Creatures, so as to prove harmless, nay, perhaps beneficial and nutritive to some, as Hemlock they say is to Goats and Starlings, and Henbane to Hogs'. Mead's authority for the beneficial effect of hemlock on starlings was Galen.

34 *Indian poisons*: Swift is almost certainly referring to the fashion for tea-drinking, whose supposed deleterious effects on health were a subject of increasing concern. *The Second Part of Whipping-Tom: or, A Rod for a Proud Lady...*, London, [1722], included on pp. 9–20 a 'discourse' entitled 'Melancholy considerations of the universal poison, or the dismal effects of tea', which described tea as 'this Indian drug' (p. 18).

Juncture, which upon many others I have so often done in vain. What will it import that half a score people in a Coffee-house may happen to read this paper, and even the Majority of those few differ in every sentiment from me. If the Farmer be not allowed to sow his Corn, If half the little money among us be sent to pay rents to Irish absentees, and the rest for forreign Luxury and Dress for the women, what will our charitable Dispositions avayl when there is nothing left to be given, when contrary to all custom and example all necessaryes of Life are so exorbitant, when money of all kinds was never known to be so scarce. So that Gentlemen of no contemptible Estates are forced to retrench in every article, (except what relates to their wives) without being able to shew any bounty to the Poor.

AN ANSWER TO SEVERAL LETTERS SENT ME FROM UNKNOWN HANDS

Headnote

Composed 1729; published posthumously, 1765; copy text *1765a* (see Textual Account); the footnotes that form part of this text were provided by the editor, Deane Swift.

The unfinished *Answer to Several Letters Sent Me from Unknown Hands* is one of the four pieces from 1729 on Irish economic questions not published in Swift's lifetime. It is notionally addressed to correspondents who had sent Swift their schemes and projections, but who have never been identified.

Although unpublished, the rhetoric of the paper moves beyond its original recipients, and reads as though intended for an audience of members of Parliament, in its listing of projects to improve Ireland: these include the construction of roads, the managing of bogland, reforestation, the spread of tillage, and the grant of an Irish mint. Of these, two, the improvement of bogland and the extension of tillage, were incorporated in the so-called 'Navigation Bill' of 1729–30 (see D. W. Hayton, 'Patriots and Legislators: Irishmen and their Parliaments, c. 1689 – c. 1740', in Julian Hoppit (ed.), *Parliaments, Nations and Identities in Britain and Ireland, 1660–1860*, Manchester: Manchester University Press, 2003, p. 116). One proposal noted by Swift – the abolition of the Irish language – did not form part of the public discussion.

AN ANSWER TO SEVERAL LETTERS SENT ME FROM UNKNOWN HANDS. WRITTEN IN THE YEAR M DCC XXIX.

I am very well pleased with the good opinion you express of me, and wish it were any way in my power to answer your expectations, for the service of my country. I have carefully read your several schemes and proposals, which you think should be offered to the parliament. In answer, I will assure you, that, in another place, I have known very good proposals rejected with contempt by public assemblies, merely because they were offered from without doors; and yours perhaps might have the same fate, especially if handed into the public by me, who am not acquainted with three members, nor have the least interest with one. My printers have been twice prosecuted, to my great expence,[1] on account of discourses I writ for the public service, without the least reflection on parties or persons; and the success I had in those of the Drapier was not owing to my abilities, but to a lucky juncture, when the fuel was ready for the first hand that would be at the pains of kindling it. It is true both those envenomed prosecutions were the workmanship of a judge, who is now gone to his own place.*,[2] But, let that be as it will, I am determined henceforth never to be the instrument of leaving an innocent man at the mercy of that bench.

It is certain, there are several particulars relating to this kingdom (I have mentioned a few of them in one of my Drapier's letters)[3] which it were heartily to be wished that the Parliament would take under their consideration, such as will nowise interfere with England, otherwise than to its advantage.

The first I shall mention is touched at in a letter which I received from one of you, Gentlemen, about the highways; which, indeed, are almost every where scandalously neglected. I know a very rich man in this city, a true lover and saver of his money, who, being possessed of some adjacent lands, hath been at great charge in repairing effectually the roads that lead

---

* Lord Chief-Justice Whitshed.

1 *My printers... to my great expence*: Edward Waters in 1720 and John Harding in 1724: see above, p. 15.

2 William Whitshed (1679–1727), chief justice of king's bench [Ire.] 1714–27 and common pleas [Ire.], 1727–d. – for whom, see above, pp. 18–19.

3 *one of my Drapier's letters*: in the *Letter to the Whole People of Ireland* (Davis, vol. X, p. 60).

to them; and hath assured me, that his lands are thereby advanced four or five shillings an acre, by which he gets treble interest. But, generally speaking, all over the kingdom, the roads are deplorable; and, what is more particularly barbarous, there is no sort of provision made for travellers on foot; no, not near this city, except in a very few places, and in a most wretched manner: Whereas the English are so particularly careful in this point, that you may travel there an hundred miles with less inconvenience than one mile here, But, since this may be thought too great a reformation, I shall only speak of roads for horses, carriages, and cattle.

Ireland is, I think, computed to be one third smaller than England; yet, by some natural disadvantages, it would not bear quite the same proportion in value, with the same encouragement. However, it hath so happened, for many years past, that it never arrived to above one eleventh part in point of riches; and, of late, by the continual decrease of trade and increase of absentees, with other circumstances not here to be mentioned, hardly to a fifteenth part; at least, if my calculations be right, which I doubt are a little too favourable on our side.

Now, supposing day-labour to be cheaper by one half here than in England, and our roads, by the nature of our carriages and the desolation of our country, to be not worn and beaten above one eighth part so much as those of England, which is a very moderate computation; I do not see why the mending of them would be a greater burthen to this kingdom than to that.

There have been, I believe, twenty acts of parliament, in six or seven years of the late King*, for mending long tracts of impassable ways in several counties of England, by erecting turnpikes,[4] and receiving passage-money in a manner that every body knows. If what I have advanced be true, it would be hard to give a reason against the same practice here, since the necessity is as great, the advantage in proportion perhaps much greater, the materials of stone and gravel as easy to be found, and the workmanship

* King George I.

4 *twenty acts of parliament... erecting turnpikes*: the Westminster Parliament passed 15 Turnpike Acts between 1720 and 1725, a further 14 in 1726, and 120 in 1727: William Albert, *The Turnpike Road System in England, 1663–1840*, Cambridge: Cambridge University Press, 1972, pp. 202–3. No Turnpike Acts were passed by the Irish Parliament under George I. Two were passed in the session of 1729–30 (3 Geo. II cc. 18, 19) (David Broderick, *The First Toll Roads: Ireland's Turnpike Roads 1729–1858*, Cork: Collins Press, 2002, pp. 34–9).

at least twice as cheap. Besides, the work may be done gradually, with allowances for the poverty of the nation, by so many perch[5] a year; but with a special care to encourage skill and diligence, and to prevent fraud in the undertakers, to which we are too liable, and which are not always confined to those of the meaner sort: But against these, no doubt, the wisdom of the nation may, and will provide.

Another evil, which, in my opinion, deserves the public care, is the ill management of the bogs,[6] the neglect whereof is a much greater mischief to this kingdom than most people seem to be aware of.

It is allowed indeed, by those who are esteemed most skilful in such matters, that the red swelling mossy bog, whereof we have so many large tracts in this island, is not by any means to be fully reduced; but the skirts, which are covered with a green coat, easily may, being not an accretion, or annual growth of moss, like the other. Now the landlords are generally too careless that they suffer their tenants to cut their turf in these skirts, as well as the bog adjoined, whereby there is yearly lost a considerable quantity of land throughout the kingdom, never to be recovered.

But this is not the greatest part of the mischief. For the main bog, although perhaps not reducible to natural soil, yet, by continuing large, deep, straight canals through the middle, cleaned at proper times, as low as the channel or gravel, would become a secure summer-pasture; the margins might, with great profit and ornament, be filled with quickins,[7] birch, and other trees proper for such a soil, and the canals be convenient for water-carriage of the turf, which is now drawn upon sled-cars with great expence, difficulty, and loss of time, by reason of the many turf-pits

---

5 *perch*: a standard measurement of length, 16 and a half feet in England, but 21 feet in Ireland, in both cases deriving its name from a stick (also known as a lug, rod or pole) by which land was measured.

6 *the ill management of the bogs*: a subject of general concern. See, for example, Samuel Peirson, *Farther Considerations for the Improvement of the Tillage in Ireland...*, Dublin, 1728; John Browne, *The Benefits Which Arise to a Trading People from Navigable Rivers. To which Are Added, Some Considerations on the Origin of Loughs, and Bogs...*, Dublin, 1729 (a copy of which Swift owned (*Library and Reading, I*, vol. I, p. 292)); George Rye, *Considerations on Agriculture...*, Dublin, 1730. The Navigation Bill introduced into the Irish Parliament in the session of 1729–30, and subsequently enacted as 3 Geo. II c. 3, included a provision for the more effectual putting into execution of a previous Act of 1716, to encourage the draining and improving of bogland (2 Geo. I c. 12), and for this reason was sometimes referred to as the 'Bog Bill' (Lord Carteret to Edward Southwell, 28 Jan. 1729/30 (BL, Southwell papers, Add. MS 38016, fo. 21)).

7 *quickins*: quicken: the mountain-ash or rowan.

scattered irregularly through the bog, wherein great numbers of cattle are yearly drowned. And it hath been, I confess, to me a matter of the greatest vexation as well as wonder, to think how any landlord could be so absurd as to suffer such havock to be made.

All the acts for encouraging plantations of forest-trees are, I am told, extremely defective;[8] which, with great submission, must have been owing to a defect of skill in the contrivers of them. In this climate, by the continual blowing of the West-south-west wind, hardly any tree of value will come to perfection that is not planted in groves, except very rarely, and where there is much land-shelter. I have not, indeed, read all the acts; but, from enquiry, I cannot learn that the planting in groves is enjoined. And, as to the effects of these laws, I have not seen the least, in many hundred miles riding, except about a very few gentlemens houses, and even those with very little skill or success. In all the rest, the hedges generally miscarry, as well as the larger slender twigs planted upon the tops of ditches, merely for want of common skill and care.

I do not believe that a greater and quicker profit could be made, than by planting large groves of ash, a few feet asunder, which in seven years would make the best kind of hop-poles,[9] and grow in the same, or less time, to a second crop from their roots.

It would likewise be of great use and beauty in our desert scenes, to oblige all tenants and cottagers to plant ash or elm before their cabbins, and round their potatoe-gardens, where cattle either do not, or ought not to come to destroy them.

The common objections against all this, drawn from the laziness, the perverseness, or thievish disposition of the poor native Irish, might be easily answered, by shewing the true reasons for such accusations, and how easily those people may be brought to a less savage manner of life: But my printers have already suffered too much for my speculations. However, supposing the size of a native's understanding just equal to that of a dog or horse, I have often seen those two animals to be civilized by rewards, at least as much as by punishments.

---

8 *All the acts ... extremely defective*: the Acts of 1699 (10 Will. III c. 12 [Ire.]), 1705 (4 Anne c. 9 [Ire.]), 1710 (9 Anne c. 5 [Ire.]) and 1722 (8 Geo. I c. 8 [Ire.]).
9 *hop-poles*: tall poles on which hop-plants were trained.

It would be a noble atchievement to abolish the Irish language in this kingdom,[10] so far at least as to oblige all the natives to speak only English on every occasion of business, in shops, markets, fairs, and other places of dealing: Yet I am wholly deceived if this might not be effectually done in less than half an age, and at a very trifling expence; for such I look upon a tax to be, of only six thousand pounds a year, to accomplish so great a work. This would, in a great measure, civilize the most barbarous among them, reconcile them to our customs and manner of living, and reduce great numbers to the national religion,[11] whatever kind may then happen to be established. The method is plain and simple; and, although I am too desponding to produce it, yet I could heartily wish some public thoughts were employed to reduce this uncultivated people from that idle, savage, beastly, thievish manner of life, in which they continue sunk to a degree,

---

10 *It would be a noble atchievement to abolish the Irish language in this kingdom*: since the reign of Queen Anne, Church of Ireland clergy and laymen had been divided over the most appropriate means of evangelising the native Catholics, whether by appointing ministers to preach to them in their native tongue, or by offering free schooling in English, which would combine basic literacy and numeracy with instruction in religion: D. W. Hayton, 'Did Protestantism Fail in Early Eighteenth-century Ireland? Charity Schools and the Enterprise of Religious and Social Reformation, c. 1690–1730', in Alan Ford, James McGuire and Kenneth Milne (eds.), *As by Law Established: The Church of Ireland since the Reformation*, Dublin: Lilliput Press, 1995, pp. 170–5. During proceedings in the Irish convocation in 1711, High Churchmen had declared it imperative that the Irish language be abolished (*Records of Convocation*, ed. Gerald Bray, 20 vols., Woodbridge: Boydell Press, 2005–6, vol. XVII, pp. 392, 413). Swift's attitude to, and knowledge of, the Irish language, has been much discussed. He may well have had 'kitchen Irish', enabling him, for example, to order food and drink where necessary from monoglot Irish speakers, and was on friendly terms with Anthony Raymond, vicar of Trim and a scholar of the Irish language, who may have assisted him in the preparation of the poem 'The description of an Irish feast', which was itself based on a translation from a Gaelic poem (Andrew Carpenter and Alan Harrison, 'Swift's "O'Rourke's Feast" and Sheridan's "Letter": Early Transcripts by Anthony Raymond', *Münster*, 1985, pp. 27–46; Alan Harrison, *The Dean's Friend: Anthony Raymond (1675–1726), Jonathan Swift and the Irish Language*, Dublin: Éamonn de Burca, 1999). In *On Barbarous Denominations in Ireland* (*CWJS*, vol. II, pp. 247–8), Swift commented, 'I am deceived, if any thing hath more contributed to prevent the Irish from being tamed, than this encouragement of their language, which might easily be abolished, and become a dead one in half an age, with little expence, and less trouble.'
11 *the national religion*: the established church (Church of Ireland). A phrase used by Swift elsewhere, in *The Sentiments of a Church of England Man with Respect to Religion and Government* (1708) (Davis, vol. II, p. 7); *Letter from a Member of the House of Commons in Ireland to a Member of the House of Commons in England, Concerning the Sacramental Test* (1708) (ibid., p. 121); and *The Advantages Proposed by Repealing the Sacramental Test, Impartially Considered* (1733) (ibid., vol. XII, p. 244).

that it is almost impossible for a country gentleman to find a servant of human capacity,[12] or the least tincture of natural honesty; or who does not live among his own tenants in continual fear of having his plantations destroyed, his cattle stolen, and his goods pilfered.

The love, affection, or vanity of living in England, continuing to carry thither so many wealthy families, the consequences thereof, together with the utter loss of all trade, except what is detrimental, which hath forced such great numbers of weavers and others to seek their bread in foreign countries, the unhappy practice of stocking such vast quantities of land with sheep and other cattle, which reduceth twenty families to one:[13] These events, I say, have exceedingly depopulated this kingdom for several years past. I should heartily wish, therefore, under this miserable dearth of money, that those who are most concerned would think it adviseable to save a hundred thousand pounds a year, which is now sent out of this kingdom to feed us with corn. There is not an older or more uncontroverted maxim in the politics of all wise nations, than that of encouraging agriculture. And, therefore, to what kind of wisdom a practice so directly contrary among us may be reduced, I am by no means a judge. If labour and people make the true riches of a nation, what must be the issue where one part of the people are forced away, and the other part have nothing to do?

If it should be thought proper by wiser heads, that his Majesty might be applied to in a national way, for giving the kingdom leave to coin halfpence for its own use; I believe no good subject will be under the least apprehension that such a request could meet with refusal, or the least delay. Perhaps we are the only kingdom upon earth, or that ever was or will be upon earth, which did not enjoy that common right of civil society, under the proper inspection of its prince, or legislature, to coin money of all usual metals for its own occasions. Every petty prince in Germany, vassal to the Emperor, enjoys this privilege.[14] And I have seen in this kingdom several

12 *to find a servant of human capacity*: in his *Sermon on the Causes of the Wretched Condition of Ireland* (Davis, vol. IX, pp. 203–4), Swift dilated upon the dishonesty (and especially the propensity to theft) of the native Irish in general, and native Irish servants in particular.
13 *the unhappy practice . . . which reduceth twenty families to one*: see above, pp. 30–1.
14 *Every petty prince . . . enjoys this privilege*: repeating, almost verbatim, a point made in *A Short View of the State of Ireland* (see above, p. 21).

silver pieces, with the inscription of *Civitas Waterford, Droghedagh,* and other towns.¹⁵

15 *Civitas Waterford, Droghedagh, and other towns*: the term 'civitas' was used to designate a city-state or a commonwealth. Coins were struck at Drogheda for Edward IV and Richard III; and at Waterford for John, Edward I, Edward IV, Richard III, Henry VII and Lambert Simnel. In the autumn of 1727, Swift had been asked by the Earl of Oxford to find some 'old Irish coins' for Oxford's collection, but had been unable to do so. The following May he wrote again: 'I have not heard of any coin in this kingdom before the conquest under Henry 2d. Those since are of no value or curiosity, not above three or four hundred years old, with the names of the cities, as Civitas Waterford, Civitas Dublin, Civitas Drogheda &c.': Swift to Oxford, 11 May 1728 (Woolley, *Corr.*, vol. III, p. 138).

A LETTER ON M'CULLA'S PROJECT ABOUT HALFPENCE, AND A NEW ONE PROPOSED

Headnote

Composed spring 1729; published posthumously, 1762; copy text SwJ 433 & *1765* (see Textual Account).

The *Letter on M'culla* was an unfinished response to James Maculla's attempt to reverse the scarcity of coins in his *A New Scheme Proposed, to the People of Ireland* (1728) and to his privately trying to gain Swift's approval for the project. The ongoing problem of Irish coinage was also tackled by Thomas Prior in 1730 (*Observations on Coin in General. With some Proposals for Regulating the Value of Coin in Ireland*). The general movement in economic thought at this time was towards an acceptance of paper currency (see James Kelly, 'Jonathan Swift and the Irish Economy in the 1720s', *ECI* 6 (1991), 7–36; Patrick Kelly, '"Conclusions by no Means Calculated for the Circumstances and Condition of Ireland": Swift, Berkeley and the Solution to Ireland's Economic Problems', in Aileen Douglas *et al.* (eds.), *Locating Swift: Essays from Dublin on the 250th Anniversary of the Death of Jonathan Swift, 1667–1745*, Dublin: Four Courts Press, 1998, pp. 47–59). Maculla was moving towards this principle, but his interim solution was the (unduly complicated) offering of promissory notes on copper; Swift (for whom the absence of an Irish mint was a prime concern) was anyway suspicious of the idea of paper currency and was unsympathetic towards the thinking behind such proposals. In the case of Maculla, the impracticality of the scheme allowed him to dismiss such projects, and to indulge in some political arithmetic of his own.

Swift's objection to the workings of the scheme, and latent suspicion of the motives behind it meant that when Maculla's plan did not succeed, the need to finish and publish the pamphlet apparently passed, after its initial composition (usually placed in spring 1729). It was first published in 1762, by George Faulkner, and reprinted three years later by Deane Swift in a text with significant differences, complicated further by an extant partial manuscript.

ON M'CULLA'S PROJECT

S^r,

You desire to know my opinion concerning M^r. M'cullas Project, of circulat^{ing} notes stampd on copper,[1] that shall pass for the value of half-pence and Pence. I have some knowledge of the Man; and about a Month ago he brought me his Book, with a Couple of his halfpenny notes, but I was then out of order, and he could not be admitted.[2] Since that time, I called at his house; where I discoursed, the whole affair with him as thorowly as I could. I am altogether a stranger to his Character. He talked to me in the usuall Style, with a great Profession of zeal for the publick good,[3] which is the common cant of all Projectors in their Bills, from a First Minister of State down to a Corn-cutter.[4] But, I stopped him short, as I would have done a better man, because it is too gross a pretence to pass at any time, and especially in this age, where we all know one another so well. Yet, whoever proposeth any Scheam which may prove to be a publick Benefit, I shall not quarrell if it prove likewise very beneficiall to the Contriver. It is certain that next to the want of silver, our greatest distress in point of coyn is the want of small change, which may be some poor Relief for the Defect of the former, since the Crown will not please to take that work upon them here as they do in England. One thing in M^r. M'culla's book is certainly right, that no law hinders me from giving a payable note upon leather, wood, Copper, Brass, Iron, or any other material (except gold and silver) as well as upon Paper.[5] The question is, whether I can

---

1 *Mr. M'cullas... circulating notes stampd on copper*: James Maculla, *A New Scheme Proposed, to the People of Ireland; for Increasing the Cash, of this Kingdom; by Making Promissary Notes of Copper, to Bear an Intrinsick Value to the British-half-pence...*, Dublin, 1728.
2 *I have some knowledge... could not be admitted*: Maculla was a Dublin 'brazier' who had previously issued copper trade tokens (Rogers Ruding, *Annals of the Coinage of Britain and Its Dependencies...*, 4 vols., London, 1817–19, vol. II, p. 460).
3 *zeal for the publick good*: presented by Maculla as his principal motive: see, e.g., *A New Scheme Proposed*, p. 2; Maculla, *A Coinage, or Mint, Proposed...*, Dublin, 1728, pp. 1, 10–11.
4 *a Corn-cutter*: a chiropodist: regarded as one of the meanest type of surgical practitioners. In Robert Manning, *England's Conversion and Reformation Compared...*, Antwerp, 1725, p. 192, a character, commenting on Henry VIII's having made Thomas Cromwell, the son of a blacksmith, his viceregent-general, says 'I should as soon have guessed that he had made a corn-cutter his prime minister of state.'
5 *One thing in M^r. M'culla's book... as upon Paper*: see Maculla, *A New Scheme Proposed*, p. 9: 'Promissary notes on copper, according to the litteral words of the said acts of parliament,

sue him on a Copper bond when there is neither his hand nor seal, nor Witnesses to prove it. To supply this, he hath proposed, that the Materials upon which his note is written shall be in some degree of value equal to the Debt. But, that is one principall matter to be enquired into. His Scheam is this.

He gives you a piece of Copper for a halfpenny or Penny, Stampt with a promissory note to pay you twenty Pence for every pound of the s^d Copper notes whenever you shall return them; eight and fourty of the halfpenny pieces are to weigh a pound, and he sells you that pound coyned and Stamped for two Shillings, by which he clearly gains a little more than 16 p. cent, that is to say, two pence in every Shilling.

This will certainly arise to a great Sum, if he should circulate as large a quantity of his notes as the kingdom, under the great dearth of silver, may very probably require: Enough indeed to make any Irish tradesman's fortune; which, however, I should not repine at in the least, if we could be sure of his fair dealing. It was obvious for me to raise the common objection, why Mr. M'culla would not give security to pay the whole sum to any man who returned him his copper notes, as my Lord Dartmouth and Colonel Moor were by their patents obliged to do.[6] To which he gave me some answers plausible enough. First, he conceived that his coins were much nearer to the intrinsic value than any of those coined by patents, the bulk and goodness of the metal equalling the best English halfpence made by the Crown. That he apprehended the ill-will of envious and designing people, who, if they found him to have a great vent for his notes, since he wanted the protection of a patent, might make a run upon him which he could not be able to support. And, lastly, that his copper, as is already said, being equal in value and bulk to the English halfpence, he did not apprehend they should ever be returned, unless a combination, proceeding from spite and envy, might be formed against him.

---

may be as lawfully made as any paper note, may be drawn, and within these statutes promissary notes of leather, past-board, parchment, steel, iron, tin, copper, or any thing else may be made and circulated, the said acts being silent as to what such notes may be made of as aforesaid, therefore every man is at his liberty to make his notes of what he pleases'.
6 *Lord Dartmouth and Colonel Moor... obliged to do*: a patent was issued on 18 May 1680 to Sir Thomas Armstrong and Colonel William Legge (later 1st Earl of Dartmouth), to coin copper halfpence for Ireland for 21 years. This patent was sold on to John Knox, then to Colonel Roger Moore, who oversupplied Ireland, resulting in a devaluation of the coin. His application in 1705 for a renewal of the patent was refused.

But there are some points in his proposal which I cannot well answer for, nor do I know whether he will be able to do it himself. The first is, whether the copper he gives us will be as good as what the Crown provided for the English halfpence and farthings?[7] And, secondly, whether he will always continue to give us as good? And, thirdly, when he will think fit to stop his hand; and give us no more? For I should be as sorry to be at the mercy of Mr. M'culla, as of Mr. Wood.

There is another difficulty of the last importance. It is known enough that the Crown is supposed to be neither gainer nor loser by the coinage of any metal: For they subtract, or ought to subtract no more from the intrinsic value than what will just pay the charges of the mint; and how much that will amount to is the question. By what I could gather from Mr. M'culla, good copper is worth fourteen pence *per* pound. By this computation, if he sells his copper notes for two shillings the pound, and will pay twenty pence back, then the expence of coinage for one pound of copper must be six pence, which is 30 *per cent*. The world should be particularly satisfied on this article, before he vends his notes: For the discount of 30 *per cent*. is prodigious, and vastly more than I can conceive it ought to be. For, if we add to that proportion the 16 *per cent*. which he avows to keep for his own profit, there will be a discount of about 46 *per cent*. Or, to reckon I think a fairer way; whoever buys a pound of Mr. M'culla's coin, at two shillings *per* pound, carries home only the real value of fourteen pence, which is a pound of copper; and thus he is a loser of 41*l*. 13 *s*. 4 *d. per cent*. But, however, this high discount of 30 *per cent*. will be no objection against M'culla's proposal; because, if the charge of coinage will honestly amount to so much, and we suppose his copper notes may be returned upon him, he will be the greater sufferer of the two; because the buyer can lose but four pence in a pound, and M'culla must lose sixpence, which was the charge of the coinage.

Upon the whole, there are some points which must be settled to the general satisfaction, before we can safely take Mr. M'culla's copper notes for value received; and how he will give that satisfaction, is not within my knowledge or conjecture. The first point is, That we shall be always sure of receiving good copper, equal in bulk and fineness to the best English halfpence.

---

7 *the English halfpence and farthings*: the copper halfpence and farthings produced by the Staffordshire ironmaster William Wood (1671–1730), under a royal patent issued in 1722, stigmatised as 'Wood's Halfpence' and denounced by Swift in the *Drapier's Letters*.

The second point is, to know what allowance he makes to himself, either out of the weight or mixture of his copper, or both, for the charge of coinage. As to the weight, the matter is easy by his own scheme: For, as I have said before, he proposes forty-eight to weigh a pound, which he gives you for two shillings, and receives it by the pound at twenty pence: So that, supposing pure copper to be fourteen pence a pound, he makes you pay 30 *per cent.* for the labour of coining, as I have already observed, besides *16 per cent.* when he sells it. But, if to this he adds any alloy, to debase the metal, although it be not above 10 *per cent.* then Mr. M'culla's promissory notes will, to the intrinsic value of the metal, be above 47 *per cent.* discount.

For, subtracting 10 *per cent.* off 60*l.* worth of copper, it will (to avoid fractions) be about five and a half *per cent.* in the whole 100*l.* which, added to

$$
\begin{array}{r}
41\ 13\ 4 \\
5\ 10\ 0 \\
\hline
\end{array}
$$

will be *per cent.*   47   3 4

That we are under great distress for change, and that Mr. M'culla's copper notes, on supposition of the metal being pure, is less liable to objection than the project of Wood, may be granted; but such a discount, where we are not sure even of our twenty pence a pound, appears hitherto a dead weight on his scheme.

Since I writ this, calling to mind that I had some copper halfpence by me, I weighed them with those of Mr. M'culla, and observed as follows.

First, I weighed Mr. M'culla's halfpenny against an English one of King Charles II. which outweighed Mr. M'culla's a fourth part, or 25 *per cent.*

I likewise weighed an Irish Patrick and David halfpenny,[8] which outweighed Mr. M'culla's 12½ *per cent.* It had a very fair and deep impression, and milled very skilfully round.

---

8 *an Irish Patrick and David halfpenny*: the copper halfpenny coinage minted in the reign of Charles II for use in Ireland, with St Patrick on the obverse and, on the reverse, a kneeling king, supposedly King David, playing the harp and gazing at the crown of England. See William Frazer, 'On the Irish "St. Patrick" or "Floreat Rex" Coinage...', *Journal of the Royal Society of Antiquaries of Ireland* 5 (1895), 338–47; Michael Sharp, 'The St Patrick Coinage of Charles II', *British Numismatic Journal* 68 (1998), 160. According to Swift's *Some Observations upon the Report of the Committee of... the Privy Council in England Relating to Woods Halfpence* (1724), 'the small St. Patrick's coin... passeth now for a Farthing' (Davis, vol. X, p. 33).

I found that even a common Harp halfpenny,[9] well preserved, weighed equal to Mr. M'culla's. And even some of Wood's halfpence were near equal in weight to his. Therefore, if it be true that he does not think Wood's copper to have been faulty, he may probably give us no better.

I have laid these loose thoughts together with little order, to give you, and others who may read them, an opportunity of digesting them better. I am no enemy to Mr. M'culla's project, but I would have it put upon a better foot. I own that this halfpenny of King Charles II. which I weighed against Mr M'culla's, was of the fairest kind I had seen. However, it is plain the Crown could afford it without being a loser. But it is probable, that the officers of the mint were then more honest than they have since thought fit to be; for I confess not to have met those of any other year so weighty, or in appearance of so good metal, among all the copper coins of the three last reigns; yet these, however, did much outweigh those of Mr. M'culla; for I have tried the experiment on a hundred of them. I have indeed seen accidentally one or two very light, but it must certainly have been done by chance, or rather, I suppose them to be counterfeits. Be that as it will, it is allowed on all hands, that good copper was never known to be cheaper than it is at present. I am ignorant of the price, further than by his informing me that it is only fourteen pence a pound; by which I observe he charges the coinage at 30 *per cent*. And therefore I cannot but think his demands are exorbitant. But, to say the truth, the dearness or cheapness of the metal do not properly enter into the question. What we desire is, that it should be of the best kind, and as weighty as can be afforded; that the profit of the contriver should be reduced from 16 to 8 *per cent*. and the charge of coinage, if possible, from 30 to 10, or 15 at most.

Mr. M'culla must also give good security that he will coin only a determinate sum, not exceeding twenty thousand pounds; by which, although he should deal with all uprightness imaginable, and make his coin as good as that I weighed of King Charles II.; he will, at 16 *per cent*. gain three thousand two hundred pounds: A very good additional job[10] to a private tradesman's fortune.

---

9 *a common Harp halfpenny*: following the minting of an Irish coinage for Henry VIII with a harp on the reverse, Irish coinage in the sixteenth and seventeenth centuries was known colloquially as 'harp coinage'.

10 *job*: private interest or advantage (*OED*).

I must advise him also to employ better workmen, and make his impressions deeper and plainer, by which a rising rim may be left about the edge of his coin, to preserve the letter from wearing out too soon. He hath no wardens nor masters, or other officers of the mint to suck up his profit;[11] and, therefore, can afford to coin cheaper than the Crown, if he will but find good materials, proper implements and skilful workmen.

Whether this project will succeed in Mr. M'culla's hands, (which, if it be honestly executed, I should be glad to see;) one thing I am confident of, that it might be easily brought to perfection by a society of nine or ten honest gentlemen of fortune, who wish well to their country, and would be content to be neither gainers nor losers, further than the bare interest of their money. And Mr. M'culla, as being the first starter of the scheme, might be considered and rewarded by such a society; whereof, although I am not a man of fortune, I should think it an honour and happiness to be one, even with borrowed money upon the best security I could give. And, first, I am confident, without any skill but by general reason, that the charge of coining copper would be very much less than 30 *per cent*. Secondly, I believe ten thousand pounds, in halfpence and farthings, would be sufficient for the whole kingdom, even under our great and most *unnecessary distress* for the want of silver; and that, without such a distress, half the sum would suffice.

For I compute and reason thus: The city of Dublin, by a gross computation, contains ten thousand families;[12] and, I am told by shopkeepers, that, if silver were as plenty as usual, two shillings in copper would be sufficient, in the course of business, for each family; but, in consideration of the want of silver, I would allow five shillings to each family, which would amount to 2,500*l*.; and, to help this, I would recommend a currency of all the genuine undefaced harp-halfpence, which are left of Lord Dartmouth's and Moor's patents under King Charles II.; and the small Patrick

---

11 *no wardens... to suck up his profit*: Sir Isaac Newton, who had given his official opinion in favour of the quality of Wood's Halfpence (Ehrenpreis, vol. III, pp. 220–1, 232) had been warden of the Mint 1696–1700 and then master from 1700 until his death in 1727.

12 *The city of Dublin... contains ten thousand families*: various contemporary computations were possible, using the revenue commissioner John South's survey published by the Royal Society, returns for the hearth tax, and other data: see Patrick Fagan, 'The Population of Dublin in the Eighteenth Century with Particular Reference to the Proportions of Protestants and Catholics', *ECI* 6 (1991), 121–56. Dobbs, *Essay*, pt 2, p. 8, estimated the number of inhabited houses in the capital at 11,086, based on hearth tax returns.

and David for farthings. To the rest of the kingdom, I would assign the 7,500*l*. remaining; reckoning Dublin to answer one fourth of the kingdom, as London is judged to answer (if I mistake not) one third of England;[13] I mean in the view of money only.

To compute our want of small change by the number of souls in the kingdom, besides being perplexed, is, I think, by no means just. These have been reckoned at a million and a half,[14] whereof a million at least are beggars, in all circumstances except that of wandring about for alms, and that circumstance may arrive soon enough, when it will be time to add another ten thousand pounds in copper. But, without doubt, the families of Ireland, who lie chiefly under the difficulties of wanting small change, cannot be above forty or fifty thousand; which the sum of ten thousand pounds, with the addition of the fairest old halfpence, would tolerably supply. For, if we give too great a loose[15] to any projector to pour in upon us what he pleases, the kingdom will be (how shall I express it under our present circumstances?) more than undone.

And hence appears, in a very strong light, the villany of Wood, who proposed the coinage of one hundred and eighty thousand pounds in copper, for the use of Ireland; whereby every family in the kingdom would be loaden with ten or a dozen shillings, although Wood might not transgress the bounds of his patent, and although no counterfeits, either at home or abroad, were added to the number; the contrary to both which would indubitably have arrived. So ill-informed are great men on the other side, who talk of a million with as little ceremony as we do of half a crown.

But, to return to the proposal I have made: Suppose ten gentlemen, lovers of their country, should raise 200*l*. apiece; and, from the time the

13 *reckoning Dublin . . . one third of England*: Charles Davenant, *An Essay upon the Probable Methods of Making a People Gainers in the Ballance of Trade*, London, 1699, p. 22, using data from the herald and pioneer demographer Gregory King, had estimated the population in the City of London and the area covered by 'the bills of mortality' at 530,000, out of a total population of 5.5 million.

14 *reckoned at a million and a half*: Swift had used the same estimate in the Drapier's *Letter to Mr. Harding . . .* (Davis, vol. X, p. 16), and was to do so again in *A Modest Proposal* (see below, p. 129). This was, in fact, some way short of the norm among contemporary commentators, which was nearer to 2 million. The way in which he may have arrived at this dubious statistic is discussed at length in C. D. Lein, 'Jonathan Swift and the Population of Ireland', *Eighteenth-Century Studies* 8 (1975), 431–53.

15 *give too great a loose*: to 'give a loose to' someone was 'to allow . . . unrestrained freedom or laxity' (*OED*).

money is deposited as they shall agree, should begin to charge it with seven *per cent.* for their own use: That they should as soon as possible provide a mint and good workmen, and buy copper sufficient for coining two thousand pounds, subtracting a fifth part of the interest of ten thousand pounds for the charges of the tools, and fitting up a place for a mint; the other four parts of the same interest to be subtracted equally out of the four remaining coinages of 2000*l.* each, with a just allowance for other necessary incidents. Let the charge of coinage be fairly reckoned, and the kingdom informed of it, as well as of the price of copper. Let the coin be as well and deeply stamped as it ought. Let the metal be as pure as can consist to have it rightly coined, (wherein I am wholly ignorant) and the bulk as large as that of King Charles II. And let this club of ten gentlemen give their joint security to receive all the coins they issue out for seven or ten years, and return gold and silver without any defalcation.[16]

Let the same club or company, when they have issued out the first two thousand pounds, go on the second year, if they find a demand, and that their scheme hath answered to their own intention as well as to the satisfaction of the public. And, if they find 7 *per cent.* not sufficient, let them subtract 8, beyond which I would not have them go. And, when they have, in two years, coined ten thousand pounds, let them give public notice that they will proceed no farther, but shut up their mint, and dismiss their workmen: Unless the real, universal, unsolicited declaration of the nobility and gentry of the kingdom, shall signify a desire that they should go on for a certain sum farther. This company may enter into certain regulations among themselves, one of which should be, to keep nothing concealed, and duly to give an account to the world of their whole methods of acting.

Give me leave to compute, wholly at random, what charge the kingdom will be at, by the loss of intrinsic value in the coinage of 10,000*l.* in copper, under the management of such a society of gentlemen.

First, it is plain that, instead of somewhat more than 16 *per cent.* as demanded by Mr. M'culla, this society desires but 8 *per cent.*

Secondly, Whereas Mr. M'culla charges the expence of coinage at 30 *per cent.* I hope and believe this society will be able to perform it at 10.

16 *without any defalcation*: without any deductions being made.

Thirdly, Whereas it doth not appear that Mr. M'culla can give any security for the goodness of his copper, because not one in ten thousand have the skill to distinguish; the society will be all engaged that theirs shall be of the best standard.

Fourthly, That, whereas Mr. M'culla's halfpence are one fourth part lighter than that kind coined in the time of King Charles II. these gentlemen will oblige themselves to the public, to give the coin of the same weight and goodness with those halfpence, unless they shall find they cannot afford it; and, in that case, they shall beforehand inform the public, shew their reasons, and signify how large they can make them without being losers; and so give over or pursue their scheme, as they find the opinion of the world to be. However, I do not doubt but they can afford them as large, and of as good metal, as the best English halfpence that have been coined in the three last reigns, which very much outweigh those of Mr. M'culla. And this advantage will arise in proportion, by lessening the charge of coinage from 30 *per cent.* to 10 or 15, or 20 at most. But I confess myself in the dark on that article; only I think it impossible it should amount to any proportion near 30 *per cent.* otherwise the coiners of those counterfeit halfpence, called *Raps*,[17] would have little encouragement to follow their trade.

But the indubitable advantages by having the management in such a society would be, the paying 8 *per cent.* instead of 16, the being sure of the goodness and just weight of the coin, and the period to be put to any further coinage than what was absolutely necessary to supply the wants and desires of the kingdom. And all this under the security of ten gentlemen of credit and fortune, who would be ready to give the best security and satisfaction, that they had no design to turn the scheme into a job.

As to any mistakes I have made in computation, they are of little moment; and I shall not descend so low as to justify them against any caviller.

The strongest objection against what I offer, and which perhaps may make it appear visionary,[18] is the difficulty to find half a score gentlemen,

---

17 *Raps*: coins of little value; Maculla, *A Coinage, or Mint, Proposed*, p. 8, refers to 'the vast quantity of raps in this kingdom, and the inconceivable loss the nation sustains, and the miseries of the poor by means thereof'.

18 *visionary*: incapable of being carried out.

who, out of a public spirit, will be at the trouble, for no more profit than one *per cent*. above the legal interest, to be overseers of a mint for five years; and perhaps, without any justice, raise the clamour of the people against them. Besides, it is most certain that many a squire is as fond of a job, and as dextrous to make the best of it, as Mr. M'culla himself, or any of his level. However, I do not doubt but there may be ten such persons in this town, if they had only some visible mark to know them at sight. Yet I just foresee another inconveniency: That knavish men are fitter to deal with others of their own denomination; while those who are honest and best intentioned, may be the instruments of as much mischief to the public, for want of cunning, as the greatest knaves; and more, because of the charitable opinion which they are apt to have of others. Therefore, how to join the prudence of the serpent with the innocency of the dove[19] in this affair, is the most difficult point. It is not so hard to find an honest man, as to make this honest man active, and vigilant, and skilful; which I doubt will require a spur of profit greater than my scheme will afford him, unless he will be contented with the honour of serving his country, and the reward of a good conscience.

After reviewing what I had written, I see very well that I have not given any allowance for the first charge of preparing all things necessary for coining, which, I am told, will amount to about 200*l*. besides 20*l*. *per annum* for five years rent of a house to work in. I can only say, that this making in all 300*l*. it will be an addition of no more than 3 *per cent* out of 10,000*l*.

But the great advantages to the public, by having the coinage placed in the hands of ten gentlemen, such as I have already described, (if such are to be found) are these:

First, They propose no other gain to themselves than 1 *per cent*. above the legal interest for the money they advance; which will hardly afford them coffee when they meet at their mint-house.

---

[19] *how to join the prudence of the serpent with the innocency of the dove*: a reference to the passage in Matthew, 10: 16, when Jesus sent out the twelve apostles to the 'lost sheep of the house of Israel': 'Behold, I send you forth as sheep in the midst of wolves: be ye therefore wise as serpents, and harmless as doves.' Swift made much of it in his sermon 'On False Witness' (Davis, vol. IX, p. 185).

Secondly, They bind themselves to make their coins of as good copper as the best English halfpence, and as well coined, and of equal weight: And do likewise bind themselves to charge the public with not one farthing for the expence of coinage, more than it shall really stand them in.

Thirdly, They will, for a limited term of seven or ten years, as shall be thought proper upon mature consideration, pay gold and silver, without any defalcation, for all their own coin that shall be returned upon their hands.

Fourthly, They will take care that the coins shall have a deep impression, leaving a rising rim on both sides, to prevent their being defaced in a long time; and the edges shall be milled.

I suppose they need not be very apprehensive of counterfeits, which will be difficult to make so as not to be discovered: For it is plain that those bad halfpence, called *Raps*, are so easily distinguished, even from the most worn genuine halfpenny, that nobody will now take them for a farthing, although under the great present want of change.

I shall here subjoin some computations relating to Mr. M'culla's copper notes. They were sent to me by a person well skilled in such calculations, and therefore I refer them to the reader.

Mr. M'culla charges good copper at fourteen pence *per* pound, but I know not whether he means Avoirdupois[20] or Troy weight.[21]

Avoirdupois is 16 ounces to a pound,	6960 grains.
A pound Troy weight	5760 grains.
Mr. M'culla's copper is fourteen pence *per* pound avoirdupois.	
Two of M'culla's penny-notes, one with another weigh	524 grains.
By which computation, 2*s*. of his notes, which he sells for 1lb. weight, will weigh	6288 grains.
But 1 lb. avoirdupois weighs, as above, - - - - -	6960 grains.
	672

---

20 *Avoirdupois*: a standard system of measuring the weight of all goods except precious metals, precious stones and medicines.
21 *Troy weight*: a standard system of measuring the weight of precious metals and precious stones.

This difference makes 10 *per cent.* to Mr. M'culla's profit, in point of weight.

The old Patrick and David halfpenny weighs	149 grains.
Mr. M'culla's halfpenny weighs	131 grains.
The difference is	18.
Which is equal to 10½ *per cent.*	
The English halfpenny of King Charles II. weighs	167 grains.
M'culla's halfpenny weighs – – – – – – – – –	131 grains.
The difference – – – – – – – – –	36
Which difference allowed a fifth part is 20 *per cent.*	

Another Computation.

Mr. M'culla allows his pound of copper (coinage included) to be worth twenty pence, for which he demands two shillings.

His coinage he computes at six pence *per* pound weight; therefore, he laying out only twenty pence, and gaining four pence. he makes *per cent.* profit.	20
The six pence *per* pound weight, allowed for coinage, makes *per cent.*	30
The want of weight in his halfpenny, compared as above, is *per cent.*	10
By all which, (*viz.* coinage, profit, and want of weight) the public loses *per cent.*	60

If Mr. M'culla's coins will not pass, and he refuses to receive them back, the owner cannot sell them at above twelve-pence *per* pound weight; whereby, with the defect of weight of 10 *per cent.* he will lose 60 *per cent.*

The scheme of the society, raised as high as it can possibly be, will be only thus:

For interest of their money, *per cent.*	8
For coinage, instead of 10, suppose, at most, *per cent.*	20
For 300*l.* laid out for tools, a mint, and house-rent, charge 3 *per cent.* upon the coinage of 10,000*l.*	3
Charges in all upon interest, coinage &c. *per cent.*	31

Which, with all the advantages above mentioned of the goodness of the metal, the largeness of the coin, the deepness and fairness of the impression, the assurance of the society confining itself to such a sum as they undertake, or as the kingdom shall approve; and, lastly, their paying in gold or silver for all their coin returned upon their hands, without any defalcation, would be of mighty benefit to the kingdom; and, with a little steadiness and activity, could, I doubt not, be easily compassed.

I would not in this scheme recommend the method of promissory notes after Mr. M'culla's manner; but, as I have seen in old Irish coins, the words *Civitas Dublin* on one side, with the year of our Lord, and the Irish Harp, on the reverse.[22]

---

22 *the words Civitas Dublin... Irish Harp, on the reverse*: the Irish coinage of Edward I and Edward IV, struck at Dublin, was marked 'civitas Dublinie' or 'civitas Dublin' on the obverse, but no coin has been identified conforming precisely to Swift's description.

A MODEST PROPOSAL FOR PREVENTING THE CHILDREN OF POOR PEOPLE FROM BEING A BURTHEN TO THEIR PARENTS, OR COUNTRY; AND FOR MAKING THEM BENEFICIAL TO THE PUBLICK

Headnote

Composed 1729; published October 1729; copy text *1729a* (see Textual Account).

A Modest Proposal has become Swift's most famous pamphlet satire, but also reflects the general direction of Swift's Irish prose writings in the years 1728–9 in its depiction of the present state of Ireland, and the impossibility of its being improved, without some fundamental reappraisal of the Anglo-Irish constitutional relationship (albeit a premise in the pamphlet veiled in complex and contentious layers of irony). It also reflects particular issues which were heavily discussed in 1729, particularly the emigration of Ulster Presbyterians to North America, as well as the ongoing problem of vagrancy in Dublin, and the countryside at large. Ironically perhaps, it appeared after the first good harvest in four years, which would in due course relieve some of the stress in the Irish economy. It may also be significant that it appeared at the beginning of the Parliamentary session of 1729–30, during which MPs would be considering a range of initiatives designed for Irish economic recovery.

It was published in Dublin before the end of October 1729, and quickly reprinted (in slightly different versions) in London; the edition reprinted in London in *A Libel on Dr Delany* (1730) was the first to add the qualifier '*in Ireland*' to its title. Henceforth the pamphlet was included in every significant edition of Swift's writings, from the *Miscellanies* of 1732 and the Faulkner *Works* of 1735 onwards. For further context and discussion, see Introduction, pp. lxxiv–lxxxvii.

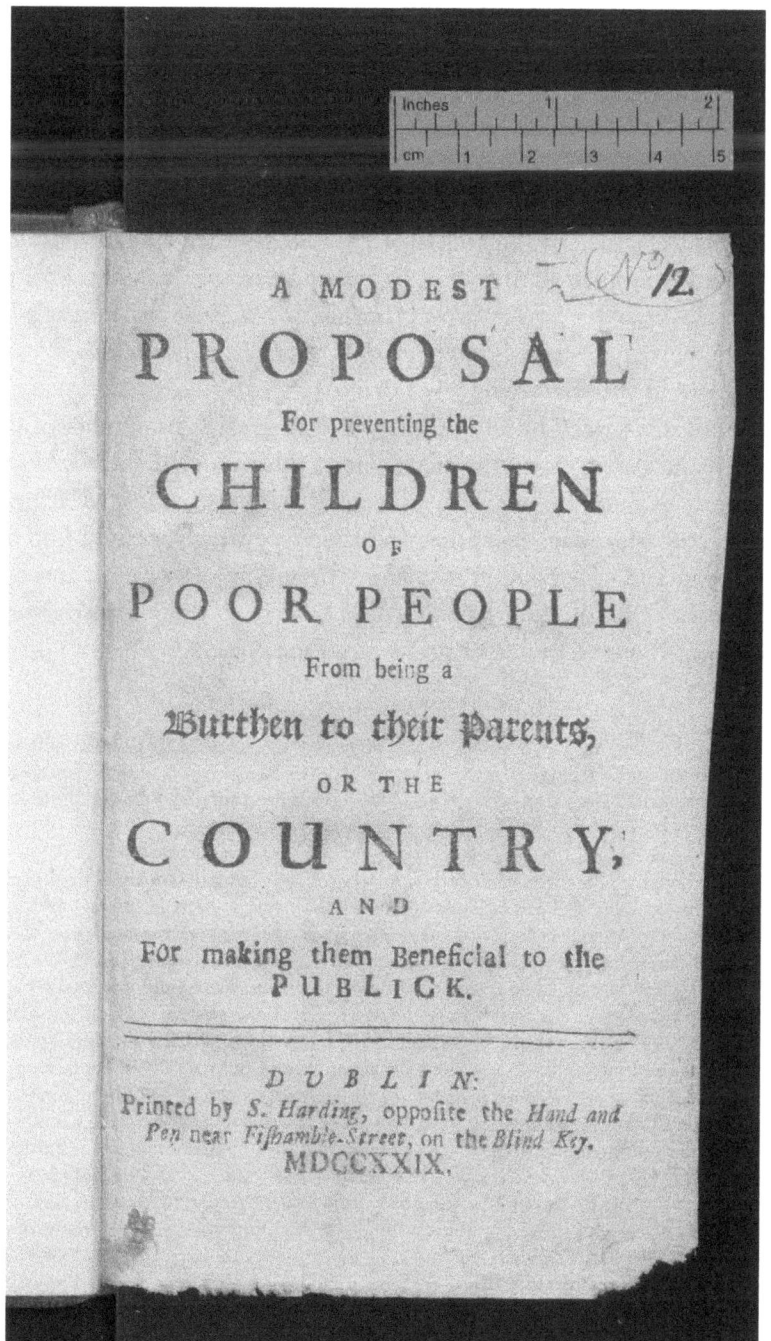

Figure 3. Jonathan Swift, *A Modest Proposal*, 1729. Title. Williams 327.

A MODEST PROPOSAL &c

It is a melancholly Object to those, who walk through this great Town, or travel in the Country, when they see the *Streets*, the *Roads*, and *Cabbin-Doors*, crowded with *Beggars* of the female Sex, followed by three, four, or six Children, *all in Rags*,[1] and importuning every Passenger[2] for an Alms. These *Mothers* instead of being able to work for their honest livelyhood, are forced to employ all their time in Stroling,[3] to beg Sustenance for their *helpless Infants*, who, as they grow up either turn *Thieves* for want of work,[4] or leave their *dear native Country*[5] *to fight for the Pretender in Spain*,[6] or sell themselves to the *Barbadoes*.[7]

I think it is agreed by all Parties, that this prodigious number of Children, in the Arms, or on the Backs, or at the *heels* of their *Mothers*, and frequently of their Fathers, is *in the present deplorable state of the Kingdom*, a very great additional grievance; and therefore whoever could find out a fair, cheap and easy method of making these Children sound and useful Members of the common-wealth would deserve so well of the publick, as to have his Statue set up for a preserver of the Nation.[8]

---

1 *all in Rags*: in the *Proposal for Giving Badges to the Beggars* (below, p. 281), Swift noted that rags were an essential part of beggars' equipment: 'their Rags are Part of their Tools with which they work'. In *A Modest Proposal* (below, p. 132) he 'compute[s] the Charge of nursing a Beggars Child' at 'about two Shillings *per Annum*, Rags Included'.
2 *Passenger*: passer-by.
3 *Stroling*: here the operative sense of the verb 'to stroll' was to roam or wander from place to place without any settled habitation, and thus a stroller was an itinerant, or vagrant.
4 *want of work*: Swift is here repeating the disdainful comments about the children of the poor, and their criminal tendencies, from *Causes of the Wretched Condition of Ireland* (Davis, vol. IX, p. 202). He was, of course, far from alone in this attitude: see above, pp. lxxxiii–lxxxiv.
5 *dear native Country*: in the voyage to Brobdingnag (*Gulliver's Travels*, pt II, ch. vi), Gulliver related 'how often I . . . wished for the tongue of Demosthenes or Cicero, that might have enabled me to celebrate the Praise of my own dear native Country' (*CWJS*, vol. XVI, p. 179).
6 *leave . . . to fight for the Pretender in Spain*: for the controversy caused in 1729 by Jacobite agents recruiting in Ireland, see L. M. Cullen, 'The Blackwater Catholics and County Cork Society and Politics in the Eighteenth Century', in Patrick Flanagan and C. G. Buttimer (eds.), *Cork: History and Society*, Dublin: Geography Publications, 1993, pp. 560–1.
7 *sell themselves to the Barbadoes*: Irish Catholics had been emigrating to Barbados and other Caribbean plantations (primarily as indentured servants) since the mid seventeenth century. See Kerby A. Miller, *Emigrants and Exiles: Ireland and the Irish Exodus to North America*, New York: Oxford University Press, 1985, pp. 139–41.
8 *to have his Statue set up for a preserver of the Nation*: Dublin city corporation had paid for the erection of statues to William III (in 1701) and George I (in 1722). Certainly in relation to the latter, Swift's observation is heavily ironical.

But my Intention is very far from being confined to provide only for the Children of *professed Beggars*, it is of a much greater extent, and shall take in the whole number of Infants at a certain Age, who are born of Parents in effect as little able to support them, as those who demand our Charity in the Streets.

As to my own part, having turned my thoughts, for many Years, upon this important Subject, and maturely weighed the several *Schemes of other Projectors*,[9] I have always found them grossly mistaken in their computation. It is true a Child, *just dropt from it's Dam*,[10] may be supported by her Milk, for a Solar year[11] with little other Nourishment, at most not above the Value of two Shillings, which the Mother may certainly get, or the Value in *Scraps*, by her lawful Occupation of begging,[12] and it is exactly at one year Old that I propose to provide for them, in such a manner, as, instead of being a Charge upon their *Parents*, or the *Parish*,[13] or *wanting Food and Raiment*[14] for the rest of their Lives, they shall, on the Contrary, contribute to the Feeding and partly to the Cloathing of many Thousands.

---

9 *the several Schemes of other Projectors*: Edward Gosnell, *Irelands Redress, from Popular Grievances Attempted; a Scheme for Employing the Poor* . . . , Dublin, 1723; Francis Hutchinson, *A Letter to a Member of Parliament, Concerning the Imploying and Providing for the Poor*, Dublin, 1723; Robert, Viscount Molesworth, *Some Considerations for the Promoting of Agriculture, and Employing the Poor*, Dublin, 1723; Sir William Fownes, *Methods Proposed for Regulating the Poor, Supporting of Some and Employing Others, According to Their Several Capacities*, Dublin, 1723–4, 1725; *Enquiries into the Principal Causes of the General Poverty of the Common People of Ireland. With Remedies Propos'd for Removing of Them*, Dublin, 1725; *Some Thoughts Concerning Government in General: and Our Present Circumstances in Great-Britain and Ireland*, Dublin, 1728; David Bindon, *A Scheme for Supplying Industrious Men with Money to Carry on Their Trades, and for Better Providing for the Poor of Ireland*, Dublin, 1729.
10 *from it's Dam*: a phrase suggesting livestock rather than humanity. The use of 'dropped' was echoed by Swift in 1737, when he told Lord Oxford that he had been 'dropped' (rather than born) in Ireland: Swift to Oxford, 14 June 1737 (Woolley, *Corr.*, vol. IV, p. 440). He had used 'dam' in a disparaging way, to refer to Lord Allen, in 'Traulus' (*Poems*, vol. III, p. 799): 'By the Dam from Lordlings sprung'.
11 *Solar year*: The time between two successive occurrences of the vernal equinox; distinct from the calendar year. Swift's ostentatious use of a precise astronomical measurement is in keeping with the pseudo-scientific nature of the proposal.
12 *her lawful Occupation of begging*: Irish statutes permitted the licensing of the impotent poor to beg within their own parishes, though Swift may also be striking a sarcastic note.
13 *a Charge upon . . . or the Parish*: money raised by the parish vestry through a levy on the inhabitants (the cess), was used to provide for poor relief: see Rowena Dudley, 'The Dublin Parishes and the Poor: 1660–1740', *Archivium Hibernicum* 53 (1999), 80–4.
14 *wanting Food and Raiment*: cf. 1 Timothy 6: 8, 'And having food and raiment, let us be therewith content'.

There is likewise another great Advantage in my Scheme, that it will prevent those *voluntary Abortions*, and that horrid practice of *Women murdering their Bastard Children*,[15] alas! too frequent among us, Sacrificing the *poor innocent Babes*,[16] I doubt, more to avoid the Expence, than the Shame, which would move Tears and Pity in the most Savage and inhuman breast. The number of Souls in this Kingdom being usually reckoned one Million and a half,[17] Of these I calculate there may be about two hundred thousand Couple whose Wives are Breeders,[18] from which number I Substract thirty Thousand Couples, who are able to maintain their own Children, although I apprehend there cannot be so many under *the present distresses of the Kingdom*,[19] but this being granted, there will remain an hundred and seventy thousand Breeders. I again Substract fifty Thousand for those Women who miscarry, or whose Children dye by accident, or disease within the Year. There only remain an hundred and twenty thousand Children of poor Parents annually born: The question therefore is, how this number shall be reared, and provided for, which, as I have already

15 *that horrid practice . . . their Bastard Children*: an Irish statute of 1707 (6 Anne c. 4 [Ire.]) made infanticide a capital offence, which seems to have inhibited juries from returning guilty verdicts where there was any ground for doubt. Nonetheless, a survey of newspaper reports in the 1720s has shown examples of convictions, all in Dublin city (James Kelly, 'Infanticide in Eighteenth-Century Ireland', *Irish Economic and Social History* 19 (1992), 5–26).

16 *poor innocent Babes*: a phrase recalling the massacre of the innocents ordered by King Herod (in Matthew, 12: 16–18). Daniel Defoe, in *Augusta Triumphans* (London, 1728), had proposed the establishment of a foundling hospital as a means of reducing the incidence of infanticide, with the argument that 'it is the height of charity and humanity, to provide against this barbarity, to prevent this crying sin, and extract good, even out of evil, by saving these innocent babes from slaughter, and bringing them up in the nurture and fear of the Lord; to be of benefit to themselves, and mankind in general' (p. 11).

17 *one Million and a half*: Swift had used this statistic in the second of the *Drapier's Letters* and in *A Letter on Mr. M'culla's Project* (above, p. 136). Other contemporary commentators, however, put the number at nearer 2 million.

18 *Breeders*: the word 'breeding' to mean reproduction (rather than in the sense of 'good breeding', in lineage or politeness), was generally confined in contemporary literature to animal husbandry. On the other hand, this usage does appear occasionally in a non-pejorative manner in the work of writers on political arithmetic: for example, in the process of attempting a calculation of the population of Ireland, Dobbs, *Essay*, pt 2, p. 11, referred to the numbers of 'breeding women' (p. 11).

19 *the present distresses of the Kingdom*: Bishop Robert Howard of Killala complained to his brother in April 1729 of conditions in Ireland: the 'universal want of money, scarcity of grain, and deadness in all trade', observing that thousands were emigrating to the West Indies, and that 'all the north [was] in motion, throwing up their leases, and some landlords forced to reduce their rents one half' (Bishop Howard to Hugh Howard, 9 Apr. 1729 (NLI, Wicklow papers, MS 38598/5)).

said, under the present Situation of Affairs, is utterly impossible by all the methods hitherto proposed, for we can *neither employ them in Handicraft*, or *Agriculture*; we neither build Houses, (I mean in the Country) nor cultivate Land? They can very seldom pick up a Livelyhood *by Stealing* till they arrive at six years Old, except where they are of towardly parts, although, I confess they learn the Rudiments much earlier, during which time, they can however be properly looked upon only as *Probationers*, as I have been informed by a principal Gentleman in the County of *Cavan*,[20] who protested to me, that he never knew above one or two Instances under the Age of six, even in a part of the Kingdom *so renowned for the quickest proficiency in that Art.*

I am assured by our Merchants, that a Boy or Girl, before twelve years Old, is no saleable Commodity, and even when they come to this Age, they will not yield above three Pounds, or three Pounds and half a Crown at most on the Exchange,[21] which cannot turn to Account either to the Parents or the Kingdom, the Charge of Nutriment and Rags having been at least four times that Value.

I shall now therefore humbly propose my own thoughts, which I hope will not be lyable to the least Objection.

I have been assured by a very knowing *American* of my acquaintance in *London*,[22] that a young healthy Child well Nursed is at a year Old a most delicious, nourishing, and wholesome Food, whether *Stewed, Roasted,*

20 *Cavan*: Swift was an occasional visitor to Thomas Sheridan at Quilca in County Cavan.
21 *Exchange*: in Jamaica at this time, an adult slave would have fetched about £25 sterling (David Richardson (ed.), *Bristol, Africa and the Eighteenth-Century Slave Trade to America*, vol. II: *The Years of Ascendancy 1730–1745*, Bristol Record Society, 39, Gloucester: Bristol Record Society, 1987, p. xxiii). Based on the accepted differential operating in the Barbados market (where an adult male slave in 1723 sold for nearly £21), this would have reduced the price for a male child to nearly £18 (D. W. Galenson, *Traders, Planters and Slaves: Market Behavior in Early English America*, Cambridge: Cambridge University Press, 1986, p. 65). In Georgia in the 1750s, the price range of an adult slave was £28–£32, and that of a child of between eight and fifteen years £10–£25 (Betty Wood, *Slavery in Colonial Georgia, 1730–1775*, Athens, GA: University of Georgia Press, 2007, p. 96).
22 *a very knowing American . . . in London*: four Iroquois chiefs had visited London during 1710 (R. P. Bond, *Queen Anne's American Kings*, Oxford: Clarendon Press, 1952). The following year, Swift confided to Esther Johnson that he had intended to write a book in the character of 'an Indian supposed to write his travels into England', but instead had passed the idea to Addison, who made use of it in the *Spectator*, to Swift's chagrin and regret: *Journal to Stella*, 28 Apr. 1711 (*CWJS*, vol. IX, p. 195); *Spectator*, vol. I, pp. 211–15. (See also the reference to the 'Iroquois Virtuosi' in *A Discourse Concerning the Mechanical Operation of the Spirit* (in *CWJS*, vol. I, p. 170.) Descriptions of cannibal practices were a feature of the travel literature relating to South American Indians, and some scholars have conjectured that the

Baked, or *Boyled*, and I make no doubt that it will equally serve in a *Fricasie*, or a *Ragoust*.[23]

I do therefore humbly offer it to *publick consideration*, that of the hundred and twenty thousand Children, already computed, twenty thousand may be reserved for Breed, whereof only one fourth part to be Males, which is more than we allow to *Sheep, black Cattle*,[24] or *Swine*, and my reason is that these Children are seldom the Fruits of Marriage, *a Circumstance not much regarded by our Savages*,[25] therefore *one Male* will be sufficient to serve *four Females*. That the remaining hundred thousand may at a year Old be offered in Sale to the *persons of Quality* and *Fortune*, through the Kingdom, always advising the Mother to let them Suck plentifully of the last Month, so as to render them Plump, and Fat for a good Table. A Child will make two Dishes at an Entertainment for Friends, and when the Family dines

---

phrase 'a very knowing American' may have been intended as a reference to the Hispanic American Garcilaso de la Vega (offspring of a Spanish father and an Inca mother), whose *Comentarios Reales*, with their accounts of the Inca practice of rearing babies for food, had been published in translation by Sir Paul Rycaut in London in 1688 (Ian Campbell Ross, '"A Very Knowing American": The Inca Garcilaso de la Vega and Swift's *A Modest Proposal*', *MLQ* 68 (2007), 493–516; Ross, 'Ottomans, Incas, and Irish Literature: Reading Rycaut', *ECI* 22 (2007), 21). Claude Rawson has suggested (*God, Gulliver and Genocide: Barbarism and the European Imagination, 1492–1945*, Oxford: Oxford University Press, 2001, p. 84) that Swift may be harking back to Montaigne's assertion of having gleaned information from an encounter with three American Indians at Rouen in 1562.

23 *a Fricasie, or a Ragoust*: fricassee and ragout: dishes in which pieces of meat are stewed and served with a sauce. Swift is suggesting that the trade in human flesh might serve the prevailing taste among the fashionable for foreign luxuries. He may also have intended a political insult at the gourmandising grandees of the Whig administration in London, among whom Sir Robert Walpole and the Duke of Newcastle both employed French cooks (Gilly Lehmann, 'The Cook as Artist?', in Harlan Walker (ed.), *Food in the Arts: Proceedings of the Oxford Symposium on Food and Cookery 1998*, Totnes: Prospect Books, 1999, pp. 127–8). Previously, Addison had implied that French cuisine exercised a debilitating effect on political virtue. In the *Tatler* 148 (21 Mar. 1710) he contrasted the salutary effects of plain English cooking with the sickliness of a French population fed with such delicacies: 'I would desire my readers to consider, what work our countrymen would have made at Blenheim and Ramillies, if they had been fed with Fricacies and Ragousts' (*Tatler*, vol. II, pp. 336–76). Swift picked up this theme in 'A Panegyrick on the Dean' (1730): 'gluttony... sent her Priests in Wooden Shoes / From haughty Gaul to make Ragous; / Instead of wholsome Bread and Cheese, / To dress their Soupes and fricassyes; / And, for our home-bred British Chear, / Botargo, catsup, and Caveer' (*Poems*, vol. III, p. 895).
24 *black Cattle*: Welsh black cattle, a native British breed, used for both beef and dairy production.
25 *Savages*: a common term of reference to the native Irish. In a letter to Pope in 1737, Swift distinguished between 'the English Gentry of this Kingdom, and the savage old Irish, (who are only the vulgar, and some gentlemen who live in the Irish parts of this Kingdom)': Swift to Pope, 23 June 1737 (Woolley, *Corr.*, vol. IV, p. 444).

alone, the fore or hind Quarter will make a reasonable Dish, and seasoned with a little Pepper or Salt will be very good Boiled on the fourth Day, especially in *Winter*.

I have reckoned upon a Medium, that a Child just born will weigh 12 pounds, and in a solar Year if tollerably nursed encreaseth to 28 Pound.[26]

I grant this food will be somewhat dear, and therefore very *proper for Landlords*, who, as they have already devoured most of the Parents, seem to have the best Title to the Children.

Infant's flesh will be in Season throughout the Year, but more plentiful in *March*, and a little before and after, for we are told by a grave Author an eminent *French* Physitian, that *Fish being a prolifick Dyet*, there are more Children born in *Roman Catholick Countries* about nine Months after *Lent*, than at any other Season,[27] therefore reckoning a Year after *Lent*, the Markets will be more glutted than usual, because the Number of *Popish Infants*, is at least three to one in this Kingdom, and therefore it will have one other Collateral advantage by lessening the Number of *Papists* among us.

I have already computed the Charge of nursing a Beggars Child (in which list I reckon all *Cottagers*, *Labourers*, and four fifths of the *Farmers*) to be about two Shillings *per Annum*, Rags included, and I believe no Gentleman would repine to give Ten Shillings for the *Carcass of a good fat Child*, which, as I have said will make four Dishes of excellent Nutritive Meat, when he hath only some particular friend, or his own Family to Dine with him. Thus the 'Squire will learn to be a good Landlord, and grow popular among his Tenants, the Mother will have Eight Shillings net profit, and be fit for Work till she produces another Child.

Those who are more thrifty (*as I must confess the Times require*) may flay the Carcass; the Skin of which, Artificially dressed, will make admirable *Gloves for Ladies*, and *Summer Boots for fine Gentlemen*.[28]

---

26 *28 Pound*: an unrealistic estimate for the average size of a new-born baby, unless Swift intended to emphasise the alien, animal, nature of the native Irish. An alternative explanation would be that he had in mind Troy weight (the system of measurement for precious stones and metals, with 12 ounces to the pound), rather than Avoirdupois. According to the standard contemporary work on obstetrics, Jane Sharp, *The Compleat Midwife's Companion*..., London, 1725, breast-feeding for a year 'is sufficient for most children' (p. 221).

27 *we are told... at any other Season*: Rabelais, *Gargantua and Pantagruel*, v, 29 (referring to the range of foods eaten in Lent, not merely fish).

28 *the Skin of which... fine Gentlemen*: Herodotus (*History*, IV, 64) had described the Scythian practices of creating garments, and covers for their quivers, from the skins of their enemies.

As to our City of *Dublin*, Shambles[29] may be appointed for this purpose, in the most convenient parts of it, and Butchers we may be assured will not be wanting, although I rather recommend buying the Children alive, and dressing them hot from the Knife, as we do *roasting Pigs.*

A very worthy Person, a *true lover of his Country*, and whose Virtues I highly esteem, was lately pleased, in discoursing on this matter, to offer a refinement upon my Scheme. He said, that many Gentlemen of this Kingdom, having of late destroyed their Deer,[30] he conceived that the want of Venison might be well supplyed by the Bodies of young Lads and Maidens, not exceeding fourteen Years of Age, nor under twelve, so great a Number of both Sexes in every County being now ready to Starve, for want of Work and Service: And these to be disposed of by their Parents if a live, or otherwise by their nearest Relations. But with due deference to so excellent a friend, and so deserving a Patriot, I cannot be altogether in his Sentiments, for as to the Males, my *American* acquaintance assured me from frequent Experience, that their flesh was generally Tough and Lean, like that of our Schoolboys, by continual exercise, and their Taste disagreeable, and to Fatten them would not answer the Charge. Then as to the Females, it would, I think with humble Submission, *be a loss to the Publick*, because they soon would become Breeders themselves: And besides it is not improbable that some scrupulous People might be apt to Censure such a Practice, (although indeed very unjustly) as a little bordering upon Cruelty, which, I confess, hath always been with me the strongest objection against any Project, however so well intended.

But in order to justify my friend, he confessed, that this expedient was put into his head by the famous *Sallmanaazor*,[31] a Native of the Island *Formosa*, who came from thence to *London*, above twenty Years ago, and

In his unpublished 'Some observations on the taxes Pay'd by Ireland to Support the Government' (1716) (TCD, Lyons (King) collection, MSS 1995–2008/1806b), Archbishop King had written, 'I cannot See how any more can be got from them [the ordinary Irish people], except we take away their potatoes and buttermilk, or flay them and Sell their Skins' (quoted in Lein, 'Swift and the Population of Ireland', p. 452).

29 *Shambles*: a place where livestock is slaughtered and meat sold.
30 *having of late destroyed their Deer*: Following the Irish Act of 1711 for the better preservation of game (11 Anne c.7), there had been six unsuccessful attempts to strengthen the law (in 1715, 1717, 1721, 1723, 1725 and 1727) but none had reached the statute book.
31 *the famous Sallmanaazor*: George Psalmanazar, the notorious impostor, whose fictitious account of what he falsely claimed to be his native country, *An Historical and Geographical Description of Formosa* (1704), had created a sensation on its publication in London, and among other things described how each year 18,000 boys would be sacrificed to the gods,

in Conversation told my friend, that in his Country when any young Person happened to be put to Death, the Executioner sold the Carcass to *Persons of Quality*, as a prime Dainty, and that, in his Time, the Body of a plump Girl of fifteen, who was crucifyed for an attempt to Poison the Emperor, was sold to his Imperial *Majesty's prime Minister of State*, and other great *Mandarins* of the Court, *in Joints from the Gibbet*, at four hundred Crowns. Neither indeed can I deny, that if the same use were made of several plump young Girls in this Town, who, without one single Groat[32] to their Fortunes, cannot stir abroad without a Chair,[33] and appear at the *Play-House*,[34] and *Assemblies*[35] in Foreign fineries, which they never will Pay for; the Kingdom would not be the worse.

Some Persons of a desponding Spirit are in great concern about that vast Number of poor People, who are aged, diseased, or maimed, and I have been desired to imploy my thoughts what Course may be taken, to ease the Nation of so grievous an Incumbrance. But I am not in the least pain upon that matter, because it is very well known, that they are every Day *dying*, and *rotting*, by *cold*, and *famine*, and *filth*, and *vermin*, as fast as can be reasonably expected. And as to the younger Labourers they are now in almost as hopeful a Condition. They cannot get Work, and consequently pine away for want of Nourishment, to a degree, that if at any time they are accidently hired to common Labour, they have not strength to perform it, and thus the Country and themselves are happily delivered from the Evils to come.

I have too long degressed, and therefore shall return to my subject, I think the advantages by the Proposal which I have made are obvious and many as well as of the highest importance.

and their raw hearts eaten by the people. Swift's sometime adversary Sir John Browne used the pseudonym Sallmanazor Histrum (Browne, *The Lucubrations of Sallmanazor Histrum, esq....*, Dublin [1730]).
32 *Groat*: fourpence.
33 *Chair*: a sedan chair.
34 *the Play-House*: the Theatre Royal in Smock Alley was at this time the only theatre in Dublin, though there were two music rooms, Mr Johnston's Room, in Dame Street, and Madam Violante's Booth, in Fownes Court: T. W. Moody and W. E. Vaughan (eds.), *A New History of Ireland*, vol. IV: *Eighteenth-Century Ireland 1691–1800*, Oxford: Clarendon Press, 1986, p. 627. 'Persons of quality and ... ladies and gentlemen of the highest rank' occupied the boxes in the Theatre Royal; 'citizens' wives and daughters' were to be found in the 'middle gallery' (*The Tricks of the Town Laid Open*, Dublin, n.d., quoted in Patrick Fagan, *The Second City: Portrait of Dublin 1700–1760*, Dublin: Branar, 1986, p. 68).
35 *Assemblies*: fashionable social gatherings.

For first, as I have already observed, it would greatly lessen the *Number of Papists*, with whom we are Yearly over-run, being the principal Breeders of the Nation,[36] as well as our most dangerous Enemies, and who stay at home on purpose with a design *to deliver the Kingdom to the Pretender*, hoping to take their Advantage by the absence *of so many good Protestants*, who have chosen rather to leave their Country, than stay at home, and pay Tythes against their Conscience, to an *Episcopal Curate*.[37]

Secondly, the poorer Tenants will have something valuable of their own, which by Law may be made lyable to Distress,[38] and help to pay their Landlord's Rent, their Corn and Cattle being already seazed, and *Money a thing unknown*.[39]

Thirdly, Whereas the Maintenance of an hundred thousand Children, from two Years old, and upwards, cannot be computed at less than Ten Shillings a piece *per Annum*, the Nation's stock will be thereby encreased fifty thousand pounds *per Annum*, besides the profit of a new Dish, introduced to the Tables of all *Gentlemen of Fortune* in the Kingdom, who have any refinement in Taste, and the Money will circulate among our selves, the Goods being entirely of our own Growth and Manufacture.

36 *Breeders of the Nation*: For contemporary concerns about the relative numbers of Catholics and Protestants in Ireland, see above, p. lix.
37 *the absence of . . . Curate*: in March 1729, it was reported that Presbyterian ministers in Ulster had been encouraging emigration by denouncing the oppressiveness of rents and tithes, and promising their congregations 'freedom from bondage' in the New World, while the 'Irish gentlemen in London are for throwing the whole occasion of this desertion on the severity of tithes': Ezekiel Stewart to Michael Ward, 25 Mar. 1729 (John Stevenson, *Two Centuries of Life in Down, 1600–1800*, Belfast: Linenhall Press, 1920, pp. 237–8); Archbishop Boulter to the Duke of Newcastle, 13 Mar. 1728[/9] (*Boulter Letters*, vol. I, pp. 231–5). The issue was raised in the Irish House of Commons in October 1729 by Colonel Alexander Montgomery, MP for Co. Donegal (Marmaduke Coghill to Edward Southwell, 23 Oct. 1729 (*Coghill Letters*, pp. 74–5)). Richard Holmes has drawn attention to this passage in order to support a suggestion that Swift may have had the Presbyterian writer James Arbuckle in mind when creating the character of the proposer ('Swift's Modest Proposer and Shaftesbury', in Brian Griffin and Ellen McWilliams (eds.), *Irish Studies in Britain: New Perspectives on History and Literature*, Newcastle: Cambridge Scholars Publishing, 2010, pp. 33–46).
38 *Distress*: the legal process (also known as distraint) by which property is seized for payment of money owed; thus the children of the poor are seen as a species of goods.
39 *Money a thing unknown*: for evidence of the general scarcity of coin in Ireland at this time, and especially silver, see Francis Annesley to Archbishop King, 15 June 1727 (TCD, Lyons collection, MS 1995–2008/2163); Archbishop Boulter to Lord Carteret, 11, 15 July 1728 (*Boulter Letters*, vol. I, pp. 198–200, 201); Bishop Robert Howard to Hugh Howard, 2 Nov. 1728 (NLI, Wicklow papers, MSS 38598/4), 9 Apr. 1729, 27 Nov. 1730 (ibid., MS 38598/5).

Fourthly, The constant Breeders, besides the gain of Eight Shillings ster. *per Annum*, by the Sale of their Children, will be rid of the Charge of maintaining them after the first Year.

Fifthly, this food would likewise bring great *Custom to Taverns*, where the Vintners will certainly be so prudent as to procure the best receipts for dressing it to perfection, and consequently have their Houses frequented by all the *fine Gentlemen*, who justly value themselves upon their knowledge in good Eating, and a skillful Cook, who understands how to oblige his Guests will contrive to make it as expensive as they please.

Sixthly, This would be a great Inducement to Marriage, which all wise Nations have either encouraged by Rewards, or enforced by Laws and Penalties. It would encrease the care and tenderness of Mothers towards their Children, when they were sure of a Settlement for Life, to the poor Babes, provided in some sort by the Publick to their Annual profit instead of Expence, we should soon see an honest Emulation among the married Women, *which of them could bring the fattest Child to the Market*, Men would become as fond of their *Wives*, during the Time of their Pregnancy, as they are now of their *Mares* in Foal, their *Cows* in Calf, or *Sows* when they are ready to Farrow, nor offer to Beat or Kick them (as it is too frequent a practice) for fear of a Miscarriage.

Many other advantages might be enumerated: For Instance, the addition of some thousand Carcases in our exportation of Barreled Beef. The Propagation of *Swines Flesh*, and Improvement in the Art of making good *Bacon*, so much wanted among us by the great destruction of *Pigs*, too frequent at our Tables, which are no way comparable in Taste, or Magnificence to a well grown, fat Yearling Child, which Roasted whole will make a considerable Figure at a *Lord Mayor's Feast*,[40] or any other Publick Entertainment. But this, and many others I omit being studious of Brevity.

Supposing that one thousand Families in this City, would be constant Customers for Infants Flesh, besides others who might have it at *Merrymeetings*,[41] particularly *Weddings* and *Christenings*, I compute that *Dublin*

---

40 *a Lord Mayor's Feast*: held annually in September to celebrate the swearing in of the new lord mayor of Dublin. From time to time Swift was invited to attend (in 1735, for example, for which see Ehrenpreis, vol. III, pp. 821–2). In *The Intelligencer*, no. 14, Sheridan depicted a group of 'clay images... stalking and staring at one another, but intirely insensible of what they were doing... like the latter end of a Lord-Mayor's Feast' (Woolley, *Intelligencer*, p. 165).

41 *Merry-meetings*: convivial gatherings.

would take off Annually about twenty thousand Carcases, and the rest of the Kingdom (where probably they will be Sold somewhat Cheaper) the remaining eighty thousand.

I can think of no one Objection, that will possibly be raised against this Proposal, unless it should be urged that the Number of People will thereby be much lessened in the Kingdom. This I freely own, and was indeed one Principal design in offering it to the World. I desire the Reader will observe, that I Calculate my Remedy *for this one individual Kingdom of IRELAND, and for no other that ever was, is, or, I think, ever can be upon Earth.*[42] Therefore let no Man talk to me of other Expedients:[43] *Of taxing our Absentees at five Shillings a pound*:[44] *Of using neither Cloaths, nor household Furniture, except what is of our own Growth and Manufacture*: *Of utterly rejecting the Materials and Instruments that promote Foreign Luxury*: *Of curing the Expenciveness of Pride, Vanity, Idleness, and Gaming in our Women*: *Of introducing a Vein of Parcimony, Prudence and Temperance*: *Of learning to Love our Country, wherein we differ even from LAPLANDERS,*[45] *and the Inhabitants of TOPINAMBOO*:[46] *Of quitting our Animosities, and*

---

42 *Earth*: the notion of Ireland's singularity was a prominent theme in Swift's writing, and manifest, for example, in this volume in the *Short View of the State of Ireland*, and *Maxims Controlled in Ireland*.

43 *Expedients*: those proposed by Swift at various times, including, in this volume in the *Short View of the State of Ireland*, and the *Proposal that All the Ladies and Women of Ireland Should Appear Constantly in Irish Manufactures*.

44 *taxing our Absentees at five Shillings a pound*: a tax on absentees had been proposed by, among others, Thomas Prior in his published *List of Absentees*, using as precedent the Irish Act of 1635 (10 Chas. I c. 21) (Prior, *Absentees*, pp. 31, 79). When Parliament opened in October, just before the appearance of *A Modest Proposal*, Archbishop Boulter reported that the hotter patriots were 'for taxing the absentees 4s. in the pound' (to Newcastle, 23 Oct. 1729 (*Boulter Letters*, vol. I, p. 263)). In the end, they had to be content with a tax of 4s in the pound on salaries and pensions paid to absentees (same to same, 13 Nov. 1729 (TNA, SP 63/391/204)).

45 *LAPLANDERS*: for Swift's assumption of the barbarism of northern lands and their inhabitants, see Dirk F. Passmann and Hermann J. Real, 'Barbarism, Witchcraft and Devil-Worship: Cock-and-Bull Stories from Several Remote Nations of the World', *SStud* 23 (2008), 94–110; Ian Higgins, *Swift's Politics: A Study in Disaffection*, Cambridge: Cambridge University Press, pp. 111–12. In *A Tale of a Tub*, he refers ironically to Lapland as 'that Polite Nation' (*CWJS*, vol. I, section VIII, p. 104).

46 *TOPINAMBOO*: the Tupi people, or Tupinamba, were indigenous inhabitants of coastal Brazil. They were first described in the sixteenth century by the German traveller Hans Staden (Johann von Staden), whose captivity among them was narrated in his *Warhaftige Historia und Beschreibung Eyner Landtschafft der Wilden, Nacketen, Grimmigen Menschfresser Leuthen, in der Newenwelt America Gelegen*, Marburg, 1557. Subsequently, the French explorer Jean de Léry published an account of the Tupi in *Histoire d'un Voyage Fait en la*

Factions, nor Act any longer like the Jews, who were Murdering one another at the very moment their City was taken:[47] *Of being a little Cautious not to Sell our Country and Consciences for nothing:*[48] *Of teaching Landlords to have at least one degree of Mercy towards their Tenants. Lastly of putting a Spirit of Honesty, Industry and Skill into our Shop-keepers, who, if a Resolution could now be taken to Buy only our Native Goods, would immediatly unite to Cheat and Exact upon us in the Price, the Measure, and the Goodness, nor could ever yet be brought to make one fair Proposal of just dealing, though often and earnestly invited to it.*

Therefore I repeat, let no Man talk to me of these and the like Expedients, till he hath at least some Glimpse of Hope, that there will ever be some hearty and sincere Attempt to put them in Practice.

But as to my self, having been wearied out for many Years with offering vain, idle,[49] visionary[50] thoughts, and at length utterly despairing of

---

Terre du Bresil, Autrement Dite Amérique..., La Rochelle, 1578. Both accounts, containing descriptions of cannibalism, were reprinted (with illustrations) in Theodore de Bry, *Americae Tertia Pars Memorabilem Provinciae Brasiliae Historiam Continens...*, Frankfurt, 1592, a copy of which is in Marsh's Library, Dublin. Though not named explicitly, the Tupi are assumed to have been the South American people whose customs are discussed in Montaigne's essay 'Des Canibales' (*Essais*, bk 1, ch. 31, a copy of which Swift owned (*Library and Reading*, *I*, vol. II, p. 1270)). By the eighteenth century, they had come to be regarded as an epitome of ignorance and savagery: see, for example, Locke, *Essay Concerning Human Understanding*, II, xvi, 6 (ed. Peter H. Nidditch, Oxford: Clarendon Press, 1975, p. 207); Swift's *Discourse Concerning the Mechanical Operation of the Spirit* (*CWJS*, vol. I, p. 170). On the earlier development of this image among Portuguese colonists, see Stuart B. Schwartz, 'The Formation of a Colonial Identity in Brazil', in Nicholas Canny and Anthony Pagden (eds.), *Colonial Identity in the Atlantic World, 1500–1800*, Princeton, NJ: Princeton University Press, 1987, p. 26. See also Claude Rawson, '"Indians" and Irish: Montaigne, Swift, and the "Cannibal Question"', *MLQ* 53 (1992), 299–363.

47 *like the Jews... their City was taken*: a reference to the violent internal conflict between Jewish factions within Jerusalem as the Roman general Titus approached in AD 70, for which see Josephus, *Wars of the Jews*, v, 1–2. The account of the siege by Josephus includes a notorious episode of cannibalism, in which a starving Jewish mother roasted her infant son, ate half the carcase herself and offered the remainder to the soldiers of the garrison (vi, 199–219).

48 *not to Sell our Country and Consciences for nothing*: in his 'Holyhead Journal' (1727), Swift had written of Ireland: 'this land of Slaves / Where all are fools and all are knaves / Where every knave & fool is bought / Yet kindly sells himself for nought' (*Poems*, vol. II, p. 421). Cf. Psalms, 44: 12–13: 'Thou sellest thy people for nought, and dost not increase thy wealth by their price', quoted by Swift in *Some Observations upon the Report of the Committee of... the Privy Council in England Relating to Woods Halfpence* (Davis, vol. X, p. 43).

49 *idle*: worthless.

50 *visionary*: incapable of being carried out. Swift had repeatedly criticised in the same terms the ideas of those who disagreed with him. His reference to his own sensible and righteous

Success, I fortunately fell upon this Proposal, which as it is wholly new, so it hath something Solid and Real, of no Expence and little Trouble, full in our own Power, and whereby we can incur no Danger in *disobliging England*. For this kind of Commodity will not bear Exportation,[51] the Flesh being of too tender a Consistance, to admit a long continuance in Salt, *although perhaps I could name a Country, which would be glad to Eat up our whole Nation without it*.[52]

After all I am not so violently bent upon my own Opinion, as to reject any Offer, proposed by wise Men, which shall be found equally Innocent, Cheap, Easy and Effectual. But before something of that kind shall be advanced in Contradiction to my Scheme, and offering a better, I desire the Author, or Authors will be pleased maturely to consider two points. *First*, as things now stand, how they will be able to find Food and Raiment for an hundred thousand useless Mouths and Backs. And *Secondly*, there being a round Million of Creatures in human Figure, throughout this Kingdom, whose whole Subsistance put into a common Stock, would leave them in Debt two Million of Pounds *Sterl*. adding those, who are Beggars by Profession, to the Bulk of Farmers, Cottagers and Labourers with their Wives and Children, who are Beggars in Effect; I desire those *Politicians*, who dislike my Overture, and may perhaps be so bold to attempt an Answer, that they will first ask the Parents of these Mortals, whether they would not at this Day think it a great Happiness to have been sold for

proposals as 'idle' and 'visionary' is a sarcastic comment on his failure to convince the powerful.

51 *bear Exportation*: as Rawson has pointed out ('A Reading of A Modest Proposal', in *Order from Confusion Sprung: Studies in Eighteenth-Century Literature from Swift to Cowper*, London: Allen & Unwin, 1985, p. 136), Swift is here taking to an extreme his own nostrum that the Irish should consume only their own produce. In this case, however, they will have no alternative and therefore will do by necessity what they should do in other instances by choice; a circumstance which, combined with the obscene nature of the consumption, serves to emphasise the disastrous consequences of continuing a wilful preference for imported goods.

52 *I could name a Country... without it*: to be able to eat someone up without salt is a proverbial expression of hatred (as used by Swift in *A Treatise on Polite Conversation* (*CWJS*, vol. II, p. 339)). In this instance, Swift is also suggesting both greed and barbarism. Since the use of salt was considered to be a sign of civilisation, the English were being presented as doubly barbarian – not only cannibals, but cannibals who do not use salt. One of Swift's *bêtes noires*, Lord Allen (attacked in the *Advertisement Against Lord Allen*, *The Substance of what was Said By The Dean* and *A Vindication of His Excellency the Lord Carteret*: see below, pp. 181–90, 200–1), was the grandson of a Dublin alderman, Sir Joshua Allen (lord mayor of the city in 1673), who was among other things an exporter of salted meat (*Poems*, vol. III, p. 795), a point to which Swift had directed attention in his poem 'Traulus' (ibid., p. 800).

Food at a year Old, in the manner I prescribe, and thereby have avoided such a perpetual Scene of Misfortunes, as they have since gone through, by the *oppression of Land-lords*, the Impossibility of paying Rent without Money or Trade, the want of common Sustenance, with neither House nor Cloaths to cover them from Inclemences of Weather, and the most inevitable Prospect of intailing the like, or greater Miseries upon their Breed for ever.

I Profess in the sincerity of my Heart that I have not the least personal Interest in endeavouring to promote this necessary Work having no other Motive than the *publick Good of my Country*, by *advancing our Trade, providing for Infants, relieving the Poor, and giving some Pleasure to the Rich.* I have no Children, by which I can propose to get a single Penny; the youngest being nine Years old,[53] and my Wife past Child-bearing.

FINIS

---

53 *nine Years old*: the proposer had previously considered and rejected an alternative scheme, of supplying the want of venison in Ireland by hunting 'young Lads and Maidens, not exceeding fourteen Years of Age, nor under twelve' (p. 133). The implication here that he might himself have children of this age would give the lie to his ethical proof, the assertion that he has no self-interest in his own scheme. Should Swift have intended the pamphlet as a satire on the altruistic Whig philosophy associated with the 3rd Earl of Shaftesbury, and represented in Ireland by the Presbyterian James Arbuckle, the notion of a bogus disinterestedness would have sharpened its edge.

A PROPOSAL THAT ALL THE LADIES AND WOMEN OF IRELAND SHOULD APPEAR CONSTANTLY IN IRISH MANUFACTURES

Headnote

Composed 1729; published posthumously, 1765; copy text *1765a* (see Textual Account).

Usually dated towards the end of 1729, and another piece that was unpublished in Swift's lifetime (eventually appearing first in Deane Swift's *Works* of 1765), the *Proposal* responded in part to the possibility of imported wine duty being increased, and its publication was partly obviated by the tax being voted through in December 1729 (see Ferguson, p. 156; Ehrenpreis, vol. III, pp. 644, 646, who finds the worry over wine duty incongruous), which is also why the pamphlet seems possibly unfinished.

Swift was not alone in his general argument about trade and patriotism, and there were many contemporaneous attempts to promote Irish manufacture: the funeral in 1729 of the Speaker of the Irish Commons, William Conolly, was marked by his wife distributing scarves as a patriotic statement (see Patrick McNally, 'William Conolly', *DIB*). Moreover, on 10 November 1731, a bill in the Irish Parliament obliging all persons to be buried in woollen cloth was introduced by Swift's friend Eaton Stannard. It was not successful.

A PROPOSAL THAT ALL THE LADIES AND WOMEN OF IRELAND SHOULD APPEAR CONSTANTLY IN IRISH MANUFACTURES. WRITTEN IN THE YEAR M DCC XXIX.

There was a treatise written about nine years ago to persuade the people of Ireland to wear their own manufactures.[1] This treatise was allowed to have not one syllable in it of party or disaffection, but was wholly founded upon the growing poverty of the nation, occasioned by the utter want of trade in every branch, except that ruinous importation of all foreign extravagancies from other countries. This treatise was presented, by the Grand-jury of the city and county of Dublin, as a scandalous, seditious, and factious pamphlet.[2] I forget who was the foreman of the city Grand-jury, but the foreman for the county, was one Doctor Seal,[3] register to the Archbishop of Dublin, wherein he differed much from the sentiments of his Lord. The Printer[4] was tried before the late Mr. Whitchet, that famous Lord Chief-Justice;[5] who, on the bench, laying his hand on his heart, declared upon his salvation that the Author was a Jacobite, and had a design to beget a quarrel between the two nations. In the midst of this prosecution, about 1500 weavers were forced to beg their bread, and had a general contribution made for their relief, which just served to make them drunk for a week; and then they were forced to turn rogues, or strolling[6] beggars, or to leave the kingdom.

The Duke of Grafton,[7] who was then Lieutenant, being perfectly ashamed of so infamous and unpopular a proceeding, obtained from

---

1 *There was a treatise... wear their own manufactures*: Swift's *Proposal for the Universal Use of Irish Manufacture* (1720).
2 *This treatise was presented... factious pamphlet*: for the proceedings, see Ehrenpreis, vol. III, pp. 128–30.
3 *Doctor Seal*: Harvey Sale or Seale (P. Beryl Eustace and Eilish Ellis, eds., *Registry of Deeds, Ireland, Abstracts of Wills*, 3 vols., Dublin: Stationery Office, 1954–84, p. 58) had held the office of registrar to the archbishop of Dublin since at least 1679 (*The Vestry Records of the Parishes of St Catherine and St James, Dublin, 1657–1692*, ed. Raymond Gillespie, Dublin: Four Courts Press, 2002, pp. 134, 143, 168, 179, 186–7, 197, 278; *Records of Convocation*, ed. Bray, vol. XVII, pt 1, pp. 143, 317; *C.J.Ire.*, vol. III, 27; Archbishop King to Francis Annesley, 22 Oct. 1711 (TCD, MS 2531, p. 358)).
4 *The Printer*: Edward Waters.
5 *the late Mr. Whitchet, that famous Lord Chief-Justice*: William Whitshed (1679–1727), chief justice of king's bench [Ire.] 1714–27, common pleas [Ire.], 1727–d. See above, pp. 15–16.
6 *strolling*: itinerant.
7 *The Duke of Grafton*: Charles Fitzroy, 2nd Duke of Grafton (1683–1757), lord lieutenant of Ireland 1720–4.

England a *noli prosequi*[8] for the Printer. Yet the Grand-jury had solemn thanks given them from the Secretary of State.[9]

I mention this passage (perhaps too much forgotten) to shew how dangerous it hath been for the best meaning person to write one syllable in the defence of his country, or discover the miserable condition it is in.

And, to prove this truth, I will produce one instance more; wholly omitting the famous case of the Drapier, and the proclamation against him, as well as the perverseness of another jury[10] against the same Mr. Whitchet, who was violently bent to act the second part in another scene. About two years ago there was a small paper printed, which was called *A Short View of the State of Ireland*,[11] relating the several causes whereby any country may grow rich, and applying them to Ireland. Whitchet was dead, and consequently the printer was not troubled. Mist,[12] the famous journalist, happened to reprint this paper in London, for which his pressfolks were prosecuted for almost a twelvemonth; and, for ought I know, are not yet discharged.[13]

This is our case; insomuch, that, although I am often without money in my pocket, I dare not own it in some company, for fear of being thought disaffected.

But since I am determined to take care, that the author of this paper shall not be discovered, (following herein the most prudent practice of the Drapier) I will venture to affirm, that the three seasons wherein our corn hath miscarried, did no more contribute to our present misery, than one

---

8 *noli prosequi*: *noli* or *nolle prosequi* (I do not wish to prosecute), a formal entry in the record of a criminal court by which the prosecutor declares that the charge will not be pursued.
9 *the Secretary of State*: in 1720, the (British) secretary of state with responsibility for Irish affairs, the secretary for the southern department, was James Craggs (1657–1727).
10 *the perverseness of another jury*: in the failed prosecution of John Harding in 1724 for publishing Swift's *Seasonable Advice*.
11 *A Short View of the State of Ireland*: see above, pp. 13–26.
12 *Mist*: Nathaniel Mist (d. 1737), an English newspaper printer and publisher of Jacobite leanings; convicted and fined in 1727 for a libel on George I; fled to exile in France in January 1728 (see *ODNB*). In 1728, he had published *The Present State of Ireland; Being Political Reflections by Mr Mist, on a Pamphlet Lately Published at Dublin* [London, 1728], which quoted extensively from Swift's original.
13 *discharged*: in fact, the prosecution of the exiled Mist's compositor, 'press men', apprentices and maid was not a consequence of the reprinting of Swift's pamphlet, but followed the publication in July 1728 of a pro-Jacobite lampoon by the Duke of Wharton on the first two Georges and their Prime Minister, in the form of a letter from Persia: Lewis Melville, *The Life and Writings of Philip Duke of Wharton*, London: Bodley Head, 1913, pp. 225–31; Michael Harris, *London Newspapers in the Age of Walpole: A Study of the Origins of the Modern English Press*, London & Toronto: Fairleigh Dickinson University Press, 1987, pp. 144–5.

spoonful of water thrown upon a rat already drowned would contribute to his death;[14] and that the present plentiful harvest,[15] although it should be followed by a dozen ensuing, would no more restore us, than it would the rat aforesaid to put him near the fire, which might indeed warm his fur-coat, but never bring him back to life.

The short of the matter is this, The distresses of the kingdom are operating more and more every day, by very large degrees, and so have been doing for above a dozen years past.

If you demand from whence these distresses have arisen, I desire to ask the following question.

If two thirds of any kingdom's revenue be exported to another country, without one farthing of value in return, and if the said kingdom be forbidden the most profitable branches of trade wherein to employ the other third, and only allowed to traffic in importing those commodities which are most ruinous to itself, how shall that kingdom stand?

If this question were formed into the first proposition of an hypothetical syllogism, I defy the man born in Ireland, who is now in the fairest way of getting a collectorship,[16] or a cornet's post,[17] to give a good reason for denying it.

Let me put another case. Suppose a gentleman's estate of 200 *l.* a year should sink to one hundred, by some accident, whether by an earthquake or inundation it matters not, and suppose the said gentleman utterly hopeless and unqualified ever to retrieve the loss; how is he otherwise to proceed in his future oeconomy, than by reducing it on every article to one half less, unless he will be content to fly his country, or rot in jail? This is a representation of Ireland's condition, only with one fault, that it is a little too favourable. Neither am I able to propose a full remedy for this, that shall ever be granted, but only a small prolongation of life, until God shall miraculously dispose the hearts of our neighbours, our kinsmen, our fellow

---

14 *his death*: from the proverb, 'Pour not water on a drowned mouse'. In 1730, Swift wrote to Bolingbroke of his fear of dying in Ireland 'like a poisoned rat in a hole': Swift to Bolingbroke, 21 Mar. 1729[/30] (Woolley, *Corr.*, vol. III, p. 294).
15 *the present plentiful harvest*: for reports of a 'bumper' harvest in 1729, see James Kelly, 'Harvests and Hardship: Famine and Scarcity in Ireland in the Late 1720s', *Studia Hibernica* 26 (1991–2), 93–4.
16 *a collectorship*: in the revenue.
17 *a cornet's post*: the lowest rank of commissioned officer in a cavalry troop.

protestants, fellow subjects, and fellow rational creatures,[18] to permit us to starve without running further in debt. I am informed that our national debt (and God knows how we wretches came by that fashionable thing a national debt) is about 250,000 *l*.;[19] which is, at least, one third of the whole kingdom's rents, after our absentees and other foreign drains are paid, and about 50,000 *l.* more than all the cash.

It seems there are several schemes for raising a fund to pay the interest of this formidable sum, (not the principal, for this is allowed impossible.) The necessity of raising such a fund is strongly and regularly pleaded from the late deficiencies in the duties and customs. And is it the fault of Ireland that these funds are deficient? If they depend on trade, can it possibly be otherwise, while we have neither liberty to trade, nor money to trade with; neither hands to work, nor business to employ them, if we had? Our diseases are visible enough, both in their causes and effects; and the cures are well known, but impossible to be applied.

If my steward comes and tells me, that my rents are sunk so low that they are very little more than sufficient to pay my servants their wages, have I any other course left, than to cashier four in six of my rascally footmen,[20] and a number of other varlets in my family, of whose insolence the whole neighbourhood complains. And I should think it extremely severe in any law, to force me to maintain a household of fifty servants, and fix their wages, before I had offered my rent-roll upon oath to the legislators.

---

18 *our neighbours... fellow rational creatures*: the English. Swift's refutation of the accepted notion that man was a 'rational creature' was a central theme of *Gulliver's Travels* (*CWJS*, vol. XVI, pp. 558–60).
19 *our national debt... is about 250,000 l.*: the Irish Parliament had first introduced the notion of a 'national debt' (then fixed at £50,000) by statute in 1716. A second loan, limited to £150,000, was sanctioned in 1729, to deal with the problem of accumulating army pay arrears, and a third, for £100,000, in 1731. See Charles Ivar McGrath, 'Money, Politics and Power: The Financial Legislation of the Irish Parliament', in D. W. Hayton, James Kelly and John Bergin (eds.), *The Eighteenth-century Composite State*, Basingstoke: Palgrave Macmillan, 2010, pp. 29–30. In the Drapier's *Humble Address to Both Houses of Parliament* (1724), Swift had estimated the annual rents in Ireland at £2 million: of this total, approximately £1,400,000 was remitted into England, half in rental income sent directly to absentees, and half through various other means, some of them indirect, including the adverse balance of trade (Davis, vol. X, pp. 128–9). See above, p. 20.
20 *my rascally footmen*: Swift details the 'rascally' behaviour of footmen in *Directions to Servants* (1745) (*CWJS*, vol. II, pp. 481–98). Cf. *The Humble Petition of the Footmen In and About the City of Dublin* (below, pp. 236–9).

To return from digressing: I am told one scheme for raising a fund to pay the interest of our national debt, is by a further duty of forty shillings a ton upon wine.[21] Some gentlemen would carry this matter much further by raising it to twelve pounds; which, in a manner, would amount to a prohibition. Thus weakly arguing from the practice of England.[22]

I have often taken notice, both in print and in discourse, that there is no topic so fallacious, either in talk or in writing, as to argue how we ought to act in Ireland from the example of England, Holland, France,[23] or any other country, whose inhabitants are allowed the common rights and liberties of humankind. I could undertake to name six or seven of the most uncontrolled[24] maxims in government, which are utterly false in this kingdom.

As to the additional duty on wine, I think any person may deliver his opinion upon it, until it shall have passed into a law; and, till then, I declare mine to be positively against it.

First, because there is no nation yet known, in either hemisphere, where the people of all conditions are more in want of some cordial,[25] to keep up

---

21 *a further duty of forty shillings a ton upon wine*: a tun was a measurement of capacity, equivalent to 252 gallons. The Additional Duties Act of 1728 (1 Geo. II c. 2 [Ire.]) had imposed a duty on imported wines of 40s a tun (excepting wines from Portugal, which paid 17s a tun). Lord Carteret was reported in November 1729 as seeking a duty of 10s per hogshead on wine (the equivalent of 40s per tun) and 4d. a gallon on brandy in order to create a fund to pay the interest on the national debt (Marmaduke Coghill to Edward Southwell, 8 Nov. 1729 (*Coghill Letters*, p. 76)).

22 *the practice of England*: prohibitive tariffs on wine imports had been introduced in late seventeenth-century England for reasons of politics and political economy, in order to reduce popular consumption of cheap imported French wine and staunch the flow of bullion from England to France. For a time, taste in wine had been a test of party, with Whigs hostile to French vintages and Tories correspondingly devoted to claret, but this distinction had disappeared by 1714 (Charles Ludington, "'Be Sometimes to Your Country True': The Politics of Wine in England, 1660–1714', in Adam Smyth (ed.), *A Pleasing Sinne: Drink and Conviviality in Seventeenth-century England*, Cambridge: D. S. Brewer, 2004, pp. 93–106). In England, the statutory customs duty on imported French wines had stood since 1686 at £8 per tun, while that on Spanish wines was higher, at £12 (3 Geo. I c. 9, continuing 9 Anne c. 21, 8 Anne c. 13, and 1 Jas. II c. 3).

23 *from the example of England, Holland, France*: as in John Browne, *An Essay on Trade in General; and, on That of Ireland in Particular*, Dublin, 1728; and John Browne, *Seasonable Remarks on Trade with Some Reflections on the Advantages that Might Accrue to Great Britain by a Proper Regulation of the Trade of Ireland*, Dublin, 1728, esp. p. 6 (Swift owned copies of both these works (*Library and Reading*, I, vol. I, pp. 293–4)). Also David Bindon, *A Scheme for Supplying Industrious Men with Money to Carry on their Trades, and for Better Providing for the Poor of Ireland*, Dublin, 1729.

24 *uncontrolled*: undisputed.

25 *cordial*: 'A medicine, food, or beverage which invigorates the heart and stimulates the circulation' (*OED*).

their spirits, than in this of ours. I am not in jest; and, if the fact will not be allowed me, I shall not argue it.

Secondly, It is too well and generally known, that this tax of forty shillings additional on every ton of wine (which will be double at least to the home-consumer) will increase equally every new session of parliament, until perhaps it comes to twelve pounds.

Thirdly, Because, as the merchants[26] inform me, and as I have known many the like instances in England, this additional tax will more probably lessen this branch of the revenue, than encrease it. And therefore Sir John Stanley,[27] a commissioner of the customs, in England, used to say, That the House of Commons were generally mistaken in matters of trade, by an erroneous opinion that two and two make four. Thus, if you should lay an additional duty of one penny a pound on raisins, or sugar, the revenue, instead of rising, would certainly sink; and the consequence would only be, to lessen the number of plum-puddings, and ruin the confectioner.

Fourthly, I am likewise assured by merchants, that, upon this additional forty shillings, the French will at least equally raise their duties upon all commodities we export thither.

Fifthly, If an original extract of the exports and imports be true, we have been gainers upon the balance by our trade with France for several years past; and, although our gain amounts to no great sum, we ought to be satisfied, since we are no losers, with the only consolation we are capable of receiving.

Lastly, The worst consequence is behind. If we raise the duty on wine to a considerable height, we lose the only hold we have of keeping among us the few gentlemen of any tolerable estates. I am confident, there is hardly a gentleman of eight hundred pounds a year and upwards, in this kingdom, who would balance half an hour to consider whether he should live here or in England, if a family could be as cheaply maintained in the one as the other. As to eatables, they are as cheap in many fine counties of England, as in some very indifferent ones here; or, if there be any difference, that vein of thrift, and prudence in oeconomy, which passes there without reproach, (and chiefly in London itself) would amply make up the difference. But the article of French wine is hardly tolerable, in any degree of plenty, to a

---

26 *merchants*: wholesale traders, especially those involved in overseas commerce.
27 *Sir John Stanley*: Sir John Stanley (1663–1744), 1st Bt, of Grangegorman, Co. Dublin, commissioner of customs [G.B.] 1708–44; chief secretary [Ire.], 1713–14, MP. [Ire.] 1713–14.

middling fortune: And this is it which, by growing habitual, wholly turns the scale with those few landed men disengaged from employments, who content themselves to live hospitably with plenty of good wine in their own country, rather than in penury and obscurity in another, with bad, or with none at all.

Having therefore, as far as in me lies, abolished this additional duty upon wine; for I am not under the least concern about paying the interest of the national debt, but leave it, as in loyalty bound, wholly to the wisdom of the Honourable House of Commons: I come now to consider by what methods we may be able to put off, and delay our utter undoing as long as it is possible.

I never have discoursed any reasonable man upon this subject, who did not allow that there was no remedy left us, but to lessen the importation of all unnecessary commodities, as much as it was possible; and likewise, either to persuade our absentees to spend their money at home, which is impossible, or tax them at five shillings in the pound during their absence, with such allowances, upon necessary occasions, as it shall be thought convenient; or, by permitting us a free trade, which is denied to no other nation upon earth. The three last methods are treated by Mr. Prior, in his most useful treatise, added to his list of absentees.[28]

It is to gratify the vanity and pride, and luxury of the women, and of the young fops who admire them, that we owe this insupportable grievance of bringing in the instruments of our ruin. There is annually brought over to this kingdom near ninety thousand pounds worth of silk, whereof the greater part is manufactured: Thirty thousand pounds more is expended in muslin, holland,[29] cambric,[30] and calico. What the price of lace amounts to, is not easy to be collected from the custom-house book,[31] being a kind

---

28 *The three last methods... added to his list of absentees*: see Prior, *Absentees*, pp. 22ff. On p. 33 Prior proposed a tax of 4s (not 5s) in the pound on absentees' estates.

29 *holland*: Dutch linen of the best quality was usually referred to simply as 'Holland' or 'Holland cloth'.

30 *cambric*: a fine white linen, originally made at Cambrai, whence its name was derived.

31 *custom-house book*: the records of duty collected, which were archived in the Custom House in Dublin, the headquarters of the customs and excise service. These were usually referred to as 'custom-house books' and frequently cited by other Irish economic writers of the time as a basis for their statistical arguments. See, for example, Browne, *Seasonable Remarks*, p. 122; Browne, *Reflections Little to the Purpose, on a Paper Less to the Purpose*, Dublin, 1729, pp. 39, 53; Dobbs, *Essay*, esp. p. 4 (in which he refers to having 'look'd over the ledgers in the Custom-House'); Prior, *Absentees*, pp. 55, 58.

of goods that takes up little room, and is easily run;[32] but, considering the prodigious price of a woman's head-dress, at ten, twelve, twenty pounds a yard, must be very great. The tea, rated at seven shillings *per* pound, comes to near twelve thousand pounds; but, considering it as the common luxury of every chambermaid, sempstress, and tradesman's wife, both in town and country, however they come by it, must needs cost the kingdom double that sum. Coffee is somewhat above 7,000 *l*. I have seen no account of chocolate, and some other Indian or American goods. The drapery imported is about 24,000 *l*. The whole amounts (with one or two other particulars) to 150,000 *l*.[33] The lavishing of all which money is just as prudent and necessary, as to see a man in an embroidered coat begging out of Newgate[34] in an old shoe.

I allow that the thrown and raw silk[35] is less pernicious; because we have some share in the manufacture;[36] but we are not now in circumstances to trifle. It costs us above 40,000 *l*. a year: And if the ladies, till better times, will not be content to go in their own country shifts, I wish they may go in rags.[37]

Let them vie with each other in the fineness of their native linen: Their beauty and gentleness will as well appear, as if they were covered over with diamonds and brocade.[38]

I believe no man is so weak, as to hope or expect that such a reformation can be brought about by a law. But a thorough, hearty, unanimous vote, in both Houses of Parliament, might perhaps answer as well: Every senator, noble or plebeian, giving his honour, that neither himself, nor any of his

32 *run*: smuggled.
33 *The whole... 150,000 l*: Dobbs, *Essay*, pp. 37–41, sets out median figures for imports for the previous seven years. His figures for particular commodities are reasonably close to Swift's: *c*. £77,000 worth of silk, *c*. £31,000 for muslin, holland and cambric, over £6,000 for lace, over £12,000 for tea, *c*. £6,000 for coffee, and *c*. £24,000 for 'drapery'. However, his overall total is much larger, at *c*. £863,000.
34 *Newgate*: Newgate prison in Dublin, the principal debtors' prison in the city, stood at the west end of the Cornmarket. Newgate prison in London served the same function.
35 *thrown and raw silk*: raw silk was produced by reeling threads onto a spindle to produce a single strand; thrown silk was a stronger thread produced by twisting together two or more single strands.
36 *we have some share in the manufacture*: for the silk-weaving industry in Ireland, see *Econ. Hist. Ire.*, pp. 208–9.
37 *go in rags*: in other words, as beggars: in *A Modest Proposal* (above, pp. 146, 149, 151) and the *Proposal for Giving Badges to the Beggars* (below, pp. 314, 318), rags were treated as synonymous with begging.
38 *brocade*: a richly decorative woven fabric, usually made from coloured silks.

family, would, in their dress, or furniture of their houses, make use of any thing except what was of the growth and manufacture of this kingdom; and that they would use the utmost of their power, influence and credit, to prevail on their tenants, dependants, and friends, to follow their example.

MAXIMS CONTROLLED IN IRELAND

Headnote

Probably composed 1729; published posthumously, 1765; copy text *1765a* (see Textual Account); the footnote that forms part of this text was provided by the editor, Deane Swift.

Hints of the process behind this unfinished essay can be found in a manuscript in the John Rylands Library, Manchester (see Associated Materials I, pp. 324–7). *Maxims* is usually dated to 1729, not least because of its connection to Swift's other writings of the time (for speculations, see Ferguson, p. 148, and Ehrenpreis, vol. III, p. 575). Swift is listing a number of supposedly axiomatic statements concerning the economy, which are inapplicable in Ireland because of the problems of governance and constitution he had previously discussed in other Irish texts of this period. The contemporary idea of using the supposedly incontrovertible maxim as a way of making plain Ireland's anomalous plight can be seen in pamphlets such as *Remarks on some Maxims, Peculiar to the Ancient, as well as Modern Inhabitants of Ireland. With a Seasonable Hint to G Bn about the Woollen trade*, Dublin, 1730, otherwise unconnected to Swift, and signed by 'Hibernicus', following the pseudonym adopted by James Arbuckle in his influential letters in the *Dublin Journal*.

MAXIMS CONTROLLED IN IRELAND.

The Truth of some Maxims in State and Government, examined with reference to Ireland.

There are certain Maxims of State, founded upon long observation and experience, drawn from the constant practice of the wisest nations, and from the very principles of government, nor ever controlled[1] by any writer upon politics. Yet all these Maxims do necessarily presuppose a kingdom, or commonwealth, to have the same natural rights common to the rest of mankind who have entered into civil society. For, if we could conceive a nation where each of the inhabitants had but one eye, one leg, and one hand, it is plain that, before you could institute them into a republic, an allowance must be made for those material defects, wherein they differed from other mortals. Or, imagine a legislator forming a system for the government of Bedlam,[2] and, proceeding upon the maxim that man is a sociable animal,[3] should draw them out of their cells, and form them into corporations or general assemblies; the consequence might probably be, that they would fall foul on each other, or burn the house over their own heads.

Of the like nature are innumerable errors, committed by crude and short thinkers, who reason upon general topics, without the least allowance for the most important circumstances, which quite alter the nature of the case.

This hath been the fate of those small dealers, who are every day publishing their thoughts either on paper or in their assemblies for improving the trade of Ireland, and referring us to the practice and example of England, Holland, France, or other nations.[4]

I shall therefore examine certain Maxims of government, which generally pass for uncontrolled in the world, and consider how far they will suit with the present condition of this kingdom.

First, it is affirmed by wise men, that the dearness of things necessary for life, in a fruitful country, is a certain sign of wealth and great commerce:

---

1 *controlled*: confuted.
2 *Bedlam*: the Bethlem Royal Hospital (for the mentally ill) in Moorfields, London.
3 *the maxim that man is a sociable animal*: from Aristotle's *Politics*, quoted by Joseph Addison in the first line of the *Spectator*, no. 9, 10 Mar. 1711 (*Spectator*, I, p. 39).
4 *those small dealers... other nations*: Swift had in mind recent pamphlets by, among others, John Browne and David Bindon (see above, pp. xl–xliv).

For, when such necessaries are dear, it must absolutely follow that money is cheap and plentiful.

But this is manifestly false in Ireland, for the following reason. Some years ago, the species of money here, did probably amount to six or seven hundred thousand pounds;[5] and I have good cause to believe, that our remittances then did not much exceed the cash brought in to us. But the prodigious discouragements we have since received in every branch of our trade, by the frequent enforcements, and rigorous execution of the navigation act,[6] the tyranny of under custom-house officers, the yearly addition of absentees, the payments to regiments abroad,[7] to civil and military officers residing in England, the unexpected sudden demands of great sums from the treasury,[8] and some other drains of perhaps as great consequence, we now see ourselves reduced to a state (since we have no friends) of being pitied by our enemies, at least, if our enemies were of such a kind as to be capable of any regards towards us, except of hatred and contempt.

Forty years are now passed since the Revolution,[9] when the contention of the British empire was, most unfortunately for us, and altogether against the usual course of such mighty changes in government, decided in the least important nation,[10] but with such ravages and ruin executed on both sides,

---

5 *six or seven hundred thousand pounds*: in the *Short View of the State of Ireland* (above, p. 24), Swift had given a figure for hard currency at 'about Five hundred thousand pounds'. John Browne, in *A Scheme of Money-Matters of Ireland*..., p. 17, assumed a circulation in Ireland of about £514,000 in specie and £400,000 in bankers' notes.

6 *the navigation act*: the English Navigation Acts of 1663 (15 Chas II c. 7), 1670 (22 & 23 Chas II c. 26) and 1696 (7 & 8 Will. III c. 22) effectively excluded Ireland from much of the transatlantic colonial trade by insisting that goods imported into England's transatlantic colonies had to be carried in English-built vessels and loaded at English ports, and goods brought from the colonies be imported only at English ports.

7 *payments to regiments abroad*: in 1727, six regiments on the Irish establishment were sent to the garrison at Gibraltar (*C.J.Ire.*, vol. V, p. 426), giving rise to discontent among Irish MPs. By 1729, three had returned to Ireland: Charles Ivar McGrath, *Ireland and Empire, 1692–1770*, London: Pickering and Chatto, 2012, pp. 156–7.

8 *the treasury*: escalating government indebtedness in Ireland in the 1720s gave rise to new financial stratagems, which in turn meant new demands on the Irish treasury; for example, in 1726, and again in 1728, £10,000 was hypothecated from the supply to pay interest to those advancing money to pay arrears of military pay: McGrath, *Ireland and Empire*, pp. 187–8.

9 *the Revolution*: the Glorious Revolution of 1688.

10 *decided in the least important nation*: in Ireland (at the battles of the Boyne in 1690, and Aughrim in 1691).

as to leave the kingdom a desert, which, in some sort, it still continues. Neither did the long rebellions in 1641[11] make half such a destruction of houses, plantations, and personal wealth, in both kingdoms, as two years campaigns did in ours, by fighting England's battles.[12]

By slow degrees, and by the gentle treatment we received under two auspicious reigns,[13] we grew able to live without running in debt. Our absentees were but few, we had great indulgence in trade, a considerable share in employments of church and state; and, while the short leases continued, which were let some years after the war ended,[14] tenants paid their rents with ease and chearfulness, to the great regret of their landlords, who had taken up a spirit of oppression that is not easily removed. And although, in these short leases, the rent was gradually to encrease after short periods; yet, as soon as the term elapsed, the land was let to the highest bidder, most commonly without the least effectual clause for building or planting. Yet by many advantages, which this island then possessed, and hath since utterly lost, the rents of lands still grew higher upon every lease

11 *the long rebellions in 1641*: the rising in Ulster in October 1641 spread quickly to the whole of Catholic Ireland, and was not finally suppressed until after Cromwell's expedition to Ireland in 1650.
12 *battles*: the prevailing Whig interpretation of the events of 1690–1 (expressed, for example, in Archbishop King's *The State of the Protestants of Ireland under the Late King James's Government*, London, 1691) emphasised the hardships suffered by Protestants in Ireland under James II, and their providential delivery by William III. Swift is not only casting aside this conventional view but inverting the arguments put forward by English MPs after 1690 in relation to Ireland, that having spent English 'blood and treasure' in rescuing Irish Protestants, the Westminster Parliament could do with the kingdom as it liked.
13 *under two auspicious reigns*: there is some ambiguity here: placing this sentence so closely after his description of the 1641 rising invites readers to infer that Swift means the reigns of Charles II and James II (until 1688), during which the Irish public revenue did indeed enjoy improving health (Seán Egan, 'Finance and the Government of Ireland, 1660–85', 2 vols. (Ph.D. thesis, TCD, 1983)); but the emphasis in the preceding paragraph on the Glorious Revolution suggests an alternative reading, that what is meant is the period 1690–1714, during which the Irish treasury was often embarrassed and Irish trade was not 'indulged', but there was no official 'national debt'. This was only instituted – in the sense that the Irish Parliament sanctioned an ongoing deficit – in 1716.
14 *the short leases... after the war ended*: in the immediate aftermath of the Jacobite war, lands were customarily set for 21 years, but within a decade the balance of advantage had switched to the tenant, and longer leases of 31 years (established by statute as the maximum term for which land could be leased to a Catholic) or three lives became usual: L. M. Cullen, *An Economic History of Ireland since 1660*, London: Batsford, 1972, p. 44; David Dickson, 'Middlemen', in Thomas Bartlett and D. W. Hayton (eds.), *Penal Era and Golden Age: Essays in Irish History 1690–1800*, Belfast: Ulster Historical Foundation, 1979, p. 171. For 'lives' leases, see above, p. 95.

that expired, till they have arrived at the present exorbitance; when the frog, overswelling himself, burst at last.[15]

With the price of land, of necessity rose that of corn and cattle, and all other commodities that farmers deal in: Hence likewise, obviously, the rates of all goods and manufactures among shopkeepers, the wages of servants, and hire of labourers. But, although our miseries came on fast with neither trade nor money left, yet neither will the landlord abate in his rent, nor can the tenant abate in the price of what that rent must be paid with, nor any shopkeeper, tradesman, or labourer live at lower expence, for food and clothing, than he did before.

I have been the larger upon this first head, because the same observations will clear up and strengthen a good deal of what I shall affirm upon the rest.

The second Maxim of those who reason upon trade and government, is to assert, that low interest is a certain sign of great plenty of money in a nation, for which, as in many other articles, they produce the examples of Holland and England.[16] But, with relation to Ireland, this Maxim is likewise entirely false.

There are two reasons for the lowness of interest in any country. First, that which is usually alleged, the great plenty of species;[17] and this is obvious. The second is the want of trade, which seldom falls under common observation, although it be equally true. For, where trade is altogether discouraged, there are few borrowers. In those countries where men can employ a large stock, the young merchant, whose fortune may be four or five hundred pounds, will venture to borrow as much more, and can afford a reasonable interest. Neither is it easy at this day to find many of those, whose business reaches to employ even so inconsiderable a sum, except among the importers of wine; who, as they have most part of the present trade in these parts of Ireland in their hands, so they are the most

---

15 *the frog... burst at last*: a reference to Aesop's fable of the ox and the frog, in which a family of young frogs returning home reported having seen a huge creature in a field – the ox – and their mother, in straining to expand to the same size, burst in the effort.

16 *they produce the examples of Holland and England*: see, for example, David Bindon, *A Scheme for Supplying Industrious Men with Money to Carry on Their Trades, and for Better Providing for the Poor of Ireland*, Dublin, 1729, pp. 6–7; Browne, *Essay on Trade*, pp. 104–5; John Browne, *Seasonable Remarks on Trade with Some Reflections on the Advantages that Might Accrue to Great Britain by a Proper Regulation of the Trade of Ireland*, Dublin, 1728, p. 63.

17 *species*: coined money.

exorbitant, exacting, fraudulent dealers, that ever trafficked in any nation, and are making all possible speed to ruin both themselves and the nation.

From this defect, of gentlemens not knowing how to dispose of their ready money, ariseth the high purchase of lands, which in all other countries is reckoned a sign of wealth. For, the frugal squires, who live below their incomes, have no other way to dispose of their savings but by mortgage or purchase, by which the rates of land must naturally encrease; and, if this trade continues long under the uncertainty of rents, the landed men of ready money will find it more for their advantage to send their cash to England, and place it in the funds; which I myself am determined to do, the first considerable sum I shall be master of.

It hath likewise been a Maxim among politicians, that the great encrease of buildings in the metropolis argues a flourishing state. But this, I confess, hath been controlled from the example of London; where, by the long and annual parliamentary sessions,[18] such a number of senators, with their families, friends, adherents, and expectants, draw such prodigious numbers to that city, that the old hospitable custom of lords and gentlemen living in their antient seats, among their tenants, is almost lost in England;[19] is laughed out of doors; in so much that, in the middle of summer, a legal House of Lords and Commons might be brought in a few hours to London from their country villas within twelve miles round.

The case in Ireland is yet somewhat worse: For the absentees of great estates, who, if they lived at home, would have many rich retainers in their neighbourhoods, having learned to rack their lands,[20] and shorten their leases, as much as any residing squire; and the few remaining of these latter, having some vain hope of employments for themselves or their children, and discouraged by the beggarliness and thievery of their own miserable farmers and cottagers, or seduced by the vanity of their wives, on

---

18 *the example of London... annual parliamentary sessions*: on the growth of London in the seventeenth and early eighteenth centuries, see A. L. Beier and R. A. P. Finlay (eds.), *London 1500–1700: The Making of the Metropolis*, London: Longmans, 1986; and George Rudé, *Hanoverian London, 1714–1808*, London: Secker & Warburg, 1971. Annual parliamentary sessions became an ingrained feature of political life in England only after the Glorious Revolution.
19 *the old hospitable custom... is almost lost in England*: for the 'fragmentation' of notions of hospitality in sixteenth- and seventeenth-century England, and the disappearance of the traditional customs of the medieval nobility, see Felicity Heal, *Hospitality in Early Modern England*, Oxford: Clarendon Press, 1990, chs. 2–3, 10.
20 *rack their lands*: impose an extortionate rent.

pretence of their children's education, (whereof the fruits are so apparent) together with that most wonderful and yet more unaccountable zeal for a seat in their assembly, though at some years purchase of their whole estates.[21] These, and some other motives better let pass, have drawn such a concourse to this beggarly city, that the dealers of the several branches of building have found out all the commodious and inviting places for erecting new houses,[22] while fifteen hundred of the old ones, which is a seventh part of the whole city, are said to be left uninhabited, and falling to ruin. Their method is the same with that which was first introduced by Doctor Barebone at London, who died a bankrupt.[23] The mason, the bricklayer, the carpenter, the slater, and the glazier, take a lot of ground,[24] club[25] to build one or more houses, unite their credit, their stock, and their money, and when their work is finished, sell it to the best advantage they can. But, as it often happens, and more every day, that their fund will not answer half their design, they are forced to undersell it at the first story, and are all reduced to beggary. In so much that I know a certain fanatic brewer,* who is reported to have some hundreds of houses in this town,[26] is said to have purchased the greater part of them at half value from ruined undertakers, hath intelligence of all new houses where the finishing is at

---

* Leeson.

21 *though at some years purchase of their whole estates*: for the rising cost of elections between 1715 and 1727, see D. W. Hayton, 'Voters, Patrons and Parties: Parliamentary Elections in Ireland, c. 1692–1727', in Clyve Jones, Philip Salmon and R. W. Davis (eds.), *Partisan Politics, Principle and Reform in Parliament and the Constituencies, 1689–1880: Essays in Memory of John A. Phillips*, Edinburgh: Edinburgh University Press, 2005, pp. 67–8.
22 *erecting new houses*: for the expansion of Dublin in the 1720s and beyond, see Edel Sheridan, 'Designing the Capital City: Dublin, c. 1660–1810', in Joseph Brady and Anngret Simms (eds.), *Dublin through Space and Time*, Dublin: Four Courts Press, 2001, pp. 88–93; Christine Casey, *The Buildings of Ireland: Dublin: The City within the Grand and Royal Canals and the Circular Road with the Phoenix Park*, New Haven & London: Yale University Press, 2005, pp. 43–5; Dickson, *Dublin*, pp. 139–42; and above, p. 24.
23 *Doctor Barebone . . . who died a bankrupt*: Nicholas Barbon (*c.* 1637–98) of Crane Court, Fleet Street, London, and Osterley Park, Middlesex, who had been involved in numerous schemes in London involving property development, insurance and banking, ended his life hopelessly in debt: see *HP 1690–1715*, vol. III, pp. 131–3.
24 *a lot of ground*: a plot or portion of land.
25 *club*: form themselves into a single body for the purpose stated; that is to say, pool their resources.
26 *a certain fanatic brewer . . . in this town*: Joseph Leeson (d. 1741) of Dublin, father of Joseph, 1st Earl of Milltown. Whether or not the elder Joseph Leeson was a Dissenter, as Swift alleges, his son certainly conformed to the established church.

a stand, takes advantage of the builder's distress, and, by the advantage of ready money, gets fifty *per cent.* at least for his bargain.

It is another undisputed Maxim in government, that people are the riches of a nation;[27] which is so universally granted, that it will be hardly pardonable to bring it in doubt. And I will grant it to be so far true, even in this island, that, if we had the African custom or privilege, of selling our useless bodies for slaves to foreigners, it would be the most useful branch of our trade, by ridding us of a most unsupportable burthen, and bringing us money in the stead.[28] But, in our present situation, at least five children in six who are born lie a dead weight upon us for want of employment. And a very skilful computer[29] assured me, that above one half of the souls in this kingdom supported themselves by begging and thievery, whereof two thirds would be able to get their bread in any other country upon earth. Trade is the only incitement to labour: Where that fails, the poorer native must either beg, steal, or starve, or be forced to quit his country. This hath made me often wish, for some years past, that, instead of discouraging our people from seeking foreign soil, that the public would rather pay for transporting all our unnecessary mortals, whether Papists or Protestants, to America, as drawbacks are sometimes allowed for exporting commodities where a nation is overstocked. I confess myself to be touched with a very sensible pleasure, when I hear of a mortality in any country-parish or village, where the wretches are forced to pay for a filthy cabin and two ridges of potatoes treble the worth, brought up to steal or beg, for want of work, to whom death would be the best thing to be wished for, on account both of themselves and the public.

Among all taxes imposed by the legislature, those upon luxury are universally allowed to be the most equitable and beneficial to the subject;[30]

---

27 *people are the riches of a nation*: an accepted dictum of mercantilist economics (see above, p. 88).
28 *in the stead*: in *A Modest Proposal* (see above, p. 146), Swift refers to Irish Catholics 'sell[ing] themselves to the Barbadoes', as indentured servants, a solution to the problem of overpopulation which is inferior to the one he is recommending.
29 *computer*: one who makes calculations.
30 *those upon luxury . . . beneficial to the subject*: for eighteenth-century views on 'luxury' and its deleterious social consequences, see John Sekora, *Luxury: The Concept in Western Thought, Eden to Smollett*, Baltimore: Johns Hopkins University Press, 1977. The author of *An Inquiry into Some of the Causes of the Ill Situation of the Affairs of Ireland*, London, 1732, declared that 'the great bane of Ireland is luxury' (p. 55). Not all contemporaries, however, regarded legislative action as feasible: for example, Bishop Francis Hutchinson's *A Letter to*

and the commonest reasoner on government might fill a volume with arguments on the subject. Yet here again, by the singular fate of Ireland, this maxim is utterly false; and the putting it in practice may have such pernicious a consequence, as I certainly believe the thoughts of the proposers were not able to reach.

The miseries we suffer by our absentees are of a far more extensive nature than seems to be commonly understood. I must vindicate myself to the reader so far, as to declare solemnly that what I shall say of those lords and squires, doth not arise from the least regard I have for their understandings, their virtues, or their persons. For, although I have not the honour of the least acquaintance with any one among them, (my ambition not soaring so high) yet I am too good a witness of the situation they have been in for thirty years past, the veneration paid them by the people, the high esteem they are in among the prime nobility and gentry, the particular marks of favour and distinction they receive from the court: The weight and consequence of their interest, added to their great zeal and application for preventing any hardships their country might suffer from England, wisely considering that their own fortunes and honours were embarked in the same bottom.[31]

---

a Member of Parliament, Concerning the Imploying and Providing for the Poor, Dublin, 1723, p. 11, had argued strongly against the introduction of 'sumptuary laws'.
31 *were embarked in the same bottom*: had a common interest (from the idea of a ship's bottom).

ADVERTISEMENT BY DR SWIFT, IN HIS DEFENCE AGAINST JOSHUA, LORD ALLEN

Headnote

Composed February 1730; published posthumously, 1801; copy text *1801* (see Textual Account).

The award of the freedom of the city of Dublin and a gold box was a recognition of Swift's status as patriot and as a defender of the interests of Ireland in general, and the Dublin manufacturing classes in particular. It is also more implicitly connected to the heightened political animation of Dublin in 1729, particularly the increased conflict originating from the rise of a patriotic lobby (see above, *Introduction*, pp. lxxxvii–xciv).

On 16 January 1730, the corporation of Dublin voted to give Swift his freedom in a gold box, but on 13 February following, when the lord mayor and sheriffs were summoned to attend the privy council to answer questions concerning riots which had occurred in the city, they were harangued over this decision by Joshua, Viscount Allen. According to Marmaduke Coghill, Allen 'wondered how they should complain of poverty, when they were so lavish as to give a gold box to a man who neither feared God nor honoured the king, who had wrote a libel on the king, queen and the government' (Coghill to Edward Southwell, 21 Feb. 1729[/30] (*Coghill Letters*, pp. 91–2)). Allen's criticism brought forth this 'Advertisement' from Swift, though there is no evidence that it was ever published or otherwise distributed in Swift's lifetime, or that Swift intended it to be.

ADVERTISEMENT BY DR. SWIFT. IN HIS DEFENCE AGAINST JOSHUA, LORD ALLEN,[1] FEB. 18, 1729.

"WHEREAS Dr. Jonathan Swift, dean of St. Patrick's Dublin, hath been credibly informed, that on Friday the 13th of this instant February, a certain person did, in a publick place, and in the hearing of a great number, apply himself to the right honourable the lord mayor of this city, and some of his brethren, in the following reproachful manner: 'My lord, you and your city can squander away the publick money, in giving a gold box to a fellow who has libelled the government!' or words to that effect. Now, if the said words, or words to the like effect,[2] were intended against him the said dean, and as a reflection on the right hon. the lord mayor, aldermen, and commons, for the decreeing unanimously, and in full assembly, the freedom of this city to the said dean, in an honourable manner, on account of an opinion they had conceived of some services done by him the said dean to this city, and to the kingdom in general: The said dean doth declare, that the said words, or words to the like effect, are insolent, false, scandalous, malicious, and in a particular manner perfidious; the said person, who is reported to have spoken the said or the like words, having for some years past, and even within some few days, professed a great friendship for the said dean; and, what is hardly credible, sending a common friend of the dean and himself, not many hours after the said or the like words had been spoken, to renew his profession of friendship to the said dean, but concealing the oratory; whereof the dean had no account till the following day, and then told it to all his friends."

---

1 *JOSHUA, LORD ALLEN*: Joshua Allen (1685–1742), 2nd Viscount Allen, formerly MP [Ire.] for Co. Kildare, 1709–26.
2 *a certain person ... words to the like effect*: on 16 Jan. 1730, the corporation of Dublin had voted to give Swift his freedom in a gold box (*Cal. Anc. Recs Dublin*, vol. VII, p. 476). Allen's hectoring speech to the lord mayor and sheriffs was delivered on 13 Feb. (see Headnote).

THE SUBSTANCE OF WHAT WAS SAID BY THE DEAN OF ST PATRICK'S TO THE LORD MAYOR AND SOME OF THE ALDERMEN, WHEN HIS LORDSHIP CAME TO PRESENT THE SAID DEAN WITH HIS FREEDOM IN A GOLD-BOX

Headnote

Composed May–June 1730; published posthumously, 1765; copy text *1765a* (see Textual Account); the footnotes that form part of this text were provided by the editor, Deane Swift.

This record of what Swift supposedly said when receiving the freedom of Dublin and a gold box on 27 May 1730 was presumably written soon after and was arguably not really intended for a wide audience; Ehrenpreis suggests it was only written for friends and allies (vol. III, p. 655).

After the corporation had voted to present Swift with his freedom, the dean proposed what Marmaduke Coghill called an 'arrogant' inscription, the terms of which gave the corporation pause, and resulted in the deferral of the presentation. The phrasing (which had probably been communicated to the corporation by Patrick Delany on Swift's behalf) would have cited the dean's 'great zeal, unequalled abilities and distinguished munificence in asserting the rights, defending the liberties, and encouraging the manufactures of the kingdom' and declared that he was 'justly esteemed the most eminent patriot and greatest ornament of his native city and country'. When the mayor and aldermen eventually presented him with his gold box, there was no inscription, and, to make matters worse, a presentation had already been made to the archbishop of Dublin. Hence Swift's self-righteous outburst, and the recitation of his achievements as an Irish 'patriot' which would otherwise have been engraved for posterity (see Coghill to Edward Southwell, 21 Feb. 1729[/30] (*Coghill Letters*, pp. 91–2); Ehrenpreis, vol. III, pp. 650–5).

THE SUBSTANCE OF WHAT WAS SAID BY THE DEAN OF ST. PATRICK'S TO THE LORD MAYOR[1] AND SOME OF THE ALDERMEN, WHEN HIS LORDSHIP CAME TO PRESENT THE SAID DEAN WITH HIS FREEDOM IN A GOLD-BOX.[2]

When his Lordship had said a few words, and presented the instrument,[3] the Dean gently put it back, and desired first to be heard. He said, He was much obliged to his Lordship and the city for the honour they were going to do him, and which, as he was informed, they had long intended him:[4] That it was true this honour was mingled with a little mortification, by the delay which attended it; but which, however, he did not impute to his Lordship or the city: And that the mortification was the less, because he would willingly hope the delay was founded on a mistake; for which opinion he would tell his reason. He said, It was well known, that, some time ago, a person with a title was pleased, in two great assemblies, to rattle bitterly some body without a name,[5] under the injurious appellations of a Tory, a Jacobite, an enemy to King George, and a libeller of the government;[6] which character, the Dean said that many people thought, was applied to him: But he was unwilling to be of that opinion, because the person who had delivered those abusive words had, for several years, caressed and courted, and solicited his friendship more than any man in either kingdom had ever done; by inviting him to his house in town and country, by coming to the Deanry often, and

---

1 *LORD MAYOR*: Sir Peter Verdoen (d. 1731), lord mayor of Dublin 1729–30.
2 *[Title]*: on 27 May 1730 (Ehrenpreis, vol. III, p. 655). The presentation of the freedom of a corporation in a gold or silver box was a special distinction commonly reserved for lords lieutenant and other dignitaries. The original vote to give Swift his freedom, in January 1730, had stipulated that the gold box containing the certificate of freedom was not to exceed £25 in value (*Cal. Anc. Recs. Dublin*, vol. VII, p. 176).
3 *instrument*: in the sense of a formal legal document.
4 *they had long intended him*: there had been talk of a presentation in 1724 in recognition of Swift's service in writing the *Drapier's Letters* (Ehrenpreis, vol. III, p. 650).
5 *a person with a title... without a name*: Joshua, 2nd Viscount Allen.
6 *to rattle bitterly ... libeller of the government*: primarily in respect of the *Drapier's Letters*. Coghill reported to Edward Southwell on 18 April that Allen 'had abused Swift in a speech he made at the privy council, and another in the House of Lords, which Swift promised to give him some return for, when the parliament was up' (*Coghill Letters*, p. 98). Swift's version of the latter speech was that Allen had denounced him as 'a Jacobite libeller &c' and had asked for the prosecution of the printer of *A Libel on Dr Delany*: Swift to Pope, 26 Feb. 1729/30 (Woolley, *Corr.*, vol. III, p. 284; Ehrenpreis, vol. III, p. 653).

calling or sending almost every day when the Dean was sick, with many other particulars of the same nature, which continued even to a day or two of the time when the said person made those invectives in the Council and House of Lords. Therefore, that the Dean would by no means think those scurrilous words could be intended against him; because such a proceeding would overthrow all the principles of honour, justice, religion, truth, and even common humanity. Therefore the Dean will endeavour to believe, that the said person had some other object in his thoughts, and it was only the uncharitable custom of the world that applied this character to him. However, that he would insist on this argument no longer: But one thing he would affirm and declare, without assigning any name or making any exception, That, whoever either did or does, or shall hereafter at any time, charge him with the character of a Jacobite, an enemy to King George, or a libeller of the government, the said accusation was, is, and will be false, malicious, slanderous, and altogether groundless. And, he would take the freedom to tell his Lordship and the rest that stood by, that he had done more service to the Hanover-title, and more disservice to the Pretender's cause, than forty thousand of those noisy, railing, malicious, empty zealots, to whom nature hath denied any talent that could be of use to God or their country, and left them only the gift of reviling, and spitting their venom, against all who differ from them in their destructive principles both in church and state. That he confessed it was sometimes his misfortune to dislike some things in public proceedings in both kingdoms, wherein he had often the honour to agree with wise and good men; but this did by no means affect either his loyalty to his prince, or love to his country. But, on the contrary, he protested that such dislikes never arose in him from any other principles, than the duty he owed to the King, and his affection to the kingdom. That he had been acquainted with courts and ministers long enough, and knew too well that the best ministers might mistake in points of great importance; and that he had the honour to know many more able, and at least full as honest as any can be at present. The Dean further said, That, since he had been so falsely represented, he thought it became him to give some account of himself for above twenty years, if it were only to justify his Lordship and the city for the honour they were going to do him. He related briefly how, merely by his own personal credit, without other assistance, and in two journeys at his own expence, he had procured a grant of the first fruits to the clergy, in the late Queen's time; for which he thought he deserved some gentle treatment from his brethren.[7] That, during said ministry, he had been a constant advocate for those who are called the Whigs; had kept many of them in their employments, both in England and here,[8] and some who were afterwards the first to lift up their heels against him. He reflected a little upon the severe treatment he had met with upon his return to Ireland after her Majesty's death, and for some years after. That, being forced to live retired, he could think of no better way to do public service, than by employing all the little money he could save, and lending it, without interest, in small sums to poor industrious tradesmen, without examining their party or their faith.[9] And God had so far pleased to bless his endeavours, that his managers tell him he hath recovered above two hundred families in this city from ruin, and placed most of them in a comfortable way of life. The Dean related how much he had suffered in his purse, and with what hazard to his liberty, by a most iniquitous judge;[10] who, to gratify his ambition and rage of party, had condemned an innocent book, written with no worse a design, than to persuade the people of this kingdom to wear their own manufactures.[11] How the said judge had endeavoured to get a jury to his mind, but they

---

7 *in two journeys... he deserved some gentle treatment from his brethren*: Swift had been in London from November 1707 to June 1709, representing the interests of the Church of Ireland in negotiations for the remission of the first fruits and twentieth parts paid by clergy from the first year's income from a benefice. Although unsuccessful on that occasion, he returned in August 1710 at the behest of Archbishop King and other bishops to press the incoming ministry on this subject, and after a personal interview with Robert Harley, chancellor of the exchequer and *de facto* 'premier minister', was informed in October that the queen had acceded to the request.
8 *during all the administration... both in England and here*: two Irish examples were the postmaster-general Isaac Manley, whom Swift once called 'the most violent party man in Ireland' (for whom, see *Hist. Ir. Parl.*, vol. V, pp. 190–1; D. W. Hayton, 'Two Ballads on the County Westmeath By-Election of 1723', *ECI* 4 (1989), 28), and the teller of the exchequer Robert Clements (for whom, see *Hist. Ir. Parl.*, vol. III, p. 431; A. P. W. Malcomson, *Nathaniel Clements: Government and the Governing Elite in Ireland, 1725–75*, Dublin: Four Courts Press, 2005, pp. 10–14): *CWJS*, vol. IX, pp. 93, 178, 185, 385.
9 *lending it... without examining their party or their faith*: by 1703, Swift had begun to lend small sums of 'industrious money' to tradespeople at low rates of interest, and he continued to do so all his life: Paul V. Thompson and Dorothy Jay Thompson (eds.), *The Account Books of Jonathan Swift*, London: Scolar Press, 1984, p. cxxvi.
10 *a most iniquitous judge*: William Whitshed (1679–1727), chief justice of king's bench [Ire.] 1714–27, common pleas [Ire.], 1727–d.
11 *an innocent book... their own manufactures*: Whitshed had presided over the trial of Edward Waters in 1720 for publishing Swift's *Proposal for the Universal Use of Irish Manufacture*.

proved so honest, that he was forced to keep them eleven hours, and send them back nine times, until, at last, they were compelled to leave the printer* to the mercy of the court.[12] And the Dean was forced to procure a *noli prosequi*[13] from a** Noble Person, then secretary of state, who had been his old friend.[14] The Dean then freely confessed himself to be author of those books called the *Drapier's Letters*, spoke gently of the proclamation offering 300 *l.* to discover the writer.[15] He said, That although a certain person was pleased to mention those books in a slight manner at a public assembly, yet he (the Dean) had learned to believe, that there were ten thousand to one in the kingdom who differed from that person; and the people of England, who had ever heard of the matter, as well as in France, were all of the same opinion. The Dean mentioned several other particulars, some of which, those from whom I had the account could not recollect, and others, although of great consequence, perhaps his enemies would not allow him. The Dean concluded with acknowledging to have expressed his wishes, that an inscription might have been graven on the box, shewing some reason why the city thought fit to do him that honour, which was much out of the common forms to a person in a private station; those

* Mr Edward Waters.
** John, Lord Carteret, afterwards Lord Lieutenant of Ireland.
12 *the said judge had endeavoured... to the mercy of the court*: in Swift's account of the trial of Waters, Whitshed repeatedly refused to accept a 'not guilty' decision from the jury until eventually a 'special verdict' was brought in, which left Waters's fate 'to the mercy of the judge' (Ehrenpreis, vol. III, pp. 128–9).
13 *noli prosequi*: or *nolle prosequi*: a formal entry in the record of a criminal court by which the prosecutor declares that the charge will not be pursued.
14 *a Noble Person... who had been his old friend*: a lapse of memory. In the summer of 1720, when the lord lieutenant, the Duke of Grafton, issued the *noli prosequi*, the secretary of state for the southern department (with responsibility for Ireland) was James Craggs, who could not have been described as Swift's 'old friend'; neither could the northern secretary, James, Earl Stanhope. Swift may have meant Lord Carteret, who became southern secretary in 1721. But in fact he had approached Grafton through the former Speaker of the House of Commons, Sir Thomas Hanmer, who was Grafton's stepfather (Ehrenpreis, vol. III, p. 130).
15 *spoke gently... to discover the writer*: at a meeting of the Irish privy council on 27 Oct. 1724, soon after his arrival in Dublin, the lord lieutenant, Lord Carteret, had prevailed on the council to agree to a proclamation offering a reward for the identification of the author of the Drapier's *Letter to the Whole People of Ireland*, despite considerable opposition: Carteret to the Duke of Newcastle, 28 Oct. 1724 (TNA, SP 63/384/984); Ehrenpreis, vol. III, pp. 268–70.

distinctions being usually made only to chief governors,[16] or persons in very high employments.

---

16 *chief governors*: the traditional title for the sovereign's deputy in Ireland, and still used alongside lord lieutenant or lord deputy. See Herbert Wood, 'The Office of Chief Governor of Ireland, 1172–1509', *Proceedings of the Royal Irish Academy* 36 (1921–4), sect. C, 206–38; Ciaran Brady, 'Viceroys? The Irish Chief Governors, 1541–1641', in Peter Gray and Olwen Purdue (eds.), *The Irish Lord Lieutenancy, c. 1541–1922*, Dublin: University College Dublin Press, 2012, pp. 15–18; Charles Ivar McGrath, 'Late Seventeenth- and Early Eighteenth-century Governance and the Viceroyalty', in Gray and Purdue (eds.), *Irish Lord Lieutenancy*, pp. 43–65.

A VINDICATION OF HIS EXCELLENCY THE LORD CARTERET, FROM THE CHARGE OF FAVOURING NONE BUT TORYES, HIGH-CHURCHMEN AND JACOBITES

Headnote

Composed April 1730; published April 1730; copy text *1730a* (see Textual Account).

Swift's friendship with John Carteret, Lord Lieutenant of Ireland from 1724 to 1730, dated back to Queen Anne's reign, when the young Carteret had been a Hanoverian Tory. It was renewed when Carteret came over to Ireland as viceroy in 1725, and Swift was able to secure from him some small items of patronage for his friends. But in general terms, Carteret pursued a political course in Ireland which involved the maintenance of local Whig interests in power; in 1730, he had ended his last parliamentary session in Ireland on a popular note.

Swift's ostensible and unnecessary defence of Carteret from the charge that he only gave advancement to Tories and Jacobites was also an opportunity to attack several enemies (Joshua Allen and Richard Tighe, appearing as Traulus and Pistorides, respectively, and unidentified in Irish editions of Swift during his lifetime) aligned to the Whig interest. Swift's pamphlet is more an attack on Whig paranoia (either real or affected) about Tory advancement under Carteret: the latter had been a Tory, and there had been a temporary recrudescence of the Tory interest in some boroughs after his arrival in 1725. By 1730, such charges were obviously unreasonable.

The pamphlet is internally dated by Swift's reference to the time of writing as 13 April 1730 (below, p. 214), and was published to coincide with the proroguing of Parliament on 15 April (see Woolley, *Corr.*, vol. III, p. 310 fn. 9, and Ehrenpreis, vol. III, p. 658).

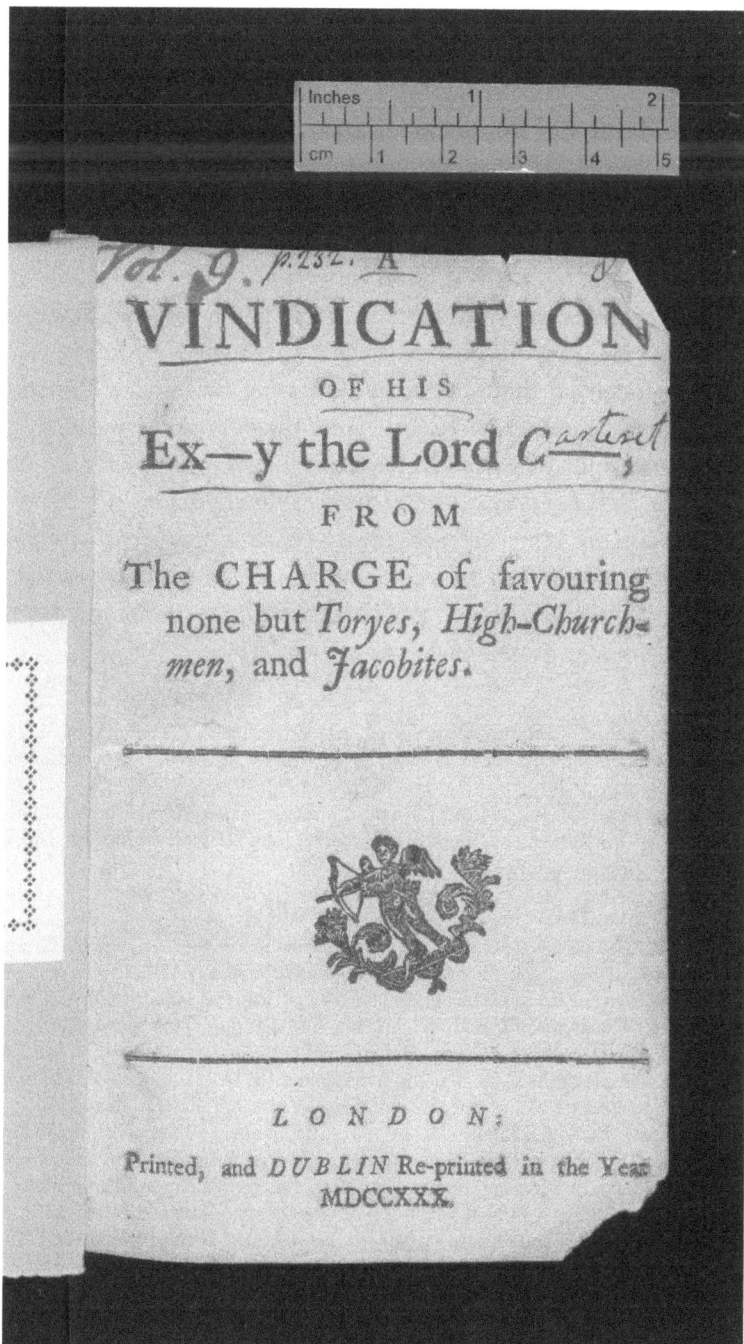

Figure 4. Jonathan Swift, *A Vindication of His Excellency the Lord Carteret*, 1730. Title. Williams 410.

A VINDICATION OF HIS EX - -Y THE LORD C—,[1] &c

In order to Treat this important Subject with the greatest Fairness and Impartiality, perhaps it may be convenient to give some Account of his E——, in whose Life and Character there are certain Particulars, which might give a very just Suspicion of some Truth in the Accusation he lyes under.

He is descended from two Noble, Antient, and most loyal Families, the *Carterets* and the *Granvilles*.[2] Too much distinguish'd, I confess, for what they acted, and what they suffer'd in defending the former Constitution in Church and State, under King *Charles* the Martyr;[3] I mean that very Prince, on Account of whose Martyrdom *a Form of Prayer with Fasting was enjoyned, by Act of Parliament, to be used on the 30th Day of* January *every Year, to implore the Mercies of God, that the Guilt of that sacred and innocent Blood, might not be visited on us or our Posterity,* as we may read at large in our *Common-Prayer-Books*.[4] Which Day hath been solemnly kept, ev'n within the Memory of many Men now alive.[5]

---

1 *His Ex—y the Lord C—*: His Excellency the Lord Carteret. John Carteret (1690–1763), 2nd Baron Carteret and later 1st Earl Granville; lord lieutenant of Ireland 1724–30 (for whom, see *ODNB*).
2 *the Carterets and the Granvilles*: Lord Carteret was the son of George Carteret, 1st Lord Carteret by his wife Grace, the daughter of Sir John Granville, 1st Earl of Bath, and later (1715) *suo jure* Countess Granville.
3 *in defending . . . King Charles the Martyr*: Carteret's paternal great-grandfather, Sir George Carteret, 1st Bt, had held Jersey for Charles I until 1651 as a privateering stronghold, before going into exile in the service of the French king. Members of the Granville (or Grenville) family had also distinguished themselves in the Royalist service, and Carteret's maternal great-grandfather, Sir Bevill Grenville, had been killed at the head of the Cornish infantry at the battle of Lansdowne in 1643. While it was true that the Granvilles had suffered financially for their loyalty, Sir George Carteret had not been impoverished; in fact, he had done rather well out of the Civil War and interregnum (B. D. Henning, *The House of Commons 1660–1690*, 3 vols., London: Secker and Warburg, 1983, vol. II, p. 28).
4 *Common-Prayer-Books*: the English Act of 1661 (12 Chas II c. 30), establishing 30 January as 'an anniversary day of fasting and humiliation', had been written so as to apply to Ireland as well as England; there was no separate Irish Act. The revised English Prayer Book, sanctioned for use in Ireland by the Irish Act of Uniformity of 1666, included the commemoration of 30 January, and this usage was confirmed by royal warrant in 1715. Irish preachers and newspapers routinely referred to 30 January sermons as prescribed by Act of Parliament. This complex story is unravelled in S. J. Connolly, 'The Church of Ireland and the Royal Martyr: Regicide and Revolution in Anglican Political Thought c. 1660–c. 1745', *Journal of Ecclesiastical History* 54 (2003), 486–7.
5 *ev'n within the Memory of many Men now alive*: the feast of the execution of King Charles the Martyr was recognised in the Church of Ireland as a day of fast and humiliation, even if the

His E——y the present Lord, was educated in the University of *Oxford*,[6] from whence, with a singularity scarce to be justifyed, he carry'd away more *Greek, Latin,* and *Philosophy*, than properly became a Person of his Rank,[7] indeed much more of each than most of those who are forced to Live by their Learning, will be at the unnecessary Pains to load their Heads with. This was the Rock he split on,[8] upon his first Appearance in the World, and just got clear of his Guardians.[9] For, as soon as he came to Town, some Bishops, and Clergymen, and other Persons most Eminent for Learning and Parts, got him among them,[10] from whom tho' he were fortunately dragg'd by a Lady[11] and the Court, yet he cou'd never wipe off the Stain,[12] nor wash out the Tincture of his University Acquirements and Disposition.

precise legal basis was unclear; however, no official commemorative sermon had been published since Carteret's chaplain, James Ward, had preached before the viceroy at Christ Church in 1725: James Ward, *A Sermon Preach'd in Christ's Church, Dublin; before His Excellency John, Lord Carteret, Lord Lieutenant General, and General Governour of Ireland...*, Dublin, 1724[/5]. Worse still, from Swift's point of view, the sermons preached after 1714, including Ward's, were ideologically Whiggish, playing down the sacrilegious aspect of the regicide and presenting Charles I as the victim of circumstances and his own misjudgements: Connolly, 'Church of Ireland and the Royal Martyr', 496–8. Swift himself partially reversed this trend in his own commemorative sermon, preached in St Patrick's in 1726 (Davis, vol. IX, pp. 219–31), which began with a riposte to those who would censure the church 'for keeping holy this day of humiliation' as themselves being 'people without any religion at all, or who derived their principles, and perhaps their birth, from the abettors of those who contrived the murder of that prince' (p. 219), and went on to observe that commemorative sermons 'of late times' had been 'of a strange nature' (pp. 226–7). See also above, p. 70.

6 *educated in the University of Oxford*: Carteret went up to Christ Church in 1706, though he did not take a degree until the conferment of a DCL by diploma in 1756 (Basil Williams, *Carteret and Newcastle: A Contrast in Contemporaries*, Cambridge: Cambridge University Press, 1943, pp. 10–11).
7 *he carry'd away... became a Person of his Rank*: for Thomas Hearne's observation that the young Carteret had been 'well versed in the best Greek and Latin authors', see Williams, *Carteret and Newcastle*, p. 11; for a sourer view, see the letters of Carteret's tutor William Stratford to Edward Harley, 25, 29 July 1710, 16 June 1711 (HMC, *Portland MSS*, vol. VII, pp. 7–8, 33).
8 *he split on*: on which he was wrecked.
9 *just got clear of his Guardians*: Carteret attained his majority in April 1711 and took his seat in the House of Lords in the following month.
10 *some Bishops... got him among them*: for evidence of Carteret's early attachment to the Tory interest, see Williams, *Carteret and Newcastle*, p. 14; Geoffrey Holmes, *British Politics in the Age of Anne*, London: Macmillan, 1967, pp. 280, 424, 426.
11 *by a Lady*: his formidable mother.
12 *wipe off the Stain*: a phrase which had been given public expression during and after the exposure of the so-called 'Atterbury Plot' and the passage of a Bill of pains and penalties against Swift's friend, Bishop Atterbury. In the context of removing the stigma of Jacobitism from the Church of England, it had appeared in a pamphlet by the royal chaplain Zachary Pearce, *A Letter to the Clergy of the Church of England: on Occasion of the*

To this another Misfortune was added; that it pleas'd God to endow him with great Natural Talents, Memory, Judgment, Comprehension, Eloquence, and Wit. And, to finish the Work, all these were fortify'd even in his Youth, with the Advantages receiv'd by such Employments as are best fitted both to Exercise and Polish the Gifts of Nature and Education; having been Ambassador in several Courts when his Age would hardly allow him to take a Degree,[13] and made Principal Secretary of State, at a Period when, according to Custom, he ought to have been busied in losing his Money at a Chocolate-House,[14] or in other Amusements equally Laudable and Epidemick among Persons of Honour.

I cannot omit another weak Side in his E——, for it is known, and can be proved upon him, that *Greek* and *Latin* Books might be found every Day in his Dressing-Room,[15] if it were carefully search'd; and there is Reason to suspect, that some of the said Books have been privately conveyed to him by *Tory* Hands. I am likewise assured, that he hath been taken in the very Fact of reading the said Books, even in the midst of a Session, to the great Neglect of publick Affairs.

I own there may be some grounds for this Charge, because I have it from good Hands, that when his E—— is at Dinner with one or two Scholars at his Elbows, he grows a most unsupportable, and unintelligible Companion to all the fine Gentlemen round the Table.

I cannot deny that his E—— lyes under another great Disadvantage. For, with all the Accomplishments abovemention'd, adding that of a most comely and graceful Person, and during the Prime of Youth, Spirits and Vigor, he hath in a most unexemplary manner led a regular domestick Life, discovers a great Esteem, and Friendship, and Love for his Lady, as well as a true Affection for his Children;[16] and when he is disposed to

Commitment of the Right Reverend the Lord Bishop of Rochester to the Tower of London, London, 1722, p. 10. Swift noted the appearance of Pearce's pamphlet when it was republished in Dublin: Swift to Robert Cope, 9 Oct. 1722 (Woolley, *Corr.*, vol. II, p. 432).

13 *when his Age would hardly allow him to take a Degree*: in fact, Carteret's first diplomatic posting, as ambassador-extraordinary to Sweden in January 1719, occurred at the age of twenty-eight.

14 *ought to have been... at a Chocolate-House*: Carteret was appointed secretary of state for the southern department in February 1721, not long before his thirty-first birthday.

15 *Greek and Latin Books... in his Dressing-Room*: for Carteret's continued enthusiasm for learning, see Williams, *Carteret and Newcastle*, p. 78.

16 *Love for... his Children*: Carteret married, in 1710, Frances (d. 1743), daughter of Sir Robert Worsley, 4th Bt, and grand-daughter of the 1st Viscount Weymouth, by whom he had one surviving son and four daughters.

admit an entertaining Evening Companion, he doth not always enough reflect whether the Person may possibly in former Days have lain under the Imputation of a *Tory*; nor at such times do the natural or affected fears of *Popery* and the *Pretender* make any part of the Conversation: I presume, because neither *Homer, Plato, Aristotle,* nor *Cicero* have made any mention of them.

These I freely acknowledge to be his E——'s Failings: Yet I think, it is agreed by Philosophers and Divines, that some Allowance ought to be given to Human Infirmity, and the Prejudices of a wrong Education.

I am well aware how much my Sentiments differ from the orthodox Opinion of one or two principal Patriots (at the head of whom I name with Honour *Pistorides*.)[17] For these have decided the matter directly against me, by declaring that no Person who was ever known to lye under the Suspicion of one single *Tory* Principle, or who had been once seen at a Great Man's Levee in the *worst of Times*,[18] should be allowed to come within the Verge of the Castle; much less to bow in the Antichamber, appear at the *Assemblees*,[19] or dance at a Birth-Night.[20] However, I dare assert, that this Maxim hath been often controlled,[21] and that on the contrary a considerable number of *early Penitents* have been receiv'd into Grace, who are now an *Ornament, Happiness,* and *Support* to the Nation.[22]

17 *Pistorides*: identified by Marmaduke Coghill (Coghill to Edward Southwell, 18 Apr. 1730 (*Coghill Letters*, p. 98)) as Richard Tighe (1678–1736), MP for Augher, Co. Tyrone. Tighe was a frequent object of Swift's satirical scorn (see 'Mad Mullinix and Timothy' and a succession of subsequent poems in 1728/9 directed specifically at Tighe (*Poems*, vol. III, pp. 782–9)), and great play was made with his supposed descent from a bread-contractor to the Cromwellian army. In 'The Character, Panegyric and Description of the Legion Club' (1735), Swift called him 'Dick Fitzbaker' (*Poems*, vol. III, p. 835). 'Pistor' was the Latin term for a baker. For Tighe, see *Hist. Ir. Parl.*, vol. VI, pp. 395–7; Ehrenpreis, vol. III, pp. 579–81.
18 *in the worst of Times*: a cant expression of the Whigs to refer to the period of the Tory ministry, 1710–14, and in Ireland, more specifically, the lord chancellorship of Sir Constantine Phipps (1656–1723), between 1711 and 1714, who may well be the 'great man' alluded to here.
19 *Assemblees*: elegant social gatherings.
20 *at a Birth-Night*: the ball held at Dublin Castle on the reigning monarch's birthday.
21 *controlled*: confuted.
22 *a considerable number of early Penitents . . . Support to the Nation*: for those former Tories who had gone over to the administration after 1715, some of whom, like the Prime Serjeant Henry Singleton, were friends of Swift, see D. W. Hayton, *Ruling Ireland, 1685–1742: Politics, Politicians and Parties*, Woodbridge: Boydell Press, 2004, pp. 212, 247; D. W. Hayton, *The Anglo-Irish Experience, 1680–1730: Religion, Identity and Patriotism*, Woodbridge: Boydell Press, 2012, p. 129.

Neither do I find any murmuring on some other Points of greater Importance, where this favourite Maxim is not so strictly observed. To instance only in one. I have not heard that any Care hath hitherto been taken to discover whether Madam *Violante*[23] be a *Whig* or *Tory* in her Principles, or even that she hath ever been *offered the Oaths to the Government*; on the contrary I am told that she openly professeth herself to be a HIGH-FLYER,[24] and it is not improbable, by her *outlandish* Name she may also be a *Papist* in her Heart, yet we see this Illustrious and Dangerous Female openly caress'd by principal Persons of both Parties, who contribute to support her in a splendid manner, without the least Apprehensions from a *Grand Jury*, or even from Squire *H— H————*[25] himself, that *zealous Prosecutor of Hawkers and Libels*. And as *Hobbes* wisely observes, *so much Money* being equivalent to *so much Power*,[26] it may deserve considering with what safety such an Instrument of *Power* ought to be trusted in the Hands of an *Alien*, who hath not given any legal Security for her good Affection to the Government.

---

23 *Madam Violante*: Signora Violante *alias* Larini (1684–?1741), the famous Italian rope-dancer, and theatrical manager, who with her husband was a well-known celebrity on the London stage. After making one of her periodical visits to Dublin in 1730, she had set up a booth theatre in Dame Street. See Grainne McArdle, 'Signora Violante and her Troupe of Dancers, 1729–32', *ECI* 20 (2005), 55–78.
24 *High-Flyer*: a pun on the adjective 'high-flying', used for extreme High Church Tories.
25 *Squire H— H————*: Hartley Hutchinson (d. by 1769) of Dublin (Sir Arthur Vicars (ed.), *Index to the Prerogative Wills of Ireland, 1536–1810*, Dublin: Stationery Office, 1897, p. 244) was an attorney who, under Queen Anne, had served as a clerk in the hanaper office (the office in Chancery into which fees were paid for the sealing and enrolment of documents), where he had established a reputation as a staunch Whig (Archbishop Synge to Archbishop King, 7 Feb. 1722/3 (TCD, MS 1995–2008/2028)). He was also a Dublin magistrate, and in 1737 appeared on the grand jury in County Armagh (Armagh Robinson Library, KH.II.3, Armagh assizes indictment book, 1735–76, p. 9). He appended 'esquire' to his name when subscribing to literary works (e.g. *A Collection of Select Aphorisms and Maxims; with Several Historical Observations, Curious Remarks, and Characters of Persons and Things*, Dublin, 1722). Hutchinson irritated Swift by repeated participation in the prosecution of persons involved in the publishing trade, the most recent instance of which had been the arrest of two newsboys for selling the *Libel on D[octor] D[elany]*, for which Hutchinson was ridiculed in [William Dunkin?], *A Vindication of the Libel: or, a New Ballad: written by a Shoe-Boy, on an Attorney, who was formerly a Shoe-Boy* [?Dublin, 1730] (printed in *Poems*, vol. III, pp. 1133–4) and James Blackwell, *A Friendly Apology for a Certain Justice of the Peace, by Way of Defence of Hartley Hutchinson, esq.* [?Dublin, 1730].
26 *Hobbes . . . so much Power*: the sentiment may be inferred from Hobbes's writings on a number of different occasions (especially *Leviathan*, pt II, ch. 24, which talks of money as 'the blood of a commonwealth'). Swift owned (and annotated) copies of *Leviathan* and Hobbes's *Opera Philosophica* (*Library and Reading, I*, vol. II, pp. 870–1).

I confess, there is one Evil which I could wish our Friends would think proper to Redress. There are many *Whigs* in this Kingdom of the *old fashioned Stamp*,[27] of whom we might make very good use; They bear the same Loyalty with us, to the *Hanoverian* Family, in the Person of King *George* the IId: The same Abhorrence of the *Pretender*, with the Consequents of *Popery* and Slavery; and the same Indulgence to *tender Consciences*; but having nothing to ask for themselves, and consequently the more leisure to think for the Publick; they are often apt to entertain Fears, and melancholly Prospects concerning the State of their Country, the decay of Trade, the want of Money, the miserable Condition of the People, with other Topicks of like Nature, all which do equally concern both *Whig* and *Tory*, who if they have any thing to lose must be equally Sufferers. Perhaps one or two of these melancholly Gentlemen will sometimes venture to Publish their Thoughts in Print; Now I can by no means approve our usual Custom of Cursing and Railing at this Species of Thinkers under the Names of *Toryes, Jacobites, Papists, Libellers, Rebels*, and the like.

This was the utter Ruin of that poor, angry, bustling, well-meaning Mortal *Pistorides*,[28] who lyes equally under the Contempt of both Parties, with no other difference than a Mixture of *Pity* on one Side, and of Aversion on the other.

How hath he been pelted, pestered, and pounded by one single Wag,[29] who promiseth never to forsake him Living or Dead?

I was much pleas'd with the Humour of a *Surgeon* in this Town,[30] who having in his own Apprehension, received some great Injustice from the

---

27 *Whigs . . . of the old fashioned Stamp*: 'country' or opposition Whigs often referred to themselves as 'old Whigs', to indicate steadfast adherence to their party's libertarian principles, in contrast to the apostasy of court Whigs. For some English examples, see Joseph Addison, *The Old Whig*, 2 parts, London, 1719; [Thomas Gordon and John Trenchard,] *Cato's Letters: or, Essays on Liberty, Civil and Religious, and other Important Subjects*, 4 vols., London, 1724; 'An Old Whig', *Reasons Against a War, in a Letter to a Member of Parliament*, London, 1727. Later in the text, Swift appears to identify himself as an 'old Whig' (see below, p. 201).
28 *This was . . . Pistorides*: for examples of Tighe's vehemence against Tories (whom he stigmatised as 'villainous rogues'), see his letters to John Baker, 5 May 1715, 14 Feb. 1714[/15] (Centre for Buckinghamshire Studies, Baker papers, D–X1069/2/50/52).
29 *one single Wag*: Swift.
30 *a Surgeon in this Town*: possibly Swift himself, who had adopted the character of an anatomist in *A Tale of a Tub* (*CWJS*, vol. I, sections V and IX, pp. 81, 112).

Earl of *Galloway*,[31] and despairing of Revenge, as well as Relief, declar'd to all his Friends that he had set apart a hundred Guineas to purchase the Earl's Carcase from the Sexton, whenever *it* should Dye; to make a Skeleton of the Bones, stuff the Hide, and shew them for three Pence; and thus get Vengeance for the Injuries he had suffered by the Owner.

Of the like Spirit too often is that implacable Race of Wits,[32] against whom there is no Defence but Innocence, and Philosophy: Neither of which is likely to be at hand; and therefore the wounded have no where to fly for a Cure, but to downright Stupidity, a crazed Head, or a profligate Contempt of Guilt and Shame.

I am therefore sorry for that other miserable Creature *Traulus*,[33] who although of somewhat a different Species, yet seems very far to outdo even the Genius of *Pistorides*, in that miscarrying Talent of railing without Consistency or Discretion, against the most innocent Persons, according to the present Scituation of his Gall and Spleen. I do not blame an *honest* Gentleman for the bitterest Invectives against one to whom he professeth the greatest Friendship; provided he acts in the Dark, so as not to be discovered. But in the Midst of *Caresses*, *Visits*, and *Invitations*, to run into the Streets, or to *as publick a place*, and without the least pretended Incitement, sputter out the basest and falsest Accusations; then to wipe his Mouth, come up smiling to his Friend, shake him by the Hand, and tell him in a Whisper, it was *all for his Service*. This proceeding, I am bold to think a great failure in Prudence; and I am afraid lest such a Practitioner, with a Body so *open*, so *foul*, and so *full of sores*, may fall under the Resentment of an incensed political *Surgeon*,[34] who is not in much Renown for his Mercy upon great Provocation: Who without waiting for his Death, will Flay, and

---

31 *Earl of Galloway*: Henri de Massue, Seigneur de Ruvigny (1648–1720), 1st Earl of Galway; a lord justice in Ireland 1697–1700, 1715–17.
32 *that implacable Race of Wits*: in *A Proposal for Correcting, Ascertaining and Improving the English Tongue* (1712) (*CWJS*, vol. II, p. 142), Swift wrote of 'that strange Race of Wits, who tell us, they Write to the Humour of the Age'.
33 *Traulus*: identified by Marmaduke Coghill (Coghill to Edward Southwell, 18 Apr. 1730 (*Coghill Letters*, p. 98)) as Joshua, 2nd Viscount Allen (1685–1742), and used again in the same year in the two-part poem 'Traulus' (*Poems*, vol. III, pp. 794–801). The word 'traulus' (from the Greek *traulos* (lisping)) meant 'a stammerer or stutterer' (Adam Littleton, *Linguæ latinæ liber dictionarius quadripartitus...*, London, 1715), a disability for which Allen was notorious ([Visct Midleton] to Thomas Brodrick, 14 Nov. 1721 (Surrey History Centre, Brodrick papers, 1248/5/142–3)). See Claude Rawson, 'Savage Indignation Revisited: Swift, Yeats, and the "Cry" of Liberty', in Rawson (ed.), *Politics and Literature in the Age of Swift: English and Irish Perspectives*, Cambridge: Cambridge University Press, 2010, p. 205.
34 *an incensed political Surgeon*: again the reference is to Swift himself.

Dissect him alive, and to the View of Mankind lay open all the disordered Cells of his Brain, the Venom of his Tongue, the Corruption of his Heart, and Spots[35] and Flatuses[36] of his Spleen – And all this for three Pence.

In such a Case what a Scene wou'd be laid open? and to drop my Metaphor what a Character of our mistaking Friend might an angry Enemy draw and expose? particularizing that unnatural Conjunction of Vices and Follies, so inconsistent with each other in the same Breast: Furious and fawning, scurrilous and flattering, cowardly and provoking, insolent and abject; most profligately False, with the strongest Professions of Sincerity, positive and variable, tyrannical and slavish.

I apprehend that if all this should be set out to the World by an angry Whig of the *old* Stamp, the unavoidable Consequence must be a Confinement of our *Friend* for some Months *more* to his Garret, and thereby depriving the publick for so long a time, and in so *important a Juncture*, of his useful Talents in their Service: While he is fed like a wild Beast thro' a Hole; but I hope with a special regard to the *quantity* and *quality* of his Nourishment.

In vain would his Excusers endeavour to palliate his Enormities, by imputing them to Madness; Because, it is well known, that Madness only operates by inflaming and enlarging the good or evil Dispositions of the Mind:[37] For the Curators of Bedlam assure us, that some Lunaticks are Persons of *Honour, Truth, Benevolence*, and many other Virtues, which appear in their highest Ravings, although after a wild incoherent manner; while others on the contrary, discover in every Word and Action the utmost *Baseness* and depravity of Human Minds; which infallibly they possessed in the same Degree, although perhaps under a better Regulation, before their Entrance into that *Academy*.

But it may be objected, that there is an Argument of much more force to excuse the overflowings of that Zeal, which our *Friend* shews or means for our Cause. And it must be confessed, that the *easy and smooth Fluency of his Elocution bestow'd him by Nature, and cultivated by continual Practice*, added to the *Comelyness of his Person*, the *Harmony of his Voice*, the *Gracefulness of his Manner*, and the *Decency of his Dress*, are Temptations too strong for such a Genius to resist upon any publick Occasion of making them appear

35 *Spots*: stains.
36 *Flatuses*: accumulations of wind.
37 *Madness only operates... Dispositions of the Mind*: cf. Swift's observations on the effects of madness in *A Tale of a Tub*, section IX (*CWJS*, vol. I, pp. 109–16).

with *universal Applause*: And if good Men are sometimes accused of loving their *Jest* better than their *Friend*,[38] surely to gain the Reputation of the first *Orator* in the Kingdom, no Man of Spirit would scruple to lose all the *Friends* he had in the World.

It is usual for Masters to make their Boys declaim on both sides of an Argument;[39] and as some kinds of Assemblies are called the *Schools of Politicks*,[40] I confess nothing can better improve political School-boys, than the Art of making plausible or implausible Harangues, against the very Opinion for which they resolve to Determine.

So Cardinal *Perron* after having spoke for an Hour to the Admiration of all his Hearers, to prove the existence of God; told some of his Intimates that he could have spoken another Hour, and much better, to prove the contrary.[41]

I have placed this reasoning in the strongest light, that I think it will bear; and have nothing to answer, but that allowing it as much weight as the Reader shall please, it hath constantly met with ill Success in the Mouth of our *Friend*, whether for want of good Luck, or good Management I suspend my Judgment.

To return from this long Digression; if Persons in high Stations have been allowed to chuse Mistresses, without regard even to difference in Religion,[42] yet never incurred the least Reflection on their Loyalty or their Protestantism; shall the chief Governor of a great Kingdom be censured for

---

38 *loving their Jest better than their Friend*: from the proverb 'Better lose a jest than a friend', originating in Quintilian, *De Institutione Oratoria*, VI. iii. 28: 'Potius amicum quam dictum perdere' (*ODEP*, p. 54).
39 *It is usual . . . both sides of an Argument*: In the teaching of rhetoric.
40 *Schools of Politicks*: the *Spectator*, no. 305 (19 Feb. 1712), had called coffee-houses, 'our British Schools of Politics' (*Spectator*, vol. III, p. 100).
41 *Cardinal Perron . . . to prove the contrary*: Jacques du Perron (1556–1618), created a cardinal in 1604. The incident, which occurred in 1583, involved King Henri III of France. See R. H. Popkin, *History of Scepticism from Erasmus to Descartes*, Assen: Van Gorcum, 1960, p. 80.
42 *if Persons in high Stations . . . difference in Religion*: Swift may be alluding to the former lord chancellor of England, John, Lord Somers (1651–1716), who was accused (by Mrs Manley in the *New Atalantis*, and by Swift himself in the *Examiner*) of keeping as his mistress a married woman, Elizabeth Blount, daughter of the diplomat Sir Richard Fanshawe, 1st Bt (1608–66). Fanshawe's various Catholic connections had meant that his own religious affiliation was not entirely clear. Swift had also made a similar accusation against Thomas, Earl of Wharton, in *A Short Character of Thomas Earl of Wharton* (Davis, vol. III, p. 179): 'He is a Presbyterian in Politics, and an Atheist in Religion; but he chuseth at present to whore with a Papist.'

chusing a *Companion*, who may formerly have been suspected for differing from the *Orthodox* in some speculative Opinions of Persons and Things, which cannot affect the Fundamental Principles of a sound *Whig*?

But let me suppose a very possible Case. Here is a Person sent to govern *I———d*,[43] whose unfortunate weak Side it happens to be, for several Reasons abovementioned, that he hath encouraged the Attendance of *one* or *two* Gentlemen distinguished for their Tast, their Wit, and their Learning; who have taken the Oaths to his Majesty, and pray heartily for him: Yet because they may perhaps be stigmatized as *quondam* Toryes by *Pistorides* and his Gang; his E———y must be forced to banish them under the Pain and Peril of displeasing the Zealots of his own Party; and thereby be put into a worse Condition than every common good-fellow;[44] who may be a sincere *Protestant*, and a loyal Subject, and yet rather chuse to Drink fine Ale at the *Pope's*-head, than muddy at the *King's*.

Let me then return to my Supposition. It is certain, the High-flown Loyalists[45] in the *present* Sense of the Word, have their Thoughts, and Studyes, and Tongues so entirely diverted by political Schemes, that the Zeal of their *Principles* hath *eaten up* their *Understandings*;[46] neither have they time from their Employments, their Hopes, and their hourly Labours for acquiring new Additions of Merit, to amuse themselves with Philological Converse, or Speculations which are utterly ruinous to all Schemes of rising in the World: What must then a Great Man do whose ill Stars have fatally perverted him to a Love, and Tast, and Possession of Literature, Politeness, and good Sense? Our thorow-sped[47] Republick of Whigs, which contains the bulk of all *Hopers, Pretenders*,[48] *Expecters and Professors*,[49] are, beyond all Doubt, most *Highly useful* to Princes, to

---

43 *I———d*: Ireland.
44 *good-fellow*: drinking companion.
45 *High-flown Loyalists*: Swift is arguing that events since 1714 have inverted the sense of these expressions. Under the Stuarts, the Tories were distinguished by loyalty to the crown (over Parliament), and by the maintenance of 'high-flying' or lofty notions of royal authority; now it is the Whigs who emphasise loyalty to the Hanoverian dynasty and support the royal prerogative.
46 *the Zeal of their Principles hath eaten up their Understandings*: John, 2: 17 (quoting Psalm 69: 9): 'And his disciples remembered that it was written, The zeal of thine house hath eaten me up.'
47 *thorow-sped*: thorough-sped, that is to say 'thoroughgoing'.
48 *Pretenders*: claimants to office.
49 *Professors*: either those who are professing principle or loyalty, or those who make office-holding their profession.

Governors, to great Ministers, and to their Country, but at the same time, and by necessary Consequence, the most disagreeable Companions to all who have that unfortunate turn of Mind peculiar to his E——, and perhaps to five or six more in a Nation.

I do not deny it possible, that an Original or Proselyte Favourer of the times,[50] might have been born to those useless Talents which in former Ages qualifyed a Man to be a Poet, or a Philosopher. All I contend for is, that where the true Genius of Party once enters, it *sweeps the House clean*, and leaves room for many *other Spirits* to take joint Possession, till the *last State of that Man is exceedingly better than the first*.[51]

I allow it a great Error in his E—— that he adheres so obstinately to his old *unfashionable* Academick Education: Yet so perverse is human Nature, that the usual Remedies for this Evil in others, have produced a contrary Effect in him; to a degree, that I am credibly informed, he will, as I have already hinted, in the middle of a Session quote Passages out of *Plato*, and *Pindar*[52] at his own Table to some *Book-learned* Companion, without blushing, even when Persons of *great Stations* are by.

I will venture one Step further; which is, freely to confess, that this mistaken Method of educating Youth in the knowledge of antient Learning and Language, is too apt to spoil their *Politicks* and *Principles*; because the Doctrine and Examples of the Books they Read, teach them Lessons *directly contrary in every Point* to the *present Practice* of the World: And accordingly, *Hobbes* most judiciously observes, that the Writings of the

50 *Original or Proselyte Favourer of the times*: those who had always been Whigs, or those former Tories (like the revenue commissioner, Marmaduke Coghill, or the Prime Serjeant, Henry Singleton) who had been Tories under Queen Anne and now supported Whig governments (Hayton, *Anglo-Irish Experience*, p. 129). In 'Mad Mullinix and Timothy', Swift puts into the mouth of Mullinix an acknowledgement that 'The Tories are gone ev'ry Man over / To our Illustrious House of Hanover', a statement that Timothy (Richard Tighe), with his obsessive suspicions of Jacobitism, cannot accept (*Poems*, vol. III, p. 773).
51 *it sweeps the House clean . . . better than the first*: Matthew, 12: 43–5: 'When the unclean spirit is gone out of a man, he walketh through dry places, seeking rest, and findeth none. Then he saith, I will return into my house from whence I came out; and when he is come, he findeth it empty, swept, and garnished. Then goeth he, and taketh with himself seven other spirits more wicked than himself, and they enter in and dwell there: and the last state of that man is worse than the first. Even so shall it be also unto this wicked generation.' (Also in Luke, 11: 24–6, with slight variations in wording.)
52 *Plato, and Pindar*: Plato (*c*. 428 – *c*. 348 BC), the philosopher, and Pindar (*c*. 522–433 BC), the poet. Swift owned editions of the works of both (*Library and Reading, I*, vol. II, pp. 1430–2, 1437–40). In the *Battle of the Books*, Pindar appears as the commander of the light horse of the ancients, while Plato and Aristotle command the archers (*CWJS*, vol. I, p. 133).

Greeks and *Romans* made young Men imbibe Opinions against absolute Power in a Prince, or even in a first *Minister*; and to embrace Notions of Liberty and Property.[53]

It hath been therefore a great Felicity to these Kingdoms, that the Heirs to Titles and large Estates, have a Weakness in their Eyes, a Tenderness in their Constitutions, are not able to bear the Pain and Indignity of whipping; and as the Mother rightly expresses it, could never take to their Book;[54] yet are well enough qualifyed to Sign a Receit for half a Year's Rent, to put their Name (*rightly spelt*) to a Warrant, and to read Pamphlets against *Religion* and *High-flying*; whereby they fill their Niches,[55] and carry themselves through the World with that Dignity which best becomes a S———r,[56] and a *Squire*.

I cou'd heartily wish his E——— would be more condescending to the *Genius* of the Kingdom he governs, to the Condition of the times, and to the Nature of the Station he fills. Yet if it be true, what I have read in old English Story-books, that one *Agesilaus* (no matter to the bulk of my Readers, whether I spell the Names right or wrong) was caught by the *Parson of the Parish*, riding on a Hobby-Horse with his Children;[57] that *Socrates* a *Heathen* Philosopher, was found dancing by himself at fourscore;[58] that a King called *Cæsar Augustus* (or some such Name) used to Play with Boys;[59] whereof some might possibly be Sons of *Toryes*;

---

53 *Hobbes most judiciously observes... Liberty and Property*: a paraphrase of *Leviathan*, pt III, ch. 29, para. 14, in which Hobbes shows how 'Greek and Latin' writers have justified tyrannicide, and have influenced 'they that live under Monarchy' to 'conceive an opinion, that the subjects in a Popular Common-Wealth enjoy Liberty, but that in a Monarchy they are all Slaves' (Thomas Hobbes, *Leviathan*, ed. Richard Tuck, Cambridge: Cambridge University Press, 1991, pp. 225–6). Hobbes says nothing of 'Property', however; nor does he mention 'absolute Power' being in the hands of a 'first Minister', an allusion to Walpole.
54 *a Weakness in their Eyes... take to their Book*: in *Directions to Servants*, Swift instructs the 'Tutoress, or Governess' to 'Say the Children have sore Eyes; Miss *Betty* won't take to her Book' (*CWJS*, vol. II, p. 524). See above, p. 81.
55 *fill their Niches*: find a suitable employment or station in life.
56 *S———r*: Senator.
57 *Agesilaus... with his Children*: a story told in Plutarch's *Life of Agesilaus*, ch. 25.
58 *Socrates... at fourscore*: the story told by Socrates against himself in Xenophon, *Symposium*, ii, 19.
59 *Caesar Augustus... with Boys*: Suetonius, *Lives of the Caesars*, Augustus, ch. 83, translated in [Jabez Hughes,] *The Lives of the XII Cæsars, or the First Twelve Roman Emperors, Written in Latin by C. Suetonius Tranquillus*, 2nd edn, London 1729, vol. I, p. 129, noted that the Emperor Augustus 'sometimes, to unbend his mind... would fish with an angle, or play at cockall, at peach-stones or cobnut with little boys'.

and, that two Great Men called *Scipio* and *Lelius* (I forget their *Christian Names*,[60] and whether they were Poets or Generals,) often play'd at Duck and Drake with smooth Stones on a River.[61] Now I say, if these Facts be true (and the Book where I found them is in Print)[62] I cannot imagine why our most zealous Patriots may not a little indulge his E———, in an Infirmity which is not morally Evil, provided he gives no publick Scandal (which is by all Means to be avoided) I say, why he may not be indulged twice a Week to converse with one or two particular Persons, and let him and them conn over their old *exploded* Readings together, after Mornings spent in hearing and prescribing Ways and Means[63] from and to his *most obedient* Politicians, for the Welfare of the Kingdom; although the said particular Person or Persons may not have made so publick a Declaration of their political Faith in all its Parts, as the Business of the Nation requires. Still submitting my Opinion to that *happy Majority*, which I am confident is *always in the right*,[64] by whom the *liberty* of the Subject hath been so frequently, so strenuously, and so successfully asserted; who by their wise

60 *their Christian Names*: a usage inappropriate to classical Rome.
61 *Scipio and Lelius... on a River*: a reference to the anecdote retailed in Cicero, *De Oratore*, II, vi, 22, that Publius Cornelius Scipio (Africanus) and his friend Gaius Laelius were used to reverting to boyhood pursuits when on holiday in the country together, such as picking up pebbles on the seashore, and engaging in various sports, however 'trifling' (see G[eorge] P[arry], *Translation of Tully de Oratore*, London, 1723, p. 14). The game of 'ducks and drakes' involves skimming flat stones across water in order to make them bounce off the surface.
62 *the Book... is in Print*: Dryden, in his 'Life of Plutarch' prefatory to the *Translation of Plutarch's Lives* (1683), groups together three of these episodes in a manner not dissimilar: 'But there is withal, a descent into minute circumstances, and trivial passages of life, which are natural to this way of writing, and which the dignity of the other two will not admit. There you are conducted only into the rooms of state; here you are led into the private Lodgings of the heroe; you see him in his undress, and are made Familiar with his most private actions and conversations. You may behold a *Scipio* and a *Lelius* gathering cockleshells on the shore, *Augustus* playing at bounding stones with Boyes; and *Agesilaus* riding on a Hobby-horse among his Children' (*The Works of John Dryden*, ed. Edward Niles Hooker, H. T. Swedenberg, jr and Vinton A. Dearing *et al.*, 20 vols., Berkeley, CA: University of California Press, 1956–2000, vol. XVII, p. 275).
    The hobby-horse (a child's toy consisting of a long stick with an imitation horse's head at one end) was a very common feature of emblem-books in sixteenth- and seventeenth-century Europe (Erika Langmuir, *Imagining Childhood*, New Haven & London: Yale University Press, 2006, pp. 147–8).
63 *Ways and Means*: in the Committee of ways and means in the Irish House of Commons, a committee of the whole House appointed to recommend the means by which the agreed supply should be raised.
64 *that happy Majority... in the right:* Locke's *Second Treatise of Civil Government*, ch. VIII, constitutes a lengthy argument for majority rule.

Councils have made *Commerce* to flourish, *Money* to abound, Inhabitants to encrease, the Value of Lands and Rents to rise;[65] and the whole Island put on a new Face of *Plenty* and *Prosperity.*

But in order to clear his E——, more fully from this Accusation of shewing his Favours to *High-flyers, Toryes,* and *Jacobites*; it will be necessary to come to Particulars.

The first Person of a Tory Denomination to whom his E—— gave any Marks of his Favour, was Doctor *Thomas Sheridan.*[66] It is to be observed, that this happened so early in his E——'s Government, as it may be justly supposed he had not been informed of that Gentleman's Character upon so *dangerous* an Article. The Doctor being well known and distinguished, for his Skill and Success in the Education of Youth,[67] beyond most of his Profession for many Years past; was recommended to his E—— on the score of his Learning, and particularly for his Knowledge in the *Greek* Tongue; whereof it seems his E—— is a great Admirer, although for what Reasons I could never imagine. However it is agreed on all hands, that his Lordship was too easily prevail'd on by the Doctor's Request, or indeed rather from the Bias of his own Nature, to hear a Tragedy acted in that *unknown* Language by the Doctor's Lads, which was written by some *Heathen* Author; but whether it contained any *Tory* or *High-Church* Principles, must be left to the Consciences of the *Boys,* the *Doctor,* and his E——: The *only* Witnesses in this Case, whose Testimonies can be depended upon.

It seems, his E—— (a thing never to be sufficiently wondered at) was so pleased with his Entertainment, that some time after he gave the Doctor a Church-living to the Value of almost one Hundred Pounds a Year,[68] and made him one of his Chaplains, from an *antiquated* Notion, that

65 *Commerce to flourish . . . Rents to rise*: all commonly accepted signs of prosperity whose application to Ireland Swift considered fallacious, as he argued *in Maxims Controlled in Ireland* (above pp. 171–80).
66 *Doctor Thomas Sheridan*: Thomas Sheridan (1687–1738), of Quilca, Co. Cavan. The principal author of the *Intelligencer*. See *DIB*; Woolley, *Intelligencer*, pp. 6–16.
67 *distinguished . . . in the Education of Youth*: Sheridan set himself up as a schoolmaster in Dublin after graduating from TCD in 1711, and soon became one of the most successful in the city. According to James Woolley's calculations, his school was the single greatest source of entrants to TCD in the period 1718–29, and by 1724 he had sent ninety-four boys to the college (Woolley, *Intelligencer*, pp. 9–10). Swift provided a more lengthy encomium on Sheridan's talents as a pedagogue in his 'Character of Doctor Sheridan' (Davis, vol. V, pp. 216–17).
68 *a Church-living . . . one Hundred Pounds a Year*: as rector and vicar of Rincurran, Co. Cork.

good Schoolmasters ought to be encouraged in every Nation, professing Civility and Religion. Yet his E—— did not venture to make this bold Step without strong Recommendations from Persons of undoubted Principles, *fitted to the Times*; who thought themselves bound in Justice, Honour, and Gratitude, to do the Doctor a good Office in return for the Care he had taken of their Children, or those of their Friends. Yet the Catastrophe was terrible: For, the Doctor in the height of his Felicity and Gratitude, going down to take Possession of his Parish,[69] and furnish'd with a few Led-Sermons,[70] whereof as it is to be supposed the Number was very small, having never served a Cure in the Church; he stopt at Cork to attend on his Bishop;[71] and going to Church on the Sunday following, was according to the usual Civility of Country Clergymen, invited by the Minister of the Parish[72] to supply the Pulpit. It happened to be the first of *August*;[73] and the first of *August* happened that Year to light upon a *Sunday*: And it happened that the Doctor's Text was in these Words; *Sufficient unto the Day is the Evil thereof*,[74] and lastly it happened, that some one Person of the Congregation, whose Loyalty made him watchful upon every Appearance of Danger to his Majesty's Person and Government, when Service was over, gave the Alarm. Notice was immediately sent up to Town, and by the Zeal of one Man of no large Dimensions of Body or Mind,[75] such a Clamour was raised, that we in *Dublin* could apprehend no less than an Invasion by the *Pretender*,[76] who must be landed in the South. The Result was, that the Doctor must be struck out of the Chaplains List, and appear no more at the Castle; yet, whether he were then, or be at this Day, a *Whig* or a *Tory*, I think is a Secret; only it is Manifest, that he is a

---

69 *going down to take Possession of his Parish*: in July 1725, shortly after his appointment.
70 *Led-Sermons*: sermons prepared in advance, to serve a turn. Swift may have adapted the term from 'led-horse', meaning a pack-horse.
71 *his Bishop*: Peter Browne (*c.* 1665–1735), bishop of Cork and Ross (*ODNB; DIB*).
72 *the Minister of the Parish*: Thomas Russell (*c.* 1693–1744), archdeacon of Cork, and minister of St Peter's church, Cork, who had entered Trinity in the same year as Sheridan (W. M. Brady, *Clerical and Parochial Records of Cork, Cloyne, and Ross...*, 3 vols., vols. I and II, London, 1864; vol. III, Dublin, 1864, vol. I, p. 318).
73 *the first of August*: the anniversary of the death of Queen Anne and the accession of the Hanoverian dynasty, in the person of George I.
74 *Sufficient unto the Day is the Evil thereof*: Matthew, 6: 34.
75 *the Zeal... no large Dimensions of Body or Mind*: Swift believed Richard Tighe to have been responsible: Swift to Thomas Tickell, 18 Sept. 1725 (Woolley, *Corr.*, vol. II, p. 599), to Sheridan, 19 Sept. 1725 (Woolley, *Corr.*, vol. II, p. 601).
76 *the Pretender*: the Stuart claimant to the throne, James Francis Edward Stuart, called 'the Old Pretender'.

zealous *Hannoverian*, at least in Poetry,[77] and a great Adorer of the present Royal Family thro' all its Branches. His Friends likewise assert, that he had preach'd this same Sermon often, under the same Text; that not having observed the Words till he was in the Pulpit, and had open'd his Notes; as he is a Person a little abstracted, he wanted presence of Mind to change them: And that in the whole Sermon there was not a Syllable relating to Government or Party, or to the Subject of the Day.

In this Incident there seems to have been an Union of Events, that will probably never happen again to the end of the World, or at least like the grand Conjunction in the Heavens, which I think they say can arrive but once in twenty thousand Years.[78]

The second Gentleman (If I am right in my Chronology) who under the suspicion of a *Tory*, received some Favour from his E—, is Mr. *James Stopford*,[79] very strongly recommended by the most eminent Whig in *England*,[80] on the Account of his Learning, and Virtue, and other Accomplishments. He had passed the greatest Part of his Youth in close Study, or in Travelling; and was either not at Home, or not at leisure to trouble his Thoughts about Party; which I allow to be a great Omission; tho' I cannot honestly place him in the List of *Toryes*, and therefore think his E— may be fairly acquitted for making him Vicar of *Finglass*, worth about one Hundred and fifty Pounds a Year.

The third is Doctor *Patrick Delany*.[81] This Divine lyes under some Disadvantage; having in his Youth received many Civilities from a certain

---

77 *at least in Poetry*: Sheridan had written a complimentary poem on the birthday of Queen Caroline (*An Ode to be Perform'd at the Castle of Dublin, on the 1st of March 1729–30...*, Dublin, 1730; *The Poems of Thomas Sheridan*, ed. R. G. Hogan, Newark, NJ: University of Delaware Press, 1994, p. 397), for which he had been reprimanded by Swift in the *History of the Second Solomon* (Davis, vol. V, p. 226).

78 *the grand Conjunction ... twenty thousand Years*: the alignment of sun, moon and earth at the centre of the Milky Way, discovered by astronomers to occur every 26,000 years.

79 *Mr. James Stopford*: (1697–1759), fellow, TCD 1717–22, vicar of Finglas, Co. Dublin in 1725, and later bishop of Cloyne. Brother-in-law of Knightley Chetwode. See J. B. Leslie, *Clergy of Dublin and Glendalough: Biographical Succession Lists*, ed. W. J. R. Wallace, Belfast: Ulster Historical Foundation, 2001, pp. 1086–7; Ehrenpreis, vol. III, pp. 335–7.

80 *the most eminent Whig in England*: William Pulteney, who had recently been persuaded by Swift's friends in England to interest himself on Stopford's behalf: Swift to John Gay and the Duchess of Queensberry, 19 Nov. 1730 (Woolley, *Corr.*, vol. III, p. 339). In fact, Swift had arranged for Stopford to be introduced to Carteret by the under-secretary Thomas Tickell: Swift to Tickell, 19 July 1725 (Woolley, *Corr.*, vol. II, p. 575).

81 *Doctor Patrick Delany*: Patrick Delany (1685/6–1768), chancellor of Christ Church cathedral, Dublin 1728, of St Patrick's 1730, and later dean of Down. See *ODNB*; *DIB*; *The Poems of Patrick Delany...*, ed. Robert Hogan and D. C. Mell, Newark, NJ: University of Delaware Press, 2006.

Person then in a very high Station here,[82] for which Reason I doubt the Doctor never drank his Confusion since;[83] And what makes the matter desperate, it is now too late; unless our Inquisitors will be content with drinking *Confusion* to his *Memory*;[84] The aforesaid eminent Person who was a Judge of all Merit but *Party*,[85] distinguished the Doctor among other Juniors in our University, for his Learning, Virtue, Discretion, and good Sense. But the Doctor was then in too good a Scituation at his College,[86] to hope or endeavour at a better Establishment, from one who had no Power to give it him.

Upon the present L—d L——t's[87] coming over, the Doctor was named to his E— by a Friend,[88] among other Clergymen of Distinction, as Persons whose Characters it was proper his E— should know: And by the Truth of which the Giver would be content to stand or fall in his E—'s Opinion; since not one of those Persons were in particular Friendship with the Gentlemen who gave in their Names. By this and some other Incidents, particularly the Recommendation of the late Arch-Bishop of *Dublin*,[89] the Doctor became known to his E—, whose fatal Turn of Mind towards *Heathenish* and *outlandish* Books and Languages, finding, as I conceive a like Disposition in the Doctor, was the Cause

---

82 *a certain Person then in a very high Station here*: Sir Constantine Phipps, lord chancellor of Ireland 1711–14. Delany had been one of his chaplains as lord chancellor, and was the author of three pamphlets published in defence of Phipps and the Tory ministry: *A Long History of a Short Session of a Certain Parliament in a Certain Kingdom*, Dublin, 1714; *The Life of Aristides, the Athenian; Who Was Decreed to be Banish'd for His Justice...*, Dublin, 1714; and *A Vindication of the Convocation and the Lord Chancellor of Ireland, in Answer to the Englishman's Defence of the C[ommons]*, Dublin, 1714.
83 *drank his Confusion since*: joined in toasts of confusion to the former chancellor, who, during and after his time in office in Ireland, had been the focus of Whig party animosity.
84 *Confusion to his Memory*: Phipps died in 1723.
85 *a Judge of all Merit but Party*: a phrase with multiple potential readings. The reader could understand Swift to mean that Phipps was able to discriminate in favour of merit, except when it came to a man of his own party; that he could judge accurately the merit in everything, except which party to support; or that, as a judge he possessed all merits, except that of belonging to the right party.
86 *in too good a Scituation at his College*: Delany had been made fellow of TCD in 1709, and Professor of Oratory and History in 1724.
87 *L—d L——t's*: Lord Lieutenant's.
88 *named... by a Friend*: Swift himself (Swift to Carteret, 3 July 1725 (Woolley, *Corr.*, vol. II, p. 567)).
89 *the late Arch-Bishop of Dublin*: William King (1650–1729), bishop of Derry 1691–1703, archbishop of Dublin 1703–29.

of his becoming so Domestick, as we are told he is, at[90] the Castle of *Dublin*.

Three or four Years ago, the Doctor grown weary of an Academick Life, for some Reasons best known to the Managers of the Discipline in that learned Society (which it may not be for their Honour to mention)[91] resolved to leave it, although by the Benefit of his Pupils, and his Senior-Fellowship with all its Perquisites, he received every Year between nine Hundred and a Thousand Pounds.

And a small Northern Living,[92] in the University's Donation, of somewhat better than a Hundred Pounds a Year, falling at the same time with the Chancellor-ship of *Christ*-Church[93] to about equal value, in the Gift of his E—:[94] The Doctor ventur'd into the World in a very scanty Condition, having squander'd away all his annual Income in a manner, which although perhaps proper enough for a Clergyman without a Family, will not be for the Advantage of his Character to discover either on the Exchange, or at a Banker's Shop.

About two Months ago, his E— gave the Doctor a Prebend in St. *Patrick*'s Cathedral;[95] which being of near the same value with either of the two former, will add a third part to his Revenues, after he shall have pay'd the great Encumbrances upon it; so that he may now be said to possess of

90 *becoming so Domestick...at*: coming to be at home in, like a member of the household.
91 *for some Reasons...to mention*: this refers to an incident in about March 1725, for which see Boulter to Newcastle, 9 Mar. 1724[/5] (*Boulter Letters*, vol. I, pp. 13–15); J. P. Mahaffy, J. W. Stubbs and T. K. Abbot, *The Book of Trinity College, Dublin, 1591–1891*, Belfast: Marcus Ward, 1892, pp. 68–9. Two undergraduates – one of whom, William Annesley, was a relation of the prominent Tory Arthur Annesley, 7th Earl of Anglesey – having entertained guests in their rooms until after the gates to the college were locked, went to the provost's lodgings in the early hours and demanded the keys in an abusive manner. The Whiggishly inclined provost, Richard Baldwin, not only refused to see them but summoned Annesley the following morning to answer for his behaviour. Having refused to submit to a public admonition in hall, and, to compound his offence, 'put on his hat before the provost', Annesley was expelled. Representations were made to the university's visitors, and to the lord lieutenant, to request his reinstatement, and one fellow (almost certainly Delany) was said by Boulter to have 'abused [Baldwin] to his face, in a sermon at the college chapel'.
92 *a small Northern Living*: the rectory of Derryvullen, Co. Fermanagh.
93 *Christ-Church*: Christ Church cathedral, Dublin.
94 *in the Gift of his E[xcellency]*: in his capacity as lord lieutenant. The chancellorship and the Donoughmore rectory were given to Delany in January 1728: Henry Cotton, *Fasti Ecclesiae Hibernicae...*, 2nd edn, 5 vols., Dublin, 1848–60, vol. II, p. 58.
95 *a Prebend in St. Patrick's Cathedral*: the vicarage of Donoughmore, Co. Wicklow, to which was attached a prebendaryship (conferring membership of the cathedral chapter). The patent was dated 3 Dec. 1729 (Cotton, *Fasti*, vol. II, p. 184).

Church Preferments in scattered Tythes,[96] three Hundred Pounds a Year; instead of the like Sum of infallible Rents from a Senior Fellowship with the Offices annexed; besides the Advantage of a free Lodging, and some other Easements.

But since the Doctor hath not in any of his Writings, his Sermons, his Actions, his Discourse, or his Company, discovered one single Principle of either *Whig* or *Tory*; and that the L— L—— still continues to admit him; I shall boldly Pronounce him *one of Us*: But like a new *Free-Mason*, who hath not yet learned all the Dialect of the Mystery.[97] Neither can he justly be accused of any *Tory* Doctrines, except perhaps some among those few, with which that *wicked Party* was charged, during the height of their Power; but have been since transferred for the most *solid Reasons*, to the *whole Body* of our firmest Friends.

I have now done with the Clergy; And upon the strictest Examination have not been able to find above one of that Order, against whom any *Party* Suspicion can lye, which is the unfortunate Gentleman, Doctor *Sheridan*, who by meer Chance-medley shot his own Fortune dead with a single *Text*.

As to the Laity I can hear of but one Person of the *Tory* Stamp, who since the beginning of his E—'s Government, did ever receive any solid Mark of his Favour; I mean Sir *Arthur Acheson*, reported to be an acknowledged *Tory*, and what is almost as bad, a *Scholar* into the Bargain.[98] It is whispered about as a certain Truth, that this Gentleman is to have a Grant of a certain Barrack upon his Estate, within two Miles of his own House; for which the Crown is to be his Tenant, at the Rent of sixty Pounds *per Annum*; he being only at the Expence of about *five Hundred* Pounds, to put the House

---

96 *Tythes*: tithes: the annual levy paid to the established church for the support of the parish incumbent, equivalent to a tenth part of agricultural produce.

97 *like a new Free-Mason . . . Dialect of the Mystery*: the Dublin Grand Lodge was established in about 1723: J. H. Lepper and Philip Crosslé, *History of the Grand Lodge of Free and Accepted Masons of Ireland*, Dublin: Lodge of Research, 1925, pp. 33–8, 52–8; Sean Murphy, 'Irish Jacobitism and Freemasonry', *ECI* 9 (1994), 76–8. Cf. Swift's *A Letter from the Grand Mistress of the Female Freemasons* (1724) (Davis, vol. V, pp. 325–33).

98 *Sir Arthur Acheson . . . into the Bargain*: Sir Arthur Acheson, 5th Bt (1688–1749) of Markethill, Co. Armagh, at whose house Swift stayed between June 1728 and February 1729, between June and October 1729, and again between June and September 1730. For Acheson's character and political inclinations, see *Hist. Ir. Parl.*, vol. III, pp. 52–3; Ehrenpreis, vol. III, pp. 600–1.

in Repair, build Stables, and other Necessaries.⁹⁹ I will place this *invidious* Mark of Beneficence, conferred on a *Tory*, in a fair light, by computing the Costs and necessary Defalcations;¹⁰⁰ after which it may be seen how much Sir *Arthur* will be annually a clear Gainer by the Publick, notwithstanding his *unfortunate* Principles, and his Knowledge in *Greek* and *Latin*.

For Repairs, &c. 500 *l.* the Interest whereof *per Ann.*	30	0	0
For all manner of Poultry to furnish the Troopers, but which the said Troopers must be at the Labour of catching, valued *per Ann.*	5	0	0
For Stragling Sheep, — — — — — — — — —	8	0	0
For Game destroyed five Miles round,) — — —	6	0	0
	49	0	0
Rent paid to Sir *Arthur*,— — — — — — — —	60	0	0
Deduct — — — — — — — — — —	49	0	0
Remains clear	11	0	0

Thus, if Sir *Arthur Acheson* shall have the good Fortune to obtain a Grant of this Barrack, he will receive net Profit annually from the Crown ELEVEN Pounds *Sterl.* to help him in entertaining the Officers, and making Provision for his younger Children.

It is true, there is another Advantage to be expected, which may fully Compensate the loss of Cattle and Poultry; by multiplying the Breed of

---

99 *It is whispered… and other Necessaries*: the proposal to convert a house on the Gosford estate (Hamilton's Bawn) to a barrack. Swift had written of this in his poem 'The Grand Question Debated. Whether Hamilton's Bawn should be turned into a Barrack or a Malt-House' (*Poems*, vol. III, pp. 863–73). On the enthusiasm of the Irish landed gentry for the building of barracks on their lands, see Edward McParland, *Public Architecture in Ireland, 1680–1760*, New Haven & London: Yale University Press, 2001, pp. 125–6; Charles Ivar McGrath, *Ireland and Empire, 1692–1770*, London: Pickering & Chatto, 2012, pp. 89–90.
100 *necessary Defalcations*: deductions, for expenses, etc.

Mankind, and particularly of *good Protestants*, in a part of the Kingdom half depopulated by the wild Humour among the Farmers thereof, leaving their Country.[101] But I am not so skillful in Arithmetick, as to compute the Value.

I have reckoned one *per Cent*. below the Legal Interest for the Money that Sir *Arthur* must expend: And valued the Damage in the other Articles very moderately. However, I am confident he may with good Management be a *Saver* at least; which is a *prodigious Instance of Moderation* in our Friends towards a professed *Tory*. Whatever Merit he may pretend by the unwillingness he hath shewn to make his E— uneasy in his Administration.

Thus I have with the utmost Impartiality collected every single Favour, (further than personal Civilities) conferred by his Excellency on *Toryes*, and reputed *Toryes*, since his first arrival hither, to this present 13*th* Day of *April*, in the Year of our Lord 1730, giving all Allowance possible to the Arguments on the other side of the Question.

And the Account will stand thus.

Disposed of Preferments and Employments to *Toryes*, or reputed *Toryes*, by his E— the L— — L— — in about the space of six Years.

To Doctor *Thomas Sheridan* in a Rectory near Kinsale, *per Ann*.	100	0	
To Sir *Arthur Acheson*, Baronet, a Barrack, *per Ann*.	11	0	0
	111	0	0

Give me leave now to compute in gross the Value of the Favours done by his E— to the *true Friends* of their K——[102] and Country, and of the *Protestant Religion*.

It is to be remembered, that although his E— cannot be properly said to bestow Bishopricks, Commands in the Army, the Place of a Judge, or Commissioner in the Revenue, and some others; yet they are, for the most

---

101 *in a part of the Kingdom . . . leaving their Country*: the wave of (mostly Presbyterian) emigration from Ulster to north America, which had reached a peak in 1728–9 (and for which, see above, p. 94).
102 *K——*: King.

part, disposed upon his Recommendation,[103] except where the Persons are immediately sent from *England* by their Interest at Court, for which I have allowed large Defalcations in the following Accounts. And it is Remarkable that the *only* considerable Station conferred on a Reputed *Tory* since his present E—'s Government was of this *latter* kind.[104]

And indeed it is but too Remarkable, that in a neighbouring Nation (where that dangerous Denomination of Men is incomparably more Numerous, more Powerful, and of consequence more Formidable) *real Toryes* can often with much less Difficulty obtain very high Favours from the Government, than their *reputed* Brethren can arrive to the lowest in ours. I observe this with all possible Submission to the Wisdom of their policy, which, however, will not I believe, dispute the praise of Vigilance with ours.

	WHIG Account.		
To Persons promoted to Bishopricks, or removed) to more Beneficial ones, computed *per Ann.*)	10050	0	0
To Civil Employments,	9030	0	0
To Military Commands,	8436	0	0
	27516	0	0
	TORY Account.		
To *Toryes*, — —	111	0	0
Balance — —	27405	0	0

I shall conclude with this Observation, That, as I think, the *Toryes* have sufficient reason to be *fully satisfied* with the share of *Trust*, and

---

103 *although his E—... disposed upon his Recommendation*: appointments were made by the monarch, but at the lord lieutenant's recommendation.
104 *it is Remarkable... of this latter kind*: Thomas Wyndham (1681–1745), appointed lord chancellor of Ireland in 1725. Little is known of his career in England, and nothing of his politics (*DIB*), but he was the son of John Wyndham, Tory MP for Salisbury in 1681 and 1685 (Henning, *Commons 1660–1690*, vol. III, p. 777), and a first cousin of the prominent English Tory Sir William Wyndham. As a fellow member of the Society of Brothers, Sir William Wyndham had been one of Swift's dining companions in 1711–13: *Journal to Stella* (*CWJS*, vol. IX, pp. 227, 276, 345, 407, 470).

Power, and *Employments* which they possess under the *Lenity* of the present Government; So, I do not find how his E— can be justly censured for favouring none but *High-Church, High-flyers, Termagants,*[105] *Laudists,*[106] *Sacheverellians,*[107] *Tip-top-gallon-men,*[108] *Jacobites, Tantivyes,*[109] *Anti-Hannoverians, Friends to Popery and the Pretender, and to Arbitrary power, Disobligers of England, Breakers of* DEPENDENCY, *Inflamers of Quarrels between the two Nations,*[110] *Publick Incendiaries, Enemies to the King and Kingdoms, Haters of* TRUE *Protestants, Lawrell-men,*[111] *Annists,*[112]

105 *Termagants*: a particularly obscure reference in this list of opprobrious names for Tories, which seems to have included some of Swift's own invention. Originally, the termagant had been a figure of a violent, overbearing nature in the mystery play, and also an imaginary deity which in medieval Christendom was thought to be worshipped by Muslims; thus, Swift may be using it in relation to Tories' supposed fanatical adherence to the doctrine of hereditary right, with further overtones of 'priestcraft'. Elsewhere his use of the word was in the customary sense of a shrewish woman, but in an allegory in the *Examiner* 32 (8 Mar. 1711), he had described 'Miss Faction' as 'termagant and froward': Ellis (ed.), *Swift vs. Mainwaring*, p. 285.
106 *Laudists*: William Laud (1573–1645), bishop of London 1628–33, archbishop of Canterbury 1633–45, the supposed progenitor of the High Church movement.
107 *Sacheverellians*: admirers of the High Church clerical hero Henry Sacheverell (1674–1724), impeached by the Whig ministry in 1710.
108 *Tip-top-gallon-men*: the expression 'tip-top' was in use at the time to indicate an extremity of height (*OED*), and thus of high-flying, while 'gallon-men' may be an allusion to the supposed drinking capacity of Tory enthusiasts.
109 *Tantivyes*: a short-hand term for High Church clergy, coined by Whigs during the Exclusion Crisis, from the hunting cry 'tantivy' and implying that those concerned were riding at full speed towards Rome.
110 *Breakers of DEPENDENCY... the two Nations*: Irish 'patriots' who protested against English policy or against the intervention by the Westminster Parliament in Irish affairs, among whom the surviving Tory oppositionists were numbered, were routinely accused of seeking to break the kingdom's 'dependency' on England. In the Drapier's *Letter to the Whole People of Ireland* (1725), one of the slurs allegedly made against those refusing Wood's Halfpence, alongside the accusation of Jacobitism, was that they were 'going to shake off their Dependance upon the Crown of England' (Davis, vol. X, p. 61).
111 *Lawrell-men*: laurel had been a Tory emblem from the days of Queen Anne (Pat Rogers, *Pope and the Destiny of the Stuarts: History, Politics, and Mythology in the Age of Queen Anne*, Oxford: Oxford University Press, 2005, p. 116), presumably as a symbol of monarchy. Tories in Dublin had worn laurels in the winter of 1713–14 as a distinguishing mark: *The World in Uproar, or the Hue and Cry after the Laurels* [Dublin, c. 1713]; Archbishop King to Swift, 13 Jan. 1713/14 (Woolley, *Corr.*, vol. I, p. 581); *An Enquiry about the Wearing of Lawrels*, [Dublin, 1714]; *Come and See, Come and See. Or, An Account of a Cruel Monster Newly Come to Town, Spew'd up by a Scotch Cod near Belfast in the North of Ireland...*, [?Dublin], 1714, p. 3; Alan Brodrick to Thomas Brodrick, 9 Feb. 1713[/14] (Surrey History Centre, Brodrick papers, 1248/3/163).
112 *Annists*: those who harked back to the Tory heyday under Queen Anne.

Complainers of the Nation's Poverty, Ormondians,[113] *Iconoclasts,*[114] *Anti-Glorious-Memorists,*[115] *White-rosalists,*[116] *Tenth-a-Junians,*[117] and the like: When by a fair State of the Account, the Balance, I conceive, plainly lyes on the other Side.

FINIS

---

113 *Ormondians*: admirers of James Butler (1665–1745), 2nd Duke of Ormond, Tory lord lieutenant in Ireland 1710–13, who had joined the Jacobites in exile in 1715.
114 *Iconoclasts*: the equestrian statue of William III in College Green, the focus of state and civic celebrations of his birthday, was occasionally subjected to malicious damage: James Kelly, '"The Glorious and Immortal Memory": Commemoration and Protestant Identity in Ireland 1660–1800', *Proceedings of the Royal Irish Academy* 94 (1994), section C, p. 32; Patrick Fagan, *The Second City: Portrait of Dublin 1700–1760*, Dublin: Branar, 1986, pp. 101–2; Éamonn Ó Ciardha, *Ireland and the Jacobite Cause, 1685–1766: A Fatal Attachment*, Dublin: Four Courts Press, 2002, pp. 173, 178.
115 *Anti-Glorious-Memorists*: those who would not drink the customary toast to the 'glorious and immortal' memory of William III.
116 *White-rosalists*: a Jacobite emblem, deriving from the white rose of York, with reference to James II in his former capacity as Duke of York.
117 *Tenth-a-Junians*: a reference to the birthday of 'the Old Pretender', evidently a frequent occasion of fighting between Catholic and Protestant mobs in Dublin (Patrick Fagan, 'The Dublin Catholic Mob (1700–1750)', *ECI* 4 (1989), 139). On 10 June 1729, the lord mayor of Dublin issued a proclamation to prohibit the wearing of white roses and other Jacobite emblems (*Faulkner's Dublin Journal*, 7–10 June 1729).

THE ANSWER TO THE CRAFTSMAN

Headnote

Probably composed November 1730; published posthumously, 1758; copy text *1758* (see Textual Account).

The context for this response is a revival in Ireland of the fear of popery at the end of the 1720s and early 1730s. Sir Robert Walpole's ministry had given permission for French recruiting officers to go to Ireland to recruit for the Irish brigade that was in French service. This necessitated their recruiting Catholics (who could not serve in British forces), which in turn led to reports that the French were actually recruiting under the name of the Pretender. The result was a scare based around common fears of Jacobite conspiracies, articulated in the paper originally titled 'The CRAFTSMAN'S First Letter of ADVICE', published Saturday 7 November 1730 (see Appendix B, pp. 333–43).

Swift's response is notable for being written by the persona of the Modest Proposer, who begins by referring to his earlier tract, and proceeds to deliver a similar extreme argument in favour of the total depopulation of Ireland, as well as using anti-Jacobite paranoia to open up the other political and economic issues concerning Ireland with which Swift was preoccupied. The *Answer* was unfinished, and unpublished in Swift's lifetime, presumably because the presence of French recruiting officers had been rescinded by the government, and the issue resolved by the end of 1730 (see Ehrenpreis, vol. III, pp. 682–5; Ferguson, p. 180).

THE ANSWER TO THE CRAFTSMAN.

SIR,

I detest reading your Papers, because I am not of your Principles, and because I cannot endure to be convinced. Yet, I was prevailed on to peruse your CRAFTSMAN of *December* the 12th,[1] wherein I discover you to be as great an Enemy of this Country, as you are of your own. You are pleased to reflect on a Project I proposed of making the Children of *Irish* Parents to be useful to the Publick instead of being burthensome;[2] and you venture to assert, that your own Scheme is more charitable, of not permitting our Popish Natives to be listed in the Service of any foreign Prince.[3]

Perhaps, Sir, you may not have heard of any Kingdom so unhappy as this, both in their Imports and Exports. We import a Sort of Goods, of no intrinsick Value, which costeth us above Forty Thousand Pounds a Year to dress, and scour, and polish them, which altogether do not yield one Penny Advantage;[4] and we annually export above Seven Hundred Thousand Pounds a Year in another Kind of Goods,[5] for which we receive not one single Farthing in Return: Even the Money paid for the Letters sent in transacting this Commerce being all returned to *England*. But, now when there is a most lucky Opportunity offered to begin a Trade,

---

1 *your CRAFTSMAN of December the 12th*: this issue was printed as No. 232, 12 Dec. 1730, in the collected edition of *The Craftsman*, 14 vols., London, 1731–7, vol. VII, pp. 139–51. The paper actually appeared on 7 November 1730. See below, Appendix B.
2 *a Project . . . burthensome*: *A Modest Proposal*.
3 *your own Scheme . . . any foreign Prince*: 'Such a method of providing for persons, whose principles render them unserviceable in our army, is indeed a little more charitable than a late project for preventing Irish children from being starv'd, by fatting them up and selling them to the butcher' (*Craftsman*, p. 146).
4 *a Sort of Goods . . . do not yield one Penny Advantage*: by 1729, the cost of the military establishment in Ireland had reached £40,726 10s (*C.J.Ire.*, vol. V, p. 675). Swift is referring to the cost of maintaining army uniforms, equipment and tack. In relation to cleaning, 'scour' could be used for clothing; for example, by Swift himself (Paul V. Thompson and Dorothy Jay Thompson (eds.), *The Account Books of Jonathan Swift*, London: Scolar Press, 1984, p. 169). In eighteenth-century slang, it also meant 'To roam about at night uproariously, breaking windows, beating the watch, and molesting wayfarers' (*OED*), behaviour for which garrison troops were notorious: T. C. Barnard, 'Athlone, 1685; Limerick, 1710: Religious Riots or Charivaris', *Studia Hibernica* 27 (1993), 61–75; D. A. Fleming, *Politics and Provincial People: Sligo and Limerick, 1691–1761*, Manchester: Manchester University Press, 2010, pp. 212–24.
5 *we annually export . . . another Kind of Goods*: the amount of money allegedly remitted to absentees, which Swift had calculated at about £700,000 in the Drapier's *Humble Address to Both Houses of Parliament* (1724) (Davis, vol. X, p. 128).

whereby this Nation will save many Thousand Pounds a Year, and *England* be a prodigious Gainer, you are pleased, without a Call, officiously and maliciously to interpose with very frivolous Arguments.

It is well known, that, about Sixty Years ago, the Exportation of live Cattle from hence to *England* was of great Benefit to both Kingdoms, until that Branch of Traffick was stopt by an Act of Parliament on your Side,[6] whereof you have had sufficient Reason to repent. Upon which Account, when another Act passed your Parliament, forbidding the Exportation of live Men to any foreign Country, you were so wise to put in a Clause, allowing it to be done by his Majesty's Permission, under his Sign Manual,[7] for which, among other great Benefits granted to *Ireland*, we are infinitely obliged to the *British* Legislature. Yet this very Grace and Favour you, Mr. *D'Anvers*,[8] whom we never disobliged, are endeavouring to prevent; which, I will take upon me to say, is a manifest Mark of your Disaffection to his Majesty, a Want of Duty to the Ministry, and a wicked Design of oppressing this Kingdom, and a traiterous Attempt to lessen the Trade and Manufacture of *England*.

Our truest and best Ally the most Christian King[9] hath obtained his Majesty's Licence, pursuant to Law, to export from hence some Thousand Bodies of healthy, young, living Men, to supply his *Irish* Regiments.[10] The

---

6 *the Exportation of live Cattle... on your Side*: the English Cattle Act of 1666 (18 Chas II c. 2), which prevented the exporting of livestock from Ireland to England.
7 *another Act... under his Sign Manual*: the Enlistment in Foreign Service Act of 1713 (12 Anne c. 11). The king's 'sign manual' was his autograph signature, authenticating a document.
8 *Mr. D'Anvers*: the pen-name Caleb D'anvers was used by the several authors of *The Craftsman*: principally, Nicholas Amhurst (1697–1742), William Pulteney and Henry St John, Viscount Bolingbroke, either working individually or together. The authorship of the *First Letter of Advice* has not been determined, although the initials 'C. D.', which appear at the end of the issue, may refer to a collaboration between Amhurst and Pulteney. See below, p. 343.
9 *the most Christian King*: the king of France (Louis XV).
10 *obtained his Majesty's Licence... Irish Regiments*: as a concession designed to forward Walpole's diplomatic initiatives in Europe, the British government had granted permission to the French to recruit up to 750 men in Ireland. The French officers involved were all of Irish extraction, and their activities in County Cork caused such outrage among local Protestants that the grant was revoked. See L. M. Cullen, 'The Blackwater Catholics and County Cork Society and Politics in the Eighteenth Century', in Patrick Flanagan and C. G. Buttimer (eds.), *Cork: History and Society*, Dublin: Geography Publications, 1993, pp. 560–1; Éamonn Ó Ciardha, *Ireland and the Jacobite Cause, 1685–1766: A Fatal Attachment*, Dublin: Four Courts Press, 2002, pp. 255–60; David Dickson, *Old World Colony: Cork and South Munster 1630–1830*, Cork: Cork University Press, 2005, pp. 266–7.

King of *Spain*, as you assert yourself, hath desired the same Civility, and seemeth to have at least as good a Claim; supposing then that these two Potentates will only desire Leave to carry off Six Thousand Men between them to *France* and *Spain*, then by computing the Maintenance of a tall, hungry, *Irish* Man, in Food and Cloaths, to be only at Five Pounds a Head, here will be Thirty Thousand Pounds *per Annum* saved clear to the Nation, for they can find no other Employment at Home beside begging, robbing, or stealing. But, if Thirty, Forty, or Fifty Thousand, (which we could gladly spare) were sent on the same Errand, what an immense Benefit must it be to us; and, if the two Princes, in whose Service they were,[11] should happen to be at War with each other, how soon would those Recruits be destroyed, then what a Number of Friends would the Pretender lose, and what a Number of Popish Enemies all true Protestants get rid of. Add to this, that then by such a Practice, the Lands of *Ireland* that want Hands for Tillage, must be employed in Grazing,[12] which would sink the Price of Wool, raw Hides, Butter, and Tallow, so that the *English* might have them at their own Rates;[13] and in Return send us Wheat to make our Bread, Barley to brew our Drink, and Oats for our Horses, without any Labour of our own.

Upon this Occasion, I desire humbly to offer a Scheme, which, in my Opinion, would best answer the true Interests of both Kingdoms: For, although I bear a most tender, filial Affection to *England*, my dear, native Country;[14] yet, I cannot deny but this noble Island hath a great Share in

---

11 *the two Princes, in whose Service they were*: the context makes it clear that Swift means Louis XV of France and his cousin Philip V of Spain, although there were Irish Catholic troops in the armies of several European rulers, including the Habsburg Emperor of Austria. During the conflict between Britain and Spain that had ended with the Treaty of Seville of 1729, France had been Britain's ally and Austria Spain's, but subsequently the French and Spanish monarchies moved closer together, and in the Treaty of Vienna of 1731 Britain made a new alliance with Austria, which prompted the conclusion of a formal Franco-Spanish agreement two years later, the so-called '*pacte de famille*'.
12 *Grazing*: for Swift's disapproval of the spread of grazing at the expense of tillage, see above, p. 30.
13 *might have them at their own Rates*: may be able to set whatever price they choose.
14 *most tender... native Country*: Swift's sense of national identity was complex. He had been born in Ireland, of English descent, and like many Irish Protestants was capable of considering himself as either Irish or English according to occasion, and sometimes as both simultaneously. See Jim Smyth, '"Like Amphibious Animals": Irish Protestants, Ancient Britons, 1691–1707', *Historical Journal* 36 (1993), 785–97; D. W. Hayton, *The Anglo-Irish Experience, 1680–1730: Religion, Identity and Patriotism*, Woodbridge: Boydell Press, 2012, pp. 25–48. This complexity is highlighted at the beginning of the *Answer* when Swift writes of 'our Popish natives', implying that he himself is Irish but distinguishing himself

my Love and Esteem, nor can I express how much I desire to see it flourish in Trade and Opulence, even beyond its present happy Condition.

The profitable Land of this Kingdom is, I think, usually computed at Seventeen Millions of Acres,[15] all which I propose to be wholly turned to Grazing. Now, it is found by Experience, that one Grazier and his Family can manage Two Thousand Acres. Thus, Sixteen Millions Eight Hundred Thousand Acres may be managed by Eight Thousand Four Hundred Families, and the Fraction of Two Hundred Thousand Acres will be more than sufficient for Cabbins, Out-Houses, and Potatoe-Gardens; because, it is to be understood, that Corn of all Sorts must be sent to us from *England*.

These Eight Thousand Four Hundred Families may be divided among the four Provinces, according to the Number of Houses in each Province; and, making the equal Allowance of Eight to a Family, the Number of Inhabitants will amount to Sixty Seven Thousand Two Hundred Souls; to these we are to add a Standing Army of Twenty Thousand *English*, which, together with their Trulls,[16] their Bastards, and their Horse-Boys, will, by a gross Computation, very near double the Count, and be very sufficient for the Defence and Grazing of the Kingdom, as well as to enrich our Neighbours, expel Popery, and keep out the Pretender. And lest the Army should be at a Loss for Business, I think it would be very prudent to employ them in collecting the publick Taxes for paying themselves and the Civil List.[17]

I advise, that all the Owners of these Lands should live constantly in *England*, in order to learn Politeness, and qualify themselves for

---

from the Gaelic Irish 'natives'. He deployed the phrase 'dear native country' in *A Modest Proposal*, to refer to the national feeling of Irish Catholics (see above, p. 146).

15 *The profitable Land... Seventeen Millions of Acres*: as with his estimates of population and the value of imported goods, Swift was a long way out of step with other contemporary writers. In the swirl of pamphlets provoked by the publication in 1728 of John Browne's *Seasonable Remarks* (which are catalogued in H. R. Wagner, *Irish Economics 1700–1783: A Bibliography with Notes*, London: Dryden Press, 1907, pp. 30–1), Browne and one of his critics presented differing accounts of Sir William Petty's computation of the profitable and unprofitable acreage of Ireland. According to Browne, Petty identified nine million acres of profitable land, and one and a half million unprofitable, of which a proportion had since been reclaimed, but a response (possibly the work of Arthur Dobbs) pointed out that Petty had actually identified seven and a half million acres of profitable land, out of a total of ten and a half million: *A Letter in Answer to a Paper, intitled, an Appeal to the Reverend Dean Swift. By the Author of Considerations on Two Papers, &c*, Dublin, 1728, pp. 8–9.

16 *Trulls*: trollops.

17 *the Civil List*: the establishment of the civil government; in Ireland, remuneration for offices of profit under the crown was divided into a military and a civil list.

Employments: But, for fear of increasing the Natives in this Island, that an annual Draught, according to the Number born every Year, be exported to whatever Prince will bear the Carriage; or transplanted to the *English* Dominions on the *American* Continent, as a Screen between his Majesty's *English* Subjects and the savage *Indians*.[18]

I advise likewise, that no Commodity whatsoever, of this Nation's Growth, should be sent to any other Country, except *England*, under the Penalty of high Treason; and that all the said Commodities shall be sent in their natural State,[19] the Hides raw, the Wool uncombed, the Flax in the Stub;[20] excepting only Fish, Butter, Tallow, and whatever else will be spoiled in the Carriage. On the contrary, that no Goods whatsoever shall be exported hither, except from *England*, under the same Penalty: That *England* should be forced, at their own Rates, to send us over Cloaths ready made, as well as Shirts and Smocks to the Soldiers and their Trulls; all Iron, Wooden, and Earthen Ware; and whatever Furniture may be necessary for the Cabbins of Graziers, with a sufficient Quantity of Gin,[21] and other Spirits, for those who can afford to be drunk on Holydays.

As to the Civil and Ecclesiastical Administration, which I have not yet fully considered, I can say little; only with Regard to the latter, it is plain, that the Article of paying Tythe[22] for supporting speculative Opinions[23] in Religion, which is so insupportable a Burthen to all true

---

18 *Indians*: see above, p. 96.
19 *no Commodity... sent in their natural State*: the English Woollen Act of 1699 (10 & 11 Will. III c. 10) prohibited the exporting of woollen cloth, and allowed exports of yarn and raw wool only to England, though not 'under the Penalty of high Treason'.
20 *the Stub*: stupe: a cloth made from the coarse fibres combed from the scutched (beaten) stems of retted (macerated) flax, which are otherwise known as tow (in Latin, *stuppa*).
21 *a sufficient Quantity of Gin*: concern at the spread of gin-drinking, especially in London, had resulted in the passage at Westminster in 1729 of an Act to regulate the trade, but this had proved ineffective, and agitation continued: Peter Clark, 'The "Mother Gin" Controversy in the Early Eighteenth Century', *Transactions of the Royal Historical Society*, ser. 5, 38 (1988), 65–7.
22 *Tythe*: tithe: the annual levy paid to the established church for the support of the parish incumbent, equivalent to a tenth part of agricultural produce.
23 *speculative Opinions*: in the *Examiner* 22 (28 Dec. 1710), Swift had asserted that the Whigs 'professed on all occasions, that they knew no reason why any one system of speculative opinions (as they term the doctrines of the church) should be established by law, more than another' (Ellis (ed.), *Swift vs. Mainwaring*, p. 131; see also no. 40 (ibid., p. 401)). He may also be alluding here to the recent appointment to the see of Killala of Robert Clayton (1695–1758), a former fellow of TCD who, while living in London prior to his return to Ireland, had been part of the intellectual circle of the Arian divine Samuel Clarke, then rector of St James's, Westminster. (For Clayton, see *ODNB*; *DIB*.)

Protestants,[24] and to most Churchmen, will be very much lessened by this Expedient; because dry Cattle pay nothing to the spiritual Hireling,[25] any more than imported Corn; so that the industrious Shepherd and Cowherd may sit, every Man under his own Blackberry Bush, and on his own Potatoe-Bed,[26] whereby this happy Island will become a new *Arcadia*.[27]

I do likewise propose, that no Money shall be used in *Ireland*, except what is made of Leather, which likewise shall be coined in *England*, and imported; and that the Taxes shall be levied out of the Commodities we export to *England*, and there turned into Money for his Majesty's Use; and the Rents to Landlords discharged in the same Manner. This will be no Manner of Grievance; for we already see it very practicable to live without Money, and shall be more convinced of it every Day. But whether Paper shall still continue to supply that Defect,[28] or whether

---

24 *all true Protestants*: a phrase often used by Whigs, including Protestant Dissenters, to distinguish themselves, and to imply that their political opponents were crypto-Catholics. For two Irish examples, both taken from sermons by Presbyterian ministers on the Hanoverian succession, see James Kirkpatrick, *God's Dominion over Kings and Other Magistrates: A Thanksgiving Sermon Preach'd in Belfast October 20. 1714. Being the Happy Day of the Coronation of His Most Excellent Majesty King George*, Belfast, 1714, p. 24; Joseph Boyse, *A Sermon Preach'd on the First of March, 1714/15. Being the Day of Publick Thanksgiving to Almighty God, for the Peaceable Accession of His Sacred Majesty King George to the Throne; and for Disappointing the Designs of the Pretender, and All his Adherents*, Dublin, 1715, p. 22.

25 *dry Cattle . . . spiritual Hireling*: although the right of the clergy to collect the tithe on pasturage (the tithe of agistment) had been confirmed by the Irish court of exchequer in 1722, there was continuing resistance from graziers, which eventually came to a head in 1735–6, when the Irish House of Commons passed a resolution condemning the tithe as a 'new demand', and as 'grievous', 'burdensome' and 'unnecessary'. In response, Swift composed his bitter satire on the Irish House of Commons, the 'Character . . . of the Legion Club': Landa, pp. 135–50; D. W. Hayton and Stephen Karian, 'Select Document: The Division in the Irish House of Commons on the "Tithe of Agistment", 18 Mar. 1736, and Swift's "Character . . . of the Legion Club"', *Irish Historical Studies* 38 (2012–13), 304–21. The term 'spiritual Hireling' is a reference to the parable of the good shepherd, in John, 10: 11–13: 'The good shepherd giveth his life for the sheep. But he that is an hireling, and not the shepherd, whose own the sheep are not, seeth the wolf coming, and leaveth the sheep, and fleeth: and the wolf catcheth them, and scattereth the sheep. The hireling fleeth, because he is an hireling, and careth not for the sheep.'

26 *every Man under his own Blackberry Bush, and on his own Potatoe-Bed*: adapting Micah 4: 4: 'they shall sit every man under his vine and under his fig-tree'.

27 *a new Arcadia*: a rural paradise of peace and simple pleasure, from the area in the Peloponnese whose inhabitants were said in classical antiquity to be remarkable for their contentment.

28 *whether Paper shall still continue to supply that Defect*: in *The Intelligencer*, no. 19 (above, p. 93) Swift had written of 'this our *blessed age of Paper*, which . . . Dischargeth all our greatest Payments'.

we shall hang up all those who profess the Trade of Bankers, (which latter I am rather inclined to)[29] must be left to the Consideration of wiser Politicians.

That which maketh me more zealously bent upon this Scheme, is my Desire of living in Amity with our neighbouring Brethren; for we have already tried all other Means, without Effect, to that blessed End: And, by the Course of Measures taken for some Years past, it should seem that we are all agreed in the Point.

This Expedient will be of great Advantage to both Kingdoms, upon several Accounts: For, as to *England*, they have a just Claim to the Balance of Trade on their Side with the whole World; and therefore our Ancestors and we, who conquered this Kingdom for them, ought, in Duty and Gratitude, to let them have the whole Benefit of that Conquest to themselves;[30] especially, when the Conquest was amicably made, without Bloodshed, by a Stipulation between the *Irish* Princes and *Henry* II. by which they paid him, indeed, not equal Homage with what the Electors of *Germany* do to the Emperor, but very near the same that he did to the King of *France* for his *French* Dominions.[31]

In Consequence of this Claim from *England*, that Kingdom may very reasonably demand the Benefit of all our Commodities in their natural Growth, to be manufactured by their People, and a sufficient Quantity of them for our Use to be returned hither fully manufactured.

This, on the other Side, will be of great Benefit to our Inhabitants the Graziers, when Time and Labour will be too much taken up in manuring their Ground, feeding their Cattle, sheering their Sheep, and sending over their Oxen fit for Slaughter; to which Employments they are turned by Nature, as descended from the *Scythians*,[32] whose Diet they are still so fond of. So *Virgil* describeth it:

29 *hang up all those who profess the Trade of Bankers, (which ... I am rather inclined to)*: in the *Short View of the State of Ireland* (above, p. 24), Swift lamented 'the daily encrease of Bankers, who may be a necessary Evil in a Trading-Country, but so ruinous in Ours'.
30 *our Ancestors and we ... Benefit of that Conquest to themselves*: here Swift appears to contradict the statement made in *The Intelligencer*, no. 19, that England had conquered Ireland (see above, p. 91).
31 *Henry II ... French Dominions*: Henry II accepted the feudal submission of many (though not all) Gaelic Irish kings during his progress through the country in 1171, as he himself acknowledged the Capetian king of France as feudal overlord in respect of the possessions he had inherited in France.
32 *the Scythians*: the supposed ancestors of the native Irish.

Et lac concretum cum sanguine bibit equino.[33]

Which, in *English*, is Bonnyclabber,[34] mingled with the Blood of Horses, as they formerly did, until about the Beginning of the last Century Luxury, under the Form of Politeness, began to creep in, they changed the Blood of Horses for that of their black Cattle; and, by Consequence, became less warlike than their Ancestors.

Although I proposed that the Army should be Collectors of the publick Revenues, yet I did not thereby intend that those Taxes should be paid in Gold or Silver; but in Kind, as all other Rent: For the Custom of Tenants makeing their Payments in Money, is a new Thing in the World little known in former Ages, nor generally practised in any Nation at present, except this Island, and the Southern Parts of *Britain*. But, to my great Satisfaction, I foresee better Times; the antient Manner beginneth to be now practised in many Parts of *Connaught*, as well as in the County of *Corke*, where the 'Squires turn Tenants to themselves, divide so many Cattle to their Slaves, who are to provide such a Quantity of Butter, Hides, or Tallow, still keeping up their Number of Cattle;[35] and carry the Goods to *Corke*, or other Port-Towns, and then sell them to the Merchants. By which Invention there is no such Thing as a ruined Farmer to be seen; but the People live with Comfort on Potatoes and Bonnyclabber, neither of which are vendible Commodities Abroad.

---

33 *Et lac... equino*: Virgil, *Georgics*, iii. 463: 'et lac concretum cum sanguine potat equino' (and he drinks milk curdled with horses' blood). The full sentence, as translated by Dryden, reads: 'This remedy the Scythian shepherds found; / Th' inhabitants of Thracia's hilly ground / And Gelons use it; when for drink and food / They mix their cruddl'd milk with horses' blood.' The burlesque poem *Hesperi-Neso-Graphia: or, A Description of the Western Isle in Eight Cantos...*, London, 1716, p. 4, described the natives of Ireland as mixing cows' blood with butter 'to make a dainty feast'.
34 *Bonnyclabber*: buttermilk, from the Gaelic *bainne clábair*. Understood to be a staple of the native Irish diet.
35 *the County of Corke... Number of Cattle*: the 'dairy agreement', popular in Cork and elsewhere in south Munster in the early eighteenth century, by which landowners or large tenants would rent herds of cows to 'dairymen' (together with sufficient grazing land), in return for a specified quantity of dairy produce: see Dickson, *Old World Colony*, pp. 201–2.

A PROPOSAL FOR AN ACT OF PARLIAMENT, TO PAY OFF THE DEBT OF THE NATION, WITHOUT TAXING THE SUBJECT, BY WHICH THE NUMBER OF LANDED GENTRY, AND SUBSTANTIAL FARMERS WILL BE CONSIDERABLY ENCREASED, AND NO ONE PERSON WILL BE THE POORER, OR CONTRIBUTE ONE FARTHING TO THE CHARGE.

Headnote

Probably composed early 1732; published February 1732; copy text *1732a* (see Textual Account).

First published in Dublin in February 1732, and reprinted in March in London, this was a contribution (in ironic mode) to Swift's campaign against the two recent bills put forward by bishops in the Irish Parliament: the first 'more effectually to enable the clergy... to reside upon their respective benefices', and the second 'for continuing and amending an act... for the real union and division of parishes'. The residence bill had been introduced into the Lords in December 1731 as 'heads', and, having been approved by both the Irish and British privy councils had been returned to the Lords on 10 Feb. 1732. The parishes bill had originated in the Irish privy council and had been brought into the Lords as a bill on 17 Feb. Both were passed by the upper house and sent down to the Commons on 21 Feb. and 24 Feb. respectively. But opponents (including Swift) were able to arouse opinion sufficiently for the Commons not to proceed. Taken together, the two bills sought to deal with the problem of non-residence among the parish clergy in an authoritarian manner by empowering bishops to force any incumbent of a benefice worth more than £100 p.a. to build a manse house; and also to divide large parishes without the incumbents' consent. Swift pursued the subject without irony in the contemporaneous *On the Bill for the Clergy's Residing on Their Livings*, and *Considerations upon Two Bills* (Davis, vol. XII, pp. 179–202). He was acutely aware of the financial difficulties of the lower clergy, caused by the poverty of many livings, the impropriation by laymen of glebe land and either the impropriation of tithes or the resistance of tithe-payers (see above, Introduction, pp. lxiv–lxviii). He was also suspicious of the arbitrary power which the bills would have given the bishops, especially with regard to the potential division of parishes which he feared would multiply opportunities for patronage and result in the creation of a horde of 'beggarly clergymen' dependent on their episcopal superior. (See Landa, pp. 111–23; D. W. Hayton, 'Parliament and the Established Church: Reform and Reaction', in D. W. Hayton, James Kelly and John Bergin (eds.), *The Eighteenth-century Composite State: Representative Institutions in Ireland and Europe, 1689–1800*, Basingstoke: Palgrave Macmillan, 2010, pp. 91–2.) In turning attention back towards the bishops' rental incomes, Swift was also referencing the ongoing efforts, both inside and outside the Irish House of Commons, to secure some amendment of the Act of 1635 (10 & 11 Chas. I c. 3) which prevented bishops from granting leases of church land for longer than 21 years. Advocates of economic development regarded this statutory limitation as a drag anchor holding tenants back from making 'improvements'. But the argument against longer leases, which Swift endorsed, was that while it would serve 'the advantage of the present bishops', who would thereby secure higher rents and fines, it would in the long run impoverish the church as a corporate body. Several Whig bishops, of whom Swift personally did not approve (Downes of Elphin, Evans of Meath, Nicolson of Derry, and even Burnet of Salisbury) in fact took the same view (Landa, pp. 97–111; Hayton, 'Parliament and the Established Church', pp. 91–2).

The significance of the pseudonym of A— P— is not entirely clear. More prosaic suggestions would include this being a contraction of 'A Proposer', or even 'A Parson' (as Ehrenpreis suggests: vol. III, p. 721). Another possibility is that Swift was making a mischievous hint at Ambrose Philips (1674–1749), satirised as 'Namby Pamby', formerly secretary to Archbishop Boulter of Armagh and a judge of the primate's prerogative court.

A PROPOSAL FOR AN ACT OF PARLIAMENT, &c.

The Debts contracted some Years past for the Service and Safety of the Nation, are grown so great, that under our present distress'd Condition by the want of Trade, the great Remittances to pay Absentees, Regiments serving Abroad, and many other drains of Money, well enough known and felt; the Kingdom seems altogether unable to discharge them by the Common Methods of Payment:[1] And either a Pole or Land Tax would be too odious to think of,[2] especially the Latter, because the Lands which have been let for these Ten or Dozen Years past, were raised so high, that the Owners can, at present, hardly receive any Rent at all. For, it is the usual Practice of an *Irish* Tenant, rather than want Land, to offer more for a Farm than he knows he can be ever able to pay, and in that Case he grows desperate, and pays nothing at all.[3] So that a Land Tax upon a rackt[4] Estate would be a Burthen wholly insupportable.

The Question will then be, how these National Debts can be paid, and how I can make good the several Particulars of my Proposal, which I shall now lay open to the Publick.

The Revenues of their Graces and Lordships the Arch-bishops and Bishops of this Kingdom, (excluding the Fines)[5] do amount by a moderate

---

1 *The Debts contracted some Years past... Methods of Payment*: The Irish Parliament had introduced the notion of a 'national debt' (then fixed at £50,000) by statute in 1716. The subsequent increase in the debt required further Acts in 1729 and 1731 to provide for loans to pay the interest.
2 *a Pole or Land Tax... to think of*: apart from the short-lived poll tax introduced in 1695 (7 Will. III c. 15 [Ire.]) and extended in the following session (9 Will. III c. 8 [Ire.]), neither a poll tax nor a land tax had been introduced in Ireland, though both had occasionally been considered – as, for example, in 1717: Martin Bladen to Charles Delafaye, 23 Mar. 1716/17 (TNA, SP 63/375/59); Charles Dering to Lord Perceval, 6 Aug. 1717 (BL, Egmont papers, Add. MS 47028, fo. 196); William Conolly to Charles Delafaye, 13 Aug. 1717 (TNA, SP 63/375/162–3).
3 *the Lands... nothing at all*: Swift is repeating views expressed by Archbishop King as early as 1719, that increases in rent disadvantaged prospective Protestant tenants, and that unscrupulous Catholics bid higher for leases with no intention of paying what they had offered (King to Archbishop Wake, 2 June 1719: Sir Charles S. King, *A Great Archbishop of Dublin William King D.D...*, London: Longmans, Green and Co., 1906, pp. 301–3). In April 1728, King wrote to Edward Southwell that Catholics were outbidding Protestants 'for all farms that are to be new set. By this means they worm out Protestant farmers, and yet run no hazard; for... when they have made the best of it the last year or two, and find they can't pay the rent, they run away and leave it' (ibid., p. 309).
4 *rackt*: rented at an exorbitant rate.
5 *the Fines*: levied by the landlord on the tenant, at fixed points in the duration of a lease, and at renewal.

Computation to 36,800 l. *per Ann.*[6] I mean the Rents which the Bishops receive from their Tenants. But the real Value of those Lands at a full Rent, taking the several Sees one with another, is reckoned to be at least three fourths more,[7] so that Multiplying 36,800 l. by 4, the full Rent of all the Bishops Lands will amount to 147200 l. *per Ann.* from which Substracting the present Rent received by their Lordships, that is, 36,800 l. the Profits of the Lands received by the first and second Tenants[8] (who both have great Bargains) will rise to the Sum of 110400 l. *per Ann.* which Lands, if they were to be Sold at Twenty Two Years Purchase,[9] would raise a Sum of 2,428,800 l. reserving to the Bishops their present Rents, only excluding Fines.

Of this Sum I propose, that out of the one half which amounts to 1,214,400 l. so much be applyed as will entirely discharge the Debts of the Nation, and the Remainder laid up in the Treasury, to supply Contingencies, as well as to discharge some of our heavy Taxes, until the Kingdom shall be in a better Condition.

But whereas, the present set of Bishops would be great Losers by this Scheme for want of their Fines, which would be hard Treatment to such Religious, Loyal, and Deserving Personages, I have therefore set a-part the other half to supply that Defect, which it will more than sufficiently do.

A Bishop's Lease for the full Term, is reckoned to be worth Eleven Years Purchase,[10] but if we take the Bishops round, I suppose, there may be Four Years of each Lease elapsed, and many of the Bishops being well stricken

---

6 *The Revenues . . . 36,800 l. per Ann.*: one contemporary estimate of the income of Irish bishoprics suggested a total of between £32,300 and £33,600 at some time in the 1720s, rising to £39,890–£41,190 in the following decade: Lambeth Palace Library, MS 2168, fos. 127–8.

7 *the real Value . . . three fourths more*: in *Some Arguments against Enlarging the Power of Bishops, in Letting of Leases, with Remarks on Some Queries Lately Published* (1723), Swift noted that in a legal case against a lease made by the bishop of Meath, the lands had not been set for a seventh of their real value (Davis, vol. IX, p. 46).

8 *the first and second Tenants*: where lands were sublet, sometimes more than once: see David Dickson, 'Middlemen', in Thomas Bartlett and D. W. Hayton (eds.), *Penal Era and Golden Age: Essays in Irish History, 1690–1800*, Belfast: Ulster Historical Foundation, 1979, pp. 162–85.

9 *at Twenty Two Years Purchase*: a calculation of the purchase price as a multiplication of the annual rental value of the property. By an Irish statute of 1635 (10 and 11 Chas. I c. 23), bishops and ecclesiastical corporations were prevented from setting leases for longer than 21 years.

10 *A Bishop's Lease . . . Eleven Years Purchase*: the Act of 1635 also required that bishops and ecclesiastical corporations set leases at not less than a half their real value.

in Years, I cannot think their Lives round to be worth more than seven Years Purchase; so that the Purchasers may very well afford fifteen Years Purchase for the Reversion, especially by one great additional Advantage, which I shall soon mention.

This Sum of 2,428,800 l. must likewise be sunk very considerably; because the Lands are to be sold only at 15 Years Purchase, and this lessens the Sum to about 1,656,000 l. of which I propose Twelve Hundred Thousand Pounds to be applyed partly for the Payment of the National Debt, and partly as a Fund for future Exigencies, and the remaining 456,000 l. I propose as a Fund for paying the present Set of Bishops their Fines, which it will abundantly do, and a great Part remain as an Addition to the Publick Stock.

Although the Bishops round do not in reality receive three Fines a Piece, which take up 21 Years,[11] yet I allow it to be so; but then I will suppose them to take but one Year's Rent, in Recompence of giving them so large a Term of Life, and thus multiplying 36800 l. by 3, the Product will be only 110400 l. so that above three fourths will remain, to be applied to Publick use.

If I have made wrong Computations, I hope to be excused, as a Stranger to the Kingdom, which I never saw till I was called to an Employment,[12] and yet where I intend to pass the Rest of my Days; but I took Care to get the best Informations I could, and from the most proper Persons; however, the mistakes I may have been guilty of, will very little affect the main of my Proposal; although they should cause a Difference of one Hundred Thousand Pounds, more or less.

These Fines, are only to be paid to the Bishop during his Incumbency in the same See: If he changeth it for a Better, the Purchasers of the Vacant See Lands, are to come immediately into Possession of the See he hath left, and both the Bishop who is removed, and he who comes into his Place, are to have no more Fines, for the removed Bishop will find his Account by a larger Revenue; and the other See will find Candidates enough. For the

---

11 *Although the Bishops ... take up 21 Years*: Dobbs, *Essay*, pt 2, p. 78, in the course of arguing that the brevity of episcopal leases was a discouragement to tenants to make improvements, had asserted that the bishops, because their time in a diocese was uncertain and often of short duration, habitually took fines every three or seven years.

12 *as a Stranger to the Kingdom ... called to an Employment*: not strictly true as applied to Swift himself, but accurate in relation to Ambrose Philips.

Law Maxim will here have place, that *Caveat*, &c.¹³ I mean the Persons who succeed, may chuse whether they will accept or no.

As to the Purchasers, they will probably be Tenants to the See, who are already in Possession, and can afford to give more than any other Bidders.

I will further explain myself. If a Person already a Bishop, be removed into a richer See, he must be content with the bare Revenues, without any Fines, and so must he who comes into a Bishoprick vacant by Death: And this will bring the Matter sooner to bear; which if the Crown shall think fit to Countenance, will soon change the present Set of Bishops, and consequently encourage Purchasers of their Lands. For Example, If a Primate should die, and the Gradation be wisely made, almost the whole Set of Bishops might be changed in a Month,¹⁴ each to his great Advantage, although no Fines were to be got, and thereby save a great Part of that Sum which I have appropriated towards supplying the Deficiency of Fines.

I have valued the Bishops Lands two Years Purchase above the usual computed Rate, because those Lands will have a Sanction from the King and Council in *England*, and be confirmed by an Act of Parliament here;¹⁵ besides, it is well known, that higher Prices are given every Day for worse Lands, at the remotest Distances, and at rack Rents, which I take to be occasioned by want of Trade: When there are few Borrowers, and the little Money in private Hands lying dead, there is no other way to dispose of it,

---

13 *Caveat, &c*: *caveat emptor* (let the buyer beware).
14 *in a Month*: this would be achieved by a series of appointments restricted to the promotion of existing Irish bishops, such as occurred in December 1729 – January 1730. Then, in two separate rounds, first Theophilus Bolton was translated from Elphin to Cashel, Robert Howard from Killala to Elphin, and Robert Clayton was nominated to Killala; and second, John Hoadly was translated from Ferns to Dublin, Arthur Price from Clonfert to Ferns, and Edward Synge the younger was nominated to Clonfert. See R. E. Burns, *Irish Parliamentary Politics in the Eighteenth Century*, 2 vols., Washington, DC: Catholic University of America Press, 1989–90, vol. I, pp. 259–60. But there was always the likelihood of English bishops being translated to Irish sees (especially the more high-ranking or lucrative), a long-standing grievance of the 'Irish party' in the episcopate and Parliament: Patrick McNally, '"Irish and English Interests": National Conflict within the Church of Ireland Episcopate in the Reign of George I', *Irish Historical Studies*, 29 (1994–5), 295–314.
15 *will have a Sanction . . . confirmed by an Act of Parliament here*: probably a reference to the legislative process in Ireland, since these sales require statutory permission. In Ireland, according to Poynings' Law, bills as such were prepared by the Irish privy council and transmitted to the privy council in England for approval, before being returned to Ireland and presented to the Irish Parliament, which had either to accept or to reject them as they stood, with no possibility of further amendment.

but in buying of Land; which consequently makes the Owners hold it so high.

Besides paying the Nation's Debts, the Sale of these Lands would have many other good Effects upon the Nation; it will considerably encrease the Number of Gentry, where the Bishops Tenants are not able or willing to Purchase; for the Lands will afford an hundred Gentlemen a good Revenue to each; several Persons from *England* will probably be glad to come over hither, and be the Buyers, rather than give thirty Years Purchase at home, under the Loads of Taxes for the Publick and the Poor, as well as Repairs, by which Means much Money may be brought among us; and probably some of the Purchasers themselves may be content to live cheap in a worse Country, rather than be at the Charge of Exchange[16] and Agencies,[17] and perhaps of Non-solvencies[18] in Absence, if they Let their Lands too high.

This Proposal will also multiply Farmers, when the Purchasers will have Lands in their own Power, to give long and easy Leases to industrious Husbandmen.

I have allowed some Bishopricks of equal Income to be of more or less Value to the Purchaser, according as they are circumstanced. For Instance, The Lands of the Primacy and some other Sees, are let so low, that they hardly pay a fifth Penny of the real Value to the Bishop, and there the Fines are the greater. On the contrary, the Sees of *Meath* and *Clonfert*, consisting, as I am told, much of Tythes,[19] those Tythes are annually Let to the Tenants without any Fines.[20] So the See of *Dublin* is said

---

16 *Exchange*: since currency values differed, there was a cost in changing Irish money into English.
17 *Agencies*: the expense of employing an agent to manage affairs in Ireland.
18 *non-solvencies*: tenants being unable to pay their rents.
19 *the Sees of Meath and Clonfert... much of Tythes*: Bishop William King of Derry wrote to Sir Robert Southwell in 1697, about the diocese of Meath: 'Tis one of the largest in Ireland, consisting anciently of five bishoprics, at least sixty miles long, in an excellent country; but the lands were mostly made away or exchanged for tithes about the Reformation' (quoted in John Healy, *History of the Diocese of Meath*, 2 vols., Dublin: Association for Promoting Christian Knowledge, 1908, vol. II, p. 27). In relation to Clonfert, King, now archbishop of Dublin, wrote to Archbishop Wake of Canterbury in 1722 that a quarter of the tithes were possessed by the bishop (quoted in Richard Mant, *History of the Church of Ireland...*, 2 vols., London, 1840, vol. II, p. 380).
20 *Let to the Tenants without any Fines*: again, Swift is contesting the arguments of Arthur Dobbs. In *Essay*, pt 2, pp. 92–3, Dobbs proposed a reform of the tithe system (which he contended was one of the reasons for Presbyterian emigration from Ulster to America, an argument Swift repeatedly rejected), including the recommendation that clergy be obliged

to have many Fee-Farms which pay no Tythes,[21] and some Leases for Lives[22] which pay very little, and not so soon nor so duly.

I cannot but be confident, that their Graces my Lords the Arch-bishops, and my Lords the Bishops will heartily join in this Proposal, out of Gratitude to his late and present Majesty, the best of Kings,[23] who have bestowed such high and opulent Stations, as well as in Pity to this Country which is now become their own, whereby they will be Instrumental towards paying the Nation's Debts, without impoverishing themselves; Enrich an Hundred Gentlemen, as well as Free them from Dependance, and thus remove that Envy which is apt to fall upon their Graces and Lordships from considerable Persons, whose Birth and Fortunes rather qualify them to be Lords of Mannors, than servile Dependents upon Churchmen, however dignified or distinguished.

If I do not flatter my self, there could not be any Law more popular than this; for the immediate Tenants to Bishops, being some of them Persons of Quality, and good Estates, and more of them grown up to be Gentlemen by the Profits of these very Leases, under a Succession of Bishops, think it a Disgrace to be Subject both to Rents and Fines, at the Pleasure of their Landlords. Then the Bulk of the Tenants, especially the Dissenters, who are our loyal Protestant Brethren,[24] look upon it both as an unnatural and

---

by law to lease their tithes to their own tenants for periods of 11, 16 or 21 years, without taking fines.

21 *Fee-Farms which pay no Tythes*: a fee-farm was a form of tenure, feudal in origin, in which land was held in consideration of an annual rent. When bishops made leases in fee farm, the property concerned was exempt from tithe.

22 *Leases for Lives*: for the lifetime of the persons named in the lease, and ending with the death of the last survivor.

23 *his late and present Majesty, the best of Kings*: George I and George II.

24 *the Dissenters... loyal Protestant Brethren*: an essential element of the case made by John Abernethy for the repeal of the sacramental test, *The Nature and Consequences of the Sacramental Test Considered*, Dublin, 1731, had been that Presbyterians were, and had always been, loyal to the Revolution settlement and Protestant succession (pp. 55, 57). This had been a long-standing point of contention. The High Church position, that Presbyterians were only concerned with their own sectarian interests, and indeed had a history of disloyalty to the monarchy, had been expressed most stridently in William Tisdall, *A Sample of True-blew Presbyterian-loyalty, in All Changes and Turns of Government*, Dublin, 1709, a pamphlet which had been answered by two Presbyterian ministers: John McBride, *A Sample of Jet-Black Pr[ela]tic Calumny, in Answer to a Pamphlet, called, A Sample of True-Bleu Presbyterian loyalty*, Glasgow, 1713, and James Kirkpatrick, *An Historical Essay upon the Loyalty of Presbyterians in Great-Britain and Ireland from the Reformation to This Present Year 1713*, Belfast, 1713.

iniquitous thing that Bishops should be Owners of Land at all;[25] (wherein I beg to differ from them) being a Point so contrary to the Practice of the Apostles, whose Successors they are deemed to be, and who although they were contented that Land should be Sold for the Common Use of the Brethren, yet would not buy it themselves, but had it laid at their Feet, to be distributed to poor Proselytes.[26]

I will add one Word more, that by such a wholesome Law, all the Oppressions felt by under Tenants of Church Leases, which are now laid on by the Bishops would entirely be prevented, by their Graces and Lordships consenting to have their Lands Sold for payment of the Nation's Debts, reserving only the present Rent for their own plentiful and honourable Support.

I beg leave to add one Particular, that, when Heads of a Bill (as I find the Style runs in this Kingdom)[27] shall be brought in for forming this Proposal into a Law; I should humbly offer that there might be a Power given to every Bishop (except those who reside in *Dublin*) for applying one Hundred Acres of profitable Land that lyes nearest to his Palace as a Demesne[28] for the Conveniency of his Family.

I know very well, that this Scheme hath been much talk'd of for some time past, and is in the Thoughts of many Patriots, neither was it properly mine, although I fell readily into it, when it was first communicated to me.

25 *look upon it... Owners of Land at all*: in 1723 a bill to permit bishops to make leases for longer than the 21 years to which they were limited by statute (thereby risking the alienation of church property) had given rise to acrimonious debates in Parliament and the press, in which Swift had taken a prominent part in defence of the church (Landa, pp. 97–111). At that time, *The History of the Popish Clergy: or, The Case of the Laity...*, Dublin, 1723, had made a strident case against clerical landownership and its deleterious effects on the Irish agrarian economy. Further attempts would be made to introduce legislation in 1735 and 1737 (D. W. Hayton, 'Parliament and the Established Church: Reform and Reaction', in Hayton *et al.* (eds.), *Eighteenth-Century Composite State*, pp. 91–2).
26 *Land should be Sold for the Common Use... to be distributed to poor Proselytes*: Acts 4: 34–5: 'Neither was there any among them that lacked: for as many as were possessors of lands or houses sold them, and brought the prices of the things that were sold, and laid them down at the apostles' feet: and distribution was made unto every man according as he had need.'
27 *Heads of a Bill... runs in this Kingdom*: Poynings' Law required that Irish statutes should originate in bills prepared by the Irish privy council, but since the Restoration the practice had arisen for Parliament to prepare drafts or 'heads of bills', identical in every respect to bills proper except for the wording of the preamble. These were presented to the lord lieutenant, in order for the council to turn them into the correct form.
28 *a Demesne*: in Ireland, that part of a landed estate immediately attached to a country house. The demesne was not leased, but set out in gardens and parkland for the use of the owner and his family.

Tho' I am almost a perfect Stranger in this Kingdom, yet since I have accepted an Employment here, of some Consequence as well as Profit; I cannot but think my self in Duty bound to consult the Interest of a People, among whom I have been so well received. And if I can be any way Instrumental towards contributing to reduce this excellent Proposal into a Law, which, being not in the least Injurious to *England*, will, I am Confident, meet with no Opposition from that Side,[29] my sincere Endeavours to serve this Church and Kingdom will be well rewarded.

FINIS

29 *no Opposition from that Side*: from England, where anticlericalism was perceived to be on the increase (J. A. I. Champion, *The Pillars of Priestcraft Shaken: The Church of England and Its Enemies, 1660–1730*, Cambridge: Cambridge University Press, 1992, pp. 173–9; William Gibson, *The Church of England 1688–1832: Unity and Accord*, London: Routledge, 2001, pp. 89–90; Stephen Taylor, 'The Bowman Affair: Latitudinarian Theology, Anticlericalism and the Limits of Orthodoxy in Early Hanoverian England', in Robert D. Cornwall and William Gibson (eds.), *Religion, Politics and Dissent, 1660–1832: Essays in Honour of James E. Bradley*, Aldershot: Ashgate, 2010, pp. 35–50). Archbishop Boulter acknowledged the hostility on both sides of the Irish Sea towards the clergy in his letter to Bishop Gibson of London, 11 May 1731 (*Boulter Letters*, vol. II, pp. 49–50), and it was discussed by Swift in *Concerning that Universal Hatred which Prevails against the Clergy* (1736) (Davis, vol. XIII, pp. 121–6).

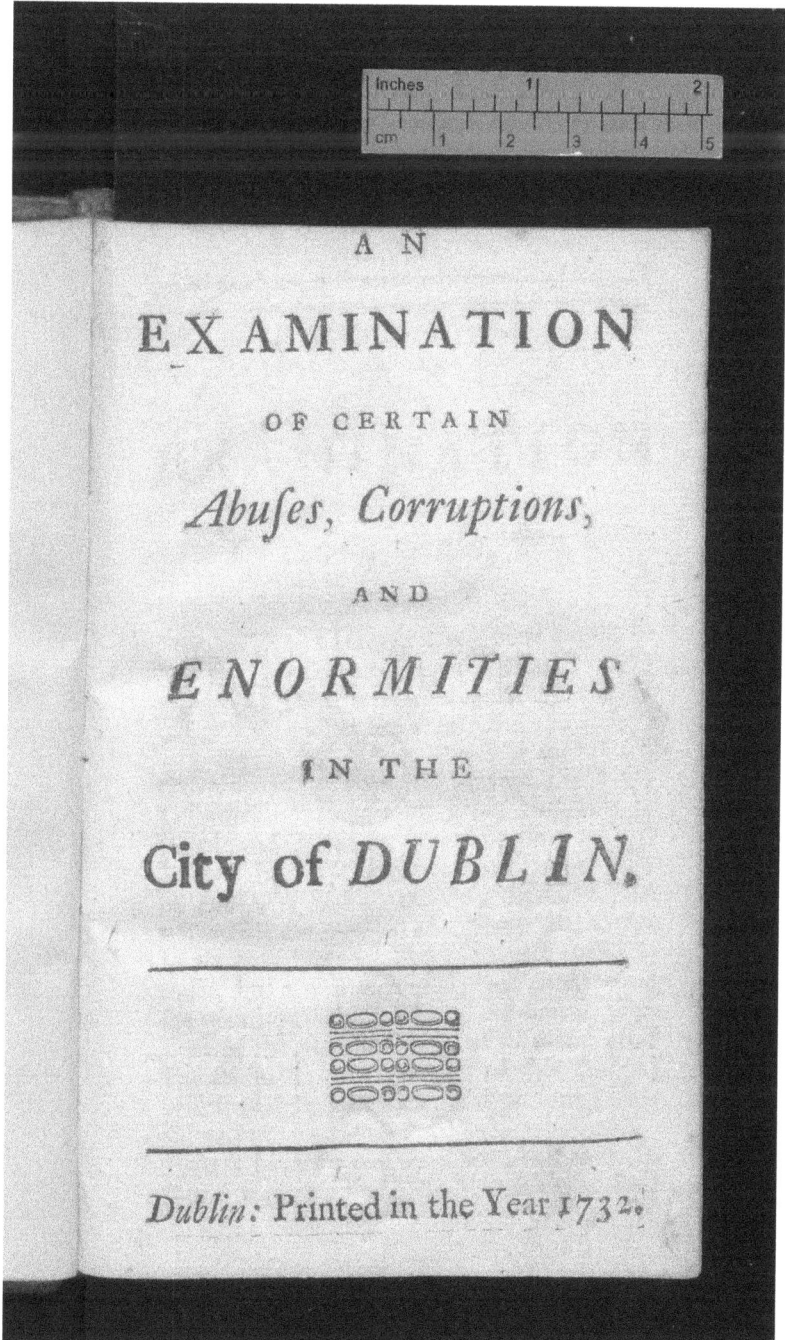

Figure 5. Jonathan Swift, *An Examination of Certain Abuses*, 1732. Title. Williams 308.

AN EXAMINATION OF CERTAIN ABUSES, CORRUPTIONS, AND ENORMITIES IN THE CITY OF DUBLIN

AN EXAMINATION OF CERTAIN ABUSES IN DUBLIN 241

Headnote

Probably composed early 1732; published *c*. March 1732; copy text *1732a* (see Textual Account).

A mock-description of supposedly treasonous Jacobite messages encoded in the cries of street-sellers and shop-signs, examined to the point of absurdity, *An Examination of Certain Abuses* is one of Swift's last prose works to be based upon the ironies that can extend from a credulous narrator. It is possible that (like the *Vindication of Carteret*) it was directed against exaggerated anti-Jacobite rhetoric, shown, for instance, in the lord mayor of Dublin's forbidding of the wearing of white roses and similar symbols on 10 June, the Pretender's birthday (see Introduction, p. xciv).

The pamphlet's general target is the Whig use of old-fashioned shibboleths to keep Tories out of office, and to advance themselves, through the indiscriminate accusation of Jacobitism against political enemies. It is not always clear whether any persons in Ireland suffered damage to their political careers as a result of such abuse: the satire is more pertinent to England than Ireland, as some of Swift's English friends (such as Bolingbroke and the second Earl of Oxford) were in permanent political exclusion because of their Toryism.

It was published in Dublin in 1732 as *An Examination of Certain Abuses, Corruptions, and Enormities in the City of Dublin*. The London edition was retitled *City Cries, Instrumental and Vocal: or, An Examination of Certain Abuses Corruptions, and Enormities in London and Dublin*. This also added three pages at the end of the pamphlet (giving another example of alleged Jacobitism, connected to London sign-posts), an addition made presumably by Swift as an acknowledgement of the different audience in England.

AN EXAMINATION OF *CERTAIN ABUSES*, &c.

Nothing is held more commendable in all great Cities, especially the Metropolis of a Kingdom, than what the *French* call the *Police*;[1] by which Word is meant the Government thereof, to prevent the many Disorders occasioned by great Numbers of People and Carriages, especially thro' narrow Streets. In this Government our famous City of *Dublin* is said to be very defective, and universally complained of.[2] Many wholesome Laws have been enacted to correct these Abuses, but are ill executed; and many more are wanting, which I hope the united Wisdom of the Nation (whereof so many good Effects have already appeared this Session) will soon take into their most profound Consideration.

As I have been always watchful over the Good of mine own Country, and particularly for that of our renowned City, where (*absit invidia*)[3] I had the Honour to draw my first Breath; I cannot have a Minute's Ease or Patience to forbear enumerating some of the greatest Enormities, Abuses, and Corruptions spread almost through every Part of *Dublin*; and proposing such Remedies as, I hope, the Legislature will approve of.

The narrow Compass to which I have confined myself in this Paper, will allow me only to touch at the most important Defects, and such as I think seem to require the most speedy Redress.

And first, perhaps there was never known a wiser Institution than that of allowing certain Persons of both Sexes, in large and populous Cities, to cry through the Streets many Necessaries of Life;[4] it would be endless to

---

1 *what the French call the Police*: in eighteenth-century France, 'police' was used to mean what the English called 'commonwealth' or 'policy' (deriving from the Greek *polis*): Clive Emsley, *Crime, Police and Penal Policy: European Experiences 1750–1940*, Oxford: Oxford University Press, 2007, p. 63. In the case of Dublin, Swift intends the agencies of maintaining public order: city constables and watchmen, under the direction of the lord mayor and sheriffs.
2 *universally complained of*: Dublin newspapers in 1729 had been full of complaints against the city constables: see, e.g., *Dublin Intelligence*, 23 Sept. 1729. Their corrupt and oppressive behaviour was sufficiently notorious to prompt the city corporation to attempt a purge of the worst offenders (*Cal. Anc. Recs. Dublin*, vol. VIII, 500). See T. D. Watt, 'The Corruption of the Law and Popular Violence: The Crisis of Order in Dublin, 1729', *Irish Historical Studies* 39 (2014–15), 1–23.
3 *absit invidia*: 'Let ill-will (or envy) be absent', often used in the sense of 'no offence meant'.
4 *to cry... Necessaries of Life*: in London in October 1712, Swift noted the 'abundance of our old criers' on the streets (*Journal to Stella*, *CWJS*, vol. IX, pp. 456–7), a subject to which Addison devoted an entire essay in the *Spectator* (*Spectator*, vol. II, pp. 474–7), noting that 'nothing more astonishes a Foreigner and frights a Country Squire, than the Cries of

recount the Conveniences which our City enjoys by this useful Invention, and particularly Strangers, forced hither by Business, who reside here but a short time; for, these having usually but little Money, and being wholly ignorant of the Town, might at an easy Price purchase a tolerable Dinner, if the several Criers would pronounce the Names of the Goods they have to sell, in any tolerable Language. And therefore till our Law-makers shall think it proper to interpose so far as to make these Traders pronounce their Words in such Terms, that a plain Christian Hearer may comprehend what is cryed; I would advise all new Comers to look out at their Garret Windows, and there see whether the Thing that is cryed be *Tripes* or *Flummery*,[5] *Buttermilk* or *Cowheels*. For, as things are now managed, how is it possible for an honest Country-man, just arrived, to find out what is meant; for Instance, by the following Words, with which his Ears are constantly stunned twice a Day, *Muggs*,[6] *Juggs and Porringers*,[7] *up in the Garret, and down in the Cellar*. I say, how is it possible for any Stranger to understand that this Jargon is meant as an invitation to buy a Farthing's worth of Milk for his Breakfast or Supper, unless his Curiosity draws him to the Window, or till his Landlady shall inform him. I produce this only as one Instance, among a Hundred much worse, I mean where the Words make a Sound wholly inarticulate, which give so much Disturbance, and so little Information.

The Affirmation solemnly made in the cry of *Herrings*, is directly against all Truth and Probability, *Herrings alive, alive here*; the very Proverb will convince us of this; for what is more frequent in ordinary Speech, than to say of some Neighbour for whom the Passing-Bell rings, that *he is*

London' (p. 474). *A Humourous Description of the Manners and Fashions of the Inhabitants of the City of Dublin*, Dublin, 1734, p. 4, referred to 'the hideous cries of those people who walk the streets to vend herbs, milk, fruit, old clothes, sand, trials, news, ghosts and bloody murthers', and Swift made them the subject for his 'Verses made for Women who cry Apples, &c.' (*Poems*, vol. III, pp. 951–3), selecting as the particular wares to be celebrated apples, asparagus, onions, oysters, herrings and oranges. Although lists of street cries were published in many European countries from *c*. 1660 onwards, none survive for Ireland before the drawings of Hugh Douglas Hamilton in 1760: Sean Shesgreen, 'Images of the Irish Underclass: The Innovative Continuity of Hugh Douglas Hamilton's "Cries of Dublin"', in William Laffan (ed.), *The Cries of Dublin &c, Drawn from the Life by Hugh Douglas Hamilton, 1760*, Dublin: Irish Georgian Society, 2003, pp. 38, 53.
5 *Flummery*: a custard or pudding, usually made with oatmeal.
6 *Muggs*: for a later eighteenth-century example of milk being sold in the streets, see Laffan (ed.) *Cries of Dublin*, pp. 64–5.
7 *Porringers*: small vessels used for eating soup or porridge.

dead as a Herring.⁸ And, pray how is it possible, that a Herring, which as Philosophers observe, cannot live longer than one Minute, three Seconds and a half out of Water,⁹ should bear a Voyage in open Boats from *Howth*¹⁰ to *Dublin*, be tossed into twenty Hands, and preserve its Life in Sieves for several Hours. Nay, we have Witnesses ready to produce that many Thousands of these Herrings, so impudently asserted to be alive, have been a Day and a Night upon dry Land. But this is not the worst. What can we think of those impious Wretches, who dare in the Face of the Sun, vouch the very same affirmative of their *Salmon*, and cry, *Salmon alive, alive*; whereas, if you call the Woman who cryes it, she is not asham'd to turn back her Mantle, and show you this individual Salmon cut into a dozen Pieces. I have given good Advice to these infamous Disgracers of their Sex and Calling, without the least appearance of Remorse, and fully against the Conviction of their own Consciences. I have mentioned this Grievance to several of our Parish Ministers, but all in vain; so that it must continue till the Government shall think fit to interpose.

There is another Cry, which, from the strictest Observation I can make, appears to be very modern, and it is that of *Sweet-hearts*,¹¹ and is plainly intended for a Reflection upon the Female Sex, as if there were at present so great a Dearth of Lovers, that the Women instead of receiving Presents from Men, were now forced to offer Money, to purchase *Sweet-hearts*. Neither am I sure, that this Cry doth not glance at some Disaffection against the Government; insinuating, that while so many of our Troops are engaged in foreign Service,¹² and such a great Number of our gallant Officers constantly reside in *England*, the Ladies are forced to take up with

---

8 *he is dead as a Herring*: proverbial (*ODEP*, p. 170). Cf. Swift's 'Verses made for Women who cry Apples, &c' (*Poems*, vol. III, p. 953).
9 *a Herring... out of Water*: Swift's source – if indeed he had one – has not been identified, but it may be worth noting that *The British Apollo: Containing Two Thousand Answers to Curious Questions in most Arts and Sciences, Serious, Comical, and Humorous*, 3rd edn, 3 vols., London, [1726]), vol. III, p. 67, poses (and answers) the question as to why, 'above all other fish', a herring dies as soon as it is lifted out of water.
10 *Howth*: the fishing village of Howth, on Howth Head, the promontory marking the north end of Dublin Bay.
11 *Sweet-hearts*: 'A sort of sugar-cakes in the shape of hearts' (Swift's note); also a form of gingerbread.
12 *while so many of our Troops are engaged in foreign Service*: in 1727, six regiments on the Irish establishment were sent to the garrison at Gibraltar (*C.J.Ire.*, vol. V, 426), giving rise to discontent among Irish MPs. Carteret reported to the Parliamentary session in 1729 that three had since returned to Ireland, but the remaining troops were still in Gibraltar in

Parsons and Attornies: But, this is a most unjust Reflection, as may soon be proved by any Person who frequents the Castle,[13] our publick Walks, our Balls and Assemblies,[14] where the Crowds of *Toupees*[15] were never known to swarm as they do at present.

There is a Cry, peculiar to this City, which I do not remember to have been used in *London*, or at least, not in the same Terms that it hath been practised by both Parties, during each of their Power; but, very unjustly by the *Tories*. While these were at the Helm, they grew daily more and more impatient to put all true *Whigs* and *Hanoverians* out of Employments. To effect which, they hired certain ordinary Fellows, with large Baskets on their Shoulders, to call aloud at every House, *Dirt to carry out*; giving that Denomination to our whole Party, as if they would signify, that the Kingdom could never be *cleansed*, till we were *swept* from the Earth like *Rubbish*. But, since that happy Turn of Times, when we were so *miraculously* preserved by just an *Inch*, from *Popery, Slavery, Massacre*, and the *Pretender*;[16] I must own it Prudence in us, still to go on with the same Cry, which hath ever since been so effectually observed; that the true *political Dirt* is wholly removed, and thrown on its proper Dunghills, there to corrupt, and be no more heard of.

But, to proceed to other Enormities: Every Person who walks the Streets, must needs observe the immense Number of human Excrements at the Doors and Steps of waste Houses, and at the Sides of every dead Wall; for which the disaffected Party have assigned a very false and malicious Cause. They would have it, that these Heaps were laid there privately by *British Fundaments*, to make the World believe, that our *Irish* Vulgar

---

1732, and funds had to be remitted from Ireland to pay them: McGrath, *Ireland and Empire*, pp. 156–7.

13 *who frequents the Castle*: Dublin Castle, whose social scene had been significantly enhanced under the patronage of the new lord lieutenant, the Duke of Dorset, and his duchess, during the winter season of 1731–2: *Pue's Occurrences*, 14 Sept., 2, 20, 23 Nov., 11 Dec. 1731, 4 Jan., 5 Feb., 25 Mar. 1732; Bishop Clayton to Lady Sundon, 9 Nov. 1731 (Katherine Thomson, *Memoirs of Viscountess Sundon*, 2 vols., London, 1847, vol. II, pp. 155–60); Edward McParland, *Public Architecture in Ireland, 1680–1760*, New Haven & London: Yale University Press, 2001, pp. 100–1.

14 *Assemblies*: elegant social gatherings.

15 *Toupees*: 'A new name for a modern periwig, and for its owner; now in fashion, Dec. 1, 1733' (Swift's note). The toupee had been favoured by young society males in London and Dublin since at least 1727, and was now synonymous with foppery and gallantry. (See above, p. 46, and *Poems*, vol. III, p. 780.)

16 *that happy Turn . . . the Pretender*: the accession of King George I in 1714.

do daily eat and drink; and, consequently, that the Clamour of Poverty among us, must be false, proceeding only from *Jacobites* and *Papists*. They would confirm this, by pretending to observe, that a *British Anus* being more narrowly perforated than one of our own Country; and many of these Excrements upon a strict View appearing Cople-crown'd,[17] with a Point like a Cone or Pyramid, are easily distinguish'd from the *Hibernian*, which lie much flatter, and with less continuity. I communicated this Conjecture to an eminent Physician,[18] who is well versed in such profound Speculations; and at my Request was pleased to make Trial with each of his Fingers, by thrusting them into the *Anus* of several Persons of both Nations, and professed he could find no such Difference between them as those ill-disposed People alledge. On the contrary, he assured me, that much the greater Number of narrow Cavities were of *Hibernian* Origin. This I only mention to shew how ready the Jacobites are to lay hold of any Handle to express their Malice against the Government. I had almost forgot to add, that my Friend the Physician could, by smelling each Finger, distinguish the *Hibernian* Excrement from the *British*, and was not above twice mistaken in an Hundred Experiments; upon which he intends very soon to publish a learned Dissertation.

There is a Diversion in this City, which usually begins among the Butchers, but is often continued by a Succession of other People, through many Streets. It is call'd the COSSING *of a Dog*;[19] and I may justly number it among our Corruptions. The Ceremony is thus: A strange Dog happens to pass through a Flesh-Market: Whereupon an expert Butcher immediately cries in a loud Voice, and the proper Tone, *Coss, Coss*, several Times: The same Word is repeated by the People. The Dog, who perfectly understands the Term of Art,[20] and consequently the Danger he is in, immediately flies. The People, and even his own *Brother Animals* pursue; the Pursuit and Cry attend him perhaps half a Mile; he is well worried in his Flight, and sometimes hardly escapes. This, our Ill-wishers of the *Jacobite* Kind, are pleased to call a *Persecution*; and affirm, that it always

17 *Cople-crown'd*: the word 'copple' denoted any object conical in shape, and was used most often in relation to the landscape.
18 *an eminent Physician:* probably Richard Helsham, MD, Professor of Physic and Natural Philosophy at TCD, and a member of the Dublin Philosophical Society; Swift's personal physician and friend (*DIB*).
19 *the COSSING of a Dog*: 'coursing', the sport of chasing an animal.
20 *Term of Art*: a term with a precise meaning in a particular field.

falls upon Dogs of the *Tory* Principle. But, we can well defend ourselves, by justly alledging that when they were uppermost, they treated our *Dogs* full as inhumanly: As to my own Part, who have in former Times often attended these *Processions*, although I can very well distinguish between a *Whig* and *Tory Dog*; yet I never carried my Resentments very far upon a *Party Principle*, except it were against certain malicious *Dogs*, who most discovered their Malice against us in the *worst of Times*.[21] And, I remember too well, that in the wicked Ministry of the Earl of *Oxford*,[22] a large Mastiff of our Party being unmercifully *cossed*, ran, without thinking, between my Legs, as I was coming up *Fishamble-street*;[23] and, as I am of low Stature, with very short Legs, bore me riding backwards down the Hill, for above two Hundred Yards: And, altho' I made use of his Tail for a Bridle, holding it fast with both my Hands, and clung my Legs as close to his Sides as I could, yet we both came down together into the Middle of the Kennel;[24] where after rowling three or four Times over each other, I got up with much ado, amidst the Shouts and Huzzas of a Thousand malicious *Jacobites*: I cannot, indeed, but gratefully acknowledge, that for this and many other Services and Sufferings, I have been since more than over-paid.

This Adventure may, perhaps, have put me out of Love with the Diversion of *Cossing*, which I confess my self an Enemy to, unless we could always be sure of distinguishing *Tory Dogs*;[25] whereof great Numbers have since been so prudent, as entirely to change their Principles, and are now justly esteemed the best *Worriers* of their former Friends.

I am assured, and partly know, that all the Chimney-Sweepers Boys, where Members of P——t[26] chiefly lodge, are hired by *our Enemies* to sculk in the Tops of Chimneys, with their Heads no higher than will just permit them to look round; and at the usual Hours when Members are

21 *the worst of Times*: a cant phrase used by Whigs to refer to the last four years of Queen Anne's reign, under a Tory administration in England and Ireland.
22 *the Earl of Oxford*: Robert Harley (1661–1724), 1st Earl of Oxford, head of the Tory ministry in England 1710–14.
23 *Fishamble-street*: the street running down from Werburgh Street, near Christ Church cathedral, to Wood Quay.
24 *Kennel*: gutter.
25 *Tory Dogs*: in his poem 'Mad Mullinix and Timothy' (1728), Swift had included the following lines: 'No more my dear Delightful way tread, / Of keeping up a party hatred. / Will none the Tory Dogs pursue, / When thro' the streets I cry holloo?' (*Poems*, vol. III, p. 779).
26 *P——t*: Parliament.

going to the House, if they see a Coach stand near the Lodging of any *loyal* Member,²⁷ they call *Coach, Coach,* as loud as they can bawl, just at the Instant when the Footman begins to give the same Call. And this is chiefly done on those Days, when any Point of Importance is to be debated. This Practice may be of very dangerous Consequence. For, these Boys are all hired by Enemies to the Government; and thus, by the Absence of a few Members for a few Minutes, a Question may be carried against the *true Interest* of the Kingdom, and very probably, not without an Eye towards the *Pretender.*

I have not observed the Wit and Fancy of this Town, so much employed in any one Article, as that of contriving Variety of Signs to hang over Houses, where *Punch* is to be sold. The Bowl is represented full of Punch, the Ladle stands erect in the Middle, supported sometimes by one, and sometimes by two Animals, whose Feet rest upon the Edge of the Bowl. These Animals are sometimes one black *Lyon,* and sometimes a Couple; sometimes a single *Eagle,* and sometimes a spread one, and we often meet a *Crow,* a *Swan,* a *Bear,* or a *Cock.*²⁸

Now, I cannot find how any of these Animals, either separate, or in Conjunction, are properly speaking, either fit Emblems or Embellishments, to advance the Sale of Punch. Besides, it is agreed among Naturalists,²⁹ that no Brute can endure the Taste of strong Liquor, except where he hath been used to it from his Infancy: And, consequently, it is against all the Rules of Hieroglyph, to assign those Animals as Patrons, or Projectors³⁰ of *Punch.* For, in that Case, we ought to suppose, that the Host keeps always ready the real Bird, or Beast, whereof the Picture hangs over his Door,

---

27 *any loyal Member*: in this context, one who was loyal to the government and the Hanoverian monarchy (though it was also used as a synonym for Tory, and even for Jacobite, in the sense of one who was loyal to the hereditary ruler).

28 *These Animals are . . . a Crow, a Swan, a Bear, or a Cock*: Sir John Gilbert's *History of the City of Dublin* recorded that there were at various times in the seventeenth and eighteenth centuries taverns called the Black Lyon on Blind Quay, in Pyed Horse Yard and Grafton Street; the Eagle on Cork Hill and Eustace Street, and the Spread Eagle, in Winetavern Street; the Swan on Blind Quay, in Fishamble Street, High Street and Swan Alley, and the Old Swan on Wood Quay; the Bear in Christ Church Yard, College Green, the Old Corn Market, Crane Lane and Pyed-Horse Yard, and the Bear and Ragged Staff in Castle Street; the Cock in St Werburgh's Street, and the Cock and Punchbowl on Cork Hill (J. T. Gilbert, *History of the City of Dublin*, 3 vols., Dublin, 1854–9, vol. I, pp. 13, 42, 65, 68, 157, 160, 223, 377; vol. II, pp. 11, 14, 119, 134, 167, 179, 313; vol. III, pp. 39, 221).

29 *Naturalists*: natural philosophers.

30 *Projectors*: those who propose or propound a venture.

to entertain his Guest; which, however, to my Knowledge, is not true in Fact. For not one of those Birds is a proper Companion for a *Christian*,[31] as to aiding and assisting in making the *Punch*. For the Birds, as they are drawn upon the Sign, are much more likely to mute,[32] or shed their Feathers into the Liquor. Then, as to the *Bear*, he is too terrible, awkard, and slovenly a Companion to converse with; neither are any of them all, handy enough to fill Liquor to the Company: I do, therefore, vehemently suspect a *Plot* intended against the Government, by these Devices. For, although the *Spread-Eagle* be the Arms of *Germany*,[33] upon which Account it may possibly be a lawful *Protestant* Sign;[34] yet I, who am very suspicious of fair Out-sides, in a Matter which so nearly concerns our Welfare, cannot but call to Mind, that the *Pretender*'s Wife is said to be of *German* Birth:[35] And that many *Popish* Princes, in so vast an Extent of Land, are reported to excel both at making and drinking Punch. Besides, it is plain, that the *Spread-Eagle* exhibits to us the perfect Figure of a *Cross*, which is a Badge of *Popery*. Then, as to the *Cock*, he is well known to represent the *French* Nation, our old and dangerous Enemy. The *Swan*, who must of Necessity cover the entire Bowl with his Wings, can be no other than the *Spaniard*, who endeavours to engross all the Treasures of the *Indies*[36] to himself. The Lyon is indeed, the common Emblem of Royal Power, as well as the Arms of *England*; but to paint him black, is perfect *Jacobitism*, and a manifest Type of those who blacken the Actions of the best Princes. It is not easy to distinguish, whether that other Fowl painted over the Punch-Bowl, be a *Crow* or *Raven*? It is true, they have both been held ominous Birds;[37] but I rather take it to be the former; because it is the Disposition of a *Crow*,

---

31 *a Christian*: that is to say, a Protestant.
32 *mute*: defecate.
33 *the Spread-Eagle be the Arms of Germany*: the spread eagle was the heraldic emblem of the Holy Roman Emperor.
34 *upon which Account it may possibly be a lawful Protestant Sign*: because the Hanoverian royal family was German (though the Holy Roman Emperor was a Catholic).
35 *of German Birth*: James Francis Edward Stuart (1688–1766), 'the Old Pretender', married Maria Clementina Sobieska (1702–35), the Polish-born daughter of the Crown Prince of Poland and his German wife.
36 *who endeavours to engross all the Treasures of the Indies*: the Americas rather than the East Indies. Hostilities with Spain, leading up to the Anglo-Spanish War of 1727–9, had arisen from rivalry in the Atlantic trade, and the various naval actions had included a failed British attempt to blockade the Spanish fleet at Porto Bello in Panama, in 1726–7.
37 *a Crow or Raven... ominous Birds*: both crows and ravens had been considered birds of ill omen in the classical world.

to pick out the Eyes of other Creatures; and often even of *Christians*, after they are dead;[38] and is therefore drawn here, with a Design to put the *Jacobites* in Mind of their old Practice, first to lull us a-sleep, (which is an Emblem of Death)[39] and then to blind our Eyes, that we may not see their dangerous Practices against the State.

To speak my private Opinion, the least offensive Picture in the whole Sett, seems to be the *Bear*; because he represents *Ursa Major*,[40] or the *Great Bear*, who presides over the *North*, where the *Reformation* first began, and which, next to *Britain*, (including *Scotland* and the North of *Ireland*)[41] is the great Protector of the *Protestant* Religion.[42] But, however, in those Signs where I observe the *Bear* to be *chained*,[43] I can't help surmising a *Jacobite* Contrivance,[44] by which these Traytors hint an earnest Desire of using all *true Whigs*, as their Predecessors did the primitive Christians;[45] I mean, to represent us as *Bears*, and then hallow their *Tory-Dogs* to bait us to Death.

Thus I have given a fair Account of what I dislike, in all those Signs set over those Houses that invite us to *Punch*: I own it was a Matter that did not need explaining, being so very obvious to the most common

---

38 *it is the Disposition... after they are dead*: a common belief, alluded to, for example in Shakespeare, *Cymbeline*, Act V, Scene iii.
39 *to lull us a-sleep, (which is an Emblem of Death)*: an emblem was a pictorial representation serving the function of a symbol. The notion that sleep resembled death was commonplace. More specifically, Cicero had written, in *De Senectute*, ch. 22, 'Iam vero videtis nihil esse morti tam simile quam somnum' (Again, you really see that nothing is so much like death as sleep), which was rendered in Samuel Parker's translation as 'the silence of sleep, the proper emblem and resemblance of death': Samuel Parker, *Tully's Two Essay* [sic] *of Old Age, and of Friendship...*, 3rd edn., London, 1727, p. 73.
40 *Ursa Major*: the constellation always visible in the northern hemisphere.
41 *(including Scotland and the North of Ireland)*: from a Whig perspective, the concentration of Presbyterians in Ulster, originally immigrants from Scotland and retaining many Scottish links (through their church, education and commerce), made the province equally a bastion of the reformed religion and Revolution principles.
42 *the North... Protestant Religion*: the kingdom of Denmark included a bear in its coat of arms from 1666. The Protestant Reformation had begun early in Denmark and, after two years of civil war, Christian III had ended the authority of the papacy in 1536.
43 *the Bear to be chained*: as in the sport of bear-baiting.
44 *a Jacobite Contrivance*: a further complexity here is that Sir Constantine Phipps, Tory lord chancellor of Ireland 1711–14, and a man of strong Jacobite sympathies, was the son of the proprietor of the Bear Inn at Reading. During his time in Ireland, Whigs reportedly drank 'confusion... to the fat bear of Reading' (*ODNB*).
45 *as their Predecessors did the primitive Christians*: as the Romans treated the early Christians (the Jacobite Pretender and many of his followers being Roman Catholics).

Understanding. Yet, I know not how it happens, but methinks there seems a fatal Blindness, to overspread our corporeal Eyes, as well as our intellectual; and I heartily wish, I may be found a false Prophet,[46] For, these are not bare Suspicions, but manifest Demonstrations.

Therefore, away with those *Popish*, *Jacobite*, and idolatrous Gew-gaws.[47] And I heartily wish a Law were enacted, under severe Penalties, against drinking any *Punch* at all. For nothing is easier, than to prove it a disaffected Liquor. The chief Ingredients, which are Brandy, Oranges, and Lemons, are all sent us from *Popish* Countries;[48] and nothing remains of *Protestant* Growth but Sugar[49] and Water. For, as to Biscuit,[50] which formerly was held a necessary Ingredient, and is truly *British*,[51] we find it is entirely rejected.

But I will put the Truth of my Assertion, past all Doubt: I mean, that this Liquor is by one important Innovation, grown of ill Example, and dangerous Consequence to the Publick. It is well known, that, by the true original Institution of making *Punch*, left us by Captain *Ratcliff*,[52] the Sharpness is only occasioned by the Juice of Lemons, and so continued till after the happy *Revolution*. Oranges, alas! are a meer Innovation, and in a Manner *but of Yesterday*. It was the Politicks of *Jacobites* to introduce them gradually: And, to what Intent? The Thing speaks it self. It was cunningly to shew their Virulence against his sacred Majesty King *William*, *of ever glorious and immortal Memory.*[53] But of late, (to shew how fast Disloyalty increaseth) they came from one to two, and then to three Oranges; nay,

---

46 *a fatal Blindness . . . a false Prophet*: an allusion to the blinding of the 'sorcerer' Elymas, a false prophet, in Acts 13: 8–11.
47 *Gew-gaws*: decorative but valueless trinkets.
48 *The chief Ingredients . . . sent us from Popish Countries*: brandy was imported from France; oranges and lemons from Spain.
49 *Sugar*: from cane grown in the British possessions in the West Indies, transported across the Atlantic as molasses and refined into sugar after its arrival in Britain.
50 *Biscuit*: 'A kind of crisp dry bread more or less hard, prepared generally in thin flat cakes' (*OED*).
51 *truly British*: See below, n. 52.
52 *the true original Institution . . . Captain Ratcliff*: Alexander Radcliffe (c. 1653 – by 1696) (*ODNB*), who published in 1680 *Bacchanalia Coelestia: A Poem in Praise of Punch*. This was reprinted in *The Works of Capt. Alex. Radcliffe*, 3rd edn, London, 1696, pp. 40–4, and gave details of ingredients: lemons, two sugar loaves, 'three gallons of trusty Langoon' (a white Bordeaux, from the area around the town of Langon), brandy, three nutmegs, and finally 'a hard sea-bisquit well bak'd by the sun'. Oranges were not included.
53 *of ever glorious and immortal Memory*: the customary loyal Protestant toast to the memory of William III.

at present we often find Punch made all with Oranges, and not one single Lemon. For the *Jacobites*, before the Death of that immortal Prince, had, by a Superstition, formed a private Prayer, that, as they *squeezed* the *Orange*, so might that *Protestant* King be *squeezed* to Death: According to that known Sorcery described by *Virgil*, *Limus ut hic durescit, & hæc ut cera liquescit*, &c.[54] And, thus the *Romans*, when they sacrificed an Ox, used this Kind of Prayer. *As I knock down this Ox, so may thou*, O Jupiter, *knock down our Enemies*.[55] In like Manner, after King *William*'s Death, whenever a *Jacobite squeezed* an *Orange*, he had a mental Curse upon the *glorious Memory*, and a hearty Wish for Power to *squeeze* all his Majesty's Friends to Death, as he *squeezed* that *Orange*, which bore one of his Titles, as he was Prince of *Orange*. This I do affirm for Truth; many of that Faction having confess'd it to me, under an *Oath of Secrecy*; which, however, I thought it my Duty not to keep, when I saw my dear Country in Danger. But, what better can be expected from an *impious* Sett of Men, who never scruple to drink CONFUSION to all *true Protestants*,[56] under the Name of *Whigs*? a most unchristian and inhuman Practice, which, to our great Honour and Comfort, was *never* charged upon us, even by our most malicious Detractors.[57]

---

54 *Limus ut hic durescit, & hæc ut cera liquescit, &c.*: Virgil, *Eclogues*, viii, 80: 'limus ut hic durescit, et haec ut cera liquescit / uno eodemque igni, sic nostro Daphnis amore' (As this clay hardens, and as this wax melts in one and the same flame, so may Daphnis melt with love for me).
55 *our Enemies*: cf. the sacrificial formula for establishing a treaty described by Livy (*Hist. Rome*, bk 1, ch. 24).
56 *all true Protestants*: a phrase used by Whigs and Protestant Dissenters, to distinguish themselves, and to imply that their political opponents were crypto-Catholics.
57 *a most unchristian and inhuman Practice... our most malicious Detractors*: Peter Browne, the bishop of Cork, had preached a sermon in 1713 to his diocesan clergy against drinking toasts to the memory of the dead (principally aimed at the practice of drinking to the 'glorious and immortal memory' of William III), in which he declared the practice to be theologically dubious almost to the point of sacrilege: *Of Drinking to the Memory of the Dead. Being the Substance of a Discourse Deliver'd to the Clergy of the Diocese of Cork, on the Fourth of November, 1713*, Dublin, 1713. He had broadened his argument in *A Discourse of Drinking Healths. Wherein the Great Evil of This Prevailing Custom is Shewn; and the Obligation Which Lieth upon All Good Christians to Suppress and Discountenance It to the Utmost of Their Power*, Dublin, 1716, in the dedication in which he referred to drinking healths as 'a relique of heathenism', and a species of 'idolatry'. For Browne, see *ODNB*; *DIB*. In his sermon on 'Brotherly Love' in 1717, Swift had pilloried Whigs and Low Churchmen, whose 'devotion consisteth in drinking Gibbets, Confusion and Damnation, in profanely idolising the Memory of one dead Prince [King William III], and ungratefully trampling upon the Ashes of another [Queen Anne]' (Davis, vol. IX, p. 178).

The Sign of two *Angels*, hovering in the Air, and with their right Hands supporting a *Crown*, is met with in several Parts of this City; and hath often given me great Offence: For, whether by the Unskilfulness, or dangerous Principles of the Painters, (although I have good Reasons to suspect the latter) those *Angels* are usually drawn with such horrid *Countenances*, that they give great Offence to every loyal Eye, and equal Cause of Triumph to the *Jacobites*, being a most infamous Reflection upon our most able and excellent Ministry.[58]

I now return to that great Enormity of City *Cries*; most of which we have borrowed from *London*. I shall consider them only in a *political* View, as they nearly affect the Peace and Safety of both Kingdoms; and having been originally contrived by wicked *Machiavels*,[59] to bring in *Popery*, *Slavery*, and *Arbitrary Power*, by defeating the *Protestant* Succession, and introducing the *Pretender*, ought, in Justice, to be here laid open to the World.

About two or three Months after the happy *Revolution*, all Persons who possest any Employment, or Office, in Church or State, were obliged by an Act of Parliament, to take the Oaths to King *William* and Queen *Mary*:[60] And a great Number of disaffected Persons, refusing to take the said Oaths, from a pretended Scruple of Conscience, but really from a Spirit of *Popery* and Rebellion,[61] they contrived a Plot, to make the swearing to those Princes odious in the Eyes of the People. To this End, they hired certain Women of ill Fame,[62] but loud shrill Voices, under Pretence of selling Fish, to go through the Streets, with Sieves on their Heads, and cry, *buy my Soul, buy my Soul*; plainly insinuating, that all those who swore to King *William*, were just ready to sell their *Souls* for an Employment.

---

58 *The Sign of two Angels... a most infamous Reflection upon our most able and excellent Ministry*: if angels is understood in the sense of 'celestial ministers' (*OED*): Gilbert, *History of the City of Dublin*, records no tavern with 'angel' in its name.
59 *Machiavels*: a type of villain in Elizabethan and Jacobean drama, named from the Florentine political theorist Niccolò Machiavelli (1469–1527).
60 *all Persons... Queen Mary*: the English statute of 1689 for abrogating the oaths of supremacy and allegiance and appointing other oaths (1 Will. & Mar. c. 8).
61 *disaffected Persons... Popery and Rebellion*: most obviously among the clergy of the established churches, for whom see J. H. Overton, *The Nonjurors: Their Lives, Principles and Writings*, London: Smith, Elder, & Co., 1902. Only three clerical dignitaries in the Church of Ireland refused to swear the oaths to William and Mary, and were deprived in consequence: William Sheridan, bishop of Kilmore; Barzillai Jones, dean of Lismore; and the pamphleteer and controversialist Charles Leslie, chancellor of Connor.
62 *Women of ill Fame*: prostitutes.

This Cry was revived at the Death of Queen *Anne*,[63] and, I hear, still continues in *London*, with great Offence to all *true Protestants*; but, to our great Happiness, seems to be almost dropt in *Dublin*.

But, because I altogether contemn the Displeasure and Resentment of *High-flyers, Tories*, and *Jacobites*, whom I look upon to be *worse even than profest Papists*, I do here declare, that those Evils which I am going to mention, were all brought upon us in the *worst of Times*, under the late Earl of *Oxford*'s Administration, during the four last Years of Queen *Anne*'s Reign. *That wicked Minister was universally known to be a Papist in his Heart.*[64] *He was of a most avaricious Nature, and is said to have dyed worth four Millions, sterl. besides his vast Expences in Building, Statues, Gold Plate, Jewels, and other costly Rarities.*[65] *He was of a mean obscure Birth, from the very Dregs of the People,*[66] *and so illiterate, that he could hardly read a Paper at the Council Table.*[67] *I forbear to touch at his open, prophane, profligate*

---

63 *revived at the Death of Queen Anne*: with the accession of a monarch who owed his title to a parliamentary statute rather than hereditary right, and whose own religious preferences were Lutheran. While Queen Anne was on the throne, nonjurors had been able to console themselves with the fact that she was at least James II's lawful daughter, as well as being a loyal and devout member of the Church of England.

64 *That wicked Minister... in his Heart*: Harley's reputation for secretiveness and trickery, combined with his departure from the godly Presbyterian ethos of his upbringing to lead a Tory ministry, encouraged many to question the sincerity of his religious allegiance, but it was rare for him to be considered a closet Roman Catholic. George Ridpath, the Scottish Whig journalist, thought him an atheist. See *HP 1690–1715*, vol. IV, pp. 244–5. However, Lady Orkney's 'character' of Harley, which Swift endorsed, presented him as devout: 'He adores God, he submits his doubts, endeavours to be perfect without presuming for perfection' (Williams, *Corr.*, vol. V, p. 224).

65 *of a most avaricious Nature... other costly Rarities*: it was Harley's boast that he had gained nothing for himself from his time in public office: 'I cannot accuse myself of any addition I have made to my fortune out of the public' (quoted in *HP 1690–1715*, vol. IV, p. 277). In 1724, in *A Letter to the Lord Chancellor Middleton* (Davis, vol. X, p. 102), Swift had contrasted Harley with Walpole, calling Harley 'the greatest, the wisest, and the most uncorrupt minister I ever conversed with'.

66 *of a mean obscure Birth... Dregs of the People*: although criticised when raised to the peerage for his temerity in reviving for his family the ancient title of Oxford and Mortimer (to which he had a distant connection by marriage), Harley came from perfectly respectable gentry stock, his father Sir Edward (a grandson, on his mother's side, of the 1st Viscount Conway) having sat in the English House of Commons as a knight of the shire. By implication, Swift is inviting comparison with the social origins of such Whig luminaries as Viscount Allen and Richard Tighe, or the former Speaker William Conolly, all of whom he had himself disparaged as upstarts (see above, pp. xxxiv, 197; and Swift to Gay and the Duchess of Queensberry, 28 Aug. 1731 (Woolley, *Corr.*, vol. III, pp. 428–9)).

67 *so illiterate... Council Table*: Harley was in fact a man of wide intellectual interests; a Fellow of the Royal Society, a bibliophile whose library constituted the greatest achievement of

Life;[68] *because I desire not to rake into the Ashes of the Dead, and therefore I shall observe this wise Maxim*: De mortuis nil nisi bonum.[69] This flagitious[70] Man, in order to compass his black Designs, employ'd certain wicked Instruments (which great Statesmen are never without) to adapt several *London* Cries, in such a Manner as would best answer his Ends. And, whereas it was upon Grounds grievously suspected, that all *Places* at Court were sold to the highest Bidder: Certain Women were employed by his Emissaries, to carry *Fish* in Baskets on their Heads, and bawl thro' the Streets, *buy my fresh Places*. I must, indeed, own that other Women used the same Cry, who were innocent of this wicked Design, and really sold their Fish of that Denomination to get an honest Livelyhood; but the rest, who were in the *Secret*, although they carried *Fish* in their Sieves or Baskets, to save Appearances; yet they had likewise, a certain Sign, somewhat resembling that of the *Free-Masons*,[71] which the Purchasers of *Places* knew well enough, and were directed by the Women whither they were to resort, and make their Purchase. And, I remember very well, how

book and manuscript-collecting in his generation, and a patron of scholars who was regarded by those who benefited from his patronage as 'the great Maecenas of English medieval learning' (*ODNB*; D. C. Douglas, *English Scholars, 1660–1730*, 2nd edn, London: Eyre & Spottiswoode, 1951, p. 263; Brian W. Hill, *Robert Harley: Speaker, Secretary of State and Premier Minister*, New Haven & London: Yale University Press, 1988, pp. 225–6). He wrote various pieces, including political pamphlets (*ODNB*), and also tried his hand at verse (John Arbuthnot to Swift, 12 June 1714; Oxford to Swift, 27 July 1714 (Woolley, *Corr.*, vol. I, p. 616; vol. II, p. 30)). In *The History of the Four Last Years of Queen Anne's Reign* (Davis, vol. VII, p. 75), Swift wrote of Harley, 'I believe there are few Examples to be produced in any Age, of a Person, who hath passed through so many Employments in the State, endowed with so great a Share both of Divine and Human learning.'

68 *his open, prophane, profligate Life*: 'open' in the sense of brazen or shameless; 'profane', meaning impious or indecent; 'profligate', licentious or debauched. In comparison with other leading figures in English politics in Queen Anne's reign (not least his great rival in the Tory ministry of 1710–14, Henry St John, Viscount Bolingbroke), Harley's private life was a model of moral rectitude, with the exception of his fondness for drink.

69 *De mortuis nil nisi bonum*: 'Let nothing be said of the dead but what is good.'

70 *flagitious*: infamous, wicked.

71 *a certain Sign, somewhat resembling that of the Free-Masons*: freemasonry was notorious for secret signs and rituals. In his infamous 'tripos' speech at the Trinity commencement in 1688, Swift's friend John Jones had referred to the discovery of a mark on the body of the freemason Ridley (John Barrett, *An Essay on the Earlier Part of the Life of Swift*, London, 1808, p. 63). Links between freemasonry and Jacobitism in Dublin are explored in Sean Murphy, 'Irish Jacobitism and Freemasonry', *ECI* 9 (1994), 75–82. The grand master elected in 1731 by the Grand Lodge in Dublin, the 4th Baron Kingston, was a Catholic convert whose father had previously been arrested on suspicion of Jacobitism (ibid., 79–80).

oddly it look't, when we observed many Gentlemen finely drest, about the Court-end of the Town, and as far as *York-Buildings*, where the Lord Treasurer *Oxford* dwelt,[72] calling the Women who cry'd *buy my fresh Places*, and talking to them in the Corner of a Street, after they understood each other's Sign; but we never could observe that any Fish was bought.

Some Years before the fine Cries last mentioned, the *Duke* of *Savoy* was reported to have made certain Overtures to the Court of *England*, for admitting his eldest Son by the Dutchess of *Orleans*'s Daughter, to succeed to the Crown, as next Heir, upon the *Pretender*'s being rejected, and that Son was immediately to turn *Protestant*.[73] It was confidently reported, that great Numbers of People disaffected to the then *Illustrious* but now *Royal*[74] House of *Hanover*, were in those Measures. Whereupon, another Sett of Women were hired by the *Jacobite* Leaders, to cry through the whole Town, *buy my* Savoys, *dainty* Savoys, *curious* Savoys.[75] But, I cannot directly charge the late Earl of *Oxford* with this *Conspiracy*, because he was not then chief Minister. However, the wicked Cry still continues in *London*, and was brought over hither, where it remains to this Day,[76] and

---

72 *York-Buildings... Oxford dwelt*: during his period in office, Oxford lived in York Buildings, near the Thames (modern Villiers Street).

73 *the Duke of Savoy... turn Protestant*: the claim of the house of Savoy to the English throne was touted at the time of the passage of the Act of Settlement in 1701 (and thus before the Hanoverians became 'Royal'). It derived from Henrietta Stuart (1644–70), Charles I's third daughter, who married Philip (1640–1701), Duke of Orléans. In turn their daughter Anne-Marie (1669–1728) married in 1684 Victor Amadeus II (1666–1732), Duke of Savoy, king of Sicily and Sardinia; in 1701 his elder son, Victor Amadeus John Philip (1699–1715), was the Savoyard claimant. In April 1701, while the English Parliament was debating the succession, the Savoyard ambassador, Count Maffei, submitted a formal protest to King William against the Bill (later Act) of Settlement (Marquis de Ruvigny, *A Legitimist Kalendar...*, 4 vols., London: Henry & Co., 1895–1910, vol. II, pp. 75–6).

74 *then Illustrious but now Royal*: before the accession of George I, the use of 'illustrious' as a description of the house of Hanover was common practice, for example in parliamentary resolutions or addresses.

75 *Savoys*: a pun on savoy cabbages. While in London in December 1712, Swift had complained to Esther Johnson that 'here is a restless dog crying Cabbage and Savoys plagues me every morning... he is now at it, I wish his largest Cabbage were sticking in his Throat' (*CWJS*, vol. IX, p. 466).

76 *where it remains to this Day*: the Duke of Savoy, Charles Emanuel III, who had succeeded to the title on the abdication of his father Victor Amadeus in 1730, was now (after the 'Young Pretender' Prince Charles Edward) second in line to the Jacobite claim to the thrones of Britain and Ireland. The phrase 'those dangerous times' refers to the period following the death of Prince William, Duke of Gloucester, Princess Anne's surviving son and heir apparent, in July 1700. Until the passage of the Act of Settlement in 1701, there was no provision for a Protestant succession.

in my humble Opinion, a very offensive Sound to every true Protestant, who is old enough to remember those *dangerous* Times.

During the Ministry of that corrupt and *Jacobite* Earl abovementioned, the secret pernicious Design of those in Power, was to sell *Flanders* to *France*; the Consequence of which, must have been the infallible Ruin of the *States-General*,[77] and would have open'd the Way for France to obtain that universal Monarchy, after which they have so long aspired;[78] to which the *British* Dominions must next, after *Holland*, have been compelled to submit. And the *Protestant* Religion would be rooted out of the World.

A Design of this vast Importance, after long Consultation among the *Jacobite* Grandees, with the Earl of *Oxford* at their Head, was at last determin'd to be carried on by the same Method with the former; it was therefore again put in Practice; but the Conduct of it was chiefly left to chosen Men, whose Voices were louder and stronger than those of the other Sex. And upon this Occasion, was first instituted in *London*, that famous Cry of FLOUNDERS. But the Cryers were particularly directed to pronounce the Word *Flaunders*, and not *Flounders*. For, the Country which we now by Corruption call *Flanders*, is in it's true Orthography spelt *Flaunders*, as may be obvious to all who read old *English* Books. I say, from hence begun that thundring Cry, which hath ever since stunned the Ears of all *London*, made so many Children fall into Fits, and Women miscarry; *come buy my fresh* Flaunders, *curious* Flaunders, *charming* Flaunders, *alive, alive, ho*; which last Words can with no Propriety of Speech, be apply'd to Fish manifestly dead, (as I observed before in *Herrings* and *Salmon*) but very

---

77 *the States-General*: the governing confederate assembly of the United Provinces (the Dutch Republic).
78 *that universal Monarchy . . . aspired*: a powerful belief current in Whig circles in the later seventeenth and early eighteenth centuries, prompted particularly, though not exclusively, by the perceived territorial aspirations of Louis XIV: see S. C. A. Pincus, 'The English Debate over Universal Monarchy', in John Robertson (ed.), *A Union for Empire: Political Thought and the British Union of 1707*, Cambridge: Cambridge University Press, 1995, pp. 37–62; John Robertson, 'Universal Monarchy and the Liberties of Europe: David Hume's Critique of an English Whig Doctrine', in N. T. Phillipson and Quentin Skinner (eds.), *Political Discourse in Early Modern Britain*, Cambridge: Cambridge University Press, 1993, pp. 349–73; Tony Claydon, 'Protestantism, Universal Monarchy and Christendom in William's War Propaganda, 1689–1697', in Esther Mijers and David Onnekink (eds.), *Redefining William III: The Impact of the King-Stadholder in International Context*, Aldershot: Ashgate, 2007, pp. 125–42.

justly to ten Provinces, which contain many Millions of living *Christians*.[79] And the Application is still closer, when we consider that all the People were to be taken like *Fishes* in a Net; and, by Assistance of the *Pope*, who sets up to be the *universal Fisher of Men*,[80] the whole innocent Nation,[81] was, according to our common Expression, to be *laid as flat as a* Flounder.[82]

I remember, my self, a particular Cryer of *Flounders* in *London*, who arrived at so much Fame for the Loudness of his Voice, that he had the Honour to be mentioned upon that Account, in a Comedy.[83] He hath disturbed me many a Morning, before he came within Fifty Doors of my Lodging. And, although I were not in those Days so fully apprized of the Designs, which our common Enemy had then in Agitation, yet, I know not how, by a secret Impulse, young as I was, I could not forbear conceiving a strong Dislike against the Fellow; and often said to my self, This Cry seems to be forged in the Jesuites School:[84] Alas, poor *England*! I am grievously mistaken if there be not some *Popish* Plot at the Bottom.[85] I communicated my Thoughts to an intimate Friend, who reproached me with being too visionary[86] in my Speculations: But, it proved afterwards, that I conjectured right. And I have often since reflected, that if the wicked Faction could have procured only a Thousand Men, of as strong Lungs

79 *ten Provinces... living Christians*: the original seventeen provinces of the Spanish Netherlands had been reduced to ten following the Dutch revolt and the Union of Utrecht of 1579, which established the United Provinces as a separate state. There remained under Habsburg control, in what was now the Austrian Netherlands, the provinces of Artois, Brabant, Cambrai, Flanders, Limburg, Luxemburg, Mechelen, Namur, Tournai and Walloon Flanders. No reliable figure has been found for the size of the population in this period, but by 1784, after a long period of growth, numbers had only reached 2,273,000: J. I. Israel, *The Dutch Republic: Its Rise, Greatness and Fall*, Oxford: Oxford University Press, 1995, p. 1011.
80 *the universal Fisher of Men*: a reference to Jesus' call to Simon Peter (John, 21: 17).
81 *the whole innocent Nation*: an adaptation of Genesis 20: 3–4, in which Abimelech appealed to God, 'Lord, wilt thou slay also a righteous nation?'
82 *as flat as a Flounder*: proverbial (*ODEP*, p. 267).
83 *that he had the Honour... in a Comedy*: in Congreve's *The Way of the World* (1700), Act V, Scene 1, a character speaks of 'the throats and lungs of hawkers, with voices more licentious than the loud Flounder-man's'. Swift owned a copy of the 1710 edition of Congreve's works (*Library and Reading*, I, vol. I, pp. 451–2).
84 *This Cry... in the Jesuites School*: Swift repeatedly ridiculed the Whig obsession with the threat posed by the Jesuits to the maintenance of the Protestant interest. He had referred explicitly to their schools in the *Examiner*, 31 and 40 (Ellis (ed.), *Swift vs. Mainwaring*, pp. 275, 401).
85 *some Popish Plot at the Bottom*: primarily with reference to the 'Popish Plot' concocted by Titus Oates and Israel Tonge in 1678.
86 *visionary*: fantastical.

as the Fellow I mentioned, none can tell how terrible the Consequences might have been, not only to these two Kingdoms, but over all *Europe*, by selling *Flanders* to *France*.[87] And yet these Cries continue unpunished, both in *London* and *Dublin*; although I confess, not with equal Vehemency or Loudness, because the Reason for contriving this desperate Plot, is, to our great Felicity, wholly ceased.

It is well known, that the Majority of the *British* House of Commons in the last Years of Queen *Anne*'s Reign, were in their Hearts directly opposite to the Earl of *Oxford*'s pernicious Measures; which put him under the Necessity of bribing them with Sallaries. Whereupon he had again Recourse to his old Politicks. And accordingly, his Emissaries were very busy in employing certain artful Women of no good Life or Conversation,[88] (as it was fully proved before Justice *P——n*)[89] to cry that Vegetable commonly called *Sollary*,[90] through the Town. These Women differed from the common Cryers of that Herb[91] by some private Mark which I could never learn; but the Matter was notorious enough, and sufficiently talked of, and about the same Period was the Cry of *Sollary* brought over into this Kingdom. But since there is not at this present, the least Occasion to suspect the Loyalty of our Cryers upon that Article, I am content that it may still be tolerated.

I shall mention but one Cry more, which hath any Reference to Politicks; but is indeed, of all others the most insolent, as well as treasonable, under our present happy Establishment. I mean that of *Turnups*; not of *Turnips*, according to the best Orthography, but absolutely *Turnups*. Although this Cry be of an older Date than some of the preceding Enormities; for it

---

87 *France*: primarily a reference to the negotiations leading up to the Treaty of Utrecht, and to a Whig canard that the Harley administration intended to give up the Spanish Netherlands to France; but also a pun on Flanders lace.
88 *of no good Life or Conversation*: using 'conversation' in the sense of sexual intimacy, Swift is again suggesting that these women are prostitutes.
89 *Justice P——n*: John Pocklington (*c*. 1658–1731), Whig MP at Westminster for Huntingdon 1695–8, and Huntingdonshire 1705–13, who served as second justice on the Chester circuit 1707–11 and as a baron of the exchequer in Ireland from 1715 until his death. In 1719, during the jurisdictional dispute between the British and Irish Parliaments over the case of *Annesley* v. *Sherlock*, he was briefly held in custody on the order of the Irish House of Lords for issuing an injunction at the behest of the Lords at Westminster (*HP 1690–1715*, vol. V, pp. 163–5; Ball, *Judges in Ireland*, vol. II, p. 192).
90 *Sollary*: celery.
91 *that Herb*: celery was known in the ancient world to have medicinal properties. It was defined as 'an herb' in, for example, John Kersey, *A New English Dictionary*, London, 1702.

began soon after the Revolution; yet was it never known to arrive at so great an Height, as during the Earl of *Oxford*'s Power. Some People, (whom I take to be private Enemies) are, indeed, as ready as my self to profess their Disapprobation of this Cry, on Pretence that it began by the Contrivance of certain old Procuresses, who kept Houses of ill Fame, where lewd Women met to draw young Men into Vice. And this they pretend to prove by some Words in the Cry; because, after the Cryer had bawled out *Turnups, ho, buy my dainty Turnups*, he would sometimes add the two following Verses.

Turn up[92] *the Mistress, and turn up the Maid,*
And turn up the Daughter, and be not afraid.

This, say some political Sophists,[93] plainly shews that there can be nothing further meant in this infamous Cry, than an Invitation to Lewdness, which indeed, ought to be severely punished in all well regulated Governments; but cannot be fairly interpreted as a Crime of State. But, I hope, we are not so weak and blind to be deluded at this Time of Day, with such poor Evasions. I could, if it were proper, demonstrate the very Time when those two Verses were composed, and name the Author, who was no other than the famous Mr. *Swan*,[94] so well known for his Talent at Quibbling, and was as virulent a *Jacobite* as any in *England*. Neither could he deny the Fact, when he was taxed for it in my Presence by Sir *Harry Dutton-Colt*, and Colonel *Davenport*, at the *Smyrna* Coffee-House,[95] on the 10th of *June*, 1701.[96] Thus it appears to a Demonstration, that those

---

92 *Turn up*: make a prostitute of.
93 *Sophists*: those who practise specious reasoning.
94 *the famous Mr. Swan*: Richard Swan, an Irishman and an habitué of Will's coffee-house, had a reputation as a minor wit (*Poems on Affairs of State: Augustan Satirical Verse, 1660–1714*, ed. G. de F. Lord et al., 7 vols., New Haven: Yale University Press, 1963–75, vol. VI, p. 255). He was a friend of Dryden, who praised his punning abilities: Swan to Dryden, n.d. (*The Letters of John Dryden*, ed. C. E. Ward, Durham, NC: Duke University Press, 1942, p. 137); Dryden, 'Discourse concerning... Satire', in *Works*, vol. IV, p. 73).
95 *Smyrna Coffee-House*: on the north side of Pall Mall, at the corner of Crown Court (Bryant Lillywhite, *London Coffeehouses...*, London: George Allen & Unwin, 1963, pp. 532–3). Swift recorded several visits in 1710–11 in the *Journal to Stella* (*CWJS*, vol. IX, pp. 41, 70, 146).
96 *he was taxed for it... 10th of June, 1701*: Sir Henry Dutton Colt, 1st Bt (c. 1646–1731) (for whom, see *HP 1690–1715*, vol. III, pp. 654–60), was a strong Whig who, along with John Arnold, made a profitable business in the 1690s from exposing Jacobite plots, often assisted by informers, with the intention of profiting from forfeited estates. Swift had satirised Colt

Verses were only a Blind to conceal the most dangerous Designs of that Party, who from the first Years after the happy Revolution, used a Cant Way of talking in their Clubs after this Manner: We hope, to see the Cards shuffled once more, and another King TURN UP[97] Trump: And, when shall we meet over a Dish of TURNUPS? The same Term of Art was used in their Plots against the Government, and in their treasonable Letters writ in Cyphers, and decyphered by the famous Dr. *Wallis*,[98] as you may read in the Tryals of those Times.[99] This I thought fit to set forth at large, and in so clear a Light, because the *Scotch* and *French* Authors have given a very different Account of the Word TURNUP, but whether out of

    in the ballad 'A Dialogue between Captain Tom and Sir Henry Dutton Colt', issued during the Westminster election of 1710, when Colt and General James Stanhope stood unsuccessfully on the Whig interest against two Tories. Of Colt's defeat, Swift observed, 'He had got a bad game, and could not turn up trumps' (Jonathan Swift, *The Complete Poems*, ed. Pat Rogers, p. 113). Colonel Sherrington Davenport (1669–1719), was a veteran of the Boyne and Aughrim, and also a committed Whig. In 1701 he was colonel of the first troop of horse guards, and was subsequently promoted to brigadier-general (1707) and major-general (1710). A military officer called Davenport was satirised in Joseph Browne's poem *St James's Park* . . . , London, 1708, as one 'who jostles the ladies on each side, / While they despise his ignorance and pride' (p. 7). The 10th of June was the birthday of the Old Pretender.
97 *King TURN UP*: the Stuart claimant.
98 *the famous Dr. Wallis*: John Wallis (1616–1703), Savilian Professor of Geometry in Oxford, was a noted cryptographer, who had lent his talents to the Parliamentarian side during the Civil War.
99 *as you may read in the Tryals of those Times*: after the Glorious Revolution, Wallis was frequently employed to decode intercepted Jacobite correspondence, including the materials relating to the supposed 'Scotch Plot' of 1703: see *Dictionary of National Biography*, 1st edn, ed. Leslie Stephen and Sidney Lee, 22 vols., London: Smith, Elder and Co., 1908–9; Henry Horwitz, *Revolution Politicks: The Career of Daniel Finch, Second Earl of Nottingham, 1647–1730*, Cambridge: Cambridge University Press, 1968, p. 191. For contemporary printed references to his work in deciphering Jacobite papers in William III's reign, see *Mr. William Fullers Third Narrative, Containing New Matters of Fact* . . . , London, 1696; *Mr. De Labadie's Letter to His Daughter . . . Nurse to the Pretended Prince of Wales* . . . , [London], 1697. The conviction of John Ashton for involvement in the so-called 'Preston plot' in 1691 was in part owing to the solving of a cipher, but Wallis's name was not mentioned in published accounts of the trial: Richard Kingston, *A True History of the Several Designs and Conspiracies against His Majesties Sacred Person and Government* . . . , London, 1698, p. 35. See also T. B. Howell, *A Complete Collection of State Trials* . . . , 21 vols., London, 1816, vol. XII, pp. 721, 1318. The reliability of decipherment, as developed by Wallis, had been a particular issue during the proceedings against Swift's friend Bishop Atterbury in 1722–3: Benjamin Hoadley, *Remarks on the Late Bishop of Rochester's Speech at the Bar of the House of Lords* . . . , London, 1723, pp. 12–13; Thomas Salmon, *Tryals for High-Treason, and Other Crimes* . . . , 9 vols., London, 1720–31, vol. IX, p. 108.

Ignorance or Partiality[100] I shall not decree; because I am sure, the Reader is convinced by my Discovery. It is to be observed, that this Cry was sung in a particular Manner by Fellows in Disguise, to give Notice where those Traytors were to meet, in Order to concert their villanous Designs.

I have no more to add upon this Article, than an humble Proposal, that those who cry this Root at present in our Streets of *Dublin*, may be compelled by the Justices of the Peace, to pronounce *Turnip*,[101] and not *Turnup*; for, I am afraid, we have still too many Snakes in our Bosom;[102] and it would be well if their Cellars were sometimes searched, when the Owners least expect it; for I am not out of Fear that *latet anguis in Herba*.[103]

Thus, we are zealous in Matters of small Moment, while we neglect those of the highest Importance. I have already made it manifest, that all these Cries were contrived in the worst of Times, under the Ministry of that desperate Statesman, *Robert* late Earl of *Oxford*, and for that very Reason ought to be rejected with Horror, as begun in the Reign of *Jacobites*,[104] and may well be number'd among the Rags of Popery[105] and Treason: Or if it be thought proper, that these Cries must continue, surely they ought to be only trusted in the Hands of true Protestants, who have given Security to the Government.

FINIS

[The London edition then continues as follows:]

Having already spoken of many Abuses relating to Sign-Posts; I cannot here omit one more, because it plainly relates to Politicks; and is, perhaps, of more dangerous Consequence than any of the City Cries, because it directly

---

100 *Ignorance or Partiality*: because of the identification of France and Scotland with support for the Jacobite cause.
101 *Turnip*: Jacobite satirists made free use of the turnip in abusive references to George I. Because the king was alleged to have been hoeing turnips at Hanover when he heard the news of Queen Anne's death, this vegetable became 'a symbol of his mediocrity': P. K. Monod, *Jacobitism and the English People, 1688–1788*, Cambridge: Cambridge University Press, 1989, pp. 57–8.
102 *Snakes in our Bosom*: in Aesop's fable, the countryman who found a serpent which was almost dead, and carried it home in his bosom, was obliged to kill it when it revived and was about to attack one of his children.
103 *latet anguis in Herba*: 'a snake lurks in the grass', from Virgil, *Eclogues*, iii, 93.
104 *in the Reign of Jacobites:* in the time of a pro-Jacobite government.
105 *the Rags of Popery*: a phrase in common use among English Protestants to denote the remnants of Roman Catholicism still to be found within the reformed Church of England.

tends to destroy the Succession. It is the Sign of his present Majesty King *George* the Second, to be met with in many Streets; and yet, I happen to be not only the first, but the only Discoverer of this audacious Instance of *Jacobitism*. And, I am confident, that if the Justices of the Peace, would please to make a strict Inspection, they might find in all such Houses, before which those Signs are hung up, in the manner I have observed, that the Landlords were malignant Papists, or which is worse, notorious *Jacobites*. Whoever views those Signs, may read over his Majesty's Head the following Letters and Cyphers, *G. R.* II. which plainly signifies *George*, King the Second; and not King *George* the Second, or *George* the Second King; but laying the Point after the Letter *G.* by which the Owner of the House manifestly shews, that he renounces his Allegiance to King *George* the Second; and allows him to be only the second King, Inuendo[1] that the Pretender is the first King; and looking upon King *George* to be only a Kind of second King, or Viceroy, till the Pretender shall come over and seize the Kingdom. I appeal to all Mankind whether this be a strained, or forced Interpretation of the Inscription, as it now stands in almost every Street; whether any Decypherer would make the least Doubt or Hesitation, to explain it as I have done; whether any other Protestant Country would endure so publick an Instance of Treason in the Capital City, from such vulgar Conspirators; and, lastly, whether some *Papists* and *Jacobites* of great Fortunes and Quality, may not probably stand behind the Curtain in this dangerous, open, and avowed Design against the Government. But I have perform'd my Duty, and leave the reforming of these Abuses to the Wisdom, the Vigilance, the Loyalty and Activity of my Superiors.

1 *Inuendo*: a medieval Latin formula, meaning 'That is to say'.

THE HUMBLE PETITION OF THE FOOTMEN IN AND ABOUT THE CITY OF DUBLIN

Headnote

Probably composed 1732; published 1733; copy text *1733*a (see Textual Account).

This satire on modern Dublin fashion is based around the genuine contemporary ambivalence towards footmen, who were regularly accused of impudence and of aping their social betters. This general attitude of dislike and suspicion is inverted into a critique of modern manners, with the earnest footmen outraged that young men about town, their alleged social superiors, are behaving like them.

The mock-solemn *Humble Petition* is an apparent *jeu d'esprit*, though there is possible contemporary political significance in the derogatory use of 'Toupees' (see above, p. 46, and below, notes, p. 266). Although the *Humble Petition* is internally dated 1732, no edition from that year has ever been found, and the first extant published version dates from 1733, printed with *A Serious and Useful Scheme to Make a Hospital for Incurables*, usually attributed to Matthew Pilkington.

TO THE HONOURABLE HOUSE OF COMMONS,
&c. *THE HUMBLE PETITION OF THE FOOTMEN
IN AND ABOUT THE CITY OF DUBLIN.*

Humbly Sheweth,

That your *Petitioners* are a great and numerous *Society*, endowed with several Privileges, Time out of Mind.

That certain *lewd, idle,* and *disorderly* Persons, for several Months past, as it is notoriously known, have been daily seen in the publick Walks of this City, habited sometimes in *Green-Coats*, and sometimes in *laced*, with long *Oaken Cudgels* in their Hands, and without Swords, in hopes to procure Favour, by that Advantage, with a great Number of Ladies who frequent those Walks, pretending and giving themselves out to be true genuine *Irish Footmen*.[1] Whereas they can be proved to be no better than common *Toupees*;[2] as a judicious Eye may soon discover, by their *aukward, clumsy, ungenteel* Gait and Behaviour; by their Unskilfulness in Dress, even with the Advantage of wearing our Habits; by their ill favoured Countenances, with an Air of *Impudence* and *Dullness* peculiar to the rest of their Brethren: Who have not yet arrived at that transcendent Pitch of

---

1 *true genuine Irish Footmen*: cf. *A Satyr on the Mall in Great Britain-Street*, [?Dublin], 1733, a verse satire on the practice of promenading, which also observed the similarity between men of fashion and footmen (p. 8): 'Others, to look more smart, turn up their Hair, / And Ape the Trooper's, or the Footman's Ayre; / So strange the Fashion! That the transform'd Beau, / You'd scarce from some Lord's Dapper Footman know.' Swift dwells on the disreputable traits of footmen in *Directions to Servants* (1745) (*CWJS*, vol. II, pp. 481–98). The view that they were as a class impudent, and even presumptuous, was common: [James Arbuckle,] *A Collection of Letters and Essays on Several Subjects, Lately Publish'd in the Dublin Journal*, 2 vols., London, 1729, vol. I, pp. 136, 255, 269, noted the propensity of footmen to 'make addresses' to the wives and daughters of their employers.
2 *Toupees*: the toupee had been favoured by young society males in London and Dublin since at least 1727, and was now synonymous with foppery and gallantry. (See above, p. 46; *A Satyr on the Mall in Great Britain-Street*, p. 8; and *A Humourous Description of the Manners and Fashions of the Inhabitants of the City of Dublin*, Dublin, 1734, p. 7.) There may also have been a political connotation, for during the 1727–8 session of the Irish Parliament it was noted by one observer that 'there are about 70 young fellows got into the House [of Commons] and carry all before them; they have entered into a combination (for the good of their country) to act in a body, and are distinguished by the name of toopees, which is no more than a particular kind of foretop which they have to their wigs, which they fancy denotes youth and smartness, upon which they place as great value as our ancestors did on their beards': Edward Cooke to [Sir Richard Cox], 22 Feb. 1727[/8] (NLI, Fownes papers, MS 8,802/11). In *Directions to Servants* (*CWJS*, vol. II, p. 495), Swift depicted the footman as spending his wages on various items of fashion, including 'second-hand Toupees'.

Assurance. Although, it may be justly apprehended, that they will do so in time, if these *Counterfeits* shall happen to succeed in their evil Design, of passing for *real Footmen*, thereby to render themselves more amiable to the Ladies.

Your *Petitioners* do further alledge, that many of the said *Counterfeits*, upon a strict Examination, have been found in the very Act of *strutting, swearing, staring, swaggering* in a manner that plainly shewed their best Endeavours to imitate us. Wherein, altho' they did not succeed, yet by their ignorant and ungainly way of copying our Graces, the utmost Indignity was endeavoured to be cast upon our whole Profession.

Your *Petitioners* do therefore make it their humble Request, that this *Honourable House* (to many of whom your *Petitioners* are *nearly allied*)[3] will please to take this Grievance into your most serious Consideration: Humbly submitting, whether it would not be proper, that certain *Officers* might, at the publick Charge, be employed to search for, and discover all such *counterfeit Footmen*, and carry them before the next *Justice* of Peace; by whose Warrant, upon the first Conviction, they should be stripp'd of their *Coats*, and *Oaken* Ornaments, and be set two Hours in the Stocks. Upon the second Conviction, besides stripping, be set six Hours in the Stocks, with a Paper pinned on their Breast signifying their Crime, in large capital Letters, and in the following Words. *A. B.* commonly called *A. B.* Esq; a *Toupee*, and a notorious *Impostor*, who presumed to personate a *true Irish Footman*.

And for any further Offence the said *Toupee* shall be committed to *Bridewell*,[4] whipp'd three times, forced to hard Labour for a Month, and not be set at Liberty, till he shall have given sufficient Security for his good Behaviour.

---

3 *to many of whom your Petitioners are nearly allied*: Swift made a point of denouncing the low social origins of Irish MPs of whom he disapproved. In the 'Legion Club', for example, Sir Thomas Prendergast was pilloried as 'Worthy Offspring of a Shoeboy, / Footman, Traytor, Vile Seducer' (*Poems*, vol. III, p. 831). It was also said (incorrectly) of Thomas Carter, the master of the rolls, that his father had been a footman (HMC, *Egmont MSS*, vol. II, p. 242; *Hist. Ir. Parl.*, vol. III, pp. 376–7). But footmen as an occupational group were also 'allied' to MPs in another sense: at Westminster, in Anne's reign, the footmen attending on members of Parliament formed themselves into a mock Parliament, a phenomenon commented on by Steele in the *Spectator*, no. 88 (11 June 1711) (*Spectator*, vol. I, p. 374), and noted by Swift in the *Journal to Stella* on 25 Nov. 1710 (*CWJS*, vol. IX, p. 74).

4 *Bridewell*: a house of correction. In 1729, the old Dublin Bridewell had been demolished and a new one built near the workhouse in St James's Street (*Cal. Anc. Recs Dublin*, vol. VII, pp. 440–1).

Your *Honours* will please to observe with what Lenity we propose to treat these enormous Offenders, who have already brought such a Scandal on our *Honourable Calling*, that several wel-meaning People have mistaken them to be of our *Fraternity*; in diminution to that Credit and Dignity wherewith we have supported our Station, as we always did, in the Worst of Times.[5] And we further beg leave to remark, that this was manifestly done with a *seditious* Design, to render us less capable of serving the *Publick* in any great Employments, as several of our *Fraternity*, as well as our *Ancestors* have done.

We do therefore humbly implore your *Honours*, to give necessary Orders for our Relief, in this present Exigency, and your *Petitioners* (as in Duty bound) shall ever pray, *&c.*

Dublin, 1732.

FINIS

---

5 *the Worst of Times*: a cant phrase used by Whigs to refer to the last four years of Queen Anne's reign, under a Tory administration in England and Ireland.

SOME CONSIDERATIONS HUMBLY OFFERED TO THE RIGHT HONOURABLE THE LORD-MAYOR, THE COURT OF ALDERMEN, AND COMMON COUNCIL OF THE HONOURABLE CITY OF DUBLIN, IN THE CHOICE OF A RECORDER

Headnote

Composed after February 1733; published 1733; copy text *1733* (see Textual Account).

The death of the incumbent, Swift's friend Alderman Francis Stoyte, in February 1733, dates this brief statement on the desired prerequisites in the Dublin Recorder, and the choice of his successor.

Swift's successful recommendation of Eaton Stannard, a lawyer and 'patriot' MP was a deliberate intervention (for Swift's wider support of Stannard, see Introduction, pp. xxxiii, lxxxviii, xci, xcviii). The Recorder's position within Dublin politics was an important one: he was not an MP, and the position was partly honorary, but for Swift the Recorder would nonetheless play an important role in representing the city during a time of considerable political agitation, and the securing of a 'patriot' as Recorder was of symbolic and possible political significance, given coming Mayoral and Aldermanic elections (and the possibility of a parliamentary election too).

SOME CONSIDERATIONS HUMBLY OFFERED TO THE RIGHT HONOURABLE THE LORD-MAYOR, THE COURT OF ALDERMEN, AND COMMON COUNCIL OF THE HONOURABLE CITY OF DUBLIN,[1] IN THE CHOICE OF A RECORDER.[2]

The Office of Recorder to this City, being vacant by the Death of a very worthy Gentleman,[3] it is said that five or six Persons are solliciting to succeed him in the Employment. I am a Stranger to all their Persons, and to most of their Characters; which latter, I hope, will, at this Time, be canvassed with more Decency, than it sometimes happens upon the like Occasions.

Therefore, as I am wholly impartial, I can with more Freedom deliver my Thoughts, how the several Persons and Parties concerned ought to proceed, in electing a Recorder for this great and antient City.

And, *first*, as it is a very natural, so I can, by no Means, think it an unreasonable Opinion, that the Sons, or near Relations of Aldermen,[4] and other deserving Citizens, should be duly regarded as proper Competitors for an Employment in the City's Disposal, provided they be equally qualified with other Candidates; and provided, that such Employments require no more than common Abilities, and common Honesty. But in the Choice of a Recorder, the Case is entirely different. He ought to be a Person of good Abilities in his Calling, of an unspotted Character, an able Practitioner, one who hath occasionally merited of this City before;

---

1 *THE COURT of ALDERMEN... CITY OF DUBLIN*: the aldermen stood at the head of the civic government of Dublin. They were elected (for life) from the members of the common council, which was in turn composed of forty-eight 'sheriffs' peers', chosen by a committee of aldermen, and ninety-two 'numbers', representatives of the various trade guilds, who were selected by the aldermen from a slate put forward by each guild master. The aldermen and common council met separately to take decisions within their own spheres of competence, but also met together on a regular basis in the general assembly to take joint decisions, including the election of the recorder.
2 *RECORDER*: a legal official within a borough, with the powers of a magistrate, responsible for overseeing the legal processes of the corporation, and for maintaining and defending its privileges.
3 *Office... the Death of a very worthy Gentleman*: Francis Stoyte, recorder of Dublin and MP for Hillsborough in the Irish Parliament, had died on 6 Feb. 1733.
4 *the Sons... of Aldermen*: John Forbes, who was standing against Swift's preferred candidate for the recordership, Eaton Stannard, was the son of Alderman George Forbes (lord mayor 1721–2).

he ought to be of some Maturity in Years, a Member of Parliament, and likely to continue so, regular in his Life, firm in his Loyalty to the *Hanover* Succession, indulgent to tender Consciences; but, at the same time, a firm Adherer to the Established Church. If he be such a one who hath already sat in Parliament, it ought to be inquired of what Weight he was there? Whether He voted on all Occasions for the Good of his Country, and particularly for advancing the Trade and Freedom of this City? Whether he be engaged in any Faction, either National or Religious?[5] And *lastly*, Whether he be a Man of Courage; not to be drawn from his Duty by the Frowns or Menaces of Power,[6] nor capable to be corrupted by Allurements or Bribes? These, and many other Particulars, are of infinitely more Consequence than that single Circumstance of being descended by a direct or collateral Line from any Alderman, or distinguished Citizen alive or dead.

There is not a Dealer, or Shop-keeper in this City, of any Substance, whose Thriving, less or more, may not depend upon the good or ill Conduct of a Recorder. He is to watch every Motion in Parliament, that may, in the least affect the Freedom, Trade, or Welfare of it.[7]

In this approaching Election, the Commoners,[8] as they are a numerous Body, so they seem to be most concerned in Point of Interest, and their Interest ought to be most regarded; because it altogether depends upon the true Interest of the City; they have no private Views, and giving their Votes, as I am informed, by balotting, they lye under no Awe, or Fear of disobliging Competitors. It is therefore, hoped, that they will duly consider which of the Candidates is most likely to advance the Trade of themselves

---

5 *any Faction, either National or Religious*: in Swift's view, there were two kinds of party division: on the one hand, the supporters of the interests of Ireland (patriots) as opposed to those of England (the court); on the other, supporters of the established church (Tories) as opposed to Dissent (Whigs).

6 *Frowns or Menaces of Power*: the phrase 'the frown (or 'frowns') of power' was in common use. Swift also employed it in his sermon on 'Brotherly Love' (1717) (Davis, vol. IX, p. 178), and in 'Verses on the Death of Dr. Swift' (*Poems*, vol. II, p. 568). The origin is unknown, but a song in Shakespeare, *Cymbeline*, Act IV, Scene ii, l. 341, includes the line 'Fear no more the frowne o' th' great'.

7 *He is to watch... Welfare of it*: besides his official municipal responsibilities, including the giving of legal advice, a borough recorder was expected to assist his corporation (and by extension his town or city) in matters relating to government and Parliament. Stoyte, for example, had drafted memorials from Dublin corporation to government in 1728 over the harbour, and in 1729 concerning the Navigation Acts and proposals to revalue the coinage (*Cal. Anc. Recs Dublin*, vol. VII, pp. 407–9, 447–8, 460).

8 *the Commoners*: the common council, sometimes referred to as 'the commons'.

and their Brother Citizens, to defend their Liberties both in and out of Parliament, against any Attempts of Encroachment or Oppression: And so GOD direct them in the Choice of a Recorder, who may for many Years supply that important Office with Skill, Diligence, Courage, and Fidelity. And let all the People say *Amen*.[9]

---

[9] *let all the People say Amen*: Psalm 106: 48.

PREFATORY LETTER TO MARY BARBER, POEMS ON SEVERAL OCCASIONS

Headnote

Probably composed 1734; published 1734 (advertised from October 1733); copy text *1734* (see Textual Account).

The Irish poet Mary Barber is mentioned frequently in Swift's correspondence in the early 1730s: he attempted to help her gain patronage, gave her contacts, letters of introduction and potential subscribers in England, and generally encouraged her work (see Woolley, *Corr.*, vol. III, p. 278; Ehrenpreis, vol. III, p. 759), above all in this letter to the Earl of Orrery. This formed the preface to her *Poems on Several Occasions*, which appeared in 1734, printed by Samuel Richardson. The volume was reprinted in 1735 and 1736, and Barber's poetry had some currency in the century, being anthologised in *Poems by Eminent Ladies*, London, 1755, and elsewhere.

TO THE RIGHT HONOURABLE JOHN, *EARL OF ORRERY*.[1]

My LORD,

I Lately receiv'd a Letter from Mrs. *Barber*,[2] wherein she desires my Opinion about dedicating her Poems to your Lordship; and seems in Pain to know how far she may be allow'd to draw your Character, which is a Right claim'd by all Dedicators. And she thinks this the more incumbent on her, from the surprizing Instances of your Generosity and Favour that she hath already receiv'd,[3] and which she hath been so unfashionable to publish where-ever she goes. This makes her apprehend, that all she can say to your Lordship's Advantage, will be interpreted as the mere Effect of Flattery, under the Style and Title of Gratitude.

I sent her Word, that I could be of no Service to her upon this Article: Yet I confess, my Lord, that all those who are thoroughly acquainted with her, will impute her Encomiums to a sincere, but overflowing Spirit of Thankfulness, as well as to the humble Opinion she hath of herself. Altho' the World in general may possibly continue in its usual Sentiments, and list her in the common Herd of Dedicators.

Therefore, upon the most mature Deliberation, I concluded that the Office of setting out your Lordship's Character, will not come properly from her Pen, for her own Reasons: I mean the great Favours you have already conferr'd on her. And God forbid, that your Character should not have a much stronger Support. You are hourly gaining the Love, Esteem, and Respect of wise and good Men: And in due Time, if Mrs. *Barber* can

---

1 *John, Earl of Orrery*: John Boyle (1707–62), 5th Earl of Orrery.
2 *Mrs. Barber*: Mary Barber (*c.* 1685 – *c.* 1755), the wife of Rupert Barber, a woollen-draper of St Werburgh St, Dublin (see *ODNB*; *DIB*). Her *Poems on Several Occasions*, to which this is a preface, were printed in London in 1734. For Swift's relationship with her, see Louise Barnett, *Jonathan Swift in the Company of Women*, Oxford: Oxford University Press, 2007, pp. 88–92, and Christopher Fanning, 'The Voices of the Dependent Poet: The Case of Mary Barber', *Women's Writing* 8 (2001), 81–97.
3 *the surprizing Instances . . . already receiv'd*: Mrs Barber, in her dedication to Orrery, spoke of 'that great goodness, wherewith you condescended to distinguish me, when I was a stranger in England; and after that, bounteously to enrich me in Ireland, at a time when my want of health, made your generosity the more valuable' (*Poems on Several Occasions*, p. xiv). In January 1733, Swift noted that 'some time' previously Mrs Barber had delivered to him birthday verses composed for him by Orrery (Swift to Orrery, 25 Jan. 1732/3 (Woolley, *Corr.*, vol. III, pp. 582–3)).

but have a little Patience, you will bring them all over in both Kingdoms, to a Man: I confess, the Number is not great; but that is not your Lordship's Fault, and therefore, in Reason, you ought to be contented.

I guess the Topicks she intends to insist on; Your Learning, your Genius, your Affability, Generosity, the Love you bear to your native Country, and your Compassion for this; the Goodness of your Nature, your Humility, Modesty, and Condescension, your most agreeable Conversation, suited to all Tempers, Conditions, and Understandings: Perhaps she may be so weak to add the Regularity of your Life, that you believe a God and Providence, that you are a firm Christian, according to the Doctrine of the Church establish'd in both Kingdoms.

These and other Topicks I imagine Mrs. *Barber* designs to insist on, in the Dedication of her Poems to your Lordship; but I think she will better shew her Prudence by omitting them all. And yet, my Lord, I cannot disapprove of her Ambition, so justly plac'd in the Choice of a Patron; and at the same Time declare my Opinion, that she deserveth your Protection on account of her Wit and good Sense, as well as of her Humility, her Gratitude, and many other Virtues. I have read most of her Poems; and believe your Lordship will observe, that they generally contain something new and useful, tending to the Reproof of some Vice or Folly, or recommending some Virtue. She never writes on a Subject with general unconnected Topicks, but always with a Scheme and Method driving to some particular End; wherein many Writers in Verse, and of some Distinction, are so often known to fail. In short, she seemeth to have a true poetical Genius, better cultivated than could well be expected, either from her Sex, or the Scene she hath acted in, as the Wife of a Citizen. Yet I am assured, that no Woman was ever more useful to her Husband in the Way of his Business.[4] Poetry hath only been her favourite Amusement; for which she hath one Qualification, that I wish all good Poets possess'd a Share of, I mean, that she is ready to take Advice, and submit to have her Verses corrected, by those who are generally allow'd to be the best Judges.

I have, at her Intreaty, suffer'd her to take a Copy of this Letter, and given her the Liberty to make it public. For which I ought to desire your

---

4 *no Woman ... in the Way of his Business*: Mary Delany described Rupert Barber as one who 'drinks his claret, smokes his pipe, and cares not a pin for his family, who if they had not met with better friends than himself, might have starved' (quoted in *DIB*).

Lordship's Pardon: But she was of Opinion it might do her some Service; and therefore I comply'd. I am, my Lord, with the truest Esteem and Respect,

> Your LORDSHIP's
> Most Obedient Servant,
> JONATHAN SWIFT.

Dublin,
August 20. 1733.

ADVICE TO THE FREE-MEN OF THE CITY OF DUBLIN IN THE CHOICE OF A MEMBER TO REPRESENT THEM IN PARLIAMENT

Headnote

Composed after July, 1733; published *c*. September 1733; copy text *1733* (see Textual Account).

The death of the incumbent Samuel Burton in July 1733 ensured the second Parliamentary by-election in Dublin in a very short time, and created a fevered political atmosphere. Humphrey French, the Lord-Mayor of Dublin from 1732 to 1733, impressed Swift greatly, as can be seen in *Advice to the Free-men of Dublin*, an endorsement of French's successful candidacy as MP for Dublin City.

The *Advice* is another example of Swift's close involvement in Dublin corporation politics: the first candidate to declare, John Macarell (who was eventually replaced by a member of the corporation), already held the office of register of the barracks, and was therefore a placeman; hence Swift's support for the 'patriot' French against him (see Introduction, p. xcviii).

The parliamentary franchise for the Dublin city constituency was in the hands of the freemen and freeholders. Although there is no surviving indication of the relative proportions of each, it may well be that freemen were in the majority. In any case, freemen, as inhabitants of the city, would be more likely to appreciate the municipal achievements of an aldermanic candidate. Moreover, Swift's constituency might have been with the freemen, as he had written so often in support of artisans.

Swift's argument first appeared as a broadsheet (its appearance was recorded in the *Dublin Journal*, 29 September 1733).

ADVICE TO THE FREE-MEN OF THE CITY OF *DUBLIN* IN THE CHOICE OF A MEMBER TO REPRESENT THEM IN PARLIAMENT.

Those few Writers, who, since the Death of Alderman *Burton*,[1] have employed their Pens in giving Advice to our Citizens how they should proceed in electing a new Representative for the next Sessions, having laid aside their Pens;[2] I have Reason to hope, that all true Lovers of their Country in general, and particularly those who have any Regard for the Priviledges and Liberties of this great and ancient City, will think a second and a third time, before they come to a final Determination upon what Person they resolve to fix their Choice.

I am told, there are only two Persons who set up for Candidates; one, is the present Lord Mayor,[3] and the other, a Gentleman, of good Esteem, an Alderman of the City, a Merchant of Reputation, and possess'd of a considerable Office under the Crown.[4] The Question is, which of these two Persons it will be most for the Advantage of the City to elect? I have but little Acquaintance with either, so that my Inquiries will be very impartial, and drawn only from the general Character and Situation of both.

---

1 *the Death of Alderman Burton*: Samuel Burton (1687–1733), an alderman of Dublin from 1728 and elected MP for the city in 1727, had died on 8 July 1733. See *Hist. Ir. Parl.*, vol. III, pp. 245–6.
2 *having laid aside their Pens*: of the surviving pamphlets and broadsides concerning the election, the following may have appeared before Swift's intervention: *Advice to the Freemen and Freeholders of the City of Dublin; in Their Choice of a Representative in the Ensuing Election*, Dublin, 1733; *A Full Vindication of Humphrey French, Late Lord Mayor of the City of Dublin*, Dublin, 1733; and *The Free-man's Letter of Advice to his Country-men and Fellow-citizens, in Behalf of the Late Lord-mayor*, Dublin, 1733. Published subsequently were *A Little More Advice to the People of Dublin*, [Dublin], 1733; and *A Great Deal More Seasonable Advice to the Freemen and Freeholders of the City of Dublin, Concerning the Choice of a Member to Represent them in Parliament*, Dublin, 1733.
3 *the present Lord Mayor*: Humphrey French (1680–1736), alderman of Dublin from 1729 and lord mayor 1732–3 (later MP Dublin city 1733–6). See *Hist. Ir. Parl.*, vol. IV, pp. 325–6. Adulatory verses, possibly by Swift, which had been originally addressed to Lord Carteret in 1729 but were rededicated to French, appeared at the end of the first London edition of Swift's pamphlet *The Presbyterian's Plea of Merit* (1733). See *Poems*, vol. III, pp. 1132–3.
4 *the other . . . Office under the Crown*: John Macarell (*c.* 1695–1757), of Lissenhall, Co. Dublin, sheriff of Dublin in 1722 and recently elected alderman, held government office as register of the barracks. See *Hist. Ir. Parl.*, vol. V, pp. 151–2. The first candidate to put up against French, Macarell was subsequently replaced by French's successor as lord mayor, Thomas Howe; see *A Full Vindication of Humphrey French*.

In order to this, I must offer my Countrymen and Fellow Citizens, some Reasons, why I think they ought to be more than ordinarily careful at this Juncture, upon whom they bestow their Votes.

To perform this with more Clearness, it may be proper to give you a short State of our unfortunate Country.

We consist of two Parties, I do not mean Popish and Protestant, High and Low Church, Episcopal and Sectarians,[5] Whig and Tory; but of these *English* who happen to be born in this Kingdom, (whose Ancestors reduced the whole Nation under the Obedience of the *English* Crown) and the Gentlemen sent from t'other Side to possess most of the chief Employments here: This latter Party is very much enlarged and strengthened by the whole Power in the Church, the Law, the Army, the Revenue, and the Civil Administration deposited in their Hands. Although out of Political Ends, and to save Appearances, some Employments are still deposited (yet gradually in a smaller Number) to Persons born here: This Proceeding fortified with good Words and many Promises, is sufficient to flatter and feed the Hopes of Hundreds, who will never be one Farthing the better, as they might easily be convinced, if they were qualify'd to think at all.

Civil Employments of all kinds, have been for several Years past, with great Prudence made precarious, and during Pleasure;[6] by which Means the Possessors are, and must inevitably be for ever dependant: Yet those very few of any Consequence, which are dealt with so sparing a Hand to Persons born among us, are enough to keep Hope alive in great Numbers who desire to mend their Condition by the Favour of those in Power.

Now, my dear Fellow-Citizens, how is it possible you can conceive, that any Person who holds an Office of some Hundred Pounds a Year, which may be taken from him whenever Power shall think fit, will if he should be chosen a Member for any City, do the least thing when he sits in the House, that he knows or fears may be displeasing to those who gave him, or continue him in that Office. Believe me, these are no times to

---

5 *Episcopal and Sectarians*: Church of Ireland and Dissenter.
6 *Civil Employments . . . during Pleasure*: in 1731, in recruiting the influential 'patriot' MP Thomas Carter to support his administration, the Duke of Dorset permitted Carter to purchase the reversion to the office of master of the rolls (then held for life by Lord Berkeley) on condition that he agreed to hold it 'during pleasure', which would permit him to be dismissed at any time (Robert E. Burns, *Irish Parliamentary Politics in the Eighteenth Century*, 2 vols., Washington, DC: Catholic University of America Press, 1989–90, vol. II, p. 6).

expect such an exalted Degree of Virtue from mortal Men. *Blazing Stars*[7] are much more frequently seen than such heroical Worthies. And I could sooner hope to find ten Thousand Pounds by digging in my Garden than such a *Phoenix*[8] by searching among the present Race of Mankind.

I cannot forbear thinking it a very erroneous as well as modern Maxim of Politicks in the *English* Nation, to take every Opportunity of depressing of *Ireland*, whereof an hundred Instances may be produc'd in Points of the highest Importance, and within the Memory of every middle-aged Man. Although many of the greatest Persons among that Party which now prevails, have formerly upon that Article much differed in their Opinion from their present Successors.[9]

But, so the Fact stands at present. It is plain, that the Court and Country Party here (I mean in the House of Commons)[10] very seldom agree in any thing but their Loyalty to his present Majesty, their Resolutions to make him and his Viceroy easy in the Government, to the utmost of their Power, under the present Condition of the Kingdom. But the Persons sent from *England*, who (to a Trifle) are possessed of the sole executive Power in all its Branches, with their few Adherents in Possession who were born here, and Hundreds of Expectants, Hopers, and Promissees, put on quite contrary Notions with regard to *Ireland*. They count upon a universal Submission to whatever shall be demanded; wherein they act safely, because none of themselves, except the Candidates, feel the least of our Pressures.

I remember a Person of Distinction[11] some Days ago affirm'd in a good deal of mixt Company, and of both Parties, That the Gentry from

---

7 *Blazing Stars*: comets.
8 *a Phoenix*: a mythical bird, said to live for 500 years in the Arabian desert, before burning itself to death on a funeral pyre and being reborn from the ashes. According to Pliny (*Natural History*, bk X, ch. 2), there was never more than one in the world.
9 *many of the greatest Persons... from their present Successors*: in the dispute over the resumption of Irish forfeited estates in 1699–1703, English Whigs supported Irish Protestant representations against the legislation of the English Parliament (see D. W. Hayton, *Ruling Ireland, 1685–1742*, Woodbridge: Boydell Press, 2004, pp. 71–84). Later, one of Swift's *bêtes noires*, Thomas, Earl of Wharton, lord lieutenant in 1708–10, claimed to have acted in Ireland's interest by promoting further popery bills and establishing an arsenal for the storage of weapons of defence (L. A. Dralle, 'Kingdom in Reversion: The Irish Viceroyalty of the Earl of Wharton, 1708–10', *HLQ* 15 (1951–2), 393–431).
10 *the Court... House of Commons*: more common in Ireland than the English terms 'Court' and 'Country' to denote government and opposition were 'Castle party' and 'patriots'.
11 *a Person of Distinction*: possibly an arch reference to Swift himself. See below, p. 287, where the author recalls hearing the Drapier 'declare... in publick Company' his support for French in the election.

England who now enjoy OUR highest Employments of all Kinds, can never be possibly Losers of one Farthing by the greatest Calamities that can befal this Kingdom, except a Plague that would sweep away a Million of our *Hewers of Wood, and Drawers of Water*.[12] Or an Invasion that would fright our Grandees out of the Kingdom. For this Person argued, that while there was a Penny left in the Treasury, the Civil and Military List must be paid; and that the episcopal Revenues which are usually farmed out at six times below the real Value,[13] could hardly fail. He insisted further, that as Money diminished, the Price of all Necessaries for Life must of Consequence do so too, which would be for the Advantage of all Persons in Employment, as well as of my Lords the Bishops, and to the Ruin of every Body else. Among the Company there wanted not Men in Office, besides one or two Expectants; yet I did not observe any of them disposed to return an Answer: But the Consequences drawn were these; That the great Men in Power sent hither from t'other Side were by no means upon the same Foot with his Majesty's other Subjects of *Ireland*. They had no common Ligament to bind them with us; they suffered not with our Sufferings, and if it were possible for us to have any Cause of Rejoycing, they could not rejoyce with us.

Suppose a Person born in this Kingdom, shall happen by his Services for the *English* Interest, to have an Employment conferred on him worth 400 l. a Year; and that he hath likewise an Estate in Land, worth 400 l. a Year more: Suppose him to sit in Parliament: Then, suppose a Land-Tax to be brought in of 5s. a Pound for ten Years; I tell you how this Gentleman will compute. He has 400 l. a Year in Land: The Tax he must pay yearly is 100 l. by which in ten Years, he will pay only 1000 l. But if he gives his Vote against this Tax, he will lose 4000 l. by being turned out of his Employment; together with the Power and Influence he hath, by Virtue or Colour of his Employment; and thus the Ballance will be against him three Thousand Pounds.

I desire, my Fellow-Citizens, you will please to call to mind how many Persons you can vouch for among your Acquaintance, who have so much Virtue and Self-Denial, as to lose 400 l. a Year for Life; together with

---

12 *Hewers of Wood, and Drawers of Water*: those condemned to menial drudgery, on the pattern of the Gibeonites in Joshua, 9: 21.
13 *the episcopal Revenues... below the real Value*: see above, pp. 231–3.

the Smiles and Favour of Power, and the Hopes of higher Advancement, meerly out of a generous Love of his Country.

The Contentions of Parties in *England*, are very different from those among us. The Battle there is fought for Power and Riches; and so it is indeed among us: But, whether a great Employment be given to *Tom* or to *Peter*, they were both born in *England*, the Profits are to be spent there. All Employments (except a very few) are bestowed on the Natives: They do not send to *Germany*, *Holland*, *Sweden*, or *Denmark*,[14] much less to *Ireland*, for Chancellors, Bishops, Judges, or other Officers. Their Salaries, whether well or ill got, are employed at home: and whatever their Morals or Politicks be, the Nation is not the poorer.

The House of Commons in *England*, have frequently endeavoured to limit the Number of Members who should be allowed to have Employments under the Crown: several Acts have been made to that Purpose, which many wise Men think are not yet effectual enough, and many of them are rendered ineffectual, by leaving the Power of Re-election:[15] Our House of Commons consists, I think, of about three Hundred Members;[16] if one Hundred of these should happen to be made up of Persons already provided for, joined with Expecters, Compliers, easy to be perswaded, such as will give a Vote for a Friend who is in Hopes to get something; if they be merry Companions, without Suspicion, of a natural Bashfulness, not apt or able to look forwards; if good Words, Smiles, and Caresses, have any Power over them, the larger Part of a second Hundred may be very easily brought in at a most reasonable Rate.

There is an *Englishman* of no long Standing among us, but in an Employment of great Trust, Power, and Profit.[17] This excellent Person did lately publish, at his own Expence, a Pamphlet printed in *England*

---

14 *Germany, Holland, Sweden, or Denmark*: Swift names three Protestant countries — the United Provinces, Sweden and Denmark — and a geographical entity, 'Germany', in which there are numerous Protestant states. Placing Germany first suggests the possibility of importing office-holders from Hanover, and placing Holland second recalls the reign of the Dutch King William III.
15 *The House of Commons... Power of Re-election*: for place legislation in England, see Betty Kemp, *King and Commons 1660–1832*, London: Macmillan, 1957, pp. 51–69.
16 *Our House of Commons... about three Hundred Members*: there were exactly 300 seats in the Irish House of Commons.
17 *an Englishman... Power, and Profit*: Edward Thompson (1696–1742) of Long Marston, near York, MP York 1722–42, who had been appointed a revenue commissioner in Ireland in 1725.

by Authority, to justify the Bill for a general *Excise*, or inland Duty, in order to introduce that blessed Scheme among us.[18] What a tender Care must such an *English* Patriot for *Ireland* have of our Interest, if he should condescend to sit in our Parliament. I will bridle my Indignation. However, methinks I long to see that Mortal, who would with Pleasure blow us up all at a Blast: But, he duly receives his Thousand Pounds a Year; makes his Progresses like a King; is received in Pomp at every Town and Village where he travels,[19] and shines in the *English* News-Papers.[20]

I will now apply what I have said to you, my Brethren and Fellow-Citizens. Count upon it, as a Truth next to your Creed, that no one Person in Office, of which he is not Master for Life, whether born here or in *England*, will ever hazard that Office for the Good of this Country. One of your Candidates is of this Kind, and I believe him to be an honest Gentleman, as the Word *Honest* is generally understood.[21] But he loves his Employment better than he does you, or his Country, or all the Countries upon Earth. Will you contribute and give him City Security, to pay him the Value of his Employment, if it should be taken from him, during his Life, for voting on all Occasions with the honest Country Party in the House; although I must question, whether he would do it, even upon that Condition.

Wherefore, since there are but two Candidates, I intreat you will fix on the present Lord-Mayor.[22] He hath shewn more Virtue, more Activity, more Skill, in one Year's Government of the City, than a Hundred Years

---

18 *did lately publish... Scheme among us*: presumably *An Appeal to the Landholders Concerning the Reasonableness and General Benefit of an Excise upon Tobacco and Wine*, London, 1733; repr. Dublin, 1733 (by Faulkner).
19 *makes his Progresses... where he travels*: in the summer of 1733, Thompson had undertaken a personal survey of several Munster ports, at the request of the English Treasury, to inquire into the prevalence of wool smuggling: see warrant, 20 Sept. 1733 (TNA, T 14/11); Marmaduke Coghill to Edward Southwell, jr, 7, 24 July 1733 (*Coghill Letters*, pp. 129, 130–1); HMC, *Egmont Diary*, vol. II, pp. 26–7.
20 *shines in the English News-Papers*: no reference to Thompson's Irish travels has been traced in a contemporary English newspaper.
21 *an honest Gentleman... generally understood*: virtuous, as contrasted with the way in which Whigs used 'honest', to convey a political position and commitment to the Protestant succession.
22 *the present Lord-Mayor*: Humphrey French (1680–1736), lord mayor of Dublin, 1732–3.

can equal. He hath endeavoured, with great Success, to banish Frauds, Corruptions, and all other Abuses from amongst you.

A Dozen such Men in Power, would be able to reform a Kingdom. He hath no Employment under the Crown; nor is likely to get or sollicite for any; his Education having not turned him that Way. I will assure for no Man's future Conduct; but he who hath hitherto practised the Rules of Virtue with so much Difficulty, in so great and busy a Station, deserves your Thanks, and the best Return you can make him; and you, my Brethren, have no other to give him; than that of representing you in Parliament. Tell not me of your Engagements and Promises to another. Your Promises were Sins of Inconsideration at best; and you are bound to repent and annul them. That Gentleman, though with good Reputation, is already engaged on the other Side. He hath 400 l. a Year under the Crown, which he is too wise to part with, by sacrificing so good an Establishment to the empty Names of Virtue, and Love of his Country. I can assure you, the *DRAPIER* is in the Interests of the present Lord-Mayor, whatever you may be told to the contrary. I have lately heard him declare so in publick Company, and offer some of these very Reasons in Defence of his Opinion; although he hath a Regard and Esteem for the other Gentleman, but would not hazard the Good of the City and the Kingdom for a Compliment.

The Lord-Mayor's Severity to some unfair Dealers, should not turn the honest Men among them against him.[23] Whatever he did, was for the Advantage of those very Trades whose dishonest Members he punished. He hath hitherto been above Temptation, to act wrong; and therefore, as Mankind goes, he is the most likely to act right as a Representative of your City, as he constantly did in the Government of it.

---

23 *The Lord-Mayor's Severity . . . against him*: French's popularity was in part owing to his paternalist interventions as lord mayor, which included taking action against 'fraudulent weights and measures' in the city markets; *A Full Vindication of Humphrey French; The Lamentation of the Poor of the City of Dublin; After the Late Lord Mayor, with a Word of Advice to the Freemen, &c. of said City*, [Dublin], 1733; *A Great Deal More Seasonable Advice . . .*; Jacqueline Hill, *From Patriots to Unionists: Dublin Civic Politics and Irish Protestant Patriotism, 1660–1840*, Oxford: Clarendon Press, 1997, p. 82. A contemporary engraved portrait of French was entitled 'The good lord mayor' (British Museum, Prints and Drawings, 1902, 1011.6984).

OBSERVATIONS OCCASIONED BY READING A PAPER, ENTITLED, THE CASE OF THE WOOLLEN MANUFACTURERS OF DUBLIN, &c.

THE CASE OF THE WOOLLEN MANUFACTURERS OF DUBLIN, &C   289

Headnote

Composed *c.* November 1733; published posthumously, 1789; copy text *1789* (see Textual Account).

Observations Occasioned by Reading the Case of the Woollen Manufacturers is a response to a piece published in November 1733 (see Appendix C, pp. 344–9), in which seven manufacturers (i.e. merchants) are named and denounced for importing foreign cloth. Swift had always been ambivalent towards the woollen manufacturers: he had written in their support, but had also criticised some of their practices and products, such as the forcing onto sellers of inferior materials at inflated prices, and drawn attention to what he regarded as their economic short-sightedness, particularly with respect to quality and pricing, which he predicted would ensure the use of foreign imports.

Swift's condemnation of the merchants was presumably written shortly after the publication of the *Case*, though not printed until John Nichols's gathering of fugitive Swift pieces in 1789.

OBSERVATIONS OCCASIONED BY READING A PAPER, ENTITLED, THE CASE OF THE WOOLLEN MANUFACTURERS OF DUBLIN, &c.

The paper called The Case of the Woollen Manufacturers, &c. is very well drawn up.[1] The reasonings of the author are just, the facts true, and the consequences natural. But his censure of those seven vile citizens,[2] who import such a quantity of silk stuffs, and woollen cloth from England, is an hundred times gentler than enemies to their country deserve; because I think no punishment in this world can be great enough for them, without immediate repentance and amendment. But, after all, the writer of that paper hath very lightly touched one point of the greatest importance, and very poorly answered the main objection, that the *clothiers are defective both in the quality and quantity of their goods.*

For my own part, when I consider the several societies of handicrafts-men in all kinds,[3] as well as shopkeepers, in this city, after eighteen years experience of their dealings, I am at a loss to know in which of these societies the most or least honesty is to be found. For instance, when any trade comes first into my head, upon examination I determine it exceeds all others in fraud. But after I have considered them all round, as far as my knowledge or experience reacheth, I am at a loss to determine, and to save trouble I put them all upon a par. This I chiefly apply to those societies of men who get their livelihood by the labour of their hands. For, as to shopkeepers, I cannot deny that I have found some few honest men among them, taking the word *honest* in the largest and most charitable sense. But as to handicrafts-men, although I shall endeavour to believe it possible to find a fair dealer among their clans, yet I confess it hath never been once my good fortune to employ one single workman, who did not cheat me at all times to the utmost of his power in the materials, the work, and the price. One universal maxim I have constantly observed among them, that they would rather gain a shilling by cheating you, than twenty in the honest way of dealing, although they were sure to lose your

---

1 *The paper... well drawn up*: see Appendix C, below, pp. 344–9.
2 *those seven vile citizens*: the seven individual merchants, or firms, named in *The CASE of the Woolen Manufacturers of the City of Dublin, and Liberties thereunto adjoyning, truly stated* (Appendix C, below, pp. 344–9).
3 *the several societies of handicrafts-men in all kinds*: see above, p. xcv.

custom, as well as that of others, whom you might probably recommend to them.

This, I must own, is the natural consequence of poverty and oppression. These wretched people catch at any thing to save them a minute longer from drowning. Thus Ireland is the poorest of all civilized countries in Europe, with every natural advantage to make it one of the richest.

As to the grand objection, which this writer slubbers[4] over in so careless a manner, because indeed it was impossible to find a satisfactory answer, I mean the knavery of our woollen manufacturers in general, I shall relate some facts which I had more opportunities to observe than usually fall in the way of men who are not of the trade. For some years, the masters and wardens, with many of their principal workmen and shopkeepers, came often to the Deanry to relate their grievances, and to desire my advice as well as my assistance.[5] What reasons might move them to this proceeding, I leave to public conjecture. The truth is, that the woollen manufacture of this kingdom sate always nearest my heart. But the greatest difficulty lay in these perpetual differences between the shopkeepers and the workmen they employed. Ten or a dozen of these latter often came to the Deanry with their complaints, which I often repeated to the shopkeepers. As, that they brought their prices too low for a poor weaver to get his bread by; and instead of ready money for their labour on Saturdays, they gave them only such a quantity of cloth or stuff, at the highest rate, which the poor men were often forced to sell one-third below the rate, to supply their urgent necessities. On the other side, the shopkeepers complained of idleness, and want of skill, or care, or honesty, in their workmen; and probably their accusations on both sides were just.

Whenever the weavers, in a body, came to me for advice, I gave it freely, that they should contrive some way to bring their goods into reputation; and give up that abominable principle of endeavouring to thrive by imposing bad ware at high prices to their customers, whereby no shopkeeper can reasonably expect to thrive. For, besides the dread of God's anger (which is a motive of small force among them) they may be sure that no buyer of common sense will return to the same shop where he was once or twice

---

4 *slubbers*: glosses over, conceals (*OED*).
5 *For some years... as well as my assistance*: Swift's efforts to help the weavers, with financial subventions as well as advice, are detailed in Ferguson, p. 59.

defrauded. That gentlemen and ladies, when they found nothing but deceit in the sale of Irish cloths and stuffs, would act as they ought to do, both in prudence and resentment, in going to those very bad citizens the writer mentions, and purchase English goods.

I went farther, and proposed that ten or a dozen of the most substantial woollen drapiers should join in publishing an advertisement, signed with their names, to the following purpose: That for the better encouragement of all gentlemen, &c. the persons undernamed did bind themselves mutually to sell their several cloths and stuffs (naming each kind) at the lowest rate, right merchantable goods, of such a breadth, which they would warrant to be good according to the several prices: and that if a child of ten years old were sent with money, and directions what cloth or stuff to buy, he should not be wronged in any one article. And that whoever should think himself ill used in any of the said shops, he should have his money again from the seller, or upon his refusal, from the rest of the said subscribers, who, if they found the buyer discontented with the cloth or stuff, should be obliged to refund the money; and if the seller refused to repay them, and take his goods again, should publicly advertise that they would answer for none of his goods any more. This would be to establish credit, upon which all trade dependeth.

I proposed this scheme several times to the corporation of weavers, as well as to the manufacturers, when they came to apply for my advice at the Deanry-house. I likewise went to the shops of several woollen-drapiers upon the same errand, but always in vain; for they perpetually gave me the deaf ear,[6] and avoided entering into discourse upon that proposal: I suppose, because they thought it was in vain, and that the spirit of fraud had gotten too deep and universal a possession to be driven out by any arguments from interest, reason, or conscience.

---

6 *gave me the deaf ear*: turned a deaf ear to; ignored.

A LETTER ON THE FISHERY

Headnote

Composed c. 1734; published 1750; copy text *1750* (see Textual Account).

Francis Grant, a London merchant who developed schemes for improving the quantity and process of fishing in British and Irish waters, had written to Swift in 1734, enclosing his pamphlet *The British Fishery Recommended to Parliament*, and asking for his support (Woolley, *Corr.*, vol. III, pp. 727–9). Grant (d. 1762) was the third son of the Scottish law lord, Lord Cullen (Sir Francis Grant, 1st Bt).

The prospect of economic gain to Ireland from the encouragement of deepsea fishing had already been discussed by pamphleteers, most recently John Knightley, *To the Honourable the Lords Spiritual, Temporal and Commons in Parliament Assembled... this Essay toward Proving the Advantages which may Arise from Improvements on Salt Works, and in the Fishing Trade of Ireland*, Dublin, 1733.

Based on his informal enquiries from MPs, Swift pessimistically predicted that the Irish Parliament would have no interest in Grant's scheme. This proved misplaced: a bill encouraging the fishery would be passed in April 1734 (7 Geo. II c. 11 [Ire.])

Dublin,
March 23, 1734.

SIR,

I return you my hearty Thanks for your Letter and Discourse upon the Fishery;[1] you discover in both a true Love of your Country, and (except your Civilities to me) a very good Judgment, good Wishes to this ruined Kingdom, and a perfect Knowledge of the Subject you treat: But as you are more temperate than I, and consequently much wiser, (for Corruptions are apt to make me impatient and give Offence, which you prudently avoid) ever since I began to think, I was enraged at the Folly of *England*, in suffering the *Dutch* to have almost the whole Advantage of our Fishery just under our Noses. The last Lord *Wemyss*[2] told me, he was Governor of a Castle in *Scotland*, near which the *Dutch* used to fish:[3] He sent to them in a civil Manner, to desire they would send him some Fish, which they brutishly refused; whereupon he ordered three or four Cannon to be discharged from the Castle, (for their Boats were in Reach of the Shot) and immediately they sent him more than he wanted. The *Dutch* are like a Knot of Sharpers[4] among a Parcel of honest Gentlemen who think they understand Play, and are bubled[5] of their Money.

I love them for the Love they have to their Country, which, however, is no Virtue in them, because it is their private Interest,[6] which is directly

---

1 *your Letter... upon the Fishery*: Swift's letter was dated 14 Mar. 1733/4 and inscribed to Grant.
2 *The last Lord Wemyss*: David Wemyss (1678–1720), 4th Earl of Wemyss [Scot.], vice-admiral of Scotland 1707–14. 'Last' here means previous, the 5th Earl having succeeded his father.
3 *Governor of a Castle... near which the Dutch used to fish*: the castle has not been identified, though Wemyss's landed property included the castles of Elcho, Burntisland (which he sold in 1700) and Wemyss itself, where he was brought up (Sir William Fraser, *Memorials of the Family of Wemyss of Wemyss*, 3 vols., Edinburgh: Privately Printed, 1888, vol. I, pp. 326, 335, 336, 339). For contemporary references to the extensive Dutch involvement in the North Sea fisheries, see [Francis Hutchinson,] *A Second Letter to a Member of Parliament, Recommending the Improvement of the Irish-Fishery*, Dublin, 1729, pp. 19, 27.
4 *Sharpers*: those who make their living by cheating others, usually at cards.
5 *bubled*: cheated (with an allusion to the South Sea Bubble).
6 *is no Virtue in them, because it is their private Interest*: one of Swift's principal arguments in *The Conduct of the Allies* (1711) was that British engagement in the War of the Spanish Succession served not merely to protect the territorial integrity of the United Provinces, but to provide the Dutch with opportunities for enrichment: for example, the terms of the Treaty of the Grand Alliance of 1701 effectively granted the Dutch control of Flanders, which would have been to their considerable economic advantage (*CWJS*, vol. VIII, p. 70).

contrary to *England*. In the Queen's Time,[7] I did often press the Lord Treasurer *Oxford*,[8] and others of the Ministry, upon this very Subject; but the Answer was, We must not offend the *Dutch*; who were at that very Time oppressing us in all our Steps towards a Peace.[9] I laught to see the Zeal that Ministry had about the Fishing of *Newfoundland*[10] (I think) while no Care was taken against the *Dutch* fishing just at our Doors. As to my native Country, (as you call it)[11] I happened indeed by a perfect Accident to be born here, my Mother being left here from returning to her House at *Leicester*, and I was a Year old before I was sent to *England*;[12]

He developed this aspect of the case for a peace in the following year in *Some Remarks on the Barrier Treaty* (ibid., pp. 123–53). In the eighteenth century, the Dutch were routinely stereotyped as greedy and money-grubbing (Douglas Coombs, *The Conduct of the Dutch: British Opinion and the Dutch Alliance during the War of the Spanish Succession*, The Hague: Martinus Nijhoff, 1958, pp. 13–15). For an instance of this stereotyping from the period of the peace negotiations, see *The Duchess of Marlborough's Vision*, [London], 1711.

7 *In the Queen's Time*: Queen Anne.
8 *the Lord Treasurer Oxford*: Robert Harley (1661–1724), 1st Earl of Oxford, lord treasurer 1711–14.
9 *the Dutch . . . our Steps towards a Peace*: for Dutch resistance in 1711 to the idea of negotiations with France, and continuing divisions between the allies thereafter over the terms of the peace, see A. D. MacLachlan, 'The Road to Peace', in Geoffrey Holmes (ed.), *Britain after the Glorious Revolution 1689–1714*, London: Macmillan, 1969, pp. 205–12; H. T. Dickinson, *Bolingbroke*, London: Constable, 1970, pp. 94–102; Brian W. Hill, *Robert Harley: Speaker, Secretary of State and Premier Minister*, New Haven & London: Yale University Press, 1988, pp. 179–80. In the *Journal to Stella* in 1711–13, Swift frequently referred to difficulties the Dutch were making over the peace (*CWJS*, vol. IX, pp. 289–90, 387, 450, 466, 467).
10 *the Zeal that Ministry had about the Fishing of Newfoundland*: Newfoundland was fought over by Britain and France throughout the War of the Spanish Succession, with English naval expeditions in 1702, 1706 and 1709, culminating in the recovery and reoccupation of St John's under the Whig ministry in 1709 (the same ministry which in the following year permitted Dutch intransigence to scupper the peace negotiations at Gertruydenberg). Although Britain secured Newfoundland itself at the peace of Utrecht, French and Spanish rights in the Newfoundland fisheries were safeguarded.
11 *my native Country, (as you call it)*: in his letter, Grant had written, 'Though I have been long an admirer of your wit and learning, I have not less valued and esteemed your public spirit and great affection to your native country' (Woolley, *Corr.*, vol. III, p. 727).
12 *I was a Year old before I was sent to England*: Swift's mother Abigail was the daughter of James Ericke, sometime vicar of Thornton, Leicestershire, who had settled with her husband in Dublin. Jonathan was born after the death of his father; and before he was a year old, and perhaps without his mother's knowledge or consent, was carried by his nursemaid to Whitehaven in Cumberland, where he remained for three years until his mother left Dublin to return to her family in Leicestershire.

thus I am a *Teague*,[13] and an *Irishman*, or what People please, although the best Part of my Life was in *England*. What I did for this Country was from perfect Hatred of Tyrany and Oppression, for which I had a Proclamation against me of 300 *l*. which my old Friend, my Lord *Carteret*, was forced to consent to, the very first or second Night of his Arrival hither.[14] The Crime was that of writing against the Project of one *Wood*, an Ironmonger, to coin One hundred and eight thousand Pounds in Halfpence, not worth a sixth Part of the Money; which was laid before the People in so plain a Manner, that they all refused it, and so the Nation was preserved from immediate Ruin.[15] I have done some small Services to this Kingdom, but I can do no more: I have too many Years upon me, and have too much Sickness. I am out of Favour at Court, where I was well received during two Summers six and seven Years ago.[16] The governing People here do not love me; for as corrupt as *England* is, it is an Habitation of Saints[17] in Comparison of *Ireland*. We are all Slaves and Knaves and Fools, and all but Bishops and People in Employments[18] Beggars. The Cash of *Ireland* does not amount to Two hundred thousand Pounds.[19] The few honest Men amongst us are dead-hearted,[20] poor, and out of Favour and Power. I talked to two or three Gentlemen of this House

---

13 *a Teague*: an abusive name for the native Irish: see, for example, the London bookseller John Dunton's memoirs of a visit to Ireland, entitled *Teague Land, or A Merry Ramble to the Wild Irish*, London, 1698.
14 *my Lord Carteret... second Night of his Arrival hither*: the reverse of the truth: on 27 Oct. 1724, the new lord lieutenant, John Carteret (1690–1763), 2nd Baron Carteret and later 1st Earl Granville, had overcome considerable opposition in the Irish privy council to push through the decision to issue a proclamation offering a £300 reward for the identification of the author of the Drapier's *Letter to the Whole People of Ireland*: Carteret to Newcastle, 28 Oct. 1724 (TNA, SP 63/384/984); Ehrenpreis, vol. III, pp. 268–70.
15 *The Crime was... from immediate Ruin*: Swift was not identified in the proclamation even though his authorship was public knowledge.
16 *I was well received during two Summers six and seven Years ago*: during Lord Carteret's viceroyalty in 1725–6 (see above, p. xxxiii).
17 *an Habitation of Saints*: an allusion to what the Irish antiquarian Aodh Mac Cruitín (Hugh MacCurtin) called the 'peculiar title' given to Ireland as 'the island of saints': Hugh MacCurtin, *A Brief Discourse in Vindication of the Antiquity of Ireland...*, Dublin, 1717, p. 144.
18 *People in Employments*: office-holders under the crown.
19 *Two hundred thousand Pounds*: in the *Short View of the State of Ireland* (above, p. 24), Swift had given a figure for hard currency at 'about Five hundred thousand pounds'.
20 *dead-hearted*: lacking in spirit.

of Commons now sitting here,[21] mentioned your Scheme, shewed how very advantageous it would be to *Ireland*; they agreed with me; but said, that if such a Thing were proposed, the Members would all go out, as a Thing they had no Concern in.[22] I believe the People of *Lapland*,[23] or the *Hottentots*,[24] are not so miserable a People as we; for Oppression supported by Power will infallibly introduce slavish Principles. I am afraid that even in *England* your Proposal will come to nothing; there is not Virtue enough left among Mankind. If your Scheme should pass into a Law, it will become a Jobb;[25] your sanguine Temper will cool, Rogues will be the Gainers; Party and Faction will intermingle, and defeat the most essential Parts of the whole Design; Standing-Armies in Time of Peace,[26] Projects of

---

21 *now sitting here*: the Irish parliamentary session that began on 4 Oct. 1733 did not end until 29 Apr. 1734.
22 *a Thing they had no Concern in*: in fact, heads of a bill 'for the further encouragement of the fishery in this kingdom' had been introduced into the Irish House of Commons on 18 Dec. 1733, and, having passed the initial stages in the legislative process, were approved by the Irish privy council and sent across to England as a bill in the following February. After approval by the British privy council, the returned bill was presented to the Irish House of Commons on 27 Mar. 1734, and eventually received the Royal Assent on 29 Apr. as 7 Geo. II c. 11 [Ire.].
23 *the People of Lapland*: Swift had compared Ireland with Lapland as an example of primitive barbarity in *A Short View of the State of Ireland* (above, p. 22), and *A Modest Proposal* (above, p. 156).
24 *the Hottentots*: an Anglicised version of a seventeenth-century Dutch term (Hodmandod) used for the Khoikhoi (or Khoekhoe) people inhabiting south-west Africa and the area around the Cape of Good Hope. The Hottentot was frequently used by early eighteenth-century writers as an archetype of the primitive; for example, the Irish essayist James Arbuckle, when wishing to indicate a people who lived in a miserable condition, without agriculture or trade (*A Collection of Letters and Essays on Several Subjects, Lately Publish'd in the Dublin Journal*, 2 vols., Dublin, 1729, vol. II, p. 379). See, in general, L. E. Merians, *Envisioning the Worst: Representations of 'Hottentots' in Early Modern England*, Newark, NJ: University of Delaware Press, 2001.
25 *Jobb*: private interest or advantage (*OED*).
26 *Standing-Armies in Time of Peace*: the argument that a standing army was inimical to liberty had been a prominent feature of English political discourse since the late seventeenth century (Lois G. Schwoerer, *No Standing Armies! The Anti-army Ideology in 17th-century England*, Baltimore & London: Johns Hopkins University Press, 1974). It retained an important place in 'patriot' denunciations of Walpole's administration, both in the Westminster Parliament (where divisions on the re-engagement of Hessian mercenaries were an annual ritual) and in the press, notably in the writings of Bolingbroke: *HP 1715–1754*, vol. I, pp. 38–40; Linda Colley, *In Defiance of Oligarchy: The Tory Party 1714–60*, Cambridge: Cambridge University Press, 1982, p. 91; Isaac Kramnick, *Bolingbroke and His Circle: The Politics of Nostalgia in the Age of Walpole*, Cambridge, MA: Harvard University Press, 1968, p. 26.

Excise,[27] and Bribing-Elections,[28] are all you are like to be employed in; not forgetting Septennial Parliaments,[29] directly against the old Whig-Principles, which always have been mine.[30]

A Gentleman of this Kingdom, about three Years ago, joined with some others in a Fishery here in the Northern Parts; they advanced only Two hundred Pounds by Way of Trial; they got Men from *Orkney* to cure the Fish, who understood it well; but the vulgar Folks of *Ireland* are so lazy and so knavish, that it turned to no Account, nor would any body join with them, and so the Matter fell, and they lost two Thirds of their Money.[31] Oppressed Beggars are always Knaves, and I believe there are hardly any other among us; they had rather gain a Shilling by Knavery, than five Pound by honest Dealing. They lost 300 *l*. a Year for ever, in the Time of the Plague, at *Marseilles*, when the *Spaniards* would have bought all their Linnen from *Ireland*; but the Merchants and the Weavers sent over such abominable Linnen, that it was all returned back, and sold for a fourth Part

---

27 *Projects of Excise*: Walpole's attempt in 1733 to introduce in Britain an excise on imported wine and tobacco provoked a storm of protest, resulting in the withdrawal of the scheme: Paul Langford, *The Excise Crisis: Society and Politics in the Age of Walpole*, Oxford: Clarendon Press, 1975.

28 *Bribing-Elections*: another traditional opposition concern at Westminster (*HP 1690–1715*, vol. I, pp. 254–61). In 1729, the Tory MP Sir Watkin Williams Wynn, 3rd Bt, had successfully introduced a bill to prevent bribery at elections (Archibald Foord, *His Majesty's Opposition 1714–1830*, Oxford: Clarendon Press, 1964, p. 185; *HP 1715–1754*, vol. II, p. 543).

29 *Septennial Parliaments*: the passage of the Septennial Act at Westminster in 1716, to extend the term of Parliaments from a maximum of 3 to a maximum of 7 years, had been opposed by Tories and 'patriot' Whigs, who saw frequent general elections as a necessary guarantee of liberty. In 1734, the cross-party opposition moved unsuccessfully for a repeal of the Act (Colley, *In Defiance of Oligarchy*, pp. 95, 216).

30 *the old Whig-Principles, which always have been mine*: Swift's earliest political associations had been with the Whigs, and, like others who had moved across the political spectrum, he argued (with some plausibility) that it was not he who had abandoned Whig principles but the 'new Whigs' of the Junto, who after the Revolution had abandoned their libertarian ideals and had become tainted by power and corruption. 'Country Whig' critics of Walpole's ministry also identified themselves as 'old' or 'real' Whigs, to deflect accusations of Toryism, or worse. For Swift's personal political trajectory, see Bertrand Goldgar, *The Curse of Party: Swift's Relations with Addison and Steele*, Lincoln: University of Nebraska Press, 1961, chs. 1–2; F. P. Lock, *Swift's Tory Politics*, London: Duckworth, 1983; Ian Higgins, *Swift's Politics: A Study in Disaffection*, Cambridge: Cambridge University Press, 1994, ch. 1.

31 *A Gentleman of this Kingdom . . . two Thirds of their Money*: no evidence has come to light to substantiate this statement, although 'projectors' were extolling the virtues of developing the Irish fishing industry: [Hutchinson,] *Second Letter to a Member of Parliament*; Knightley, *Essay toward Proving the Advantages*.

Value.[32] This is our Condition, which you may please to pity, but never can mend. I wish you good Success with all my Heart. I have always loved good Projects, but have always found them to miscarry.

> *I am, Sir,*
> *with true Esteem for your good*
> *Intentions,*
> *your most obedient humble Servant.*

P. S. I would subscribe my Name, if I had not a very bad one, so I leave you to guess it. If I can be of any Service to you in this Kingdom, I shall be glad you will employ me.

---

32 *in the Time of the Plague... sold for a fourth Part Value*: in 1720 (see above, p. 10).

THE REV. DEAN SWIFT'S REASONS AGAINST LOWERING THE GOLD AND SILVER COIN

Headnote

Composed April 1736; published April 1736; copy text *1736* (see Textual Account).

This printing of a speech by Swift raises the perennial problem of Irish currency, specifically what Swift and others perceived as the draining away of bullion to England. The scarcity of coin in Ireland led to an attempt to revalue the Irish currency in 1736 in order to compensate for a difference in value: gold was worth more in Ireland than England, leading to the use of silver by the Irish to pay English bills. Added to this was the use of foreign gold coins in Ireland, and the importation of gold, rather than silver, where possible. The outgoing viceroy, the Duke of Dorset, proposed pragmatically to reconcile the value of gold, in order to alleviate the problem of the shortage of currency.

Swift's opposition recalled the furore against Wood's halfpence, though in this instance much less successfully, as he tried to inflame public opinion in Dublin against the imposition of such a step by officials, bishops, absentee landlords and other misguided or oppressive figures. His speech, *Reasons Against Lowering the Gold and Silver Coin*, was given on 24 April 1736, at the Guildhall, Dublin, and published shortly afterwards (alongside an unattributed paper which shares its argument), in a pamphlet entitled *Reasons Why We Should not Lower the Coins now Current in this Kingdom*. The speech was not republished until 1905.

THE REV. DEAN *SWIFT*'S REASONS AGAINST LOWERING THE GOLD AND SILVER COIN.

GENTLEMEN,

I *Beg* you will consider, and very well weigh in your hearts what I am going to say, and what I have often said before. There are several Bodies of Men, among whom the Power of this Kingdom is divided. 1st, *The Lord-Lieutenant, Lords-Justices and Council*, next to these, *my Lords the Bishops*; there is likewise *my Lord Chancellor, and my Lords the Judges of the Land*, with other eminent Persons in the Law, who have Employments and great Salaries annexed. To these must be added the Commissioners of the Revenue, with all their under Officers: *And lastly, their Honours of the Army, of all Degrees*.

Now, *Gentlemen*, I beg you again to consider, that none of these Persons above-named, can ever suffer the loss of one Farthing *by all the Miseries under which the Kingdom groans at present*. For, first, until the Kingdom be *intirely Ruined*, the Lord Lieutenant and Lords-Justices must have their *Salaries*. My Lords the Bishops, whose Lands are set at a fourth part value,[1] will be sure of their *Rents* and their *Fines*. My Lords the Judges and Those of other *Employments* in the Courts, must likewise have their *Salaries*. The Gentlemen of the Revenue will pay Themselves;[2] and as to the Officers of the Army, *the Consequences of not paying Them, is obvious enough;* Nay, so far will those *Persons* I have already mentioned be from suffering, that, on the contrary their *Revenues* being no way lessen'd by the fall of Money, and the *prices* of all *Commodities* considerably sunk thereby, they must be great *Gainers*. Therefore *Gentlemen*, I do entreat you that, as long as you live, you will look upon all *Persons* who are for lowering the Gold, or any other Coin, *as no Friends to this poor Kingdom*, but such who find their private account in what will be most detrimental to *Ireland*.[3] And, *as the Absentees are in the strongest views, our greatest Enemies*, first, by consuming above

---

1 *the Bishops, whose Lands are set a fourth part value*: in *A Proposal for an Act of Parliament to Pay Off the Debt of the Nation*, Swift provided a figure for the annual rents received for bishops' lands in Ireland as £36,800, adding 'But the real Value of those Lands at a full Rent, taking the several Sees one with another, is reckoned to be at least three fourths more' (above, p. 232).
2 *will pay Themselves*: their salaries will be paid from the produce of the duties they collect.
3 *all Persons . . . most detrimental to Ireland*: Swift's principal target is Archbishop Boulter, publicly perceived to be the chief architect of the new monetary policy.

one half of the *Rents of this Nation Abroad*.[4] And, secondly, by turning the Weight, by their Absence, so much on the Popish side, by weakning the Protestant Interest. Can there be a greater folly than to pave a Bridge of Gold[5] at your own Expence, to support them in their Luxury and Vanity abroad, while hundreds of thousands are starving at home for want of Employment.

---

4 *by consuming above one half of the Rents of this Nation Abroad*: in the Drapier's *Humble Address to Both Houses of Parliament* (1724) Swift had estimated the annual rents in Ireland at £2 million, of which approximately £700,000 was remitted directly to absentees (Davis, vol. X, pp. 128–9).
5 *a Bridge of Gold*: from the proverb 'For a flying enemy make a bridge of gold' (see *ODEP*, p. 316). When the Prince of Orange addressed his supporters at Exeter on 15 Nov. 1688, in a speech which was subsequently printed, he proclaimed, 'Let the whole world now judge if our pretences are not sincere, since we might have even a bridge of gold to return back; but it is our principle and resolution rather to die in a good cause than to live in a bad one' (repr. in *Harleian Miscellany*, 12 vols., London, 1808–11, vol. VII, p. 131).

A PROPOSAL FOR GIVING BADGES TO THE BEGGARS IN ALL THE PARISHES OF DUBLIN

Headnote

Composed before 24 April 1737; published *c.* April–May 1737; copy text *1737a* (see Textual Account).

Dated 22 April 1737, and (unusually) acknowledged on its title page by Swift, *A Proposal for Giving Badges to the Beggars* returns to the concerns of the unfinished *Upon Giving Badges to the Poor*, of 1726 (see above, pp. 1–4). For Swift's attitude towards badging, and his plan for the controlled expulsion of beggars who were not from Dublin back to their own parishes, see Introduction, pp. lxxii–lxxiv.

Swift's revisiting of the subject shows that the problem of the poor in Dublin had obviously not been solved: he accordingly begins with the problems faced by the workhouse, and expands to a description of the same questions surrounding the indigent and vagrant, and his proposed solution.

It is not immediately clear why Swift returned to the question of badging eleven years after drafting his initial scheme. The subject was very much alive, and in 1735 the Irish Parliament had passed the Cork Workhouse Act (9 Geo. II c. 25). Among contemporary publications referring to the large number of beggars in Ireland, Samuel Madden, *Reflections and Resolutions Proper for the Gentlemen of Ireland*..., Dublin, 1738, proposed a scheme of national workhouses (pp. 146, 154–60). (See also the anonymous *Agriculture the Surest Means of National Wealth*..., Dublin 1738; Jean-François Melon, *A Political Essay upon Commerce*, trans. David Bindon, Dublin, 1738, 'Preface', p. xiii.) Swift may also have been prompted by the publication of George Berkeley's *The Querist* (1735–7), with its proposal of enforced labour for the able-bodied poor, and by the death in 1735 of Sir William Fownes, who had explored the subject extensively (Mary Carter, 'Swift and the Scheme for Badging Beggars in Dublin, 1726–1737', *Eighteenth-Century Life* 27 (2013), 106–7). Whatever the reason behind its composition, it would be Swift's last substantial prose intervention in Irish affairs.

Figure 6. Jonathan Swift, *A Proposal for Giving Badges to the Beggars*, 1737. Title. Williams 339.

A PROPOSAL FOR GIVING BADGES, &c.

It hath been a general Complaint, that the Poor-House, especially since the new Constitution by Act of Parliament, hath been of no Benefit to this City, for the Ease of which it was wholly intended.[1] I had the Honour to be a Member of it many Years before it was new modelled by the Legislature;[2] not from any personal Regard, but meerly as one of the two Deans, who are of Course put into most Commissions that relate to the City; and I have likewise the Honour to have been left out of several Commissions upon the Score of Party, in which my Predecessors, Time out of Mind, have always been Members.

The first Commission was made up of about fifty Persons, which were the Lord Mayor, Aldermen, and Sheriffs, and some few other Citizens: The Judges, the two Arch-Bishops, the two Deans of the City, and one or two more Gentlemen.[3] And I must confess my Opinion, that the dissolving the old Commission, and establishing a new One of near three Times the Number, have been the great Cause of rendering so good a Design not only useless, but a Grievance instead of a Benefit to the City. In the present Commission all the City-Clergy are included, besides a great Number of 'Squires, not only those who reside in *Dublin*, and the Neighbourhood, but several who live at a great Distance, and cannot possibly have the least Concern for the Advantage of the City.[4]

---

1 *the Poor-House... wholly intended*: the Act of 1728 for better regulating the Dublin workhouse (1 Geo. II c. 27 [Ire.]); further amended by an Act of 1732 (5 Geo. II c. 14 [Ire.]).
2 *I had the Honour... before it was new modelled by the Legislature*: the Act of 1704 that first established the Dublin workhouse (2 Anne c. 19 [Ire.]) had included the deans of Christ Church (dean of Kildare) and St Patrick's, *ex officio*, as members of the governing corporation.
3 *The first Commission... one or two more Gentlemen*: besides the two deans, the corporation named by the 1704 Act included the following Irish office-holders: the chief governor(s), lord chancellor, three lord chief justices, attorney- and solicitor-general, state physician, surgeon-general, surveyor-general, together with the archbishops of Armagh and Dublin, lord mayor, recorder, aldermen and sheriffs of the city, high sheriff of the county, seneschals of St Sepulchre's and Thomas Court, and three named JPs from the county (to be replaced, when required, by election by their fellow magistrates).
4 *In the present Commission... the Advantage of the City*: the 1728 Act added to the list of dignitaries and officials named in the 1704 Act a number of other Irish office-holders (such as the chancellor of the exchequer and prime serjeant), four bishops (Clogher, Elphin, Ferns and Leighlin, and Meath), twelve temporal lords, and sixty-one commoners, mostly MPs, a great many of whom had their principal estates not only outside county Dublin but outside the province of Leinster. The MPs (and others) would of course have maintained Dublin residences as well.

At the few General Meetings that I have attended since the new Establishment, I observed very little was done, except one or two Acts of extream Justice,[5] which I then thought might as well have been spared: And I have found the Court of Assistants usually taken up in little Brangles[6] about Coachmen, or adjusting Accounts of Meal and Small-Beer;[7] which, however Necessary, might sometimes have given Place to Matters of much greater Moment, I mean some Schemes recommended to the General Board, for answering the chief Ends in erecting and establishing such a Poor-House, and endowing it with so considerable a Revenue: And the principal End I take to have been that of maintaining the Poor and Orphans of the City, where the Parishes are not able to do it; and clearing the Streets from all Strollers,[8] Foreigners,[9] and sturdy Beggars,[10] with which, to the universal Complaint and Admiration, *Dublin* is more infested since the Establishment of the Poor-House, than it was ever known to be since its first Erection.

As the whole Fund for supporting this Hospital is raised only from the Inhabitants of the City; so there can be hardly any Thing more absurd than to see it misemployed in maintaining Foreign Beggars and Bastards, or Orphans, whose Country Landlords never contributed one Shilling towards their Support. I would engage, that half this Revenue, if employed with common Care, and no very great Degree of common Honesty, would maintain all the real Objects of Charity in this City, except a small Number of Original Poor in every Parish, who might without being burthensome to the Parishioners find a tolerable Support.

I have for some Years past applied my self to several Lord Mayors, and to the late Arch-Bishop of *Dublin*,[11] for a Remedy to this Evil of Foreign Beggars; and they all appeared ready to receive a very plain Proposal, I

---

5 *extream Justice*: often used as a synonym for capital punishment, but used here in the classical sense of 'summum ius', the imposition of the full rigour of the law, which, according to the legal saying quoted in Cicero, *De Officiis*, bk I, ch. x, l. 30, results in the greatest injustice: 'summum ius, summa iniuria'. Swift's copy of Cicero included this work (*Library and Reading, I*, vol. I, p. 406).
6 *Brangles*: wrangles.
7 *Small-Beer*: beer of weak or inferior quality.
8 *Strollers*: vagrants.
9 *Foreigners*: beggars from outside the parish.
10 *sturdy Beggars*: able-bodied beggars, who were specifically excluded by law from receiving poor relief, and from being licensed to beg in a parish.
11 *the late Arch-Bishop of Dublin*: William King (1650–1729), archbishop of Dublin 1703–29.

mean, that of badging the Original Poor of every Parish, who begged in the Streets; that, the said Beggars should be confined to their own Parishes; that, they should wear their Badges well sown upon one of their Shoulders, always visible, on Pain of being whipt and turned out of Town; or whatever legal Punishment may be thought proper and effectual.[12] But, by the wrong Way of thinking in some Clergymen, and the Indifference of others, this Method was perpetually defeated to their own continual Disquiet, which they do not ill deserve; [13] and if the Grievance affected only them, it would be of less Consequence; because the Remedy is in their own Power. But, all Street-walkers,[14] and Shop-keepers, bear an equal Share in this hourly Vexation.

I never heard more than one Objection against this Expedient of badging the Poor, and confining their Walks to their several Parishes. The Objection was this: What shall we do with the Foreign Beggars? Must they be left to starve? I answered, No; but they must be driven or whipt out of Town; and let the next Country Parish do as they please, or rather after the Practice in *England*, send them from one Parish to another, until they reach their own Homes.[15] By the old Laws of *England* still in Force, and

---

12 *a very plain Proposal... proper and effectual*: parishes in Dublin, and several in Counties Antrim, Armagh and Down were operating badging schemes in the late seventeenth and early eighteenth centuries: Rowena Dudley, 'The Dublin Parishes and the Poor: 1660–1740', *Archivium Hibernicum* 53 (1999), 89; David Dickson, 'In Search of the Old Irish Poor Law', in Rosalind Mitchison and Peter Roebuck (eds.), *Economy and Society in Scotland and Ireland 1500–1939*, Edinburgh: John Donald, 1988, p. 151. Sir William Fownes, a former lord mayor of Dublin, discussed extending the practice in a pamphlet in 1724, and not long afterwards Swift persuaded Archbishop King to attempt its introduction in the Dublin diocese by clerical initiative. This proved a failure. See Fownes, *Methods Proposed for Regulating the Poor, Supporting of Some, and Employing Others: According to their Several Capacities*, Dublin, 1723–4; Davis, vol. XIII, pp. 172–3; Joseph O'Carroll, 'Contemporary Attitudes towards the Homeless Poor 1725–1775', in David Dickson (ed.), *The Gorgeous Mask: Dublin 1700–1850*, Dublin: Trinity History Workshop, 1987, p. 68.
13 *to their own continual disquiet, which they do not ill deserve*: because there are still large numbers of beggars, those who oppose the scheme remain unhappy.
14 *Street-Walkers*: Those who sell goods in the street, hawkers (with a subsidiary sense of those who sell themselves, prostitutes).
15 *after the Practice in England... their own Homes*: in 1537, the Irish Parliament had replicated the English vagrancy Act of 1531, by which the impotent poor were licensed to beg only within the town or parish in which they resided, and were liable to punishment if they begged elsewhere (O'Carroll, 'Contemporary Attitudes towards the Homeless Poor', pp. 64–5; Dickson, 'In Search of the Old Irish Poor Law', p. 148). Severe punishment of those transgressing the law had been strongly defended in Francis Hutchinson, *A Letter to a*

I presume by those of *Ireland*, every Parish is bound to maintain its own Poor;[16] and the Matter is of no such Consequence in this Point as some would make it, whether a Country Parish be rich or poor. In the remoter and poorer Parishes of the Kingdom, all Necessaries for Life proper for poor People are comparatively cheaper; I mean Buttermilk, Oatmeal, Potatoes, and other Vegitables; and every Farmer or Cottager who is not himself a Beggar, can sometimes spare a Sup or a Morsel, not worth the fourth Part of a Farthing, to an indigent Neighbour of his own Parish, who is disabled from Work. A Beggar Native of the Parish is known to the 'Squire, to the Church Minister, to the Popish Priest, or the Conventicle Teachers,[17] as well as to every Farmer: He hath generally some Relations able to live, and contribute something to his Maintenance. None of which Advantages can be reasonably expected on a Removal to Places where he is altogether unknown. If he be not quite maimed, he and his Trull,[18] and Litter of Brats (if he hath any) may get half their Support by doing some Kind of Work in their Power, and thereby be less burthensome to the People. In short, all Necessaries of Life grow in the Country, and not in Cities, and are cheaper where they grow; nor is it equal that Beggars should put us to the Charge of giving them Victuals, and the Carriage[19] too.

But, when the Spirit of wandring takes him, attended by his Female, and their Equipage[20] of Children, he becomes a Nuisance to the whole Country: He and his Female are Thieves, and teach the Trade of stealing to their Brood at four Years old; and if his Infirmities be counterfeit, it is dangerous for a single Person unarmed to meet him on the Road. He wanders from one County to another, but still with a View to this Town, whither he arrives at last, and enjoys all the Priviledges of a *Dublin* Beggar.

Member of Parliament, Concerning the Imploying and Providing for the Poor, Dublin, 1723, p. 18. For the development of the English poor law system, see Paul Slack, *The English Poor Law 1531–1782*, Basingstoke: Palgrave Macmillan, 1990.
16 *By the old Laws... its own Poor*: in fact, Ireland differed from England in that until the statute of 1665, parish vestries were not legally permitted to raise money from the inhabitants in order to relieve the poor, earlier Irish Acts having only provided for the licensing of beggars: Dudley, 'Dublin Parishes and the Poor', 81.
17 *the Conventicle Teachers*: those who ministered to Dissenting congregations.
18 *Trull*: trollop.
19 *the Carriage*: the cost of transporting food supplies to the city.
20 *Equipage*: a retinue. The term was commonly reserved for a royal or aristocratic household. The lord lieutenant of Ireland was specifically provided with funds for his equipage.

I do not wonder that the Country 'Squires should be very willing to send up their Colonies;[21] but why the City should be content to receive them, is beyond my Imagination.

If the City were obliged by their Charter to maintain a thousand Beggars, they could do it cheaper by eighty per Cent. a hundred Miles off, than in this Town, or any of its Suburbs.

There is no Village in *Connaught*, that in Proportion shares so deeply in the Daily increasing Miseries of *Ireland*, as its Capital City; to which Miseries there hardly remained any Addition, except the perpetual Swarms of Foreign Beggars, who might be banished in a Month without Expence, and with very little Trouble.

As I am personally acquainted with a great Number of Street Beggars, I find some weak Attempts have been made in one or two Parishes to promote the wearing of Badges; and my first Question to those who ask an Alms, is, *Where is your Badge?* I have in several Years met with about a Dozen who were ready to produce them, some out of their Pockets, others from under their Coat, and two or three on their Shoulders, only covered with a Sort of Capes which they could lift up or let down upon Occasion. They are too lazy to work; they are not afraid to steal, nor ashamed to beg, and yet are too proud to be seen with a Badge, as many of them have confessed to me, and not a few in very injurious Terms, particularly the Females. They all look upon such an Obligation as a high Indignity done to their Office. I appeal to all indifferent People, whether such Wretches deserve to be relieved. As to myself, I must confess, this absurd Insolence hath so affected me, that for several Years past, I have not disposed of one single Farthing to a Street Beggar, nor intend to do so until I see a better Regulation; and I have endeavoured to persuade all my Brother-walkers to follow my Example, which most of them assure me they do. For, if Beggary be not able to beat out Pride, it cannot deserve Charity. However, as to Persons in Coaches and Chairs, they bear but little of the Persecution we suffer, and are willing to leave it intirely upon us.

To say the Truth, there is not a more undeserving, vicious Race of human Kind than the Bulk of those who are reduced to Beggary, even

---

21 *their Colonies*: used here in the sense of an occupational group (in this case beggars) residing in a particular locality, but deriving from the Latin 'colonus', meaning agricultural worker or farmer, or 'colonia', a Roman settlement, often of military veterans (with an obvious resonance for the Irish situation). Cf. below, p. 314.

in this beggarly Country. For, as a great Part of our publick Miseries is originally owing to our own Faults (but, what those Faults are I am grown by Experience too wary to mention) so I am confident, that among the meaner People, nineteen in twenty of those who are reduced to a starving Condition, did not become so by what Lawyers call the Work of GOD,[22] either upon their Bodies or Goods; but meerly from their own Idleness, attended with all Manner of Vices, particularly Drunkenness, Thievery, and Cheating.

Whoever inquires, as I have frequently done, from those who have asked me an Alms, what was their former Course of Life, will find them to have been Servants in good Families, broken Tradesmen, Labourers, Cottagers, and what they call decayed Housekeepers;[23] but (to use their own Cant) reduced by Losses and Crosses,[24] by which nothing can be understood but Idleness and Vice.

As this is the only Christian Country, where People, contrary to the old Maxim, are the Poverty and not the Riches of the Nation,[25] so, the Blessing of Increase and Multiply[26] is by us converted into a Curse: And, as Marriage hath been ever countenanced in all free Countries, so we should be less miserable if it were discouraged in ours, as far as can be consistent with Christianity. It is seldom known in *England*, that the Labourer, the lower Mechanick,[27] the Servant, or the Cottager, thinks of marrying until he hath saved up a Stock of Money sufficient to carry on his Business; nor takes a Wife without a suitable Portion;[28] and as seldom fails of making a yearly Addition to that Stock, with a View of providing

22 *what Lawyers call the Work of GOD*: an act of God, for which no human being may be held responsible.
23 *decayed Housekeepers*: impoverished householders (or former householders).
24 *Losses and Crosses*: a common phrase of Puritan divines, found in the biblical commentaries of Matthew Henry and others, denoting man's trials and afflictions.
25 *People . . . Riches of the Nation*: an accepted dictum of mercantilist economics which Swift repeatedly challenged.
26 *the Blessing of Increase and Multiply*: in Genesis, God blessed Adam and Eve (Gen., 1: 22), Noah and his sons (Gen., 9: 1) and Jacob (Gen., 35: 11) with the same phrase, 'Be fruitful, and multiply'. In the Irish Book of Common Prayer, the collect for the fourth Sunday after Trinity included the words: 'Increase and multiply upon us thy mercy; that, thou being our ruler and guide, we may so pass through things temporal, that we finally lose not the things eternal' (*The Book of Common Prayer, and Administration of the Sacraments, and Other Rites and Ceremonies of the Church, According to the Use of the Church of Ireland . . .*, Dublin, 1716, n.p.).
27 *Mechanick*: a manual worker.
28 *Portion*: dowry.

for his Children. But, in this Kingdom the Case is directly contrary, where many thousand Couples are yearly married, whose whole united Fortunes, bating[29] the Rags on their Backs, would not be sufficient to purchase a Pint of Buttermilk for their Wedding Supper, nor have any Prospect of supporting their *honourable State* but by Service, or Labour, or Thievery. Nay, their *Happiness* is often deferred until they find Credit to borrow, or Cunning to steal a Shilling to pay their Popish Priest, or infamous Couple-Beggar.[30] Surely no miraculous Portion of Wisdom would be required to find some kind of Remedy against this destructive Evil, or at least, not to draw the Consequences of it upon our decaying City, the greatest Part whereof must of Course in a few Years become desolate, or in Ruins.

In all other Nations, that are not absolutely barbarous, Parents think themselves bound by the Law of Nature and Reason to make some Provision for their Children; but the Reasons offered by the Inhabitants of *Ireland* for marrying, is, that they may have Children to maintain them when they grow old and unable to work.

I am informed that we have been for some Time past extremely obliged to *England* for one very beneficial Branch of Commerce: For, it seems they are grown so Gracious as to transmit us continually Colonies of Beggars,[31] in Return of a Million of Money they receive Yearly from hence.[32] That I may give no Offence, I profess to mean real *English* Beggars in the literal Meaning of the Word, as it is usually understood by Protestants.[33] It seems, the Justices of the Peace and Parish-Officers in the Western Coasts of *England*, have a good while followed the Trade of exporting hither

---

29 *bating*: excepting.
30 *Couple-Beggar*: an itinerant priest who survived on fees for marriages, usually from the poorest classes.
31 *Colonies of Beggars*: in the straightforward sense of colonial settlers. Cf. above, p. 312.
32 *Return... from hence*: in the Drapier's *Humble Address to Both Houses of Parliament* (1724), Swift had estimated that two-thirds of the annual revenues of Ireland were remitted into England, totalling about £1,400,000 (Davis, vol. X, pp. 128–9). Other writers offered lower estimates (see above, pp. 20, 25, 113).
33 *real English Beggars ... understood by Protestants*: that is to say, English by birth, and in contrast to the way in which Irish Protestants would themselves be described as English by the native Catholics on account of their family origins, however historically distant. The process by which, in the late seventeenth and early eighteenth centuries, Irish Protestants were ceasing to regard themselves as the representatives of the 'English interest' in Ireland is related in D. W. Hayton, *The Anglo-Irish Experience, 1680–1730: Religion, Identity and Patriotism*, Woodbridge: Boydell Press, 2012, pp. 25–48.

their supernumerary Beggars, in order to advance the *English* Protestant Interest among us; and, these they are so kind to send over *Gratis*, and Duty-free. I have had the Honour more than once to attend large Cargoes of them from *Chester* to *Dublin*:[34] And I was then so ignorant as to give my Opinion, that our City should receive them into *Bridewell*,[35] and after a Month's Residence, having been well whipt twice a Day, fed with Bran and Water, and put to hard Labour, they should be returned honestly back with Thanks as cheap as they came: Or, if that were not approved of, I proposed, that whereas one *English* Man is allowed to be of equal intrinsick Value with twelve born in *Ireland*, we should in Justice return them a Dozen for One, to dispose of as they pleased. But to return.

As to the native Poor of this City, there would be little or no Damage in confining them to their several Parishes. For Instance; A Beggar of the Parish of St. *Warborough's*,[36] or any other Parish here, if he be an Object of Compassion, hath an equal Chance to receive his Proportion of Alms from every charitable Hand; because the Inhabitants, one or other walk through every Street in Town, and give their Alms, without considering the Place, wherever they think it may be well disposed of: And, these Helps, added to what they get in Eatables by going from House to House, among the Gentry and Citizens, will, without being very burthensome, be sufficient to keep them alive.

It is true, the Poor of the Suburb Parishes will not have altogether the same Advantage, because they are not equally in the Road of Business and Passengers:[37] But here it is to be considered, that the Beggars there have not so good a Title to Publick Charity, because most of them are Strollers

---

34 *from Chester to Dublin*: in the late seventeenth and early eighteenth centuries, the port of Chester was in decline, with commercial traffic to Ireland increasingly concentrated in Liverpool, and the passenger packet-boat leaving from Parkgate on the western side of the Wirral. From the 1660s onwards, Royal Navy yachts, provided for the government of Ireland, had sailed between Chester and Dublin, carrying ordinary passengers by arrangement: *Victoria County History, Cheshire*, ed. A. T. Thacker, B. E. Harris, C. P. Lewis *et al.*, 5 vols. so far, Oxford & Woodbridge: Oxford University Press, Boydell & Brewer, 1979-2005, vol. V, pt 1, pp. 137–45. Swift may therefore be intending to identify immigrant 'beggars' with English office-holders, who would have travelled to Ireland on the viceregal yacht.
35 *Bridewell*: a house of correction. In 1729, the old Dublin Bridewell had been demolished and a new one built near the workhouse in St James's Street (*Cal. Anc. Recs Dublin*, vol. VII, pp. 440–1).
36 *St. Warborough's*: St Werburgh's, close by St Patrick's cathedral.
37 *Passengers*: passers-by.

from the Country, and compose a principal Part of that great Nuisance, which we ought to remove.

I should be apt to think, that few Things can be more irksome to a City-Minister than a Number of Beggars which do not belong to his District, whom he hath no Obligation to take Care of, who are no Part of his Flock, and who take the Bread out of the Mouths of those, to whom it properly belongs. When I mention this Abuse to any Minister of a City-Parish, he usually lays the Fault upon the Beadles,[38] who he says are bribed by the foreign Beggars; and as those Beadles often keep Ale-Houses, they find their Account in such Customers. This Evil might easily be remedyed, if the Parishes would make some small Addition to the Salaries of a Beadle, and be more careful in the Choice of those Officers. But, I conceive there is one effectual Method, in the Power of every Minister to put in Practice; I mean, by making it the Interest of all his own original Poor, to drive out Intruders: For, if the Parish-Beggars were absolutely forbidden by the Minister and Church-Officers, to suffer Strollers to come into the Parish, upon Pain of themselves being not permitted to beg Alms at the Church-Doors, or at the Houses and Shops of the Inhabitants; they would prevent Interlopers more effectually than twenty Beadles.

And, here I cannot but take Notice of the great Indiscretion in our City-Shopkeepers, who suffer their Doors to be daily besieged by Crowds of Beggars, (as the Gates of a Lord are by Duns,)[39] to the great Disgust and Vexation of many Customers, whom I have frequently observed to go to other Shops, rather than suffer such a Persecution; which might easily be avoided, if no foreign Beggars were allowed to infest them.

Wherefore, I do assert, that the Shopkeepers who are the greatest Complainers of this Grievance, lamenting that for every Customer, they are worried by fifty Beggars, do very well deserve what they suffer, when a 'Prentice with a Horse-Whip is able to lash every Beggar from the Shop, who is not of the Parish, and doth not wear the Badge of that Parish on his Shoulder, well fastned and fairly visible; and if this Practice were universal in every House, to all the sturdy Vagrants, we should in a few Weeks clear

38 *he usually lays the Fault upon the Beadles*: parish officials. The Irish Act of 1724 'for continuing and amending an act, entitled, an act for the better regulating of the parish-watches' (10 Geo. I c. 3) had blamed the influx of vagrants into Dublin partly on the beadles' neglect of their duties: see O'Carroll, 'Contemporary Attitudes towards the Homeless Poor', p. 68.
39 *Duns*: debt-collectors, bailiffs.

the Town of all Mendicants, except those who have a proper Title to our Charity: As for the Aged and Infirm, it would be sufficient to give them nothing, and then they must starve or follow their Brethren.

It was the City that first endowed this Hospital, and those who afterwards contributed, as they were such who generally inhabited here; so they intended what they gave to be for the Use of the City's Poor. The Revenues which have since been raised by Parliament, are wholly paid by the City,[40] without the least Charge upon any other Part of the Kingdom; and therefore nothing could more defeat the original Design, than to misapply those Revenues on strolling Beggars, or Bastards from the Country, which bears no Share in the Charges we are at.

If some of the Out-Parishes be over-burthened with Poor, the Reason must be, that the greatest Part of those Poor are Strollers from the Country, who nestle themselves where they can find the cheapest Lodgings, and from thence infest every Part of the Town, out of which they ought to be whipped as a most insufferable Nuisance, being nothing else but a profligate Clan of Thieves, Drunkards, Heathens, and Whore-mongers, fitter to be rooted out of the Face of the Earth,[41] than suffered to levy a vast annual Tax upon the City, which shares too deep in the publick Miseries brought on us by the Oppressions we lye under from our Neighbours, our Brethren, our Country-men, our Fellow Protestants, and Fellow Subjects.

Some Time ago I was appointed one of a Committee to inquire into the State of the Work-house;[42] where we found that a Charity bestowed by a

---

40 *The Revenues... wholly paid by the City*: the Act of 1704 establishing the workhouse empowered the governors to raise funds by licensing hackney carriages and other carriers plying their trade in Dublin and by raising a tax on property-owners in the city; this was reaffirmed in the Act of 1728.
41 *the Face of the Earth*: Gen., 6: 7: 'And the Lord said, I will destroy man whom I have created from the face of the earth; both man, and beast, and the creeping things, and the fowls of the air; for it repenteth me that I have made them.' For another example of Swift's use of this quotation, God's announcement of the imminent great flood, see *Gulliver's Travels*, part IV, ch. ix (*CWJS*, vol. IX, p. 408), and for a discussion of the significance, see Claude Rawson, *God, Gulliver and Genocide: Barbarism and the European Imagination, 1492–1945*, Oxford: Oxford University Press, 2001, pp. 264–8.
42 *Some Time ago... State of the Work-house*: the details of this inquiry are obscure. The Irish House of Commons set up two committees of inquiry into the workhouse, one in 1725 and another in 1727, both of which produced a damning report leading to legislation (*C.J.Ire.*, vol. IV, pp. 264, 367, 450, 516) and ultimately, in 1728, the amending Act, but Swift cannot mean either of these. However, there is evidence that Archbishop King was taking a strong critical interest in the workhouse in the spring of 1726, following the failure of the

great Person for a certain Time,[43] which in its Consequences operated very much to the Detriment of the House: For, when the Time was elapsed, all those who were supported by that Charity, continued on the same Foot with the rest on the Foundation; and being generally a Pack of profligate vagabond Wretches from several Parts of the Kingdom, corrupted all the rest; so partial, or treacherous, or interested, or ignorant, or mistaken, are generally all Recommenders, not only to Employments, but even to Charity it self.

I know it is complained, that the Difficulty of driving Foreign Beggars out of the City, is charged upon the *Bellowers*[44] (as they are called) who find their Accounts best in suffering those Vagrants to follow their Trade through every Part of the Town. But, this Abuse might easily be remedyed, and very much to the Advantage of the whole City, if better Salaries were given to those who execute that Office in the several Parishes, and would make it their Interest to clear the Town of those Caterpillars,[45] rather than hazard the Loss of an Employment that would give them an honest Livelyhood. But, if that should fail, yet a general Resolution of never giving Charity to a Street Beggar out of his own Parish, or without a visible Badge, would infallibly force all Vagrants to depart.

There is generally a Vagabond Spirit in Beggars, which ought to be discouraged and severely punished. It is owing to the same Causes that drove them into Poverty, I mean, Idleness, Drunkenness, and rash Marriages, without the least Prospect of supporting a Family by honest Endeavours,

---

first amending bill (brought in by the ecclesiastical lawyer Thomas Trotter, King's vicar-general). Marsh's Library, MS Z3.1.1, contains three documents, probably from King's personal papers, relating to the workhouse: 'A list of the poore in the city work-house, from their several parishes', 20 Mar. 1725/6; 'Observations on the present state and condition of the workhouse' [a list of major donations], 6 Apr. 1726; and 'The present state of the work house' [current financial accounts], 6 Apr. 1726. In May he wrote to the lord mayor of Dublin to report the views of clergy and churchwardens whom he had canvassed on the operation of the workhouse scheme (King to Joseph Kane, 10 May 1726 (TCD, MS 750/8, p. 96)).

43 *we found... for a certain Time*: possibly Mary, Lady Lanesborough (the wife of the 2nd Viscount), who had made a donation of £200 to the workhouse in 1705: John Page to Archbishop King, 20 Jan. 1705 (Marsh's Library, MS Z3.1.1); D. W. Hayton, 'Did Protestantism Fail in Early Eighteenth-century Ireland? Charity Schools and the Enterprise of Religious and Social Reformation, c. 1690–1730', in Alan Ford, James McGuire and Kenneth Milne (eds.), *As by Law Established: The Church of Ireland since the Reformation*, Dublin: Lilliput Press, 1995, p. 173.

44 *Bellowers*: town criers.

45 *Caterpillars*: a pejorative term, indicating persons who prey on society.

which never came into their Thoughts. It is observed, that hardly one Beggar in twenty, looks upon himself to be relieved by receiving Bread or other Food; and they have in this Town been frequently seen to pour out of their Pitcher, good Broth that hath been given them, into the Kennel;[46] neither do they much regard Cloaths, unless to sell them; for their Rags are Part of their Tools with which they work: They want only Ale, Brandy, and other strong Liquors, which cannot be had without Money; and, Money as they conceive, always abounds in the Metropolis.

I had some other Thoughts to offer upon this Subject. But, as I am a Desponder in my Nature, and have tolerably well discovered the Disposition of our People, who never will move a Step towards easing themselves from any one single Grievance; it will be thought, that I have already said too much, and to little or no Purpose; which hath often been the Fate, or Fortune of the Writer.

J. SWIFT[47]

April 22, 1737.

---

46 *Kennel*: gutter.
47 *J. SWIFT*: Swift's signature at the end of the work is unusual, and complements the invocation on the title page of his own name and of the Drapier, all of which are presumably intended to enhance the impact of the pamphlet.

ASSOCIATED MATERIALS

I. Hints for Intelligencer *Papers, and* Maxims Examined

Headnote

Composed 1728–9; copy text Rylands English MS 659 (see Textual Account).

These extant manuscript notes and ideas date from 1728–9, and are part of the Piozzi papers in the John Rylands Library, Manchester (Rylands English MS 659). Included in the possible ideas for issues of the *Intelligencer*, and the origins of *Maxims Controlled in Ireland*, are incidental proverbial observations and aphorisms.

The notes and their origins are discussed by J. L. Clifford and Irvin Ehrenpreis, 'Swiftiana in Rylands English MS 659 and Related Documents', *Bulletin of the John Rylands Library* 37 (1955), 368–92.

HINTS FOR *INTELLIGENCER* PAPERS

[MSS 659 (9)]

No great matter for the bulk of women, since the Men are as foolish & ignorant.

Begin. A person of Quality a little absolute,[1] a man of tact and letters who well knew how to support his opinions, which were generally right, fell into one, which I thought he held in a sense not sufficiently limited., although he had many old proverbs and maxims on his side, which carry the authority of ages with him that women shoud only regard their Children & family &c.

---

1 *a little absolute*: possible relevant meanings would be: independent or independent-minded; positive in his opinions without harbouring reservations; authoritarian.

My practice of advising Ldys to read, and what;[2] and my way of instructing young Misses.

―――

I used to stay a month or two. the Country desolate, the Neighbourhood scarce and not very inviting.

―――

A Companion for life[3] to a man of Sense especially without Employ^mnt, and violent lover of the Country, should have a reasonable companion., who could distinguish a man of Sense &c, and relish good conversation without being talkative, positive or assuming

―――

It would make the women love home better, and able to teach their Daughters.

―――

The Lady was a considerable heiress used too fondly, live in Town had that kind of Education which is called the best, learning Italian, French, Musick and Singing, all wch she forgot &c. | fell into play, visits, assemblies[4] &c.

―――

No French Romances.[5], and few plays, for young Ladyes

―――

How hard for a woman to live solitary and not read;

―――

2 *My practice of advising Ldys to read, and what*: cf. Swift's citation, among the standard arguments used by opponents of women's education, of the allegation that 'a humour of reading books, excepting those of devotion or housewifery, is apt to turn a woman's brain', in *Of the Education of Ladies* (*CWJS*, vol. II, p. 214).
3 *A Companion for life*: cf. the description of the Lilliputian nurseries in *Gulliver's Travels*, part I, ch. vi (*CWJS*, vol. XVI, p. 91): 'For, their Maxim is, that among People of Quality, a Wife should be always a reasonable and agreeable Companion, because she cannot always be young.' Swift had also emphasised companionship in *A Letter to a Young Lady, on her Marriage* (Davis, vol. IX, pp. 89–90).
4 *assemblies*: elegant social gatherings.
5 *No French Romances*: Swift's disapproval of romances as inappropriate for young ladies (expressed, for example, in *A Letter to a Young Lady, on Her Marriage* (Davis, vol. IX, p. 89)), was extended in *Gulliver's Travels* to their being permitted as reading matter for servants, a maid of honour in the Lilliputian court having fallen asleep over a romance and allowed her mistress's apartment to catch fire (part I, ch. v: *CWJS*, vol. XVI, p. 79).

A generall inspection into family affairs right: but not to be a Hous keeper[6] &c. any more than an Architect should have his hand: in mortar.

———

I have often thanked God that custom has made it detestable otherwise, otherwise they have a good plea to keep a Gallant[7] rather than marry, I mean a great heiress, who when she is marryd can call nothing her own, & may want common necessaryes, by the churlishness of a husband &c. therefore I was never a against what they call pin-money,[8] nor see the reason why people should not part when all agreem^{nt} is desperate

———

Women I own do often want balast[9] &c. but it is often through ignorance or half knoledge.

———

A shame that not one woman in a million can properly be said to read or write, or understand.

INTELLIGEN[C]ER

[MSS 659 (10)]

Beau's dresses

———

Clergy preaching, bad Engl &c

———

Universal Knavery of all handicrafts & Shopkeepers, and in th Country of all farmers Cottagers, &c. Scotch worse than Irish, but worst when partake of both nations[1]

———

Building, and praise of Pearce[2]

6 *a Hous keeper*: one who is responsible for the running of a household.
7 *a Gallant*: a man of fashion and pleasure.
8 *pin-money*: money given by a man to his wife for personal expenses.
9 *balast*: presumably Swift is using 'ballast' to mean stability. balast] r batP *MS del.*
1 *worst when partake of both nations*: Presbyterians in Ulster, of Scottish extraction but settled in Ireland, could be said to 'partake of both nations'; otherwise, the reference must be to those of mixed parentage.
2 *Pearce*: presumably Sir Edward Lovett Pearce (1699–1733), the architect of the Dublin Parliament House, for whom see *ODNB*; *DIB*.

Improvem^{nt}, penal clause, as to time &c for Improvemnt. & preservation of trees, & their kind – abuse Squires on this head

———

Knavery the effect of poverty and oppression: they steal or cheat, as the quickest way to live, when industry is not encouraged.: therefore they do not stand on credit or y^r buying anoth^r time. Sacrifice your custom for cheating you half a Crown.

———

That great rogue Badgers[3]

———

Stuff gowns what I did, and how the weavers acted.

———

Peter Walters[4]

HINTS FOR MAXIMS EXAMINED

Not [get th] redress their grievances before they | pass their money bills. should [?] We cannot | pretend to that &c[1]

———

[Leasers[2] way of buying]

———

3 *Badgers*: hucksters: those who buy commodities (especially corn) in one place to sell in another (*OED*).
4 *Peter Walters*: Peter Walter (?1664–1746), scrivener, money-lender and steward to the Duke of Newcastle (for whom, see Howard Erskine-Hill, *The Social Milieu of Alexander Pope: Lives, Example and the Poetic Response*, New Haven & London: Yale University Press, 1975, ch. IV): a hate-figure to both Swift and Alexander Pope, who saw him as the archetype of the unscrupulous, money-grubbing parvenu 'new Whig'. In his poem 'To Mr Gay on his being steward to the duke of Queensberry' (1731), Swift described Walter as 'that rogue of genuine ministerial kind' (*Poems*, vol. II, p. 534). See also Swift's characterisation of Walter in *The Answer of the Right Honourable William Pulteney, Esq.; to the Right Honourable Sir Robert Walpole* (Davis, vol. V, p. 117), and the marginal annotation to his copy of the 1735 edition of Pope's works (*Library and Reading, I*, Vol. II, pp. 1490–2).
1 *Not [get th] . . . We cannot | pretend to that &c*: members of the English House of Commons had traditionally claimed to make the redress of grievances a prerequisite for the granting of supply, though this was honoured increasingly in the breach after 1689: *HP 1690–1715*, vol. I, p. 395.
2 *Leasers*: the MS word is hardly legible, and may read 'Leeson', a reference to the Dublin brewer and property speculator Joseph Leeson (1660–1741), for whom see above, p. 178.

[horses] [?]
───

Not so among us till we can sell them as the Africans do.³
───

Nations encourage marriage
───

The Engl contempt for absentees.
───

I speak not this from any regard to their persons.⁴
───

If they had stayd, an assembly of great revenues might have prevented some fatal events. I know their contempt well, these 30 years past &c
───

Encouraging marriage, as all wise nations did, is an appendix to th Maxim of people the riches of a Nation;⁵ we ought to discourage it. The wretches we see with children
    Maxims examnd.
    [Dearness of things] necessary for Life.   X
───

Lowness of Interest   X
───

High purchase of Land.   X
───

Buildings added to the Metropolis   X
───

People the Riches of a Nation.   X
───

Tax upon Luxury.⁶
───

3 *Not so ... Africans do*: a reference to the selling of children into slavery, a means of securing an economic return from surplus population, which in *A Modest Proposal* is considered inferior to raising children for meat (see above, p. 149).
4 *their persons*: i.e. the persons of absentees.
5 *Maxim of people the riches of a Nation*: a mercantilist precept which Swift had mimicked in *A Modest Proposal* and elsewhere: L. A. Landa, '"A Modest Proposal" and Populousness', *Modern Philology* 40 (1942), 16; and above, pp. 36, 102, 179, 313.
6 *Tax upon Luxury*: in *Maxims Controlled in Ireland*, Swift observed that 'Among all taxes imposed by the legislature, those upon luxury are universally allowed to be the most equitable and beneficial to the subject' (see above, p. 179).

326 ASSOCIATED MATERIALS

Res nolunt diu male administrari[7]

Parlmt not minding any thing printed; tis but a Pamph^{lt}

[Folly of those who argue] from Engl^d, Holl^d, &c[8]

[Whoever would write on] Bedlam,[9] that Society is a good [thing: Tis otherwise there, they would] burn th house

Accidental and unprecedented [?impedimenti][10]

[So if a Legislator] should form a Scheam for the [Governm^t of Bedlam,] and upon th Principle tht Man being [a Sociable Creatur,][11] they ought to go into Councils &c

Parlm^{nt} not minding Pamphlets, made me write this when all was over, that they may judge from effects
Nothing will do but wearing our own growth &c[12]

I have talked & writ a little on this Subject before

Nevr love our Country
  I write this on purpose when it is too late Because there is no arguing with them

7 *Res nolunt diu male administrari*: a Latin proverb, meaning 'things refuse to be mismanaged for long'. Swift wrote to Bolingbroke and Pope on 5 Apr. 1729: 'Pray will you please to take your pen, and blot out that political maxim from whatever book it is in, *Res nolunt diu male administrari*; the commonness makes me not know who is the author, but sure he must be some modern' (Woolley, *Corr.*, vol. III, p. 230). Walter Moyle, in 'An Essay on the Lacedaemonian Government' (printed in *The Whole Works of Walter Moyle, Esq* . . . , London, 1727, p. 60) noted that it was a favourite saying of Robert Harley, Earl of Oxford.
8 *[Folly of those who argue] from Engl^d, Holl^d, &c*: authors like John Browne or David Bindon, for whom see above, p. 116. Swift found this form of reasoning not only specious but also particularly irritating.
9 *Bedlam*: the Bethlem Royal Hospital (for the mentally ill) in Moorfields, London.
10 The word is not clear, hence disputed readings: Clifford and Ehrenpreis, 'Swiftiana in Rylands English MS 659 and Related Documents', 380, has 'administrari'; Davis, vol. XII, p. 309, 'impediments'.
11 *a Sociable Creatur*: the maxim that man is a sociable animal was taken from Aristotle's *Politics*. See above, p. 173.
12 *wearing our own growth &c*: wearing clothes manufactured in Ireland.

Who would live in Irelnd, without a great balance[13] The can live saving in Engl^d yet honorable, nor need invite as here,[14] & have many dishes[15]

August Assembly[16]

Lost all Idea of Liberty

Of those vermin writers too low to answer, yet lye so horridly of mere Clergy in Je. [?] London from Irl^d and that if Linnen Scarves hurt Eng^d we should not wear them, sure they are not heard. Like Rats in a house[17]

These Singularityes of Govm^{nt} have turned the very | heads of th people, made them think themselves not upon the foot with others of their own Species,[18] & | a Spirit of Servitude

I own that in Scot^{ld} & some Towns in Italy, Interest is low, & land dear, but want trade.

Bad Seasons[19] a trifle, where are they not ?

---

13 *a great balance*: a great income.
14 *invite as here*: entertain on the same scale.
15 *dishes*: courses at dinner.
16 *August Assembly*: a cliché, originating in classical descriptions of the Roman senate.
17 *Like Rats in a house*: fighting with each other: the proverbial phrase is 'like rats in a bag', and the last word in the MS is not clear.
18 *others of their own Species*: the English.
19 *Bad Seasons*: Ireland had endured bad summer weather and consequently poor harvests in four successive years, beginning in 1725, but experienced an improvement in 1729. For a detailed discussion of the repercussions for the Irish economy, see James Kelly, 'Harvests and Hardship: Famine and Scarcity in Ireland in the Late 1720s', *Studia Hibernica* 26 (1991–2), 72–94.

II. Letter to the Printer of Thoughts on the Tillage of Ireland

Headnote

Composed (and dated) 13 December 1737; published 1738; copy text 1738 (see Textual Account).

Swift's letter forms the preface to Alexander MacAulay, *Some Thoughts on the Tillage of Ireland* ..., Dublin, 1738. MacAulay (d. 1766) was an Irish MP (*Hist. Ir. Parl.*, vol. V, pp. 162–3), a civil lawyer and a judge of the Dublin consistorial court. He was also one of the executors of Swift's will; Swift left him the gold box containing the freedom of the city of Dublin that he had been given in 1730 (see above, p. 182).

MacAulay's argument in *Some Thoughts* complements Swift's earlier comments about tillage in works such as *An Answer to a Paper* (see above, pp. 27–39). Most significantly, MacAulay's pamphlet, *Property Inviolable: or, Some Remarks upon a Pamphlet Entituled, Prescription Sacred*, Dublin, 1736, had justified the rights of the clergy to claim the so-called 'tithe of agistment', which would have particularly endeared him to Swift (see Introduction, pp. lxvii–lxviii).

A LETTER TO THE PRINTER.

Mr. Faulkner,[1]

I received from you, a Manuscript, sent, as you tell me, by some unknown Hand, entitled, A Discourse upon the Tillage of Ireland;[2] of which you desire my Judgment: In Answer, I do assure you, I think it extremely well writ, and might be of the greatest Advantage to the Kingdom, if there

---

1 *Mr. Faulkner*: George Faulkner (?1703–75), Swift's publisher since 1726, for whom see the biographical entries in M. Pollard, *A Dictionary of Members of the Dublin Book Trade 1550–1800* ..., London: Bibliographical Society, 2000, pp. 198–205; *DIB*.
2 *A Discourse upon the Tillage of Ireland*: Alexander MacAulay, *Some Thoughts on the Tillage of Ireland: humbly Dedicated to the Parliament. To which is Prefixed, a Letter to the Printer, from the Reverend Doctor Swift, Dean of St. Patrick's, Recommending the Following Treatise*, Dublin, 1737.

were Virtue enough among us to follow the Author's Advice, as I heartily wish.

                      I am, Sir,
                      Your assured Friend,
                      and Servant,
                      J. SWIFT.

Deanry-House,
Dec. 13, 1737.

APPENDICES

A. The Memorial of the Poor Inhabitants, Tradesmen, and Labourers of the Kingdom of Ireland

Published in 1728, and the impetus behind Swift's *An Answer to a Paper, Called A Memorial* (above, pp. 27–39).

THE
MEMORIAL
Of the Poor INHABITANTS, TRADESMEN,
and LABOURERS of the Kingdom of IRELAND.

Most Humbly sheweth,

That last Year, 1727, there was a very great Scarcity of Bread Corn That the Grainerys were exhausted; and were it not for the Supplys from Great-Britain, many of the Poor would have perished for want of Bread,[1] which was so Dear in most Places, that Multitudes have sunk themselves so far in Debt for the support of their Familys, that they are now reduced to Beggary.

A Famine among the Poor, has often been the Occasion of Pestilential and contagious Distempers, whereby the Rich have become sharers in the general Calamity, as it happened of late in some of the Danish and Swedish Dominions,[2] and other Places.

1 *That last Year... want of Bread*: see Archbishop Boulter to the Duke of Newcastle, 7 Mar. 1727[/8] (*Boulter Letters*, vol. I, pp. 181–2); James Kelly, 'Harvests and Hardship: Famine and Scarcity in Ireland in the Late 1720s', *Studia Hibernica* 26 (1991–2), 78–9.
2 *The general Calamity... Danish and Swedish Dominions*: an outbreak of plague had occurred in Denmark and Sweden in 1710–11, aggravated by the disorder produced by the Great Northern War: Peter Christensen, 'Copenhagen 1711: Danish Authorities Facing the Plague', in Sally Sheard and Helen Power (eds.), *Body and City: Histories of Urban Public*

When Provisions fail, Trade and Industry ceases, Lands become waste; thus Landlords and Rich Men may soon be on the Level with the Poor Tennants and Cottiers.[3]

People in Extremity often Robb, Plunder and Steal, rather than Starve; so that few will Escape it's dismal Effects.

Many were forced last Year to fall too soon upon their early Corn and Potatoes; and it is certain, that by the Wetness of the Season, heavy Rains, and other Accidents, a great part of the last Year's Crop of Corn was so hungary and Weak, that there is more than a third Part wanting of the usual Product as in other Years; and it is fear'd, that encouraging Tillage for the time to come, will not relieve the present Necessities of the Poor;[4] and that the Merchants will not of themselves Import in due time, such Quantities of Grain, as may be Sufficient.

That the Price of Corn is risen so high in Great-Britain,[5] that there is no hopes of Relief from thence as formerly; and we will need many more, than was last Year imported.

There is a good Premium offered for Exportation of Corn out of Great-Britain, and there is something allowed to that Purpose in this Kingdom, in favour of Tillage, when Corn is very Cheap.[6]

Surely, there is as much Reason for this Nation to give a Premium for its Importation for a few Months, now in the time of Scarcity, until the Danger of a Famine be over: It is good to provide in Time, considering that the

---

Health, Aldershot: Ashgate, 2000, pp. 50–8; Christensen, '"In These Perilous Times": Plague and Plague Policies in Early Modern Denmark', *Medical History* 47 (2003), 443–5.

3 *Cottiers*: agricultural labourers, occupying a cottage and working a small plot of land in return for labour services.

4 *encouraging Tillage... Necessities of the Poor*: in advance of the calling of the Irish Parliament in 1727, the Irish privy council had prepared a bill 'For regulating abuses committed in the buying and selling of corn and for increase of tillage', but this had been suppressed by the British privy council; a second bill, 'For regulating abuses committed in the buying and selling of corn and for increase of tillage' was prepared by the council during the session of 1727–8 and eventually passed into law as 1 Geo. II c. 10 [Ire.].

5 *the Price of Corn is risen so high in Great-Britain*: in early January 1728, wheat was fetching 36s to 46s a quarter in London, in the following June 40s to 50s, and at the end of August, 38s to 40s, as compared with 26s to 38s in August of the previous year (*Gloucester Journal*, 9 Jan., 4 June, 27 Aug. 1728; 1 Aug. 1727).

6 *There is a good Premium... when Corn is very Cheap*: an English Act of 1689 (1 Will. & Mary c. 12) provided for the payment of a bounty on corn exported when the price fell below 48s a quarter. It is noteworthy that Archbishop Boulter, in recommending to the British ministry in February and March 1728 the Tillage Bill prepared by the Irish privy council, noted specifically that it sought to encourage arable farming by setting a minimum of land to be ploughed, not by offering a premium on the export of crops (Boulter to Newcastle, 24 Feb., 7 Mar. 1727[/8]: *Boulter Letters*, vol. I, pp. 177, 181).

Winds do not always serve to bring in our Ships when there is Occasion for them.

It is certain, that the Price of Corn, is now Risen higher, than ever it was known to be,[7] so early in the Year; especially, in many of the Country Villages, which increases the fears and Crys of the Poor; who cannot gain by their Labour, what will feed them and their Familys.

There is plenty of Corn in our Plantations abroad, and in some of our neighbouring Countries; so that if a Premium of about two Shillings per Barrel of Wheat, & c, and some ease in the Duty was allowed in due Time, it would encourage Merchants and others to turn themselves that way; Ten thousand Pounds, which is no heavy Sum upon a whole Nation under such Circumstances, would by good Management be sufficient to encourage the Importation of One hundred thousand Barrels, which destributed by prudent Managers into the Ports nearest to the Places where there is the greatest Necessity, under proper Restrictions, would (under God) be a means to prevent the great Danger that threatens Us; then the Rich Farmers, the Ingrosers,[8] and such as keep up their Grain, hearing of a Supply from abroad, would find it convenient to be selling off their Stores at the current Price, so the Markets would in a great Measure be kept down; Perhaps a lesser Premium per Barrel would be Sufficient, then more Corn (if needfull) may be imported.

To raise a Fund for this charitable Use, if a further Tax was laid upon Tea, Coffee, Sugar, Spices, Wine, foreign Cloaths, and other foreign Things, as are chiefly for the use of the Great and Wealthy,[9] or on any Thing whatsoever, whereby the Money would be advanced on this pressing Occasion. That it may be considered how strange and suprizing it would be in foreign Parts to hear that the Poor was Starving in a rich Country,[10] where such immence Sums were daily laid out on several Occasions, where there was timely warning, even to a Demonstration of the approaching Danger.

And there are presidents of Money being rais'd to prevent eminent Dangers. These and all other Things are most humbly submitted to the great Care and Wisdom of those in Power and Trust in this Nation.

7 *the Price of Corn... than ever it was known to be*: between 1726 and 1727, the price of grain in Ireland had risen by 140 per cent (Kelly, 'Harvests and Hardship', p. 78).
8 *Ingrosers*: engrossers, monopolists.
9 *a further tax... Great and Wealthy*: for Swift's attitude to the vice of 'luxury', and the possibility of sumptuary laws to repress it, see above, pp. 179–80.
10 *That it may be considered... in a rich Country*: a central theme of Swift's writings in this period was that Ireland was in fact much poorer than other economic writers (such as Sir John Browne) asserted: see Ferguson, pp. 145–8, and above, Introduction, pp. xxxvii, xlii–xliii.

May it therefore please you to consider this Case, and as you find proper, to recommend to his Excellency, the Lord Lieutenant and Council, and to the Right Honourable the Lords and Commons in Parliament.

B. *The Craftsman's First Letter of Advice, Saturday 7 November 1730*

The issue of the journal that was the origin of Swift's *The Answer to the Craftsman* (above, pp. 218–27).

CRAFTSMAN's First Letter of *ADVICE*,

To the People of GREAT-BRITAIN, and IRELAND, with Respect to some *French-Officers* being arrived in that Kingdom, in order to raise Recruits, for his *Gallick* Majesty.

By CALEB D'ANVERS of *Gray's Inn*, Esq.; Saturday *November 7th.* 1730

The following Article, which hath lately appeared in the News-Papers,[1] deserveth our immediate Consideration, *viz.*

"THEY write from *Dublin*, that an Officer from every Regiment in the *French* Service is arrived there, in order to raise Recruits for their respective Corps;[2] which is not to be done in a *clandestine Manner* as formerly, when several Persons suffer'd Death for it, but *publickly*. These Gentlemen are to disperse themselves into the several Counties, where They have the *best Interest*;[3] and a *Field Officer*[4] is to reside constantly at *Dublin*, to hear all Complaints, which may be made by any of the Recruits against their Officers; and also to prepare for sending them off – Count *Broglio*[5] hath been solliciting an Order, to this Purpose, these two Years."[6]

1 *News-papers*] New-papers, *1731.*
2 *respective Corps*: as a concession designed to forward Walpole's diplomatic initiatives in Europe, the British government had granted permission to the French to recruit up to 750 men in Ireland. See above, pp. lx, 146, 221.
3 *where They have the best Interest*: the officers were themselves Irish Catholics.
4 *a Field Officer*: one ranked higher than a captain (but lower than a general).
5 *Count Broglio*: François-Marie de Broglie (1671–1745), comte (and later duc) de Broglie, French envoy in Britain.
6 *"THEY write from Dublin ... these two Years."*: a report to this effect, dated 10 Oct., but worded differently, appeared in the *Daily Courant*, 20 Oct. 1730, and was picked up in other English newspapers.

When I first read this Account in the publick Prints, I look'd upon it as a common Piece of *false Intelligence*, and was in full Expectation of seeing it contradicted in the next Day's Papers, according to frequent Custom; but having since heard it confidently affirm'd to be true, (although I can hardly believe it; especially, as to *every Part*) the Duty, which I owe my *Country*, and my Zeal for the *present Establishment* oblige me to take some Notice of an Affair, which I apprehend to be of very great Importance to *both*.

It will be necessary, in the first Place, to give the Reader a short Account of the Nature of *these Troops*, as They are now established in *France*.

They consist, as we have been infor'ed, of one Regiment of *Horse*, and five Regiments of *Foot*, all *doubly* or *trebly Officer'd*;[7] so that They are, of Themselves, a very considerable Body of Men.

But their *Number* is the least Point to be consider'd in this Affair. There are other Circumstances, which render *these Troops* infinitely more formidable to *Great Britain*. They are not only all *Roman-Catholicks*, but the most dangerous of that Communion, with respect to us. I mean *Roman-Catholick Subjects of our own Dominions*; many of whom have been oblig'd to fly their native Country, on Account of *Rebellions* or *Conspiracies*, in which They have been engag'd; and all of them, devoted by Inclination, by Interest, by Conscience, by every Motive human and divine, to the Service of the *Pretender*, in Opposition to the *Protestant Succession in his Majesty's Royal Family*.

To This We may add, that They are generally esteem'd the best Forces in the *French Service*; that They have always behav'd Themselves as such in the late Wars;[8] and are commanded by *Officers* of approv'd Courage, as well as great Skill and Experience in military Affairs.

It is said likewise, that the *Serjeants, Corporals* and *private Men*, are so well seasoned to Danger, and expert in their Duty, that by a gradual Promotion, They could furnish *Officers* for a very formidable Army, in case of any sudden Invasion or Insurrection.

---

7 *They consist... all doubly or trebly Officer'd*: since 1715, the Irish infantry regiments had been reduced from six to five, under the command in 1730 of the Duke of Berwick, Lord Clare, Arthur Dillon, and Colonels Lee and Roth. In addition, there was a single cavalry regiment, commanded by Christopher Nugent: David Murphy, *The Irish Brigades, 1685–2006: A Gazetteer of Irish Military Service, Past and Present*, Dublin: Four Courts Press, 2007, pp. 10–28.

8 *in the late Wars*: the War of the League of Augsburg or Nine Years' War (1688–97), the War of the Spanish Succession (1702–13) and the War of the Quadruple Alliance (1718–20), in which only Berwick's regiment had participated (Murphy, *Irish Brigades*, p. 24).

In the next Place, it will not be improper to examine this Affair with Regard to our *Laws*.

It is made *Felony*, by Act of Parliament in *Ireland*, for any Subject of that Kingdom to inlist Himself, or to inlist others, in the Service of any *foreign State*;[9] and it is well known that Multitudes of poor Wretches have suffer'd *Death* upon that Account.

We know it may be said, that a Power is reserv'd to his Majesty, by a Clause in *that Act*, to dispense with it, by granting any *foreign Prince* a Licence to raise Forces in his *Dominions*, and indemnifying his Subjects from the Penalties of the *Law*.

Though it is far from my Intention to dispute any of his Majesty's *legal Prerogatives*, or to call the Wisdom of the *Legislature* in Question; yet I must take the Liberty to observe, that *such Powers* have been sometimes granted out of Complaisance to the *Crown*, that the Prince's Hands may not be absolutely ty'd up, and in full Confidence that They will never be exerted but for the Benefit of *this Nation*, or possibly of some *Protestant Ally*, upon great Emergencies of State. The Exercise of the *Prerogative*, in these Cases, is therefore meerly a *prudential* Part, which is left to the Discretion of the *Prince* and his *Minister*, who has the sole Management of these Affairs; and therefore how ridiculous would it be to send to the *Attorney-General* for his Opinion in such a Case, who can be a competent Judge of nothing but the *Legality* of it, and whether the Affair be *Actionable* or not; but *Ministers* ought to regulate their Conduct, in these Respects, according to the Situation of Affairs, and the Exigencies of Government.

I must therefore beg Leave to consider the present Subject, of the *Irish Forces*, in this Light.

It will not be deny'd, I presume, that a Licence to recruit *Roman-Catholick* Regiments of *English* Subjects, in *Foreign* Service, and in the Interest of the *Pretender* to the Crown, (which is *Death* by the *Law*, without his Majesty's Permission) is a Favour of a very extraordinary Nature, and ought to be attended with some extraordinary Circumstances. – I confess that I can see no such extraordinary Circumstances at present; unless it should be said that *this Favour* was granted, in order to engage our *good Allies* in the Demolishing of *Dunkirk*;[10] but I hope they have more Generosity, than to insist upon such

---

9 *It is made Felony... foreign State*: by the British Act of 1722 (8 Geo. I c. 9), 'For amending an act, entitled, for the better and more effectual apprehending and transporting felons and others... and also to prevent the enlisting of his majesty's subjects to serve as soldiers in foreign service, without his majesty's licence'.

10 *this Favour... Demolishing of Dunkirk*: the Treaty of Utrecht had required the French to remove the fortifications at Dunkirk, but since 1725 these had been restored, a grievance

hard Terms for the effectual Performance of that, which they are obliged by *Treaty* to do. I am sure, such Conditions seem unreasonable on *our Part*, after we have made them so many other Concessions; particularly with relation to the *Flag* and *Santa Lucia*;[11] which, I think, are sufficient to make them comply with all our Demands, without expecting any farther Favours, and even Superogations of Friendship.

Perhaps my *Adversaries* (if they have any Conceit) may take an Opportunity of ridiculing me for writing in this Strain; but as it sometimes serves their Turn to make me a *great Man*, and to argue against me as such, I will for once suppose myself so; and, methinks, if I had the Honour of being but half an Hour in that Station, I could reason against such an Order, for the Good of my King and my Country, in the following Manner:

1. *These Troops* have always been made Use of, whenever there hath been any Attempt in Favour of the *Pretender*; and indeed, they are, upon many Accounts, the fittest for this Purpose. They are our Fellow-Subjects; they speak our Language; are acquainted with our Manners; and do not raise that Aversion in the People, which they naturally conceive against *other foreign Troops*, who understand neither. – I am afraid I may add, that they are kept up, for *this Purpose*, in *intire Regiments*, without suffering them to be mix'd with the Troops of any *other Nation*. It is well known, at least, that they supplied the late King *James* with a Nursery of Soldiers, who were always ready for his Service, whenever any Opportunity offer'd itself for his Restoration; and that, at this Time, the *Pretender* is always the Bait made use of by their Officers to raise Recruits. They never mention the King of *France*, or the King of *Spain*, upon these Occasions, but list the poor Wretches under an Assurance that they are enter'd into the Service of *Him*, whom they call their *natural* and *rightful* King. – I will not suspect the present Fidelity of *France*, and their Cordiality to the

---

which British representatives in Paris had been pressing since 1727. The French ministry had eventually responded early in 1730 with assurances that the work had been undertaken without Louis XV's knowledge and would be demolished, though this was not enough to prevent complaints by the parliamentary opposition at Westminster, leading in March to a House of Commons inquiry: Jeremy Black, *The Collapse of the Anglo-French Alliance 1727–1731*, Gloucester: Alan Sutton, 2004, pp. 166–9.

11 *we have made... Santa Lucia*: festering grievances over the refusal of French naval captains to acknowledge the flag of Royal Navy ships, even in British ports, and the dispute between the British and French for control of the island of St Lucia in the Lesser Antilles, the right to ownership of which was 'obscure and contested': Jeremy Black, *Parliament and Foreign Policy in the Eighteenth Century*, Cambridge: Cambridge University Press, 2004, p. 59.

Protestant Establishment;[12] yet methinks we might easily excuse ourselves from furnishing them with *Instruments*, which they may employ against us, whenever *Ambition*, or *Reason of State* shall dissolve their present Engagements, and induce them to espouse the Cause of the *Pretender* again.

2. It is very probable that his *Catholick Majesty*[13] (who hath likewise several Regiments of *this Kind* in his Service) will expect the same Favour in recruiting them in *Ireland*; and that he may, in case of Refusal, make it a Pretence, at any Time, for quarrelling with us, interrupting our Commerce, and disturbing us again in the Possession of *Gibraltar*; and here it is proper just to take Notice, that *these Troops* did his *Catholick Majesty* the most eminent Service in the last Siege of that important Place.[14] – He may complain, perhaps, of our Partiality to *France*, and alledge that we do not treat *Spain*, in the same Manner we expect to be treated by them, as *one of the most favour'd Nations*.

3. The Kingdom of *Ireland* seems, at this Time, in a very ill Condition to admit of any such Draughts out of her Dominions. She hath been already so much exhausted by the voluntary Transportation of Multitudes of her Inhabitants, (who have been prevailed upon, by the Encouragements promis'd them abroad, to transport themselves into other Parts of the World) that the Interposition of *Parliament* was found necessary to put a Stop to it;[15] and shall We suffer any foreign Power to drain her still farther under such Circumstances; especially in this Manner, and for this Purpose? – I do not hear that this Licence is confined to any particular Number of Men.

It is confess'd, I think, that They want above *Two Thousand Men* to compleat their Corps; and who knoweth but They may design to raise a great many more than they care to own; or even, to form some *new Regiments* of these Troops? But supposing they are confined to a *certain*

---

12 *I will not suspect... to the Protestant Establishment*: in fact, diplomatic relations between France and Britain were shifting. During Britain's recent conflict with Spain, France and Britain had been allies, with Austria supporting Spain, but following the cessation of hostilities the French and Spanish monarchies moved closer together. In the Treaty of Vienna of 1731, Britain made a new alliance with Austria, which prompted the conclusion of a formal Franco-Spanish agreement.
13 *his Catholick Majesty*: the King of Spain.
14 *the last Siege of that important Place*: the British garrison at Gibraltar had been besieged by the Spanish between February and June 1727.
15 *She hath been already... put a Stop to it*: a reference to the emigration of Protestants (mostly Presbyterians) from the north of Ireland to the north American colonies, for which see above, p. 95.

Number of Recruits, and that *Ireland* were in a Capacity to spare them; it is well known how easily such Limitations are evaded, and how difficult it is to know when People conform exactly to the Terms of their Commission. This was sufficiently explained in the late, famous Controversy, concerning Mr. *Wood's* Patent for supplying *Ireland* with a particular Sum of *Copper Half Pence*; and the Arguments upon *that Subject* may be applied to *This*, with some Allowances for the Difference between the two Cases. – It may, perhaps, be said likewise, that all the Vigilance of the Ministry hath been hitherto found ineffectual to prevent the *French* from *clandestinely* recruiting these Regiments with *Irish* Catholicks; and, therefore, that we may as well allow them to do it openly; nay, that it is our Interest to let them purge *Ireland* of her *Popish* Inhabitants as much as they please; but I deny This for several Reasons, which I shall mention presently; and if it were really the Case, that the *French* can at any Time recruit these Troops *clandestinely*, I cannot see any Reason why they should solicit an *Order* so pressingly, for *two Years* together, to do it *openly*, unless they have some other *Design*. – Ought not even this Consideration to put us, at least, a little upon our Guard; and is it not a tacit Confession, that *these Troops* are thought to be of more Importance to *Them* than *We* ought to wish. – Besides, are We to licence and authorise a *mischievous Practice*, because we cannot *totally prevent* it? – Every Body justly applauded his Majesty's singular Firmness and Resolution in supporting the Rights of his *German Subjects*, when an Attempt was made to seduce some of them into the King of *Prussia's* Service,[16] although perhaps it is impossible to prevent that Practice intirely. We all remember that the inlisting a *Miller's Son*, and a few other ordinary Peasants, occasion'd such a Misunderstanding between the two Crowns, as proceeded almost to a Rupture. Nor was the Zeal of the *English Parliament* backward on this Occasion; but, on this Consideration, amongst others, resolved to keep up a Body of 12000 *Hessian* Troops in our Pay, which have already cost us above a *Million* of Money.[17] I am confident, therefore, that the same paternal Care will always influence his Majesty to guard and protect his

16 *Every Body justly applauded . . . the King of Prussia's Service*: a decision by Frederick William I of Brandenburg-Prussia to authorise his agents to operate in other German states, including Hanover, had so outraged George II that he had retaliated in July 1729 by ordering the arrest of the Prussian recruiting officers, provoking a crisis between the two powers which threatened war.
17 *Nor was the Zeal . . . a Million of Money*: the cost of employing Hessian troops was a particular grievance of the English parliamentary opposition, and on 4 February 1730 the House of Commons at Westminster had voted that the estimate for 12,000 Hessian troops be referred to the committee of supply, in a division that gave rise to a published division list: *HP 1715–54*, vol. 1, pp. 42, 128–9.

British Subjects in the same Manner; and if any Measure should be taken, which favours too much of the *French Interest*, and seems of dangerous Consequence to the Interest of *his Family*, the World can impute it to nothing, but the deceitful Representations of *Those*, who lye under such particular Obligations to the Court of *France*, that They can refuse them nothing.

4. Such a *Licence* seems to give Encouragement to the People of *Ireland*, to continue *Roman Catholicks*; since they are sure to meet with a Provision both in the *French* and *Spanish Service*; whereas We always reject them in *our Troops*, and absolutely prohibit our Officers to recruit in *Ireland*. Now, though it may not be safe to trust them in our Armies; yet certainly We ought not to give the least Encouragement to their entering into *foreign Service*; especially into such compact Bodies as *these Regiments*; and here it will not be amiss, to relate a Story much to the Honour of an *English Nobleman*, who hath also, one of the Largest Estates in *Ireland*, of any Man in the Kingdom.[18] When he went to visit the *Invalides*[19] in *France*, a Place in the Nature of our *Chelsea College*[20] here, all the *Irish* Officers and Soldiers of that Hospital drew out in a Body to do him particular Honours. We can make no Question that their chief View was to have some *Present* from his Lordship; but though he hath an *Heart* as well disposed to generous Charity as any Man, and a *Purse* well able to answer the Dictates of it; yet out of Regard to his Country, for which he seems to have the utmost Respect, he was pleased to return them the following Answer, "Gentlemen, I am very sensible of the Honour you have done me, and heartily pity your Misfortunes; but as you have drawn them upon your selves, by *serving against your Country*, you must not expect any Relief, or Reward from *me*, for having suffer'd in a Service, in which I wish you had never engaged."

5. Is there not some Reason to apprehend that *this Licence* may, at one Time or other, prove a Snare to that Country, and draw many People into their Destruction; for, unless it is made *perpetual*, can it be suppos'd that all the poor, ignorant Wretches in the Kingdom, should be appris'd how long *this Licence* is to be in Force; or when they may list with *Impunity*, and when they may not? Besides, as it may be presum'd that *these Officers* will never go, for the future, upon such Errands, without some *pretended*

---

18 *an English Nobleman . . . in the Kingdom*: presumably Richard Boyle (1694–1753), 3rd Earl of Burlington, the virtuoso and architect, who had visited Paris several times, most recently in 1726.
19 *the Invalides*: the (Hôpital des) Invalides, established by Louis XIV in Paris in 1670 as a hospital for elderly and infirm soldiers.
20 *Chelsea College*: the Royal Hospital.

Orders, when the *real One* is expired; so they will find it no difficult Matter to impose such a Counterfeit upon illiterate People; who may thus incur the Penalties of the *Law*, without knowing any Thing of the Matter – Such a Method of providing for Persons, whose Principles render them unserviceable in *our Army*, is indeed a little more charitable than a *late Project* for preventing *Irish Children* from being starved, by fatting them up and selling them to the Butcher.[21]

6. I have often heard that *these Troops* have been made use of, in Parliament, as an Argument for keeping up a *standing Army* in *England*; and I think We need not take any Measures to render that *Argument* stronger. – God knows, there are too many Arguments always ready upon *such Occasions*.

I might insist upon some other Points, which this Affair naturally suggests to a considering Mind; particularly the Danger of suffering several *bigotted*, *Irish Papists*, in *foreign Service*, to disperse Themselves into those Counties, where they have the *best Interest*, and to stroll about *Ireland*[22] amongst their Relations and old Acquaintance, of the *same Principles* with Themselves – Are We sure that They will not make a bad Use of this Liberty, by enquiring into the Strength of their *Party*; by giving them *Hopes*, and taking an Opportunity to concert Measures for the Advantage of their *Cause*? Have We no Reason to apprehend that They may endeavour to raise *Seamen*, as well as *Soldiers*, under Colour of *this Order*; or engage great Numbers of their Countrymen to transport themselves over to the *French Colonies* and *Plantations* in the *West-Indies*, which are already grown formidable to the trading Interest of *Great Britain* in *those Parts*?

But whatever may be the Motives to such an *extraordinary Favour*, or the Consequence of it, I am sure it is the strongest Mark of our Confidence in *France*, and such a one as, I believe, They would not place in us, upon any Occasion – I will illustrate this by a parallel Case.

The *French Protestants*, who fled over hither from a Persecution, on Account of Religion,[23] never discovered any Principles, which are incompatible with the Civil Government of *France*, nor ever set up any *Pretender* to the *present Royal Family* of that Kingdom; and yet, if We should think fit to form any considerable Number of them into *compleat, distinct Regiments*, to be composed of *French Protestants* only, and commanded by

---

21 *a late Project . . . selling them to the Butcher*: *A Modest Proposal*.
22 *to stroll about Ireland*: the verb 'to stroll' also carried a pejorative meaning, implying the lack of any settled habitation, and was applied to itinerant beggars. The usage was picked up from *A Modest Proposal* (see above, p. 146).
23 *The French Protestants . . . on Account of Religion*: the Huguenots who left France after the revocation of the Edict of Nantes in 1685, for a refuge abroad.

French Officers, without any Incorporation of *British Soldiers*; I fancy it would give our *good Allies*[24] some Umbrage. But I am almost confident that they would never permit us to send over a *Protestant French Officer* from every Regiment, to recruit their respective Corps, by dispersing themselves into those Provinces, where They have the *best Interest*; or suffer a *Field Officer*, in *English* Pay, to reside constantly in *Paris*, and exercise a Sort of martial Law in the Capital of their Dominions; I say they would hardly suffer this, even tho' *our Ambassador* should solicit such an Order, with the utmost Application, for twenty Years together.

And yet the Case of these *Irish Forces* is much stronger with respect to *Us*. They do not differ with us only in Matters of Religion; but hold Principles, absolutely destructive of our *civil Government*; and are generally look'd upon abroad, as a *standing Army*, kept on Foot to serve the *Pretender* upon any Occasion.

I must ask a Question or two, which naturally offer themselves in this Place.

What Power is this *Field Officer* to exercise during his Residence in *Dublin*? – Is the *French martial Law* to take Place, if any of these *Recruits* should happen to repent of what they have done, and think fit to *desert*?

Troops are generally *arm'd* as soon as they are listed – Is this Rule to be observ'd in the present Case? If so, another Question occurs. – It hath been found necessary, for the Security of *Ireland*, to restrain all *Roman Catholicks* from wearing, or keeping any *Arms* in their Houses.[25] I ask, therefore, whether the Authority of *this Licence* is to supersede the *Laws of the Land*? – I may go farther.

The Garrison of *Dublin* seldom consisteth of above 800 Men, for the Duty of the Place. – Supposing double that Number of *Popish Recruits* should be brought thither, in order to be view'd by their Field Officer; will it be said that there is no just Apprehension of Danger? – But as these Suggestions may appear to be founded on the Infidelity of *France* (a Case not to be suppos'd at present)[26] I will press them no farther.

I must however repeat it, that this *Order* is the fullest Demonstration of the *Confidence* we repose in them; and I hope they will scorn to make any bad Use of it; but if it were possible to suspect that they could have any Design to play the Knave with us, they could not wish for a better Opportunity to promote it than by such a *Power*, as is now said to be put into their Hands.

24 *our good Allies*: ironical: see above, pp. 335–7.
25 *It hath been found necessary... Arms in their Houses*: by the Disarming Act of 1695 (7 Will. III c. 5 [Ire.]).
26 *a Case not to be suppos'd at present*: another ironical reference to deteriorating Anglo-French relations.

I hope my Remarks on this *Article of News* will not be construed in a *Jacobite Sense*, even by the most prostitute Scribblers of the present Times; but I must beg Leave to expostulate a little with the Publick, on that mean and infamous Practice, which *these Writers* have lately used, in explaining some of my Papers into treasonable Libels; taking an Occasion from hence to appear formally in Defence of the *Throne*, and laying it down, as a Point granted, that there is an actual, concerted Design, of setting aside the *present Establishment*. This is a Practice, which may be of great Service to the *real Enemies* of the present Government; and every *Jacobite* in the Kingdom may make Use of it to publish the most *explicit Invectives* on the King and his Government, under the Pretence of interpreting the *implicit Design* of other Writings. It is a Practice, which was never allow'd of till now, and ought never to be allow'd; for whatever may be the *secret Meaning* of any Author, *such Explanations* are certainly *Libels*, which may have a very bad Effect upon weak Minds, and are punishable by the *Laws*, without any extraordinary Methods of Construction. – These *Writers* ought to remember the Case of Sir *Richard Steele*, who published the *Pretender's Declaration*, at the Beginning of the late Reign, with an *Answer* annex'd; and though he did it with a very good Design, yet it was universally allow'd to be contrary to *Law*; and, if his Principles of Loyalty had not been very well known, might have involved him in a severe Prosecution.[27] – I shall make no Reflections on *those*, who encourage such scandalous *Explanations*; and *those*, who are hired to do it, are beneath my Notice. Let them empty all the trite Common-Places of *servile, injudicious Flattery*, and endeavour to make their Court by such *nauseous, dishonest Adulation*, as, I am sure, gives the most Offence to *those Persons*, to whom it is paid. – Let them throw as much foul Dirt at *me* as they please; and charge me with Designs, which never enter'd into my Thoughts, and cannot justly be imputed to me from any Part of my Conduct. – God knows my Heart, I am as zealous for the Welfare of the *present Royal Family* as the most sordid of *these Sycophants*. – I am sensible that our Happiness dependeth on the Security of his *Majesty's Title*, and the Preservation of the *present Government*, upon *those Principles*, which established them, at the late *glorious Revolution*; and which, I hope, will continue to actuate the Conduct

27 *These Writers... in a severe Prosecution*: Sir Richard Steele (1672–1729), Whig writer and politician. The landing of the Pretender in Scotland in January 1716 had been marked by the issuing of a printed 'Declaration' on his behalf. Steele immediately produced a response, *The British Subject's Answer, to the Pretender's Declaration* (originally published as no. 5 of *Town Talk* and reissued separately), which included a copy of the original Declaration (*The Correspondence of Richard Steele*, ed. Rae Blanchard, Oxford: Clarendon Press, 1941, p. 311).

of *Britons* to the latest Generations. These have always been my *Principles*; and whoever will give himself the Trouble of looking over the Course of these Papers, will be convinced that *they have been* my Guide: But I am a blunt, plain-dealing, old Man, who am not afraid to speak the *Truth*; and as I have no Relish for Flattery myself, I scorn to bestow it on others. I have not however, been sparing of *just Praise*, nor slipt any seasonable Opportunity to distinguish the royal Virtues of their *present Majesties*. – More than this I cannot do; and more than this, I hope, will not be expected. – Some of my Expressions, perhaps, may have been thought too rough and unpolished for the Climate of a *Court*; but they flow'd purely from the Sincerity of my Heart; and the Freedom of my Writings hath proceeded from my Zeal, for the Interest of my King and my Country.

With Regard to my *Adversaries*, I will leave every impartial Reader to judge whether, even in *private Life*, that Man is not most to be depended upon, who being inwardly convinced of the great and good Qualities of his Friend, never loadeth him with *fulsome Flatteries*, but taketh the honest Liberty of warning him against the Measures of *those* who are endeavouring to mislead him. – The Case is much stronger in *publick Life*; and a *Crown* is beset with so many Difficulties, that even a Prince of the most *consummate Wisdom* is not always sufficiently guarded against the Dangers which surround him, from the Stratagems of *artful Ministers*, or the Blunders of *weak ones*. Both of them may be equally *bad Ministers*, and pursue the *same Methods* of supporting themselves, by flattering him into *Measures*, which tend to his Destruction.

But it is Time to draw to a Conclusion; and I can only add, that if I were really engaged in any Design, contrary to the Interest of the *present Establishment*, I should have sate down contented, and secretly rejoyced at the *Affair*, which occasioned this Paper, instead of giving myself and the Reader so much Trouble.

C. D.[28]

---

28 *C. D.*: Caleb D'anvers, the pseudonymous author of *The Craftsman*, was a composite identity. The principal authors were in fact Nicholas Amhurst, William Pulteney and Henry St John, Viscount Bolingbroke, working either individually or together. Allocation of responsibility for individual contributions has been a subject of much controversy, in particular over the usefulness of the initial or initials customarily appended to each issue. Isaac Kramnick (*Bolingbroke and His Circle: The Politics of Nostalgia in the Age of Walpole*, Cambridge, MA: Harvard University Press, 1968, pp. 273–4) considered 'the game of "initialmanship"' to be ultimately futile. Simon Varey has since suggested that 'C' may indicate Amhurst, 'D' Pulteney, and a combination of these letters a collaboration between the two: Lord Bolingbroke, *Contributions to The Craftsman*, ed. Simon Varey, Oxford: Clarendon Press, 1982, pp. xxiii–xxiv.

C. The Case of the Woollen Manufacturers

The 1733 broadsheet that produced Swift's *Observations Occasion'd by Reading a Paper* (above pp. 288–92).

The CASE of the *Woolen* Manufacturers of the City of *Dublin*, and Liberties thereunto adjoyning, truly stated.

To the Nobility, and Gentlemen, and other Well-wishers to the Happiness and Prosperity of this Kingdom.

Cari sunt Parentes, cari Liberi, Propinqui, Familiares; sed omnes omnium Caritates Patria una complexa est. Tul. Offic. Cap. xvii.[1]

Nothing is more apparent, at the first View, than that the Employment of the Hands of the Poor, in any Nation, in some useful Manufacture, is highly conducive to the Welfare and Happiness of that Nation: There is an Interest attends it, which diffuses itself through the whole Community; because, by this Means, the remitting of several Sums of Money to other Countries, in order to be furnished with Conveniencies, is prevented; which helps to keep the Ballance of Trade[2] as it should be.

Whereas, if the Imports of a Nation be more than its Exports, the Ballance of Trade must be consequently against it; which, in Time, will consume its Vitals, as it drains, by Degrees, its Substance from it.

Nothing is also more apparent, than that the greater the Encouragement is, which is given to the Consumption of any Manufacture, the greater Improvement will be made in that Manufacture; Poverty, and the Consequence of this, the Want of sufficient Materials, being grand Impediments in the Way of any Business.

---

1 *Cari... complexa est*: Cicero, *De officiis*, I, 57–8: 'Parents are dear; dear are children, relatives, friends; but one native land embraces all our loves.'
2 *Ballance of Trade*: a phrase in common use on both sides of the Irish Sea. In Ireland, it may be found, for example, in John Browne, *Seasonable Remarks on Trade with Some Reflections on the Advantages that Might Accrue to Great Britain by a Proper Regulation of the Trade of Ireland*, Dublin, 1728, pp. 18, 42, 64; Browne, *A Reply to the Observer on Seasonable Remarks*, Dublin, 1728, p. 14; 'Isaac Broadloom, clothier', *The Hue and Cry of the Poor of Ireland for Small Change*, Dublin, 1731, p. 6; *The Drapier Reviv'd: or, Considerations on the Inconveniences which the People of Ireland Labour under for the Want of Small Change*, Dublin, 1731, p. 6; [?Sir Richard Cox], *Some Observations on the Present State of Ireland, Particularly with Relation to the Woollen Manufacture*, Dublin, 1731, p. 5; and very frequently in Prior, *Absentees*, and Dobbs, *Essay*, and *Essay*, pt 2.

C. THE CASE OF THE WOOLLEN MANUFACTURERS 345

This, your late Experience has fully proved to be true, since you were pleased to enter into that noble Agreement to countenance our Undertakings, and encourage the Industry of your own Poor.[3]

Every Thing was going on successfully with us, and we thought ourselves extremely happy in your Benevolence; but there is a Storm now rising, which, we are greatly afraid, will turn all that Happiness we proposed to our selves into Misery; our Sun will soon set in Darkness, unless we can perswade you to interpose in our Behalf, and hinder our impending Ruin.

No doubt, ye are surprized at this, and cannot imagine what can alarm us now: But, the Custom-House Entries[4] will soon discover the Occasion of it.

There it will appear, that too many make their own particular Interest the Measure of all their Actions, and care not how many starve, and perish, so they can but fill their own Pockets, and compleat their mercenary Projects.

There it will appear, that a vile, base, private Spirit reigns in the Hearts of many Woollen-Drapers in this City; who, this Moment, are endeavouring to sacrifice that Branch of Trade to their Avarice and Ambition.

As we maintain a good Cause, the Cause of our Country, we are neither afraid, or ashamed to let you know their Names.

The Principal then of them, are these following, viz. Mr. *Hinde*,[5] and Mess. *Bradshaw* and *Company*,[6] in *Castle-street*; Mr. *Dobson*,[7]

---

3 *that noble Agreement... your own Poor*: possibly a reference to the bill attempted in the Irish House of Commons in November 1731 to require the use of domestically produced woollens for the burial of 'all persons'; this was reintroduced in December 1733 and passed into law in the following year as 7 Geo. II c. 13 [Ire.] (*C.J.Ire.*, vol. VI, pp. 96, 315). In December 1733, one of the MPs for Dublin, Humphrey French (for whom, see above, pp. xcvii–xcviii) presented a bill 'For the more effectual employment of the poor, by prohibiting the use and wear of all wrought silks, bengals, and stuffs mixed with silk, cotton, or herba of the manufacture of Persia, China, or the East India, and of all painted, stained, or dyed calicoes in apparel, household stuff or furniture'. It was rejected by the British privy council.
4 *Custom-House Entries*: the Custom House on Essex Quay, Dublin, accommodated the offices of the commissioners of customs and excise (usually referred to as the revenue commissioners). Prior, *Absentees*, p. 39, included a calculation of the yearly value of imports and exports 'taken from the Custom House books in Dublin'. Dobbs, *Essay*, p. 5, claimed that 'whilst in the committee of trade, I carefully look'd over the ledgers in the Custom House, and took extracts from them for seven or eight years, of the most material imports, and all the exports; in order to form proper calculations upon them, and to set our trade in a full and fair light'.
5 *Mr. Hinde*: probably John Hinde (d. *c*. 1737), woollen draper of Dublin (lease, 24 Nov. 1719: Registry of Deeds, Dublin, xxiv, 498, no. 14514); Sir Arthur Vicars (ed.), *Index to the Prerogative Wills of Ireland, 1536–1810*, Dublin: E. Ponsonby, 1897, p. 232.
6 *Mess. Bradshaw and Company*: unidentified.
7 *Mr. Dobson*: possibly William Dobson (d. *c*. 1737), of Dublin, one of the sheriffs of the city in 1710: Vicars (ed.), *Index to Prerogative Wills*, p. 136.

Mr. Card,[8] Mr. Lombard,[9] and Mr. Richard Eustace,[10] in *High-street*, as also, Mr. Mc. Kenzie,[11] on *Essex-Bridge*: These, in Conjunction with some other Merchants in this City, we affirm, have imported into this Kingdom, within these four Months past, 15000 Yards of Woollen Commodities, and several Thousand Yards of rich foreign Silks, and other Manufactures, to the Value of 14000 *l. Sterl.*

Now, *my Lords and Gentlemen*, as your Estates are in this Kingdom, and as in Consequence of this, your Interest is interwoven with that of the Publick; we hope you will take Notice of the pernicious Practices of those Enemies to the Commonwealth.

Certainly, should their Designs, so detrimental to our *Irish* Manufacture, succeed; that is, if those Goods are bought, and thereby these Drapers be encouraged to continue their Scheme; several Thousands of the inferior Sort of People, that are now supported, and maintained by the Woollen Trade at home, and that rely entirely upon your kind Disposition towards them, as breathing the same Air with you in poor *Ireland*, must inevitably come to great Want.

Their Cries can scarce be out of your Ears yet, since the last low Ebb of Trade.

Were they not then the most miserable Spectacles? The greatest Objects of Compassion and Charity? In short, it is impossible to have a just Idea of their Calamity, unless ye had been Eye-Witnesses of it.

Were we not then forced to apply for the *Concordatum* Money,[12] to keep them from starving? And were there not publick Collections made throughout the whole City, for their Relief?[13]

---

8 *Mr. Card*: probably Samuel Card (d. *c.* 1732), merchant of Dublin (lease, 4 Dec. 1721: Registry of Deeds, xxx, 60, no. 19658; mortgage, 7 July 1726: NLI, Dunalley papers, MS 29,806/108; Vicars (ed.), *Index to Prerogative Wills*, p. 75).
9 *Mr. Lombard*: possibly James Lombard of Skinner Row, Dublin (d. aft. 1743) (lease, 2 Aug. 1743: Registry of Deeds, cx, 266, no. 77127).
10 *Mr. Richard Eustace*: presumably the Dublin mercer of that name whose will was proved in 1755 (*Cal. Anc. Recs Dublin*, vol. VIII, p. 137; P. Beryl Eustace and Eilish Ellis (eds.), *Registry of Deeds, Ireland, Abstracts of Wills*, 3 vols., Dublin: Stationery Office, 1954–84, vol. II, p. 55; Vicars (ed.), *Index to Prerogative Wills*, p. 158).
11 *Mr. Mc. Kenzie*: unidentified.
12 *Concordatum Money*: a small fund in the Irish treasury, at the disposal of the Irish chief governor, originally established for charitable purposes; the Irish equivalent of the English 'secret service' fund.
13 *And were there not . . . for their Relief*: the acute distress suffered by weavers and their families in the winter of 1720–1 had prompted the Irish government to order a charity sermon to be preached in Dublin churches for their benefit: Courtenay Moore, 'An Old Dublin Remembrancer', *Journal of the Royal Society of Antiquaries of Ireland* 14 (1904), 75.

Now, will not the same Cause produce the same Effects again? Will not their Miseries increase, in Proportion to the Encouragement given to foreign Manufacturers, 'till at last they are reduced to the same deplorable Circumstances, and in the same melancholly Condition beg Relief at your Hands?

But this is not the only Evil that will be the Consequence.

We need not inform you, that the Heads of the Populace are extremely giddy; that they are ever prone to Mischief when idle; so that it was always accounted, if it was only for Peace Sake, an excellent Piece of Policy to keep them employed.

But what Disorders, and what Rapine would ensue, if they should not only be idle, but also want Bread? This would be a Spur to their depraved Inclinations; and would assuredly urge many of them on to injure their Neighbours, as often as Opportunity served.

But, perhaps, those Drapers, that would starve our Poor, or subject them to such Temptations, as Flesh and Blood would find difficult to resist; may say, as we hear they frequently do, by Way of Excuse, that they would not import a Yard of foreign Cloth, if the Clothiers here were not defective both in the Quality and Quantity of their Goods.

To this we answer, and say, We appeal to their own Consciences, whether we have not made Goods, for several Years past, equal to any that have come from Abroad.

To prove this farther, we are willing to produce them this present Time, if any Gentleman will be so curious as to make an Enquiry.

The Truth then, as to the Quality of them, fairly appearing, it will consequently follow, that it is in our Power to have any Quantity, if proper Encouragement be given, and the Natives and Inhabitants of *Ireland*, like so many worthy Patriots, join in the Consumption of it.

We can with Confidence assure those, that are Lovers of their Country, that no Pains or Expence has been spared by some industrious Men amongst us, to bring this Manufacture to the greatest Perfection in all its Branches.

But this is not the only Piece of Craft they have devis'd; for we have Reason to believe they have sold several foreign Cloths of a middle Price for our superfine; and so have abused many well-dispos'd Gentlemen, who honestly intended to have serv'd the Nation.

Nay, to shew their Deceit more plainly, and that nothing is too difficult for Minds prone to Mischief to get over, we can even prove they have attempted to corrupt our Seal-master, and endeavour'd to perswade him to seal their foreign Cloths with the Seal of *Ireland*.

So that we desire all those who sincerely wish well to the Land they live in, to take Notice, that the *Irish* Seal, which is the Harp,[14] is fixed at the Head End of all our Pieces. This will continue till we agree upon some common Mark, to prevent all Counterfeits; which shall be carefully advertis'd.

This Caution, together with your Encouragement, we presume, will restore Trade; and the Price of Wool, which falls and sinks under such wicked, and destructive Practices as are mention'd in this Paper. By which Means your Rents will be better paid, and the Kingdom in general will flourish.

We shall beg Leave to mention one Thing more; which is, to let you know how these Men, with many other Shop-keepers in Town, serve us in point of Payment.

All our Money, which we should lay out for Wool in proper Seasons of the Year, is employ'd in the Payment of foreign Bills; so that we seldom get a Sum together that is of any Service: In short, they keep us standing at their Doors (like poor Petitioners) till meer Necessity will oblige us sometimes to take a Moydore[15] or two, where fifty or a hundred are due; and that for nine, twelve, or eighteen Months together. A Practice shameful to the last Degree, and we hope will be resented by you in a proper Manner.

It is the Business of every worthy Patriot to support the publick Good.

He should ever lay this down as a fundamental Maxim, *viz.* That he thrives in the Prosperity, and suffers in the Loss and Damage of his Country.

The Streams therefore of his Affection and Love should always direct their Current thither, as to their ultimate End, and be all swallowed up in that Ocean.

Since it is plain, that no Kingdom, or State can subsist, unless the Members thereof are engaged with a commendable Zeal mutually to promote the Interest of their respective Establishments, it may be fairly inferr'd, that it is the indispensable Duty of every one of them, to apply the Use of those Means, without which, this noble End will be entirely frustrated.

We conclude all with our unfeigned, and hearty Thanks to you, for the Encouragement given hitherto to our *Irish* Woollen Drapery,[16] and hope your kind Dispositions towards us will be continued, while we take Care to deserve them.

---

14 *the Harp*: the heraldic emblem of Ireland, incorporated into the royal arms by Henry VIII on the declaration of the kingdom of Ireland in 1541.
15 *Moydore*: the moidore was a Portuguese gold coin worth £1 10s Irish.
16 *the Encouragement given hitherto to our Irish Woollen Drapery*: see above, n. 3.

This will animate us to prosecute our Trade with Vigour, and put it in our Power to improve it daily.

This will keep our Poor continually employ'd, hinder them from becoming Robbers or Objects of Charity, and prevent a great deal of Money from being sent out of the Kingdom.

Dublin: Printed in the YEAR M,DCC,XXXIII.

D. *To The Author of those Intelligencers Printed at Dublin*

This 1733 pamphlet attempts to refute the claims made in *Intelligencer* 19 concerning Irish emigration to America (above pp. 94–7). It was published in New York, and thus represents an unusually early American response to Swift. Although its authorship is unknown, it is possible that it was written by James Alexander, the editor of the *New York Journal* (which shared the same publisher, John Peter Zenger), and a supporter of the Lewis Morris faction, or 'Country party', in New York, which had a strong Dissenting constituency. See Michael Kammen: *Colonial New York: A History*, New York: Charles Scribner's Sons, 1975, pp. 203–7. An abridged version was printed as Appendix K of Woolley, *Intelligencer*.

To the Author of those Intelligencers printed at *Dublin*, to which is prefixed the following Motto,

> *Omne vafer vitium ridenti Flaccus amico*
> *Tangit, & admissus circum præcordia ludit.*
> *Persius.*[1]

Being a Defence of the Plantations against the virulent Aspersions of that Writer, and such as copy after him.

> *Non pugnam aspicere hanc oculis, non fædera possum,*
> *Tu pro Germano, si quid præsentius audes*
> *Perge, decet.- - - - - -*[2]

Though your Works put in a noisy Claim to a Resemblance of this Masterly Picture, yet they can have no Title to it in the Eyes of competent Judges, if from Distance or Misinformation you suffer your self to be deceived in Facts:

---

1 *Omne... Persius*: Aulus Persius Flaccus, *Satires*, I, ll. 116–17: 'Horace the rogue, manages to probe every fault while making his friend laugh; he gains his entrance, and plays about the innermost feelings.'
2 *Non pugnam... decet.- - - - - -*: Virgil, *Aeneid*, xii, 151–3: 'My eyes refuse to look upon such fight, such fatal league. If for thy brother's life thou couldst be bold to venture some swift blow, go, strike it now.'

For then, what you would seem to intend for gentle pleasing Reformation, becomes undeserved Scandal and bitter Reproach; and consequently, Reflections arising from Facts falsely introduced, such as have no Foundation in Truth, will destroy the Character which they are meant to support.

I SHALL make no Apology for so late an Answer, because it was promised that the Cause of the Plantations should have been undertaken by a more able Pen; but that Promise is not perform'd as yet: And moreover you will please to observe, that this Letter is from North *America*, where we receive all the Productions of *Europe* from the last Hand;[3] and the Fame of your *Intelligencers* had reach'd me long before I could obtain a Sight of them.

Your *6th* and *19th* Numbers contain a melancholy Description of *Ireland* and its Inhabitants; but upon this Subject, and without one just Cause assign'd. His Majesty, the Ministry, and the People of *England* appear to be the principal Objects of your Wrath and Indignation, and when you have wearied your self and your readers with those offensive Ideas, which Rags, Filth, and the most abject Poverty is wont to infuse, you rake all together into one Dunghill, mount the dirty Eminence, and bespatter the Crown and its best Friends.

To so much of your Works you have had your Answer already (as I am inform'd:) But as I am an Inhabitant of the Plantations, which are seldom considered at home any otherwise than as one large Tract of Infant Countries, some whereof are often wanting, and in their Turns as frequently receiving the most tender Marks of Goodness and Compassion, from the Hand of their immediate Lord and Royal Master;[4] and as we well know that we shall never want his Protection, so long as we take Care to deserve it, we ought to be very much in Earnest in order to obviate those vile and scandalous Aspersions, which your *19th Intelligencer* endeavours to fix upon this Continent: For while you spread the grossest Misrepresentations, and wickedly toil to make the World believe, that we are a Clan of *Kidnappers*, *Pickpockets*, *Knaves*, and *Villains*, you give (as far as in you lyes) the worst Impressions of us to those whose Patronage is no otherways to be obtain'd than by Virtue and Integrity.

---

3 *from the last Hand*: 'to put the last hand to' something meant to apply the finishing touch; presumably what is meant here is that the north American market is the last to be supplied.
4 *their immediate Lord and Royal Master*: King George II. Britain's north American colonies were of three types: royal colonies (including, from 1685, New York) which were ruled directly by a governor appointed by the crown, and corporate and proprietary colonies, the government of which depended on a royal charter (see L. W. Labaree, *Royal Government in America: A Study of the British Colonial System before 1783*, New Haven: Yale University Press, 1930, p. 2).

It would require more Sheets to shew the unchristian Treatment you have dealt to us, than I at present intend; but it is impossible to be wholley silent upon so unjust Provocation, especially at a Time when we seem to want Friends; and that it is publickly imputed to some of us, as if we were departing from that Zeal and affectionate Regard which our Actions can only express, for our Mother Country, and for those wise and well concerned Measures, which in Times of the greatest Peril and Danger have enabled the best of Kings to preserve us, His far distant Subjects, in profound Peace and Tranquillity.[5] Our Gratitude to so good a Prince should ever appear suitable and proportion'd to the great Occasion, and then, whatever may be the Machinations of our open or secret Enemies, certainly our common Interest will excite the best and ablest amongst us to explain our Conduct, and by setting that in a true Light, effectually contradict all Insinuations to our disadvantage.

That we should to a Man be unanimous in Sentiments which are the Result of common Prudence, or that the Opinion of every Individual should center in the same Point of Loyalty, is as little to be hoped for, as to see an universal Conformity in religious Tenets, Forms and Ceremonies: Yet in contradiction to those Indignities which you have laid at our Doors, I can with Truth affirm, That we are all as far removed from those savage and barbarous Manners with which you charge us, as is any the most civiliz'd Nation upon Earth; Accusations of this Kind, if true, would and are by you intended to render us unworthy of the protection of our King, and therefore it behoves us by all just and fair Methods, to free our selves of that Load of Scandal, under which we shall deservedly sink, if nothing can be said in our Defence.

To give our People a just figure of your Mind, to form a true Pourtraiture of your Heart, swoln with Envy, Rancour and Malice towards an

---

5 *especially at a Time... profound Peace and Tranquillity*: for the disturbances in American colonial government and politics in the late 1720s and early 1730s, particularly in New England, and their repercussions in English political discourse, see Alison Gilbert Olson, *Anglo-American Politics 1660–1775: The Relationship between Parties in England and Colonial America*, Oxford: Clarendon Press, 1973, pp. 115–18; Jack P. Greene, *Peripheries and Center: Constitutional Development in the Extended Politics of the British Empire and the United States 1607–1788*, Athens, GA: University of Georgia Press, 1986, pp. 60–1. English opinion was subject to the arguments of West Indian sugar interests, whose economic rivalry with the New England colonies, focused in 1732 on the struggle in the Westminster Parliament over the bill to regulate the trade between New England and the West Indies, led them to assert the disloyalty of the north American plantations. For examples, see *The British Empire in America, Consider'd. In a Second Letter, from a Gentleman of Barbadoes, to His Friend in London*, London, 1732; *A Comparison between the British Sugar Colonies and New England, as They Relate to the Interest of Great Britain*, London, 1732.

Administration, under which the Kingdom of *Ireland* at this day enjoys as great Ease, Plenty and Security as any Part of the Earth, and where those Poor whom their avaritious Landlords had laid under some pressing, or rather new, but legal Hardships, were immediately relive'd by his Excellency the Lord Lieutenant, the pious Lord Primate, and Lord Chancellor, in Consultation with the principal Nobility and Gentry of that Kingdom,[6] which at that Time, when you were sullenly retir'd, and were describing Calamities which it never knew nor ever felt, was supplying a Hundred foreign Markets with the Superfluities of its native Product, and at that very Juncture saw remarkably rising under the Care and Encouragement of a great and generous Legislature, a Manufacture, which now and in so short a Space rivals that rich and only one which can ever stand in Competition with it:[7] To shew you thus, (I say) and as in Truth you are, I must first expose that untrue, that ugly deform'd Picture which you give of your own Country, and to do this I take your *6th* and *19th Intelligencers* together, as of one Thread and one Piece, that like Figures in old Hangings explain great Designs wretchedly executed.

In your *6th Intelligencer, fol. 36*[8] you tell us, *'That the Natives of* Ireland *are sunk to the lowest Degree of Misery and Poverty, their Houses are Dunghills, their Victuals the Blood of their Cattle, or the Herbs of the Field, and their* CLOATHING *(to the Dishonour of God and Man) NAKEDNESS: That in your late Journey from* Dublin *to* Dundalk *you went into the House of a principal Farmer, where you took an Inventory of his Goods and Chattels; and his whole Stock within Doors,* you describe in the following Manner, *instead of Glass, the Panes of the Window were of brown Paper, because the Owner could not afford White; by the Hearth lay a Log of Wood, which supply'd the Place of Chairs; there was one black Jug, one greasy Bowl, three horn Spoons, one split Stick for a Candlestick, one rotten Bedstead, three Blankets, one for the Farmer and the Wife, one for the Children, and one for the Man and the Maid: That the Families of Farmers who pay great Rents, live in Filth and Nastiness, upon Butter-Milk and Potatoes, without a Shoe or Stocking to their Feet, and in Houses not so convenient as* English *Hogsties: That upon this Road the Signs of Inns are all taken from the*

6 *where those Poor . . . the principal Nobility and Gentry of that Kingdom*: a reference to the actions of the Irish lords justices Archbishop Boulter and Lord Chancellor Wyndham, in response to the subsistence crisis of winter 1728–9 (for which, see Dickson, 'In Search of the Old Irish Poor Law', pp. 152–3). These included a public subscription for poor relief. See also below, p. 371.
7 *a Manufacture . . . Competition with it*: the linen manufacture, whose development was supported by the Linen Board, established under statute in 1711.
8 *In your 6th Intelligencer, fol. 36*: 'folio' in the old sense of 'page'; '36' is an error for '46': the passage is on p. 46 of the 1729 edition (Woolley, *Intelligencer*, p. 282).

Posts, lest the Wind should shake them down, and the Houses with them, which are now distinguish'd by a Rag or a Wisp of Straw, stuck upon a Pole in some adjoining Heap of Dung. Then in this Journey you saw Twenty Jockies[9] *going to Fair with eight Horses, the Men had no Boots, and their Garrons*[10] *no Shoes, amongst them all no more than four Saddles and those of Straw, and bridles of Wythys: Two Families driving one Cow and a Calf; and a Deal more of such lamentable Description, as a great Multitude of Poor People going to Dublin, in a tatter'd ragged Condition, without Cloths, Money or Sustenance, who had no other Dependance upon Earth, but the Charity of the good People of that City;'* and here you conclude with a wicked Irony, *"That these wretched People are the Riches of a Country which the* English *Plunderers have reduced to so distress'd a Condition."* But when you arrive at Drogheda, there your pious Compassion overflows all Bounds; for, *'after you had travell'd through a Country, esteem'd* (as you say) *the most fruitful Part of the Kingdom, and so by Nature intended to be, no Ornaments or Improvements of such a Scene were visible, no Habitations fit for Gentlemen, no Farmers Houses, few Fields of Corn, and almost a bare Face of Nature, without new Plantations of any Kind, only a few miserable Cottages:* But this passed over, it was at Drogheda *'you were mortified, and your heart pierc'd with the sad Contemplation of a most deplorable, most melancholy Scene of Woe and Horrour, rising from the Destruction of Churches, made by that Usurper* Cromwell *and his phanatick Zeal."*

As *Cromwell's Zeal* is not propos'd to be the Subject of this Paper, I shall drop it with a short Digression, and then return to my first purpose; you know that Seventy and more Years have pass'd, since that Restoration which introduced again the Modes and Ceremonies of a Primitive Apostolic Church,[11] and strange it is, that the pious Zeal of *Charles* the second, a Prince of a most primitive Constitution too, should have done nothing towards re-edifying those his beloved religious Structure, which had sunk in the Defence of his Father's and his own Cause: To him Succeeded a Brother of less publick Spirit[12] indeed, yet a Bigot to the Religion whose Votaries had ever enjoyd the Offices exercised in, and the benefices apply'd to these Structures, but nothing is done for them yet; the next was a most glorious

---

9 *Jockies*: horse-dealers.
10 *Garrons*: a small and inferior breed of horse common in Ireland.
11 *the Modes and Ceremonies of a Primitive Apostolic Church*: presumably the author intends this as an ironical commentary on the claims of the Church of Ireland to be the true heir of the early church. Assertions of congruity with the practices of the 'primitive' church were a common feature of Anglican polemic.
12 *a Brother of less publick Spirit*: King James II.

Reign,[13] but it was burthened with foreign War and homebred division, and therefore the Amount of all publick Expence was requir'd for the Support of one, and Reconciling the other; next came that immortal Queen[14] to the Throne, whose Virtue, Wisdom and Piety, have erected Monuments of everlasting Honour to her Memory.[15] To Her succeeded King GEORGE the first, renown'd for Arms and Councils which govern'd and preserv'd the Peace of Europe, so happily, and amidst the greatest Struggles so wisely maintain'd and continued to us by His present most illustrious, most sacred Majesty; yet the roads from *Dublin* to *Dundalk* afford, you tell us (and so does *Drogheda*) as pityfull a Prospect as ever? but he must read you with little Observation who does not remark, that here, all the intermediate time between *Cromwell* a Tyrant Usurper, and the Reign of our lawfull sovereign Lord King *GEORGE* the second is forgotten, or to speak the Truth, willfully and maliciously omitted, and so much Shade, so little Light do you throw into this and the following part of your Work, that ignorant People are insensibly led to believe, that their Excellencies the late and present Lord Lieutenant of *Ireland*[16] had carried off the Rubbish of their Ruins, and built Palaces out of their remains; or that at least the present Ministry of *Great Brittain*, had so influenc'd the Councils of that Kingom, as to have it enacted, that no Churches in *Ireland* should be built, rebuilt, or repair'd for the future; and as your Papers at first came hither in single Pieces to be scatter'd and retail'd as best serv'd a Faction, I should have found it the other Day a very hard Task, to convince an honest plain Neighbour, who brought your Number 6 in his Pocket[17] to my House, of the Falshood of your Remarks upon *Ireland*, and the malignant Design of them, if from Number

---

13 *a most glorious Reign*: that of King William III.
14 *that immortal Queen*: Queen Anne.
15 *erected Monuments of everlasting Honour to her Memory*: in England, twelve new churches had been constructed in London and its environs by 1733 under the auspices of the Commission for Building Fifty New Churches, established by Act of Parliament in 1710 (9 Anne c. 17). The author may also have been referring to the activities of the Board of First Fruits in Ireland, which had been established to provide grants for the improvement of church buildings and the purchase of glebe land, from Queen's Anne's remission of the 'first fruits and twentieth parts', respectively the tax paid by incumbents on taking up their benefices, and the rents from church lands reserved to the crown at the Reformation. For the important role played by Swift in securing this advantage to church and clergy, see Landa, pp. 44–67.
16 *the late and present Lord Lieutenant of Ireland*: the Duke of Dorset, lord lieutenant in 1733, and his predecessor, Lord Carteret.
17 *who brought your Number 6 in his Pocket:* the original printings of *The Intelligencer*, by Sarah Harding in Dublin, in separate numbers.

19 of the stitch'd Volume,[18] and from his own Knowledge and Experience of this Country, by you so lately traduc'd, I could not have demonstrated, that the Truth is not in you, and that your Writings have no Tendency to the Relief of those Poor, or the restoring those Churches whose Decay you would be thought to mourn, but are calculated for Raising groundless and unreasonable Discontents, in order to disturb the Peace of that Government, in the Administration of which it is the Prayer of every good Man, that such turbulent and seditious Spirits as your Papers declare you to possess, may never have the least Share or Shadow of Power.

I now return my first and principal Motive for thus appearing against you in the most publick Manner I am able; in the last mentioned Intelligencer you tell the World, *'That notwithstanding the Misery of your own Country,* which by the way, you most falsely exaggerate, *'you cannot account for that Enthusiasm which has of late prevail'd upon so many Thousand Irish to flock over to the Plantations, for that all who go thither are immediately sent up to the Frontiers, there to remain as a Barrier between the Planters and wild Indians, in order to be first devour'd;*[19] *a Cruelty, say you, taken from the like Practice amongst the Romans, who were wont to place certain barbarous Nations, Prisoners of War in the Front of the Battle, in order to take off the Fury of the first Onset, or to Hurt the Edge of the Enemy's Sword.* This Story, or one like it, you found some where, but if you find it in the Roman History between the first Year of *Romulus,* and the first Year of the first Christian Emperour,[20] I confess it will be a new Discovery to me, unless this Station was assign'd by the *Lex Talionis*[21] or for the Punishment of notorious Malefactors, but I am not farther concern'd in this Point than to let you know, *That it is a scandalous and intolerable Abuse upon the Sense of Mankind, to impose one Lye upon them by the Authority of another,* it is no Entertainment to a generous Mind, to see the greatest Infamy cast upon the greatest, wisest, and most human People, that the World ever saw, nor is it easily to be born, that a living People, who have a great Share of the Roman Spirit, who are as fond of their Mother

---

18 *Number 19 of the stitch'd Volume*: one of the consolidated, single-volume editions, the first printed by William Bowyer in Dublin in 1729 and reprinted in London; the second printed by Francis Cogan in London in 1730.
19 *devour'd*: consumed, or destroyed, but also alluding to tales of cannibalism among American Indians (for which, see above, pp. 149–50).
20 *the first Year of Romulus, and the first Year of the first Christian Emperour*: Romulus, the mythical founder of Rome, dated by historians to the eighth century BC, and Constantine the Great, the first emperor to embrace Christianity, whose reign began in AD 306.
21 *Lex Talionis*: Talion law: the principle in biblical and early Roman law that the punishment inflicted on a criminal should be precisely the same as the injuries or damages suffered by the victim.

Country, and of the Laws, Liberties and Priviledges which they inherit from her Bounty as the *Romans* themselves were of Rome, and the Advantage of that most honourable Birth-right insulted, for no better Reason than for the Resemblance they bear to a Nation, which not only civilizd *Great Brittain*, but all Europe beside; it is not improper in this Place to let you see, that Animosity and party Rage have carried you to a Length, which lays your unhappy Talent naked and exposed to one who is resolv'd not to spare you, upon a Point of such Importance to the Honour and Wellfare of *America*; I am therefore going to relate to you a known Truth (and I appeal to every Native of *Ireland* upon this Continent whether it be not so) *viz*. That some of the Colonies have laid a Tax of Twenty-Shillings per Head upon every Irish Servant imported,[22] so far are they from wanting any Guards upon their Frontiers, or endeavouring to expose their fellow Subjects for their own Preservation, and you know, I hope you have Ingenuity enough to acknowledge it, that such as are not Servants, whether *Irish*, *Scotch* or *English*, have Priviledges here equal to any which they enjoy in their native Countries respectively; I doe not intend to enter into particular Instances except such as I can give in the Provinces of *New-York*, and *New-Jersey*, where I am well acquainted with many of your Nation who have purchas'd unsettled and uncultivated Lands at their first coming over, and made such Improvements in a few Years, as give great Pleasure to those who have Minds capable of enjoying the Happiness and Prosperity of their Neighbours, in one part of this Country we have a considerable Settlement of them situated near a large navigable River, where they purchas'd Woodlands not long since, at the rate of Thirty, Thirty five, and Forty Pounds the Hundred Acres, and in five or six Years Time have made such Farms as afford them all the Necessaries of Life in plenty, nor doe they want the Conveniencies of it, if you will allow clean warm Houses, neat, though homely, Furniture, commodious Barns, and a sufficient stock of Horses, Cows, Hogs, Poultry, *&c*. To be such, and all this rising from a principal Fund of no more than Forty or Fifty Pounds Sterling; for so far are the People here from oppressing these new Commers, who never refuse to meet at their own Expence in small Companies, or by turns, and give them the Labour of as much Time as is sufficient to put up a warm comfortable Habitation for them, for the five

22 *upon every Irish Servant imported*: in 1704, an Act of the Maryland Assembly imposed a levy of 20s a head on Irish servants 'to prevent the Importing too great a number of Irish papists into this province' (Thomas Bacon, *Laws of Maryland at Large...*, Annapolis, 1765). More recently, in May 1729, a statute had been passed in Pennsylvania 'laying a duty on foreigners, and Irish servants, imported into this province' (*Laws of the Commonwealth of Pennsylvania*, 4 vols., Philadelphia, 1795–1801, vol. I, p. xix).

or six first Years, 'though for their credit it must be said, that they seldom content themselves with it for long, but build a better and convert the former to such use as the Enlargement of the Family, and a better Way of Living requires, if they happen to be Tradesmen, as many of them are, 'tis their own Fault if they ever want Work, and ready Payment equal to more than double the Value of what they receive for the same in their own Country, if they come over under Obligations for a Term of Years, they are bound by Indentures made in *Ireland*,[23] and if their Accommodation in the Passage be bad, the Buyer here is not accountable for it, such Fault or misfortune is only chargeable on the Merchant who sends them, or on the common Accident: of all Navigation, and when we receive them into our Families It is well known to all Merchants, factors, Captains of Ships, and others who deal with us from Europe, that they have plenty of good wholesome Provisions, warm Clothing, and such Lodgings as might content their Betters, and when a servitude of four Years is expired they are as free as the Air which they[24] breath, and this is the[25] true State of the Case between the Inhabitants of *New-Jersey*, and *New-York*, and such *English*, *Scotch*, and *Irish*, (for they are all upon a Footing) as come over to us in any of the Circumstances above mention'd: But no Man whatsoever, unless he voluntarily lists himself in His Majesty's Troops, is sent to the Frontiers, nor do we want in Time of Peace any other forces, than what are maintain'd here by the Bounty Of His Majesty, who is so exceeding Gracious to these his Dominions, as to support four independent Companies of an Hundred effective Men each,[26] with their proper Officers, besides Storekeepers, Gunners, and Mattrosses,[27] in several Garrisons, for the security of a Frontier which of our selves we are not able to cover upon any sudden Rupture, tho' the Incursions of the Savages are always

---

23 *if they come over under Obligations for a Term of Years, they are bound by Indentures made in Ireland:* on indentured servitude in general, see D. W. Galenson, *White Servitude in Colonial America: An Economic Analysis*, Cambridge: Cambridge University Press, 1981; and for its prevalence among early eighteenth-century migrants from Ireland to the American plantations, J. G. Leyburn, *The Scotch-Irish: A Social History*, Chapel Hill: University of North Carolina Press, 1962, pp. 176–9; R. J. Dickson, *Ulster Emigration to Colonial America 1718–1775*, London: Routledge and Kegan Paul, 1966, pp. 87–97.
24 *they*] the *1733*. Emended.
25 *the*] they *1733*. Emended.
26 *four independent Companies of an Hundred effective Men each*: the garrison of New York was manned by the 'Four Independent Companies', infantry companies paid for by the government of the colony and recruited mostly from European mercenaries. See Stanley M. Pargellis, 'The Four Independent Companies of New York', in *Essays in Colonial History Presented to Charles McLean Andrews by His Students*, New Haven: Yale University Press, 1931, pp. 96–123.
27 *Mattrosses*: gunners' mates.

made by small Parties; and that we may receive no Damage in our Trade, or be surpris'd from Sea, His several Station Ships are ever cruising upon our Coasts, which would otherwise be infested by Pirates to the Destruction of all Commerce; but if His Majesty's Royal Mind were capable of receiving those Impressions which you would industriously infuse, or if his great and wise Ministry could stoop to read your Works, and be prevail'd upon to believe that we were Brutes, and Monsters, and were no more than the outward Form and Visage of Man; might we not expect in an Instant to be depriv'd of that Protection which is our best Security; and not only so, but is likewise real visible Wealth to two great and Neighbouring Colonies,[28] whose Trade and necessary Intercourse, whose Frontiers (the Result of our scituation) are such, that the same Guard and Defence which he has given, the same Royal Appointments which he has made for the one, seem by his extensive Wisdom, most Gracious and most Provident Care of all his People, equally intended the Safety and Preservation of both, while the Sum of 20,000 l. at least is annually expended amongst us by these His Majesty's Forces belonging to the Sea and Land, and the Trade and consumption of both Colonies would soon feel the vast Loss of this Advantage if withdrawn or transferr'd to any other Part of the American Dominions, which, as is well known has been more than once Attempted.

And now I have gone thus far, it is absolutely necessary that I should refute that Obloquy and Scandle with which you falsely and audaciously charge the Government here, for in that one comprehensive Word you sum up the King, the Ministry, the Governour, and the whole legislature of both Colonies, at this Mark all your envenom'd Arrows are shot, and neither *Jersey* or *York*, had been the Subject of your Papers, if tired with many impotent Efforts to blacken the Administration at Home, you had not thereby lost all Credit in the three Kingdoms, and were compell'd to shift the Scene to a Country where perhaps your Works might not appear to admit of Contradiction, till the intended Mischief had taken Effect; therefore you affirm, '*That altho' the Miseries of Ireland* (which are in Reality the Forgeries of your own Brain) *are insupportable, yet such of its natives as have exchang'd that Country for the Plantations, would be glad to return, if they were not condemn'd and chain'd to the Frontiers; and no more would now embark for those Northern Colonies*, if the GOVERNMENT HAD NOT WISELY TAKEN *Care, That no Letters whatsoever should be suffered to be put on Board any Ship or other Vessel, bound for* Ireland, *before they were read and examined by the Boards of Council of the several Provinces.*"

28 *two great and Neighbouring Colonies*: New York and New Jersey.

I verily believe when this Assertion took hold of you, the foul Fiend[29] had deserted your Elbow, and that you were left entirely to the Conduct of your own evil Genius; for it is so gross a Blunder, so apparent a Falshood, as the reputed Subtilty of the Divil could not have committed; yet I am willing to allow you as great a Share of Probability in this Case as I possibly can. Let us suppose then that the Sea-Coast extends no farther along the Inhabited Part of the Continent than seven Hundred Miles, from *North* to *South*, and that such *Irish* as came over Free-men, or have been emancipated within these Twenty Years, are admitted to the free Use of Pen, Ink and Paper, that no more than one Hundred Ships are constantly passing between this Continent and *England*, *Scotland* and *Ireland*, that amongst all those who navigate them, there are no more than two Hundred *Irish* Sailors, and that not above Fifty Thousand Men are kept in constant Pay, for no other purpose but to seize all Letters and Pacquets which have not the Pasport of the several Governours and Council, for they must secure all Letters, at least open all for every Part of *Europe*, there being a considerable Correspondence held with *Ireland* by *Italy*, *Spain*, *Portugal*, *France* and *Germany*; yet so worthy and so wise a Project could have no Effect, and in so many Years, at least a Dozen or more Letters, besides that single one which a poor old Man, with so great Care, and Caution, at the Peril of his Life transmitted to *Dublin*, would have escaped this Search either by Day or Night: But it is, I own, as weak to engage in this Part of the Controversy with you, as you your self could wish; therefore I shall not call the common Sence of Mankind so much in Question as to reply any farther to it; however, give me Leave to shew, *That you in Person, all who are confederated, and every Paper of yours which comes from the Press, are so many Instances of the Folly and Madness of this Accusation.* If the Government of *England* could possibly entertain a Thought of *destroying* Ireland by *depopulating that Kingdom*, which is the wild Principle upon which your whole mad Argument is built, *what Reason can be assigned, that a Wretch as you, who have by this Discovery destroy'd so wonderful a Scheme, and broke in upon all Measures form'd to give it ample Execution, should not by Measures much less arbitrary be depriv'd of the Power of Opposition?* But the Truth is, that the Rancour of your Heart has corrupted your Head, and while you are charging the Ministry with *an Intent to destroy Ireland*, you forget your self, and lay the Charge at the Doors of its own Natives; you tell us, *That they are gone to* America *in great Numbers, and we know that they were not sent for, and for the 'Fox's Reason*, you tell us (*for a certain Fox it seems had lost*

---

29 *the foul Fiend*: Satan. In *Pilgrim's Progress*, ch. 16, Christian meets and fights the 'foul fiend' Apollyon, the destroying angel, sometimes used as a synonym for the Devil himself.

his tail, and would have persuaded all of his Kind to take off theirs too, for tails were out of Fashion, and very Troublesome beside,)[30] *they tell fine Stories of their New World, and draw their old Neighbours, Friends and Relations in the same Snare with themselves.* Thus after all, and upon second Thoughts, Letters do pass from hence to *Ireland,* and the *Irish* are their own Butchers:[31] But this is one of those general Accusations, which shew *That one man may be found so depraved in his own nature, so abandon'd by all Goodness, as to believe that there is neither Honour, Honesty, Love, Friendship or Affection to be found in the Universe.* I shall always believe, thank God I know, *That these are not words of Art, but are the greatest and best Gifts which Heaven bestows in this Life.* The *Sinon* of *Virgil*[32] was a Knave, and what he said of himself is a fine Image of a deceitful Heart, yet the same Thing in Words less elegant, may be truly spoken in another Case,

- - - - - - *Miseram si tristis Iernem,*
Non etiam Vanum, mendacemque improbe finxit,
Fortuna. - - - - - - - - - [33]

And of a Country, which for many Ages has Produced as wise, as valiant, as good, and as great Men as any Age or History can shew; of this we have a noble and near Example, and at a very little Distance from us is to be found the richest Magazine of all useful Knowledge, polite Learning, antient and modern Science, in the single Person of a Native of that Country,[34] who seems by Providence and the happy Auspices of the wise Founder of *Pensylvania*[35] to have been introduc'd there to give Birth, Continuance, and Establishment to all those Arts which were the Glory of *Rome*:

---

30 *a certain Fox . . . very Troublesome beside*: the fox in Aesop's fable, who lost his tail in a trap, and sought to persuade the other foxes to get rid of theirs.
31 *the Irish are their own Butchers*: a reference to *A Modest Proposal*.
32 *The Sinon of Virgil*: According to the *Aeneid*, a Greek warrior named Sinon persuaded the Trojans to bring the wooden horse into the city, having ingratiated himself with them in the guise of a deserter.
33 *Miseram . . . Fortuna*: 'Though cruel Fortune has made sad Ireland miserable, she has not also made her false and lying'; adapted from Virgil, *Aeneid*, ii, 79–80 (Woolley, *Intelligencer*, p. 282). The original quotation, 'nec si miserum Fortuna Sinonem finxit, vanum etiam mendacemque improba finget' (Though Fortune has made Sinon wretched, she has not made him untrue and a liar), appears at a significant point in *Gulliver's Travels* (pt IV, ch. xii; *CWJS*, vol. XVI, p. 437) to emphasise Gulliver's veracity.
34 *a Native of that Country*: William Tennent (1673–1746), a Scotsman by birth, but who had lived in the north of Ireland. Having first been admitted as a Presbyterian minister, he was subsequently ordained into the Church of Ireland. In 1727, he established an academy at Neshaminy, Pennsylvania, which came to be known as the 'Log College'. See J. R. F. Watson, *Annals of Pennsylvania*, Philadelphia, 1830, pp. 246–7.
35 *the wise Founder of Pensylvania*: William Penn.

and *Athens*; nor can an honest Mind be insensible of the most pleasing Emotion, while an *English* Gentleman,[36] adorn'd with those Accomplishments which have acquir'd him the Affection and Esteem of all Mankind, whose Conversation is form'd to win universal Love and Admiration, is often heard with unaffected Modesty to say, *That to this great Man his kind praeceptor, invaluable Friend, he owes the Blessings of his Education.* As I at first intended to confine this Defence to *New-Jersey* and *New-York*, I shall in few Words shew you, *That it is not in the Power of the Enemies of their King and Country to mislead or render disaffected a People whose Interest Duty and Inclination are united to keep them steady, and to preserve them loyal to the illustrious House of* Hanover:[37] *Under the Influence of his Majesty's righteous Government we enjoyed the Liberties, Rights, Priviledges, Laws, Usages and Customs of* England, *which now are all dispensed to us with a just and equal Hand, both in Law and Equity; the best Acknowledgement which an Infant Country can make for so great Blessings, is that Respect, Duty, Fidelity, Esteem and Regard which would pay to the worthy Representative of his Majesty's Royal Person, by such a Support as that great Dignity requires, and our Circumstances will admit; in this we are not wanting to Him, or to our selves, for we look upon the Honour and Interest of the Crown and these two Colonies as inseparable.*[38] *And this amiable Harmony it is which has hitherto supported our Credit at Home and Abroad; while our near Neighbours to the Eastward, and others farther to the Southward, have by Personal Animosities, private Feuds and publick Opposition to His Majesty's most just and reasonable Expectations, well nigh reduced themselves to Poverty,*

---

36 *an English Gentleman*: unidentified, though a possible candidate is Jonathan Dickinson (1688–1747), the first president of Princeton, an American Congregationalist much influenced by Tennent.
37 *illustrious house of Hanover*: the adjective 'illustrious' was commonly applied to the Hanoverian royal family (in, for example, parliamentary addresses) before George I's accession to the throne.
38 *is that Respect . . . as inseparable*: written with some circumspection, given the political situation in New York in 1733. The governor of New York and New Jersey was the Irishman William Cosby (1690–1736), of Stradbally Hall, Queen's County. He had been appointed in 1732 but during the following winter stirred up popular hostility and fell out with the 'Country party' headed by chief justice Lewis Morris. After a dispute with the chairman of the council, Rip Van Dam, over perquisites, Cosby created a chancery court to adjudicate the dispute in his favour. Morris denounced this as unconstitutional, and Cosby dismissed him. By the latter part of 1733, Morris and his supporters established an opposition newspaper, edited by James Alexander and printed by John Peter Zenger, which bombarded the governor with hostile invective. Eventually Cosby ordered this newspaper to be burned, and Zenger to be arrested, in what became a *cause célèbre* of colonial American politics (Michael Kammen, *Colonial New York: A History*, New York: Charles Scribner's Sons, 1975, pp. 206–7, 212–13).

Anarchy and Confusion.[39] *But it will be a Part of his Majesty's Glory, and to the Honour of the Ministry, that the more we strive to excell in Loyalty, and to give the surest Demonstrations of our Attachment to the Crown, by Actions which best speak for themselves, the more signal and distinguishing other Marks of Royal Favour which are conferr'd upon us. And as His Majesty's Ear is ever open to the Addresses of His Subjects, so is he pleas'd that ours should be transmitted to Him, by Persons remarkable for their Merit and Services, in whose honour he can confide, and whose former Attendance upon His Royal Person, or the high Trusts that have enjoy'd in in Employments which required try'd and experience Valour and Prudence, have given Him satisfactory Proofs how fully He may depend upon the Representations.*[40] *To these His Majesty's most intelligent Considerations and Condescensions, and to our own ready chearful Obedience and habitual Loyalty, these Provinces owe their present flourishing unhappy Condition, and a more weak or wicked Attempt can never be made, than to divide us from our true Interest by false and scandalous Misrepresentations. The King and all His Princely Thoughts appear transcendently in our Favour, His great and eminent Ministry, who have a watchful Eye upon these Colonies, and under him, are upon every Emergency our surest Sanctuary, a Branch of whose high Office is to weigh all Acts which have the publick Sanction in the Balance,*[41] *and by the same Scale to try the Sincerity of our Intentions, will know from thence and from the Testimony of the honourable Person who has more than equal Charge over us, that we are faithful and true Servants of our Lawful Prince, affectionate to those great Persons who have so long serv'd, and do still continue to serve him in the most exalted Stations; and that our Loyalty is such, as will never give us leave to think, that our utmost Endeavours to serve Him, or the most solid Honours we can pay to his excellent Representative and his noble Family, are Works of Supererogation.*[42] *To be good Subjects is one sure sign that we are good Christians, and as good Christians we never can deserve to be stigmatiz'd with the black Characters of Unhospitable,* Brutal, Savage, Covetous *and* Barbarous, *Epithets which you so freely bestow.*

39 *our near Neighbours... Anarchy and Confusion*: to the east, Massachusetts (for which, see below, p. 363), and to the south New Jersey, where successive governors John Montgomerie and William Cosby had become embroiled in political difficulties, largely of their own making, and where there was also an economic crisis, marked by high interest rates and rising prices (John E. Pomfret, *Colonial New Jersey: A History*, New York: Charles Scribner's Sons, 1973, pp. 144–5).
40 *And as His Majesty's... Representations*: addresses from representative assemblies and other colonial bodies were generally, though not invariably, transmitted by the governor.
41 *His great and eminent Ministry... in the Balance*: Acts passed in colonial assemblies required the approval of the British privy council.
42 *Works of Supererogation*: acts performed beyond the requirements of duty; more particularly, acts of piety beyond what God requires.

To conclude, I desire you would not be surpris'd, if after all I have said, I now in the Name of the whole Continent return your hearty Thanks for your Performance; and you will certainly think better of us, when you see, *That we look only upon the Effect, but despite the Intention of it.* We who live remote from the great Scene of Action, and are ignorant of the true Springs of every considerable Movement in *England,* are apt to take Things too much upon trust from Pamphlets, Party Papers, and private Advices; but you for your Part, who for the sake of publishing and supporting a fractious and seditious Fiction concerning your own Country, have falsely introduced us, as Parties concern'd, must henceforth with all your Tribe of foul Mouth'd Hirelings[43] expect no Credit here; which will not a little contribute to the Continuance of that Felicity we have so many years enjoy'd. To your Honour be it said, *That in one Libel you have done more for the Satisfaction and Conviction of all* America, *than if you had spent your past Life in the honest and faithful Service of its Inhabitants; and while King* GEORGE *the second sits upon the Throne of* Brittain, *and moves the great Machine of Government, yours, and the Writings of your Party will have no other Influence here, than to give us just Reason to believe, that the contrary of all you say is true.*

I have now only to wish, that one certain Colony, whose fatal Politics have brought it to near the Brink of Ruin,[44] would, e'er it[45] be too late bethink themselves proper Measures to retrieve their sinking Affairs, and that Character in the World which they once so fairly maintain'd. Their Ancestors (as is[46] well known) left their Native Country upon Terms which will ever be mention'd to their Honour;[47] for no greater Testimony of Virtue and Piety can be given, than the Sacrifice of all Worldly Possessions to the Dictates of a good Conscience; and agreeable to this great and good Foundation have these people stood and encreas'd ever since in Trade and

---

43 *Tribe of foul Mouth'd Hirelings*: in the second of the *Drapier's Letters* (*To Mr Harding*), Swift had referred to Wood's 'tribe of accomplices' (Davis, vol. X, p. 17), and in the fourth (*To the Whole People of Ireland*), to 'Wood and his hirelings' (Davis, vol. X, p. 66).
44 *one certain Colony... Brink of Ruin*: Massachusetts, whose Assembly had been convulsed since 1728 by a dispute over the governor's salary and whether the Assembly had the right to determine when and how this would be paid. See L. W. Labaree, *Royal Government in America: A Study of the British Colonial System before 1783*, New Haven: Yale University Press, 1930, pp. 360–5; Benjamin W. Labaree, *Colonial Massachusetts: A History*, Milwood, NY: KTO Press, 1979, pp. 138–9; Richard L. Bushman, *King and People in Provincial Massachusetts*, Chapel Hill: University of North Carolina Press, 1985, pp. 29–30, 67–8, 119–20, 125–7.
45 *it*] it it *1733*. Emended.
46 *is*] is is, *1733*. Emended
47 *Their Ancestors... their Honour:* the 'Pilgrim Fathers' who had founded a colony at Plymouth, Massachusetts, in 1620.

Numbers, which incited some of our Kings to distinguish them by peculiar Favours and Concessions, such as they well deserved, *for by Actions only can the Heart be known*; and surely no people ever gave greater Evidence of Virtue, Justice, Temperance, Religion and Loyalty than do the People of that Country, and no Man who knows them can imagine, but that the Person, the Crown, and Dignity of *King GEORGE the Second*, and His illustrious House, are as dear to them (and that universally) as their Liberties, Lives and Fortunes: but most unhappily for this Country, and at a Time too when they have a most worthy Gentleman at their Head,[48] a man of Merit, Ability, Virtue, Honesty and Integrity, equal to that of any his worthiest Predecessors. From a chain of evil Accidents has this Misfortune befallen them; His Excellency found the Coals blown into a flame, he strove to throw cold Water on them both at Home in *England*, and his just and worthy Endeavours were in both Places well received, and those great Men in the latter, who saw and knew his Qualifications and admirable Disposition, his Loyalty and Love for his Sovereign, and his deep Affection for his Native Country, recommended and presented him to the King, as the Person most likely to succeed in healing those Breaches which by ill Conduct had been already too much widened. Under these Circumstances, and equally engag'd in the Service of the Crown and the Colony, he enter'd upon this eminent but difficult Station; and as he now might well have appeal'd to all the World, and to his own Country in particular, for an honourable Justification of his Conduct, the People have taken that Talk upon themselves, and in their own behalf; but it is to be hoped, *That before another eighth of May comes about*,[49] *they will, while they are straining at Gnats, consider, how difficult it will be to swallow the uncontroulable Edict of a British Parliament*,[50] *or to leave you and the Enemy of Mankind to Triumph in that sad Catastrophe, which seems to be too nearly impending over all those parts of America, where a few malignant Spirits are corrupting the Minds of the People, and the common*

---

48 *they have a most worthy Gentleman at their Head*: Jonathan Belcher (1682–1757), a Bostonian, succeeded in 1730 to the governorship of Massachusetts on the death of William Burnet, of whose administration he had been a leading opponent.

49 *before another eighth of May comes about*: presumably the date at which the Massachusetts Assembly was scheduled to meet (*Journal of the Commissioners for Trade and Plantations, 1729–54*, p. 356; Governor Belcher to the Commissioners for Trade and Plantations, 28 June 1733 (*Calendar of State Papers, Colonial America and the West Indies, 1733*, p. 132)).

50 *straining at Gnats . . . British Parliament*: Matthew, 23: 24: 'Ye blind guides, which strain at a gnat and swallow a camel'. At various stages in the dispute over the governor's salary, the British administration threatened Parliamentary action at Westminster to enforce its wishes (Labaree, *Royal Government*, pp. 360, 362–3, 364).

licentiousness Voice is allowed against Law and all that circumscribes their lawless Passions.

That you may be soon restored to your Senses, and calmly set about a speedy Reformation, is what I sincerely wish; in the mean Time I think I have discover'd an Expedient which may be of great Use to you: Be so good, Sir, to make one Voyage to *New-Jersey* or *New-York*, and there you will see what Reception is given to your own Works, as well as to those of the wretched few who are Copying after you. Yours indeed make a pretty Amusement for the Boys, being almost always upon the Wing by Day Light, and 'tis diverting enough to observe how much they are the Emblem of your self;[51] for by how much the more Line their Directors give them, so much the sooner are they out of Sight and lost to all Notice and Observation: But your Copyers take their Excursions by Twylight, and spread their dabbled[52] Wings in Dusk or utter Darkness, and like *Æsop's* Bat, *having deserted the standard of the Royal Bird, are listed with the Beasts.*[53]

Farewell, but still remember Milo's *End,*
Wedg'd in the Timber which he strove to rend.
Roscommon.[54]

E. *From* The Dublin Weekly Journal, *Saturday, June 7th. 1729*

This letter from 'Andrew Trueman' and 'Patrick Layfield', sent to Swift in April or May 1729, then printed in the *Dublin Weekly Journal* by its pseudonymous author or authors, is the origin of Swift's *An Answer to Several Letters from Unknown Persons* (above, pp. 108–18); the correspondents appear to be differently named versions of 'Andrew Dealer' and 'Patrick Pennyless', whose

---

51 *the Emblem of your self*: emblem books, which originated in Germany in the 1530s, were a popular literary form in sixteenth- and seventeenth-century Europe, and popularised the idea that an image (emblem) could stand as a symbol for a person or persons, an object or an idea.
52 *dabbled*: not necessarily a misprint for 'dappled', since one of its meanings was splashed or spattered (literally with liquid, and figuratively with light).
53 *Æsop's Bat... listed with the Beasts*: in Aesop's fable, 'The Birds, the Beasts, and the Bat', the bat at first refused to join the birds in their war with the beasts, but then was himself rejected by the beasts, and ended up belonging to neither side; his conclusion was that 'he that is neither one thing nor the other has no friends'.
54 *Farewell... Roscommon*: quoted from Wentworth Dillon (1637–85), 4th Earl of Roscommon, *An Essay on Translated Verse*, London, 1684, p. 6. Milo of Croton, a wrestler in the sixth century BC, met his end when his hands became trapped in a cracked tree trunk which he was attempting to rip apart, and he was attacked and killed by a pack of wolves.

previous writings to Swift, which have not survived, inspired the writing of *Intelligencer 19*.

To the Publisher of the *Dublin Weekly Journal*.[1]

Sir,

The following is from a Country Farmer as you may observe by its plainness; its View seems intended as a Warning to remove the Cause of the Things complained of, which is hardly wished for by all true Lovers of their Country. Your inserting it in your Paper will be grateful to several, and in particular to

Your very humble Servant
J.W.

A Letter from some Farmers in the Country to a Gentleman in Dublin, shewing their Reasons for removing to the British Plantations in America, with other remarks & c.

SIR,

We receiv'd your Letter, wherein you desired to know the Cause why so many are grown fond of transporting themselves to *America*.[2] in Obedience to your Commands we made Enquiry, and here send you as many of the Reasons as we could discover in the Country where we live, and hope you will pardon our Freedom, in expressing ourselves in the plain Terms and Language of the people.

About fifteen Years ago, many of our Friends and Acquaintance went with their Families to *Pensilvania*, from whom we have received many inviting Letters, which gave a fair Description of that Country, and much the same with a Book Entituled, *An Account of the British Empire in America*. Printed

---

1 *the Publisher of the Dublin Weekly Journal*: James Carson (d. 1765). The *Dublin Weekly Journal* was established in 1725 as Ireland's first literary journal. To begin with, its concerns were strongly political, but after 1727 the articles it contained were usually of a more general nature, though its political bent remained Whiggish (Robert Munter, *The History of the Irish Newspaper 1685–1760*, Cambridge: Cambridge University Press, 1967, pp. 160–2; Munter, *A Dictionary of the Print Trade in Ireland 1550–1775*, New York: Fordham University Press, 1988, p. 50; M. Pollard, *A Dictionary of Members of the Dublin Book Trade 1550–1800...*, London: Bibliographical Society, 2000, p. 91).
2 *grown fond of transporting themselves to America*: for the wave of emigration from Ulster to north America in the 1720s, which reached a peak in 1729, see above, pp. 94–5.

at London in the Year, 1708.³ These Letters fraught with Invitations and Encomiums on that happy Settlement, assure us of the abundance of all Necessaries, and Conveniences of Life, and that without the Dread of the *Racking Landlord*,⁴ and *Griping Tythmaster*.⁵ The Tenures of land are to them and their Posterity for ever; so that there are no vexatious Covenants in Leases, *No: mina penas*,⁶ *Heriots*,⁷ *Duties*, or such base Impositions. no tedious Law Suits, nor exorbitant Fees, and, but few Lawyers; their Laws are excellent, being carefully Collected by the judicious Sir *William Penn*;⁸ the Native Indians are said to be there very much civilised,⁹ and that the Conqueror's do not become Tyrants as in other Nations we have known;¹⁰ and there is great care taken of the Poor.¹¹

Our neighbour *William* has bought home the Maps of the whole World, where we find *Pensilvania* about the Centre of the *British* Settlements, and under the same Degree of Latitude with *Italy*, and the South of *France*, Countries always renowned for great Fertility.

Here, in the North of *Ireland*, we can easily observe the Country seems to be over peopled already, and that if the Number increases but Six or Eight

---

3 *a Book Entituled . . . 1708*: John Oldmixon, *The British Empire in America, Containing the History of the Discovery, Settlement, Progress and Present State of All the British Colonies, on the Continent and Islands of America*, 2 vols., London, 1708.
4 *Racking Landlord*: one who imposes an exorbitant rent.
5 *Griping Tythmaster*: tithes (originally levied as a tenth part of agricultural produce, but sometimes transmuted into a money payment) were duties paid for the upkeep of the parish church and the maintenance of the minister. Since the Reformation, some tithes had been impropriated (so that the right to collect them had passed to lay proprietors). While some owners (clerical and lay) levied tithes themselves, others employed 'tithe-proctors' to undertake the collection for them, and others sold the right to collect to 'tithe-farmers' or 'tithe-jobbers'. See above, pp. lxvii–lxviii.
6 *mina penas*: as well as being an ancient coin, a mina was 'a measure of grain or corn' (Bryan A. Garner (ed.), *Black's Law Dictionary*, 10th edn, London: Thomson-Reuters, 2014, p. 1145). *Penas* (from Lat. *poenas*): punishments or penalties. The phrase therefore seems to refer to a penalty applied to a crop or yield.
7 *Heriots*: a heriot was a financial obligation of manorial tenants: originally a feudal service, since transmuted into a money payment.
8 *Sir William Penn*: William Penn (1644–1718), the founder of Pennsylvania.
9 *the Native Indians . . . very much civilised*: Nathaniel Crouch, *The English Empire in America. Or, a View of the Dominions of the Crown of England in the West-Indies . . .* , Dublin, 1729, contained a detailed, and generally favourable, account of the Pennsylvania Indians (pp. 103–10).
10 *Conqueror's do not become Tyrants . . . we have known*: as the English have in Ireland.
11 *great care taken of the Poor*: the Act for the Relief of the Poor, passed in the Pennsylvania Assembly in 1705, provided for the appointment of overseers of the poor for each township, whose responsibility it was to raise funds by assessment for poor relief, and to indenture poor children as apprentices: *The Laws of the Province of Pennsylvania: Now in Force*, Philadelphia, 1728, pp. 81–4.

Thousand Yearly, (which will be found to be a moderate Computation in the whole Kingdom) our Butter, Beef, and Leather, which used to bring us a little Mony, will scarce suffice the Inhabitants, and we may in time be obliged to send to *America* for such Things as we have formally exported, as we do now for part of our Timber and Corn.

The Linen Trade, our chief Support, although under the best Regulation,[12] is very much decayed.[13]

Our Youth lye under great Discouragements, and Complain that few of them are preferred in the Church or Revenue, or admitted even to serve in the Army.[14]

We are allowed but very little for the Benefit of Forreign Trade, nor are we even allowed a Mint for any sort of Coyn, a Priviledge seldom denied the meanest Principalities.[15] 'Tis said there is above five hundred thousand pounds carryed yearly, most part in Specie, out of this Kingdom,[16] and most of that for things that might as well be wanted. What Money comes to us, is privately, or chiefly by Stealth, which is given for a Reason why Gold is so much more plenty than Silver, yet our silver is not raised to make it equal to the Gold, nor any Method taken to keep our little Gold at home, or from going to those Places where it passes at a larger Value.[17]

We, to supply the want of Change, would cut part of the forreign Gold and Silver into small Pieces, to be passed by Weight, but the Treasury will not receive them, although it would be both acceptable to the Army, and beneficial to all Degrees, by the present supply of Change.

But what we suffer from many of our Landlords is very intolerable, they seem ambitious only of out doing one another in the Oppression of their

---

12 *under the best Regulation*: the so-called 'Linen Board', established by an Act of the Irish Parliament in 1711. For its work, see *Precedents and Abstracts from the Journals of the Trustees of the Linen and Hempen manufactures of Ireland*, Dublin, 1784.

13 *very much decayed*: in fact, the linen industry in Ulster had entered on a period of sustained growth (L. M. Cullen, *An Economic History of Ireland since 1660*, London: Batsford, 1972, p. 48), and its profitability was noted in John Browne, *Reflections Little to the Purpose, on a Paper Less to the Purpose*, Dublin 1729, p. 21.

14 *or admitted even to serve in the Army*: as commissioned officers. See above, p. 112. On the disposal of Irish patronage in general, see McNally, *Parties, Patriots and Undertakers*, ch. 5, and for the army in particular, ibid., pp. 95, 102–6.

15 *nor are we even allowed a Mint . . . the meanest Principalities*: a point made repeatedly by Swift; see above, p. 21.

16 *'Tis said there . . . out of this Kingdom*: see above, pp. 21, 89–91. Thomas Prior calculated that over £620,000 a year was carried out of Ireland (*Absentees*, p. 14).

17 *What Money comes to us . . . where it passes at a larger Value*: a problem with which Thomas Prior wrestled in *Observations on Coin in General. With Some Proposals for Regulating the Value of Coin in Ireland*, Dublin, 1729.

Tenants, by exorbitant Rents, Leases for short Terms of Years,[18] filled with a Train of the hardest Covenants, the Lawyer's Wit can contrive; and after all, what Duties the Steward, the Lady, or the Cookmaid shall think needful: Thus must we spend our Lives and Fortunes in improving these Lands, which cost our Forefathers so much Time to Cultivate, and bring in from Woods and Boggs, which now from time to time are to be raised higher and higher, to supply some Prodigal, or gratify some covetous Landlord; and in these calamitous Times, Landlords are unwilling to lessen their Rent Roll, by giving an abatement of Rent to their Needy Tenants, or to accept of a surrender of their dear Leases, so that many of the poor People, are under a Necessity of running away, either to *America*, or to some other part of the World; to shelter themselves from Imprisonment, for Debts and Arrears of Rent.

The Books of the *Judges* on their Circuits shew the vast Numbers of Civil Bills and Decrees for Debt against poor People, many of whom choose rather to go any where than starve in Prison, and there are great Complaints that the Cost or Fees of every Decree, for the smallest uncontested Sum of Money (though fairly due by Bill or Bond) will be at least Nine Shillings; this and the unequal Tax called *Hearth Money*,[19] is very heavy upon the Poor.

Some of the Reverend Clergy have been so far imposed upon, as to put their Tyths into the Hands of very ill Men,[20] who do so overaw us by the Interest they pretend to have in the Courts, and by having a hank over us, for small Dues, or old Debts, that we are sometimes glad to please them with a seventh part of the Value, instead of a Tenth, and besides, they often threaten us with Law Suits for the Tyths of the little Gardens of Flax and Potatoes,[21] and Christning, and Burial Money,[22] by which Means the poorest People are great Sufferers.

The great scarceity of Fewel puts us in mind, that the sinking of very deep Pits of fifty or sixty Fathom, (as in other Countries) in proper Places to

---

18 *Leases for short Terms of Years*: see above, p. 175. In the period immediately after the Williamite revolution, leases for 21 years had been common, but by this time a longer period of 31 years or three lives was usual.
19 *Hearth Money*: a tax levied on the number of hearths per household, first levied in Ireland in 1663.
20 *to put their Tyths into the Hands of very ill Men*: see above, n. 5.
21 *Flax and Potatoes*: for the 'small' tithes of flax and potatoes, see Maurice Bric, 'The Tithe System in Eighteenth-Century Ireland', *Proceedings of the Royal Irish Academy* 86 (1986), sect. C, 273.
22 *Christning, and Burial Money:* the so-called 'book money': charges made by Church of Ireland clergy for christenings, marriages and burials.

discover Coals, or other Mines, which have appear'd almost above Ground in many parts of this Kingdom, to employ our Poor, and save a good part of our Money at home, is not practiced by our Great Men, or modern Projectors.

Instead of beneficial Projects, for the Good of the Nation, the Heads of our Men of Fortune run upon little else, but buying Estates, to be in a condition to Rack and Oppress the poor Tenants, who for want of Trade and Business, are bred for the most part to Husbandry alone, so that they eat up the Product of their little Farms.

Some of our Neighbours, who are but too superstitious, prognosticate strange Things, from these unusual Appearances in the Sky, and Lights in the North:[23] And indeed all of us, when we observe the Sun's usual Heat, or Influence, so much abated, can't help thinking, it looks but too like the Frowns of Heaven; and when we see the Earth for these three Years past, refuse its former Encrease, though equally Tilled, we are apt to think our Land like that of *Canaan*, is cursed for the Sins of the People.[24]

Now should a Famine, the forerunner of a Plague, or Pestilence afflict us, as there is now the most apparent Danger, we fear they would be as few *Joseph's* to provide for our Sustenance,[25] as there are Drapers to take our Interests.[26] It was a great Mortification to see our little Corn and Provision sold off publickly to other Countries, whilst our poor and honest Housekeepers[27] are almost starving, in Countries where there are more Hands than Business, and more Mouths than Meat, its undoubtedly better, that considerable Numbers go Yearly Abroad, than be idle at Home, helping to starve their Neighbours.

The *Israelites* when oppressed by a Famine, removed to the Land of *Egypt*.[28] Even Bees, are taught by Instinct, when crowded, to send off their Superfluous Numbers in Swarms; the people of the *Swiss Cantons* ramble to all Countries for Bread and Pay;[29] and wou'd it not be prudent in us to withdraw upon these Accounts and also avoid the threatening Arm of

---

23 *unusual Appearances in the Sky, and Lights in the North*: the comet of 1729, possibly the largest on record, which was eventually identified in August of that year.
24 *our Land ... cursed for the Sins of the People*: a reference to Noah's cursing of his son Ham ('the father of Canaan'): 'Cursed be Canaan; a servant of servants shall he be unto his brethren' (Gen., 9: 20).
25 *as few Joseph's to provide for our Sustenance*: the story, told in Gen., 45: 23, of Joseph sending supplies to Canaan from Egypt to relieve his father and family from famine, which was also cited by Swift in *An Answer to a Paper* ... (above, p. 33).
26 *Drapers to take our Interests*: Swift, in the persona of 'The Drapier'.
27 *Housekeepers*: householders.
28 *removed to the Land of Egypt*: at Joseph's bidding (Gen., 45: 18).
29 *the people of the Swiss Cantons ... Bread and Pay*: as mercenary soldiers.

Providence, which seems now impending over our Nation, ready to punish its Pride, Vanity, Avarice, Infidelity, Oppression, and other Crimes.

Is it not very surprizing, to see many of our Great Men and Ladies, as if they were under an Infatuation, and insensible of the Miseries coming upon us, who, instead of laying out Money in Charity, or in contributing to the Importation of Corn; either hoarding up their Money, or passing it off in costly Apparel, fine Equipage, luxurious Dainties, Gaming, or feeding up Stables of Horses, Kennels of Dogs, and useless Creatures, at a Time when thousands of poor People are ready to starve.

We must not omit the great Goodness and Charitable Endeavours of his Grace the Lord Primate of all *Ireland*, in relieving the Poor of the City of *Armagh*, and other Places last Year, with Money and Corn, nor those good Men, who have this Year, subscribed very large Sums of Money, in conjunction with his Grace, to be laid out in the Importation of Corn, to be distributed at a moderate price, for the Relief of the Poor in the Province of *Ulster*.[30]

It is believed, that if all our Landlords were like those Good Men, many of the People that intend for *America*, would alter their Minds.

It is reported, that the Landlords are drawing up Memorials, to prevent our going; in which they alledge, we carry off a great deal of the current Coin, but we beg of them to consider, that few but poor People are yet gone, who do not carry off even one tenth part of what they themselves *melt down* into Plate, or send abroad Yearly, for Wine, Tea, Spices, and foreign Cloaths, which at this Time, might be better spared.

And if it be true, that every Hand will earn in *America*, three Times as much Wages, as here, they will rather buy their Linen from us, where it is cheap, than to bestow their Time in making it here.

It was seldom known among our Forefathers, that they should be hindred of a Passage from any part of his Majestys Dominions to another, except when *Oliver Cromwel* was stopped in his intended Voyage to *New England*,[31] the consequence of which, any one that reads the History of those Times may find, besides, might it not be against the Interest of *Ireland*

---

30 *Relief of the Poor... Ulster*: for Archbishop Boulter's charitable activities in Armagh, see *DIB*; for the subscription opened in 1729 to purchase corn in Munster to supply the needs of the population in the north, see Boulter to the Archbishop of Canterbury, 13 Feb. 1728[/9] (*Boulter Letters*, vol. I, p. 224), and to Newcastle, 13 Mar. 1728[/9] (vol. I, p. 230).

31 *Oliver Cromwel was stopped in his intended Voyage to New England*: supposedly in 1634 (see *ODNB*), a story to be found in Cotton Mather, *Magnalia Christi Americana: or, The Ecclesiastical History of New-England, from Its First Planting in the year 1620. unto the Year of Our Lord, 1698*, London, 1702, p. 23.

to make it a place of Confinement, or if it be so, we wish it was for the Rich, who carry or send away vast Sums of Money, to be spent in foreign Countries.

Some alledge, That the Protestants ought to be kept at home, as a Security for us against the Papists, least they[32] should joyn our Enemies, or rise in Arms as they did in the Year, 1641. Now, in *Ulster*, the Number of Papists are not very considerable;[33] and it is believed, if there were more Encouragement given to *Charity Schools*,[34] and if the Clergy would spend a little Time in Conversing more freely with them, and treat them in a courteous and kind Manner, many of them would be brought over.

But if the Landlords fear anything from that Quarter, why don't they give us better Bargains, to Encourage our Stay, for a Security to them, and their Estates.

It is observed, that when very great Tracts of Land are granted in Lease by the Nobility and Bishops, the Chief Tenants become Landlords,[35] and there is no great care taken to secure the Poor Inhabitants that labour the Ground, from the Oppression of rack rents, and severe Duties, even of unseasonable Days Work,[36] and in the time of their Harvest.

Ireland was once covered with Wood, 'till cleared by the Industry of our Forefathers, whose Posterity are now, in like manner, for the Reasons aforesaid, inclined to clear their Way in forreign Countries; and since his Majesty's Plantations want Numbers of People to secure them against their Enemies, our Removal seems no less for the Interest of the King, than of Us, besides, the Service that would be done to the Church and State, by the propagation of the Protestant Religion, and the *British* interest, in that *Great Continent*.

---

32 *they*: the Catholics.
33 *in Ulster, the Number of Papists are not very considerable*: a point which was by no means universally accepted, but which would be reiterated within three years in a published analysis of the Hearth Money returns: David Bindon, *An Abstract of the Number of Protestant and Popish Families in the Several Counties and Provinces of Ireland, Taken from the Returns made by the Hearthmoney Collectors...*, Dublin, 1736.
34 *Charity Schools*: the charity school movement was in serious decline from the mid-1720s: D. W. Hayton, 'Did Protestantism Fail in Early Eighteenth-century Ireland? Charity Schools and the Enterprise of Religious and Social Reformation, c. 1690–1730', in Alan Ford, James McGuire and Kenneth Milne (eds.), *As by Law Established: The Church of Ireland since the Reformation*, Dublin: Lilliput Press, 1995, p. 182.
35 *become Landlords*: by subletting. On this phenomenon, see David Dickson, 'Middlemen', in Thomas Bartlett and D. W. Hayton (eds.), *Penal Era and Golden Age: Essays in Irish History 1690–1800*, Belfast: Ulster Historical Foundation, 1979, pp. 162–85.
36 *unseasonable Days Work*: the statutory requirement that all 'housekeepers' provide six days' labour each year to repair roads (W. E. H. Lecky, *History of Ireland in the Eighteenth Century*, 5 vols., London, 1892, vol. II, p. 45).

Some of our Knights and Squires have courted our Interest,[37] with pretended Love, and fair Promises of representing our Grievances in order to have them redressed, but no sooner have they gained their point, than they become Lazy, Heedless, or too Proud and Haughty, to mind us, or the Grievances of their afflicted Country, and consequently mute as Fish[38] in moveing ought that may tend to its Benefit, and, in truth some of them seem as if they never thought of it, but preferment for themselves, or their Friends, or to be of some Party, or be skreend from Debts, seem to be some of their chiefest aims, whereas would they, with Spirit and Conduct, joyn heartily in a fair Representation of our Grievance to his sacred Majesty, there is no room to doubt of speedy Redress from so good a Sovereign.

It is observed, that Merchants, and Owners of Ships make such Advantage by the Fraught of Passengers to those Countries, that they frequently send Emissaries abroad[39] to Entice and Ensnare the unwary People, who out of Hopes of becoming very Great, because some few, as in other Places, were successful there, they are often overperswaded to quit their Farmes, and comfortable Livings, for mere Uncertainties, to the hazard of their Lives, and the lives of their Wives and Children.

To conclude, if the Landlords, and others, who are unwilling to part with us, will in a proper Manner lay before his Majesty the National Grievances, so that by their Redress there may be Encouragement of Trade and Employing of the Poor, who now, as an Instance of their Poverty, go yearly to *England* in Crowds, to look for a Day's Labour, and many of them die in the Fields by the Way; and in the Province of *Ulster*, there are great Numbers of Labouring Men and Women, going about the Country, in a starving Condition, Begging to get Meal alone for their Labour. Now if they will let us have fair Leases of our Land, at a moderate Rent, free from those barbarous Covenants and Impositions, and for such Terms of Years as our Children may reap some Benefit of our Improvements: And if the Clergy will be more moderate in their Dues, and not give them into the Hands of Racking Farmers, they may be well assured, we would not for the short Space that remains of our Lives, leave our Relations, our Friends, and our Native Soil, in search of distant Lands, to undergo the various Toyles, Hardships and Dangers of the Seas, by Storms, Shipwracks, Turks[40] and Pyrates, to be

37 *Some of our Knights and Squires have courted our Interest*: in standing for election to Parliament.
38 *mute as Fish*: proverbial (*ODEP*, p. 552).
39 *abroad*: about the country.
40 *Turks*: the Barbary corsairs, pirates operating from the Berber (Barbary) coast of north Africa and sometimes known as Ottoman Corsairs. The Muslim inhabitants of the region were referred to as Moors or Turks.

starved, or cast away by the Villainy of Shipmasters, or when safely landed to be liable to many Troubles, and Disappointments; the Sickness and Seasonings of the Country, the fatigue of clearing Woods and Forrests, before we can sow our Corn, and the Incursions and Insurrection of the *Indians*, Civil Wars, or Invasions. We run upon these Hazards and Dangers (as we think) to avoid Landlords and other Afflictions. Tho' perhaps at length there may arise in those Countries Landlords, oppressors and devourers of Mankind,[41] as in these; so that if we could be Easy at home, we should think it by much the best, to stay where we are, in hopes of better Times, and be buried with our Forefathers.

We are, SIR,
Your most obedient humble Servants,
Andrew Trueman,
Patrick Layfield.

Lisburn,
May, 31st. 1729.

---

41 *oppressors and devourers of Mankind*: Proverbs, 30: 14: 'There is a generation, whose teeth are as swords, and their jaw teeth as knives, to devour the poor from off the earth, and the needy from among men.'

GENERAL TEXTUAL INTRODUCTION AND TEXTUAL ACCOUNTS OF INDIVIDUAL WORKS

GENERAL TEXTUAL INTRODUCTION

Swift's Irish prose writings after the *Drapier's Letters* were often works of controversy or addressed to a particular debate (some more successfully so than others), and thus frequently written with an immediate purpose. As such, their dissemination in Dublin was often relatively straightforward, using the same printers, and often not requiring a particularly high standard of printing: the work needed to be published, not refined and endlessly revised. Unpublished works, polemics that were not finished or whose time quickly passed, were collected posthumously by later editors. London printings and reprintings complicated matters somewhat, but, nevertheless, none of the works included in this volume offer the sort of intractable textual problems that make the choice of a copy text in itself an act of conjecture as much as judgment.

The transmission of Swift's prose pamphlets in this period can be thought about with reference to his own view of his writing at this time. Stephen Karian has suggested that Swift's 'late period' begins around September 1727 (the end of his final visit to England). It was at this time, Karian argues, that he 'was no longer seeking patronage that might alter his residence and ecclesiastical position in Ireland. That acceptance of his professional status seems to have liberated him toward being quite politically outspoken as a writer, even more outspoken than earlier.'[1] Although Karian's argument is applied to Swift's increased poetic output from this point, the mixture of apparent resignation (as his writings will avail him little personally) and liberation (as he has little to fear from the consequences) can be applied to his polemical prose in these years, and the manner of its arrival into the world.

Swift was apparently very ambivalent about the value of his topical writings from this time onwards, most explicitly in telling Pope (in 1731) that 'I write

[1] Stephen Karian, *Jonathan Swift in Print and Manuscript*, Cambridge: Cambridge University Press, 2010, p. 3.

Pamphlets and follys meerly for amusement, and when they are finished, or I grow weary in the middle, I cast them into the fire, partly out of dislike, and chiefly because I know they will signify nothing.' A year later he described how 'As to Ireland... I remember to have published nothing but what is called the Drapier's letters, and some few other trifles relating to the affairs of this miserable and ruined Kingdom.'[2] This is somewhat disingenuous, as for all this supposed state of apathy and resignation, Swift still completed and published many of these writings, and still wanted them to appear in Dublin (for their immediate purpose) and London (at least partly for the sake of maintaining his reputation, and for posterity).

The period of writing covered in this volume (from 1726 to 1737) saw Swift's publishing and printing practices go through certain quite clearly delineated phases. This introduction will detail these in turn, concluding on a description of this volume's editorial and textual principles.

1 Sarah Harding

This volume begins with *Upon Giving Badges to the Poor* and its companion, *Considerations about Maintaining the Poor*, works presumed to have been written in 1726, both of which were published posthumously. Swift's earliest published Irish prose writings in this volume (and his first since the *Drapier's Letters*) were his contributions concerning contemporary Irish economic problems in 1728 (*A Short View of the State of Ireland* and *An Answer to a Paper, Called A Memorial of the Poor Inhabitants of Ireland*), angry expressions of Swift's perception of the ruin of Irish trade and agriculture. These were printed and sold by Sarah Harding, widow of John Harding, veteran printer of the *Drapier's Letters* and thus a trusted figure for Swift. The reasons for this, and for her subsequent publication of Swift and Sheridan's journal *The Intelligencer*, have been summarised by James Woolley. Whilst her 'unimpressive printing' raises the question why she was chosen, this is 'answered only in part by the fact that she succeeded her husband John as Swift's printer'. It was at least in part a question of loyalty: her husband had been imprisoned for publishing the fourth *Drapier's Letter* in 1724, and had died in April 1725, having been a significant figure in the Drapier's campaign, and his widow had been willing to continue the publication. Swift, as Woolley suggests, also needed to work with people likely to be discreet: these works were often politically contentious, to say the least, and were all

2 Swift to Pope, 15 January 1730-1 (Woolley, *Corr.*, vol. III, p. 355); Swift to Rev Henry Henney, 8 June 1732 (ibid., p. 484).

published anonymously, so 'Swift evidently valued deniability', particularly 'expecting that the bookseller would absorb the risks of prosecution or other legal harassment'.[3] As Swift wrote in 1732:

> no Printer or Bookseller hath any kind of property here. I have writ some things that would make people angry[.] I have always sent them by unknown hands, the Printer might guess, but he could not accuse me[,] he ran the whole risk, and well deserved the property, if he could carry it to London and print it there, but I am sure I could have no property at all.[4]

By 'Property' here, Swift means that the Irish publisher could not enforce any claim or right to publish a work, in terms of ownership. In contrast to the more regulated London trade, no printer or bookseller could hope to maintain their property against piracy. If they were willing to run the risk of publishing such material, they were welcome to the rewards; Sarah Harding, like her husband and other printers and booksellers, was willing to take such risks.

In the printings of *A Short View* and *An Answer to a Paper* (both octavo, like all Harding's work for Swift), polemic intent was uppermost, at the expense of quality. As Woolley summarised (and it is true of all of Harding's printings of Swift's works in this period, to a greater or lesser extent), 'Crude typography, cheap paper, shabby makeready, and at times careless proofreading were standard in the Harding shop.'[5] This is especially noticeable in *An Answer*, which uses italic for some stretches, not for emphasis but to supply missing roman type, as well as random switching of type sizes, uneven margins, and repeated errors and misprints.

Harding continued to print Swift's next important work, the twenty numbers of the jointly written *Intelligencer* from May 1728 to February 1729. Her printing of the short numbers of *The Intelligencer* (few of which run to more than eight pages, and which were in Woolley's words 'well within the normal range of ephemeral Dublin printing') shows what Swift wanted: he never used Harding for books, or anything extensive and lengthy,

---

3 James Woolley, 'Sarah Harding as Swift's Printer', in Christopher Fox and Brenda Tooley (eds.), *Walking Naboth's Vineyard: New Studies of Swift*, Notre Dame, IN: University of Notre Dame Press, 1995, pp. 164–77 (pp. 164, 165). For her willingness to carry on publishing the letters after her husband's demise, see p. 167. Woolley also notes (p. 164) that Sarah had been arrested for printing *On Wisdom's Defeat in a Learned Debate* (1725), ascribed to Swift by Ehrenpreis (vol. III, pp. 314–16).
4 Swift to Benjamin Motte, 4 November 1732 (Woolley, *Corr.*, vol. III, p. 556).
5 Woolley, 'Sarah Harding', p. 168.

presumably as it was beyond her scope and means.[6] Secrecy was supposedly served by the papers being copied 'into an unknown hand' and then taken to the bookseller.[7] Swift did complain that readers were offended with the continual nonsense made by Harding's printers' errors, whilst refusing (naturally) to acknowledge authorship.[8] Aside from the vagaries of printing, highlighted by the many variants in issues of such small pieces, another quirk was rhetorical: the pointing of *The Intelligencer* was based around the spoken, rather than the written, sentence, though the punctuation errors of Harding's press cannot always be explained away because of this. These and other qualities specific to Harding's Dublin *Intelligencer* were smoothed out in the editions collected in London in 1729 and 1730, the papers by Swift included in the third Volume of the Pope–Swift *Miscellanies* (1732) and in Faulkner's 1735 Dublin *Works*.

Harding's last printing in October 1729 was one of Swift's most notorious works: *A Modest Proposal*. The quality of printing was somewhat better compared to the efforts of the previous year, but Swift's use of her was coming to an end. It has been suggested that her business had gone through some change, and perhaps reduced its operations (the imprint for *A Modest Proposal* had changed to 'Fishamble Street', an evident move from the 'Crown in Copper-Alley' of the works of the previous year). She then 'drops from sight', in terms of publishing; it is more than likely that she remarried.[9] For these and perhaps other reasons, she no longer needed the financial boost of Swift's printings. At this time, Swift's printing was taken over by the figure who would become the most significant publishing connection of his career.

2 George Faulkner, William Bowyer, Dublin and London

George Faulkner had previously printed the collection and reprint of the *Drapier's Letters* entitled *Fraud Detected, or the Hibernian Patriot* (1725), as the celebrity of the endeavour required a larger-scale edition and more durable printing than Harding's pamphlets could provide. From October 1729, he became Swift's Dublin printer, a relationship that would include

---

6 See ibid., p. 169. For Dublin edition sizes, see Mary Pollard, *Dublin's Trade in Books, 1500–1800*, Oxford: Oxford University Press, 1989, pp. 116–20.
7 For the alleged transmission of the papers, see Woolley, 'Sarah Harding', p. 165; Swift to Motte, 4 November 1732 (Woolley, *Corr.*, vol. III, p. 308).
8 Swift to Rev. John Worrall, January 13 1728–9 (Woolley, *Corr.*, vol. III, p. 206).
9 Woolley, 'Sarah Harding', p. 169. For the remarriage, see Woolley, *Intelligencer*, p. 38.

selected pamphlets, the four-volume *Works* of 1735 and its subsequent augmentations, and almost every significant posthumous publication of Swift. His printing is more uniform in style and quality than the more basic versions of Harding, and his responsibility for many of the works in this volume ensures their textual problems, errors and variants are far less pronounced than in the Harding printings. He also became a crucial conduit in the transmission of Swift's works to London.

London publication was important to Swift in terms of his canon, and the mark it made in the future: his often-stated ambivalence towards Ireland suggests that, whilst he needed to publish his controversial works anonymously in Dublin, as contributions to public debate, he also needed them to be reprinted in London, for the sake of their wider dissemination, to satisfy his need for continued recognition as a significant public and intellectual figure, and because he could avoid certain measures of censorship practised upon their publication in Dublin.

The strengths and weaknesses of publishing in Dublin during the first half of the century are summarised by Máire Kennedy:

> Books cost less in Dublin than in London. Dublin printers were able to undercut their London rivals by reprinting in smaller formats, using cheaper paper, and not needing to purchase copyright. Advertisers were careful to point out the saving achieved by the purchase of an Irish edition, usually claiming that the production was as good, if not better, than the London edition.[10]

Yet, as this implies, the factors that made Dublin such a source of possible profit also made piracy more likely; though lack of copyright was not perhaps the most telling factor, Swift needed a reliable method of publishing in London, not least to maintain some presence in a cultural climate he found inherently more sophisticated and of more significance than his own.

The only control over material in Dublin was the signal of a bookseller's intention to publish: this system of so-called 'posting' was all that resembled copyright.[11] Given this, it was to the advantage of Dublin and London publishers to work together – the absence of copyright in the former meant that

---

10 Máire Kennedy, 'Reading Print, 1700–1800', in Raymond Gillespie and Andrew Hadfield (eds.), *The Oxford History of the Irish Book*, vol. III: *The Irish Book in English 1550–1800*, Oxford, Oxford University Press, 2006, p. 151.
11 For this system of claiming copyright, see Pollard, *Dublin's Trade in Books*, pp. 169–72, though she admits that 'How this posting-up worked in practice is not clear' (p. 170), and it probably used a mixture of notices posted at Stationers Hall, and newspaper advertisements.

cheap reprintings were legion, and, to prevent these, agreements between publishers were desirable.[12]

Swift and Faulkner found a method of London publication that suited their separate needs: William Bowyer, the London printer. Faulkner had befriended Bowyer, worked in his shop in 1726, and was exactly placed to pass on Swift's writings to him, after printing them in Dublin, and taking some share of the profit.[13] As Keith Maslen has described, 'between 1729 and 1767 Bowyer printed some three score editions of Irish origin', many of them from Faulkner: 'Bowyer was certainly or probably indebted to his Dublin friend for a steady supply of mostly little pieces from which Bowyer might derive a double profit, from printing and from selling.'[14] Maslen estimates that at least twenty-four of such printings were from Faulkner. The *Bowyer Ledgers*, which record the business of the print shop in these years, list the works by Swift reprinted by Bowyer with Faulkner, and also include a list of the type sold by Bowyer to Faulkner, another sign of the closeness of their relationship. Swift also assigned to Matthew Pilkington copyright of works which 'were printed in Dublin, by Mr George Faulkner, some of which were sent in Manuscript to Mr William Bowyer of London, Printer'.[15] Faulkner was, to a large degree, acting as a conduit for Swift in passing on works to London.

These works were often published under the pseudonymous imprint of 'A Moor', or a 'trade' publisher, such as James Roberts, owner of what Michael Treadwell describes as 'by far the largest trade publishing shop in London. For the first twenty years after taking over the business in 1713, James Roberts put his name to more books, pamphlets and periodicals than anyone else in the trade', and for good reason: 'It was simply one of the trade

---

12   For Dublin and London's mutual need for each other, and deals to obviate cheaper Irish reprints, see ibid., pp. 87–96.
13   The first Bowyer–Faulkner work was the 1729 London edition of *The Intelligencer*. Keith Maslen lists them all in 'George Faulkner and William Bowyer: The London Connection', in *An Early London Printing House at Work: Studies in the Bowyer Ledgers*, New York: Bibliographical Society of America, 1993, pp. 223–33, p. 231, where he also describes the history of the professional relationship between the two printers. In the following, and in the individual textual accounts, we have given the work by number in Keith Maslen and John Lancaster (eds.), *The Bowyer Ledgers: The Printing Accounts of William Bowyer, Father and Son*, London: Bibliographical Society, 1991, and add date and original ledger-page number. See also Woolley, *Corr.*, vol. III, p. 464, n. 5, for the ordering of works of 1732 'implicating variously Swift as author, Faulkner as printer publisher and Irish go-between, Bowyer as London printer and proprietor'.
14   'George Faulkner and William Bowyer', pp. 224, 227–8.
15   The account is between 1735 and 1737. See *Ledger* A340. For the assigning to Pilkington, see 22 July 1732, in Woolley, *Corr.*, vol. III, p. 508.

publisher's functions (and not the least important) to stand mute between the real proprietors and the authorities in time of any slight unpleasantness.'[16] Conversely, Roberts's productions were so numerous that he was perhaps simply the most convenient publisher, and politics did not come into it: a trade publisher was the primary means of distribution for a great many works, rather than a publisher *per se*, and therefore lacked the individuality (and responsibility) associated with the role. As for 'A Moor, near St Pauls', supposed publisher of the first Bowyer–Faulkner work, the 1729 collection of *The Intelligencer*, as David Foxon put it: 'whether or not any such person existed, the imprint was regularly used, fictitiously'.[17] Such pseudonyms and large-scale 'trade' publishers became the primary means for distributing Swift's prose pamphlets in London.

There were advantages for all parties in this system: Bowyer received exclusive editions of Swift's work, Faulkner could profit from selling works in two places, and Swift could publish in London. A good example of this process in action is *A Vindication of His Excellency the Lord Carteret*, first published in Dublin in 1730, and reprinted in London, for all the claims of its imprint 'London printed and Dublin re-printed'. It appeared in Dublin in April 1730 directly after the closing of Parliament, and was entered in the Bowyer paper ledgers for 30 April 1730. It was, as Maslen argues, 'evidently first printed by Faulkner', and the claim of a Dublin reprint a feint in case of trouble.[18] A feature of the London version that backs up this reading is the identification, in the 1730 London edition, of Swift's enemies Joshua Allen and Richard Tighe, albeit through the use of blanks and suggestive footnotes. The supposed Dublin 'reprint' does not gloss them at all, suggesting Faulkner's understandable reluctance to increase the offensiveness of an outspoken pamphlet. Whereas it would place a burden on Faulkner (or any printer) to run the risk of libel by identifying publicly figures already tacitly known to readers (and, indeed, Faulkner did not identify them in the

16 Michael Treadwell, 'London Trade Publishers 1675–1750', *The Library* 4 (1982), 99–134, pp. 110, 125.
17 David F. Foxon, *English Verse 1701–1750: A Catalogue of Separately Printed Poems with Notes on Contemporary Collected Editions*, 2 vols., London: Cambridge University Press, 1975, vol. II, p. 172.
18 Maslen, 'George Faulkner and William Bowyer', p. 227. There is a reference in the pamphlet to writing on 13 April (see above, p. 214). Ehrenpreis posits that 'he might have added this sentence while the essay was in the press'. Carteret would be leaving for England soon after the end of Parliament, 'yet what Swift wished to write would have been risky during Parliament time' (vol. III, p. 658). Parliament was prorogued on Wednesday 15 April 1730. The London printings are TS 697 (Bowyer 1545, 24 April 1730), and 2nd edn, Bowyer 1576, 25 July 1730 (not in TS). See Maslen, 'George Faulkner and William Bowyer', p. 231.

1735 Dublin *Works* reprint), the London edition could be more explicit, and these two versions of the *Vindication of Carteret* are thus presented slightly differently to these two audiences.

There are also works that may well have been part of the Faulkner–Bowyer axis, but for which proof is elusive. The most outstanding of these is *An Examination of Certain Abuses, Corruptions, and Enormities In the City of Dublin* (1732), reprinted in London in the same year but retitled *City Cries, Instrumental and Vocal, or An Examination of Certain Abuses, Corruptions, and Enormities in London and Dublin*, with an extra ending more appropriate to the London edition of the satire (see the Textual Account below, pp. 468–70), offering a fine example of how Swift was tailoring his work for different milieus.

The Faulkner–Bowyer relationship, and the sale of their output to trusted booksellers, guaranteed a certain quality of printing and similarity of format in the majority of the works in this volume: there are cases where the variants in London cannot be associated with Swift directly (*A Modest Proposal* is an interesting example, in terms of its first London printing, and other later reprints), but generally the textual problems found here are not profound. The complication, as Faulkner developed his printing of the Swift canon, is his four-volume Dublin *Works* of 1735, which reprinted many of the pamphlets in this volume with locally small but cumulatively significant changes, and Faulkner claimed that these revisions were at Swift's instigation. The argument ever since has concerned what form this instigation took, and its thoroughness (it is entirely possible that Swift revised parts of his work decisively, but hardly glanced at a short pamphlet on a now obsolete Irish political question published seven years before). It is also the case that Swift's public attitude towards Faulkner's edition was deliberately ambiguous. Consequently, whereas it was once almost an assumption about the edition of 1735 that (in Herbert Davis's words) 'many of its variants must result from authorial intervention', that view has now been replaced by a greater scepticism about what exactly Swift revised, and where he intervened. Stephen Karian's description of 'the extent of Swift's involvement, and the reliability of Faulkner's conflicting accounts' of it, concludes that 'The goal of extracting purely authentic Swift versions from Faulkner's texts can never be achieved', in part because Faulkner admitted adding notes at least to the texts, and therefore it is possible that he revised some texts himself.[19] For reasons fully

---

19 *The Drapier's Letters*, ed. Herbert Davis, Oxford: Clarendon Press, 1935, p. 39. Karian, *Jonathan Swift in Print and Manuscript*, p. 42. See also his discussion of the context of Faulkner's disparate comments on the edition (pp. 30–43).

explained in the editorial principles below, therefore, this volume always chooses the earliest possible text, rather than the 1735 *Works*.

3 Miscellaneous and Posthumous Printings

The majority of the works in this volume were printed in Dublin by Sarah Harding or George Faulkner, and then reprinted in London. There are a number of pieces, though, that were unpublished in Swift's lifetime; some were unfinished. There are extant manuscripts of four of these pieces in the Forster Collection of the V & A (the transcription of one of which, the fragment 'Upon Giving Badges to the Poor', has never been published before). All of these pieces first appeared in posthumous collected editions of Swift's writings, which (starting with Faulkner's in 1735) were augmented as the century went on, and more uncollected pieces became available. There was one premiered by John Nichols as late as 1801, but, generally, the last significant tranche of unpublished prose pieces was included by Swift's cousin once removed, Deane Swift, in his 1765 revised edition of John Hawkesworth's collection of Swift; most were reprinted in Dublin by Faulkner soon after, by agreement. Deane Swift had inherited various Swift papers from Martha Whiteway, Swift's cousin. He therefore had propinquity to enable his publication of manuscript and unpublished material, but even though the works may have been printed from manuscript, they were published first as part of a uniform edition, with all the lack of individually distinctive textual qualities, in terms of typography, capitals, spelling and accidentals that this entails. Ultimately, though, Deane Swift is the only authority for these works, and how Swift wanted them to appear cannot be known.

The pieces collected here appeared, for the most part, in all post-1765 collected editions of Swift, up to Herbert Davis's two volumes containing them (vol. XII and XIII, 1955 and 1959). Significant printings of them (chiefly those that might have textual authority) are discussed in the individual textual accounts for each work.

4 Rationale for Texts Included and Excluded

This volume collects all of Swift's non-religious prose writing on Irish subjects after the publication of the *Drapier's Letters*. Its chronology runs from the fragmentary *Upon Giving Badges to the Poor* (1726) to the similarly themed *Proposal for Giving Badges to the Beggars* (1737). It includes associated and ancillary materials, such as manuscript fragments, or pamphlets which generated responses from Swift in the works in the volume proper. It does not include Swift's ecclesiastical writings from this period (which are collected elsewhere in the Cambridge edition), or works by Swift in which the mixture of prose and poetry predominates towards the latter. This is of most relevance with regard to *The Intelligencer*, partly because the journal was jointly authored with Thomas Sheridan, creating potential complications regarding attribution. Two numbers of *The Intelligencer* are known to be in part by Swift, but are made up primarily of verse. These are: no. 8 (*c*. 29 June – 2 July 1728), which contains 'Mad Mullinix and Timothy', and no. 10 (*c*. 13–16 July 1728), which consists partly of 'Tim and the Fables'. Both papers feature prose introductions to the poems by Sheridan, who also adds 'the four last slovenly lines' of 'Tim and the Fables', according to Swift's summary of the authorship of the journal (Swift to Pope, 12 June 1732; see Woolley, *Corr.*, vol. III, p. 489). Since Swift's hand in these papers is entirely poetic, they are not included here, but will instead appear in the volumes of this edition that collect Swift's *Poems*.

Also not included here, for related but slightly different reasons, is the final *Intelligencer*, no. 20, 'Dean Smedley Gone to Seek His Fortune' (*c*. 8–19 May 1729). This last paper is a mixed prose and poetic attack on Jonathan Smedley (1671–1729), until recently Dean of Clogher, who had received a chaplaincy in Madras; unbeknown to Swift or Sheridan, he died en route to India in March 1729 (Woolley, *Intelligencer*, p. 218). An inveterate enemy of Swift, Smedley had been lampooned by Sheridan in *Intelligencer* no. 11 (*c*. 8–12 October 1728), and had in 1728 published *Gulliveriana*, attacking Pope and Swift. The textual history of no. 20 is somewhat confusing, in that it was printed by John Nichols in one edition of *A Supplement to Swift's Works* (1779; see Woolley, *Intelligencer*, p. 336), but has not been consistently included by editors since: in the last century it has been overlooked (or silently excluded) by Temple Scott and Herbert Davis.

James Woolley, including no. 20 in his comprehensive *Intelligencer* edition, admits that 'the attribution to Swift is, it must be conceded, conjectural', though he puts forward some possible thematic and stylistic reasons for it, alongside some aspects of the work that could equally be attributed to Sheridan (*Intelligencer*, p. 217). Woolley also hypothesises that no. 20 was published too late to be included in the first collected London edition of the journal (1729), and was subsequently not noticed by Faulkner when checking for inclusions for the 1735 works, or by Swift when listing his involvement to Pope (Woolley, *Corr.*, vol. III, p. 489). This may well be the case, as it was included in the second London collected edition of 1730, though it is unusual for a work to fall through so many cracks for decades, if it was freely acknowledged by Swift in his lifetime.

Ultimately, the attribution of no. 20, 'Dean Smedley', remains ambiguous: neither Swift, nor the indefatigable Faulkner, Deane Swift and Hawkesworth (whose editions between them gathered up the vast majority of Swift's fugitive pieces in the decades following his death), managed to include it in any post-1730 collection, yet had various opportunities to do so. Practically, the nature of the majority of its original material – poetic satire – means that it too has been excluded from this volume, and will be included in the volumes that collect Swift's poetry.

5 Editorial Principles and Textual Policy

The principles of this volume follow the guidelines of the General Editors of this Cambridge edition: as these polemical tracts were written for a specific historical moment and purpose, the first published text will be deemed more suitable as copy text than one revised for later publication. The copy texts in this volume adhere to this policy strictly, and always take the first possible published version as copy text, as these represent Swift's intentions at the moment of greatest relevance to the immediate circumstances. Similarly, in cases where the choice is between a manuscript and a posthumous publication, the manuscript has been chosen as copy text.

Adherence to this policy sometimes leads to a certain level of emendation – particularly in Sarah Harding's most error-strewn printings, such as *An Answer to the Memorial*, where the misprints and homophones in her edition have to be rectified quite often. For the most part, though, the choice between the earliest text and those later revised and collected (most frequently by Faulkner, in his 1735 *Works*) neither affects the quality of the text presented, nor confuses the reader.

The occurrence of two very different posthumously published texts and a partial manuscript makes the *Letter on M'culla* somewhat more complicated, but the great virtue of having full textual accounts, and a comprehensive listing of significant variants, offers the reader all alternatives. Where there are appended or extra sections in other versions not in the copy text, discretion has been exercised: Sheridan's introduction to *A Short View of the State of Ireland*, for its reprinting as *Intelligencer*, no. 15, is included in the historical collation, as it is known not to be by Swift; conversely, the extra paragraphs at the end of *City Cries*, the London version of *An Examination of Certain Abuses*, are also included in full at the end of the main text, to make both versions of Swift's work easily accessible to the interested reader.

The individual textual accounts describe (where possible and known) the origins and composition of each work, the publication of each significant edition, and of those with possible authority. The choice of copy text is explained and justified, and (where relevant) the later history of the text discussed. (One exception is Swift's contributions to *The Intelligencer*, which are considered in one account.) The bibliographical descriptions of each significant edition then follow for each work, providing descriptions of title pages, collations, contents, pagination, type and page measurements, variants, failures of catchwords to catch, word division for compound words, and locations of copies examined and collated. We have personally looked at every copy listed here, and have, where possible, collated several copies, though there are some cases (particularly broadsheets and half-sheets) where copies of any work are scarce, and comparison of multiple copies impossible. These are followed in each account by the list of emendations from the copy text, and the historical collation, which details every significant substantive difference between texts with potential authority, thus allowing the reader to reconstruct the original text of any of these editions. When in the list of emendations no source follows the bracket, the emendation is editorial; similarly, when in the historical collations the lemma is not from the copy text, the source of the emendation is given immediately after the bracket. For the ease of the reader, and to avoid repetition, the relevant numbers of each publication in the *Teerink Scouten* bibliography of Swift's writings (TS) and the ESTC number follow directly after the title of its listing in the bibliographical description.

Swift's texts are reprinted without preservation of the long-s, ligatures, drop capitals and lineation (including spacing between paragraphs). This edition preserves the copy text's punctuation, italicization, spelling, em-dashes, multiple hyphens, elisions and footnotes. Black letter has been reproduced in title pages, headings and texts. Works using a manuscript as copy text print a clean-text version, but include superscript and do not expand contractions or emend abbreviated forms.

TEXTUAL ACCOUNTS OF INDIVIDUAL WORKS

Upon Giving Badges to the Poor

Textual Account

Dated 26 September 1726, and belonging to the aftermath of the *Drapier's Letters*, this fragment shares ideas with the *Proposal for Giving Badges to the Beggars*, published eleven years later.

It was previously included by Davis (vol. XIII, pp. 172–3), who used the first printed version (Deane Swift's *Works*, 1765), and was seemingly not aware of the manuscript, alongside others from Swift, in the Forster Collection of the Victoria and Albert Museum (for the history of these, see David Woolley, 'Forster's *Swift*', *The Dickensian* 70 (1974) 191–204); this is SwJ 479, entitled 'About Beggars &c' at its end. This manuscript is thus printed here for the first time, as copy text, collated against Deane Swift (1765a) and Faulkner's reprint in *Works*, in the same year (1765b).

The manuscript is a fair copy, likely the last version of the text before Swift stopped composition, with the left-hand side of each page left blank for insertions. It would seem that these were added at the stage of composition: the inking on all insertions longer than one word, and their placing on the blank left-hand of the page suggests authorial additions immediately after the reading through of this final draft of the fragment (and its unfinished state explains why such variants and revisions are sparse). These insertions, along with deletions, are listed separately below as variants. Apart from the adoption of the more conventional titles, there are no emendations; the Historical Collation adds later variants from the published versions.

Copy Text
V & A, Forster MS 518, F.48.G.6/2 Item 6.

Manuscript
SwJ 479
Location: V & A, Forster MS 518, F.48.G.6/2 Item 6.
Description: autograph hand, 2 leaves, 194 × 154 mm; cropped and mounted on card by page. Fos. 1^v–2^r paginated 2–3 in pen, by Swift. Fos. 1^r–2^v paginated 1–4 (added later in pencil, in middle of top of card). Foliation '6' on first leaf added later in pencil, on right of top of card.
Contents: fo. 1^r 'Badges to the Poor' (added later to card, bottom middle); '2 L' (added later to card in same hand, bottom right); 1^r–2^v: text in right-hand column; additions on left. 2^v: 'About Badges' added in Swift's hand, under text in left-hand column, and at the foot of the same column, inverted, 'Badges to the Poor'.

Alterations to the Manuscript
3.2 Concourse of] *before del.* Poor
3.4 according to the antient Laws of the Land.] *ins. with caret from left-hand margin*
3.6 Grace] *interlineated with caret after* His
3.7 of Brass, Copper, or Pewter] *ins. with caret from left-hand margin*
3.9 each] *before del.* of
3.11 distinguished.] *before del.* It was before ordered
3.11 And] *interlineated before* that none
3.12 Parish] *before del.* or
3.16 of them] *before del.* It
3.17 of] *interlineated with caret before* those
3.19 fasten them] *before del.* with
3.20 Coats] *before del.* so as
3.21 walk] *before del.* the
4.5 to put] *interlineated with caret before del.* had

Deane Swift, *Works*, 1765a
TS 87. *ESTC* T52748
Title: THE | WORKS | OF | Dr. JONATHAN SWIFT, | Dean of St. Patrick's, Dublin. | VOLUME VIII. Part I. | COLLECTED AND REVISED | By DEANE SWIFT, Esq; | of Goodrich, in Herefordshire. | *Hæ tibi erunt artes*. Virgil. | [double-rule] | LONDON: | Printed for W. Johnston, in Ludgate-Street. | M DCC LXV
Collation: 4°: A^4 a–b^4 B–2N^4
Pagination: *i–xxiv*, 1–278

Contents: A1ʳ title page; A1ᵛ 'ERRATA'; A2ʳ–b2ᵛ 'SUBSCRIBER'S NAMES'; b3ʳ⁻ᵛ contents; b4ʳ 'THE EDITORS TO THE READER'; b4ᵛ blank; B1ʳ–2N3ᵛ text
Errata (A1ᵛ): 'for *Whitchet* read *Whitshed*'
Upon Giving Badges: 220–1; 2F2ᵛ–3ʳ.
Typography: 36 lines per page (2A1ᵛ); type-page 200 (257) × 136 mm; 20 lines of roman type 116 mm
Copies consulted: BL, 90.d.8 (with vol. VIII pt ii).

Faulkner, *Works*, 1765b
TS 47. *ESTC* N31130
Title: VOLUME XII. | OF THE | Author's WORKS. | COLLECTED AND REVISED | By DEANE SWIFT, Esq. | of Goodrich in Herefordshire. | *Hae tibi erunt artes.* Virgil. | [ornament] | DUBLIN: | Printed by GEORGE FAULKNER | [short rule] | MDCCLXV.
Collation: 8°: A⁴ B–2E⁸
Pagination: *i–ii* iii–v *vi* vii–viii *1* 2–429 *430–2*
Contents: A1ʳ title page; A1ᵛ blank. A2ʳ–3ʳ contents; A4ʳ⁻ᵛ 'The Editors to the Reader'; A4ᵛ blank; B1ʳ–2E7ʳ text; 2E7ᵛ–8ᵛ 'A Catalogue of Books' printed and sold by Faulkner
Upon Giving Badges: Y2ᵛ–3ʳ; 331–3
Typography: 31 lines per page (S7ʳ); type-page 145 (156) × 83 mm; 20 lines of roman type 94 mm
Copies consulted: Bodl., Vet. A5 e. 4858; Bodl., Vet. A4 e. 3055/12.

Emendations
[None]

Historical Collation
3.1 UPON GIVING BADGES TO THE POOR] *om.* SwJ 479; About Badges SwJ 479, 2ᵛ [*alternate title added on MSS*]
3.1 TO THE POOR] See a Treatise on this Subject, vol. VI, p. 157. *1765a*; See a Treatise on this Subject, vol. VI. part I, p. 42. *1765b* [*added footnotes*]
3.6 in] of *1765a*+
3.9 sewn] sewed *1765a*+
4.14 All] And that all *1765a*+

Word Division
Copy Text
None

Edited Text
None

Considerations About Maintaining the Poor

Textual Account

First printed along with *Upon Giving Badges* in Deane Swift's *Works*, 1765, and presumed to have been written around the same period of 1726. Like that work, it is an adjunct to the later *Proposal for Giving Badges to the Beggars*, being an unfinished draft concerning topics that were of concern to Swift during the period covered by this volume.

It was reprinted in the same year by Faulkner, *Works*, vol. XII, pp. 335–40. There are no variants. Deane Swift, as first publication, is the printing used here.

Copy Text

BL, 90.d.8.

Deane Swift, *Works*, 1765
TS 87. *ESTC* T52748
Title: THE | WORKS | OF | Dr. JONATHAN SWIFT, | Dean of St. Patrick's, Dublin. | VOLUME VIII. Part I.
[see entry under *Upon Giving Badges to the Poor* for full description]
Contents: Considerations: 222–5; 2F3^v–2G1^r

Emendations

[None]

Word Division
Copy Text
None

Edited Text
None

A Short View of the State Of Ireland

Textual Account

Oliver Ferguson, amongst others, suggested that the initial impetus for *A Short View* was John Browne's pamphlet, *Seasonable Remarks on Trade* (see Ferguson, pp. 144–6, 189–90). This premise, though, is 'not conclusive' (Woolley, *Intelligencer*, p. 170). David Woolley describes *A Short View* as 'published coincidentally in the same week with Browne's two pamphlets' (*Corr.*, vol. III, p. 177 n. 2). These were *Seasonable Remarks* and *An Essay Upon Trade* (both Dublin: Ewing, 1728), and were 'both in print by 23 March 1728' (Woolley, *Corr.*, vol. III, p. 177 n. 1, citing *The Dublin Intelligence*), and sent to Swift before Browne's letter to him, mentioning them (4 April 1728, Woolley, *Corr.*, vol. III, pp. 174–8).

Swift's pamphlet was published in Dublin on 19 March 1728 (*Mist's*, 30 March 1728, quotes a Dublin report from 20 March, referring to its publication 'Yesterday'). It was printed by Sarah Harding, whose relationship with Swift's works in this period is discussed in the General Textual Introduction. James Woolley discovered that Harding's original printing has two issues: an uncorrected (hereafter 1728a) and (rare) corrected outer forme (1728b), with three substantive variants, all apparent errors (Woolley, *Intelligencer*, p. 326). A corrected state of the pamphlet has therefore been chosen as copy text here.

There was a reprint of 1728a by Combra Daniell, in Cork in 1728 (TS 664); very little is known of Daniell, and it is a relatively clumsy affair (though hardly less so than Harding's original) of no textual value, though the effort shows the apparent popularity of Swift's pamphlet. In London, it was partially reprinted in *Mist's*, 20 April 1728, which quotes Swift's fourteen main points and paraphrases his general conclusions. Most of this was separately published as the (undated) *The Present STATE IRELAND; BEING Political Reflections by Mr. MIST, on a Pamphlet lately published at Dublin.* Swift would later claim that Mist's 'press-folks were prosecuted for almost a twelve month' for this printing (above, p. 163). As with the Daniell printing, this has been collated, but not added to the textual accounts.

Later in 1728, *A Short View* became *The Intelligencer* no. 15 (hereafter 1728c), with an added introduction by Sheridan (attributed by Swift in a letter to Pope, 12 June 1732; see Woolley, *Corr.*, vol. III, p. 489). The Introduction is printed in the Historical Collation. It was subsequently included in the collected London *Intelligencers* of 1729 and 1730 (the details of which are discussed more fully in the Textual Accounts of the *Intelligencer*

TEXTUAL ACCOUNT: A SHORT VIEW OF THE STATE OF IRELAND 393

papers). Faulkner reprinted it in the *Works* of 1735 as *A Short View*, returning to the 1728 pre-*Intelligencer* text.

We have collated all of these versions, and the following textual accounts include all editions with the possibilities of variants having authority: chiefly the Harding original (*1728a* and *b*), the reprints in *The Intelligencer* (*1728c*, *1729*, *1730*) and Faulkner (*1735*). *A Short View* offers a choice of two alternatives, in terms of copy text: the authority of the original, more basic (and often shabby) printing (1728), or the revisions of Faulkner's much more polished reprint (1735). While this last edition appears to have been produced, in James Woolley's usefully inclusive phrase, 'with Swift's co-operation' (Woolley, *Intelligencer*, p. 40), the corrected *1728b* is chosen as copy text in line with the edition policy of adopting the earliest printing of a polemical work. Moreover, despite Sarah Harding's 'generally untidy presswork' (Woolley, *Intelligencer*, p. 40), the earlier text loses little in terms of substantives, when compared with Faulkner's later corrections (even if they were abetted by Swift); the variants are never profound, and there are only five (emended) errors. A quality of the original text is its sense of immediacy: the retention of local detail, altered in small ways for 1735 (where 'this kingdom' became 'Ireland', for example) compensates for using a printing which has its share of inconsistencies and inaccuracies.

Copy Text
Bodl. Godw: Pamph. 2753(1).

Dublin, 1728a & 1728b
TS 663. *ESTC* T1868
Title: A | Short VIEW | OF THE | STATE | OF | IRELAND. | [ornament] | *DUBLIN*: | Printed by *S. HARDING*, next Door to | the *Crown* in *Copper-Alley*, 1727-8.
Collation: 8°: A⁸
Pagination: *1-2*, 3-15, *16* [3 misnumbered as 1]
Contents: A1ʳ title page; A1ᵛ blank; A2ʳ-8ʳ text; A8ᵛ blank
Typography: 30 lines per page (A2ᵛ); type-page 120 (130) × 70 mm; 20 lines of roman type 80 mm
Failure of catchwords to catch:
A2ʳ tradictors] dictors
Copies consulted: Bodl., Godw. Pamph. 2753(1), bound with fourteen other pamphlets on contemporary Ireland; corrected state (*1728b*); BL, 8145.a.28, uncorrected state (*1728a*); CUL, Williams 349, uncorrected

state (*1728a*); CUL, Hib.8.724.7.14, bound as no. 14 in collection of pamphlets by various authors on Irish politics and economics, 1726–30, uncorrected state (*1728a*).

Intelligencer, Number 15, 1728c
TS 666. *ESTC* P2223

Title: THE | Intelligencer, | [rule] | NUMB. XV. | [rule] Lamentations, Chap. 2. v. 19. | *Arise, cry out in the Night: in the begin-* | *ning of the Watches, pour out thine Heart like* | *Water, before the Face of the Lord: lift up* | *thy Hands towards him, for the Life of thy* | *Young Children that faint for Hungar, in the* | *Top of every Street.* | [rule] | [ornament] | [double rule] | *DUBLIN* | Printed by S. HARDING next Door to | the *Crown* in *Copper-Alley*.
Collation: 8°: A^8
Pagination: *1*, 2–16
Contents: A1^r title page; A1^v–A8^v text
Typography: 32 lines per page (A3^v); type-page 137 (155) × 71 mm; 20 lines of roman type 80 mm
Failure of catchwords to catch:
A2^r *om.*] tradictors
Copies consulted: TCC, Rothschild no. 2114; V & A, Forster 8544.

Intelligencer, 1729
TS 34. *ESTC* T135902

Title: THE | INTELLIGENCER. | [rule] | *Omne vafer vitium ridenti Flaccus amico* | *Tangit, & admissus circum præcordia ludit.* | Pers. | [rule] | [ornament] | [rule] | Printed at *DUBLIN*. | *LONDON* | Reprinted, and sold by *A. Moor* in St. *Paul*'s | Church-yard, and the Booksellers of | *London* and *Westminster*. MDCCXXIX.
Collation: 8°: A^3 B–O^8 P^5
Pagination: *i–vi*, 1–217
Contents: A1^r title page; A1^v blank; A2^r–A3^v 'To the Reader'; A3^r–A3^v contents; B1^r–P5^r text; P5^v blank; *No. 15*: 156–75; L6^v–M8^r [167 – M4 signed M3]
Typography: 25 lines per page (B2^r); type-page 130 (140) × 77 mm; 20 lines of roman type 104 mm
Failure of catchwords to catch:
166 M3^v It] I⊤

Copies consulted: Bodl., 8° B 441 Linc; V & A, Forster 8543.34.B.32; BL, PP.6177.

Intelligencer, 1730
TS 35. *ESTC* T130870
Title: THE | INTELLIGENCER. | [rule] | *Omne vafer vitium ridenti Flaccus amico* | *Tangit, & admissus circum præcordia ludit.* | Pers. | [rule] | *By the Author of a* TALE *of a* TUB. | [rule] | *The* SECOND EDITION. | [rule] | [ornament] | [rule] | *LONDON:* | Printed for FRANCIS COGAN, at the | *Middle-Temple-Gate* in *Fleet-street.* | MDCCXXX.
Collation: 12°: A⁴ B–M¹² N²
Pagination: *i–viii*, 1–268
Contents: A1ʳ title page; A1ᵛ blank; A2ʳ–A3ʳ 'To the Reader'; A3ᵛ–A4ᵛ contents; B1ʳ–N2ᵛ text [running head of p. 253 mistakenly titles *No. 19* as *No. 1*; that of pp. 54–5 likewise refers to *No. 6* as *No. 5*]; *No.15*: I6ʳ–K5ᵛ; 179–202
Typography: 23 lines per page (B2ʳ); type-page 115 (125) × 73 mm; 20 lines of roman type 99 mm
Copies consulted: Bodl., Douce S647; Bodl., Hope. 8° 530, pp. 83–6 (E6ʳ–E7ᵛ) missing; V & A, Forster 8544.

Works, 1735
TS 41. *ESTC* T52771
Title: VOLUME IV. | Of the AUTHOR's | WORKS. | CONTAINING, | A Collection of TRACTS relating to | *Ireland*; among which are, The | *Drapier's Letters* to the People of | *Ireland*, against receiving *Wood*'s | Halfpence: Also, two Original | *Drapier's Letters*, never before | published. | [double-rule] | [ornament] | [double-rule] | *DUBLIN:* | Printed by and for GEORGE FAULKNER, Printer | and Bookseller, in *Essex-Street*, opposite to the | Bridge. MDCCXXXV.
Collation: 8°: *A*⁴ B–2B⁸ 2C²
Pagination: *i–x*, *i* ii, *1* 2–58 *59–60* 65–388
Contents: A1ʳ title page; A1ᵛ blank; A2ʳ⁻ᵛ Advertisement; A3ʳ–4ᵛ Contents; B1ʳ–2C2ᵛ text
Short View: R5ᵛ–S2ᵛ; 250–260
Typography: 33 lines per page (BB2ᵛ); type-page 145 (155) × 83 mm; 20 lines of roman type 90 mm
Copies consulted: CUL, Williams 4; CUL, Hib.5.735.13; Bodl., Radcliffe. e.234.

Emendations
15.9 Contradictors] *1729*; Condictors
26.6 Kingdom] *1728c*; Kindgom

Historical Collation
15.1 A SHORT VIEW OF THE STATE OF IRELAND] A | Short VIEW | OF THE | State of *IRELAND*. | [rule] | Written in the Year 1727. *1735*
15.1 [*In* Intelligencer, *no. 15, Thomas Sheridan provides the following introduction to the reprinting of* A Short View]

NUMBER XV. | Lamentations, Chap. 2. v. 19. |

Arise, cry out in the Night: in the beginning of the Watches, pour out thine Heart like Water, before the Face of the Lord: lift up thy Hands towards him, for the Life of thy Young Children that faint for Hungar, in the Top of every Street.

    I Do remember to have Read an Account, that an Ode which *Pindar* Writ, in honour to the Island *Delos*, was Inscribed in the Temple of *Minerva*, at *Athens*, in large Letters of Gold; A publick and very laudable acknowledgment for the Poet's Ingenuity, and for no more than a bare Compliment! Such was the encouragement given by the great, and publick Spirited *Athenians*. Had the same Poet, inspired by a Noble and Heroick Ardor, by another Ode, awakened and rouzed their whole State against an invading Enemy; or opened their Eyes against any Secret and Wicked Contrivers of their Destruction, they would have erected him a Statue at least. But Alass that Spirit is fled from the World! and, long since neglected Virtue is become her own Pay-master. My *Country-men*, I hope, will forgive me, if I complain there has been so little Notice taken of a small, but most excellent *Pamphlet*, written by the DRAPIER. It is Intitled, *A SHORT VIEW OF THE STATE OF IRELAND.* There never was any Treatise yet published, with a Zeal more generous for the Universal good of a Nation, or a design more seasonable, considering our present lamentable Condition, yet we listen not to the Voice of the Charmer. Whereas it should have been Inscribed in Capital Letters (as Glorious as those of the Poet) in the most publick part of every *Corporation-town*, through this whole *Kingdom*, that People might behold the several unprovoked causes of their Poverty, our Offences towards Heaven excepted.

    Nay, I will proceed farther, and say, that every Head of every Family, ought to instruct the Children so far in this most *incomparable Pamphlet*, that they should not only understand, but be able, to repeat by Heart every single *Paragraph*, through the Whole. This was the Method laid down by the wisest Law-giver, that ever the World produced; To gain the Hearts of the People, by working upon their Memories.

Deut. chap. 6. v. 7. And thou shalt Teach them diligently unto thy Children, and shalt talk of them, when thou sittest in thine House, and when thou walkest by the Way, and when thou liest down, and when thou risest up.

8. *And thou shalt bind them for a Sign upon thine Hand, and they shall be as frontlets between thine Eyes.*
9. *And thou shalt Write them upon the Posts of thy House, and on thy Gates.*

And, where would be the great Trouble, since we have little else to do, if every Man would read a Lecture of the *Short View* every Day in his Family, after Reading Prayers? Nor do I think the expence would be extravagant, if he should have every Page of it Re-printed, to be hung up in Frames, in every Chamber of his House. That it might be as evident, as, the *Hand Writing on the Wall.*

And, since I have ventured thus far, to praise and recommend this most inimitable Piece, let me Speak a few Words in favour of it's AUTHOR.

I would propose to *My Country-men*, before all their MONY goes off, (it is going as fast as possible) to convert it into a few Statues to the DRAPIER, in those Memorable parts of this Kingdom, where our Heroes have shone with the greatest Lustre, in Defence of our *Liberty*, and the PROTESTANT RELIGION over all *Europe*. At *DERRY*, at *ENNISKILLEN*, at *BOYN*, at *AUGHRIM*. Nor would it be amiss, to set up a few more about our *Metropolis*, with that Glorious Inscription *Libertas et Natale Solum.*

If our MONY were metamorphosed upon such a good occasion, as this, it would not be in the Power of any * *Cypselus*, to get it into his own Coffers, and it would be the only method, to prevent it's being carry'd off, except our *Vice-roys*, should act like the *Roman Prefects*, and Run away with our very Statues.

Courteous READER, Mark well what follows.

* Cypselus, a *Governor of* Corinth, *who contrived a Tax, which brought all the Mony of that State to himself in ten Years Time.* Vid. Aristot. polit. *1728c.*

15.7 happens] happen *1735*
15.9 Contradictors] *1729*; Condictors *1728a–c*
15.10 cordially] *cordially 1735*
15.10 or] and *1729–1730*
15.11 Kingdom] Kindgom *1728a*
15.20 into other] others *1728c*; to other *1730*
15.29 Liberty] Priviledge *1735*
16.8 Eighth] Eight *1728c*

16.8 Princes] Prince *1735*
16.8 Administrators] Administrator *1735*
16.20 Revenues] Revennes *1735* [*turned letter*]
16.22 a People] the People *1735*
17.24 of which however we are only defective in] *om. 1728c–1730*
17.26 Discouragements] Discouragemts *1730*
18.1 bestowed us so liberally] hath bestowed so liberally on this Kingdom *1735*
18.4 this Kingdom] *Ireland 1735*
18.11 this] this Privilege *1735*
18.15 unto] on to *1729–1730*
18.18 uncontroverted] unconverted *1728a*
18.19 my] *om. 1735*
18.19 L– C– J– W–'s] Lord Chief Justice *Whitshed*'s *1735*; L– C– J– W–'s *1728c*
18.19 *LIBERTAS ET NATALE SOLUM*] **Libertas & natale Solum* [*Fn:*] **Liberty and my native Country. 1735*
19.6 divide] decide *1728c, 1729, 1735*
20.10 Court] Courts *1728c, 1729–1730*
21.12 in great quantity] *om. 1735*
21.19 half of] half *1735*
22.1 C———rs] *Commissioners 1735*
22.12 these] those *1735*
22.15 Irony] Journey *1728a*
22.17 *Ysland*] Island *1728a*; Iceland *1730*
23.8 *miseriâ magnus es*] miseriâ magna es *1735*
24.3 they] themselves *1735*
24.7 *Bankers*] *Bankiers 1729*
25.4 BANKERS] Bankiers *1729*
25.6 that] who *1735*
25.8 *Bankers*] *Bankiers 1729*
25.10 *Pharoah*] Pharoach *1728c*
25.13 these] those *1735*
26.6 Kingdom] *1728c*; Kindgom *1728a, 1728b*

Word Division
Copy Text
Custom-house

Edited Text
None

An Answer to a Paper, Called a Memorial

Textual Account

It would seem that, directly after the publication of *A Short View* in March 1728, Swift received a short pamphlet, *To the R—d Dr. J—n S—t, The Memorial of the Poor Inhabitants, Tradesmen, and Labourers of the Kingdom of Ireland* (see Appendix A, pp. 330–3). This is usually attributed to John Browne, whose *Seasonable Remarks* may have inspired *A Short View*. In a letter to Swift of 4 April 1728, Browne tried to justify himself against Swift's earlier charges in the third *Drapier's Letter*, *Some Observations upon a Paper*, of 1724 (Woolley, *Corr.*, vol. III, pp. 174–7).

Swift's angry riposte to the pamphlet, *An Answer to a Paper*, is dated 25 March 1728, less than a week after the publication of *A Short View*, and it was quickly printed, by Sarah Harding: *Mist's*, 4 May 1728 (reporting news from Dublin of 23 April), noted that, soon after *A Short View*, 'came out another intitled *A Memorial address'd to the Reverend Dean S*—— [...] In a few Days after, a third Pamphlet was publish'd, being an Answer to the said *Memorial*.' *Mist's* then reprinted *An Answer* in the next issue, 11 May. An answer to Swift's *Answer* (which may also have been by Browne) duly emerged, as *To the R—d Dr. J—n S—t. A Reply, to the Answer Given to the Memorial*, Dublin: Thomas Walsh, 1728. Pope wrote to Harley on 17 May 1728, asking him to make a copy or pass on the original, 'wherever you can procure (or I) the Other pamphlet in answer to the Memorial'; he is sending 'the Deans first book', which could be *A Short View* (Pope, *Correspondence*, vol. II, p. 493, where it is speculated that Pope refers to the first book of the *Four Last Years*), showing the effect of the pamphlets beyond their immediate environment.

The alacrity with which the first edition (hereafter *1728*) was produced perhaps contributed to its number of errors and misreadings; it is the most uneven of Sarah Harding's printings for Swift, containing considerable variations in type size (on pp. 6–8) in an apparent attempt to fit the text into the one sheet of which its eight leaves consist. There are also many mundane errors ('two' for 'too', 'excuse' for 'excise'). These might be partly due to misreadings of Swift's manuscript, which was presumably copied and sent to Harding by the 'unknown hands' which Swift described in a later letter on the *Intelligencers* to Motte (4 November 1732; Woolley, *Corr.*, vol. III, p. 556; see also Woolley, 'Sarah Harding as Swift's Printer', p. 165). The suggestion of generally hasty production is supported by the problems of pointing, with barely impressed periods and commas (as well as erroneously placed ones) leading to moments of syntactic confusion.

Swift's *Answer* was next reprinted by Faulkner, alongside other Irish writings, in the *Works* of 1735. Faulkner's text tidied up the errors of the first edition considerably, incorporated some revisions which may be directly from Swift, and followed a consistent policy towards capitalized nouns, italics, and small capitals to begin paragraphs. The choice of copy text in this case is thus not straightforward. Despite the greater polish of Faulkner's reprint, in the interests of consistency with the edition's policy of printing Swift's earliest possible text in cases of contemporary intervention, the copy text is Harding's 1728 edition, though this necessitates emending in favour of the 1735 text on a number of occasions.

Copy Text

CUL, Williams 290.

Dublin, 1728

TS 665. *ESTC* T21996

Title: AN | ANSWER | TO A | PAPER, | CALLED | A **Memorial** | Of the Poor *Inhabitants, Tradesmen* and | *Labourers* of the KINGDOM of | *IRELAND*. | [rule] | By the AUTHOR of the SHORT VIEW of the | State of *IRELAND*. | [rule] | [ornament] | [double rule] | *DUBLIN*: | Printed by S. HARDING, next Door to the | *Crown* in *Copper-Alley*, 1728.

Collation: 8°: A⁸

Pagination: 1, 2–16

Contents: A1ʳ title page; A1ᵛ–A8ᵛ text

Typography: type is mixed on some pages (A4ᵛ, A5, A7ᵛ); some pages in smaller type (A7ʳ–8ᵛ). 26 lines per page (A2ʳ), then 30 lines per page where type is mixed (A5ᵛ). Type-page 130 (140) × 75 mm; 20 lines of roman type 94 mm; 84 mm for smaller type on mixed pages.

Failure of catchwords to catch:

A2ʳ Master-] Master

A6ʳ lion] they

Copies consulted: CUL, Williams 290; CUL, x.172820/12; Bodl., Don.e.462 (3) [collected as 'Four Pamphlets', with 'A LETTER To THE AUTHOR OF THE SHORT VIEW OF THE State of *IRELAND*. By the Author of SEASONABLE REMARKS.' (1); 'TO THE R——d Dr. J——n S——t. THE MEMORIAL OF THE POOR INHABITANTS OF IRELAND' [John Browne] (2); and 'TO THE R——d D—n S - -t, A REPLY TO THE ANSWER GIVEN IN THE MEMORIAL' (4)]; TCC, Rothschild 2112.

Works, 1735
TS 41. *ESTC* T52771
Title: VOLUME IV. | Of the Author's | WORKS.
[see entry under *Short View of the State of Ireland* for full description]
Contents: *Answer*: S3ʳ–S8ᵛ; 261–72.

Emendations

30.8 too] *1735*; two
30.18 are too] *1735*; were two
33.9 Victuals.] *1735*; ~ₐ
33.22 District] *1735*; Distinct
35.5 of] *1735*; if
35.13 than] *1735*; then
35.13 encreased.] *1735*; ~ₐ
35.15 on a] *1735*; one a
35.15 Hunger)] *1735*; ~ₐ
35.28 excise] *1735 [Excise]*; excuse
37.12 called on ye] *1735*; called, and ye
39.4 must] *1735*; mnst
39.10 hunc tu Romane cavetto] *1735*; hanc tu Romane eaveto
39.12 if] *1735*; of
39.17 sleep)] *1735*; ~ₐ

Historical Collation

30.8 too] two *1728*
30.11 were] are *1735*
30.13 such] some *1735*
30.16 are] were *1735*
32.4 till] until *1735*
32.8 it,] them; *1735*
33.9 Victuals.] *1735*; ~ₐ *1728*
33.22 District] *1735*; Distinct *1728*
33.26 particular] particularly *1735*
35.5 of] *1735*; if *1728*
35.7 happend] happens *1735*
35.8 And at least] At least *1735*
35.10 Husband] Husbands *1735*
35.11 few] small *1735*
35.13 than] *1735*; then *1728*
35.13 encreased.] *1735*; ~ₐ *1728*

35.15 on a] *1735*; one a *1728*
35.15 Hunger)] *1735*; Hunger *1728*
35.17 even] *om. 1735*
35.28 excise] excuse *1728*; Excise *1735*
36.12 Million] they *1728* [*failure to catch*]
36.21 thousand] Thousands *1735*
36.26 would] could *1735*
37.12 called on ye] *1735*; called, and ye *1728*
37.20 sent] lately sent *1735*
37.20 some days ago] *om. 1735*
37.22 a departed J——ge] the late Lord Chief Justice *Whitshed 1735*
38.7 Virtues,] *Virtues* have from the other; *1735*
39.4 must] *1735*; mnst *1728* [*turned letter*]
39.10 hunc tu Romane cavetto] *1735*; hanc tu Romane eaveto *1728*
39.12 if] *1735*; of *1728*
39.17 sleep)] *1735*; ~∧ *1728*

Word Division
Copy Text
None

Edited Text
None

Papers from the Intelligencer

Textual Account

Of the twenty *Intelligencer* papers published in 1728–9 in Dublin, in the journal jointly written by Swift and Thomas Sheridan, Swift's prose contributions amounted to seven, one of which (no. 15) was a reprint of *A Short View of the State of Ireland*, 'merely for laziness not to disappoint the town', with an introduction by Sheridan (for attributions, see Swift's letter to Pope, 12 June 1732: Woolley, *Corr.*, vol. III, p. 489). The Dublin printings were by Sarah Harding, with each number published as a separate pamphlet, often in a variety of slightly different impressions. The first collected London edition of 1729 (printed by 'A. Moor') was part of the reprinting of Swift's Irish publications by William Bowyer, as was the second edition (printed by Francis Cogan) of 1730; numbers 5, 7 and 9 were included in the so-called 'Third' volume of the Pope–Swift *Miscellanies*; all numbers authored by Swift (bar the first) were collected in the first and fourth volumes of Faulkner's

1735 *Works*. Fragmentary plans of potential *Intelligencer* papers have been preserved in manuscript (see Associated Materials I, pp. 321–4, 'Hints for *Intelligencer* Papers').

The texts of *The Intelligencer* raise considerable problems: no. 1, for instance, appeared in eight different impressions by Harding in Dublin in 1728 alone, yet most of the differences are very minor typographical features, and have been comprehensively detailed by James Woolley, in his definitive edition of the journal (1992). The textual accounts here, accordingly, record and collate major variants between the 1728 editions, the London versions of 1729 and 1730, the *Miscellanies* of 1732, and the 1735 *Works*, and do not attempt to replicate Woolley's invaluable bibliographical accounts, which record the minute differences between the Dublin impressions of 1728. Instead, the copies examined are related to the order of impressions in Woolley's edition.

The possible reasons behind Swift's use of Sarah Harding's services are discussed in the General Textual Introduction (above, pp. 377–9). Her printing of *The Intelligencer* shows what Woolley describes as 'her generally untidy presswork', but also a scheme of capitalisation that 'may seem chaotic', in which 'capitals reflect emphasis or parallelism' (Woolley, *Intelligencer*, p. 40). Punctuation, similarly, is more rhetorical than grammatical, in many ways, and used 'to signal the length of pause if the text were being read aloud' (p. 41), with commas, semi-colons and periods thus becoming markers of the quantity of a pause, rather than serving their standard grammatical function (see Woolley, *Intelligencer*, p. 41, for examples, to which can be added Gildon and Brightland's *A Grammar of the English Tongue*, 3rd edn (1714), pp. 127–8). The text, in this sense, was an intended indication of itself as a spoken performance, as much as a written one. Moreover, there were many archaic spellings, which can usually be justified, but sometimes appear to be errors.

Amidst this apparent chaos, there were the real slips and inconsistencies in Harding's texts that Swift commented upon, and subsequently criticised. A letter of 13 January 1729 finds him instructing John Worrall to pass on his enclosed writing to Harding 'in an unknown hand', and to desire her to 'make her people be more correct, and that the Intelligencer himself may look over it, for that every body who reads those papers, and are very much offended with the continual nonsense made by her printers' (Woolley, *Corr.*, vol. III, p. 206). Apart from the conventional fiction of his not knowing the author, this is rare evidence of Swift both acknowledging authorship (if tacitly) and being aware of the flaws of its production: Harding's printing was indeed uneven, in terms of consistency of type, occasional use of italic as filler, and punctuation which seemed mistaken even within the rhetorical scheme of the pamphlets – as well as irregular italics and apostrophes.

Such flaws were ironed out in the far more regularised texts reprinted in London, where general consistency of spelling, type size and inking quality, and a more orthodox scheme of punctuation and capitalisation, generally resulted in a lighter pattern of commas, in particular, along with less apparently eccentric use of capitals, with their role as emphatic indicators removed; and standard use of drop capitals and small capitals to begin paragraphs. The 1729 and 1730 London editions are examples of William Bowyer's printing: the 1729 version was advertised very widely from 13 May (see Woolley, *Intelligencer*, p. 292), and can be found in the Stationers' Register (20 May 1729) and Bowyer's paper-ledger for 17 May (see Keith Maslen, 'George Faulkner and William Bowyer: The London Connection', in *An Early London Printing House at Work: Studies in the Bowyer Ledgers*, New York: Bibliographical Society of America, 1993, pp. 223–33, pp. 226–7); it is number 1446 (Ledger A25) in the printed account of *The Bowyer Ledgers*, ed. Maslen and Lancaster. It was published by 'A Moor', the usual fake imprint for controversial or contentiously copyrighted works. With regard to the question of copyright, Woolley notes that Swift 'thought of the *Intelligencer* as Sheridan's property' (p. 292). The 1730 edition was entered into Bowyer's ledger on 29 June (number 1570; A27), and advertised in the *Evening Post* for 2 July.

The 1730 edition raises the important question regarding all Bowyer's reprinting of Swift's Irish writings: that of George Faulkner's involvement (discussed in general in the General Textual Introduction above, pp. 379–83). By 1730, Faulkner had become Swift's main printer, and had worked in previous years in Bowyer's shop; his relationship with Bowyer involved importing the latter's works to Dublin, and reciprocating with his own publications. The degree to which he was passing on corrections from Swift in the London texts is thus unclear: as Woolley notes, almost all of the 1730 *Intelligencer* reprints the collection of 1729, except for some cases, where it 'introduced readings which appear authorial' and 'may have been transmitted to Bowyer' through Faulkner (p. 293). This is particularly the case with no. 5, and these potential revisions are discussed in the collation and emendation tables.

The texts in the *Miscellanies* of 1732 are based on the 1729 London edition, presumably chosen and revised by Alexander Pope, as part of his work for that complicated joint endeavour. Not all the *Intelligencers* by Swift are included: nos. 5 and 7 are combined, and (along with no. 9) given new titles (an arrangement maintained by Faulkner, in 1735). The copy of this volume, with Swift's autograph corrections, in the Rothschild Collection suggests that (to a certain degree) Swift approved (or did not actively disapprove) of the texts: Woolley argues that 'Faulkner – presumably with Swift's approval – used this text' as his basis for the 1735 *Works* (p. 294). Moving onto 1735, he also posits that, whilst it is possible that some of the revisions in 1735 are authorial, it is highly unlikely that Swift altered the pointing or emphasis of the capitals, during the sessions where Faulkner would read his texts aloud to him for revision (p. 39). The vexed question of Swift's involvement in these texts aside, the choice of copy text in the case of *The Intelligencer* is clear: the Harding texts are the original version of the pamphlets, following a rhetorical scheme (howsoever flawed, at points) intended to be disseminated and read in Dublin in 1728; the London texts follow a different, somewhat more grammatically and orthographically orthodox route, which culminates in the 1735 *Works*. The aims of the present edition mean that the Harding 1728 printings are used as copy texts, given their immediacy and unique textual status; where necessary, they have been emended to correct an obvious error, rather than to supply a later revision.

The major editions referred to here are the 1728 Harding pamphlets (*1728*); the first London edition (*1729*); the second London edition (*1730*); the 'Third' volume of *Miscellanies* (*1732*, and Swift's copy with autograph notes, *1732a*) and Faulkner's *Works* (*1735*). For the sake of convenience, there is a summary of the reprinting history of each pamphlet below. The Textual Accounts follow each individual *Intelligencer*, rather than collected editions; to avoid repetition, when the details of a collection have been fully described once, each collection is summarised by title page and the pages of the particular pamphlet, on subsequent mentions.

Intelligencer:

1:	appears in	*1728, 1729, 1730.*
3:		*1728, 1729, 1730, 1735.*
5:		*1728, 1729, 1730, 1732, 1735.*
7:		*1728, 1729, 1730, 1732, 1735.*
9:		*1728, 1729, 1730, 1732, 1735.*
19:		*1728, 1729, 1730, 1735.*

The dates of publication for each 1728 Dublin number, some of which are conjectural, are taken from James Woolley's edition (*Intelligencer*, p. 32).

Copy Text

1, 3, 5: CUL, Hib.8.728.5.
7, 9: TCC, Rothschild 2114.
19: V & A, Forster 8544 [seventh impression, 28g].

406 GENERAL TEXTUAL INTRODUCTION AND TEXTUAL ACCOUNTS

Intelligencer, Number 1
Dublin, 1728 (Sat. 11 May)
TS 666. *ESTC* P2223. Fourth impression, 28d (Woolley, *Intelligencer*, p. 300).
Title: THE | Intelligencer, | [rule] | NUMB. I. | [rule] | Saturday, May 11. To be Continued Weekly. | [rule] | [ornament] | [double rule] | *DUBLIN*: | Printed by S. HARDING, next Door to | the *Crown* in *Copper-Alley*, 1728.
Collation: 8°: *A*⁴
Pagination: *1–2* 3–7 *8*
Contents: A1ʳ title page; A1ᵛ blank; A2ʳ–4ʳ text; A4ᵛ blank
Typography: 30 lines per page (A2ᵛ); type-page 121 (130) × 71 mm; 20 lines of roman type 82 mm
Copies consulted: CUL, Hib.8.728.5; TCC, Rothschild 2114 [sixth impression, 28f]; V & A, Forster 8544 [seventh impression, 28g].

London, 1729
TS 34. *ESTC* T135902
Title: THE | INTELLIGENCER.
[see entry under *Short View of the State of Ireland* for full description]
Contents: *Number* 1: B1ʳ–3ʳ; 1–5

London, 1730
TS 35. *ESTC* T130870
Title: THE | INTELLIGENCER
[see entry under *Short View of the State of Ireland* for full description]
Contents: *Number* 1: B1ʳ–B3ᵛ; 1–6
Failure of catchwords to catch:
B3ʳ us] us,

Emendations
[None]

Historical Collation
45.26 *Kingdom*] ~? *1730*
45.27 sent] lately sent *1735*
46.14 shall have] have *1730*

Word Division
Copy Text
Parliament-house

Edited Text
None

Intelligencer, Number 3
Dublin, *1728 (c. 25 May)*
TS 666. *ESTC* P2223. First edition, 28a (Woolley, *Intelligencer*, p. 302).
Title: THE | Intelligencer, | [rule] | NUMB. III. | [rule] | *Ipse per Omnes ibit Personas,* | *Et turbam reddet in uno.* | [rule] | [ornament] | [double rule] | *DUBLIN*: | Printed by S. HARDING, next Door to | the *Crown* in *Copper-Alley*, 1728.
Collation: 8°: A⁴
Pagination: *1–2* 3–8
Contents: A1ʳ title page; A1ᵛ blank; A2ʳ–4ᵛ text
Typography: 40 lines per page (A3ʳ); type-page 128 (141) × 73 mm; 20 lines of roman type 66 mm
Copies consulted: CUL, Hib.8.728.5; Rothschild 2114 [later impression]; V & A, Forster 8544 [28g, third edition].

London, 1729
TS 34. *ESTC* T135902
Title: THE | INTELLIGENCER.
[see entry under *Short View of the State of Ireland* for full description]
Contents: Number 3: B8ʳ–C5ʳ; 15–25
Failure of catchwords to catch:
18 (C1ᵛ) Writer;] Writer,

London, 1730
TS 35. *ESTC* T130870
Title: THE | INTELLIGENCER
[see entry under *Short View of the State of Ireland* for full description]
Contents: Number 3: B9ʳ–C3ʳ; 17–29

Works, 1735
TS 41. *ESTC* T52771
[see entry under *Short View of the State of Ireland* for full description]
Number 3: S6ʳ–T1ᵛ; 267–74

Emendations

49.7 London] Londen
55.10 it doth] itdoth
55.12 takes] taekes

Historical Collation

47.3 uno] unam 1729+; Written in *Ireland* in the Year 1728. *1735*.
49.3 this] the *1735*
49.4 and the manner,] and Manner, *1735*
49.18 a Hundred] an ~ *1735*
50.9 succeeds] succeed *1735*
51.16 Corruption] Corruptions *1735*
51.19 personal] the private *1735*
52.5 Corner.] Corner? *1729+*
52.11 an high] a high *1729+*
52.16 Reflections] Reflection *1728Roths+*
52.24 M———] * Minister *1735*, [*with footnote*]: * Sir *Robert Walpole*
52.24 great M———] Prime Minister *1735*
53.6 D.] Duke *1729+*
53.8 *Courtiers*] the *Courtiers 1735*
53.8 is] be *1735*
53.20 more immediately] *om. 1735*
54.8 among] with *1735*
54.8 would] might *1735*
54.9 and at such lewd *Comedies*] at such *Comedies. 1735*
54.16 goes] comes *1735*
54.18 P——e] P - - - - te *1729*; Prelate *1735*
54.22 COURT-CHAPLAIN] *Court Chaplain* [*with footnote:*] *Dr. Herring, Chaplain to the Society at* Lincoln's-Inn *1735*
55.1 Gay,] GAY's *1729+*
55.9 these] those *1735*
55.10 although it doth by no means affect the present Age, yet might have been useful in the former and may possibly be so in Ages to come] without enquiring whether it affects the present Age, may possibly be useful in Times to come *1735*
55.12 occasion] the occasion *1735*
55.13 common *Robbers* to *Robbers of the Publick*] Common *Robbers of the Publick 1729+*

55.19 that many Years ago] many Years ago *1729+*
55.20 so] *om. 1735*
55.21 that many] and many *1735*
56.1 a Fore-runner] the Fore-runner *1729–1735*
56.1 want] have *1735*

Word Division
Copy Text
None

Edited Text
None

Intelligencer, Number 5
Dublin, 1728 (*c.* 8 June)
TS 666. *ESTC* P2223. First impression, 28a (Woolley, *Intelligencer*, p. 307)
Title: THE | Intelligencer, | [rule] | NUMB. V. | [rule] | Describ'd it's thus: Defin'd would you it have? | Then the World's honest Man's an errant Knave. | BEN JOHNSON | [rule] | [ornament] | [double rule] | *DUBLIN*: | Printed by S. HARDING, next Door | to the *Crown* in *Copper-Alley*, 1728.
Collation: 8°: *A*⁴
Pagination: *1–2* 3–8 [4 misnumbered as 3]
Contents: A1ʳ title page; A1ᵛ blank; A2ʳ–4ᵛ text
Typography: 30 lines per page (A2ᵛ); type-page 121 (132) × 72 mm; 20 lines of roman type 82 mm
Copies consulted: CUL, Hib.8.728.5; TCC, Rothschild 2114; V & A, Forster 8544.

London, 1729
TS 34. *ESTC* T135902
Title: THE | INTELLIGENCER.
[see entry under *Short View of the State of Ireland* for full description]
Contents: Number 5: D3ᵛ–7ʳ; 38–45

London, 1730
TS 35. *ESTC* T130870
Title: THE | INTELLIGENCER
[see entry under *Short View of the State of Ireland* for full description]
Contents: Number 5: C10ᵛ–D2ᵛ; 44–52

Miscellanies, 1732

TS 25 (4a). *ESTC* N62568
Title: MISCELLANIES | [rule] | THE | THIRD VOLUME. [rule] | [Ornament] | [double-rule] | *LONDON:* | Printed for BenJ. MOTTE at the *Middle | Temple-Gate*, and LAWTON GILLIVER | at *Hormers's Head*, against St. *Dunstan*'s | Church in *Fleetstreet*, 1732.
Collation: π² ᵗA³, A–R⁸ S⁴, ²A–F⁸ G²
Pagination: *i–iv*, *i* ii, *1* 2–4, 1–254, *1–2*, 255–76, *277–8*, 1–100 642
Contents: π1ʳ⁻ᵛ Adverts; π2ʳ title page; π2ᵛ blank; ᵗA2ʳ⁻ᵛ Advert; ᵗA3ʳ–Q7ᵛ text; Q8ʳ⁻ᵛ Advert; R1ʳ–S3ᵛ texts; S4ʳ errata; S4ᵛ blank; ²A1ʳ–G2ᵛ text Numbers 5 & 7 (combined, and renamed 'AN ESSAY ON THE *Fates of Clergymen*'): N7ᵛ–O7ʳ; 206–21
Typography: 28 lines per page (L2ʳ); type-page 156 (190) × 70 mm; 20 lines of roman type 97 mm
Copies consulted: V & A, Forster 8573.34.C.36.

Miscellanies, 1732a

TS 25 (4a). *ESTC* N62568.
[a copy of 1732, with Swift's autograph corrections]
Copies consulted: TCC, Rothschild 1422.

Works, 1735

TS 41. *ESTC* T52771
Title: VOLUME IV. | Of the AUTHOR's | WORKS.
[see entry under *Short View of the State of Ireland* for full description]
Contents: Numbers 5 & 7 (combined, and renamed 'AN ESSAY ON THE *Fates of Clergymen*'): T2ʳ–7ʳ; 275–85

Emendations

59.3 reach] *1729*; rech
59.10 greatest] *1729*; gratial
59.18 require] reqnine
59.29 and] *1729*; and and
60.7 this.] this
60.12 true, *when*] true, that, *when*
60.12 World] *1729*; Word
62.8 Gentleman] *1729*; Gentlemen
62.9 understanding] nnderstanding
63.2 heartily] heartly
63.11 Resty] resty *1732a*; Rusty

Historical Collation

57.1 Numb. V.] AN ESSAY ON THE *Fates of Clergyman 1732* [*title added*]
57.2 would you it have?] it would you have? *1729*
57.3 honest Man's] honest, Man's *1730*
57.3 errant] arrant *1729–1730*
57.3 Describ'd... JOHNSON] *om. 1732+*
59.3 reach] rech *1728*
59.4 People] Men *1735*
59.4 is in common] in common *1735*
59.13 present] the present *1732*
59.16 that] the *1735*
59.17 means to meddle] Means, meddle *1735*
59.18 require] reqnire *1728*
59.27 further] farther *1729+*
59.29 nor] or *1730, 1735*
59.29 and] *1729*; and and *1728*
59.30 to do so] *om. 1735*
59.32 the *Courts*] *Courts 1732a+*
60.10 great Affairs] Affairs *1730*
60.11 a One] an One *1729–1732*
60.11 occurs. For, if] occurs; if *1729+*
60.12 certain Writer] *certain Writer [*with footnote:*] *Vide *the Author's Thoughts on various Subjects. 1735*
60.12 when] that, when *1729+*
60.13 And thus although] And, if this be his Fate, when *1735*
60.15 Avarice; what must he expect] Avarice, he is sure to raise the Hatred of the noisy Croud, who envy him the quiet Enjoyment of himself. What must such an one expect *1730*
60.17 and every hand] every Hand *1730*
60.17 ready] will be ready *1730*
60.17 when] as soon as *1730*
60.18 And in] In *1730*
61.9 Stations] Station *1735*
61.14 Promotions] Promotion *1735*
61.15 Regulations] Observations *1735*
61.20 World] *1729+*; Word *1728*
61.24 Man] Men *1729+*
61.24 *A.B.C.T.*] an Archbishop *1732+*; [*with footnote:*] Dr. Tenison, *Late Archbishop of* Canterbury. *1735*
61.25 Clergy-Man] Clergymen *1730*

62.2 S——rs] Summers *1735*
62.3 Pr——] Prelate *1732+*
62.8 ——Shire] Yorkshire *1735*
62.8 Gentleman] *1729+*; Gentlemen *1728*
62.9 understanding] nnderstanding *1728*
63.2 heartily] heartly *1728*
63.4 happen] happens *1729+*
63.4 usually] generally *1730*
63.5 be] me *1729+*
63.11 Resty] resty *1732a+*; Rusty *1728, 1732*; rusty *1730*
63.12 In some following Paper, I will give] I will here give *1732+*

Word Division
Copy Text
None

Edited Text
None

Intelligencer, Number 7
Dublin, 1728 (*c.* 22–25 June)

TS 666. *ESTC* P2223. First impression, 28a (Woolley, *Intelligencer*, p. 311).
Title: THE | Intelligencer, | [rule] | NUMB. VII. | [rule] | ——*Probitas laudatur & alget.* | [rule] | [ornament] | [double rule] | *DUBLIN*: | Printed by S. HARDING, next Door to | the *Crown* in *Copper-Alley*, 1728. |
Collation: 8°: A^4
Pagination: *1* 2–8
Contents: A1^r title page; A1^v–4^v text
Typography: 32 lines per page (A2^r); type-page 141 (153) × 74 mm; 20 lines of roman type 80 mm
Copies consulted: TCC, Rothschild 2114; V & A, Forster 8544.

London, 1729
TS 34. *ESTC* T135902
Title: THE | INTELLIGENCER.
[see entry under *Short View of the State of Ireland* for full description]
Contents: Number 7: E5^r–F1^v; 57–66

London, 1730
TS 35. *ESTC* T130870
Title: THE | INTELLIGENCER
[see entry under *Short View of the State of Ireland* for full description]
Contents: Number 7: D9^v–E2^v; 66–76

Miscellanies, 1732
TS 25 (4a). *ESTC* N62568
Title: MISCELLANIES | [rule] | THE | THIRD VOLUME.
[see entry under *Intelligencer*, Number 5 for full description]
Contents: Numbers 5 & 7 (combined, and renamed 'AN ESSAY ON THE *Fates of Clergymen*'): N7^v–O7^r; 206–21

Works, 1735
TS 41. *ESTC* T52771
Title: VOLUME IV. | Of the Author's | WORKS.
[see entry under *Short View of the State of Ireland* for full description]
Contents: Numbers 5 & 7 (combined, and renamed 'AN ESSAY ON THE *Fates of Clergymen*'): T2^r–7^r; 275–85

Emendations
68.12 Promotion.] *1729*; Promotion
68.15 *Corusodes*,] *1729*; ~$_\wedge$
69.10 their faults] *1729*; the faults
69.16 and *quod*] *1729*; and *Quod*
70.12 set] Set
71.8 Church] ~:
72.9 Words.] *1729*; ~,

Historical Collation
64.1 ——Probitas laudatur & alget.] *om. 1732+*
66.2 at] an *1728*
66.8 dagling] dragling *1729+*
67.3 *perceived*] perceive *1729+*
67.5 *myself*] my self *1730*
67.6 and got] got *1729+*
67.8 Waiting-woman] a Waiting Woman *1730*
67.10 fourteen] Ten *1735*
67.16 House] Houses *1735*

67.16 his] his own *1730*
68.8 disposed] disposed of *1729+*
68.12 Promotion.] *1729*; Promotion, *1728*
68.13 high] great *1732a*
68.15 *Corusodes,*] *1729–1732*; ~∧ *1728*
69.10 their faults] *1729*; the faults, *1728*
69.16 and *quod*] *1729*; and *Quod 1728*
69.16 *nihil*] *nil 1732*
69.21 his] in *1730*
69.23 Mitre,] Mitre, (in which he succeeded) *1732a*
70.3 Carrier] Career *1729*
70.9 be not] be *1730*
71.3 Streets] Street *1735*
71.6 a good] good *1732a*
71.7 fortune] Estate *1735*
71.8 Church at] Church: at *1728*
71.10 the Men of Wit] Men of Wit *1729+*
72.7 this] the *1735*
72.9 his] this *1735*
72.9 Words.] *1729*; Words, *1728*
72.12 Father] Father's *1729*
72.13 pound] Pounds *1735*

Word Division
Copy Text
Waiting-woman
Lincoln-shire

Edited Text
None

Intelligencer, Number 9
Dublin, 1728 (*c*. 6–9 July)
TS 666. *ESTC* P2223. First impression, 28a (Woolley, *Intelligencer*, p. 316).
Title: THE | Intelligencer, | [rule] | NUMB. IX. | [rule] | [ornament] | [double rule] | *DUBLIN*: | Printed by S. HARDING, next Door to | the Crown in *Copper-Alley*, 1728.
Collation: 8°: A⁸
Pagination: *1–2* 3–16

Contents: A1ʳ title page; A1ᵛ blank; A2ʳ–8ᵛ text
Typography: 31 lines per page (A2ᵛ); type-page 135 (155) × 70 mm; 20 lines of roman type 80 mm
Copies consulted: TCC, Rothschild 2114; V & A, Forster 8544.

London, 1729
TS 34. *ESTC* T135902
Title: THE | INTELLIGENCER.
[see entry under *Short View of the State of Ireland* for full description]
Contents: Number 9: F8ᵛ–G8ᵛ; 80–96
Failure of catchwords to catch:
95 (G8ʳ) his] for his

London, 1730
TS 35. *ESTC* T130870
Title: THE | INTELLIGENCER
[see entry under *Short View of the State of Ireland* for full description]
Contents: Number 9: E10ᵛ–F8ʳ; 92–111

Miscellanies, 1732
TS 25 (4a). *ESTC* N62568
Title: MISCELLANIES | [rule] | THE | THIRD VOLUME.
[see entry under *Intelligencer*, Number 5 for full description]
Contents: Number 9 (renamed 'AN ESSAY ON *Modern Education*'): O7ᵛ–P7ʳ; 222–37

Works, 1735
TS 41. *ESTC* T52771
Title: VOLUME IV. | Of the Author's | WORKS.
[see entry under *Short View of the State of Ireland* for full description]
Contents: Number 9: T7ᵛ–U4ᵛ; 286–96

Emendations
76.12 Minors had] *1729*; Minors have or had
76.23 Coventry] Coonuley
77.3 Vernon] *1732+*; Vernor
78.1 Allyance] *1732a*; allowance
78.6 important] *1732a*; compatent
79.27 is he] *1729*; he is
81.9 other] *1729*; othet

81.15 Age adding only to] *1729+*; being
82.8 *Great*] *1729*; great
82.10 own] *1729*; one
82.18 acquired] *1729*; required
82.21 important... Gentleman] *1729*; important... Gentlemen
83.29 misled] *1732a*; Mild
84.20 Wealth?] *1729*; ~:

Historical Collation

75.1 [*Heading:*] AN ESSAY ON *Modern Education*] *1732*
75.5 Wealth and Grandeur] *Wealth* of and *Grandeur 1732*
75.12 I.] [*begins a new paragraph*] *1732+*
75.26 some Additional] *some 1735*
76.1 a Neighbouring Kingdom, from whence the Chief among us are descended, and whose manners we most affect to follow] *England 1732+*
76.4 in that Kingdom] *om. 1732+*
76.5 the Hands of] *om. 1735*
76.6 very few] few *1735*
76.7 supported] supplied *1735*
76.11 Ormonde] Ormond *1729+*
76.12 Minors had] *1729–1732*; Minors having *1735*; Minors have or had; *1728*
76.17 chief Conduct of publick Affairs] highest Employments of State *1735*
76.21 good Estates] ample Fortunes *1735*
76.23 *Bridgman*] Bridgeman *1732+*
76.23 *Coventry*] Coonuley *1728–1730*; *om. 1732+*
77.2 *Summers*] Sommers *1729+*
77.3 *Vernon*] *1732+*; Vernor *1728–1730*
77.3 *Harry*] *om. 1732*
77.4 *Harcourt*] Harcout *1735*
77.4 *Trevers*] Trevor *1732+*
77.5 last] following *1732*
77.6 understood for many Years, to be] for many years *1732+*
78.1 *Craiggs*] Craggs *1729+*
78.1 Allyance] *1732a+*; Allowance *1728–1732*
78.6 great share] great a Share *1735*
78.6 important] *1732a+*; compatent *1728*; *competent 1729–1732*
78.12 Noble and Wealthy] noble wealthy *1735*
78.13 Body] Bodies *1730*
78.18 a universal] an universal *1730*; a *1735*

78.19 fault on] fault in *1732a*
78.24 the least expence] the Expence *1730*
79.2   publick] the publick *1735*
79.16 were] was *1730+*
79.17 Standard-Patterns] Standard-Pattern *1730+*
79.27 is he] *1729+*; he is *1728*
80.2   Blockado] Blockade *1729+*
80.2   recountring] rencountring *1729–1732*; reconoitring *1735*
80.6   contempt of Learning] Contempt *1730*
80.7   many, and some even in this Kingdom] many *1732*; a few *1735*
80.14 been likewise] likewise been *1729+*
80.15 a humorous] an humorous *1730*
80.16 *Le-Sac*] *Le-Sack* 1732; *Le Sac* 1735
81.2   *Well*,] **Well*, [*with footnote:*] **The Author's Friends have heard him tell this Passage as from the Earl himself. 1735*
81.9   other] othet *1728*
81.10 the Dancing-master] Dancing-master *1729, 1732*
81.15 Age adding only to] *1729+*; being *1728*
81.16 Vice] Vices *1732a+*
81.20 and posture] and the Posture *1735*
81.20 change] Changes *1735*
81.21 knowlidge] knowledge *1729+*
81.23 Nursary] Nursery *1729+*
82.1   Lord] *Lord [*with footnote:*] **The Author is supposed to mean the Lord Viscount* Montcassel, *of* Ireland. *1735*
82.8   *Great*] *1729*; great *1728*
82.10 own] *1729*; one *1728*
82.13 removal,] Removal to the University; *1735*
82.14 very Worthy] *om. 1735*
82.18 acquired] *1729*; required *1728*
82.20 important . . . Gentleman] *1729*; important . . . Gentlemen *1728*
83.8   them to] ~ in *1735*
83.10 that] who *1735*
83.12 a Patron] Patron *1735*
83.15 *Schools*] *School 1732+*
83.24 out of] by *1735*
83.27 for] But *1735*
83.29 never] ever *1732*
83.29 misled] *1732a*; Mild *1728–1732*
84.15 cause] *1728–1732*; Course *1735*

84.18 calls] calleth *1735*
84.20 Wealth?] *1729*; ~: *1728*
85.2 the] their *1735*
85.3 enervated] enervate *1730*
85.3 thorough] through *1729+*

Word Division
Copy Text
Coffee-house
Dancing-master
Bosom-friend

Edited Text
None

Intelligencer, Number 19
Dublin, 1728 (*c.* 3–7 Dec.)

TS 666. *ESTC* P2223. First impression, 28 (Woolley, *Intelligencer*, p. 332)
Title: THE | Intelligencer. | [rule] | NUMB. XIX. | [rule] | *Having on the 12th of* October *last, receiv'd* | a *LETTER Sign'd* Andrew Dealer, *and* | Patrick Pennyless; *I believe the following* | PAPER, *just come to my Hands, will be* | *a sufficient Answer to it.* | [rule] | *Sic vos non vobis vellera fertis ovos.* | Virg. | [rule] | [ornament] | [rule] | *DUBLIN* | Printed by S. HARDING, next Door to | the *Crown* in *Copper-Alley* 1728
Collation: 8°: A⁸
Pagination: *1–2*, 3–15 16
Contents: A1ʳ title page; A1ᵛ blank; A2ʳ–8ʳ text; A8ᵛ blank
Typography: 30 lines per page (A2ᵛ); type-page 130 (155) × 70 mm; 20 lines of roman type 80 mm
Copies consulted: V & A, Forster 8544; TCD, OLS B-10–237.

London, 1729

TS 34. *ESTC* T135902
Title: THE | INTELLIGENCER.
[see entry under *Short View of the State of Ireland* for full description]
Contents: Number 19: O5ᵛ–P5ʳ; 202–17
Failure of catchwords to catch:
208 (O8ᵛ) I know] I Know

London, 1730

TS 35. *ESTC* T130870

Title: THE | INTELLIGENCER
[see entry under *Short View of the State of Ireland* for full description]
Contents: Number 19: L10ʳ–M7ᵛ; 235–54 [running head of 253 mistitles it Number 1]

Miscellanies, 1732

TS 25 (4a). *ESTC* N62568
Title: MISCELLANIES | [rule] | THE | THIRD VOLUME.
[see entry under *Intelligencer*, Number 5 for full description]
Contents: Number 19: O5ᵛ–P5ʳ; 202–17

Works, 1735

TS 41. *ESTC* T52771
Title: VOLUME IV. | Of the Author's | WORKS.
[see entry under *Short View of the State of Ireland* for full description]
Contents: Number 19: Z2ʳ–7ʳ; 339–349

Emendations

88.5 oves] *1729*; ovos
90.1 so often] *1729*; soo ften
92.18 lest] *1735*; lesty
92.20 Disaffection.] *1729*; ~∧
93.1 *Crowley*] Cowley
95.17 come] *1730*; came
95.27 satisfactory] *1729*; satisactory
96.5 Tract of] Tractof
96.11 Insults] *1729*; Insulst
96.13 Now] *1729*; now

Historical Collation

88.1 [*Note added after title:*] N. B. In the following Discourse the Author personates a Country Gentleman in the North of Ireland. And this Letter is supposed as directed to the Drapier. *1735*
88.5 oves] *1729*; ovos *1728*
88.6 Virg.] *om.* [*note added:*] Written in the Year 1728. *1735*
88.11 till] until *1735*
88.11 to be not] not to be *1729+*

88.19 Conveniencies] Conveniences *1730*
89.1 kinds] Kind *1735*
89.1 till] until *1735*
89.3 among us] us *1735*
89.9 other] *om. 1735*
89.14 though] although *1735*
89.20 of] They consider not *1735*
89.21 of half] that half *1735*
89.21 sent annually] are annually sent *1735*
89.21 and] with *1735*
89.22 excepted for our Sins] except ~ ~ ~ *1729–1730*; *om. 1735*
89.23 keeps] keep *1729+*
90.1 so often] soo ften *1728*
90.7 too] so *1735*
90.9 inconveniences] Inconveniencies *1729–1730*
90.10 timely] tamely *1735*
90.16 *Lord Lieutenant*] * Lord Lieutenant [*with note:*] * The Lord Carteret. *1735*
90.19 *easy upon that*] made easy upon this *1735*
91.5 6 *d.*] and 6 *d. 1735*
91.8 dare] dares *1729–1730*
91.11 to] in *1735*
92.18 lest] *1735*; lesty *1728*; least *1729–1730*
92.19 politick] *1728–1729*; Politicks *1730+*
92.20 *Disaffection.*] *1729+*; ~ₐ *1728*
93.1 *Crowley*] Cowley *1728*; Crawley *1729+*
93.8 degree] Degrees *1730*
93.9 greatest] gratial *1728*
93.11 till] until *1735*
93.14 conveniences] Conveniencies *1735*
94.4 would never] could never *1735*
94.24 to] of *1730*
95.8 at all] all *1730*
95.17 come] *1730*; came *1728–1729*
95.27 satisfactory] *1729*; satisactory *1728*
96.5 Tract of] Tractof *1728*
96.11 Insults] *1729*; Insulst *1728*
96.13 Now] *1729*; now *1728*
96.14 inclines] incline *1730*

96.16 so,] *om. 1735*
96.17 have] have also *1735*
96.25 discourage] discourse *1730*
96.26 effects] Effect *1735*

Word Division
Copy Text
Shop-keepers
Shop-keepers
Rack-rent

Edited Text
Rack-rent

A Letter to the Archbishop of Dublin, Concerning the Weavers

Textual Account

One of four pieces (along with the *Answers* to *Unknown Persons* and an *Unknown Hand*, and the *Letter on M'culla*) written in the spring of 1729 concerning Irish economic and agricultural problems, and not published in Swift's lifetime, the *Letter to the Archbishop* can be dated reasonably accurately: it was composed in response to an appeal from a spokesman for the Irish weavers, asking Swift to 'publish a recommendation that the Irish people should wear cloth made in their own country' (Ehrenpreis, vol. III, p. 614; see also Ferguson, pp. 153–5). The appeal was made in the *Dublin Intelligence*, 29 April 1729. The nominal recipient of Swift's polemic, Archbishop William King, died on 8 May. Swift's opening reference to a visit from the Weavers on 'Thursday last' (probably 28 April) suggests a hasty composition around the end of April or early May.

On the reasons behind the non-publication of the *Letter to the Archbishop*, along with the other pieces, the speculation of Ehrenpreis is sound: 'they were either too offensive or not finished enough' (vol. III, p. 610).

The *Letter to the Archbishop* would appear posthumously, first in Deane Swift's 1765 London *Works* (hereafter *1765a*) and then in Faulkner's Dublin *Works* of the same year (*1765b*), in an identical text, in terms of variants. Yet both differ in some small respects from the autograph manuscript of the *Letter to the Archbishop*, in the Forster Collection at the Victoria and Albert

Museum (hereafter SwJ 436; for the provenance of these manuscripts, which came originally from Martha Whiteway via Deane Swift, and were donated by John Forster in 1876–7, see Woolley, 'Forster's *Swift*'). The manuscript is dated 'April 1729', albeit by 'a hand that is not Swift's' (Ehrenpreis, vol. III, p. 611). The manuscript is a fair copy, with the left-hand side of the page left blank for insertions, but used very infrequently; the consistency of inking suggests that revisions belong to the initial point of composition.

This complete manuscript is the obvious choice of copy text for this edition, given the absence of any variation or authorial revision in the texts of Faulkner or Deane Swift. It has not needed much emendation, beyond common manuscript absences – missing periods, the odd tautology or repetition, grammatical non-agreement and the wrong tense – and represents Swift's response in 1729 perfectly adequately, allowing for some necessary tidying. Swift's manuscript insertions and deletions are listed below as variants, along with any regularising of contractions, spellings and superscript. The historical collation compares the manuscript with the print versions.

Copy Text
V & A, Forster MS 520, F.48.G.6/2 Item 7.

Manuscript:
SwJ 436
Location: V & A, Forster MS 520, F.48.G/2 Item 7
Description: autograph hand, 10 leaves, 205 × 160 mm; cropped and mounted on card by page. Fos. 1^r–9^r paginated by Swift, 1, 3, 5, 7, 9, 11, 13, 15, 17, top right-hand side of page. Fos. 1^r–10^v paginated 1–18, 20 (added later in pencil, on middle of top of card).
Contents: fo. 1^r 'About Weavers &c. Apr 1729' (added later to card, bottom middle); fos. 1^r–9^v, text in right-hand column, additions on left: 2^v, 8^r, 9^v – 10^r missing; 10^v, 'Lettr to the A B P Apr 1729. / About Weavers &c.' (endorsement 'probably by Deane Swift': Davis, vol. XII, p. 329)

Alterations to the Manuscript
100.10 Nation] *above del.* Kingdom
100.17 clad, and erect] *interlineated after* faces
101.1 Courage,] *interlineated with caret after* Property
101.2 wt] *del. before* whether
101.4 would] *del. after* whoever
101.10 force] *interlineated over del.* oblige

101.13 evil] *interlineated with caret above* Condition
101.15 not] *interlineated with caret before* enter
101.21 called] *del. before* entitled
101.25 But our [. . .] never be less exacting.] *ins. in left-hand margin*
101.25 the] *interlineated over del.* our
101.27 own] *ins. after* our
102.3 abortive] *after del.* crude
102.6 to] *after del.* for the
102.8 People] *after del.* Rich
102.18 numerous] *after del.* me
102.20 by] *interlineated with caret after* least
102.22 Trade.] *before del.* Tho
102.26 the] *interlineated with caret before* intolerable
103.1 luxury] *after illegible del.*
103.4 husband] *before illegible del.*
103.7 parts] *after del.* countryes
103.9 directly] *after del.* from
103.11 Tea] *before del.* (Coffee and
104.7 devouring] *ins. with caret above* poysonous
104.8 mischief,] *before del.* and
104.8 but] *ins. above with caret above* with
104.12 deciding] *before del.* of
104.13 no more] *interlineated with caret after* hear
104.20 selling] *before del.* in our markets at home
104.23 Woollen] *after del.* Woll
104.25 known.] *interlineated with caret before* About
104.29 Brethren in] *interlineated with caret above del.* Clergy of
104.30 Citizens] *ins. with caret above del.* Cityes
104.30 Corporations who appear] *before extraneous* who *and del.* notably
104.31 a kind] a *interlineated with caret above del.* I
104.32 a yard] *interlineated with caret after* pence
105.2 appoint as] *before illegible del.*
105.3 Opinions] *before del.* but instead
105.4 seeing] *before del.* woul
105.5 consequence] *before del.* to begin
105.11 step] *interlineated with caret after* least
105.12 more] *before del.* for Your Visitation passed without any overture at all from the Weavers
105.18 undersigned] *before del.* did bind themselves
105.19 other] *interlineated with caret after* each

105.25 if any person] *after del.* then
105.27 satisfied] *before del.* either
105.28 unless] *before del.* there *and ins. it above*
106.9 such] *after del.* this
106.11 persuade] *with del. last letter* persuaded
106.14 digest] *before del.* the
106.18 weavers] Linnen-weavers *del.*
106.19 notwithstanding all the [. . .] the Spaniards] *ins. with caret from left-hand margin*
106.20 when we had an offer of] *del.*
106.20 commerce with] *before del.* them
106.21 a year] *before del.* notwithstanding all the care taken by the Governors of that Board.
106.24 an] *ins. above illegible del. before* answer
106.25 Weavers] *interlineated above del.* weavers; *before del.* linnen-weavers
106.25 that I would] *ins. from left-hand margin*
106.25 offer] *after del.* To
106.25 that I should] *interlineated above* offer *and del.*
106.27 Commons] *before del.* for
106.27 one] *interlineated above del.* a
107.1 shall] *interlineated above del.* should
107.1 still] *after del.* were
107.2 a] *interlineated with caret before* vote
107.3 wear] *interlineated with caret after* future
107.8 and China ware] *interlineated with caret after* Coffee
107.14 and receiving from thence and all other Countryes nothing but what is fully manufactured,] *ins. with caret from left-hand margin*
107.15 Oatmeal] *ins. above del.* butter
107.20 hath] *interlineated with caret before* spent
107.22 Cottager] *before del.* complaining
107.23 ill] *interlineated with caret before del.* bad
107.23 Clymats] *interlineated after* better
107.24 exposed to] *before del.* than ours

Deane Swift, *Works*, 1765a
TS 87. *ESTC* T52748
Title: THE | WORKS | OF | Dr. JONATHAN SWIFT, | Dean of St. Patrick's, Dublin. | VOLUME VIII. Part I.
[see entry under *Upon Giving Badges to the Poor* for full description]
Contents: Letter to the Archbishop: 2A1ʳ–4ᵛ;177–84

Faulkner, *Works*, 1765b
TS 47. *ESTC* N31130.
Title: VOLUME XII. | OF THE | Author's WORKS.
[see entry under *Upon Giving Badges to the Poor* for full description]
Contents: Letter to the Archbishop: S4^r–T1^v; 263–74

Emendations

101.1 by] *1765a*; by by
101.30 they] *1765a*; the
102.3 of so] *1765a*; so
102.10 neither manufactures to] *1765a*; neither to
102.12 other] *1765a*; order
103.11 Sum] *1765a*; some
104.16 our selves.] ourselves. *1765a*; our selves
104.22 Proceedings.] *1765a*; ~$_\wedge$
104.23 who] *1765a*; ~ ~
105.12 more.] *1765a*; ~$_\wedge$
105.23 Monopoly] *1765a*; Monpoly
105.29 Mistake.] *1765a*; ~$_\wedge$
106.13 first.] *1765a*; ~$_\wedge$
107.6 Friends] *1765a*; Frends
107.11 Travellers, Students] *1765a*; Travellers, Colliers, Students
107.26 warning.] *1765a*; ~$_\wedge$

Historical Collation

100.1 [A LETTER...WEAVERS] *om.* SwJ 436
100.4 wollen] woollen *1765a*
100.9 the] this *1765a*
100.9 Manufacture] Manufactures *1765a*+
101.1 by] by by SwJ 436
101.6 Governmt] government *1765a*+
101.7 this many year] these many years *1765a*+
101.17 *Short View of the State of Ireland*] *1765a*+; Short view of the State of Ireld SwJ 436
101.18 utmost] the utmost *1765a*+
101.25 can ly] labour *1765a*+
101.25 Trade] *1765a*+; Trad SwJ 436
101.30 they] *1765a*+; the SwJ 436
102.3 of so] *1765a*+; so SwJ 436

102.5 the raising] raising *1765a+*
102.7 so] *om. 1765a+*
102.10 neither manufactures to] *1765a+*; neither to SwJ 436
102.12 other] *1765a+*; order SwJ 436
102.15 the] a *1765a+*
103.5 theory] thing *1765a+*
103.11 sum] *1765a+*; some SwJ 436
103.17 over reckoning] over-reaching *1765a*
104.16 our selves.] ourselves. *1765a+*; our selves SwJ 436
104.22 Proceedings.] *1765a+*; ~∧ SwJ 436
104.23 This] The *1765a+*
104.29 their Brethren] the Clergy of SwJ 436 *del*
105.3 Visitations] Visitation *1765a+*
105.9 Manufacture] Manufactures *1765a+*
105.10 whether] if *1765a+*
105.12 more.] *1765a+*; ~∧ SwJ 436
105.16 Purpose.] [new paragraph] *1765a*
105.23 Monopoly] *1765a+*; Monpoly SwJ 436
105.26 or] and *1765a+*
105.29 Mistake.] *1765a+*; ~∧ SwJ 436
106.4 till] until *1765a*
106.5 in] into *1765a+*
106.13 first.] *1765a+*; ~∧ SwJ 436
106.19 the whole trade with Spain for our Linnen,] *om. 1765a+*
106.21 Spaniards to the value] Spaniards for our linen to the value *1765a+*
106.27 H.] House *1765a+*
107.2 *nemine contradicente*] *1765a+*; nemine contradicente SwJ 436
107.11 Travellers, Students] *1765a+*; Travellers, Colliers, Students SwJ 436
107.18 every] any *1765a+*
107.25 inconveniency] inconvenience *1765a+*
107.26 warning. *1765a+*; ~∧ SwJ 436

Word Division
Copy Text
None

Edited Text
None

An Answer to Several Letters from Unknown Persons

Textual Account

Another of the four unpublished pieces on contemporary Irish problems written in the spring of 1729. Ferguson thinks it was written in 'late April or early May' (Ferguson, p. 161). Like the *Letter to the Archbishop*, it refers to William King as still living, and therefore predates 8 May 1729; Ehrenpreis (vol. III, p. 611) notes that it also refers to William Burnet and his difficulties in Massachusetts; Burnet went there in 'mid April 1728'. It was a response to a letter from 'Andrew Trueman' and 'Patrick Layfield', sent to Swift, then printed in the *Dublin Weekly Journal* (7 June 1729; see Appendix E, above, pp. 365–74). The correspondents are usually assumed to be the same source that had produced 'Andrew Dealer' and 'Patrick Pennyless', whose previous writings to Swift, which have not survived, inspired the writing of *Intelligencer*, no. 19. Ferguson thinks the pseudonyms mask one author, perhaps a Scottish Presbyterian, from the comments on paying tithes to the Anglican church; see Ferguson, pp. 161–2.

Like its companion pieces, the *Answer to Several Letters from Unknown Persons* would not appear in Swift's lifetime; it also shares the publication history of the *Letter to the Archbishop*, appearing in Deane Swift's 1765 London *Works* (hereafter *1765a*) and in Faulkner's Dublin *Works* of the same year (*1765b*). Moreover, it is also to be found in an autograph manuscript in the Forster collection, amongst others which can be traced from Martha Whiteway via Deane Swift: see Woolley, 'Forster's *Swift*'.

The copy text for this edition is this manuscript: neither Faulkner nor Deane Swift show any evidence of working from any later authorially revised text, in their small variations. There is one interesting deviation, though, which suggests that an alternative source was available to them: both 1765 editions include a passage deleted in the manuscript (see the Historical Collation, p. 386), suggesting either that Deane Swift, the first editor, was using a different, possibly earlier manuscript source, or that, when transcribing this manuscript, he thought that including this passage would clarify Swift's argument. Herbert Davis suggested that 'it was possible that Swift was copying out this manuscript with his own hand from a "foul copy", and that some of these insertions and deletions are not really deliberate alterations or later corrections' (vol. XII, p. 331). Yet the passage crossed out in the manuscript and reproduced by Deane Swift would seem to contradict this, as it is unlikely Swift would transcribe a long sentence already deleted. It would seem more probable that Swift crossed it out after transcription, and that Deane Swift was either working from an earlier manuscript, where many small alterations had been made, but the passage was not yet marked for deletion, or that he decided to include it for the sake of clarity.

Swift followed his usual practice of leaving the left-hand side of the manuscript blank for additions. The neatness of the text signals that this was intended as a fair copy (as Davis suggests). The state of the (sparse) alterations suggests they are slightly later corrections, probably on completion of the draft. These manuscript variants are listed separately below.

Emendations mainly rectify the absence of periods, and the odd slip or misspelling. These are included in the historical variants, as is any regularising of contractions, spellings and superscript.

Copy Text
V & A, Forster MS 546, F.48.G.6/2 Item 19.

Manuscript:
SwJ 390
Location: V & A, Forster MS 546, F.48.G.6/2 Item 19
Description: autograph hand, 8 leaves, 205 × 153 mm; cropped and mounted on card by page. Fos. 1ʳ–8ʳ paginated by Swift, 1, 3, 5, 7, 9, 11, 13, 15, top right-hand side of page. Fos. 1ʳ–8ᵛ paginated 1–16 (added later in pencil, on middle of top of card). Foliation 19/1–19/4 every four leaves added later in pencil, on right of top of card.
Contents: fo. 1ʳ 'Answer to Several Letters from unknown Persons. 8 leaves' (added later to card, bottom middle); fos. 1ʳ–8ᵛ text in right-hand column; 8ᵛ 'Answer to several Letters from Unknown Persons', very faded addition below in different hand: 'this is in my grandfather Mr Deane Swift's handwriting' – presumably written by E. Lewenthal Swifte, Deane Swift's grandson.

Alterations to the Manuscript

110.12 is not to be had but by] *ins. from left-hand margin, after del.* we cannot expect without
110.19 intend that] *before del.* the *and two illegible words*
110.22 in] *interlineated above del.* under
110.22 directed] *interlineated above del.* sent
110.24 tonight,] *before del.* kn
111.4 conjecture] *after two illegible del. words*
111.4 I] *interlineated with caret after* was

111.9 thither.] *before illegible del.*
111.16 Praise] *after del.* the
111.19 open] *after illegible del.*
112.4 seem not to] *before illegible del.*
112.7 or the Army] *interlineated with caret after* Revenue
112.13 but as] *before del.* they do not
112.13 these Speculations may probably not much] *ins. with caret from left-hand margin*
112.15 observe] *final letter in* observed *del.*
112.16 hitherto] *before del.* prevailed
112.17 oratory] *before del.* under
112.19 one] *interlineated with caret before del.* many
112.21 having] *interlineated above del.* had
113.7 three] *interlineated above del.* two
113.9 Natives] *before del.* in
113.14 Landlords] *before del.* is in
113.16 fault] *before illegible del.*
114.2 experience] *final letter in* experienced *del.*
114.3 any] *interlineated above del.* a
114.7 firm] *before del.* clauses for
114.9 Ireland] *before del.* in twenty years time
114.12 exactions] *after illegible del.*
114.14 in] *interlineated with caret before del.* of
115.6 making] *after del.* not
115.16 continued] *after del.* Dear
115.16 in] *after del.* of
115.17 chief] *before del.* of
115.17 Expedition;] *before del.* but, there is likewise another temptation which is not of inconsiderable weight, which is their itch of living in a Country where their Sect is predominant, and where their eyes and consciences will not be offended by the Stumbling block of Ceremonyes, habits and spiritual Titles.
115.22 rent,] *before illegible del.*
116.3 sufficient] *before del.* reasons
116.5 become] *ins. before del.* grow
116.9 Maxims,] *before illegible del.*
116.10 understanding] *interlineated with caret above del.* knowing
116.14 short] *before illegible del.*
116.16 few] *after del.* many
116.17 by] *interlineated with caret after* attained

116.18 of our own wooll] *interlineated above* Cloth
117.1 men] *before illegible del.*
117.6 whole] *final letters in* wholely *del.*
117.13 few] *interlineated with caret after* those
117.19 exigency] *after del.* eg
117.23 our] *interlineated with caret above del.* their
117.25 ever] *interlineated with caret after* can
117.28 well-meaning] *interlineated with caret before* People
118.3 differ] *last three letters in* differing *del.*
118.4 half] *interlineated with caret after* if
118.5 and the rest] *after illegible del.*

Deane Swift, *Works*, 1765a
TS 87. *ESTC* T52748
Title: THE | WORKS | OF | Dr. JONATHAN SWIFT, | Dean of St. Patrick's, Dublin. | VOLUME VIII. Part I.
[see entry under *Upon Giving Badges to the Poor* for full description]
Contents: An Answer to Several Letters: BB1^r–4^r; 185–91

Faulkner, *Works*, 1765b
TS 47. *ESTC* N31130
Title: VOLUME XII. | OF THE | Author's WORKS.
[see entry under *Upon Giving Badges to the Poor* for full description]
Contents: An Answer to Several Letters: T2^r–7^r; 275–85

Emendations

110.24 with.] *1765a*; ~∧
110.27 Kingdom.] *1765a*; ~∧
111.2 Sincerity.] *1765a*; ~∧
112.6 Church,] *1765a*; ~∧
112.6 Sixthly] *1765a*; Seventhly
112.9 money.] *1765a*; ~∧
113.1 they] *1765a*; the
115.1 than his] *1765a*; than is
115.10 Landlord] *1765a*; Landed
118.5 and the rest] *1765a*; and and the rest
118.10 (except] *1765a*; except
118.12 Poor.] *1765a*; ~∧

Historical Collation

110.2 Answer to several Letters from unknown Persons]; AN ANSWER TO SEVERAL LETTERS from unknown PERSONS., *1765a+*
110.4 last] * last [with footnote added:] * Trueman and Layfield *1765a+*
110.10 so] too *1765a*
110.24 with.] *1765a+*; ~∧ SwJ 390
110.27 Kingdom.] *1765a+*; ~∧ SwJ 390
111.2 Sincerity.] *1765a+*; ~∧ SwJ 390
111.9 do] *om. 1765a*
112.6 Sixthly] *1765a+*; Seventhly SwJ 390
112.9 money.] *1765a+*; ~∧ SwJ 390
112.22 is] was *1765a*
113.1 markets] market *1765a*
113.1 they] *1765a+*; the SwJ 390
113.10 Revenues] Revenue *1765a+*
113.10 As to the first,] As to the first and second, *1765a*
113.12 till] until *1765b*
114.11 Clergymen] Clergyman *1765a*
114.17 tithing-table] tithing-teller *1765a*
115.10 Landlord] *1765a+*; Landed SwJ 390
115.17 Expedition] but, there is likewise another temptation which is not of inconsiderable weight, which is their itch of living in a Country where their Sect is predominant, and where their eyes and consciences will not be offended by the Stumbling block of Ceremonyes, habits and spiritual Titles.] *1765a+*; SwJ 390 *del.*
116.16 necessityes] necessaries *1765a*
116.18 Cloth of our] Cloth made of our *1765a*
117.18 Does] Doth *1765a*
118.5 and the rest] *1765a+*; and and the rest SwJ 390
118.10 (except] *1765a+*; except SwJ 390
118.12 Poor.] *1765a+*; ~∧ SwJ 390

Word Division
Copy Text
None

Edited Text
None

An Answer to Several Letters Sent Me from Unknown Hands

Textual Account

Of the four pieces from 1729 not published in Swift's lifetime, the unfinished *Answer to Several Letters Sent Me from Unknown Hands* is the least complicated, textually: no manuscript survives, and there is no variation between its two authoritative versions, one of which is a reprint of the other.

Deane Swift, its first editor, affixed the date of 1729 beneath its title, and it is indeed of a piece with other works of that period in its concerns, though underneath its despair and complaint, it is also, as Ehrenpreis says, 'a survey of proposals that might help the nation', albeit a 'fragmentary' one (vol. III, p. 617). Indications of its time of composition cannot narrow it down overmuch: it mentions the death of Swift's old bugbear, Justice Whitshed, which dates it after August 1727; it refers to the (unidentified) correspondents' proposals to help the Irish economy, and their desire that Swift somehow aid them in getting these considered by the Irish Parliament. That Parliament commenced on 23 September 1729, and Ehrenpreis assumes that, as the essay 'recommends policies for an imminent Parliament', it 'was probably written not long before that date' (vol. III, p. 611). It can be countered that the *Answer to Several Letters Sent Me from Unknown Hands* uses Parliament as an opening rhetorical gesture and reason for Swift to air his grievances and suggestions for amelioration; it does not necessarily suggest immediacy and direct purpose in so doing. The (traditional) alternative is to place it in spring 1729, partly because Swift left Dublin in June for an extended visit to the Achesons at Markethill (writing on 9 August, he says he has been there 'these ten weeks', and did not return until October (Woolley, *Corr.*, vol. III, p. 243)).

It first appeared in Deane Swift's 1765 London *Works* (hereafter *1765a*) and was then reprinted in Faulkner's Dublin *Works* of the same year (*1765b*). Given that Faulkner used the same text for his edition, with (very) minor changes (two variant spellings and one difference in paragraphing), Deane Swift's edition is the copy text chosen for this volume. A work appearing in a collection in this period would be made to conform to the style of the edition with regard to punctuation, spelling and typography. With many of the posthumously published works, it is simply not possible to gauge the degree to which Deane Swift imposed a house style, and regularised Swift's spelling, punctuation, capitalisation and italicisation; in the case of the *Answer to Several Letters Sent Me from Unknown Hands*, the 1765 editions refrain from using capitals or italics beyond the essential, and some of the

TEXTUAL ACCOUNT: LETTERS SENT FROM UNKNOWN HANDS 433

hyphenation seems more likely to have been imposed than in the original text. The absence of capitalised nouns and the reduction of semi-colons are in some ways an indication of a more modern printing style, and the decades that have passed since Faulkner's 1735 *Works* presented Swift's texts rather differently.

Copy Text

BL, 90.d.8 (with vol. VIII, pt ii).

Deane Swift, *Works*, 1765a

TS 87. *ESTC* T52748

Title: THE | WORKS | OF | Dr. JONATHAN SWIFT, | DEAN OF ST. PATRICK'S, DUBLIN. | VOLUME VIII. PART I.

[see entry under *Upon Giving Badges to the Poor* for full description]

Contents: *An Answer to Several Letters from Unknown Hands*: 192–7; 2B4^v–2C3^r

Faulkner, *Works*, 1765b

TS 47. *ESTC* N31130

Title: VOLUME XII. | OF THE | AUTHOR'S WORKS.

[see entry under *Upon Giving Badges to the Poor* for full description]

Contents: *An Answer to Several Letters from Unknown Hands*: T8^r–U4^r; 287–95

Emendations

[None]

Historical Collation

121.3 Written in the Year 1729. *1765a*; ~~~~ MDCCXXIX. *1655b*
123.14 other.] [*new paragraph*] *1765b*
124.11 enjoined] joined *1765b*
126.2 does] doth *1765b*

Word Division
Copy Text
water-carriage
West-south-west
hop-poles

Edited Text
None

A Letter on M'culla's Project

Textual Account

James Maculla's attempt to alleviate the drastic shortage of coins in Ireland is outlined in his pamphlet of 1728, *A New Scheme Proposed, to the People of Ireland: For Increasing the Cash, of this Kingdom, by Making Promissory Notes of Copper* ... (mentioned in the *Dublin Intelligence*, 8 February 1729). He attempted to gain Swift's aid for his scheme, as Swift recalled in the *Letter on M'culla*, and as Ferguson summarises: 'Maculla called on him some time during February, with a copy of his book and some of the counters. Swift was ill at the time, and could not receive him, but in March or April Swift returned the visit and discussed Maculla's project with him' (Ferguson, p. 160). Swift was therefore writing in Dublin, and his response is usually dated before his departure for Markethill in early June (see the letter of 9 August: Woolley, *Corr.*, vol. III, p. 243), and more specifically to March or April, given that he states that Maculla had visited him a month before.

The year 1729 was affixed to the title by Faulkner, the first editor of the work. He also added Delany as the intended recipient. The non-publication of the *Letter* in Swift's lifetime can be ascribed partly to the moment having passed, given the immediacy of the subject (Maculla's scheme did not come to fruition; see Ferguson, p. 160, quoting the *Dublin Intelligence*, 29 April, that the 'Prospect' of the plan 'seems to be almost over').

The relative clarity of the context of its composition is not matched by the textual history of the *Letter on M'culla*, which is more complicated, in terms of choices of text, than any other work in this volume. There are two posthumous printed versions: Faulkner first published it in 1762, in Volume X of his *Works* (1751–63), an edition eventually extended to eleven volumes (*1762* in the Historical Collation). Deane Swift included it in his 1765 *Works* (*1765* in the Collation) alongside other Irish writings. The differences between these two texts are significant and frequent, going well beyond standard editorial intervention, and it is evident that the editors use different manuscript sources.

Deane Swift's text follows an extant autograph manuscript, in the Forster Collection (for the history of which, as with other manuscript works located there, see Woolley, 'Forster's *Swift*'). Unfortunately, this is only a short fragment of two leaves, though it shows the origin of Deane Swift's text. It also indicates, through Faulkner's text's absorbing its changes without replicating any deleted parts, that Faulkner's manuscript was probably a later draft than the fragment. Faulkner's variants include apparent corrections of some of the figures offered in Deane Swift's text, and some refinements of phrasing; both of these may, of course, be authorial in origin, rather than editorial.

Faulkner's text exhibits certain qualities that seem very much imposed upon it by an editor: insistent capitalisation of all nouns, greater frequency of colons and semi-colons, many new paragraphs, and some variant spellings, particularly the addition of 'eth' to verbs in the present tense. The result is a consistent style, but not one that resembles Swift's (albeit brief) manuscript, and is highly unlikely to have been a replication of Faulkner's manuscript source. Therefore, the copy text for this edition is the manuscript fragment for its brief span, then Deane Swift's much plainer text (which is devoid of extra capitals, variant spellings and -eth verb endings). This offers the complete text closest to Swift's original intentions (the manuscript and Deane Swift's text), with Faulkner's apparently later version, and its small number of possibly authorial revisions available via the Historical Collation.

Herbert Davis uses an issue of 'Faulkner, *Works*, vol. X, 1759', but also claims elsewhere in his edition that the *Letter* was 'first printed by Faulkner in 1758' (vol. XII, pp. 332, xvi). We have not been able to locate a Volume X with either of those dates (Temple Scott, the previous editor, used Volume X of Faulkner's 1772 edition, a reprint of the volume described below), nor does Teerink–Scouten list one. The confusions caused by Faulkner's multiple reprintings are myriad. Inasmuch as it is possible to verify, the Faulkner volume and text used here is identical to Davis's, in every bibliographic and textual detail, save its apparent date.

The unfinished Forster collection manuscript follows Swift's rule in leaving a blank left side for insertions and corrections. Both the relative roughness of the handwriting (when contrasted with similar manuscripts from the year) and the large number of alterations indicate that this was an early draft: sections of the argument are removed, or heavily revised, and there is the continual attention to local prose detail expected in an early or first draft. The inking suggests that the one longer insertion comes from the stage of revision that probably followed the initial drafting.

In the copy text, manuscript contractions and superscript have been retained, along with Swift's insertions. His deletions (along with his additions) are noted in the separate list of manuscript variants below. For purposes of clarity, the present edition uses M'culla, the most common spelling of the name in SwJ 433, in the copy text and in references not directly to the texts by Deane Swift and Faulkner.

Copy Text
V & A, Forster MS 523, F.48.G.6/2 Item 8, & BL, 90.d.8.

Manuscript
SwJ 433
Location: V & A, Forster MS 523, F.48.G.6/2 Item 8
Description: autograph hand, 2 leaves, 205 × 153 mm; cropped and mounted on card by page. Fos. 1ʳ–2ᵛ paginated 1–4 (added later in pencil, on middle of top of card). Foliation '8' on first leaf added later in pencil, on right of top of card.
Contents: fo. 1ʳ 'M'culla's Project – about Halfpence, & a new one proposd | 1729', top left-hand side of text (not in Swift's hand), 'MᶜCulla's Project – About Halfpence, 1729.' (added later to card, bottom middle), '2 leaves' (added later to card in same hand, bottom right); 1ʳ–2ᵛ, text in right-hand column, additions on left: 1ᵛ

Alterations to the Manuscript
130.3 of] *interlineated after del.* and
130.4 circulating] ing *added to* circulate *with last letter del.*
130.4 shall] *before del.* be
130.4 pass] *before del.* of
130.9 Character.] *before del.* I happened indeed to hear last Summer while I was in the Country that he was under some trouble in England upon which I examined him, [*del.* and *ins. above* when] he charged it all upon the malice of an [*ins. with caret* Irish] Attorney, [*in left-hand margin intended to be ins. in main text with caret, but del.*] However, his shop is well-furnished, and he see [*illegible*] of with goods, and if his report of the Circumstances be true, it was as thorow a masterpiece of villany as I have heard of.
130.9 He] *interlineated above del.* Mr M'culla
130.10 style,] *before del.* of other Projectors
130.10 Profession] *interlineated above del.* appearance
130.11 which is the common cant of all Projectors in their Bills, from a First Minister of State down to a Corn-cutter. But,] *ins. with caret from left-hand margin*
130.14 age] *interlineated above del.* era
130.15 proposeth] *interlineated with caret before del.* backs
130.21 payable] *after del.* note pay
130.23 whether] *after del.* onely
131.3 value] *after del.* one

131.4   one] *interlineated after del.* the
131.7   pence] *before del.* a Pound
131.7   every pound of] *interlineated with caret after* for
131.7   Copper] *after del.* piece of
131.8   notes] *interlineated with caret after* Copper
131.8   the pieces] *last letter of* them *del. in* the
131.8   halfpenny] *interlineated with caret before* pieces
131.9   pound] *before del.* those
131.12 sum] *before del.* and
131.12 circulate] *before del.* fifty or sixty thousand
131.12 circulate as] *SwJ 433 ends after* 'as'
132.3   good] *before del.* wherein
132.8   another] *interlineated with caret above del.* and know
134.14 Yet] *interlineated above del.* But
134.20 which] *interlineated above del.* and
136.15 please] *after del.* place
136.17 in] *interlineated with caret before* England

Faulkner, *Works*, 1762

TS 45A (6a). *ESTC* N31128
Title: VOLUME X. | OF THE | Author's WORKS | CONTAINING, | Sermons on several Subjects; | AND | Other PIECES on different | Occasions. | [rule] | [ornament] | [double rule] | *DUBLIN*: | Printed by GEORGE FAULKNER. | M,dcc,lxii.
Collation: 8°: A³ B–2E⁸ 2F¹
Pagination: i–iii iv–v vi, 3 4–436
Contents: A1ʳ title page; A1ᵛ blank; A2ʳ–A3ʳ Contents; A3ᵛ blank; B1ʳ–2F1ᵛ text
Letter on M'culla's Project: Y3ᵛ–Z5ᵛ; 328–48
Typography: 31 lines per page (Y4ʳ); type-page 142 (154) × 85 mm; 20 lines of roman type 91 mm
Failure of catchwords to catch:
Z2ᵛ Credit,] Credit
Copies consulted: Bodl., Vet. A5 e. 4856; Bodl., Vet. A4 e.3055/10.

Deane Swift, *Works*, 1765

TS 87. *ESTC* T52748
Title: THE | WORKS | OF | Dr. JONATHAN SWIFT, | Dean of St. Patrick's, Dublin. | VOLUME VIII. Part I.

[see entry under *Upon Giving Badges to the Poor* for full description]
Contents: Letter on M'culla's Project: U2ᵛ–X4ᵛ; 148–60
Copies consulted: BL, 90.d.8 (with vol. VIII, pt ii).

Emendations
[None]

Historical Collation
130.1 On M'culla's Project] A Letter concerning Mr. MACULLA's Project about Copper Notes to pass for Pence and Half-pence; with a Proposal for another Scheme for providing Copper Change in this Kingdom. To the Rev. Dr. DELANY. *1762*; A LETTER ON Mr. M'culla's Project about HALFPENCE, and a new one proposed. Written in MDCCXXIX. *1765*.
130.1 M'culla's] Maculla's *1762*
130.4 circulatⁱⁿᵍ notes] circulating-notes *1762*
130.13 pretence] practice *1765* [*a misreading of SwJ 433*]
130.15 well.] [*new paragraph*] *1762*
130.16 the Contriver] himself *1765*
130.17 Contriver.] [*new paragraph*] *1762*
130.18 poor] *om. 1762*
130.19 that] the *1762*
130.20 England.] [*new paragraph*] *1762*
130.21 hinders] hindereth *1762*
130.23 Paper.] [*new paragraph*] *1762*
131.1 when] where *1765*
131.2 witnesses] Witness *1762*
131.2 it.] [*new paragraph*] *1762*
131.4 into.] [*new paragraph*] *1762*
131.6 gives] giveth *1762*
131.7 the 5d] *om. 1765*
131.9 sells] selleth *1762*
131.10 gains a little more than 16 p. cent, that is to say, two pence in every Shilling.] gaineth 20*l. per Cent.* that is to say, four Pence for laying out twenty Pence; allowing his Copper at fourteen Pence, and the Coinage at six Pence *per* Pound. *1762*
131.16 sure] secure *1762*
131.19 Colonel Moor] Col. *Moore 1762*
131.19 to do.] [*new paragraph*] *1762*
131.22 metal equalling] metal fully equalling *1762*

131.26 support.] [*new paragraph*] *1762*
131.29 formed] framed *1762*
132.1   proposal] Proposals *1762*
132.2   will] would *1762*
132.2   himself.] [*new paragraph*] *1762*
132.3   provided] provideth *1762*
132.4   farthings?] [*new paragraph*] *1762*
132.5   good?] [*new paragraph*] *1762*
132.6   be] lie *1762*
132.11 pay the] pay all the *1762*
132.12 question.] [*new paragraph*] *1762*
132.13 this] *om. 1762*
132.14 sells] selleth *1762*
132.16 30 *per cent*] 30*l.* per Cent *1762* [*new paragraph*]
132.17 vends] vendeth *1762*
132.19 16] 20 *1762*
132.19 avows] owneth *1762*
132.20 of about 46 *per cent.*] of 50 per Cent. *1762* [*new paragraph*]
132.21 buys] buyeth *1762*
132.21 *per* pound] *om. 1762*
132.23 41*l.* 13*s.* 4*d. per cent*] ten Pence in every two Shillings *1762* [*new paragraph*]
132.24 proposal] proposals *1762*
132.25 coinage.] But Maculla hath still 30*l.* per Cent. by the same, if they be returned. *1762*
132.32 conjecture.] [*new paragraph*] *1762*
132.33 fineness] in fineness *1762*
133.1   makes] maketh *1762*
133.2   of] of his *1762*
133.4   proposes] proposeth *1762*
133.5   gives] giveth *1762*
133.5   receives] receiveth *1762*
133.6   makes] maketh *1762*
133.7   30] 30*l. 1762*
133.8   16 *per cent.*] 20*l. per cent. 1762*
133.8   sells] selleth *1762*
133.9   10] 10*l. 1762*
133.10 will, to] will, as to *1762*
133.10 47 *per cent.*] 55*l. per cent. 1762*
133.12 60*l.*] 50*l. 1762*

133.12 will (to avoid fractions) be about five and a half *per cent.*] will be 5 *per cent. 1762*
133.13 41 13 4] 50 *1762*
133.16 5 10 0] 5 *1762*
133.17 47 3 4] 55 *1762*
133.24 M'culla] *Maculla's 1762*
133.26 Mr.] *om. 1762*
133.26 a fourth part, or 25 *per cent.*] above a fifth Part, or 20*l. per cent. 1762*
133.29 milled] was milled *1762*
134.2 Mr.] *om. 1762*
134.3 his.] [*new paragraph*] *1762*
134.3 does] doth *1762*
134.6 an] *om. 1762*
134.8 foot.] [*new paragraph*] *1762*
134.9 fairest] finest *1762*
134.10 loser.] For, the Benefit of defrauding the Crown never accrueth to the Publick, but is wholely turned to the Advantage of those whom the Crown employeth: *1762*
134.11 the] these *1762*
134.14 did much] *om. 1762*
134.18 good] * good [*with footnote:*] *This Letter was written in the Year* 1729, *when copper was* 14*d. a Pound, but in this Year* 1762, *it is* 16*d. Halfpenny. 1762*
134.19 present.] [*new paragraph*] *1762*
134.20 by] from *1762*
134.24 and] *om. 1762*
134.25 16] 20 *1762*
134.31 three thousand two hundred] four thousand *1762*
135.3 letter] Letters *1762*
135.16 give.] [*new paragraph*] *1762*
135.18 cent.] [*new paragraph*] *1762*
135.21 the] that *1762*
135.29 Moor's] Mr. Moor's *1762*
136.6 These] They *1762*
136.18 eighty] eight *1762*
136.20 although] altho' *1762*
136.23 arrived] happen'd *1762*
137.5 a] the *1762*

137.8   incidents.] [*new paragraph*] *1762*
137.8   of] *om. 1762*
137.10 as well and deeply] well and as deeply *1762*
137.12 II.] [*new paragraph*] *1762*
137.18 public.] [*new paragraph*] *1762*
137.19 8] 3 *1762*
137.20 two] five *1762*
137.21 farther] further *1762*
137.22 unsolicited] and unsolicited *1762*
137.24 farther.] [*new paragraph*] *1762*
137.31 of somewhat more than 16 *per cent.*] of 20 per Cent. *1762*
137.32 desires] desireth *1762*
138.5   one fourth part] above one-fifth *1762*
138.7   the] their *1762*
138.11 so] to *1762*
138.12 be.] [*new paragraph*] *1762*
138.16 most.] [*new paragraph*] *1762*
138.22 16] 20 *1762*
138.28 computation] computations *1762*
138.31 perhaps may] may perhaps *1762*
139.6   level.] [*new paragraph*] *1762*
139.7   sight.] [*new paragraph*] *1762*
139.14 point.] [*new paragraph*] *1762*
139.15 and] *om. 1762*
139.19 written] writ *1762*
139.22 in.] [*new paragraph*] *1762*
139.23 all] all but *1762*
140.4   shall] shall still *1762*
140.19 reader.] reader, it being a matter wholly out of my trade. *1762*
140.20 charges] chargeth *1762*
140.20 pound, - - -] pound, equal to *1762*
140.21 weight] weight is *1762*
140.27 sells] selleth *1762*
140.30 672] ——— *1762*
141.5   is] *om. 1762*
141.6   Which is equal] The difference is equal *1762*
141.13 allows] alloweth *1762*
141.15 computes] computeth *1762*
141.22 *(viz.* coinage] *(viz.)* coinage *1762*

141.24 refuses] refuseth *1762*
141.27 possibly] probably *1762*
141.32 3] *om. 1762*

Word Division
Copy Text
None

Edited Text
None

A Modest Proposal

Textual Account

What would become Swift's most widely read and notorious pamphlet satire was published by Sarah Harding before the end of October 1729; it was advertised in the *Dublin Intelligence* of 8 November (see Ehrenpreis, vol. III, p. 629). There seems to have been relatively fierce competition over publishing a London version, suggesting that the pamphlet had quickly gained recognition: the first London edition, sold by Roberts, was advertised in the *Daily Journal* for Saturday 22 and Monday 24 November; also on Monday 24, Weaver Bickerton's London edition was advertised in the *Daily Post*: 'From the original correct edition Printed at Dublin, and Published by Dr. Swift'. Moreover, by Friday 28, Bickerton again used the *Daily Post* to promote another Irish pamphlet, *The Present State of Ireland Considered* (which would soon be collected with Swift's pamphlet) with the reminder 'from whom may be had *A Modest Proposal*, the second edition, Printed from the correct copy printed at Dublin'. The 'second edition' suggests considerable English interest, if literally true (and not, that is, meaning second because a London reprint). Bickerton's version would run to three apparently new editions by the end of 1730, all impressions of the same setting of type (thus only the first is textually significant); it is commonly thought to have been printed that year, rather than 1729, but the frequency of advertisements suggests a late 1729 printing, in order to challenge the Roberts edition.

The interest in the work in England was confirmed by its appearance in a collection of writings published in London: *A Libel on Dr Delany* reprinted a Dublin printing of Swift's poem, supplemented by two other poems and Swift's pamphlet, and appeared in two competing editions in 1730. In the same year, *A Modest Proposal* also appeared in another supposed London reprint of a Dublin book, *A View of the Present State of Affairs*, alongside two rather more earnest pamphlets on Irish absenteeism (including *The Present State of Ireland Considered*). The next edition, the 'Third Volume' of the Pope–Swift *Miscellanies* of 1732, was also probably the copy text for Faulkner's printing in Volume IV of the 1735 *Works*; the copy of the *Miscellanies* text in the Rothschild Collection has two pencil marks and corrections in Swift's hand (included in the Historical Collation). Matthew Pilkington promised William Bowyer on 17 August 1732 that 'I shall get you the right of printing *The Proposal for Eating Children*', in the attempted assigning of Swift's copyright that was pre-empted by Alexander Pope (see Woolley, *Corr.*, vol. III, pp. 509, 527, 531–2). Faulkner's 1735 text is the last considered to have any possible authorial intervention.

Swift's relationship with Sarah Harding, a continuation of his work with her late husband, is discussed in the Textual Introduction (see above, pp. 377–9). *A Modest Proposal* was the last work she printed for him; it is likely that she remarried and retired from printing soon afterwards (see Woolley, *Intelligencer*, p. 38). Woolley suggests that using her was of some possible value: 'the imprint of a London edition of *A Modest Proposal* mentioned her, suggesting that her name carried significance', as it was 'highly unusual for London reprinters to mention the name of the original printer' (p. 38).

Her printing of *A Modest Proposal* is an improvement over the earlier *Intelligencer* papers, the *Short View* and *An Answer to a Paper, Called A Memorial*, and has few of their shortcomings, being clearly inked, with consistent use of somewhat worn type, italics (which are frequent, for rhetorical emphasis, and contribute to the tone of the piece) and capitals, and is regular in its spellings. The Roberts London reprint of 1729 was described by Davis thus: 'the number of printer's errors suggest this was set up very hurriedly' (vol. XII, p. 335). These 'errors' are few, however; more importantly, this is not, as Davis implies, a simple London reprint of Harding's pamphlet, and it opens up a record of the transmission of the text that is more complex than previously realised.

The Roberts edition possesses some variants from the Harding edition that would be followed in the texts of *A Libel* and the 1732 *Miscellanies*, but, equally, there are also places where it does not anticipate these texts (such as lacking the addition of '*in* Ireland' to the title). It also contains variants that are in many respects a tidying of the text, and cannot necessarily be seen as authorial. The title page is the first to identify Swift as the author.

The Roberts text copies the essential presentational features of Harding's text, with notably less punctuation, as do the three Bickerton reprints of the following year (with small modifications for house style, such as the use of full capitals at the opening of paragraphs); Bickerton does not follow the Roberts text, in terms of variants, but adds a couple of changes. *A View of the Present State of Affairs* reprints different editions of Bickerton from 1730. Conflicting extant copies reprint the title pages and text from the first and second editions of Bickerton's printings, and Teerink saw a printing that used Bickerton's third edition (see TS, pp. 337–8), but the text used is anyway identical with that of his first edition, and has no authority. *A Libel on Dr Delany*, printed by 'Capt Gulliver;' was first advertised in the *Morning Chronicle*, 12 February; a week later in the *Grub Street Journal*, Thursday 19 February, it denounced its rival edition, printed by the pseudonymous 'A Moor', as spurious: the 'Gulliver' edition is 'Printed together in 8vo exactly from the Dublin copies'. 'Capt. Gulliver' is presumably Lawton Gilliver, one of the proprietors of the *Grub Street Journal*, who used that alias in its imprint; Sam Aris, who printed the *Journal*, was the likely printer of *A Libel*. We are indebted to James McLaverty for this information, and for the suggestion that, as Gilliver was working closely with Alexander Pope at this time, the latter poet might have some role to play in the textual revisions of this version (see also McLaverty, 'Lawton Gilliver: Pope's Bookseller', *Studies in Bibliography* 32 (1979), 101–24).

The text of *A Modest Proposal* included in *A Libel* is from the same setting of type as the 1729 Roberts edition, and anticipates the substantive (though not accidental) variants of the 1732 *Miscellanies*. It would seem possible (given that the poem *A Libel on Dr Delany* had been published separately in Dublin beforehand by Faulkner) that this volume was published in London with Swift's cognisance: as well as anticipating the variants of 1732, it is the first text before that edition to add '*in* Ireland' to the title, signifying its English printing, and tailoring its meaning slightly for its different audience.

The text of *A Libel* is thus a re-impression of Roberts with some small but important additions (as well as a few slips). It also identified Swift as the pamphlet's author, albeit through blanks. The editions for the *Miscellanies* (1732) and *Works* (1735) are, as larger-scale works, equivalent in standards of printing and presentation: both replicate the heavy italic phrasing and the capitals of the text; Faulkner in 1735 begins paragraphs with small capitals, but the differences between his text and Harding's are more variants of content than features of print, pointing or emphasis.

There are therefore two lines of transmission of *A Modest Proposal*: (a) the Harding Dublin version, largely reprinted in London by Bickerton; (b) the Roberts London edition, reprinted in *A Libel*, the *Miscellanies* and Faulkner's 1735 *Works*. Any debate over which version of *A Modest Proposal* is most suitable for a copy text is concerned chiefly with the efficacy of Harding's 1729 text, contrasted with Faulkner's 1735 revisions (which integrate the changes made in 1729 in the first London edition, in *A Libel*, and in the 1732 *Miscellanies*). It is the origin of these that is the problem: the text of the 1735 *Works*, Herbert Davis assumed in 1955, 'contains alterations clearly due to Swift himself' (XII, p. 335), and Davis accordingly bases his text on Faulkner. More recently, there has been greater questioning of the degree and nature of Swift's revisions to Faulkner's volumes.

If the tendency to view Faulkner's 1735 texts automatically as Swift's last revision has passed, the choice for the present volume is in many ways simple for another reason: the 1729 Harding printing is taken as copy text, partly because it has the most undoubted authority of any edition, and chiefly in support of the editorial aim of this edition, whereby the first published version of a work is used when the text in question is polemical or an intervention in contemporary debate. The success of *A Modest Proposal* has ensured that it swiftly developed an audience far beyond its immediate context, but it originated as part of Swift's writing about Ireland in the 1720s, and shares the concerns of all this writing, which is what the copy text reflects: the version in *A Libel on Dr Delany*, and all texts after 1732, may change the title, adding a qualifier for the reader to make clear that the reference is to 'Poor People in Ireland', yet the 1729 Harding edition, like its author, had no such geographical distance from its subject.

Although all the editions described above have been collated, some are direct reprints, and make no appearance in the Historical Collation. Those texts that do are referred to thus: Harding's 1729 Dublin text (*1729a*); Roberts's London text (*1729b*); Bickerton's London reprint (*1730a*); *A Libel on Dr Delany* (*1730b*); the Third Volume of *Miscellanies* (*1732*, and *1732a* for Swift's annotations to this volume); and Volume IV of Faulkner 1735 *Works* (*1735*). The present edition is the first collation to include the variants from *1729b* and *A Libel*, and to show the ways in which they complicate the previously assumed pattern of revision in *A Modest Proposal*.

Copy Text

TCC, Rothschild 2116.

Dublin, 1729a

TS 676. *ESTC* N5335

Title: A MODEST| PROPOSAL | For preventing the | CHILDREN | OF | POOR PEOPLE | From being a | Burthen to their Parents, | OR THE | COUNTRY, | And | For making them Beneficial to the | PUBLICK. | [double-rule] | *DUBLIN*: | Printed by *S. Harding*, opposite the *Hand and* | *Pen* near *Fishamble-Street*, on the *Blind Key*. | MDCCXXIX.
Collation: 8°: A^8
Pagination: 1–2, 3–16
Contents: A1^r title; A1^v blank; A2^r–A8^v text
Typography: 32 lines per page (A2^v); type-page 129 (138) × 80 mm; 20 lines of roman type 81 mm
Copies consulted: TCC, Rothschild 2116; V & A, Forster 8562.

London, 1729b

TS 677. *ESTC* T70428

Title: A MODEST| PROPOSAL | For preventing the | CHILDREN | OF | POOR PEOPLE | From being a Burthen to | Their Parents or Country, | AND | For making them Beneficial to the | PUBLICK. | [rule] | By Dr. SWIFT. | [rule] | *Dublin*, Printed by *S. Harding*: | *London*, Re-printed; and sold by *J. Roberts* | in *Warwick-lane*, and the Pamphlet-Shops. | M. DCC. XXIX.
Collation: 8°: *A*^{4} B^4 C^2
Pagination: 1–5, 6–19 *20*
Contents: A1^r half title; A1^v blank; A2^r title; A2^v blank; A3^r–C2^r text; C2^v advert for 'The Tribunes'
Typography: 31 lines per page (B2^v); type-page 120 (130) × 80 mm; 20 lines of roman type 83 mm
Copies consulted: CUL, Williams 409.

London, 1730a

TS 678. *ESTC* T41350

Title: A MODEST| PROPOSAL | For preventing the | CHILDREN | OF | POOR PEOPLE | From being a Burthen to their PA- | RENTS or the COUNTRY,| And for making them Beneficial to the | PUBLICK | [rule] | [ornament] | *DUBLIN:* | Printed: And Reprinted at *LONDON*, for | WEAVER BICKERTON, in *Devereux-Court* | near the *Middle-Temple*. M.DCC.XXX.
Collation: 8°: *A*^{4} B–C^4

Pagination: 1–4 5–23 24
Contents: A1ʳ half-title; A1ᵛ advert for Bickerton; A2ʳ title page; A2ᵛ blank; A3ʳ–c4ʳ text
Typography: 29 lines per page (B3ʳ); type-page 140 (150) × 80 mm; 20 lines of roman type 93 mm
Copies consulted: BL, 1080.i.15 (14).

A Libel on Dr Delany, 1730b
TS 36. *ESTC* N5048
Title: A | LIBEL | ON | Dr. D———NY, | And a certain Great LORD. | By Dr Sw—t, | *Occasion'd by a certain* EPISTLE. | [rule] | To which is Added | I. An Epistle to his Excellency *John* Lord| *Carteret*, by Dr. D—*ny*. | II. An Epistle on an Epistle; or, a *Christmas* | *Box* for Dr. D———*ny* | III. Dr. Sw—*t's* Proposal for preventing the | Children of Poor People being a Burthen | to their Parents or Country, and for ma- | king them beneficial to the Public. | [rule] | *DUBLIN*: Printed, | *LONDON*: Reprinted for *Capt. Gulliver* | near the *Temple*, MDCCXXX. | (Price Sixpence.)
Collation: 8°: *A*⁴ B–D⁴ [D signed B]
Pagination: 1–3 4–32
Contents: *A*1ʳ title; *A*1ᵛ blank; A2ʳ–D4ᵛ text
A *Modest Proposal*: C2ʳ–D4ᵛ [sig. D signed B]; 25–32
Typography: 34 lines per page (C3ʳ); type-page 145 (188) × 78 mm; 20 lines of roman type 80 mm
Failure of catchwords to catch:
C4ʳ Infant,] Infant's
Copies consulted: BL, RB.23a.28477; Bodl., Vet.A4e.1335.

A View of the Present State of Affairs, 1730
Referenced as reprint of TS 678; see TS, pp. 337–8. T86135
Title: A | VIEW | OF THE | Present State of Affairs | In the KINGDOM of | *IRELAND*; | In Three DISCOURSES. | VIZ. | I. A LIST of the ABSENTEES of *Ireland*, and the | *Yearly Value* of their ESTATES and INCOMES spent | abroad. With Observations on the present TRADE and | CONDITION of that Kingdom. | II. The PRESENT STATE of *Ireland* Consider'd: | Wherein the LIST of the ABSENTEES of *Ireland* is | occasionally Answer'd. | III. A MODEST PROPOSAL for Preventing the | Children of *Poor People* from being a *Burthen* to their | PARENTS or the COUNTRY, and for making them | Beneficial to the Publick. By Dr. Sw-*ft*. | [double-rule] | Printed at *DUBLIN*: | Reprinted at *LONDON*,

for WEAVER BICKERTON, | in *Devereux-Court*, near the *Middle-Temple*. | M.DCC.XXX. | [rule] | (Price Two Shillings.)
Collation: 8°: works are separately paginated; for *Modest Proposal*, as 1730a.
Pagination: 1–4 5–23
Contents: A1^r half-title; A1^v '*BOOKS printed for and sold by* WEAVER BICKERTON in Devereux-Court.'; A2^r title page; A2^v blank; A3^r–c4^r text
Typography: 29 lines per page (B3^r); type-page 150 (192) × 78 mm; 20 lines of roman type 93 mm
Copies consulted: BL, 8145.b.53 [Evidence of rebinding in stub between B4^v and C1^r (pp. 16–17)]; Cam. Queens, p. 71 [1–3]; University of London Libraries, Senate House, [G.L] 1730 [reprinted in *Eighteenth Century Collections Online*].

Miscellanies, Third Volume, 1732

TS 25 (4a). *ESTC* N62568
Title: MISCELLANIES | [rule] | THE | THIRD VOLUME.
[see entry under *Intelligencer*, Number. 5 for full description]
Contents: *A Modest Proposal*: K5^v–L6^v;154–72

Miscellanies, 1732a

TS 25 (4a). *ESTC* N62568
[a copy of 1732, with Swift's autograph corrections]
Copies consulted: TCC, Rothschild 1422.

Works, 1735

TS 41. *ESTC* T52771
Title: VOLUME IV. | Of the AUTHOR's | WORKS.
[see entry under *Short View of the State of Ireland* for full description]
Contents: *A Modest Proposal*: T1^r–7^r; 273–85

Emendations

148.7 about] *1729b*; abont
149.3 *Agriculture*;] *1729b*; ~$_\wedge$
152.20 Breeders] *1729b*; Breedders
155.2 ster.] sterl. *1730a*; Ster. *1729a, 1729b, 1730b*; Sterling *1732+*
155.20 Miscarriage.] ~$_\wedge$ *1729a*
156.6 thereby be] *1729b*; be thereby be
158.5 too] *1729b*; two
159.9 Work] *1729b*; Works

Historical Collation
146.1 A MODEST PROPOSAL...] A MODEST PROPOSAL For *preventing the Children of poor People in* Ireland, *from being a Burden to their Parents or Country, and for making them Beneficial to the Publick.* By Dr. Sw——t. *1730b*; A MODEST PROPOSAL For *Preventing the Children of poor People in* Ireland, *from being a Burden to their Parents or Country, and for making them Beneficial to the Publick. 1732, 1735*
146.3 Cabbin-Doors] Cabbins-Doors *1735*
147.7 of other] for no *1732a*
147.9 It is] 'Tis *1730a*
148.6 this Kingdom] Ireland *1735*
148.7 about] abont *1729a*
148.9 Couples,] Couple *1732a*
148.11 an] One *1730a*
148.12 Breeders.] [*new paragraph*] *1730*
149.3 *Agriculture*;] *1729b+*; ~∧ *1729a*
149.5 till] until *1735*
149.16 the] om. *1729b, 1730b, 1732+*
150.6 than] *1729b*; that *1729a*
150.11 of] in *1729b, 1730b, 1732+*
151.5 Pound] Pounds *1730a+*
151.10 Author] * Author [*with footnote:*] * Rabelais *1735*
151.23 'Squire] Esquire *1730a*
151.25 net] *1735*; neat *1729a+*
151.25 till] until *1735*
151.25 produces] produceth *1735*
152.11 County] Country *1729b, 1730b, 1732*
152.13 a live] alive *1730a+*
152.20 Breeders] *1729b*; Breedders *1729a*
152.24 however so well] however well *1730a*; how well so ever *1729b, 1730b, 1732+*
152.26 Sallmanaazor] Psalmanaazar *1730a*
153.10 the] a *1729b, 1730b, 1732+*
153.22 happily] in a fair way of being *1735*
154.7 an *Episcopal*] an idolatrous *Episcopal 1735*
155.2 ster.] sterl. *1730a*; Ster. *1729a, 1729b, 1730b*; Sterling *1732+*
155.16 *Market*] Market; *1730a*; Market. *1729b, 1730b, 1732+*
155.19 as it is] as is *1729b, 1730b, 1732*
155.25 Tables, which] Tables, and *1735*
155.26 Yearling] Yearly *1729b, 1730b, 1732+*

155.31 particularly] particularly at *1729b, 1730b, 1732*+
156.6 thereby be] *1730a*; be thereby be *1729a*; be thereby *1729b, 1730b, 1732*+
156.6 and was] and 'twas *1730b, 1732*; and it was *1735*
156.7 World.] [*new paragraph*] *1730a*
157.8 earnestly] in earnest *1730a*
157.11 some Glimpse] a Glimpse *1735*
158.5 too] *1729b*+; two *1729a*
158.10 Effectual.] [*new paragraph*] *1730a*
158.12 points.] [*new paragraph*] *1730a*
158.14 an] One *1730*; a *1729b, 1730b, 1732*+
158.14 Backs.] [*new paragraph*] *1730a*
158.15 human] humane *1729b*
158.17 *Sterl.*] Ster. *1729b, 1730b*; Sterling *1732*+
158.19 Effect;] Effect. [*new paragraph*] *1730a*
159.2 through] thro' *1730a*
159.5 from Inclemences] from these Inclemencies *1729b*; from the Inclemencies *1730b, 1732*+
159.9 Work] *1729b*; Works *1729a*
159.13 FINIS.] *om. 1732*+

Word Division
Copy Text
School-boys
Merry-meetings
TO-PINAMBOO
Shop-keepers
Child-bearing

Edited Text
None

A Proposal that All the Ladies and Women of Ireland Should Appear Constantly in Irish Manufactures

Textual Account

Unpublished in Swift's lifetime, the *Proposal that Ladies Should Appear* belongs to the end of 1729, after the four earlier unpublished writings of the year and *A Modest Proposal*. It can be dated generally through the affixing of

1729 to the title page of its first publications in 1765, and more specifically through its context: Swift was responding to a plan put forward by the Irish Parliament to increase duty on imported wine, and, as Ferguson puts it, 'Because the tax was voted before Swift could get his tract into print, he did not publish it' (Ferguson, p. 156). Ehrenpreis presumes it to be written after Swift's return to Dublin in 1729, and before the Bill received royal assent (i.e. 22 December), and also suggests that it 'may be unfinished', perhaps because its argument, criticising the very action recommended by Swift so many times in his Irish writings, of putting extra duty on an import, was both self-seeking and redundant (vol. III, pp. 644, 646).

The *Proposal* was first published by Deane Swift in the 1765 quarto edition, and reprinted by Faulkner in Dublin the same year; apart from three misspellings (acknowledged in the errata for Deane Swift's volume) and one different paragraph break, there are no variants, and very little difference (beyond format) in print, layout, capitalisation, italics or other features, between the two texts. Deane Swift's volume (*1765a*) serves as copy text, as first printing, and has been collated with Faulkner (*1765b*).

Copy Text
BL, 90.d.8.

Deane Swift, *Works*, 1765a
TS 87. *ESTC* T52748
Title: THE | WORKS | OF | Dr. JONATHAN SWIFT, | DEAN OF ST. PATRICK'S, DUBLIN. | VOLUME VIII. PART I.
[see entry under *Upon Giving Badges to the Poor* for full description]
Contents: Proposal that all Ladies should Appear: Z1ᵛ–4ᵛ; 170–6

Faulkner, *Works*, 1765b
TS 47. *ESTC* N31130
Title: VOLUME XII. | OF THE | AUTHOR'S WORKS.
[see entry under *Upon Giving Badges to the Poor* for full description]
Contents: Proposal that all Ladies should Appear: R6ʳ–S3ʳ; 251–61

Emendations
[None]

Historical Collation
162.15 Whitchet] Whitshed *1765b*
163.9 Whitchet] Whitshed *1765b*

163.12 Whitchet] Whitshed *1765b*
165.10 duties] duites *1765b*
166.14 till] until *1765b*
169.15 till] until *1765b*
169.17 rags.] [*new paragraph*] *1765b*

Word Division
Copy Text
custom-house

Edited Text
None

Maxims Controlled in Ireland

Textual Account

This unfinished essay is usually assigned a date of 1729; for possible evidence of a composition date, see Ferguson, p. 148, and Ehrenpreis, vol. III, p. 575 (who finds anticipations of the ironies of *A Modest Proposal*, thus pre-dating *Maxims* to before November 1729). There are some hints of the argument sketched out in manuscript Eng. 659 (11) in the John Rylands Library, Manchester (see Associated Materials, pp. 324–7). Like so much of Swift's posthumous prose, it was first published in Deane Swift's quarto edition of 1765 (hereafter *1765a*) and reprinted by Faulkner in Dublin the same year (*1765b*); the copy text is Deane Swift, though the differences in type, punctuation and presentation are slight, as can be seen in the handful of variants in the Historical Collation, and the absence of emendations.

Copy Text
BL, 90.d.8.

Deane Swift, *Works*, 1765a
TS 87. *ESTC* T52748
Title: THE | WORKS | OF | Dr. JONATHAN SWIFT, | Dean of St. Patrick's, Dublin. | VOLUME VIII. Part I.
[see entry under *Upon Giving Badges to the Poor* for full description]
Contents: *Maxims Controlled in Ireland*: S4^v–T3^v; 136–42

Faulkner, *Works*, 1765b
TS 47. *ESTC* N31130
Title: VOLUME XII. | OF THE | Author's WORKS.
[see entry under *Upon Giving Badges to the Poor* for full description]
Contents: *Maxims Controlled in Ireland*: P5ʳ–Q1ᵛ; 217–26

Emendations
[None]

Historical Collation
177.3 gentlemens] gentlemen's *1765b*
179.4 a nation] the nation *1765b*
179.8 unsupportable] insupportable *1765b*
180.4 pernicious a] a pernicious *1765b*

Word Division
Copy Text
over-stocked

Edited Text
None

Advertisement Against Lord Allen

Textual Account

For the context of this short outburst against Joshua, Viscount Allen, who had criticised the planned award of a gold box and the freedom of the city of Dublin to Swift, while at a meeting of the privy council of Ireland (13 February 1730), see Ehrenpreis, vol. III, pp. 650–3. Swift's response was 'to put into circulation' this advertisement, dated 18 April 1730 (p. 652). The nature of that circulation is vexed: as both Ehrenpreis and Davis (vol. XII, p. 337) suggest, no evidence of its being published at the time has ever emerged, and the present editors have been as unable as predecessors to locate any newspaper copy of it. It is probable that Swift wrote it, then thought better of publishing it.

It was first collected in John Nichols's 1801 edition, which presented Swift's prose in modern printing style, devoid of capitalised nouns, light on italics and semi-colons, with Swift's idiosyncrasies presumably regularised (assuming that Nichols was working from a manuscript, or a non-extant printed copy). This is the sole, and thus obvious, copy text.

BL, G.18036.   Copy Text

                              Nichols, 1801
TS 129
Title: THE | WORKS | OF THE | REV. JONATHAN SWIFT, D.
D., | DEAN OF ST. PATRICK'S, DUBLIN. | *ARRANGED BY
THOMAS SHERIDAN, A.M.* | WITH | NOTES, HISTORICAL
AND CRITICAL. | [double-rule] | A NEW EDITION, IN NINE-
TEEN VOLUMES; | CORRECTED AND REVISED | *BY JOHN
NICHOLS, F.S.A. EDINBURGH AND PERTH.* | [double-rule] | VOL-
UME XIII. | [double-rule] | *LONDON:* | PRINTED FOR J. JOHN-
SON, J. NICHOLS, R. BALDWIN, | OTRIDGE AND SON, J.
SEWELL, F. AND C. RIVINGTON, T. | PAYNE, R. FAULDER,
G. AND J. ROBINSON, R. LEA, J. | NUNN, W. CUTHELL, T.
EGERTON, CLARKE AND SON, | VERNOR AND HOOD, J.
SCATCHERD, T. KAY, LACKING- | TON ALLEN AND CO.,
CARPENTER AND CO., MURRAY | AND HIGHLEY, LONG-
MAN AND REES, CADELL JUN. AND | DAVIES, T. BAGSTER,
J. HARDING, AND J. MAWMAN. | [rule] | 1801.
Collation: 8°: a⁴ B–2G⁸ 2H⁴
Pagination: *i–iii* iv–viii, 1–472
Contents: A1ʳ title; A1ᵛ blank; A2ʳ–A4ᵛ contents; B1ʳ–2H4ᵛ text
Advertisement: 2H4ʳ⁻ᵛ; 471–2
Typography: 33 lines per page (FF1ʳ); type-page 154 (166) × 88 mm; 20
lines of roman type 98 mm
Copies consulted: BL, G.18036; BL, 633 k. 15.

                              Emendations
[None]

Word Division
Copy Text
None

Edited Text
None

The Substance of What Was Said By The Dean

Textual Account

The record of what Swift claims to have said upon being given the freedom of Dublin and a gold box on 27 May 1730 must have been written soon after; Ehrenpreis (vol. III, p. 655) thinks it was probably shown to friends and well-wishers; as a somewhat self-aggrandising record of what Swift felt to be his due, a lack of wider appeal probably explains it not being published in his lifetime.

Posthumously published by Deane Swift (*1765a*) and reprinted in the same year by Faulkner (*1765b*), the texts are almost entirely uniform, and share all the other qualities of these editions; the only variants are additional identifying footnotes by Faulkner, who also (as Davis noted, vol. XII, p. 337) corrected Deane Swift's error, and identified the 'printer' referred to as Waters, and not Harding. The copy text is taken from Deane Swift's edition.

Copy Text
BL, 90.d.8.

Deane Swift, *Works*, 1765a
TS 87. *ESTC* T52748
Title: THE | WORKS | OF | Dr. JONATHAN SWIFT, | DEAN OF ST. PATRICK'S, DUBLIN. | VOLUME VIII. PART I.
[see entry under *Upon Giving Badges to the Poor* for full description]
Contents: Substance of what was Said: S4^v–T3^v; 136–42

Faulkner, *Works*, 1765b
TS 47. *ESTC* N31130
Title: VOLUME XII. | OF THE | AUTHOR'S WORKS.
[see entry under *Upon Giving Badges to the Poor* for full description]
Contents: Substance of what was Said: U5^r–7^v; 297–302

Emendations
189.19 Mr. Edward Waters] *1765b*; Harding

Historical Collation
186.14 person] person* [*with footnote:*] *Joshua, Lord Viscount Allen. *1765b*

189.18 a] a* [*with footnote:*] *John, Lord Carteret, afterwards Lord Lieutenant of Ireland. 1765*b*
189.19 Mr. Edward Waters] Harding *1765a*

Word Division
Copy text
None

Edited text
None

A Vindication of His Excellency the Lord Carteret

Textual Account

This pamphlet is internally dated by Swift's reference to the time of writing as 13 April 1730, and was published to coincide with the proroguing of Parliament on 15 April (see Woolley, *Corr.*, vol. III, p. 310 fn. 9, and Ehrenpreis, vol. III, p. 658). In a letter to Pope of 2 May, Swift remarked how his recent enemy Joshua, Lord Allen 'without the least provocation rayl'd at me in the Privy Council and the H. of Lords as a Jacobite, and Libeller of the Government &c. he hath been worryed by some well-wisher of mine in a Paper called a Vindication of Lord Carteret &c. and all this is lay'd on me' (Woolley, *Corr.*, vol. III, pp. 308–9).

A Vindication is an example of the system that George Faulkner and William Bowyer developed for reprinting Swift's Dublin texts in London (discussed in the General Textual Introduction, pp. 381–3). *A Vindication* was first published in Dublin in 1730 (hereafter *1730a*), and reprinted in London (*1730b*), despite the claims of its imprint 'London printed and Dublin re-printed' which seems to be placed there to deflect attention and avoid potential controversy. As Keith Maslen explains:

> The first two London editions... carry the imprint 'London: printed for T Warner'. The corresponding Dublin edition of the *Vindication*, although carrying the imprint 'London printed and Dublin re-printed', was evidently first printed by Faulkner... these Bowyer printings are entered into the customer accounts, not to Warner, but to 'Faulkner and WB'. Faulkner, as printer of a Dublin edition... would have stood to gain from sales in both Dublin and London.
> (Keith Maslen, 'George Faulkner and William Bowyer: The London Connection', in *An Early London Printing House at Work: Studies in the Bowyer Ledgers*, New York: Bibliographical Society of America, 1993, pp. 223–33, p. 227)

The use of Warner conceals the presence of Faulkner and Bowyer reprinting the Irish text, presumably on Swift's authority, and this provenance is only revealed by its being entered in the Bowyer ledgers for 24 April 1730 (number 1545; A26). It was advertised in the *Daily Journal* for 25 April; a second edition followed two months later (Bowyer number 1576, 25 July 1730; A27). It was also included in the 1732 'Third' volume of *Miscellanies* (a copy in the Rothschild collection has Swift's autograph corrections), and thereafter by Faulkner in the 1735 *Works*.

Changes in the different versions of *A Vindication* are not radical, with the London reprint allowing for extra information, such as the identifications of '*Traulus*' and '*Pistorides*' as Allen and Richard Tighe respectively, albeit through the customary use of initials and blanks in the footnotes to the 1730 London edition. Such identifications were not possible in Dublin, even for Faulkner in 1735, suggesting a reticence to call further legal attention to the pamphlet. It would have placed a burden on Faulkner (or any printer) to run the risk of libel by identifying publicly figures already tacitly known to readers. The London edition could afford to be more detached. It is therefore possible to see the London and Dublin versions of the *Vindication of Carteret* as discreetly different versions of the same text, with some features tailored to these different audiences.

In terms of typography and printing, the London version follows the Dublin edition faithfully, with regard to capitals, punctuation and paragraphing. Most of the variants are to do with house style: a different number of em-dashes, to indicate blanks, and no final letter in blanked names in the Dublin edition. This is refined subsequently in the 1730 London editions, and names are spelt out from 1732 onwards. The occasional mistake in the first Dublin edition is corrected in the London texts, along with the addition of footnotes and a different scheme of blanks and contractions. In 1732, there are many small changes, though not in agreement with the London versions; in 1735, amongst Faulkner's revisions, extensions of contractions, small changes of style, and polishing, rarely are any variants from 1732 accepted and absorbed. The conclusion that can be drawn, given knowledge of the Faulkner–Bowyer connection, is that both the Dublin and London editions have Swift's authority (the second London edition of 1730 has been collated, but offers no variants, and is not included in the Historical Collation). The reviser of the text for the *Miscellanies* (*1732*) cannot be confirmed, nor are the revisions significant, or consistent (though the autograph copy, with Swift's annotations, is included as *1732a*). Faulkner's changes (*1735*) are both, but the uncertainty over Swift's level of involvement in them, combined with their being made in all likelihood four years after the initial publication of a pamphlet written precisely to a moment, means that the 1730 Dublin edition, very obviously the work of Faulkner, is the most appropriate copy text. Emendation has been kept to a minimum, partly because many of the later variants are minor revisions of slight syntactic vagary, or second thoughts, rather than corrections.

Copy Text
CUL, Williams 410.

Dublin, 1730a

TS 698. *ESTC* T73031
Title: A | VINDICATION | OF HIS | Ex—y the Lord *C*—, | FROM | The CHARGE of favouring | none but *Toryes, High-Church-* | *men,* and *Jacobites.* | [rule] | [ornament] | [rule] | *LONDON:* | Printed, and *DUBLIN* Re-printed in the Year | MDCCXXX.
Half-title: A | VINDICATION | OF HIS | EX—Y | THE | Lord C—T, &c. | [row of flowers]
Collation: 8°: *A*⁴ B–D⁴ E³
Pagination: *1–4* 3 4–37 *38*
Contents: A1ʳ half-title; A1ᵛ blank; A2ʳ title page; A2ᵛ blank; A3ʳ–E3ʳ text; E3ᵛ blank
Typography: 25 lines per page (A3ʳ); type-page 125 (135) × 75 mm; 20 lines of roman type 93 mm
Failure of catchwords to catch:
D2ᵛ one] *om.*
Copies consulted: CUL, Williams 410 [on cover is written (presumably by Harold Williams) 'This Dublin reprint is rare. I have not been able to find the BM copy shown by Spencer Jackson.']; BL, 8145.a7.

London, 1730b

TS 697. *ESTC* T50820
Title: A | VINDICATION | OF HIS | EXCELLENCY | THE | Lord *C– – – –T,* | FROM THE | CHARGE | OF favouring none but | Tories, High-Churchmen and | Jacobites. | [rule] | By the Reverend Dr. *S — T.* | [rule] | *LONDON:* | Printed for T. Warner at the *Black-Boy* | in *Pater-Noster-Row.* M DCC XXX. | (Price 6 *d.*)
Collation: 8°: A² B–D⁴ E²
Pagination: *1–4* 1–27 *28*

TEXTUAL ACCOUNT: A VINDICATION OF LORD CARTERET 459

Contents: A1^r title page; A1^v blank; B1^r–E2^r text; E2^v advert for *The Hibernian Patriot* and other Irish writings
Typography: 32 lines per page (B1^v); type-page 149 (159) × 82 mm; 20 lines of roman type 93 mm
Failure of catchwords to catch:
B2^r I own] I own,
B4^r madness] ~,
D1^r of] ~,
D2^v The] the
Copies consulted: CUL, Hib 7.730.12.

Miscellanies, 1732
TS 25 (4a). *ESTC* N62568
Title: MISCELLANIES | [rule] | THE | THIRD VOLUME.
[see entry under *Intelligencer*, Number 5 for full description]
Contents: *Vindication*: L7^r–N7^r; 173–205

Works, 1735
TS 41. *ESTC* T52771
Title: VOLUME IV. | Of the AUTHOR's | WORKS.
[see entry under *Short View of the State of Ireland* for full description]
Contents: *Vindication*: T7^v–X3^r; 286–309

Emendations
196.8 according to] *1730b*; according
197.11 Patriots (at] Patriots. (at
197.12 Pistorides.)] *Pistorides*,)
213.19 net Profit] *1735*; neat profit

Historical Collation
194.1 A VINDICATION ... &c] A VINDICATION OF THE Lord Lieutenant of *Ireland*, THE Lord *CARTERET*, From the Charge of favouring *Tories, High-Church-Men*, and *Jacobites. 1732*+
194.5 E——,] E——y *1730b*; Excellency, *1732*+
194.6 give] suggest *1732*
194.15 Blood,] Blood, &c. *1730a, 1732*
194.16 Books. Which] Books, Which *1730b, 1732*
195.1 E——y] Excellency *1732*+
195.2 whence] thence *1730b*+

195.7 and just] just *1732*
195.9 tho'] although *1735*
196.8 according to] according *1730a*
196.11 E———] E———y *1730b*; Excellency *1732+*
196.20 unsupportable] insupportable *1730b*
196.22 E———] E———y *1730b*; Excellency *1732+*
196.23 with] besides *1732*
196.23 adding] having *1732*
196.24 Person, and] Person, he hath, *1732*
196.25 Vigour, he hath in] Vigour, in *1732*
196.25 unexemplary] exemplary *1732+*
196.26 discovers] discover'd *1732*
197.7 E———] E———y *1730a*; Excellency *1732+*
197.11 Patriots (at the head of whom I name with Honour *Pistorides*,) For] Patriots; for *1732*
197.12 *Pistorides*] *Pistorides* [*with footnote:*] * The Rt Hon. R—d T—gh, Esq; whose Grandfather was a Baker. *1730b*
198.4 Madam] *Madam [*with footnote:*] *A famous Rope-dancer. 1732*; *A famous Italian Rope-dancer 1735*
198.7 improbable,] improbable, but *1730b, 1732*
198.11 *H— H*———] *H—ly H-tch—n 1730b*; Hartly Hutcheson *1735*
198.11 *Jury*, or even from Squire *H— H*——— himself, that *zealous Prosecutor of Hawkers and Libels.* And] *Jury.* And *1732*
199.5 IId] Second *1730b+*
199.6 Popery and Slavery] Popery Slavery *1732* ['and' *added in pen in 1732a*]
199.7 consequently] therefore *1735*
200.2 a] one *1735*
200.5 the Owner] its Owner *1735*
200.7 Innocence] Innocence *1732*
200.11 *Traulus*] *Traulus [*with footnote:*] *L—d V———t A———n, who spoke against the Libel in the Privy Council, and likewise in the House of Lords. 1730b, 1732*
200.14 according to] *1730b, 1732a, 1735*; according *1730a, 1732*
201.5 mistaking] mistaken *1730b, 1732*
201.11 I apprehend that ... *quality* of his Nourishment.] *om. 1732*
201.28 much more] much *1730b, 1735*
201.31 *bestow'd*] bestowed on *1730b+*
202.7 *Politicks*] *Principles 1732*
202.14 I have placed ... suspend my judgement] *om. 1732*
202.17 whether] but whether *1735*

202.20 Mistresses] *Wenches 1735*
203.1   who] and who *1730b*
203.5   I——d] *Ireland 1732+*
203.10 E——y] Excellency *1732+*
203.15 Supposition] Suppositions *1735*
203.22 must then] then must *1735*
203.26 *Professors*] *Possessors 1730b+*
204.3   E——] E——y *1730b*; Excellency *1732+*
204.6   those] these *1730b, 1732*
204.9   till] until *1735*
204.11 E——] E——y *1730b*; Excellency *1732+*
204.18 further] farther *1730b, 1732*
205.5   Eyes,] Eyes, and *1732*
205.8   Book] Books *1730b*
205.12 S——r] Senator *1732+*
205.13 E——] E——y *1730b*; Excellency *1732+*
205.17 Names] Name *1732*
206.5   E——] E——y *1730b*; Excellency *1732+*
206.6   morally] mortally *1730b, 1732*
207.4   E——] E——y *1730b*; Excellency *1732+*
207.7   E——] E——y *1730b*; Excellency *1732+*
207.9   E——'s] E——y's *1730b*; Excellency's *1732+*
207.13 E——] E——y *1730b*; Excellency *1732+*
207.15 E——] E——y *1730b*; Excellency *1732+*
207.22 E——] E——y *1730b*; Excellency *1732+*
207.24 E——] E——y *1730b*; Excellency *1732+*
207.26 of almost] almost of *1730b, 1732*
208.2   E——] E——y *1730b*; Excellency *1732+*
209.13 E—] E——y *1730b*; Excellency *1732+*
209.20 E—] E——y *1730b*; Excellency *1732+*
210.1   Person] †Person [*with footnote:*] † *Sir* Constantine Phipps, *Lord Chancellor of* Ireland *when Queen* Anne *died. 1730b+*
210.2   drank] drunk *1730b, 1732*
210.5   but] except that of *1735*
210.10 L—d L——t's] Lord Lieutenant's *1732+*
210.11 E——] E——y *1730b*; Excellency *1732+*
210.11 Friend] †*Friend* [*with footnote:*] † *The Author 1735*
210.12 E——] E——y *1730b*; Excellency *1732+*

210.14 E——'s] E——y's *1730b*; Excellency's *1732+*
210.15 Gentleman] *1730, 1732a, 1735*; Gentlemen *1730b, 1732*
210.17 E——] E——y *1730b*; Excellency *1732+*
211.12 E——] E——y *1730b*; Excellency *1732+*
211.17 E——] E——y *1730b*; Excellency *1732+*
212.3 Lodging, and] Lodging, a great Number of Pupils, and *1735*
212.7 L—d L——t] Lord Lieutenant *1732+*
212.11 height] Heighth *1735*
212.16 *Sheridan*] *Sheridau 1732*
212.20 E——'s] Excellency's *1732+*
213.19 net Profit] *1735*; neat profit *1730a, 1730b, 1732*
213.20 *Sterl.*] *Sterling 1730b*
214.1 particularly of] particularly that of *1735*
214.9 *Tory.* Whatever] *Tory*, whatever *1732*
214.10 E——] E—— *1730b*; Excellency *1732+*
214.19 E—— the L— L—— E——] Excellency the Lord Lieutenant *1732+*
214.25 E——] Excellency *1732+*
214.25 K——] King *1732*
214.27 E——] Excellency *1732+*
215.5 E——'s] Excellency's *1732+*
215.7 that dangerous] this dangerous *1735*
216.2 E——] E——y *1730b*; Excellency *1732+*
217.2 *White-rosalists*] *Anti-Revolutioners, White-rosalists 1735*
217.3 plainly lyes] plainly lies *1730b, 1732*; seems to lie *1735*

Word Division
Copy Text
Chocolate-House
good-fellow

Edited Text
None

The Answer to the Craftsman

Textual Account

As an ironic response to the *Craftsman*, 7 November 1730 (see Appendix B, pp. 333–43), the *Answer* is usually dated soon after this; it is unfinished, and was unpublished in Swift's lifetime, partly because the situation to which it responded – the tacitly agreed presence of French recruiting officers in Ireland – had been rescinded by the government, and the officers left near the end of the year (see Ehrenpreis, vol. III, pp. 682–5; Ferguson, p. 180).

Faulkner first published it in 1758, as Volume IX of his augmented *Works*: he claimed that it was printed 'from the original Manuscript, that was sent to *England*, and handed about there' and 'hath been highly approved of by Men of the greatest Wit and taste in that Nation; and particularly by a Nobleman as remarkable for his Genius and Learning, as for his excellent Government during his Administration in this Kingdom' ('To the Reader', A2^v). This high praise (probably referring to Carteret) suggests the pamphlet could have achieved a large readership.

The *Answer* was responding in part to the mention in the *Craftsman* of *A Modest Proposal*; Ehrenpreis rated it almost as highly, in terms of irony, as that piece, claiming 'it would now be one of his best-known works', if not for being fragmentary and locked into its historical frame of reference (vol. III, p. 684).

Faulkner's 1758 text was followed by the reprinting, albeit with many small variants, by Deane Swift in his quarto edition of 1764; the presentation of the texts is similar, except for the Faulkner's capitalisation, not present in the later text. Otherwise, both follow the same patterns of spelling and emphasis, down to replicating small capitals and italics. Whatever the veracity of the claim for the manuscript being widely read, Faulkner's version, as the earliest, is the obvious choice of copy text, though the amount of minor revision in the 1764 text is interesting, and produces more variants than would normally be expected in an unfinished essay-pamphlet. On the other hand, emendation has been avoided, chiefly because the revisions in 1764 appear to be minute polishing of phrases and syntactic structures (such as 'shall continue' for 'shall still continue', and 'have sufficient' for 'have had sufficient') rather than significant changes of meaning; even if (as seems unlikely) Deane Swift was working from a different manuscript, it seems to be somebody's later thoughts rather than corrections, and not necessarily Swift's at that.

Copy Text

Bodl., Vet. A5 e.4855.

Faulkner, *Works*, 1758

TS 45A (4b). *ESTC* T184756

Title: VOLUME IX. | OF THE | Author's WORKS, | CONTAINING | LETTERS to Governor Hunter. | The HISTORY of the last Session

of | PARLIAMENT, and the PEACE OF | UTRECHT. Written at WINDSOR in | the Year 1713. | The CRAFTSMAN of December 12, 1730. | And the Answer thereto. | A TREATISE on GOOD MANNERS and | GOOD BREEDING. | [rule] | By the Rev. Dr. J. SWIFT, D.S.P.D. | [rule] | [ornament] | [double-rule] | DUBLIN: | Printed by GEORGE FAULKNER in Essex-street. | M,DCC,LVIII.
Collation: 8°: A–I⁸ K⁸ (±K3[= X4]) L–U⁸ X⁴(–X4) Y–2A⁸
Pagination: *1–5* 6–14 *15–16, 1* 2–310, *1–3* 4–47 *48*
Contents: A1ʳ title page; A1ᵛ blank; A2ʳ⁻ᵛ 'To the Reader'; A3–2A8ᵛ text
Answer to the Craftsman: Appendix, Z4ʳ–2A1ʳ; 23–33
Typography: 28 lines per page (Z5ᵛ); type-page 152 (164) × 85 mm; 20 lines of roman type 105 mm
Failure of catchwords to catch:
Z4ʳ Perhaps] ~,
Copies consulted: Bodl., Vet. A5 e.4855; Bodl., Vet A4 e.3055/9; Bodl., Vet. A5 e.6570 (with cancellandum K3 in place and cancellans K3 at X4).

Deane Swift, *Works*, 1764

TS 87. *ESTC* T52747
Title: THE | WORKS | OF | Jonathan Swift, D. D. | Dean of St. Patrick's, Dublin. | VOLUME VII. PART I. | [double-rule] | LONDON, | Printed for W. BOWYER, R. and J. DODSLEY, and L. DAVIS | and C. REYMERS. | MDCCLXIV.
Collation: 4°: A–2F⁴ 2G³
Pagination: *i–viii*, 1–221
Contents: A1ʳ title page; A1ᵛ blank; A2ʳ⁻ᵛ contents; A3ʳ 'Advertisement'; A3ᵛ blank; B–2G1ᵛ text
Answer to the Craftsman: O4ʳ–P2ᵛ; 103–8
Typography: 33 lines per page (O4ᵛ); type-page 200 (255) × 140 mm; 20 lines of roman type 116 mm
Copies consulted: BL, 90.d.7 (with vol. VII, pt ii).

Emendations

[None]

Historical Collation

220.13 costeth] it costeth *1764*
220.14 polish them] polish *1764*
220.17 for the Letters] for letters *1764*
221.7 have had] have *1764*

221.13 D'*Anvers*] D'ANVER *1764*
221.17 Manufacture] manufactures *1764*
222.9 must it] it must *1764*
222.22 to] for *1764*
223.24 the] our *1764*
224.12 exported] imported *1764*
224.17 be] get *1764*
225.9 to] for *1764*
225.13 shall still] shall *1764*
226.14 by a] by *1764*
227.2 Bonnyclabber] Bonnyclabber* [*with footnote:*] *Thick, sour milk. *1764*
227.2 mingled] milk mingled *1764*
227.3 as they formerly did] as it formerly was *1764*
227.3 Century Luxury] century; when, luxury *1764*
227.4 began] beginning *1764*
227.18 to the] to *1764*

Word Division
Copy Text
Port-Towns

Edited Text
None

Proposal to Pay Off the Debt of the Nation

Textual Account

On 28 August 1732, as Ehrenpreis points out, this was included in the list of works by Swift that Matthew Pilkington intended to publish, as he tells Bowyer (Woolley, *Corr.*, vol. III, pp. 530–1; see Ehrenpreis, vol. III, p. 721, where he also mentions 'a similar project' described in the *Dublin Journal*, 15 September 1730). It was first published much earlier in the year in Dublin by Faulkner (though with no name on the imprint) with 'By A – – P – – Esq;' on the title page, and reprinted in London, along with *Considerations Upon Two Bills*, and published by James Roberts, as part of the arrangement between Faulkner and Bowyer (see Textual Introduction, p. 343), being number 1785 (6 March 1732) in the *Bowyer Ledgers*, though the wrong text is attributed to the Bowyer printing, and it is the Roberts and not the 'A. Moore' printing of this pamphlet (TS 716, which does not include the

Proposal) that was printed by John Purser, in agreement with Bowyer. It was reprinted by Faulkner in the 1735 *Works*.

The date of the Bowyer entry means the Dublin printing certainly appeared before March; Faulkner, in 1762, recalled printing parts of it in the *Dublin Journal* of 26 February 1732, and being 'ordered into Custody by the House of Lords' for so doing: see *Works* (Dublin: Faulkner, 1762), vol. I, 'To the Reader', pp. xi–xii. Barry Slepian points out that, as the *Dublin Journal* prints direct quotations from the pamphlet, 'the extract must have been made by someone who had a manuscript before him', assuming it had yet to appear ('George Faulkner's *Dublin Journal* and Jonathan Swift', *Library Chronicle of the University of Pennsylvania* 31 (1965), 97–116, p. 104).

Given that all three editions with any authority show Faulkner's involvement, the choice of copy text is straightforward: the Dublin edition of 1732 (hereafter *1732a*) has the greatest prominence, and most exactly reflects Swift's intentions. The 1732 London Roberts reprint (*1732b*) is identical with the Faulkner text in all features, from capitals and italics to paragraphing, and must have been set from the same type, or followed with an extraordinary exactitude, as each line is equivalent in letters and spacing (the occasional insertion of two lines more text at the bottom of the page is the only difference between the two). The 1735 reprint adds the squared bracket disclaimer before the title, '*The Reader will perceive the following Treatise to be altogether ironical*', showing how the work is positioned differently when appearing in a collected edition, and makes some minor changes and revisions, all of which are noted in the Historical Collation, but none of which invite emendation.

Copy Text

NLI, LO Swift 165.

Dublin, 1732a

TS 717a. *ESTC* T219081

Half title: A | PROPOSAL | FOR AN | A— of p————, &c. | To sell the BISHOPS LANDS. | [rule]

Title: A | PROPOSAL | FOR AN | Act of PARLIAMENT, | To pay off the | DEBT | OF THE | NATION, | Without taxing the SUBJECT, by | which the Number of landed Gentry, and sub- | stantial Farmers will be considerably encreased, and | no one Person will be the poorer, or contribute | one Farthing to the Charge. | [rule] | *By* A — P —, *Esq*; | [two rules] | *D U B L I N*: | Printed in the Year M,DCC,XXXII.

Collation: 8°: A⁸
Pagination: *i–iv*, 5, 6–16
Contents: A1ʳ half title; A1ᵛ blank; A2ʳ title page; A2ᵛ blank; A3ʳ–8ʳ text; A8ᵛ advertisement: 'Speedily will be publish'd', *An Examination of Certain Abuses*
Typography: 28 lines per page (A6ᵛ); type-page 140 (150) × 80 mm; 20 lines of roman type 93 mm
Copies consulted: NLI, LO Swift 165.

London, 1732b

TS 717. *ESTC* T145270
Title: CONSIDERATIONS | UPON TWO | BILLS, | Sent down from the | Rt. Hon. the HOUSE of LORDS | TO THE HONOURABLE | House of Commons of *Ireland*, | RELATING TO THE | CLERGY | Of That KINGDOM. | [rule] | *By the Rev. Dr. SWIFT, D.S.P.D.* | [rule] | To which is added, | A PROPOSAL for an Act of Parliament, | to pay off the DEBT of the NATION, | without taxing the Subject, by which the | Number of Landed Gentry, and substantial | Farmers will be considerably encreas'd, and | no one Person will be the poorer, or contri- | bute one Farthing to the Charge. | [rule] | *By* A— P—, *Esq*; | [rule] | *DUBLIN*, Printed; | *LONDON*, Re-printed for J. Roberts at the *Oxford* | *Arms* in *Warwick-Lane*. 1732. | (Price Six-pence.)
Collation: 8°: A–D⁴
Pagination: *1–2*, 3–32
Contents: A1ʳ title page; A1ᵛ blank; A2ʳ–C3ᵛ *Considerations*; C4ʳ–D4ᵛ *Proposal*
Typography: 28 lines per page (D3ᵛ); type-page 150 (160) × 82 mm; 20 lines of roman type 96 mm
Copies consulted: BL, 116.g.6.

Works, 1735

TS 41. *ESTC* T52771
Title: VOLUME IV. | Of the Author's | WORKS.
[see entry under *Short View of the State of Ireland* for full description]
Contents: *Proposal to Pay off Debt*; 310–17; X3ᵛ–7ʳ.

Emendations

232.3 three fourths more; so that multiplying] three fourths more, so that Multipling
235.9 Loads of Taxes] *1732b*; Loads of of Taxes

Historical Collation
231.1 [above title] *The Reader will perceive the following Treatise to be altogether Ironical 1735*
234.1 Caveat, &c.] *Caveat Emptor 1735*
235.22 Tythes] *Fines 1735*
236.5 bestowed such high] bestowed on them such high *1735*
236.20 loyal] *true loyal 1735*
237.8 on by the] on the *1735*
238.1 Tho'] ALTHOUGH *1735*

Word Division
Copy Text
None

Edited Text
None

An Examination of Certain Abuses

Textual Account

Written from the persona of a credulous Whig, this satiric mock catalogue of the supposed codes and treasonable secret messages conveyed by Tory and Jacobite supporters through absurd examples of street cries has not been the recipient of much critical attention, yet is one of the more intriguing of Swift's later Irish works, in terms of the nature of its publication. *An Examination of Certain Abuses, Corruptions, and Enormities in the City of Dublin* was published in Dublin in 1732 in a printing which bears all the characteristics of George Faulkner (it was advertised at the end of Faulkner's edition of *A Proposal to Pay off the Debt of the Nation*, published before March 1732; see Textual Account, above, pp. 465–6). The London edition, retitled *City Cries, or, An Examination of Certain Abuses Corruptions, and Enormities in London and Dublin*, was advertised in the *Daily Post* for 11 March, thus making the Irish edition likely to have preceded that by a couple of weeks. It was reprinted (in its original Dublin form and title) by Faulkner in the 1735 *Works*.

The satire was revised for its London publication in a curious manner. In London it appeared under the imprint of James Roberts, the biggest 'trade publisher' of the period; this was presumably a distribution route for William Bowyer, and it seems an obvious example (along with *A Vindication of Carteret* and others) of the Bowyer–Faulkner relationship, whereby Swift's Dublin printings were reliably reprinted in London (discussed in the Textual Introduction, pp. 381–2). Unfortunately, there is no direct evidence, whether in the Bowyer ledgers, or in terms of bibliographical scrutiny, for this implied relationship.

The revisions to the London edition are significant: as well as the title being altered to 'Dublin and London', changing the satiric reference of the piece, it is noteworthy that, after the conclusion to the 1732 Dublin edition, the London reprint has additional pages adding yet another instance of the perniciousness of secret Jacobitism, in the sign-posts bearing the mark of George the Second (meaning the second king, after the Pretender, the true monarch). The Dublin version ends at the bottom of p. 27 of the Dublin edition and p. 28 of the London edition, which then adds two further pages. Herbert Davis claimed that 'After the pamphlet had been printed in Dublin Swift gave [Matthew] Pilkington a copy to arrange for its printing in London. The copy contained an extra paragraph.' If this is the case, rather than an educated and highly plausible speculation, alas Davis left no reference to support it (vol. XII, pp. xxxiv–xxxv).

It might be asked why this conclusion was only included in London editions. Ostensibly, Swift was able to publish in London ideas or statements that would be too inflammatory for Dublin, yet this added conclusion would not seem to offend more than any other page of a work based upon irreverent and ridiculous examples of treason. It seems, paradoxically, to have been thought potentially libellous to the King in Dublin, but much safer when republished in London. It is possible to view the conclusion as an addition that shows Swift (or his representative editor) tailoring his message to an audience, and evincing an awareness of a different reading culture, as with the change in title of the pamphlet. There is also the practical question of signs with 'Geo II' upon them being present in London, but not Dublin, making the London conclusion not specifically Irish.

Although it is not possible to say precisely how Faulkner managed the two texts, it can be suggested that the longer London printing must have been the text that was reduced (by Swift, Pilkington, Faulkner or some other agency) for the Dublin version before either was published (there are neither variants nor other differences to suggest two different sources). While the greater leading of the Roberts text soon changes the parallels, the two 1732 texts share so many features – identical in capitals and italics, with the odd difference in pointing, and the occasional variant for the London audience – that it would seem inconceivable that one does not derive from the other: the choice of which text to print is then between the fullest text (London, hereafter *1732b*) or the Dublin original (*1732a*). Faulkner, publishing in Dublin in 1735, revised his printing of 1732, making small adjustments and revisions which may or may not be authorial, as is the case with the *Works* generally. This volume is concerned with Swift's Irish writings of the period, and thus the original Dublin edition is chosen as copy text, having precedence over both the London reprint (even if its revisions and additional ending are assumed to be authorial) and the 1735 *Works*, as the first and only definitive authorial version, and as a text intended for publication solely in Ireland. The ending to the London version is added after the end of the Dublin text.

Copy Text
CUL, Williams 308.

Dublin, 1732a

TS 718. *ESTC* T81147
Title: AN | EXAMINATION | OF CERTAIN | *Abuses, Corruptions,* | AND | *ENORMITIES* | IN THE | City of *DUBLIN*. | [rule] | [flower] | [rule] | *Dublin:* Printed in the Year 1732.
Collation: 8°: A^4 B–C^4 D^2
Pagination: 1–2, 3–27 28
Contents: A1^r title page; A1^v blank; A2^r–D2^r text; D2^v blank
Typography: 32 lines per page (A3^r); type-page 133 (143) × 75 mm; 20 lines of roman type 85 mm
Failure of catchwords to catch:
C1^v *om.*] dently
D1^r Author] Author,
Copies consulted: CUL, Williams 308. Handwritten note (presumably by Harold Williams) at front: 'An extremely rare pamphlet. Copies traced, BM, National Library Dublin. Reprinted as *City Cries, Instrumental and Vocal*: London, J. Roberts, 1732.'; TCC, Rothschild 2138; TCC, Rothschild 2139.

London, 1732b

TS 719. *ESTC* T30787
Title: *CITY CRIES*, | INSTRUMENTAL and *VOCAL*: | OR, AN | EXAMINATION | OF CERTAIN | Abuses, Corruptions, | AND | ENORMITIES, | IN | *London* and *Dublin*. | [rule] | By the Rev. Dr. Swift, D.S.P.D. | [rule] | *DUBLIN*, Printed; | *LONDON*, Re-printed

TEXTUAL ACCOUNT: AN EXAMINATION OF CERTAIN ABUSES 471

for J. ROBERTS at the *Oxford* | *Arms* in *Warwick-Lane*. 1732. | (Price Six-pence.)
Collation: 8°: A^4 B–D^4
Pagination: *1–2* 3–30 *31–2*
Contents: A1^r title page; A1^v blank; A2^r–D3^v text; D4^{r-v} 'BOOKS *printed for* J. ROBERTS *at the* Oxford-Arms *in* Warwick-Lane.'
Typography: 30 lines per page (B1^r); type-page 185 (196) × 82 mm; 20 lines of roman type 99 mm
Failure of catchwords to catch:
C1^v succession] succession,
Copies consulted: CUL, Williams 409; Bodl., G. Pamph. 1154 (16); Bodl., G. Pamph. 393 (4).

Works, 1735
TS 41. *ESTC* T52771
Title: VOLUME IV. | Of the AUTHOR's | WORKS.
[see entry under *Short View of the State of Ireland* for full description]
Contents: *An Examination of Certain Abuses*: X3^v–Z1^v; 318–38.

Emendations
243.2 Business, who] *1732b*; Business. who

Historical Collation
242.1 AN EXAMINATION Of *certain Abuses*, &c.] CITY CRIES: OR AN Examination *of certain Abuses, Corruptions, &c. 1732b*; AN EXAMINATION OF *Certain Abuses, Corruptions, and Enormities, in the City of Dublin. Written in the Year 1732. 1735*
242.8 these Abuses] those Abuses *1735*
242.11 their most profound] their profound *1735*
242.19 touch at the] touch the *1735*
243.2 Business, who] Business. who *1732a*; Business, and who *1732b*
243.6 till] until *1735*
243.7 these Traders] those Traders *1735*
243.13 meant; for] meant, for *1732b*; meant? For *1735*
243.18 till] until *1735*
244.3 Howth] *Howth [*with footnote:*] * The Sea about eight Miles from *Dublin*, where they fish for Herrings. *1732b*
244.17 Observation] Observations *1732b*
244.18 and it is] which is that *1732b*

244.18 Sweet-hearts] *Sweet-hearts [with footnote:] *A Sort of Sugar-Cakes in the Shape of Hearts. 1735
245.3 Toupees] *Toupees [with footnote:] A new Name for a modern Periwig, and for its Owner, now in Fashion. Dec. I, 1733. 1735
245.13 till] until 1735
245.21 the] an 1735
245.23 have] hath 1735
246.10 his] their 1732b
246.15 Malice] Enmity 1735
247.14 together into] together in 1732b
248.17 Cock.] Cock, in the same Posture. 1735
248.19 either fit] fit 1735
248.23 Hieroglyph] Hieroglyphics 1732b
249.1 Guest] Guests 1735
249.2 For not one] Not one 1735
249.2 is] being 1735
249.3 Punch] Liquor 1732b
249.3 For the Birds, as they] For, as they 1735
249.4 are much] they are much 1735
249.8 intended against the Government, by] against the present Government, intended by 1732b
250.10 the Protestant] the true Protestant 1735
250.14 hallow] halloo 1735
250.16 those Signs] the Signs 1735
250.18 most common Understanding] common Understandings 1732b; common Understanding 1735
251.5 those] these 1735
252.4 that known] the known 1735
252.7 may] mayst 1732b
253.5 horrid Countenances] horrid, or indeed rather diabolical Countenances 1735
254.7 worst of Times] *worst of Times [with footnote:] *A Cant-Word used by Whigs for the four last Years of Queen Anne's Reign, during the Earl of Oxford's Ministry; whose Character here is an exact reverse in every Particular. 1735
254.11 sterl.] sterling 1732b
254.11 Gold Plate] Plate 1735
255.6 Grounds] good grounds 1735
256.6 the fine Cries] the Cries 1735
256.8 Orleans's] Orleance's 1732b

256.17 and in] and is in *1735*
257.7 after which they have so long aspired] they have so long aimed at *1735*
257.9 And] And that *1732b*; Whereby *1735*
258.8 to be] of being *1735*
258.18 have often since] have since *1735*
259.3 these Cries] these *1732b*
259.13 P——n] *Peyton [*withfootnote:*] *A famous Whig Justice in those Times. *1735*
260.15 but] yet *1735*
260.18 the Author] the very Author *1732b*
261.4 King TURN UP] King (Inuendo the Pretender) TURN UP *1732b*
262.20 FINIS] Having already spoken... the Loyalty and Activity of my Superiors. *1732b*

Word Division
Copy Text
Fishamble-street

Edited Text
None

The Humble Petition of the Footmen of Dublin

Textual Account

Despite being internally dated 1732, no edition of that year has ever been located; instead, there were two 1733 editions, in Dublin and London – both accompanying the *Serious and Useful Scheme*, usually attributed to Matthew Pilkington (see Davis, vol. XII, p. 345) – with a second issue in Dublin, a reprint of it in 1734, and the inclusion by Faulkner in *Works*, 1735. The order of the 1733 editions is ambiguous, mainly because they involve George Faulkner and a possible channel (though unrecorded in this instance) via his relationship with William Bowyer, using the trade publisher James Roberts. The advertisement for Faulkner's edition of *Works* at the end of the pamphlet is dated '21 November 1733'. Davis (vol. XII, p. 345) claims that Pilkington 'might have been responsible for providing copy for Curll for the 1733 volume', though no other evidence of Curll's responsibility can be found.

Faulkner's 'London: printed and Dublin reprinted' on the title page might be a way of disowning responsibility for the publication, an inversion, for example, of *The Dunciad*'s false 'Dublin, Printed, London Reprinted'. In this period, Faulkner's Dublin editions generally take precedence over the London versions, and, therefore, the likelihood is that the London text is the reprint. In practical terms, there is only one variant. The second Dublin issue of 1733 mentions Faulkner alone on the title page, and identifies Swift as author by initials. The reprint of 1734 has been collated, but not included in the Textual Accounts, given the absence of other variants. Copy text is the first Dublin edition (*1733a*), with reference also made to the London edition (*1733b*), the second Dublin edition (*1733c*) and *Works* (*1735*).

Copy Text
BL, 1163111.47.10.

Dublin, 1733a

TS 732. *ESTC* T452

Title: A | SERIOUS and USEFUL | SCHEME. | To make an | Hospital for Incurables, | OF | Universal Benefit to all His Ma- | jesty's Subjects. | [rule] | Humbly addressed to the Rt. Hon. the Lord ⁂ ⁂ ⁂, | the Rt. Hon Sir ⁂ ⁂ ⁂, and to the Rt. Hon. | ⁂ ⁂ ⁂ ⁂, Esq; | [rule] | To which is added, | A Petition of the Footmen in and about *Dublin*. | [rule] | *Fœcunda Culpæ Secula !*———— Hor. | [rule] | Printed at *LONDON:* And, | *DUBLIN:* | Printed by *GEORGE FAULKNER*, and Sold at his Shop | in *Essex-Street*, opposite to the *Bridge*, and by *G.* | *Risk, G. Ewing* and *W. Smith*, Booksellers in *Dame-* | *Street*, 1733.

Collation: 8°: A^4 B–D^4 E^2

Pagination: 1–34, 35–6

Contents: $A1^r$ title page; $A1^v$ blank; $A2^r$–$D4^r$ (1–31) text: *Serious and Useful Scheme*; $D4^v$–$E1^v$ (32–4) text *Humble Petition*; $E2^{r-v}$ Advertisement for Swift's *Works*, dated Dublin November 21, 1733

Typography: 33 lines per page ($E1^r$); type-page 135 (145) × 78 mm; 20 lines roman type 83 mm

Copies consulted: BL, 1163.aa.47(10); Bodl., Vet. A4 f.846(12).

London, 1733b

TS 730. *ESTC* N21200

Title: A | SERIOUS and USEFUL | SCHEME, | To make an | Hospital for Incurables, | OF | Universal Benefit to all His Majesty's | Subjects. |

TEXTUAL ACCOUNT: PETITION OF THE FOOTMEN OF DUBLIN 475

Occasioned by a Report, that the Estate of | RICHARD NORTON Esq; was | to be appointed by Parliament | for such an Endowment. | To which is added, | A Petition of the Footmen in and about *Dublin*. | [rule] | By a Celebrated Author in *Ireland*. | [rule] | *Fœcunda Culpæ Secula!* —— Hor. | [rule] | *LONDON:* | Printed for J. ROBERTS, at the *Oxford Arms* in | *Warwick-Lane*. MDCCXXXIII. | Price 6 d. |
Collation: 8°: A^1 B–E^4 F^1
Pagination: i–ii 1–30 *31* 32–4
Contents: A1^r title page; A1^v blank; B1^r–E3^v (1–30) *Serious and Useful Scheme*; E4^r–F1^v (31–4) *Humble Petition*; F2^{r-v} advertisement
Typography: 30 lines per page (E4^v); type-page 145 (155) × 82 mm; 20 lines of roman type 92 mm
Copies consulted: CUL, Williams 345; CUL, Hib .7.733.12.

Dublin, 1733c, Second Issue
TS 731. *ESTC* T451
Title: A | SERIOUS and USEFUL | SCHEME | To make an | Hospital for Incurables, | OF | Universal Benefit to all His Ma- | jesty's Subjects. | [rule] | Humbly addressed to the Rt. Hon. the Lord *̈ * * *̈*, | the Rt. Hon Sir *̈ * * *̈*, and to the Rt. Hon. | *̈ * * * *̈*, Esq; | [rule] | *Fœcunda Culpæ Secula!* —— Hor. | [rule] | To which is added, | A Petition of the Footmen in and about *Dublin*. | [rule] | By the Revd. Dr. *J. S. D. S.P. D.* | [rule] | Printed at *LONDON:* And, | *DUBLIN:* | Printed by *GEORGE FAULKNER*, in *Essex-Street*, | opposite to the Bridge. 1733.
Collation: 8°: A^4 B–D^4 E^2
Pagination: 1–34, *35–6*
Contents: A1^r title page; A1^v blank; A2^r–D4^r (1–31) text: *Serious and Useful Scheme*; D4^v–E1^v (32–4) text *Humble Petition*; E2^{r-v} Advertisement for Swift's *Works*, dated Dublin November 21, 1733
Typography: 33 lines per page (E1^r); type-page 135 (145) × 78 mm; 20 lines roman type 83 mm
Copies consulted: BL, 11631.aa.63 (5); CUL, Williams 346.

Works, 1735
TS 41. *ESTC* T52771
Title: VOLUME IV. | Of the AUTHOR'S | WORKS.
[see entry under *Short View of the State of Ireland* for full description]
Contents: *Humble Petition*: BB2^r–3^v; 371–74.

Emendations

268.8 as] *1733b*; at

Historical Collation

266.3 Dublin.] [*added*] Written in the Year 1732 *1733b, 1735*
266.16 of wearing our] of our *1735*
267.7 swearing, staring] staring, swearing *1735*
268.8 as] at *1733a*

Word Division
Copy Text
None

Edited Text
None

Some Considerations in the Choice of a Recorder

Textual Account

The death of Francis Stoyte (1733), the eponymous Recorder, dates this brief statement to that year: the Dublin half-sheet (without imprint) which formed its only lifetime printing declares that it was printed in 1733. In Dublin, it was collected by Faulkner in the augmentation of the *Works* (*1746*), and subsequently in the next reprint of the edition (*1751*). In London, it was reprinted from Faulkner in the *Miscellanies* of C. Hitch *et al.*, and then in the quarto edition (*1755*). All of these have been collated, and are described below (with the exception of Faulkner, 1751, a straightforward reprint).

The differences between the post-1746 versions are very slight: the 1755 modernised printing relegates almost all of the capitalised nouns of *1733* and 1746 to lower case. Otherwise, it is clear that the few variants all emerge in Faulkner's first 1746 printing; every edition follows them literally (including the headnote explaining the context of the piece), meaning that the only two texts with possible authority are 1746 and the original half-sheet. The half-sheet is the obvious choice of copy text, given its appearance in Swift's lifetime, and its propinquity.

Copy Text

NLI, LO Swift 356.

Dublin, 1733

Not in TS. *ESTC* T207966

Title: SOME | CONSIDERATIONs | Humbly offered to the Right Honourable the | LORD-MAYOR, | The COURT of ALDERMEN, and COMMON | COUNCIL of the Honourable City of *Dublin*, | in the Choice of a RECORDER.
Collation: half-sheet; 2 columns, one side only.
Contents: A1^r text
Typography: 45 lines per page (A1^r); type-page 277 (315) × 150 mm; 20 lines of type 84 mm
Copies consulted: NLI, LO Swift 356.

Works, 1746

TS 44. *ESTC* T228839

Title: VOLUME VIII. | OF THE | AUTHOR's WORKS, | CONTAINING | Directions to Servants; | AND | Other Pieces in PROSE and VERSE, | published in his Life-time; with several | Poems, Letters, and other Pieces never be- | fore printed. | [rule] | [ornament] | [rule] | *DUBLIN:* | Printed by and for GEORGE FAULKNER, | M,DCC,XLVI.
Collation: 8°: $^\pi A^9\ ^\pi B^8$ (–B8), A–E^8 F–I^4 K–2K^8 L^3 [?$^\pi$A1 = B8]
Pagination: *i–xviii* 1–14 *15–16 i* ii 1–25 *26* 1–6 33–77 *78 81–2* 83–466 (324, 362, 466 as 224, 162, 366)
Contents: $^\pi A1^r$ title page; $^\pi A1^v$ advertisement; $^\pi A2^r$–3^r dedication; $^\pi A3^v$ blank; $^\pi A4^r$–7^r preface; $^\pi A7^v$ advertisement; $^\pi A8^r$–9^v contents; $^\pi B1^r$–7^v Swift's Will; A1^r–2L3^v text
Some Considerations: 2A4^v–5^v; 308–10
Typography: 32 lines per page (2A5^r); type-page 150 (160) × 84 mm; 20 lines of roman type 93 mm
Copies consulted: CUL, Williams 20; Bodl., 12 Theta 1302.

London, *Miscellanies*, 1746

TS 66. *ESTC* T39445

Title: MISCELLANIES. | [rule] | By *Dr.* SWIFT. | [rule] | THE | ELEVENTH VOLUME. | [rule] | [ornament] | [double-rule] | *LONDON:* | Printed for C. HITCH, C. DAVIS, R. DODS- | LEY, and M. COOPER. | [rule] | MDCCXLVI.
Collation: 8°: A^4 B–U^8 X^2 [2 leaves music]
Pagination: *i–viii*, *1–2*, 3–304, *305–8*
Contents: A1^r title page; A1^v blank; A2^r–4^v contents; B–X4^v text
Some Considerations: O6^r–7^v; 203–6

Typography: 31 lines per page (O7^r); type-page 116 (125) × 66 mm; 20 lines of roman type 79 mm
Copies consulted: CUL, Williams 188; Bodl., 2699f.199.

London, *Works*, 1755

TS 87. *ESTC* T52755
Title: THE | WORKS | OF | Jonathan Swift, D. D. | Dean of St. Patrick's, Dublin. | VOLUME VI. PART II. | [double-rule] | LONDON, | Printed for C. DAVIS, C. HITCH and L. HAWES, J. HODGES, C. BATHURST, | R. and J. DODSLEY, and W. BOWYER. | [rule] | MDCCLV.
Collation: 4°: π^1 a^2 B–2E^4 2F^1
Pagination: *1–2* i–iii iv *1* 2–218
Contents: π1^r title page; π1^v blank; a1^r–a2^r contents; a2^v blank; B1^r–2F1^v text
Some Considerations: 2D4^{r-v}; 207–8
Typography: 33 lines per page (2D1^r); type-page 195 (209) × 140 mm; 20 lines of roman type 116 mm
Copies consulted: CUL, Williams 54. With Vol. VI, pt I; BL, 90.d.6. With Vol. VI, pt i.

Emendations

[None]

Historical Collation

271.1 [*Before Title*] *Upon the Death of Mr.* STOYTE, *Recorder of the City of Dublin, in the Year* 1733, *several Gentlemen declared themselves Candidates to succeed him; upon which the Dean wrote the following Paper, and* EATON STANNARD, *Esq;* (*a Gentleman of great Worth and Honour, and very knowing in his Profession*) *was elected.*] *1746*
271.18 an] any *1746+*
272.13 alive or dead] dead or alive *1746+*
272.18 Commoners] Commons *1746+*
273.2 any] all *1746+*

Word Division
Copy Text
None

Edited Text
None

Prefatory Letter to Mary Barber, *Poems on Several Occasions*

Textual Account

Swift often mentioned Mary Barber and her struggle for patronage of her verse in his correspondence; he wrote to Pope (6 February 1729–30) of 'one Mrs Barber, wife to a Wollen Draper, who is our chief Poetess, and upon the whole hath no ill Genius' (Woolley, *Corr.*, vol. III, p. 278). Her *Poems on Several Occasions* were advertised from 20 October 1733 (though not entered into the Stationers' Register until 17 May 1735; see Woolley, *Corr.*, vol. III, p. 685 n. 2); Swift gave Barber letters of introduction to friends in England, to help swell the subscription list (see Ehrenpreis, vol. III, p. 759).

The *Poems* appeared by 1734, printed by Samuel Richardson for Rivington, with Swift's prefatory remarks attached. They were reissued in the same edition in 1735 and 1736, with revised title pages and supplemented booksellers, but without any changes to Swift's brief puff. The copy text is the 1734 edition of *Poems*; the italic and roman text has been reversed.

Poems, 1734

ESTC T42622

Title: POEMS | ON | SEVERAL OCCASIONS | [double-rule] | [ornament] | [double-rule] | *LONDON*: | Printed for C. Rivington, at the Bible | and *Crown* in St. *Paul's Church-Yard.* | [rule] | M.DCC.XXXIV.
Collation: 4°: A^4 a–e^4 B–2N^4 2O^2 2P^4
Pagination: *i–ii* iii–xlviii, *1* 2–283 *284–92*
Contents: A1^r title page; A1^v blank; A2^r–4^v Swift's Letter; a1^r–4^v dedication; b1^r–c3^v preface; c4^r–e2^v subscribers; e3^r–4^v Verses to the Author; B1^r–2O2^r text; 2O2^v blank; 2P1^r–4^r index; 2P4^v blank
Swift's 'Letter': A2^r–4^v; iii–viii
Typography: 21 lines per page (A3^r); type-page 203 (287) × 139 mm; 20 lines of roman type 170 mm
Copies consulted: BL, 77.k.8; BL, 642.1.3.

Emendations

[None]

Word Division
Copy Text
where-ever

Edited Text
None

Advice to the Free-men of Dublin

Textual Account

Swift's promotion of Humphrey French's candidacy as MP for Dublin was first published in 1733; Ehrenpreis finds it 'probably published in September', on the grounds that the *Dublin Journal* of 29 September denied supressing it (vol. III, p. 761). It was collected by Faulkner in a volume of additional Dublin *Works* (*1746*), and reprinted in 1751; in London, it was reprinted in the 1746 *Miscellanies*, and the 1755 quarto *Works*. There are minor differences between 1746 and the texts of the 1746 *Miscellanies* (hereafter *1746a*) and *1755*; all of these have been collated, and are described below (except for Faulkner's reprint of his own text in 1751). The London and Dublin texts follow their own path, and both differ, though not to a great degree, from the original broadsheet – most of the variants can be seen as editorial polishing, rather than shifts in meaning (e.g. Faulkner's characteristic 'hath' for 'has' and 'doth' for 'does'). The 1755 text does not replicate the capitalised nouns of all previous versions, and is more heavily punctuated.

The copy text is the broadsheet of 1733: it is the most immediate intervention, a respectable (if anonymous) printing and an appropriate form for a short piece of exhortation for a specific occasion. The posthumous alternatives (the 1746 and 1755 *Works*, the 1746 *Miscellanies*) do not have the authority of appearing in Swift's lifetime, and it would be hard to make the case that their variations are authorial revisions or corrections, rather than editorial.

Copy Text
RIA, SR 24 C 32 (6).

Broadsheet, Dublin, 1733
TS 739
Title: ADVICE | TO THE | Free-Men of the City of *Dublin*, in the Choice of a Member to | Represent them in PARLIAMENT.
Collation: half-sheet
Pagination: none
Typography: 57 lines per page; type-page 290 (300) × 150 mm; 20 lines of roman type 82 mm
Copies consulted: RIA, SR 24 C 32 (6).

Works, 1746
TS 44. *ESTC* T228839
Title: VOLUME VIII | OF THE | Author's WORKS,
[see entry under *Some Considerations* for full description]
Contents: *Advice to the Free-men*: R4ᵛ–S1ʳ; 196–205

Miscellanies, 1746a
TS 66. *ESTC* T39445
Title: MISCELLANIES | [rule] | *By Dr.* SWIFT.
[see entry under *Some Considerations* for full description]
Contents: *Advice to the Free-men*: N5ʳ–O3ʳ; 187–97

London, *Works*, 1755
TS 87. *ESTC* T52755
Title: THE | WORKS | OF | Jonathan Swift, D. D.
[see entry under *Some Considerations* for full description]
Contents: *Advice to the Free-men*: 2D4ʳ⁻ᵛ; 200–6

Emendations
282.15 Number)] *1746*; Number
283.21 safely] *1746*; sefely

Historical Collation
281.3 PARLIAMENT] ** The following Piece was published in the Year 1733; and, as it may be useful upon a like Occasion, we think proper to insert it here.* [*note in* 1746+]
281.13 Mayor] **Humphry French.* [*note in* 1746+]
281.13 other] **John Macarall.* [*note in* 1746+]
281.15 Office] *Register to the barracks.* [*note in* 1746+]
282.8 these] those *1746a*; those of *1755*
282.13 out of] for *1755*
282.22 are] being *1746a, 1755*
283.6 depressing of] depressing *1746a, 1755*
283.21 safely] *1746*; sefely *1733*
284.2 never be possibly] never possibly be *1746*
284.15 t'other] the other *1746+*
284.25 has] hath *1746+*
285.2 of] for *1746+*

482 GENERAL TEXTUAL INTRODUCTION AND TEXTUAL ACCOUNTS

285.25 Englishman] * EDWARD THOMPSON, Esq; Member of Parliament for *York*, and a Commissioner of the Revenue in *Ireland*. [*note in* 1746]; ~ in *Ireland. 1755*
286.6 up all] all up *1746*
286.7 Progresses] progress *1746a*, *1755*
286.7 received] *Mr. THOMPSON was presented with his Freedom of several Corporations in Ireland. [*note in* 1746+]
286.16 does] doth *1746+*
287.12 though] although *1746+*
287.20 hazard] answer *1746*, *1755*
287.23 Trades] Traders *1746*, *1746*; traders *1755*

Word Division
Copy Text
Vice-roy

Edited Text
None

Observations Occasioned by Reading a Paper, Entitled, the Case of the Woollen Manufacturers of Dublin, &c

Textual Account

The '*Paper*' to which this responds (see Appendix C, pp. 344–9) was a half-sheet, published in November 1733; one of the merchants criticised in it published a rejoinder in the *Dublin Journal* in December, and it is around this time that Swift's response, excoriating the said manufacturers for importing and selling foreign goods, was presumably written (see Davis, vol. XII, pp. xxvi–xxvii).

No printing from this time has been found, and it was not published until 1789, when John Nichols put it in his volume of works explicitly not included in Sheridan's edition of 1784; it is presumed that Nichols, as an indefatigable literary historian, had access to a manuscript, though the reasons why it was not included previously, and evaded Sheridan, Deane Swift, Hawkesworth and Faulkner before him, are likely to remain mysterious. Lacking a mode of comparison, it can only be assumed that Nichols modernised some features, such as capitals and spellings that had become slightly obscure.

Copy Text
BL, 633.g.18.

Pieces, 1789

TS 121. *ESTC* T39427

Title: MISCELLANEOUS | PIECES, | IN PROSE AND VERSE. | BY | The Rev. Dr. JONATHAN SWIFT, | DEAN OF ST. PATRICK'S, DUBLIN. | NOT INSERTED IN MR. SHERIDAN's EDITION | OF THE DEAN's WORKS. | L O N D O N: | PRINTED FOR C. DILLY, IN THE POULTRY. | MDCCLXXXIX.

Collation: 8°, A^4 B–P^8 Q^7 R^8 S^4

Pagination: *i–v* vi *vii–viii 1* 2–262

Contents: A1^r title page; A1^v blank; A2^{r-v} advertisement; A3^{r-v} 'LIST of DESIDERATA in SWIFT's WORKS'; A4^{r-v} contents; B1^r–S4^v text

Observations: I8^r–K2^r; 127–31

Typography: 32 lines per page (I8^v); type-page 185 (200) × 91 mm; 20 lines of roman type 106 mm

Copies consulted: BL, 633.g.18.

Emendations

[None]

Word Division
Copy Text
handicrafts-men

Edited Text
None

A Letter on the Fishery

Textual Account

Francis Grant, a London businessman interested in the effect of fishing upon the British and Irish economies, had written to Swift soliciting his support in 1734, enclosing his pamphlet of the same year, *The British Fishery Recommended to Parliament.* Swift's letter in reply was absorbed by Grant sixteen years later into his *Letter to a Member of Parliament* (1750), where it is used to bolster his argument and authority. It was first reprinted and called *A Letter on the Fishery* in *A Supplement to The Works of Dr. Swift* (London: Francis Cogan, 1752; TS 83), pp. 70–4, a replication of Grant's text, down to capitals and pointing, and then in the *Gentleman's Magazine* for 1762 (vol. 32, pp. 111–14). It was included by Faulkner the same year in volume X of his ongoing *Works* (distinctively, this edition contains a mistaken opening note about Admiral Vernon, erroneously thought by Faulkner to be Swift's correspondent because of his authorship of *Considerations upon the White Herring and Cod Fisheries* in 1749; see Davis, vol. XII, p. xxxii). It was then reprinted in London in 1765, in Deane Swift's quarto edition.

The copy text for this short work is Grant's pamphlet of 1750, as the first printing; it has been collated with both Faulkner and Deane Swift, and with the versions in *A Supplement* and the *Gentleman's Magazine*, though they lack authority, and are not detailed in the following descriptions. The variants are neither numerous, profound nor significant, and Grant's printing of his copy of Swift's letter, separated from the house style and polish of Faulkner and Deane Swift, remains probably the most accurate representation of Swift's epistolary intentions.

Copy Text
CUL, ddd.25.58.

London, 1750

ESTC T38049

Title: A | LETTER | TO A | Member of Parliament, | Concerning the | *Free British Fisheries*; | WITH | Draughts of a Herring-Buss and Nets, and | the Harbour and Town of *Peterhead*. | – – – – – - With adventurous Oar, | How to dash wide the Billow; nor look on, | Shamefully passive, while *Batavian* Fleets | Defraud us of the glittering finny Swarms, | That heave our Firths, and crowd upon our Shores: | How all-enlivening Trade to rouse, and wing, | The prosperous Sail from every growing Port, | Unchalleng'd, round the sea-incircled Globe; | And thus, in Soul united as in Name, | Bid *Britain* reign the Mistress of the Deep. | Thomson's *Seasons*. | *LONDON*: | Printed for R. Spavan, in *Ivy-Lane, Pater-* | *Noster-Row*, 1750.

Collation: 8° A, B–G⁴

Pagination: *1–2* 1–44 *48*

Contents: A1ʳ title page; A1ᵛ blank; B1ʳ–G4ᵛ text

Letter on the Fishery: C1ᵛ–3ᵛ; 10–14

Typography: 30 lines per page (C2ʳ); type-page 141 (156) × 79 mm; 20 lines of roman type 94 mm

Copies consulted: CUL, ddd.25.58 [bound with nine contemporary pamphlets on questions of economics, trade and industry]; BL, 808.2 (9) [one of eleven briny contemporary pamphlets].

Works, 1762
TS 45a (6a). *ESTC* N31128
Title: VOLUME X. | OF THE | Author's WORKS. | CONTAINING, | Sermons on several Subjects; | AND | Other PIECES on different | Occasions. | [rule] | [ornament] | [double rule] | *DUBLIN*: | Printed by GEORGE FAULKNER | M, dcc, lxii
Collation: 8°: A^3 B–2E^8 2F1 [2F1 printed as A1]
Pagination: i–iii iv–v vi *3* 4–436
Contents: A1^r title page; A1^v blank; A2^r–A3^r contents; A3^v blank; B1^r–2F1^v text
Letter on the Fishery: 2E7^r–2F1^v; 431–6
Typography: 31 lines per page (EE8^v); type-page 144 (155) × 85 mm; 20 lines of roman type 91 mm
Copies consulted: Bodl., Vet. A5 e. 4856; Bodl., Vet. A4 e.3055/10.

Deane Swift, *Works*, 1765
TS 87. *ESTC* T52748
Title: THE | WORKS | OF | Dr. JONATHAN SWIFT | Dean of St. Patrick's, Dublin. | VOLUME VIII. Part II. | COLLECTED AND REVISED | By DEANE SWIFT, Esq; | of Goodrich, in Hereford-shire. | *Hæ tibi erunt artes.* Virgil. | [double-rule] | LONDON: | Printed for W. Johnston, in Ludgate-Street | M DCC LXV.
Collation: 4°: A–2N^4
Pagination: i–ii iii–vii viii *1* 2–279 *280*
Contents: A1^r title page; A1^v 'ERRATA'; A2^r–A4^r contents; A4^v blank; B–2N4^r text; 2N4^v blank
Letter on the Fishery: 2M1^v–2M3^r; 266–9
Typography: 34 lines per page (2M2^r); type-page 200 (257) × 136 mm; 20 lines of roman type 104 mm
Copies consulted: BL, 90.d.8.

Emendation
297.7 not worth] *1762*; no worth

Historical Collation
295.1 [*Before Title*] EDWARD VERNON, Esq; the brave *English* Admiral, who, with six Ships only, took the Town, Citadel and Port of *Portobello* in *America*, in the Year 1739, from the *Spaniards*; having the *British* Fishery much at Heart, in Opposition to the *Dutch*, wrote a Letter to Dr. SWIFT,

D. S. P. D. on that Occasion, to which the following is an Answer. A Letter on the Fishery. *1762*
295.1 To FRANCIS GRANT, Esq; MERCHANT in LONDON. *1765*
295.3 1734] 1733–4 *1765*
295.12 our] their *1762*
296.4 oppressing] opposing *1765*
296.7 (as you call it)] *om. 1765*
297.7 no worth] not worth *1762*
297.13 six and seven] six or seven *1762*
299.10 are hardly] hardly are *1765*
299.12 300] 30,000 *1765*
299.15 Part Value] part of the value *1765*
300.7 *obedient humble Servant*] obedient servant *1765*

Word Division
Copy Text
None

Edited Text
None

The Rev. Dean Swift's Reasons Against Lowering the Gold and Silver Coin

Textual Account

Swift's speech against lowering the value of Irish coin was given, as its title page suggests, on 24 April 1736, and published to accompany an unattributed paper arguing the same. It was published by Edward Waters, printer of previously controversial works, including Swift's *Proposal for the Universal Use of Irish Manufacture* (1720), for which he was briefly imprisoned (see Ehrenpreis, vol. III, pp. 128–30, and Ferguson, pp. 49–59). The use of Waters rather than Faulkner at this point suggests either that Swift was not behind the publication, or that it was a by-product rather than an intention. The printing by Waters is not a thing of beauty: using the sort of rhetorical italic emphasis redolent of the *Drapier's Letters* and Harding's printing of *A Modest Proposal*, it squeezes the subtitle and all of Swift's badly-inked text onto one page. It resembles a memorial record of the speech, rather than a carefully written version, and is marked by printing errors and failures of plural agreement.

TEXTUAL ACCOUNT: REASONS AGAINST LOWERING THE COIN 487

It would seem that lack of authorial acknowledgement, and the absence of any manuscript to support its attribution, kept the work from Faulkner, Deane Swift, Nichols and other editors of the burgeoning Swift canon in the eighteenth century. As Davis points out (vol. XIII, p. 223), the work was 'overlooked' by editors until mentioned in Craik's *Life* (1882) and included in vol. VII of Temple Scott's edition (London: George Bell and Sons, 1905). The copy text is 1736, the only pre-twentieth-century printing. This edition follows one of Temple Scott's emendations of *Reasons against Lowering the Coin* in his edition (vol. VII, pp. 357–8).

Copy Text

BL, 8225.aa7.

Dublin 1736

TS 754. *ESTC* T46482
Title: REASONS | Why we should not | Lower the COINS | Now current in this | KINGDOM. | Occasioned by a Paper Intituled | *REMARKS on the* Coins current *in this* | KINGDOM. | To which is added, | *The Rev.* Dean SWIFT'*s* | OPINION, | Delivered by him, in an Assembly of above | One hundred and Fifty eminent Merchants | who met at the Guild Hall, on *Saturday* | the 24th of *April*, 1736, in order to draw | up their Petition, and Present it to his Grace | the Lord-Lieutenant against lowering said | Coin. | [rule] | *Dublin*: Printed and sold by *E. Waters* in *Dame-street.*
Collation: 8°: A^4
Pagination: *1–2*, 3–8
Contents: A1^r title page; A1^v Swift's Speech; A2^r–4^v text
Typography: 41 lines per page (A1^v); type-page 141 (151) × 81 mm; 20 lines of roman type 67 mm
Copies consulted: BL, 8225.aa7.

Emendations

303.4 hearts] heart [*Temple Scott*]
303.6 Power] Bower

Word Division
Copy Text
None

Edited Text
None

A Proposal for Giving Badges to the Beggars

Textual Account

This pamphlet is dated 22 April 1737, and highly unusual in being acknowledged by its author. Swift's ideas about badging the itinerant population of Dublin were deep-seated, as can be seen in the unfinished *Upon Giving Badges to the Poor*, begun in 1726. The *Proposal* was published soon after its date of composition by Faulkner in Dublin in 1737, and reprinted in London that year, as part of the Faulkner–Bowyer arrangement (see Textual Introduction, pp. 381–2): it was entered as number 2379, A39 (6 May 1737) in the Bowyer ledgers, and published by T. Cooper (and was advertised in the *Craftsman* for 28 May). It is near identical to Faulkner's text, save for two errors in the latter, within three lines of each other ('word' for 'world', and a non-plural agreement, both corrected in subsequent editions).

It was reprinted by Faulkner in a new volume of the *Works* (1738), and in the same year in London as part of *Political Tracts*, a Faulkner–Bowyer work, number 2601 (21 September 1738), where *A Proposal* is a reprint in every detail of the text of Faulkner's 1738 *Works*, down to pagination and signatures. All these editions have been collated, though the spartan Historical Collation will indicate how little they differ: Faulkner's 1737 Dublin edition (with a splendid illustration of M. B. Drapier as the title page ornament) is the copy text, given the alacrity with which Swift must have delivered and authorised it, along with its status as the first published text. The 1737 London edition does not follow it in commencing paragraphs with small capitals, is less inclined to hyphenate or italicise, and re-punctuates according to its own scheme, yet, like the other editions that follow Faulkner (including his own reprint in 1738), it is nearly identical in terms of substantives. Texts are identified as follows: Faulkner, Dublin (1737a); Cooper, London (1737b); Faulkner, *Works* (1738).

Copy Text

CUL, Williams 339.

Dublin, 1737a

TS 755. *ESTC* N12214

Title: A | PROPOSAL | FOR GIVING | BADGES | TO THE | BEGGARS | IN ALL THE| Parishes of *DUBLIN.* | [rule] | By the Dean of St. PATRICK's. | [rule] | [ornament labelled 'M. B. Drapier'] | [double-rule] |

DUBLIN: | Printed by GEORGE FAULKNER, Bookseller, in | *Essex-Street*, opposite to the Bridge, | M DCC XXX VII.
Collation: 8°: A^8 B^4 C^2
Pagination: *1–2*, 3–25, *26–8*
Contents: A1^r title page; A1^v blank; A2^r–C1^r text; C1^v–2^v advertisement for Faulkner
Typography: 27 lines per page (A3^r); type-page 128 (140) × 70 mm; 20 lines of roman type 94 mm
Copies consulted: CUL, Hib.8.737.13; CUL, Williams 339; TCC, Rothschild 27.2; TCC, Rothschild 27.3.

London, 1737b

TS 756. *ESTC* T146620
Title: A | PROPOSAL | FOR GIVING | BADGES | TO THE | BEGGARS | IN ALL THE| PARISHES of *DUBLIN*. | BY THE | DEAN of St. PATRICK's | [flower] | *LONDON*, | Printed for T. COOPER at the *Globe* in *Pater Noster Row*. | MDCCXXXVII. | Price Six Pence.
Collation: 4°: A–B^4
Pagination: *1–2*, 3–16
Contents: A1^r title page; A1^v blank; A2^r–B4^v text
Typography: 29 lines per page (A2^v); type-page 174 (184) × 115 mm; 20 lines of roman type 117 mm
Copies consulted:
CUL, Williams 340 [Typewritten note posted onto front r: 'A / Proposal / For Giving / Badges / To The / Beggars / In All The / Parishes of Dublin. / By The Dean of St. Patrick's. / ornament / London, / Printed for T. Cooper at the Globe in Pater Noster Row. / MDCCXXXVII. / Price Six Pence. First Edition. Small 4to, half calf. A very rare tract of Swift. It was also published in Dublin, 1737, 8vo., and was reprinted in Faulkner's edition of Swift's Works, vol.vi (1738). Collation: A & B in fours. Contents: Title, A1 [a inserted in ink]; Blank, A 2 crossed out and 1b written over; Text, A2 to B4; 8 leaves, 16pp. including title.']
CUL, Hib.5.737.4

Works, 1738

TS 42. *ESTC* T139456
Title: VOLUME VI. | OF THE | AUTHOR's WORKS. | CONTAINING | The PUBLICK SPIRIT of the | WHIGS; and other Pieces of Politi- | cal

Writings, &c. With POLITE | CONVERSATION, &c. | [double-rule] | [ornament] | [double-rule] | *DUBLIN:* | Printed by and for GEORGE FAULKNER. | M,DCC,XXX,VIII.
Work title: (L7ʳ): A | PROPOSAL | FOR GIVING | BADGES | TO THE | BEGGARS | IN ALL THE| Parishes of *DUBLIN.* | [rule] | By the Dean of St. PATRICK's. | [rule] | [ornament] | [double-rule] | *DUBLIN:* | Printed by and for GEORGE FAULKNER. | [rule] | M,DCC,XXXVIII.
Collation: 8°: π² A⁸ B–O⁸ P² Q–2B⁸ 2C⁷
Pagination: *i–xx, 1–3* 4–386
Contents: π1ʳ title page; π1ᵛ blank; π2ʳ preface; π2ᵛ contents; A1ʳ–8ʳ subscribers; A8ᵛ blank; B1ʳ–2C7ᵛ text
Proposal for Giving Badges: L7ʳ–M6ʳ; 157–71
Typography: 36 lines per page (M2ʳ); type-page 150 (160) × 82 mm; 20 lines of roman type 83 mm
Copies consulted: CUL, Williams 22; CUL, Hib.7.738.14; Bodl., Rad. e. 236.

Political Tracts, 1738
TS 25 (7). *ESTC* T43973
Title: POLITICAL | TRACTS. | [rule] | VOL. II. | [rule] | By the AUTHOR of | *GULLIVER's* TRAVELS. | [rule] | [ornament] | [rule] | *LONDON*, | Printed for C. DAVIS in *Pater-Noster-Row.*| MDCCXXXVIII
Collation: 8°: A² B–U⁸ X²
Pagination: *i–iv, 1–288, 289–308*
Contents: A3ʳ title page; A3ᵛ blank; A4ʳ⁻ᵛ contents; B–T8ᵛ text; U–X2ʳ index; X2ᵛ blank
Proposal for Giving Badges: L7ʳ–M6ʳ; 157–71
Typography: 36 lines per page (M2ʳ); type-page 150 (160) × 82 mm; 20 lines of roman type 83 mm
Copies consulted: BL, 1477.dd.48.

Emendations

312.13 find some weak Attempts have] *1738*; had some weak Attempts to have
313.13 be understood] be be understood
314.23 Word] *1737b*; World
314.24 Justices] *1737b*; Justice
317.23 was bestowed] *1738*; Charity bestowed

Historical Collation

312.13 had some weak Attempts to have] *1737a, 1737b*; find some weak Attempts have *1738*

314.23 Word] *1737b*+; World *1737a*
314.24 Justices] *1737b*+; Justice *1737a*

Word Division
Copy Text
Street-walkers
Butter-milk
Whore-mongers

Edited Text
None

Associated Materials

Textual Accounts

I. *Hints for Intelligencer Papers, and Maxims Examined*

From the Piozzi papers, in the John Rylands Library, Eng. MSS. 659, in three parts:

1. 659 (9) 'Hints Education of Ldyes'. *Description*: autograph hand, folded to make 2 leaves, 149 × 92 mm. Endorsed 2^v: Hints / Eductn de dames / pour une Intelligencer

    Contents: fo. 1^r–1^v, text ['Hints']; 2^r text [draft of 'To Mr Gay on his being Steward to the Duke of Queensbury']; 2^v endorsement

2. 659 (10) 'Intelligencer'. *Description*: autograph hand, 2 leaves, 151 × 92 mm; endorsed on 2^v

    Contents: fo. 1^r text. 1^v–2^r blank. 2^v endorsement

3. 659 (11a & b) 'Maxims Examind'. *Description*: autograph hand, 3 leaves, 159 × 103 mm. 3 leaves on 3pp. – one leaf torn and pasted to other sheet of writing paper; folded to make two leaves

    Contents: fo. 1^r text; 1^v blank; 2^{r-v} text

II. *'A Letter to the Printer'*

Dated 13 December 1737, and published as a preface to Alexander MacAulay's *Some Thoughts on the Tillage of Ireland* (Dublin: Faulkner, 1738; TS 769, T122646), from which the text here is taken. Despite the earlier date, the London edition (printed for T. Cooper; TS 770, T49412) is a reprint, and part of the Faulkner–Bowyer arrangement of reprinting Irish texts in England (see *Bowyer Ledgers*, number 2498; 31 January 1738).

Copy Text

CUL, Williams 461.

Appendices

Textual Accounts

A. To the R—d Dr. J—n S—t, The Memorial of the Poor Inhabitants, Tradesmen, and Labourers of the Kingdom of Ireland.

Printed from the first edition of the pamphlet (Dublin: Thomas Walsh, 1728; T1996). Published in March; see Textual Account of *An Answer to a Paper*, above, pp. 360–1).

Copy Text

CUL, Williams 290.

B. *The* CRAFTSMAN'S *First Letter of* ADVICE, *Saturday 7 November 1730*

This paper from the *Craftsman* was followed by a second *Letter of Advice* on the same subject on Wednesday 18 November. In the first collected edition of the *Craftsman* (London, 1731, vol. VII, p. 139), the 'First Letter of *ADVICE*' was removed as a title. It was placed in sequence, but given the wrong date '12 Dec. 1730', and numbered 232. It was first republished in relation to Swift's response in Faulkner's 1758 *Works*, vol. IX, where it appears at the end of the volume in an Appendix, consisting of itself and the *Answer* (for description, see the Textual Account, above, pp. 413–14).

Copy Text

TCD, Press A.7.2./98.

C. *The Case of the Woolen Manufacturers of the City of Dublin, and Liberties Thereunto Adjoyning, Truly Stated...*

Dublin: Printed in the year, 1733; T.189440. Printed from this 1733 broadsheet, the only edition of this work.

Copy Text

NLI, ILB.04. p2 (9).

D. *To the Author of those Intelligencers printed at Dublin*

Taken from the only edition of this anonymous pamphlet (New York: Printed and Sold by J. Peter Zenger, 1733; W4428). Zenger is better known as the printer and publisher of the *New York Weekly Journal*, the subject of a historically important libel trial in 1735. The 'Roscommon' classmark is the result of a quotation from a poem by Wentworth Dillon, 4th Earl of Roscommon, appearing at the pamphlet's end, and subsequent misidentification of him as its author.

Copy Text

New York Public Library, *KD 1733 (Roscommon...).

E. Dublin Weekly Journal, *Saturday, June 7th. 1729.*

Taken from the first uncollected edition of the journal.

Copy Text

BL, PENN.NT16 NPL.

BIBLIOGRAPHY

This bibliography excludes single-work editions of Swift, but does include items listed in the abbreviations and the relevant Swift collected works. Publishers' details have been omitted for all works published before 1900, except where relevant.

Primary Sources

Manuscript

British Library, London:
 Egmont papers (Add. MSS 46978–89, 47000–1B, 47089, 47009OB, 47013A, 47032–3)
 Hardwicke papers (Add. MSS 35585–6, 35892, 36134–5, 36138–9)
 Newcastle papers (Add. MSS 32687–92)
 Southwell papers (Add. MSS, 21122–3, 38016)
 Lady Suffolk papers (Add. 22625–6)
 Lady Sundon papers (Add. MSS 20102–5)
 Wentworth papers (Add. MS 22222, 22228)

Christ Church, Oxford:
 Wake papers (Arch Epist. W. xiv)

Dublin City Library and Archive, Dublin:
 Dublin Corporation 'Monday books'

Irish Architectural Archive, Dublin:
 Castletown papers

Marsh's Library, Dublin:
 MS Z. 3.1.1

The National Archives [of the UK], Kew:
 State Papers (Ireland) 1727–38 (SP 63/388–401)

National Art Library, Victoria & Albert Museum, London:
  'Answer to several letters from unknown hands', Forster MS 546, F.48.G/2 Item 19
  'Letter on Maculla's project', Forster MS 523, F.48.G/2 Item 8
  'Letter to Archbishop', Forster MS 520, F.48.G.6/2 Item 7
  'Upon giving Badges to the Poor', Forster MS 518, F.48.G/2 Item 6

National Library of Ireland, Dublin:
  Bayly letterbook (MS 16,139)
  Castle Durrow papers (MS 11,478)
  De Vesci papers (MS 38,869, 38,876, 38,881–2, 38,900)
  Dodington papers (MS 16,139)
  Fownes papers (MS 8,801–2)
  Lane papers (MS 8,645)
  Mahon papers (MS 47,891/1)
  Shannon papers (MS 13,297)
  Smythe of Barbavilla papers (MS 41,577–82, 41,585–7)
  Southwell papers (MS 875)
  Talbot-Crosbie papers (unsorted collection, P.C. 188)
  Wicklow papers (MSS 38,593, 38,597–9, 38,632)

National University of Ireland, Galway, Hardiman Library:
  Galway Corporation archives

Public Record Office of Northern Ireland, Belfast:
  Armagh diocesan registry papers (DIO/4)
  Chatsworth papers (T/3158/13)
  Dobbs papers (D/162)
  Foster/Massereene papers (D/207, D/562)
  Shannon papers (D/2707)
  Wilmot papers (T/3019)

Royal Dublin Society, Dublin:
  Dublin Society minute books, 1731–41 (nos. 1–2)

Royal Society of Antiquaries of Ireland, Dublin:
  'Book of Brothers', Guild of the Blessed Virgin Mary, 1722–43 (RSAI/BV/WVRS/009)
  Minute book of Guild of the Blessed Virgin Mary, 1734–60 (RSAI/BV/WVRS/007)

John Rylands Library, Manchester:
'Hints for Intelligencer and Maxims', Rylands English MS 659

Surrey History Centre, Woking:
Brodrick papers (MS 1248/7)

Trinity College Dublin:
Archbishop King letterbooks (MSS 750/8–9)
Lyons collection (MSS 1995–2008)

Printed

A. Newspapers and periodicals

Castle Courant (Dublin)
The Craftsman (London)
Daily Courant (London)
Daily Journal (London)
Daily Post (London)
Daily Post Boy (London)
Dublin Gazette
Dublin Intelligence
Dublin Journal
Dublin Mercury
Dublin Post Man
Dublin Weekly Journal
Evening Journal (London)
Evening Post (London)
Flying Post (London)
Fog's Weekly Journal (London)
London Daily Post
London Evening Post
London Intelligence
Mist's Weekly Journal (London)
Post Boy and Historical Account (London)
Post Man and Historical Account (London)
Pue's Occurrences (Dublin)
St James's Evening Post (London)

B. Books, Pamphlets and Editions

Abernethy, John, *The Nature and Consequences of the Sacramental Test Considered*, Dublin, 1731.

An Account of the Journey-men Weavers Grateful Congratulation of the Rev. Dr. Swift Dean of St. Patrick's Safe Arrival, with his Kind Answer, and Bounty to Their Corporation, Sep. the 5th 1726, [Dublin], 1726.
Addison, Joseph, *The Old Whig*, 2 parts, London, 1719.
An Address Humbly Offered to the Mature Consideration of the Right Honourable the Lord Mayor, Aldermen, Common Council, and Citizens of the City of Dublin, Dublin, 1733.
Address to Humphrey French esq; Late Lord Mayor of the City of Dublin. From the hon. Senate of Trinity College, Dublin, Dublin, [1733].
Address of the Society of Yellows, to Alderman Humphry French, Late Lord Mayor of the City of Dublin, [Dublin], 1733.
Advice from the Bear in Crane-Lane, [Dublin, 1729].
Advice to the Free-men of the City of Dublin; in The Choice of a Member to Represent Them In Parliament, [Dublin], 1733.
Advice to the Industrious Tradesmen and Manufacturers of Ireland, upon the Present Regulation of the Coin, [Dublin, 1737].
An Answer to the Remonstrances of the People of Ireland, against Making any Alteration in the Coin, London, 1736.
An Apology for the Clergy of Ireland in Respect of their Civil Rights, Especially as to Agistment for Dry and Barren Cattle, Dublin, 1737/8.
An Argument upon the Woollen Manufacture of Great Britain: Plainly Demonstrating, that Ireland Must be Speedily Employ'd Therein, as the Only Means to Recover its Decay and Prevent its Ruin, 2nd edn, Dublin, 1737.
'An Old Whig', *Reasons Against a War, in a Letter to a Member of Parliament*, London, 1727.
Arbuckle, James, *A Collection of Letters and Essays on Several Subjects, Lately Publish'd in the Dublin Journal*, 2 vols., Dublin, 1729.
[Arbuckle, James], *The Tribune*, London, 1729.
[Arnall, William], *The Free Briton, Number 50, Containing Reflections on the Irish Troops in the Service of France; with a Defence of Royal Licences to Raise Recruits in Ireland ...*, London, 1730.
Aston, Miles, *An Heroick Poem on the Weaving Trade Setting Forth its Antiquity and Use, Humbly Inscribed to, its Great Patron Doctor Swift*, Dublin, [1734].
Astræa's Congratulation: an Ode upon Alderman Humphrey French being Elected Representative for the City of Dublin, [Dublin], 1733.
Atterbury, Francis, *The Epistolary Correspondence ... of the Right Reverend Francis Atterbury, D.D. Lord Bishop of Rochester ...*, 3 vols., London, 1783–4.
Bacon, Thomas, *Laws of Maryland at Large ...*, Annapolis, 1765.
Barber, Mary, *The Poetry of Mary Barber*, ed. Bernard Tucker, Lampeter: Edwin Mellen Press, 1992.

Berkeley, George, *The Works of George Berkeley, Bishop of Cloyne*, ed. A. A. Luce and T. E. Jessop, 9 vols., London: Nelson, 1948–57.
Bindon, David, *A Scheme for Supplying Industrious Men with Money to Carry on their Trades, and for Better Providing for the Poor of Ireland*, Dublin, [1729].
An Abstract of the Number of Protestant and Popish Families in the Several Counties and Provinces of Ireland, Taken from the Returns made by the Hearthmoney Collectors ... in the years 1732 and 1733, Dublin, 1736.
A Letter from a Merchant who has Left off Trade to a Member of Parliament. In which the Case of the British and Irish Manufacture of Linen, Threads, and Tapes, is Fairly Stated, 1738.
Blackwell, James, *A Friendly Apology for a Certain Justice of the Peace, by way of Defence of Hartley Hutchinson, esq.*, [?Dublin, 1730].
Bolingbroke, Henry St John, Viscount, *Contributions to The Craftsman*, ed. Simon Varey, Oxford: Clarendon Press, 1982.
The Book of Common Prayer, and Administration of the Sacraments, and Other Rites and Ceremonies of the Church, According to the Use of the Church of Ireland ..., Dublin, 1716.
Boulter, Hugh, *Letters Written by His Excellency, Hugh Boulter, D.D. Lord Primate of All Ireland ...*, 2 vols., Dublin, 1770.
Boyse, Joseph, *A Sermon Preach'd on the First of March, 1714/15. Being the Day of Publick Thanksgiving to Almighty God, for the Peaceable Accession of His Sacred Majesty King George to the Throne; and for Disappointing the Designs of the Pretender, and All his Adherents*, Dublin, 1715.
Brady, W. M., *Clerical and Parochial Records of Cork, Cloyne, and Ross*, 3 vols., vols. I and II, London, 1864; III, Dublin, 1864.
Brewster, Sir Francis, *Essays on Trade and Navigation ...*, London, 1695.
A Discourse Concerning Ireland and the Different Interests Thereof ..., London, 1698.
New Essay's on Trade ..., London, 1702.
A Brief Character of Ireland, with Some Observations on the Customs &c. of the Meaner Inhabitants of That Kingdom, London, 1692.
A Brief Journal of What Passed in the City of Marseilles, While It Was Afflicted with the Plague, in the Year 1720 ..., London, [1721].
The British Empire in America, Consider'd. In a Second Letter, from a Gentleman of Barbadoes, to His Friend in London, London, 1732.
Browne, Sir John, *An Essay on Trade in General; and, on That of Ireland in Particular*, Dublin, 1728.
A Reply to the Observer on Seasonable Remarks, Dublin, 1728.
Seasonable Remarks on Trade, with Some Reflections on the Advantages that Might Accrue to Great Britain, by a Proper Regulation of the Trade of Ireland, Dublin, 1728.

The Benefits Which Arise to a Trading People from Navigable Rivers. To which Are Added, Some Considerations on the Origin of Loughs, and Bogs ..., Dublin, 1729.

The Drapier Reviv'd: or, Considerations on the Inconveniences Which the People of Ireland Labour Under for the Want of Small Change, [Dublin, 1729; 2nd edn, Dublin, 1731].

Reflections Little to the Purpose, on a Paper Less to the Purpose, Dublin, 1729.

A Scheme of the Money-matters of Ireland, in which the Consequences of Raising or Lowering the Coin, are Impartially Consider'd, Dublin, 1729.

The Lucubrations of Sallmanazor Histrum, esq. ..., Dublin, 1730.

[Browne, Sir John], *To the R——d Dr. J—n S—t; the Memorial of the Poor Inhabitants, Tradesmen, and Labourers of the Kingdom of Ireland*, [Dublin], 1728.

Browne, Joseph, *St James's Park*, London, 1708.

Browne, Peter. *A Discourse of Drinking Healths. Wherein the Great Evil of This Prevailing Custom is Shewn; and the Obligation Which Lieth upon All Good Christians to Suppress and Discountenance It to the Utmost of Their Power*, Dublin, 1716.

Of Drinking to the Memory of the Dead. Being the Substance of a Discourse Deliver'd to the Clergy of the Diocese of Cork, on the Fourth of November, 1713, Dublin, 1713.

Bruce, Edward, *A Letter to a Member of Parliament, Concerning the Late Reduction of the Gold-coin*, Dublin, 1738.

Calendar of the Ancient Records of Dublin, ed. J. T. Gilbert and R. M. Gilbert, 17 vols., Dublin: Joseph Dollard, 1889–1921.

Calendar of State Papers, Colonial Series: America and the West Indies, 45 vols., London: HMSO, 1860–1994.

Clayton, Robert, *A Sermon Preach'd in the Parish Church of St. Mary, Dublin: March the 22d. 1729[/30]. At the General Meeting of the Children Educated in the Charity-Schools in Dublin*, Dublin, 1730.

Coghill, Marmaduke, *Letters of Marmaduke Coghill, 1722–1738*, ed. D. W. Hayton, Dublin: Irish Manuscripts Commission, 2005.

A Collection of Select Aphorisms and Maxims; with Several Historical Observations, Curious Remarks, and Characters of Persons and Things, Dublin, 1722.

Come and See, Come and See. Or, An Account of a Cruel Monster Newly Come to Town, Spew'd up by a Scotch Cod near Belfast in the North of Ireland ..., [?Dublin], 1714.

The Comical Pilgrim; or, Travels of a Cynick Philosopher, London, 1722.

A Comparison between the British Sugar Colonies and New England, as They Relate to the Interest of Great Britain, London, 1732.

A Congratulatory Speech of the Loyal and Charitable Society of Woollen Broad-Cloath-Weavers, in Honour to the Reverend Doctor Jonathan Swift, [Dublin, 1727].
The Conolly Archive, ed. Patrick Walsh and A. P. W. Malcomson, Dublin: Irish Manuscripts Commission, 2010.
Considerations on Two Papers lately Published. The First call'd, Seasonable Remarks ... and the Other, An Essay on Trade in General, and That of Ireland in Particular, Dublin, [1728].
Considerations upon Two Bills Sent Down from the R[ight] H[onourable] the H[ouse] of L[ords] to the H[onoura]ble H[ouse] of C[ommons] Relating to the Clergy of I[relan]d, London, 1732.
[?Cox, Sir Richard], *Some Observations on the Present State of Ireland, Particularly with Relation to the Woollen Manufacture*, Dublin, 1731.
Crisis; or, The Last Stake: being Impartial Advice, to the Citizens of Dublin, on the Election &c., [Dublin, 1730].
Crouch, Nathaniel, *The English Empire in America. Or, a View of the Dominions of the Crown of England in the West-Indies*, Dublin, 1729.
D'anvers, Caleb, *The Twickenham Hotch-Potch ...*, London, 1728.
Davenant, Charles, *An Essay upon the Probable Methods of Making a People Gainers in the Ballance of Trade*, London, 1699.
de Bry, Theodore, *Americae Tertia Pars Memorabilem Provinciae Brasiliae Historiam Continens*, Frankfurt, 1592.
Defoe, Daniel, *Augusta Triumphans*, London, 1728.
Delany, Patrick, *The Poems of Patrick Delany ...*, ed. Robert Hogan and D. C. Mell, Newark, NJ: University of Delaware Press, 2006.
Dennis, John, *An Essay on the Operas after the Italian Manner, Which Are About to Be Establish'd on the English Stage: with Some Reflections on the Damage Which They May Bring to the Public*, London, 1706.
The Stage Defended, from Scripture, Reason, Experience, and the Common Sense of Mankind, for Two Thousand Years ..., London, 1726.
The Critical Works of John Dennis, ed. E. N. Hooker, 2 vols., Baltimore: The Johns Hopkins Press, 1939–43.
A Description of the City of Dublin in Ireland, wherein, Besides taking Notice of Every Thing Remarkable in the City, and the Grandeur of the Court, is Represented the Happy Situation of Ireland for Commerce ..., London, 1732.
Dobbs, Arthur, *An Essay on the Trade and Improvement of Ireland*, Dublin, 1729.
An Essay on the Trade and Improvement of Ireland. Part II, Dublin, 1731.
[?Dobbs, Arthur], *A Letter in Answer to a Paper, intitled, an Appeal to the Reverend Dean Swift. By the Author of Considerations on Two Papers, &c*, Dublin, 1728.

The Drapier's Advice to the Freemen and Freeholders of the City of Dublin, [Dublin, 1729].
The Drapier's Miscellany, in Verse and Prose ..., Dublin, 1733.
Dryden, John, *The Letters of John Dryden*, ed. C. E. Ward, Durham, NC: Duke University Press, 1942.
The Works of John Dryden, ed. Edward Niles Hooker, H. T. Swedenberg, jr and Vincent A. Dearing *et al.*, 20 vols., Berkeley, CA: University of California Press, 1956–2000.
The Duchess of Marlborough's Vision, [London], 1711.
D'Urfey, Thomas, *The English Stage Italianiz'd, in a New Dramatic Entertainment, Called Dido and Æneas*, London, 1727.
[?Dunkin, William], *A Vindication of the Libel: or, a New Ballad: written by a Shoe-Boy, on an Attorney, who was formerly a Shoe-Boy*, [?Dublin, 1730].
An Elegy. On the Much Lamented Death of Alderman John Stoyte, esq; Member of Parliament for this City, Dublin, 1727.
An Elegy on the Much Lamented Death of Alderman Paeter Verdoen, Kt, Dublin, 1731.
Elegy on the Much Lamented Death of the Right Honourable William Whitshed, [Dublin, 1727].
Enquiries into the Principal Causes of the General Poverty of the Common People of Ireland. With Remedies Propos'd for Removing of Them, Dublin, 1725.
An Enquiry about the Wearing of Lawrels, [Dublin, 1714].
Error in Choice, or A Mistake on the Right Side, [Dublin, 1729].
An Essay, or, Modest Proposal, of a Way to Encrease the Number of People, and Consequently the Strength of this Kingdom ... [?London, 1693].
An Essay upon the Taste and Writings of the Present Times ..., London, [1728].
Eustace, P. Beryl, and Eilish Ellis, eds., *Registry of Deeds, Ireland, Abstracts of Wills*, 3 vols., Dublin: Stationery Office, 1954–84.
Forman, Charles, *A Letter to the Right Honourable Sir Robert Sutton, for Disbanding the Irish Regiments in the Service of France and Spain*, London, 1728.
A Letter to the Right Honourable Sir Robert Walpole, for Re establishing the Woollen Manufacturies of Great Britain upon their Ancient Footing, by Encouraging the Linen Manufacturies of Ireland, London, 1732.
Defence of the Courage, Honour and Loyalty of the Irish Nation, in Answer to the Scandalous Reflections of the Free-Briton and Others, 5th edn, London, 1735.
Fownes, Sir William, *Methods Proposed for Regulating the Poor. Supporting of Some, and Employing Others: According to Their Several Capacities*, Dublin, 1723–4; repr. 1725.
The Free-Man's Letter of Advice to his Country-men and Fellow-citizens, in Behalf of the Late Lord-mayor, Dublin, 1733.

A Full Vindication of Humphry French, Late Lord Mayor of the City of Dublin ..., Dublin, 1733.
Fuller, William, Mr. *William Fullers Third Narrative, Containing New Matters of Fact* ..., London, 1696.
A General History of the Turks, Moguls, and Tatars, Vulgarly called Tartars, together with a Description of the Countries they Inhabit, 2 vols., London, 1729.
Gervaise, Isaac, *The System or Theory of the Trade of the World*, London, 1720.
Gillespie, Raymond, ed., *Settlement and Survival on an Ulster Estate: The Brownlow Leasebook 1667–1711*, Belfast: PRONI, 1988.
Godwin, Francis, *The Man in the Moone: or A Discourse of a Voyage Thither by Domingo Gonsales the Speedy Messenger*, London, 1638.
[Gordon, Thomas, and John Trenchard], *Cato's Letters: or, Essays on Liberty, Civil and Religious, and other Important Subjects*, 4 vols., London, 1724.
Gosnell, Edward, *Irelands Redress, from Popular Greivances Attempted; a Scheme for Employing the Poor* ..., Dublin, 1723.
Grant, Francis, *The British Fishery Recommended to Parliament*, London, 1734.
Granville, Mary, *The Autobiography and Correspondence of Mary Granville, Mrs. Delany*, ed. Lady Llanover, 2nd ser., 6 vols., London, 1861–2.
A Great Deal More Seasonable Advice to the Freemen and Freeholders of the City of Dublin, Concerning the Choice of a Member to Represent them in Parliament, Dublin, 1733.
Hannibal Not at Our Gates, London, 1714.
Hesperi-Neso-Graphia: or, A Description of the Western Isle in Eight Cantos ..., London, 1716.
The Hibernian Patriot: Being a Collection of the Drapier's Letters to the People of Ireland, Dublin, 1729; repr. London, 1730.
Historical Manuscripts Commission reports:
  Egmont Diary, vols. I–II
  Stopford-Sackville MSS
  Various collections, vol. VI
The History of the Popish Clergy: or, The Case of the Laity, Dublin, 1723.
Hoadley, Benjamin, *Remarks on the Late Bishop of Rochester's Speech at the Bar of the House of Lords* ..., London, 1723.
Hobbes, Thomas, *Leviathan*, ed. Richard Tuck, Cambridge: Cambridge University Press, 1991.
A Humourous Description of the Manners and Fashions of the Inhabitants of the City of Dublin, in a Letter from a Gentleman to his Friend in ... Drogheda, Dublin, 1734.
Hutchinson, Francis, *A Letter to a Member of Parliament, Concerning the Imploying and Providing for the Poor*, Dublin, 1723.
[Hutchinson, Francis], *A Second Letter to a Member of Parliament, Recommending the Improvement of the Irish-Fishery*, Dublin, 1729.

An Inquiry into Some of the Causes of the Ill Situation of the Affairs of Ireland; with some Reflexions on the Trade, Manufactures, &c. of England, London, 1732.
Ireland's Mourning Flagg ... Some Queries Occasion'd by the Lowering of the Gold Coin, Dublin, 1737.
'Isaac Broadloom, Clothier', *The Hue and Cry of the Poor of Ireland for Small Change*, Dublin, 1731.
J.W., *A Military Dictionary, Explaining All Difficult Terms in Martial Discipline, Fortification, and Gunnery...*, 4th edn, London, 1730.
Journal of the Commissioners for Trade and Plantations, 14 vols., London: HMSO, 1920–38.
The Journals of the House of Commons of the Kingdom of Ireland, 2nd edn, 19 vols., Dublin, 1753–76.
Kennett, White, *A Compassionate Enquiry into the Causes of the Civil War. In a Sermon Preached in the Church of St. Botolph Aldgate, on January XXXI, 1703/4...*, London, 1704.
Kersey, John, *A New English Dictionary*, London, 1702.
Kingston, Richard, *A True History of the Several Designs and Conspiracies against His Majesties Sacred Person and Government...*, London, 1698.
Kirkpatrick, James, *An Historical Essay upon the Loyalty of Presbyterians in Great-Britain and Ireland from the Reformation to This Present Year 1713*, Belfast, 1713.
God's Dominion over Kings and Other Magistrates: a Thanksgiving Sermon Preach'd in Belfast October 20. 1714. Being the Happy Day of the Coronation of His Most Excellent Majesty King George, Belfast, 1714.
Knightley, John, *To the Honourable the Lords Spiritual, Temporal and Commons in Parliament Assembled ... this Essay toward Proving the Advantages which may Arise from Improvements on Salt Works, and in the Fishing Trade of Ireland*, Dublin, 1733.
Laffan, William, ed., *The Cries of Dublin &c, drawn from the life by Hugh Douglas Hamilton, 1760*, Dublin: Irish Georgian Society, 2003.
The Lamentation of the Poor of the City of Dublin; After the Late Lord Mayor, with a Word of Advice to the Freemen, &c. of said City, [Dublin], 1733.
Laws of the Commonwealth of Pennsylvania, 4 vols., Philadelphia, 1795–1801.
The Laws of the Province of Pennsylvania: Now in Force, Philadelphia, 1728.
A Letter ... from a Country Gentleman ... concerning the Growth of Wool, and the Nature of the Woollen Trade in Ireland, Dublin, 1732.
A Letter Concerning the Bankers of Dublin, Dublin, 1737.
Letter from Dermott Mac-Poverty to the Author of the Intelligencer, Dublin, 1728.
A Letter from a Gentleman in the North of Ireland, to a Person in an Eminent Post under His Majesty, Concerning the Transportation of Great Numbers from that Part of the Kingdom to America, Dublin, 1729.
A Letter from Patrick O Saplin President of the Kevin-Bail to John Crabb-Tree, Captain of the London-Mob, Dublin, 1736.

A Letter in Answer to a Paper, intitled, an Appeal to the Reverend Dean Swift. By the Author of Considerations on Two Papers, &c, Dublin, 1728.
A Letter to the Author of a Pamphlet, entitled, An Enquiry into the Reasons of the Decay of Credit, Trade, and Manufactures in Ireland, Dublin, 1735.
A Letter, to M. B. Drapier, Occasionally Writ, on the Late Oppressive Villainy of the Br[ewer]s, in Raising the Price of their Malt-liquors, Dublin, 1729.
A Letter to the People of Ireland. By M.B. Draper, Dublin, 1729.
A Letter to the Right Honourable Humphrey French, Esq., Present Lord Mayor of the City of Dublin, Dublin, 1733.
A Letter to the Right Honourable Sir Ralph Gore, Bart. Speaker of the Honourable House of Commons, [Dublin, 1732].
A Little More Advice to the People of Dublin, [Dublin], 1733.
Littleton, Adam, *Linguæ latinæ liber dictionarius quadripartitus* ..., London, 1715.
Locke, John, *An Essay Concerning Human Understanding*, ed. Peter H. Nidditch, Oxford: Clarendon Press, 1975.
Some Thoughts on Education, ed. John W. and Jean S. Yolton, Oxford: Clarendon Press, 1989.
Two Treatises of Government, ed. Ian Shapiro, New Haven & London: Yale University Press, 2003.
MacAulay, Alexander, *Property Inviolable: or, Some Remarks upon a Pamphlet Entituled, Prescription Sacred*, Dublin, 1736.
Some Thoughts on the Tillage of Ireland: humbly Dedicated to the Parliament. To which is Prefixed, a Letter to the Printer, from the Reverend Doctor Swift, Dean of St. Patrick's, Recommending the following Treatise, Dublin, 1737.
MacCurtin, Hugh, *A Brief Discourse in Vindication of the Antiquity of Ireland*, Dublin, 1717.
Maculla, James, *A New Scheme Proposed, to the People of Ireland; for Increasing the Cash, of this Kingdom; by Making Promissary Notes of Copper, to Bear an Intrinsick Value to the British-half-pence* ..., Dublin, 1728.
Madden, Samuel, *Reflections and Resolutions Proper for the Gentlemen of Ireland, as to their Conduct for the Service of their Country*, Dublin, 1738.
Maple, William, *A Method of Tanning without Bark*, Dublin, 1729.
Mather, Catton, *Magnalia Christi Americana: or, The Ecclesiastical History of New-England, from Its First Planting in the year 1620. unto the Year of Our Lord, 1698*, London, 1702.
Mattaire, Michel, *Opera et Fragmenta Veterum Poetarum Latinorum Profanorum & Ecclesiasticorum*, London, 1713.
Maxwell, Henry, *An Essay upon an Union of Ireland with England* ..., Dublin, 1704.
Mr Maxwell's Second Letter to Mr Rowley; Wherein the Objections Against the Bank are Answer'd, Dublin, 1721.

Reasons Offer'd for Erecting a Bank in Ireland; in a Letter to Hercules Rowley, Esq., Dublin, 1721.
McBride, John, *A Sample of Jet-Black Pr[ela]tic Calumny, in Answer to a Pamphlet, called, A Sample of True-Bleu Presbyterian loyalty*, Glasgow, 1713.
Mead, Richard, *A Mechanical Account of Poisons in Several Essays*, 3rd edn, Dublin, 1729.
Mist, Nathaniel, *The Present State of Ireland; Being Political Reflections by Mr Mist, on a Pamphlet Lately Published at Dublin*, [London, 1728].
Molesworth, Robert, Viscount, *Some Considerations for the Promoting of Agriculture, and Employing the Poor*, Dublin, 1723.
Moryson, Fynes, *An Itinerary ... Concerning His Ten Yeeres Travel through the Twelve Dominions of Germany ... Scotland and Ireland*, London, 1617.
Moyle, Walter, *The Whole Works of Walter Moyle, Esq ...*, London, 1727.
Mr. De Labadie's Letter to His Daughter ... Nurse to the Pretended Prince of Wales, [London] 1697.
The Munster Combat, or The Invasion of the Moors ..., [Dublin, 1722]
The Nature and Consequences of the Sacramental Test Considered, Dublin, 1731.
O'Brien, William, *An Epick Poem on ... William Leigh*, Dublin, 1727.
Oldmixon, John, *The British Empire in America, Containing the History of the Discovery, Settlement, Progress and Present State of All the British Colonies, on the Continent and Islands of America*, 2 vols., London, 1708.
Orrery, John Boyle, Earl of, *Remarks on the Life and Writings of Dr. Jonathan Swift*, London, 1752; ed. João Frées, Newark: University of Delaware Press, 2000.
Parker, Samuel, *Tully's Two Essay [sic] of Old Age, and of Friendship ...*, 3rd edn, London, 1727.
P[arry], G[eorge], ed., *Tully de Oratore*, London, 1723.
Pearce, Zachary, *A Letter to the Clergy of the Church of England: on Occasion of the Commitment of the Right Reverend the Lord Bishop of Rochester to the Tower of London*, London, 1722.
Peirson, Samuel, *Farther Considerations for the Improvement of the Tillage in Ireland ...*, Dublin, 1728.
A Poem Occasion'd by the Lord Mayor's Reducing the Price of Coals &c., Dublin, 1729.
Poems on Affairs of State: Augustan Satirical Verse, 1660–1714, ed. G. de F. Lord, William J. Cameron, Galbraith M. Crump, Frank H. Ellis, Elias F. Mengel, jr and Howard H. Schless, 7 vols., New Haven: Yale University Press, 1963–75.
The Poor Man's Case Consider'd; or a Pill for Colts and Cure for the Publick: Being the Address of All and Singular the Journeymen of the City of Dublin, Dublin, 1732.

Pope, Alexander, *The Correspondence of Alexander Pope*, ed. George Sherburn, 5 vols., Oxford: Clarendon Press, 1956.
The Twickenham Edition of the Poems of Alexander Pope, ed. John Butt, Maynard Mack and Geoffrey Tillotson *et al.*, 3rd edn, 11 vols., London: Methuen, 1962–9.
Prescription Sacred: or, Reasons for Opposing the New Demand of Herbage in Ireland, [Dublin?], 1736.
The Present Miserable State of Ireland. In a Letter from a Gentleman in Dublin, to his Friend S R W in London, Dublin, 1735.
The Present State of Ireland Consider'd, Dublin, 1730.
Prior, Thomas, *A List of the Absentees of Ireland, and the Yearly Value of their Estates and Incomes spent abroad*, Dublin, 1729.
Observations on Coin in General. With some Proposals for Regulating the Value of Coin in Ireland, Dublin, 1729.
A Proposal for the Relief of Ireland, by a Coinage of Monies, of Gold and Silver; and Establishing a National Bank, Dublin, 1734.
Queries concerning the Lowering of the Gold Coin, [Dublin, 1737].
Queries relating to the New Half-pence, and Lowering the Coin, [Dublin], 1737.
Ralph, James, *The Touch-Stone: or, Historical, Critical, Political, Philosophical, and Theological Essays on the Reigning Diversions of the Town*, London, 1728.
Ratcliffe, Alexander, *The Works of Capt. Alex. Radcliffe*, 3rd edn, London, 1696.
Remarks on some Maxims, Peculiar to the Ancient, as well as Modern Inhabitants of Ireland. With a Seasonable Hint to G Bn about the Woollen trade. In A Letter from a Gentleman in the County of Kerry, Dublin, 1730.
Remarks upon a Paper just Publish'd, intitled, Some Considerations on Lowering the Gold, Dublin, 1736.
A Reply to the Principal Arguments for the Reduction of the Gold Coin, and some Considerations on the Consequences thereof, Dublin, 1737.
Robinson, Bryan, *An Appendix to A Short Essay on Coin*, Dublin, 1737.
A Short Essay on Coin, Dublin, 1737.
Rye, George, *Considerations on Agriculture* ..., Dublin, 1730.
Salmon, Thomas, *Tryals for High-Treason, and Other Crimes* ..., 9 vols., London, 1720–31.
A Satyr on the Mall in Great Britain-Street, [?Dublin], 1733.
Scheme of the Proportions which the Protestants of Ireland may probably bear to the Papists; Humbly Offer'd to the Public, [Dublin, 1732].
The Second Part of Whipping-Tom: or, A Rod for a Proud Lady ..., London, [1722].
Sharp, Jane, *The Compleat Midwife's Companion*, London, 1725.

Sheridan, Thomas, *An Ode to be Perform'd at the Castle of Dublin, on the 1 of March 1729–30* ..., Dublin, 1730.
The Poems of Thomas Sheridan, ed. R. G. Hogan, Newark, NJ: University of Delaware Press, 1994.
A Short Answer to Short Reasons why our Gold-money in Ireland should not be Lower'd, Dublin, 1737.
Some Thoughts concerning Government in General: and our Present Circumstances in Great-Britain and Ireland, Dublin, 1728.
The Spectator, ed. Donald F. Bond, 5 vols., Oxford: Clarendon Press, 1965.
Spenser, Edmund, *The Works of Edmund Spenser*, ed. Edwin Greenlaw, Charles Grosvenor Osgood, Frederick Morgan Padelford and Ray Heffner, 11 vols., Baltimore: Johns Hopkins Press, 1943–57.
Steele, Richard, *The Correspondence of Richard Steele*, ed. Rae Blanchard, Oxford: Clarendon Press, 1941.
The Tracts and Pamphlets of Richard Steele, ed. Rae Blanchard, Baltimore: Johns Hopkins Press, 1944.
Swift, Jonathan, *The Works of J.S, D.D, D.S.P.D.*, 4 vols., Dublin, 1735 [TS 41].
Political Tracts, 2 vols., London, 1738 [TS 25 (6–7)].
The Works of J.S, D.D, D.S.P.D., 6 vols., Dublin, 1738 [TS 42].
The Works of Jonathan Swift, D.D, D.S.P.D., 8 vols., Dublin, 1741–6 [TS 44].
The Works of Jonathan Swift, D.D, D.S.P.D ... The Sixth Edition, 8 vols., Dublin, 1741–8 [TS 51].
A Supplement to the Works of Dr. Swift, London: Francis Cogan, 1752 [TS 83].
The Works of Jonathan Swift, D.D., 25 vols., London, 1754–79 [TS 88].
The Works of Jonathan Swift, D.D., 14 vols., London, 1755–79 [TS 87].
The Works of the Reverend Dr. Jonathan Swift, Dean of St. Patrick's, Dublin, 19 vols., Dublin, 1756–68 [TS 53].
The Works of Dr. Jonathan Swift, Dean of St. Patrick's, Dublin, 26 vols., London, 1760–79 [TS 90].
The Works of the Reverend Dr. J. Swift, D.S.P.D., 20 vols., Dublin, 1763–71 [TS 52].
The Works of the Reverend Dr. Jonathan Swift, Dean of St. Patrick's, Dublin, 20 vols., Dublin, 1765–71 [TS 47].
The Works of Dr. Jonathan Swift, Dean of St. Patrick's, Dublin, 27 vols., London, 1765–79 [TS 92].
Miscellaneous Pieces in Prose and Verse by the Rev. Jonathan Swift, ed. John Nichols, London, 1789 [TS 121].
The Works of the Rev. Jonathan Swift, D.D., ed. John Nichols, 19 vols., London, 1801 [TS 129].

The Prose Works of Jonathan Swift, ed. Temple Scott, 12 vols., London, 1897–1908.
The Drapier's Letters, ed. Herbert Davis, Oxford: Clarendon Press, 1935.
The Prose Writings of Jonathan Swift, ed. Herbert Davis, Irvin Ehrenpreis, Louis Landa and Harold Williams, 16 vols., Oxford: Basil Blackwell, 1939–74.
Journal to Stella, ed. Harold Williams, 2 vols., Oxford: Clarendon Press, 1948.
The Poems of Jonathan Swift, ed. Harold Williams, 2nd edn, 3 vols., Oxford: Clarendon Press, 1958.
The Correspondence of Jonathan Swift, ed. Harold Williams, 5 vols., Oxford: Clarendon Press, 1963–5.
Poetical Works, ed. Herbert Davis, London: Oxford University Press, 1967.
The Complete Poems, ed. Pat Rogers, Harmondsworth: Penguin, 1983.
The Correspondence of Jonathan Swift, D.D., ed. David Woolley, 5 vols., Frankfurt am Main: Peter Lang, 1999–2014.
The Cambridge Edition of the Works of Jonathan Swift, ed. Claude Rawson, Ian Higgins, James McLaverty, *et al.*, Cambridge: Cambridge University Press, 2008–.
Swift's Irish Writings: Selected Prose and Poetry, ed. Carole Fabricant and Robert Mahony, Basingstoke: Palgrave Macmillan, 2010.
Swift, Jonathan, and Thomas Sheridan, *The Intelligencer*, ed. James Woolley, Oxford: Clarendon Press, 1992.
Synge, Edward, *Two Affidavits in Relation to the Demands of Tythe-agistment in the Diocese of Leighlin; with an Introduction*, Dublin, 1736.
The Tatler, ed. Donald F. Bond, 3 vols., Oxford: Clarendon Press, 1987.
Temple, Sir William, *The Works of Sir William Temple*, 2 vols., London, 1740.
Thomson, Katherine, *Memoirs of Viscountess Sundon*, 2 vols., London, 1847.
Tisdall, William, *A Sample of True-blew Presbyterian-loyalty, in All Changes and Turns of Government*, Dublin, 1709.
To the Right Honourable the Lord Viscount Mont-Cassel: This Fable is Most Humbly Dedicated by a Person Who Had Some Share in His Education, Dublin, 1727.
To the Worthy Freemen and Freeholders of this City . . . October 11, 1729, [Dublin, 1729].
Two and Two Make Four: in a Letter to the Honest Traders of Ireland, Dublin, 1737.
The Vestry Records of the Parishes of St Catherine and St James, Dublin, 1657–1692, ed. Raymond Gillespie, Dublin: Four Courts Press, 2002.
A View of the Present State of Affairs in the Kingdom of Ireland; in Three Discourses, London, 1730.

Ward, James, *A Sermon Preach'd in Christ's Church, Dublin; before His Excellency John, Lord Carteret, Lord Lieutenant General, and General Governour of Ireland*, Dublin, 1724[/5].
Weaver, James, *Irelands Hue and Cry after the Gold Coin; in a Letter from Belfast to the Castle of Comfort*, Dublin, 1737.
Webb, Daniel, *An Enquiry into the Reasons of the Decay of Credit, Trade, and Manufactures in Ireland*, Dublin, 1735.
Wilkins, John, *The Discovery of a World in the Moone. Or, A Discourse Tending, to Prove, That 'Tis Probable There May Be Another Habitable World in That Planet*, London, 1638.
Wilson, Robert, *The Interest and Trade of Ireland Consider'd*, Dublin, 1731.
The Wooden-Man in Essex-Street's Memorial, and Reasons against Lowering the Gold Coin, Dublin, 1737.
The World in Uproar, or the Hue and Cry after the Laurels, [Dublin, c. 1713].

Secondary Sources

Albert, William, *The Turnpike Road System in England, 1663–1840*, Cambridge: Cambridge University Press, 1972.
Baker, D. C., 'Tertullian and Swift's "A Modest Proposal"', *Classical Quarterly* 52 (1957), 219–20.
Ball, F. E., *The Judges in Ireland, 1221–1921*, 2 vols., London: John Murray, 1926.
Baltes, Sabine, '"The Grandson of that Ass Quin": Swift and Chief Justice Whitshed', *SStud* 23 (2008), 126–46.
Barnard, T. C., 'Athlone, 1685; Limerick, 1710: Religious Riots or Charivaris', *Studia Hibernica* 27 (1993), 61–75.
 'Protestants and the Irish Language, c. 1675–1725', *Journal of Ecclesiastical History* 44 (1993), 243–72.
 'Improving Clergymen, 1660–1760', in Alan Ford, James McGuire and Kenneth Milne (eds.), *As by Law Established: The Church of Ireland since the Reformation*, Dublin: Lilliput Press, 1995, pp. 136–51.
 'Considering the Inconsiderable: Electors, Patrons and Irish Elections 1659–1761', in D. W. Hayton (ed.), *The Irish Parliament in the Eighteenth Century: The Long Apprenticeship*, Edinburgh: Edinburgh University Press, 2001, pp. 107–27.
 '"Grand Metropolis" or "the Anus of the World"? The Cultural Life of Eighteenth-century Dublin', in Peter Clark and Raymond Gillespie (eds.), *Two Capitals: London and Dublin 1500–1840: PBA*, 107 (2001), pp. 185–210.
 A New Anatomy of Ireland: The Irish Protestants, 1649–1770, New Haven & London: Yale University Press, 2003.

Irish Protestant Ascents and Descents, 1641–1770, Dublin: Four Courts Press, 2004.
The Kingdom of Ireland, 1641–1760, Basingstoke: Palgrave Macmillan, 2004.
Making the Grand Figure: Lives and Possessions in Ireland, 1641–1770, New Haven & London: Yale University Press, 2004.
'"Almoners of Providence": The Clergy, 1647 to c. 1780', in T. C. Barnard and W. G. Neely (eds.), *The Clergy of the Church of Ireland, 1000–2000: Messengers, Watchmen, and Stewards*, Dublin: Four Courts Press, 2006, pp. 78–105.
'Print Culture, 1700–1800', in Raymond Gillespie and Andrew Hadfield (eds.), *The Oxford History of the Irish Book*, vol. III: *The Irish Book in English, 1550–1800*, Oxford: Oxford University Press, 2006, pp. 34–58.
Improving Ireland? Projectors, Prophets, and Profiteers, 1641–1786, Dublin: Four Courts Press, 2008.
'St Patrick's Cathedral in the Age of Swift, 1690–1745', in John Crawford and Raymond Gillespie (eds.), *St Patrick's Cathedral, Dublin: A History*, Dublin: Four Courts Press, 2009, pp. 197–218.
'The Dublin Society and Other Improving Societies, 1731–85', in James Kelly and Martyn Powell (eds.), *Clubs and Societies in Eighteenth-century Ireland*, Dublin: Four Courts Press, 2010, pp. 53–88.
Barnett, Louise, *Jonathan Swift in the Company of Women*, Oxford: Oxford University Press, 2007.
Barrett, John, *An Essay on the Earlier Part of the Life of Swift*, London, 1808.
Beckett, J. C., *Protestant Dissent in Ireland 1687–1780*, London: Faber and Faber, 1948.
'Swift and the Anglo-Irish Tradition', in Claude Rawson (ed.), *The Character of Swift's Satire: A Revised Focus*, Newark, NJ: University of Delaware Press, 1983, pp. 151–65.
Belcher, T. W., *Memoir of Sir Patrick Dun Knt.*, 2nd edn, Dublin, 1866.
Bennett, G. V., *White Kennett*, London: SPCK, 1957.
The Tory Crisis in Church and State, 1688–1730: The Career of Francis Atterbury, Bishop of Rochester, Oxford: Clarendon Press, 1975.
Bergin, John, 'The Irish Catholic Interest at the London Inns of Court, 1674–1800', *ECI* 24 (2009), 36–61.
Black, Jeremy (ed.), *Britain in the Age of Walpole*, London: Macmillan, 1984.
'An Underrated Journalist: Nathaniel Mist and the Opposition Press during the Whig Ascendancy', *British Journal for Eighteenth-Century Studies* 10 (1987), 27–41.
'Swift and Foreign Policy Revisited', in *Münster* (1993), pp. 61–70.

The Collapse of the Anglo-French Alliance 1727–1731, Gloucester: Alan Sutton, 2004.
Parliament and Foreign Policy in the Eighteenth Century, Cambridge: Cambridge University Press, 2004.
Bond, R. P., *Queen Anne's American Kings*, Oxford: Clarendon Press, 1952.
Booth, Wayne C., *A Rhetoric of Irony*, Chicago: University of Chicago Press, 1974.
Boyce, D. G., *Nationalism in Ireland*, Dublin: Gill & Macmillan, 1982.
Brewer, John, *The Sinews of Power: War, Money and the English State, 1688–1783*, London: Routledge, 1989.
Bric, Maurice, 'The Tithe System in Eighteenth-century Ireland', *Proceedings of the Royal Irish Academy* 86 (1986), sect. C, 271–88.
Briggs, P. M., 'John Graunt, Sir William Petty, and Swift's *Modest Proposal*', *Eighteenth Century Life*, 29 (2005), 3–24.
Broderick, David, *The First Toll Roads: Ireland's Turnpike Roads 1729–1858*, Cork: Collins Press, 2002.
Brown, Michael, *Francis Hutcheson in Dublin, 1719–1730: The Crucible of his Thought*, Dublin: Four Courts Press, 2001.
Burke, W. P., *History of Clonmel*, Clonmel: Neil Harvey, 1907.
Burns, Robert E., *Irish Parliamentary Politics in the Eighteenth Century*, 2 vols., Washington DC: Catholic University of America Press, 1989–90.
Bushman, Richard L., *King and People in Provincial Massachusetts*, Chapel Hill: University of North Carolina Press, 1985.
Carpenter, Andrew, 'Two Possible Sources for Swift's "A Modest Proposal"', *Irish Booklore* 2 (1992), 147–8.
Carpenter, Andrew, and Alan Harrison, 'Swift's "O'Rourke's Feast" and Sheridan's "Letter": Early Transcripts by Anthony Raymond', in *Münster* (1985), pp. 27–46.
Carpenter, Andrew, and Richard Harrison, 'Swift, Raymond, and a Legacy', *SStud* 1 (1986), pp. 57–60.
Carroll, Clare, *Circe's Cup: Cultural Transformations in Early Modern Ireland*, Cork: Cork University Press, 2002.
Carter, Mary, 'Swift and the Scheme for Badging Beggars in Dublin, 1726–1737', *Eighteenth-Century Life*, 27 (2013), 97–118.
Casey, Christine (ed.), *The Buildings of Ireland: Dublin: The City within the Grand and Royal Canals and the Circular Road with the Phoenix Park*, New Haven & London: Yale University Press, 2005.
The Eighteenth-century Dublin Townhouse: Form, Function and Finance, Dublin: Four Courts Press, 2010.
Champion, J. A. I., *The Pillars of Priestcraft Shaken: The Church of England and Its Enemies, 1660–1730*, Cambridge: Cambridge University Press, 1992.

Chowdhury, Ahsan, 'Splenetic Ogres and Heroic Cannibals in Swift's Modest Proposal', *English Studies in Canada* 34 (2008), pp. 131–57.
Clark, Peter, 'The "Mother Gin" Controversy in the Early Eighteenth Century', *Transactions of the Royal Historical Society*, ser. 5, 38 (1988), 63–84.
Clarke, Desmond, *Thomas Prior, 1681–1751, Founder of the Royal Dublin Society*, Dublin: Royal Dublin Society, 1951.
— *Arthur Dobbs, Esquire, 1689–1765: Surveyor-general of Ireland, Prospector and Governor of North Carolina*, Chapel Hill: University of North Carolina Press, 1957.
Clifford, J. L., and Irvin Ehrenpreis, 'Swiftiana in Rylands English MS 659 and Related Documents', *Bulletin of the John Rylands Library* 37 (1955), 368–92.
Cole, Shaun, *The Story of Men's Underwear*, New York: Parkstone, 2007.
Coleborne, Bryan, '"We Flea the People & Sell their Skins": A Source for *A Modest Proposal*', *Scriblerian* 15 (1983), 132–3.
— 'The Dublin Grub Street: The Documentary Evidence in the Case of John Browne', *SStud* 2 (1987), 12–24.
— 'Jonathan Swift and the Literary World of Dublin', *Englische Amerikanische Studien* 10 (1988), pp. 6–88.
Colley, Linda, *In Defiance of Oligarchy: The Tory Party 1714–60*, Cambridge: Cambridge University Press, 1982.
Connolly, S. J., 'Law, Order and Popular Protest in Early Eighteenth-century Ireland: The Case of the Houghers', in P. J. Corish (ed.), *Radicals, Rebels and Establishments*, Belfast: Appletree Press, 1985, pp. 51–68.
— 'The Houghers: Agrarian Protest in Early Eighteenth-century Connacht', in C. H. E. Philpin (ed.), *Nationalism and Popular Protest in Ireland*, Cambridge: Cambridge University Press, 1987, pp. 139–62.
— 'Violence and Order in the Eighteenth Century', in Patrick O'Flanagan, Paul Ferguson and Kevin Whelan (eds.), *Rural Ireland: Modernisation and Change 1600–1900*, Cork: Cork University Press, 1987, pp. 42–61.
— 'Albion's Fatal Twigs: Justice and Law in the Eighteenth Century', in Rosalind Mitchison and Peter Roebuck (eds.), *Economy and Society in Scotland and Ireland, 1500–1939*, Edinburgh: John Donald, 1988, pp. 117–39.
— *Religion, Law and Power: The Making of Protestant Ireland, 1660–1760*, Oxford: Clarendon Press, 1992.
— 'Eighteenth-century Ireland: Colony or Ancien Régime', in D. G. Boyce and Alan O'Day (eds.), *The Making of Modern Irish History: Revisionism and the Revisionist Controversy*, London: Routledge, 1996, pp. 15–33.
— 'Swift and Protestant Ireland: Images and Realities', in Aileen Douglas, Patrick Kelly and Ian Campbell Ross (eds.), *Locating Swift: Essays from Dublin on the 250th Anniversary of the Death of Jonathan Swift, 1667–1745*, Dublin: Four Courts Press, 1998, pp. 28–46.

'The Church of Ireland and the Royal Martyr: Regicide and Revolution in Anglican Political Thought, c. 1660 – c. 1745', *Journal of Ecclesiastical History* 54 (2003), 484–506.

Coombs, Douglas, *The Conduct of the Dutch: British Opinion and the Dutch Alliance during the War of the Spanish Succession*, The Hague: Martinus Nijhoff, 1958.

Cowan, Brian, *The Social Life of Coffee: The Emergence of the British Coffeehouse*, New Haven & London: Yale University Press, 2005.

Craig, Maurice, *Dublin 1660–1860*, Dublin: Allen Figgis, 1980.

Craik, Henry, *The Life of Jonathan Swift*, London: John Murray, 1882.

Crawford, John, and Raymond Gillespie, *St Patrick's Cathedral, Dublin: a History*, Dublin: Four Courts Press, 2008.

Crawford, W. H., 'Landlord–Tenant Relations in Ulster 1609–1820', *Irish Economic and Social History* 2 (1975), 5–21.

Cruickshanks, Eveline, Stuart Handley and D. W. Hayton (eds.), *The House of Commons 1690–1715*, 5 vols., Cambridge: Cambridge University Press, 2002.

Cullen, L. M., 'Five Letters Relating to Galway Smuggling in 1737', *Journal of the Galway Historical and Archaeological Society* 27 (1959), 10–25.

Anglo-Irish Trade 1660–1800, Manchester: Manchester University Press, 1968.

'The Smuggling Trade in Ireland in the Eighteenth Century', *Proceedings of the Royal Irish Academy* 67 (1969), sect. C, 149–75.

An Economic History of Ireland since 1660, London: Batsford, 1972.

The Emergence of Modern Ireland 1600–1900, London: Batsford, 1981.

'Landlords, Bankers and Merchants: The Early Irish Banking World 1700–1820', *Hermathena* 135 (1983), 25–44.

'Catholics under the Penal Laws', *ECI* 1 (1986), 23–36.

'The Growth of Dublin, 1600–1900: Character and Heritage', in F. H. Aalen and Kevin Whelan (eds.), *Dublin City and County from Prehistory to the Present: Studies in Honour of J. H. Andrews*, Dublin: Geography Publications, 1992, pp. 252–77.

'The Blackwater Catholics and County Cork Society and Politics in the Eighteenth Century', in Patrick Flanagan and C. G. Buttimer (eds.), *Cork: History and Society*, Dublin: Geography Publications, 1993, pp. 535–84.

'The Irish Food Crises of the Early 1740s: The Economic Conjuncture', *Irish Economic and Social History*, 37 (2010), 1–23.

Damrosch, Leo, *Jonathan Swift: His Life and His World*, New Haven & London: Yale University Press, 2013.

Deane, Seamus, 'Swift and the Anglo-Irish Intellect', *ECI* 1 (1986), pp. 9–22.

Dickinson, H. T., *Bolingbroke*, London: Constable, 1970.

Dickson, David, 'Middlemen', in Thomas Bartlett and D. W. Hayton (eds.), *Penal Era and Golden Age: Essays in Irish History 1690–1800*, Belfast: Ulster Historical Foundation, 1979, pp. 162–85.
'In Search of the Old Irish Poor Law', in Rosalind Mitchison and Peter Roebuck (eds.), *Economy and Society in Scotland and Ireland 1500–1939*, Edinburgh: John Donald, 1988, pp. 148–59.
New Foundations: Ireland 1660–1800, 2nd edn, Dublin: Irish Academic Press, 2000.
'Jacobitism in Eighteenth-century Ireland: a Munster Perspective', *Éire-Ireland* 39 (2004), 38–99.
Old World Colony: Cork and South Munster 1630–1830, Cork: Cork University Press, 2005.
Dublin: The Making of a Capital City, London: Profile Books, 2014.
Dickson, R. J., *Ulster Emigration to Colonial America, 1718–1775*, London: Routledge and Kegan Paul, 1966.
Doody, M. A., 'Swift among the Women', *Yearbook of English Studies* 28 (1988), 68–92.
Douglas, D. C., *English Scholars, 1660–1730*, 2nd edn, London: Eyre and Spottiswoode, 1951.
Downie, J. A., *Jonathan Swift, Political Writer*, London: Routledge and Kegan Paul, 1984.
'Walpole, "the Poet's Foe"', in Jeremy Black (ed.), *Britain in the Age of Walpole*, Basingstoke: Macmillan, 1984, pp. 171–88.
Doyle, Mel, 'The Dublin Guilds and Journeymen's Clubs', *Saothar: Journal of the Irish Labour History Society* 3 (1977), 6–14.
Dudley, Rowena, 'The Dublin Parishes and the Poor: 1660–1740', *Archivium Hibernicum* 53 (1999), 80–94.
'The Dublin Parish, 1660–1730', in Elizabeth FitzPatrick and Raymond Gillespie (eds.), *The Parish in Medieval and Early Modern Ireland: Community, Territory and Building*, Dublin: Four Courts Press, 2006, pp. 277–96.
Dunlevy, Mairead, 'Samuel Madden and the Scheme for the Encouragement of Useful Manufactures', in Agnes Bernelle (ed.), *Decantations: A Tribute to Maurice Craig*, Dublin: Lilliput Press, 1992, pp. 21–8.
Edie, Carolyn A., 'The Irish Cattle Bills: a Study in Restoration Politics', *Transactions of the American Philosophical Society*, new ser., 60 (1970), 1–66.
Ehrenpreis, Irvin, *Swift: The Man, His Works, and the Age*, 3 vols., London: Methuen, 1962–83.
Eilon, Daniel, 'Swift's Burning the Library of Babel', *MLR* 80 (1985), pp. 269–82.
Elias, A. C., 'Senatus Consultum: Revising Verse in Swift's Dublin Circle, 1729–1735', *Münster* (1998), pp. 249–67.

Ellis, F. H. (ed.), *Swift vs. Mainwaring: The Examiner and The Medley*, Oxford: Clarendon Press, 1985.
Ellis, Markman, *The Coffee-house: A Cultural History*, London: Weidenfeld & Nicolson, 2004.
Emsley, Clive, *Crime, Police and Penal Policy: European Experiences 1750–1940*, Oxford: Oxford University Press, 2007.
Erskine-Hill, Howard, *The Social Milieu of Alexander Pope: Lives, Example and the Poetic Response*, New Haven & London: Yale University Press, 1975.
Fabricant, Carole, *Swift's Landscape*, Baltimore: Johns Hopkins University Press, 1982.
'Speaking for the Irish Nation: The Drapier, the Bishop and the Problems of Colonial Representation', *ELH* 66 (1999), 337–72.
Fagan, Patrick, *The Second City: Portrait of Dublin 1700–1760*, Dublin: Branar, 1986.
'The Dublin Catholic Mob (1700–1750)', *ECI* 4 (1989), 133–42.
Dublin's Turbulent Priest: Cornelius Nary, 1658–1738, Dublin: Royal Irish Academy, 1991.
'The Population of Dublin in the Eighteenth Century with Particular Reference to the Proportions of Protestants and Catholics', *ECI* 6 (1991), 121–56.
Catholics in a Protestant Country: The Papist Constituency in Eighteenth-century Dublin, Dublin: Four Courts Press, 1998.
Fanning, Christopher, 'The Voices of the Dependent Poet: The Case of Mary Barber', *Women's Writing* 8 (2001), 81–97.
Fauske, C. J., *Jonathan Swift and the Church of Ireland 1710–1724*, Dublin: Irish Academic Press, 2002.
A Political Biography of William King, London: Pickering & Chatto, 2011.
Fennelly, Teddy, *Thomas Prior: His Life, Times, and Legacy*, Port Laoise: Arderin Publishing, 2001.
Ferguson, Oliver W., *Jonathan Swift and Ireland*, Urbana, IL: University of Illinois Press, 1962.
Fleming, D. A., *Politics and Provincial People: Sligo and Limerick, 1691–1761*, Manchester: Manchester University Press, 2010.
Flinn, M. W., *Men of Iron: The Crowleys in the Early Iron Industry*, Edinburgh: Edinburgh University Press, 1962.
Foord, Archibald, *His Majesty's Opposition 1714–1830*, Oxford: Clarendon Press, 1964.
Fox, Christopher (ed.), *The Cambridge Companion to Jonathan Swift*, Cambridge: Cambridge University Press, 2003.
Foxon, David F., *English Verse 1701–1750: A Catalogue of Separately Printed Poems with Notes on Contemporary Collected Editions*, 2 vols., London: Cambridge University Press, 1975.

Frazer, William, 'On the Irish "St. Patrick" or "Floreat Rex" Coinage ...', *Journal of the Royal Society of Antiquaries of Ireland* 5 (1895), 338–47.
Galenson, D. W., *White Servitude in Colonial America: An Economic Analysis*, Cambridge: Cambridge University Press, 1981.
Garnham, Neal, *The Courts, Crime and the Criminal Law in Ireland 1692–1760*, Blackrock, Co. Dublin: Irish Academic Press, 1996.
'The Short Career of Paul Farrell: A Brief Consideration of Law Enforcement in Eighteenth-century Ireland', *ECI* 11 (1996), 46–52.
'How Violent was Eighteenth-century Ireland?', *Irish Historical Studies* 30 (1996–7), 377–92.
Gerrard, Christine, *The Patriot Opposition to Walpole: Politics, Poetry, and National Myth, 1725–1742*, Oxford: Clarendon Press, 1994.
Gibson, William, *The Church of England 1688–1832: Unity and Accord*, London: Routledge, 2001.
Gilbert, J. G., *Jonathan Swift: Romantic and Cynical Moralist*, Austin, TX: University of Texas Press, 1966.
Gilbert, J. T., *A History of the City of Dublin*, 3 vols., Dublin, 1854–9.
Gill, Conrad, *The Rise of the Irish Linen Industry*, Oxford: Oxford University Press, 1923.
Gillespie, Raymond, *Reading Ireland: Print, Reading and Social Change in Early Modern Ireland*, Manchester: Manchester University Press, 2005.
Goldgar, Bertrand, *The Curse of Party: Swift's Relations with Addison and Steele*, Lincoln: University of Nebraska Press, 1961.
Gray, Peter, and Olwen Purdue, eds., *The Irish Lord Lieutenancy, c. 1541–1922*, Dublin: University College Dublin Press, 2012.
Greene, Jack P., *Peripheries and Center: Constitutional Development in the Extended Politics of the British Empire and the United States 1607–1788*, Athens, GA: University of Georgia Press, 1986.
Gregori, Flavio, 'The Italian Reception of Swift', in Hermann J. Real (ed.), *The Reception of Jonathan Swift in Europe*, London: Thoemmes Continuum, 2005, pp. 17–56.
Griffin, Patrick, *The People with No Name: Ireland's Ulster Scots, America's Scots Irish, and the Creation of a British Atlantic World*, Princeton: Princeton University Press, 2001.
Hardie, Philip, *Rumour and Renown: Representations of Fama in Western Literature*, Cambridge: Cambridge University Press, 2012.
Harris, Michael, *London Newspapers in the Age of Walpole: A Study of the Origins of the Modern English Press*, London & Toronto: Fairleigh Dickinson University Press, 1987.
Harrison, Alan, *The Dean's Friend: Anthony Raymond (1675–1726), Jonathan Swift and the Irish Language*, Dublin: Éamonn de Burca, 1999.

Hart, A. Tindal, *The Life and Times of John Sharp Archbishop of York*, London: SPCK, 1949.
Hartle, P. N., 'A New Source for Swift's "Modest proposal"', *SStud* 7 (1992), 97–100.
Hayton, D. W., 'Anglo-Irish Attitudes: Changing Perceptions of National Identity among the Protestant Ascendancy in Ireland, ca. 1690–1750', *Studies in Eighteenth-Century Culture* 17 (1987), 151–2.
'Did Protestantism Fail in Early Eighteenth-century Ireland? Charity Schools and the Enterprise of Religious and Social Reformation, c. 1690–1730', in Alan Ford, James McGuire and Kenneth Milne (eds.), *As by Law Established: The Church of Ireland since the Reformation*, Dublin: Lilliput Press, 1995, pp. 166–86.
'The Stanhope/Sunderland Ministry and the Repudiation of Irish Parliamentary Independence', *English Historical Review* 113 (1998), 610–36.
'Patriots and Legislators: Irishmen and their Parliaments, c. 1689 – c. 1740', in Julian Hoppit (ed.), *Parliaments, Nations and Identities in Britain and Ireland, 1660–1860*, Manchester: Manchester University Press, 2003, pp. 103–23.
Ruling Ireland, 1685–1742: Politics, Politicians and Parties, Woodbridge: Boydell Press, 2004.
'Voters, Patrons and Parties: Parliamentary Elections in Ireland, c. 1692–1727', in Clyve Jones, Philip Salmon and R. W. Davis (eds.), *Partisan Politics, Principle and Reform in Parliament and the Constituencies, 1689–1880: Essays in Memory of John A. Phillips*, Edinburgh: Edinburgh University Press, 2005, pp. 44–70.
'"Paltry Underlings of State"? The Character and Aspirations of the "Castle" Party, 1715–32', in Claude Rawson (ed.), *Politics and Literature in England and Ireland in the Age of Swift*, Cambridge: Cambridge University Press, 2010.
'Parliament and the Established Church: Reform and Reaction', in D. W. Hayton, James Kelly and John Bergin (eds.), *The Eighteenth-century Composite State: Representative Institutions in Ireland and Europe, 1689–1800*, Basingstoke: Palgrave Macmillan, 2010, pp. 78–106.
The Anglo-Irish Experience, 1680–1730: Religion, Identity and Patriotism, Woodbridge: Boydell Press, 2012.
Hayton, D. W., and Stephen Karian, 'Select Document: The Division in the Irish House of Commons on the "Tithe of Agistment", 18 Mar. 1736, and Swift's "Character ... of the Legion Club"', *Irish Historical Studies* 38 (2012–13), 304–21.
Heal, Felicity, *Hospitality in Early Modern England*, Oxford: Clarendon Press, 1990.
Healy, John, *History of the Diocese of Meath*, 2 vols., Dublin: Association for Promoting Christian Knowledge, 1908.

Higgins, Ian, *Swift's Politics: A Study in Disaffection*, Cambridge: Cambridge University Press, 1994.

'The Afterlife of *A Modest Proposal*', in *Dean Swift's Modest Proposal at 280: A Symposium on Swift and Ireland*, Dublin: Deanery of St Patrick's Cathedral, 2009, www.iol.ie/~rjtechne/swift/2009/higins09.htm.

Hill, Brian W., *Robert Harley: Speaker, Secretary of State and Premier Minister*, New Haven & London: Yale University Press, 1988.

Hill, Jacqueline, 'Corporate Values in Hanoverian Edinburgh and Dublin', in S. J. Connolly, R. A. Houston and R. J. Morris (eds.), *Conflict, Identity and Economic Development: Ireland and Scotland, 1600–1939*, Preston: Carnegie, 1995, pp. 114–24.

'Dublin Corporation, Protestant Dissent, and Politics, 1660–1800', in Kevin Herlihy (ed.), *The Politics of Irish Dissent 1650–1800*, Dublin: Four Courts Press, 1997, pp. 28–39.

From Patriots to Unionists: Dublin Civic Politics and Irish Protestant Patriotism, 1660–1840, Oxford: Clarendon Press, 1997.

Hindle, Steve, 'Dependency, Shame and Belonging: Badging the Deserving Poor, c.1550–1750', *Cultural and Social History* 1 (2004), 6–35.

On the Parish? The Micro-politics of Poor Relief in Rural England c.1550–1750, Oxford: Clarendon Press, 2004.

Holmes, Geoffrey, *British Politics in the Age of Anne*, London: Macmillan, 1967.

Holmes, Richard, 'James Arbuckle and Dean Swift: Cultural Politics in the Irish Confessional State', *Irish Studies Review* 16 (2008), 431–44.

'Swift's Modest Proposer and Shaftesbury', in Brian Griffin and Ellen McWilliams (eds.), *Irish Studies in Britain: New Perspectives on History and Literature*, Newcastle: Cambridge Scholars Publishing, 2010, pp. 33–46.

Horwitz, Henry, *Revolution Politicks: The Career of Daniel Finch, Second Earl of Nottingham, 1647–1730*, Cambridge: Cambridge University Press, 1968.

Howell, T. B., *A Complete Collection of State Trials* ..., 21 vols., London, 1816.

Hughes, Leo, 'Attitudes of Some Restoration Dramatists toward Farce', *Philological Quarterly* 19 (1940), pp. 268–87.

Hughes, S. C., *The Church of S. Werburgh, Dublin*, Dublin: Hodges Figgis, 1889.

Israel, J. T., *The Dutch Republic: Its Rise, Greatness and Fall*, Oxford: Oxford University Press, 1995.

James, F. G., 'Irish Smuggling in the Eighteenth Century', *Irish Historical Studies* 12 (1960–1), 219–317.

'The Irish Lobby in the Early Eighteenth Century', *English Historical Review* 81 (1966), 543–57.

Ireland in the Empire 1688–1770: A History of Ireland from the Williamite Wars to the Eve of the American Revolution, Cambridge, MA: Harvard University Press, 1973.
Johnson, J. W., 'Tertullian and *A Modest Proposal*', *MLN* 73 (1958), 561–3.
Johnston, Joseph, *Bishop Berkeley's Querist in Historical Perspective*, Dundalk: Dundalgan Press, 1970.
Johnston-Liik, Edith Mary, *History of the Irish Parliament 1692–1800*, 6 vols., Belfast: Ulster Historical Foundation, 2002.
Jones, Clyve, '"Venice Preserv'd; or A Plot Discovered": The Political and Social Context of the Peerage Bill of 1719', in Clyve Jones (ed.), *A Pillar of the Constitution: The House of Lords in British Politics, 1640–1784*, London & Ronceverte WV: Hambledon Press, 1989, pp. 79–112.
Kammen, Michael, *Colonial New York: A History*, New York: Charles Scribner's Sons, 1975.
Karian, Stephen, *Jonathan Swift in Print and Manuscript*, Cambridge: Cambridge University Press, 2010.
Kelly, James, 'Jonathan Swift and the Irish Economy in the 1720s', *ECI* 6 (1991), 7–36.
  'Harvests and Hardship: Famine and Scarcity in Ireland in the Late 1720s', *Studia Hibernica* 26 (1991–2), 65–105.
  '"The Glorious and Immortal Memory": Commemoration and Protestant Identity in Ireland 1660–1800', *Proceedings of the Royal Irish Academy* 94 (1994), section C, 25–52.
  'Political Publishing, 1700–1800', in Raymond Gillespie and Andrew Hadfield (eds.), *The Oxford History of the Irish Book*, vol. III: *The Irish Book in English, 1550–1800*, Oxford: Oxford University Press, 2006, pp. 215–33.
Kelly, Patrick, 'William Molyneux and the Spirit of Liberty in Eighteenth Century Ireland', *ECI* 3 (1988), 133–48.
  'Archbishop William King (1650–1729) and Colonial Nationalism', in Ciaran Brady (ed.), *Worsted in the Game: Losers in Irish History*, Dublin: Lilliput Press, 1989, pp. 84–94.
  'Industry and Virtue versus Luxury and Corruption: Berkeley, Walpole and the South Sea Bubble Crisis', *ECI* 7 (1992), 57–74.
  '"Conclusions by no Means Calculated for the Circumstances and Condition of Ireland": Swift, Berkeley and the Solution to Ireland's Economic Problems', in Aileen Douglas, Patrick Kelly and Ian Campbell Ross (eds.), *Locating Swift: Essays from Dublin on the 250th Anniversary of the Death of Jonathan Swift, 1667–1745*, Dublin: Four Courts Press, 1998, pp. 47–59.
  'The Politics of Political Economy in Mid-eighteenth-century Ireland', in S. J. Connolly (ed.), *Political Ideas in Eighteenth-century Ireland*, Dublin: Four Courts Press, 2000, pp. 105–29.

'Conquest versus Consent as the Basis of the English Title to Ireland in William Molyneux's *Case of Ireland . . . Stated* (1698)', in Ciaran Brady and J. H. Ohlmeyer (eds.), *British Interventions in Early Modern Ireland*, Cambridge: Cambridge University Press, 2005, pp. 334–56.
Kemp, Betty, *King and Commons 1660–1832*, London: Macmillan, 1957.
Kendrick, T. F. J., 'Sir Robert Walpole, the Old Whigs and the Bishops, 1733–1736: A Study in Eighteenth-Century Parliamentary Politics', *Historical Journal* 11 (1968), 421–35.
Kennedy, Máire, 'Reading Print, 1700–1800', in Raymond Gillespie and Andrew Hadfield (eds.), *The Oxford History of the Irish Book*, vol. III: *The Irish Book in English 1550–1800*, Oxford: Oxford University Press, 2006, pp. 146–66.
Kiernan, T. J., *History of the Financial Administration of Ireland to 1817*, London: T. S. King, 1930.
King, Sir Charles S., *A Great Archbishop of Dublin William King D.D . . .*, London: Longmans, Green and Co., 1906.
Kohn, G. C., *Encyclopedia of Plague and Pestilence: From Ancient Times to the Present*, New York: Infobase Publishing, 2008.
Kramnick, Isaac, *Bolingbroke and his Circle: The Politics of Nostalgia in the Age of Walpole*, Cambridge, MA: Harvard University Press, 1968.
Labaree, Benjamin W., *Colonial Massachusetts: A History*, Milwood, NY: KTO Press, 1979.
Labaree, L. W., *Royal Government in America: A Study of the British Colonial System before 1783*, New Haven: Yale University Press, 1930.
Landa, L. A., '"A Modest Proposal" and Populousness', *Modern Philology* 40 (1942), 161–70.
'Jonathan Swift and Charity', *Journal of English and German Philology* 44 (1945), 337–50.
Swift and the Church of Ireland, Oxford: Clarendon Press, 1954.
Langford, Paul, *The Excise Crisis: Society and Politics in the Age of Walpole*, Oxford: Clarendon Press, 1975.
Laprade, W. T., *Public Opinion and Politics in Eighteenth Century England*, New York: Macmillan, 1936.
Leavis, F. R., *The Common Pursuit*, London: Chatto & Windus, 1934.
Lecky, W. E. H., *History of Ireland in the Eighteenth Century*, 5 vols., London, 1892.
Lehmann, Gilly, 'The Cook as Artist?', in Harlan Walker (ed.), *Food in the Arts: Proceedings of the Oxford Symposium on Food and Cookery 1998*, Totnes: Prospect Books, 1999, pp. 125–33.
Lein, C. D., 'Jonathan Swift and the Population of Ireland', *Eighteenth-Century Studies* 8 (1975), 431–53.
Lennon, Colm, 'The Print Trade, 1700–1800', in Raymond Gillespie and Andrew Hadfield (eds.), *The Oxford History of the Irish Book*, vol. III:

The Irish Book in English, 1550–1800, Oxford: Oxford University Press, 2006, pp. 74–87.
Lepper, J. H., and Philip Crosslé, *History of the Grand Lodge of Free and Accepted Masons of Ireland*, Dublin: Lodge of Research, 1925.
Leslie, J. B., *History of Kilsaran Union of Parishes in the County of Louth*, Dundalk: William Tempest, 1908.
Lester, Katherine Morris, and Bess Viola Oerke, *Accessories of Dress*, Peoria, IL: Manual Arts Press, 1940.
Leyburn, J. G., *The Scotch-Irish: A Social History*, Chapel Hill, NC: University of North Carolina Press, 1962.
Lillywhite, Bryant, *London Coffeehouses*, London: George Allen & Unwin, 1963.
Lindsay, Alexander, *Index of English Literary Manuscripts*, vol. III, pt 4, London: Mansell, 1997.
Livesey, James, 'The Dublin Society in Eighteenth-Century Irish Political Thought', *Historical Journal* 47 (2004), 615–40.
  Civil Society and Empire: Ireland and Scotland in the Eighteenth-Century Atlantic World, New Haven & London: Yale University Press, 2009.
Lock, F. P., *Swift's Tory Politics*, London: Duckworth, 1983.
Ludington, Charles, '"Be Sometimes to Your Country True": The Politics of Wine in England, 1660–1714', in Adam Smyth (ed.), *A Pleasing Sinne: Drink and Conviviality in Seventeenth-century England*, Cambridge: D. S. Brewer, 2004, pp. 93–106.
Mack, Maynard, *Alexander Pope*, New Haven & London: Yale University Press, 1985.
MacLachlan, A. D., 'The Road to Peace', in Geoffrey Holmes (ed.), *Britain after the Glorious Revolution 1689–1714*, London: Macmillan, 1969, pp. 197–215.
Magennis, Eoin, 'Whither the Irish Financial Revolution? Money, Banks, and Politics in Ireland in the 1730s', in Charles Ivar McGrath and C. J. Fauske (eds.), *Money, Power and Print: Interdisciplinary Studies on the Financial Revolution in the British Isles*, Newark: University of Delaware Press, 2008, pp. 198–208.
  'Regulating the Market: Parliament, Corn and Bread in Eighteenth-Century Ireland', in Michael Brown and S. P. Donlan (eds.), *The Laws and other Legalities of Ireland, 1679–1850*, Farnham: Ashgate, 2011, pp. 209–30.
Mahaffy, J. P., J. W. Stubbs and T. K. Abbot, *The Book of Trinity College, Dublin, 1591–1891*, Belfast: Marcus Ward, 1892.
Mahony, Robert, *Jonathan Swift: The Irish Identity*, New Haven & London: Yale University Press, 1995.
  'The Irish Colonial Experience and Swift's Rhetorics of Perception in the 1720s', *Eighteenth-Century Literature* 22 (1998), 63–75.

'Swift's *Modest Proposal* and the Rhetoric of Irish Colonial Consumption', *Ideas, Aesthetics and Inquiries into the Early Modern Era* 4 (1998), 205–14.
'Protestant Dependence and Consumption in Swift's Irish Writings', in S. J. Connolly (ed.), *Political Ideas in Eighteenth-century Ireland*, Dublin: Four Courts Press, 2000, pp. 83–104.
Malcomson, A. P. W., 'Absenteeism in Eighteenth Century Ireland', *Irish Economic and Social History* 1 (1974), pp. 15–35.
Archbishop Charles Agar: Churchmanship and Politics in Ireland, 1760–1810, Dublin: Four Courts Press, 2002.
Nathaniel Clements: Government and the Governing Elite in Ireland, 1725–75, Dublin: Four Courts Press, 2005.
Malek, J. S., 'Swift's "Vindication of Lord Carteret": Authorial Intention and Historical Context', *Rocky Mountain Review of Language and Literature* 29 (1975), 10–23.
Mant, Richard, *History of the Church of Ireland* . . . , 2 vols., London, 1840.
Maslen, Keith, 'George Faulkner and William Bowyer: The London Connection', in *An Early London Printing House at Work: Studies in the Bowyer Ledgers*, New York: Bibliographical Society of America, 1993, pp. 223–33.
Maslen, Keith, and John Lancaster (eds.), *The Bowyer Ledgers: The Printing Accounts of William Bowyer, Father and Son*, London: Bibliographical Society, 1991.
Matthew, H. C. G., and Brian Harrison (eds.), *The Oxford Dictionary of National Biography*, 60 vols., Oxford: Oxford University Press, 2004.
Maxwell, Constantia, *Dublin under the Georges 1714–1830*, London: Faber and Faber, 1956.
McArdle, Grainne, 'Signora Violante and her Troupe of Dancers, 1729–32', *ECI* 20 (2005), 55–78.
McBride, Ian, *Eighteenth-century Ireland: The Isle of Slaves*, Dublin: Gill and Macmillan, 2009.
'Catholic Politics in the Penal Era: Father Sylvester Lloyd and the Delvin Address of 1727', in John Bergin, Eoin Magennis, Lesa Ní Mhunghaile and Patrick Walsh (eds.), *New Perspectives on the Penal Laws*, *ECI*, special issue, 1 (2011), 115–48.
McGrath, Charles Ivar, 'The Provisions for Conversion in the Penal Laws, 1695–1750', in Michael Brown, Charles Ivar McGrath and Thomas Power (eds.), *Converts and Conversion in Ireland, 1650–1850*, Dublin: Four Courts Press, 2005, pp. 35–59.
'Money, Politics and Power: The Financial Legislation of the Irish Parliament', in D. W. Hayton, James Kelly and John Bergin (eds.), *The Eighteenth-century Composite State: Representative Institutions in Ireland and Europe, 1689–1800*, Basingstoke: Palgrave Macmillan, 2010, pp. 21–43.

Ireland and Empire, 1692–1770, London: Pickering and Chatto, 2012.
McGuire, James, and James Quinn (eds.), *Dictionary of Irish Biography*, 9 vols., Cambridge: Cambridge University Press, 2009.
McLaverty, James, 'Lawton Gilliver: Pope's Bookseller', *Studies in Bibliography* 32 (1979), 101–24.
McMinn, Joseph, 'A Weary Patriot: Swift and the Formation of an Anglo-Irish Identity', *ECI* 2 (1987), 103–13.
'Jonathan's Travels: Swift's Sense of Ireland', *SStud* 7 (1992), 36–53.
Jonathan's Travels: Swift and Ireland, Belfast: Appletree Press, 1994.
McNally, Patrick, '"Irish and English Interests": National Conflict within the Church of Ireland Episcopate in the Reign of George I', *Irish Historical Studies* 29 (1994–5), pp. 295–314.
Parties, Patriots and Undertakers: Parliamentary Politics in Early Hanoverian Ireland, Dublin: Four Courts Press, 1997.
'Wood's Halfpence, Carteret, and the Government of Ireland, 1723–56', *Irish Historical Studies*, 30 (1996–7), 354–76.
McParland, Edward, *Public Architecture in Ireland, 1680–1760*, New Haven & London: Yale University Press, 2001.
'Building the Parliament House in Dublin', *Parliamentary History* 21 (2002), 131–40.
Melville, Lewis, *The Life and Writings of Philip Duke of Wharton*, London: Bodley Head, 1913.
Merians, Linda E., *Envisioning the Worst: Representations of 'Hottentots' in Early Modern England*, Newark, NJ: University of Delaware Press, 2001.
Miller, Kerby A., *Emigrants and Exiles: Ireland and the Irish Exodus to North America*, New York: Oxford University Press, 1985.
Milne, Kenneth, *The Irish Charter Schools 1730–1800*, Dublin: Four Courts Press, 1997.
Monod, P. K., *Jacobitism and the English People, 1688–1788*, Cambridge: Cambridge University Press, 1989.
Moody, T. W., and W. E. Vaughan (eds.), *A New History of Ireland*, vol. IV: *Eighteenth-century Ireland 1691–1800*, Oxford: Clarendon Press, 1986.
Moore, Courtenay, 'An Old Dublin Remembrancer', *Journal of the Royal Society of Antiquaries of Ireland* 14 (1904), 74–5.
Moore, S. D., 'Devouring Posterity: *A Modest Proposal*, Empire, and Ireland's "Debt of the Nation"', *PMLA* 122 (2007), 679–95.
Swift, the Book, and the Irish Financial Revolution: Satire and Sovereignty in Colonial Ireland, Baltimore: John Hopkins University Press, 2010.
Munter, Robert, *The History of the Irish Newspaper 1685–1760*, Cambridge: Cambridge University Press, 1967.
A Dictionary of the Print Trade in Ireland 1550–1775, New York: Fordham University Press, 1988.

Murphy, David, *The Irish Brigades, 1685–2006: A Gazetteer of Irish Military Service, Past and Present*, Dublin: Four Courts Press, 2007.
Murphy, Sean, 'Charles Lucas and the Dublin Election of 1748–1749', *Parliamentary History* 2 (1983), 93–111.
'The Corporation of Dublin, 1660–1760', *Dublin Historical Record* 38 (1984), 22–35.
'Irish Jacobitism and Freemasonry', *ECI* 9 (1994), 75–82.
Nokes, David, *Jonathan Swift, a Hypocrite Reversed: A Critical Biography*, Oxford: Oxford University Press, 1985.
O'Brien, George, *The Economic History of Ireland in the Eighteenth Century*, Dublin: Maunsell, 1918.
O'Brien, Gerard (ed.), *Catholic Ireland in the Eighteenth Century: Collected Essays of Maureen Wall*, Dublin: Geography Publications, 1989.
O'Carroll, Joseph, 'Contemporary Attitudes towards the Homeless Poor 1725–1775', in David Dickson (ed.), *The Gorgeous Mask: Dublin 1700– 1850*, Dublin: Trinity History Workshop, 1987, pp. 64–85.
Ó Ciardha, Éamonn, *Ireland and the Jacobite Cause, 1685–1766: A Fatal Attachment*, Dublin: Four Courts Press, 2002.
Olson, Alison Gilbert, *Anglo-American Politics 1660–1775: The Relationship between Parties in England and Colonial America*, Oxford: Clarendon Press, 1973.
O'Regan, Philip, *Archbishop William King ... and the Constitution in Church and State*, Dublin: Four Courts Press, 2000.
Osborough, W. N., 'The Failure to Enact an Irish Bill of Rights: A Gap in Irish Constitutional History', *Irish Jurist* 33 (1998), 392–415.
Overton, J. H., *The Nonjurors: Their Lives, Principles and Writings*, London, 1902.
Pargellis, Stanley M., 'The Four Independent Companies of New York', in *Essays in Colonial History Presented to Charles McLean Andrews by His Students*, New Haven: Yale University Press, 1931, pp. 96– 123.
Passmann, Dirk F., '"Many Diverting Books of History and Travels" and "A Modest Proposal"', *ECI* 2 (1987), 167–76.
Passmann, Dirk F., and Hermann J. Real, 'Barbarism, Witchcraft and Devil-Worship: Cock-and-Bull Stories from Several Remote Nations of the World', *SStud* 23 (2008), 94–110.
Passmann, Dirk F., and H. J. Vienken, *The Library and Reading of Jonathan Swift: A Bio-bibliographical Handbook. Part I, Swift's Library in Four Volumes*, 4 vols., Frankfurt am Main: Peter Lang, 2004.
Paterson, T. G. F., 'The Black Bank and Fews Barracks', *Ulster Journal of Archaeology* 1 (1938), 108–12.
Phiddian, Robert, 'Have you Eaten Yet? The Reader in "A Modest Proposal"', *SEL 1500–1900* 36 (1996), 603–21.

'Political Arithmetick: Accounting for Irony in Swift's *A Modest Proposal*', *Accounting Auditing and Accountability Journal* 9 (1996), 71–83.

Plumb, J. H., *Sir Robert Walpole: The King's Minister*, London: Cresset Press, 1960.

Pollard, Mary, *Dublin's Trade in Books 1550–1800*, Oxford: Oxford University Press, 1989.

A Dictionary of Members of the Dublin Book Trade 1550–1800 Based on the Records of the Guild of St Luke the Evangelist Dublin, London: The Bibliographical Society, 2000.

Pomfret, John E., *Colonial New Jersey: A History*, New York: Charles Scribner's Sons, 1973.

Potter, Tiffany, 'A Colonial Source for Cannibalistic Breeding in Swift's "A Modest Proposal"', *Notes and Queries* 244 (1999), 347–8.

Power, T. P., 'Converts', in T. P. Power and Kevin Whelan (eds.), *Endurance and Emergence: Catholics in Ireland in the Eighteenth Century*, Blackrock, Co. Dublin: Irish Academic Press, 1990, pp. 101–27.

Probyn, Clive, 'Jonathan Swift at the Sign of the Drapier', in *Münster* (1998), pp. 225–37.

Rankin, Helen, and Charles Nelson (eds.), *Curious in Everything: The Career of Arthur Dobbs of Carrickfergus, 1689–1765*, Carrickfergus: Carrickfergus and District Historical Society in association with Society for the History of Natural History, 1990.

Rawson, Claude, *Order from Confusion Sprung: Studies in Eighteenth-Century Literature from Swift to Cowper*, London: George Allen & Unwin, 1985.

'"Indians" and Irish: Montaigne, Swift, and the "Cannibal Question"', *MLQ* 53 (1992), 299–363.

God, Gulliver, and Genocide: Barbarism and the European Imagination, 1492–1945, Oxford: Oxford University Press, 2001.

Swift and Others, Cambridge: Cambridge University Press, 2015.

(ed.), *Politics and Literature in England and Ireland in the Age of Swift*, Cambridge: Cambridge University Press, 2010.

Records of Convocation, ed. Gerald Bray, 20 vols., Woodbridge: Boydell Press, 2005–6.

Reilly, Patrick, 'The Displaced Person: Swift and Ireland', *SStud* 8 (1993), 68–83.

Reilly, Susan, 'William King and the Idea of "Improvement"', in C. J. Fauske (ed.), *Archbishop William King and the Anglican Irish Context, 1688–1729*, Dublin: Four Courts Press, 2004, pp. 148–59.

Rogers, Nicholas, 'Riot and Popular Jacobitism in Early Hanoverian England', in Eveline Cruickshanks (ed.), *Ideology and Conspiracy: Aspects of Jacobitism, 1689–1759*, Edinburgh: John Donald, 1982, pp. 70–88.

'Policing the Poor in Eighteenth-century London: The Vagrancy Laws and their Administration', *Social History* 24 (1991), 127–47.

Rogers, Pat, *A Political Biography of Alexander Pope*, London: Pickering & Chatto, 2010.
(ed.), *The Cambridge Companion to Alexander Pope*, Cambridge: Cambridge University Press, 2007.
Rosenheim, E. W., *Swift and the Satirist's Art*, Chicago: University of Chicago Press, 1963.
Ross, Ian Campbell, *Swift's Ireland*, Dublin: Eason, 1983.
'"More to Avoid the Expence than the Shame": Infanticide in the Modest Proposer's Ireland', *SStud* 1 (1986), 75–6.
'Ottomans, Incas, and Irish Literature: Reading Rycaut', *ECI* 22 (2007), 11–27.
'"A Very Knowing American": The Inca Garcilaso de la Vega and Swift's *A Modest Proposal*', *MLQ* 68 (2007), 493–516.
Ross, Ian Campbell, and Anne Markey, 'From Clonmel to Peru: Barbarism and Civility in *Vertue Rewarded; Or, the Irish Princess*', *Irish University Review* 38 (2008), 179–202.
Ruding, Rogers, *Annals of the Coinage of Britain and Its Dependencies...*, 4 vols., London, 1817–19.
Ryder, Michael, 'The Bank of Ireland, 1721: Land, Credit and Dependency', *Historical Journal* 25 (1982), 557–82.
Sahlins, Peter, *Boundaries: The Making of France and Spain in the Pyrenees*, Berkeley: University of California Press, 1989.
Schultz, W. E., *Gay's Beggar's Opera: Its Content, History and Influence*, New Haven: Yale University Press, 1923.
Schwartz, Stuart B., 'The Formation of a Colonial Identity in Brazil', in Nicholas Canny and Anthony Pagden (eds.), *Colonial Identity in the Atlantic World, 1500–1800*, Princeton, NJ: Princeton University Press, 1987, pp. 15–50.
Schwoerer, Lois G., *No Standing Armies! The Anti-army Ideology in 17th-century England*, Baltimore & London: Johns Hopkins University Press, 1974.
Seaby, W. A., and T. G. F. Paterson, 'Ulster Beggars' Badges', *Ulster Journal of Archaeology* 3rd ser., 3 (1970), 95–106.
Sedgwick, Romney, *The House of Commons 1715–1754*, 2 vols., London, HMSO, 1970.
Sekora, John, *Luxury: The Concept in Western Thought, Eden to Smollett*, Baltimore: Johns Hopkins University Press, 1977.
Sharp, Michael, 'The St Patrick Coinage of Charles II', *British Numismatic Journal* 68 (1998), 160.
Sheridan, Edel, 'Designing the Capital City: Dublin, c. 1660–1810', in Joseph Brady and Anngret Simms (eds.), *Dublin through Space and Time*, Dublin: Four Courts Press, 2001, pp. 66–135.

Shesgreen, Sean, 'Images of the Irish Underclass: The Innovative Continuity of Hugh Douglas Hamilton's "Cries of Dublin"', in William Laffan (ed.), *The Cries of Dublin &c, Drawn from the Life by Hugh Douglas Hamilton, 1760*, Dublin: Irish Georgian Society, 2003, pp. 38–55.

Simms, J. G., 'Historical Revision: X, Irish Catholics and the Parliamentary Franchise, 1692–1728', *Irish Historical Studies* 12 (1960–1), 28–37.

'The Irish Parliament of 1713', in G. A. Hayes-McCoy (ed.), *Historical Studies*, vol. IV, London: Bowes and Bowes, 1963, pp. 82–92.

'Dean Swift and County Armagh', *Seanchas Ardmhacha* 6 (1971), 131–40.

Colonial Nationalism, 1698–1776: Molyneux's 'The Case of Ireland ... Stated', Cork: Mercier Press, 1976.

'Dean Swift and the Currency Problem', *Numismatic Society of Ireland: Occasional Papers* 20 (1978), 8–18.

William Molyneux of Dublin: 1656–1698, ed. P. H. Kelly, Dublin: Irish Academic Press, 1982.

Slack, Paul, *The English Poor Law 1531–1782*, Basingstoke: Palgrave Macmillan, 1990.

Smithers, Peter, *The Life of Joseph Addison*, Oxford: Clarendon Press, 1968.

Smyth, Jim, '"Like Amphibious Animals": Irish Protestants, Ancient Britons, 1691–1707', *Historical Journal* 36 (1993), 785–97.

Sneddon, Andrew, 'Bishop Francis Hutchinson (1660–1739): A Case Study in the Eighteenth-century Culture of Improvement', *Irish Historical Studies* 35 (2006–7), 289–310.

Witchcraft and Whigs: The Life of Bishop Francis Hutchinson, 1660–1739, Manchester: Manchester University Press, 2008.

'Legislating for Economic Development: Irish Fisheries as a Case Study in the Limitations of "Improvement"', in D. W. Hayton, James Kelly and John Bergin (eds.), *The Eighteenth-century Composite State: Representative Institutions in Ireland and Europe, 1689–1800*, Basingstoke: Palgrave Macmillan, 2010, pp. 136–59.

Speck, William, 'Whigs and Tories Dim Their Glories', in John Cannon (ed.), *The Whig Ascendancy: Colloquies on Hanoverian England*, London: Edward Arnold, 1981, pp. 51–70.

Stephen, Leslie, *Swift*, London, 1882.

Stevenson, John, *Two Centuries of Life in Down, 1600–1800*, Belfast: Linenhall Press, 1920.

Stubbs, W. C., 'The Weavers Guild, the Guild of the Blessed Virgin Mary, Dublin, 1446–1840', *Journal of the Royal Society of Antiquaries of Ireland* 49 (1919), 60–88.

Sundell, Kirsten Ewart, '"A Savage and Unnatural Taste": Anglo-Irish Imitations of *A Modest Proposal*, 1730–31', *SStud* 18 (2003), 80–98.

Survey of London, 47 vols., London: Athlone Press, 1900–2012, vol. XXXIII.
Sykes, Norman, *William Wake, Archbishop of Canterbury, 1657–1737*, 2 vols., Cambridge: Cambridge University Press, 1957.
Tave, S. M., *The Amiable Humorist: A Study of the Comic Theory and Criticism of the Eighteenth and Early Nineteenth Centuries*, Chicago: University of Chicago Press, 1960.
Taylor, Stephen, 'Sir Robert Walpole, the Church of England, and the Quakers' Tithe Bill of 1736', *Historical Journal* 28 (1985), 51–77.
'Whigs, Tories and Anticlericalism: Ecclesiastical Courts Legislation in 1733', *Parliamentary History* 19 (2000), 329–56.
'The Bowman Affair: Latitudinarian Theology, Anti-clericalism and the Limits of Orthodoxy in Early Hanoverian England', in Robert D. Cornwall and William Gibson (eds.), *Religion, Politics and Dissent, 1660–1832: Essays in Honour of James E. Bradley*, Aldershot: Ashgate, 2010, pp. 35–50.
Teerink, H., *A Bibliography of the Writings of Jonathan Swift*, 2nd edn, revised and corrected by Arthur H. Scouten, Philadelphia: University of Pennsylvania Press, 1963.
Thirsk, Joan, ed., *The Agrarian History of England and Wales*, vol. V: *1640–1750*, Cambridge: Cambridge University Press, 1985.
Thompson, Paul V., and Dorothy Jay Thompson (eds.), *The Account Books of Jonathan Swift*, London: Scolar Press, 1984.
Treadwell, Michael, 'London Trade Publishers 1675–1750', *The Library* 4 (1982), 99–134.
Tucker, Bernard, '"Our Chief Poetess": Mary Barber and Swift's Circle', *ECI* 7 (1992), 43–56.
Twomey, Brendan, *Smithfield and the Parish of St. Paul, Dublin, 1698–1750*, Maynooth Studies in Local History, 63, Dublin: Four Courts Press, 2005.
Varey, Simon, 'The Craftsman', in J. A. Downie and T. N. Corns (eds.), *Telling People What to Think: Early Eighteenth-century Periodicals from 'The Review' to 'The Rambler'*, London: Cass, 1993, pp. 58–77.
Vicars, Sir Arthur, ed., *Index to the Prerogative Wills of Ireland, 1536–1810*, Dublin: E. Ponsonby, 1897.
Victoria County History, Cheshire, ed. A. T. Thacker, B. E. Harris, C. P. Lewis *et al.*, 5 vols. so far, Oxford & Woodbridge: Oxford University Press, Boydell & Brewer, 1979–2005.
Victory, Isolde, 'The Making of the Declaratory Act of 1720', in Gerard O'Brien (ed.), *Parliament, Politics and People: Essays in Eighteenth-century Irish History*, Blackrock, Co. Dublin: Irish Academic Press, 1989, pp. 9–29.
Wagner, H. R., *Irish Economics 1700–1783: A Bibliography with Notes*, London: Dryden Press, 1907.

Walsh, Patrick, 'Free Movement of People? Responses to Emigration from Ireland, 1718–30', *Journal of Irish and Scottish Studies* 3 (2009), 221–36.
'Club Life in Late Seventeenth- and Early Eighteenth-Century Ireland: In Search of an Associational World, c. 1680 – c. 1730', in James Kelly and Martyn Powell *(eds.)*, *Clubs and Societies in Eighteenth-Century Ireland*, Dublin: Four Courts Press, 2010, pp. 44–8.
The Making of the Irish Protestant Ascendancy: The Life of William Conolly, 1662–1729, Woodbridge: Boydell Press, 2010.
Walsh, T. J., *Opera in Dublin 1705–1797: The Social Scene*, Dublin: Allen Figgis, 1973.
Ward, James, 'Which Crisis? A Politics of Distress in *A Modest Proposal*', *SStud* 21 (2006), 76–86.
Watson, R. F., *Annals of Pennsylvania*, Philadelphia, 1830.
Watt, T. D., 'The Corruption of the Law and Popular Violence: The Crisis of Order in Dublin, 1729', *Irish Historical Studies* 39 (2014–15), 1–23.
Whan, Robert, *The Presbyterians of Ulster, 1680–1730*, Woodbridge: Boydell Press, 2013.
White, Terence de Vere, *The Story of the Royal Dublin Society*, Tralee: The Kerryman, 1955.
Williams, Basil, *Carteret and Newcastle: A Contrast in Contemporaries*, Cambridge: Cambridge University Press, 1943.
Wilson, F. P., *The Oxford Dictionary of English Proverbs*, 3rd edn, Oxford: Clarendon Press, 1970.
Wittkowsky, George, 'Swift's *Modest Proposal*: The Biography of an Early Georgian Pamphlet', *Journal of the History of Ideas* 4 (1943), 75–104.
Wood, Herbert, 'The Office of Chief Governor of Ireland, 1172–1509', *Proceedings of the Royal Irish Academy* 36 (1921–4), sect. C, 206–38.
Woodward, Donald, 'The Anglo-Irish Livestock Trade in the Seventeenth Century', *Irish Historical Studies* 18 (1972–3), 489–523.
Woolley, David, 'Forster's *Swift*', *The Dickensian* 70 (1974), 191–204.
Woolley, James, 'Sarah Harding as Swift's Printer', in Christopher Fox and Brenda Tooley (eds.), *Walking Naboth's Vineyard: New Studies of Swift*, Notre Dame, IN: University of Notre Dame Press, 1995, pp. 164–77.

Unpublished Theses

Burke, Nuala, 'Dublin 1600–1800: A Study in Urban Morphogenesis', Ph.D., TCD, 1972.
Chapman, Paul, 'Jacobite Political Argument in England, 1714–1766', Ph.D., University of Cambridge, 1983.
Coleborne, Bryan, 'Jonathan Swift and the Dunces of Dublin', Ph.D., University College Dublin, 1982.
Egan, Seán, 'Finance and the Government of Ireland, 1660–85', 2 vols., Ph.D., TCD, 1983.

Flanagan, C. M. "'A Merely Local Dispute?" Partisan Politics and the Dublin Mayoral Dispute of 1709–1715', Ph.D., University of Notre Dame, 1983.
Griffin, Joseph, 'Parliamentary Politics in Ireland during the Reign of George I', MA, University College Dublin, 1977.
Holmes, Richard, 'The Literary Career of James Arbuckle 1717–30', Ph.D., University of Bristol, 2012.
McCoy, J. G., 'Court Ideology in Mid-Eighteenth-century Ireland', MA, St Patrick's College, Maynooth, 1990.
'Local Political Culture in the Hanoverian Empire: The Case of Ireland, 1714–1760', D.Phil., University of Oxford, 1994.
McNally, Patrick, 'Patronage and Politics in Ireland, 1714–1727', Ph.D., Queen's University Belfast, 1993.
Rees, G. A., 'Pamphlets, Pamphleteers and the Problems of Irish Society, c. 1727–1749', Ph.D., Queen's University Belfast, 2011.
Victory, Isolde, 'Colonial Nationalism in Ireland, 1692–1725: From Common Law to Natural Right', Ph.D., Trinity College Dublin, 1995.

INDEX

Abernethy, John, 236
Acheson, Sir Arthur, xxxii, 110, 212, 213, 214
Acheson, Sir Arthur, and Lady Ann, xxxi, xxxii, 88, 432
Act of Settlement (1701), 256
Act of Uniformity, Irish, the (1666), 194
Acts (of the Apostles), 111, 237, 251
Addison, Joseph, 23, 37, 43, 45, 59, 71, 77, 149, 150, 173, 199, 242
Aeacus, 92
Aesop (fables of), 25, 96, 104, 176, 262, 360, 365
Agesilaus, 205, 206
Ajax (of Telamon), 32
Albert, William, 122
Alexander, James, 349, 361
Allen, Joshua, Viscount, xxxiv, lxxxvii, lxxxviii, xciii, xcix, c, 147, 158, 182, 183, 186, 192, 200, 254, 382, 453, 456, 457
'Traulus', xxxiv, xcix, 457
Allestree, Richard, lxxvii, 79
Amhurst, Nicholas, 221, 343
Anglo-Spanish War (1727–9), 249
Anne, Queen of England, xxvi, xxxiii, xxxv, l, lxv, xc, 24, 71, 77, 125, 192, 198, 204, 208, 216, 247, 252, 254, 255, 259, 262, 268, 296, 354
Annesley, Arthur, 5th Earl of Anglesey, lii
Annesley, Arthur, 7th Earl of Anglesey, 211
Annesley, William, 211
Annesley v. Sherlock, xxxix, 259
Antrim, Presbytery of, lxiii
Anytus, 39

Apology for the Clergy of Ireland in Respect of their Civil Rights, An, lxv, lxviii
Arbuckle, James, xxviii, lxxxvi, 154, 159, 172, 266, 298
Arctic Ocean, 111
Aristides ('the Just'), 60
Aristotle, 61, 66, 80, 173, 197, 204, 326
Armstrong, Sir Thomas, 131
Arnold, John, 260
Ashley Cooper, Anthony, 1st Earl of Shaftesbury, 77
Ashley Cooper, Anthony, 3rd Earl of Shaftesbury, 154, 159
Ashton, John, 261
Atterbury, Francis, Bishop of Rochester, xxxv, 60, 65, 66, 67, 69, 70, 71, 72, 195, 261
Atterbury, Lewis, 71
Aughrim (Battle of), 261
Augustus, Roman Emperor, 53, 205, 206
Austria, 222, 337
Austrian Netherlands, 258
Avoirdupois, 140, 151

Bacon, Francis, 60, 78
Bacon, Thomas, 356
badging (in Ireland), lxxiii, 2, 3, 306, 310, 488
Baker, John, 199
Baldwin, Richard, 211
Ball, F. Elrington, 259
Baltes, Sabine, 19, 38
Barbary corsairs, 373
Barber, Mary, xxxii, 275–7, 479
Poems on Several Occasions, 276
Barber, Rupert, 276, 277
Barbon, Nicholas, lxxv, 178

531

INDEX

Barnard, T. C., xxviii, xlix, l, lviii, lxv, lxvii, lxxiii, xci, 114, 220
Barnett, Louise, 276
Barrett, John, 255
Bath, 1st Earl of. *See* Granville, Sir John
Baxter, Richard, 26
Bayly, John, xxxii, cvi, cvii
Beckett, J. C., lxiii
Beckett, John V., 31
Bedlam (Bethlem Royal Hospital), 173, 201, 326
Beier, A. L., 177
Belcher, Jonathan, 364
Belcher, T. W., 9
Belfast, corporation of, lxii
Benjamin Burton, xxxvi
Bennett, G. V., 66
Bentley, Richard, 71
Bergin, John, lvi
Berkeley, George, Bishop, xliv, 19, 93, 306
Berkeley, James, 3rd Earl of, 282
Bettesworth, Richard, xxxiv, lxvi, xcvi, c, civ
Bible
  Colossians, 26
  Ecclesiastes, 84
  Ephesians, 26
  Exodus, 25, 84
  Galatians, 26
  Genesis, 33, 92, 258, 313, 317, 370
  John (gospel of), 203
  Lamentations, 396
  Luke (gospel of), 204
  Matthew (gospel of), 110, 139, 204, 364
  New Testament, lvii
  Proverbs, 37, 374
  Psalms, 80, 157, 203, 273
  Thessalonians, 54
Bickerton, Weaver, lxxxv, lxxxvi, 442, 444, 445
Bill of Rights (English, 1689), 92
Bill of Rights, Irish, lack of, 92
Bindon, David, xxxvii, xli, xliv, xlv, lix, xcvi, ciii, 116, 147, 166, 173, 176, 306, 326, 372

Black, Jeremy, 336
Black-Cattle, 31, 32
Bladen, Martin, 231
Blount, Elizabeth, 202
Bolingbroke, Viscount. *See* St John, Henry
Bolton, 2nd Duke of. *See* Paulet (Powlett), Charles
Bolton, Theophilus, Bishop of Clonfert, xxxi, 234
Bolton, William, l
Bond, R. P., 149
Bonnell, Jane, liv, lxiv, cvi
Book of Common Prayer, lvii, 54, 313
Boulter, Hugh, Archbishop of Armagh, xlvi, li, liii, lvi, lix, lxi, lxv, lxvii, xcviii, cvi, 28, 66, 68, 69, 90, 94, 114, 154, 156, 211, 230, 238, 303, 330, 331, 352, 371
Bowyer, William, 355, 381
Bowyer ledgers, 381, 404
Boyce, D. G., lxxxii
Boyle, Henry, xxxiii, xlvi, xlix, xcix, c, cii, 77
Boyle, John, 4th Earl of Orrery, 71
Boyle, John, 5th Earl of Orrery, xxvii, xxxii, 116, 275, 276
Boyle, Richard, 3rd Earl of Burlington, 339
Boyne, Battle of the (1690), 174, 261
Boyse, Joseph, 225
Brady, W. M., 208
Bray, Alan, 55
Brewer, John, 9
Brewster, Sir Francis, xl
Bric, Maurice, 114, 369
Bridewell (Dublin), lxix, lxxii, xcvii, 267, 315
Bridgeman, Orlando, 1st Baronet, 76
British Apollo: Containing Two Thousand Answers to Curious Questions, The, 244
'Broadloom, Isaac', 344
Broderick, David, 122
Brodrick, Alan, 1st Viscount Midleton, xxxvii, xlvii, lii, c, 200
Brodrick, St John, xlvii, xlviii, lii

Brodrick, Thomas, xxxvii, 200, 216
Broglie, François-Marie de, 333
Browne, John, xxviii, xxxvii, xli, xlii, xliii,
    xliv, lxxv, lxxxvii, 14, 18, 20, 24,
    26, 28, 30, 34, 46, 89, 93, 116,
    123, 153, 166, 168, 173, 174,
    176, 223, 326, 332, 344, 368,
    392, 399
Browne, Joseph, 261
Browne, Peter, Bishop of Cork and
    Ross, 208, 252
bugles (beads), 94
Bunyan, John
    Pilgrim's Progress, The, 359
Burke, Nuala, 24
Burke, W. P., xlix
Burlington, 3rd Earl of. *See* Boyle,
    Richard
Burnet, William, 112, 364, 427
Burns, Robert E., xlviii, 282
Burrows, Henry, xcii
Burton, Francis, liv
Burton, Samuel, 280
Bushman, Richard L., 363
Butler, James, 1st Duke of Ormond, 76
Butler, James, 2nd Duke of Ormond,
    217

Caesar, Julius, 53
Campbell Ross, Ian, lxxix, 150
Canaan, 370
Card, Samuel, 346
Caroline, Queen of England, 52, 53, 209
Carpenter, Andrew, lviii, 125
Carrion-Row, 33
Carson, James, xxviii, 366
Carter, Mary, 306
Carter, Thomas, c, 267, 282
Carteret, Sir George, 1st Baronet, 194
Carteret, George, 1st Lord, 194
Carteret, John, 2nd Lord, xxxiii, xxxiv,
    xlvi, xlvii, xlviii, l, li, lii, liii, lvii,
    lxv, lxvii, lxxxvi, xciii, xciv, xcviii,
    xcix, 8, 19, 53, 90, 123, 154, 166,
    189, 192, 194, 195, 196, 209,
    210, 241, 244, 281, 297, 354,
    382, 383, 455, 456, 457, 463, 469

Case of the Woollen Manufacturers, The,
    344–9, 492
Casey, Christine, 24, 178
Cattle Act, 18, 32, 221
Cavendish, William, 3rd Duke of
    Devonshire, xxxiii, cii, civ, cv,
    cvi, cvii
Cervantes Saavedra, Miguel de, 50
Chamberlayne, John, 56
Champion, J. A. I., 238
Charles I, King of England, 60, 70, 76,
    194, 195, 256
Charles II, King of England, 71, 133,
    134, 135, 137, 138, 141, 175
Chaucer, Geoffrey, 38
Chelsea College, 339
Cherry, Francis, 68
Chetwode, Knightley, xxvi, xxxii, xxxiii,
    li, 209
Christ Church Cathedral, Dublin, 211
Christensen, Peter, 330
Church party, xxvi
Churchill, John, 1st Duke of
    Marlborough, 65
Cicero, Marcus Tullius, 23, 53, 146,
    197, 206, 250, 309, 344
Clarendon, 1st Earl of. *See* Hyde,
    Edward
Clarendon, 2nd Earl of. *See* Hyde,
    Henry
Clark, P. O., 22
Clark, Peter, xxviii, 224
Clarke, Desmond, xli
Clarke, Henry, 82
Clarke, Samuel, 224
Claydon, Tony, 257
Clayton, Robert, Bishop of Clogher, lxx,
    224, 234, 245
Clifford, James, 321, 326
Clifford, Thomas, 1st Baron, 76
Clonmel, corporation of, xlix
Cogan, Francis, 355
Coghill, Marmaduke, xxiv, xli, xlvi,
    xlviii, liii, liv, lvi, lxvii, lxxxvi,
    lxxxviii, xci, ci, ciii, 22, 154, 166,
    182, 185, 186, 197, 200, 204, 286
coining, 21, 92

Cole, Shaun, 82
Colley, Linda, xxxv, 298, 299
comet (of 1729), 370
Commission for Building Fifty New
    Churches, 354
Commissioner of the Treasury, 34
Concordatum Money, 346
Congreve, William
    The Way of the World, 258
Connolly, S. J., xli, lvii, lviii, lxiii, lxxxii,
    28, 194, 195
Conolly, William, xxxiii, xxxix, xlvii,
    xlviii, l, li, lii, liii, liv, lxiv, xcix, c,
    ci, cii, 22, 161, 231, 254
Constantine the Great, 355
Convocation, English, 66, 69
Convocation, Irish, li, lviii, 125
Cooke, Edward, liii, 266
Coombs, Douglas, 296
Cork Workhouse Act [Ire.], 306
Corn Act (1689), 331
corn-cutter, 130
Corusodes, 66
Cosby, William, 361, 362
Cotton, Henry, 211
Court, Thomas, 308
Coventry, Henry, 76
Coventry, William, 76
Cowan, Brian, xxix, 71
Cox, Sir Richard, 2nd Bt, xlii, cii
Craftsman's First Letter of Advice, The,
    333-43, 492
Craggs, James (*fils*), 78, 163, 189
Craggs, James (*père*), 78
Crawford, W. H., 88
Crofton, Henry, xxxvii, lxviii
Cromwell, Thomas, 130
Crosslé, Philip, 212
Crotty, Andrew, xlvi, c
Crouch, Nathaniel, 367
Crowley, Sir Ambrose, 93
Crowther, Samuel, 62
Cullen, L. M., xxxii, xxxvii, lx, 19, 20,
    23, 24, 93, 146, 175, 221, 294,
    368
Cumberland, William Augustus, Duke
    of, 53

Custom House (Dublin), 22, 345

D'anvers, Caleb, 46, 195, 295
D'Urfey, Thomas, 55
Daily Courant, lxxxix, xci, xcii, 286,
    333
Damrosch, Leo, 62
Danby, 1st earl of. *See* Osborne, Sir
    Thomas
Daniell, Combra, 392
Dartmouth, 1st Earl of. *See* Legge,
    William
Davenant, Charles, xli, 136
Davenport, Colonel Sherrington, 261
Davis, Herbert, xlix, lii, liv, lviii, lxv,
    lxxiii, lxxxiii, lxxxiv, 16, 19, 20,
    21, 23, 24, 25, 30, 32, 46, 47, 58,
    60, 85, 94, 102, 121, 125, 126,
    133, 136, 139, 146, 157, 165,
    195, 202, 207, 209, 212, 216,
    220, 229, 232, 238, 252, 254,
    255, 272, 304, 310, 314, 322,
    324, 326, 363, 383, 384, 385,
    388, 422, 427, 428, 435, 443,
    445, 453, 455, 469, 473, 482,
    484, 487
Davys, Edward, 3rd Viscount
    Mountcashel, 82
de Bry, Theodore, 157
De Quincey, Thomas, lxxiv
Declaratory Act, xxxix, 16, 19, 93, 107
Defoe, Daniel, 46, 148
Delafaye, Charles, 231
Delany, Mary, 277
Delany, Patrick, xxxii, li, lii, 49, 144,
    185, 209, 210, 211, 434, 442,
    444, 445
Delvin, Lord, lvi
Delvin, Thomas, 9th Baron, lvi
Denmark, 250, 285, 330
Dennis, John, 51, 55
Derry, corporation of, lxii
Derry, siege of, 1689, 94
Devonshire, 3rd Duke of. *See*
    Cavendish, William
di Passerana, Adalberti Radicati, lxxxvi
Dickinson, H. T., 296

INDEX 535

Dickinson, Jonathan, 361
Dickson, David, xxix, xxxvii, lx, lxix, lxx, lxxi, lxxiii, 24, 30, 113, 175, 178, 221, 227, 232, 310, 352, 372
Dickson, R. J., 95, 357
Dillon, Wentworth, 4th Earl of Roscommon, 365
Diphilus, 23
Disarming Act [Ire.] (1695), 341
Dissenters, xxv, lxi–lxiv, lxvi, xc, xci, xcix, 69, 115, 178, 225, 236, 252, 282
  in Dublin, lxii, xc, xci, 178
Dobbs, Arthur, xxiv, xli, xliii, xliv, xlv, lxvii, lxxv, ciii, 30, 103, 135, 148, 168, 169, 223, 233, 235, 344, 345
Dobson, William, 345
Dodington, George, xxxii, cvi, cvii
Donatus, Tiberius Claudius, 88
Dorset, 1st Duke of. *See* Sackville, Lionel
Douglas, Catherine, Duchess of Queensberry, 209, 254
Douglas, D. C., 255
Doyle, Mel, xciv
Dralle, L. A., 283
Dryden, John, 45, 51, 206, 227, 260
Dublin, corporation of, lxx, lxxxvii–xciii, xcvi, xcvii, xcviii, 146, 182–3, 242, 270–3
  aldermen, lxxxvii–xcii, xcv, xcvi, xcviii, cv, 44, 183, 269–71, 308
  common council ('commons'), lxxxvii, lxxxviii, lxxxix, xc, xci–xcii, xcv–xcvi, xcvii, cv, 183, 269, 271–2
  guilds, xxvi, xcii, xcv–xcvii, 100, 106, 271
Dublin Intelligence, xxvii, xxxvii, xci, xcii, xciii, xciv, xcv, 49, 50, 99, 242, 392, 421, 434, 442
Dublin Journal, xciv, xcv, 41, 172, 217, 266, 280, 298, 465, 466, 480, 482
Dublin Society, The, xxiii, xxiv, xli, xlv, xlvi, lxi, 32
Dublin Weekly Intelligence, xxviii
Dublin Workhouse Act
  1704 [Ire.], lxxv, 6, 7, 8, 11, 308
  1728 [Ire.], lxxi–lxxii, 11, 308
  1732 [Ire.], lxxii, 308
Dudley, Rowena, lxix, lxxiii, 3, 9, 147, 310, 311
Dunkirk (demolition of), 335
Dunlevy, Mairead, xlvi
Dunton, John, 297
Dutton Colt, Sir Henry, 260, 261

Edie, Carolyn A., 32
Edward I, King of England, 127, 142
Edward IV, king of England, 127, 142
Egan, Seán, 175
Egmont, 1st and 2nd Earls of. *See* Perceval, John
Egypt, 32, 33, 370
Ehrenpreis, Irvin, xxvi, xxvii, xxxi, li, lii, lxxi, lxxvi, lxxxvii, lxxxviii, civ, cvi, 72, 83, 103, 135, 155, 161, 162, 172, 185, 186, 189, 192, 197, 209, 212, 219, 230, 275, 297, 321, 326, 378, 382, 421, 422, 427, 432, 442, 451, 452, 453, 455, 456, 463, 465, 479, 480, 486
Eilon, Daniel, 92
Elias, A. C., xxxiii
Ellis, Markman, 71
emigration (from Ireland to North America), xxiii, xxiv–xxv, xxxii, xlii, lxii, lxiii, lxxxv, 95, 102, 111, 113, 115, 148, 154, 214, 235, 337, 349–74
Emsley, Clive, 242
English Prayer Book (revised), 194
Ericke, James, 296
Erskine-Hill, Howard, 324
Eustace, Richard, 346
Evans, John, Bishop of Meath, lxvi
Exchange (Dublin), 17
excise, xxvii, 35, 36, 286, 299
Excise Crisis (1733), xxvii, xcix, 299

Fabricant, Carole, lxxx
Fagan, Patrick, xxxiv, lvii, lix, 135, 153, 217
Fanning, Christopher, 276
Fanshawe, Sir Richard, 202

Faulkner, George, xxvii, xciv, xcv, 19,
    29, 60, 62, 90, 129, 217, 286,
    328, 379, 381, 383, 384, 385,
    386, 388, 391, 393, 400, 402,
    404, 421, 422, 427, 432, 433,
    434, 435, 443, 444, 445, 451,
    452, 455, 456, 457, 458, 463,
    465, 466, 468, 469, 470, 473,
    474, 476, 480, 482, 483, 484,
    486, 487, 488, 492
  works with Bowyer, 381
Fauske, Christopher, 3
Fennelly, Teddy, xli
Ferguson, Oliver, lxxv, lxxviii, 28, 87, 88,
    161, 172, 219, 291, 332, 392,
    421, 427, 434, 451, 452, 463, 486
First Fruits in Ireland, Board of, 354
First Fruits in Ireland (remission of), 188
Fitzroy, Charles, 2nd Duke of Grafton,
    xlvii, 162, 189
Flanagan, C. M., lx, xc, 146
Fleming, D. A., xlix, 220
Flinn, M. W., 93
Flower, Colonel William, xcix
Foord, Archibald, 299
Forbes, George, 271
Forbes, John, xci, xcii, 271
Ford, Charles, xxxii, 85
Forfeitures Resumption Act, xxxix
Fownes, Sir William, xxx, liii, lxxi, lxxiii,
    lxxvi, lxxxiii, xc, xcvi, 2, 7, 147,
    153, 266, 306, 310
Foxon, David, 382
France, xxv, xxxv, xxxvii, 10, 50, 66, 77,
    103, 163, 166, 167, 173, 189,
    221, 222, 226, 242, 251, 257,
    259, 262, 296, 334, 336, 337,
    339, 340, 341, 359, 367
Francis I, Holy Roman Emperor, 126
Frankland, Sir Thomas, 22
Fraser, Sir William, 295
Frazer, William, 133
Frederick William I, King of Prussia, 338
French, Humphrey, xxviii, lxxii, lxxvi,
    lxxxviii, lxxxix, xcvi, xcvii, xcviii,
    280, 286, 287, 345, 480

Gaius Laelius, 206
Galen, 117
Galenson, D. W., 149, 357
Galway, corporation of, xlix–l
Galway, 1st Earl of. *See* Massue, Henri
    de
Garnham, Neal, xxxii
Gay, John, xxxii, 48, 52, 53, 209,
    254
  Beggar's Opera, The, xxix, 49, 55
Gee, Joshua, xli
General Synod of Ulster, lxii
George I, King of England, xlix, li, lii,
    52, 68, 77, 122, 163, 208, 236,
    245, 256, 262, 361
George II, King of England, lv, lvi, 52,
    53, 54, 126, 186, 236, 263, 338,
    350
Gerald of Wales, 19
Germain, Lady Elizabeth, 52, 53
Germany, lxxix, 91, 126, 226, 249, 285,
    359, 365
Gertruydenberg, 296
Gervaise, Isaac, 103
Gherardi, Evaristo, 50
Gibraltar, siege of (1727), 337
Gibson, Edmund, 54
Gibson, William, 238
Gilbert, J. G., 66
Gilbert, J. T. (Sir John), 9, 248, 253
Gill, Conrad, xxxvii
Glastonbury (thorn at), 21
Glorious Revolution, the, lxxxi, 174,
    175, 177, 261
Glynne, Sir William, 2nd Bt, 68
Godolphin, Sidney, 1st Earl, 77
Godwin, Francis, 103
Goldgar, Bertrand, 299
Gordon, Thomas, 199
Gore, Sir Ralph, xxvii, xxxiii, liii, liv,
    xcviii, xcix, c, ci, ciii
Gosnell, Edward, 7, 147
Grafton, 2nd Duke of. *See* Fitzroy,
    Charles
Graham, Richard, 1st Viscount Preston,
    67

Grant, Francis, civ, 294, 483
  The British Fishery Recommended to Parliament, civ, 294, 483
Granville, Sir John, 1st Earl of Bath, 194
Grattan, Richard, cv
graziers, xxxi, 24–5, 26–8, 197, 198, 199, 200
Greene, Jack P., 351
Gregori, Flavio, lxxxvi
Grenville, Sir Bevill, 194
Griffin, Patrick, 95
guinea (value of), 91
Gwithers, Charles, 9

Ham (son of Noah), 370
Hamilton, Elizabeth, Countess of Orkney, 254
Hamilton, Hugh Douglas, 243
Han, Ebülgâzî Bahadir, 33
Harcourt, Simon, Viscount, 77
Hardie, Philip, 38
Harding, John, 18, 38, 121, 163, 377
Harding, Sarah, 41, 354, 377, 378, 379, 384, 386, 392, 393, 399, 402, 403, 442, 443
Harley, Sir Edward, 254
Harley, Robert, 1st Earl of Oxford, xxiii, xxxii, xxxv, 60, 77, 80, 92, 127, 188, 241, 247, 254, 255, 256, 257, 259, 260, 262, 296, 326
Harris, Michael, 163
Harrison, Alan, lviii, 22, 125
harvest failures, 89
Hawkesworth, John, 17, 384
Hawkins, John, xcii
Hayton, D. W., xxiv, xxxviii, xxxix, xl, xlix, lii, liv, lviii, lix, lxii, lxiii, lxxxi, cii, 29, 99, 113, 114, 120, 125, 175, 178, 188, 197, 204, 222, 225, 229, 230, 232, 237, 283, 314, 318, 372
Heal, Felicity, 177
Healy, John, 235
Hearne, Thomas, 195
hearth tax, lix, 9, 135, 369, 372
Helsham, Richard, 246

Henning, B. D., 194
Henri III, King of France, 202
Henrietta Maria, Queen of England, 70
Henry II, King of England, 226
Henry VII, King of England, 127
Henry VIII, King of England, 130, 134, 348
Herbert, Robert Sawyer, 22
Herodotus, lxxix, 151
Herring, Thomas, 54
Hesperi-Neso-Graphia, 62, 227
Hick, Vivien, 8
Higgins, Francis, li
Higgins, Ian, lxxiv, 156, 299
High Church party, li
Hill, Arthur, xlix
Hill, Brian W., 296
Hill, J. R., xc, 287
Hinde, John, 345
Hoadley, Benjamin, 261
Hoadly, John, 234
Hobbes, Thomas, 198, 204, 205
Hoey, James, xxvii
Hogan, R. G., 209
Holland, 7, 116, 166, 173, 176, 257, 285
Holmes, Geoffrey, 195
Holmes, Richard, lxxxvi, 154
Holy Roman Emperor, 21, 249
Homer, Sidney, 23
Horace, 51, 77, 349
  Satires, 39
Horwitz, Henry, 261
Hottentots, the, 297–8
houghing, 28
House of Lords (Irish), xxv, xxxix, lvii, lxxxviii, 259
Howard, Henrietta, Countess of Suffolk, 21
Howard, Hugh, xxxvii, xlviii, lxxxix, cvii, 148, 154
Howard, Robert, Bishop of Elphin & of Killala, xxxvii, xlviii, lxx, lxxxvi, lxxxix, cvii, 148, 154, 234
Howard, William, xci
Howe, Thomas, xcviii, 281
Howell, T. B., 261

Hughes, Leo, 50
Huguenots, 340
Humourous Description of the Manners and Fashions of the Inhabitants of the City of Dublin, A, xxix, 215, 237
Hutchinson, Francis, Bishop of Down, lxxii, ciii, 7, 10, 147, 179, 295, 310
Hutchinson, Hartley, 198
Hyde, Edward, 1st Earl of Clarendon, 60, 76
Hyde, Henry, 2nd Earl of Clarendon, 76

Iceland, 22
Incorporated Society in Dublin for Promoting English Protestant Schools in Ireland, xxv
infantry regiments, Irish, 334
Intelligencer, no, 20, 'Dean Smedley Gone to Seek His Fortune', 385
Invalides, Hôpital des, 339
Irish brigades, xxv, 296
Isle of Man, 21, 25
Israel, J. I., 258

James II, King of England, xl, 77, 175, 217, 254, 353
James, F. G., xlvi, 99
John, King of England, 127
Johnson, Esther ('Stella'), xxxi, xxxii, 149, 256
Johnston, John, xxxii
Jones, Barzillai, Dean of Lismore, 253
Jones, Clyve, 84
Jones, Mary, lxiv
Jonson, Ben, 57
Joseph of Arimathea, 21
Josephus, 157
Jupiter, 92, 252
Juvenal, 51, 64

Kammen, Michael, 349, 361
Kane, Joseph, xc
Karian, Stephen, cii, 29, 225, 376, 383
Keating, Geoffrey, 19
'Keeper of the King's Conscience', 54

Kelly, James, xxviii, xxxvii, xli, xlii, xliv, lx, xcv, cv, 89, 129, 148, 164, 217, 327, 330, 332
Kelly, Patrick, xxxviii, xl, xli, lxxxii, ciii, 129
Kemp, Betty, 285
Kendrick, T. F. J., lxvi
Kennedy, Máire, 380
Kennett, White, 57–58, 59–60, 66
Kersey, John, 259
Kevan Bail, the, xciii, xcv
Kidd, Colin, 113
Kiernan, T. J., 9
King, Sir Charles S., lviii, 231
King, Gregory, 136
King, James, 4th Baron Kingston, 255
King, John, ci
King, William, Archbishop of Dublin, xxxiii, l, li, lvii, lviii, lix, lxxiii, lxxxii, 2, 3, 19, 99, 100, 110, 152, 154, 162, 175, 188, 198, 210, 216, 231, 235, 309, 310, 317, 318, 421, 427
Kingston, 4th Baron. *See* King, James
Kingston, Richard, 261
Kirkpatrick, James, 225, 236
Knightley, John, ciii, 294
Knox, John, 131
Kohn, G. C., 10
Kramnick, Isaac, 298, 343

Labaree, Benjamin W., 363, 364
Labaree, L. W., 350, 363
Laffan, William, 243
Lambert, Ralph, Bishop of Meath, lxi
Landa, Louis, lxvi, lxvii, 29, 102, 225, 229, 230, 237, 325, 354
Lane, James, 2nd Viscount Lanesborough, lxx–lxxi
Lane, Mary, Viscountess Lanesborough, lxx–lxxi, 318
Langford, Paul, 35, 299
Langmuir, Erika, 206
Lapland, 22, 156, 298
Larini. *See* Violante
Laud, William, 60, 216

'Lawrell-men', 216
'Layfield, Patrick', 88, 109, 365, 374, 427
Lecky, W. E. H., 372
Leeson, Joseph, 178, 324
Legge, William, 1st Earl of Dartmouth, 131, 135
Lein, C. D., 16, 136, 152
Lepper, J. H., 212
Léry, Jean de, 156
'Le-Sac' (dancing master), 80
Leslie, Charles, 253
Leslie, J. B., 9, 209
Lester, Katherine Morris, 82
Letter from Dermott Mac-Poverty to the Author of the Intelligencer, xxvii
Letter from Some Farmers in the Country, to a Gentleman in Dublin, A, 366–74
Leyburn, J. G., 95, 357
Lillywhite, Bryant, 71, 260
Linen Board, xlv, 106, 352, 368
linen manufacture (Irish), xxxii, xxxvii, xlv, liv, lxvii, lxx, 10, 106, 168, 169, 352, 368, 371
Littleton, Adam, 200
Lock, F. P., 299
Locke, John, 16, 74, 79, 91, 157, 206
Lombard, James, 346
London Assurance Company, 8
Louis XIV, King of France, 257, 339
Louis XV, King of France, 221, 222, 336
Lowther, Anthony, 22
Lucas, Charles, lxxxviii, lxxxix
Lucretius, 61
Ludington, Charles, 166
Lyon, John, 17

Macarell, John, xcviii, 280, 281
MacAulay, Alexander, xxiv, lxviii, 328
MacCurtin, Hugh (Aodh Mac Cruitín), 297
Machiavelli, Niccolò, 253
MacLachlan, A. D., 296
Maculla, James, lxxv, 21, 93, 129, 130, 138, 434
Madden, Samuel, xlv, xlvi, lxvii, 306

Maffei, Count, 256
Magennis, Eoin, lvi, cv
Malcomson, A. P. W., lxvi, 20, 188
Malek, J. S., lii
Malone, Anthony, xcvi, ci, cii
Mandeville, Bernard de, lxxvii
Manilius, 47
Manley, Delarivier, 202
Manning, Robert, 130
Maple, William, xli, 32
Marlborough, 1st Duke of. *See* Churchill, John
Marshall, P. J., 113
Marshalsea (prison), xcvii
Martial, 44, 45
Maryland, 356
Maslen, Keith, 381, 382, 404
Massue, Henri de, 1st Earl of Galway, 174
Mather, Cotton, 371
Mattaire, Michel, 47
Maule, Henry, Bishop of Cloyne, lxi, lxx
Maurice, Edward, lii
Maxwell, Henry, xl
Maynwaring, Arthur, 102
McArdle, Grianne, 198
McBride, Ian, lvi, lxxxii
McBride, John, 236
McGrath, Charles Ivar, xxxvi, lv, cv, 8, 165, 174, 190, 213, 245
McIlwaine, H. R., 93
McMinn, Joseph, xxxi
McNally, Patrick, xlviii, 112, 161, 234, 368
McParland, Edward, xxx, 8, 213, 245
Mead, Richard, 117
Medley, 102
Mell, D. C., 209
Melon, Jean-François, 306
Memorial of the Poor Inhabitants of Ireland, The, 330–3, 492
Merians, Linda E., 298
Micah, 225
Midleton, 1st Viscount. *See* Brodrick, Alan
Miller, Kerby A., 146

Milne, Kenneth, lviii, lxi, 125
Milo (of Croton), 365
Minos, 92
Mint (lack of one in Ireland), xxxvi, xxxviii, 16, 21, 87, 91, 92, 94, 120, 129, 130, 139, 368
Minucius Felix, 69
Miscellanies (Pope–Swift), 41, 46, 58
Mist, Nathaniel, xxvii, 163, 392, 399
Molesworth, Robert, 1st Viscount, xl, xlv, lxxviii, lxxxiii, ciii, 7, 16, 102, 114, 147
Molyneux, William, xxxviii, xxxix, 16
Monod, P. K., xciv, 262
Montagu, Charles, 77
Montaigne, Michel de, 150, 157
Montgomery, Alexander, 154
Moore, Courtenay, 346
Moore, Colonel Roger, 131, 135
Moore, Sean D., xxxvi
More, Sir Thomas, 32
Morris, Lewis, 349, 361
mortmain, lxvi
Moryson, Fynes, lxxix
Mountcashel, Edward Davys, 3rd Viscount, 82
Moyle, Walter, 326
Munter, Robert, xxviii, 366
Murphy, David, 334
Murphy, Sean, lxxxix, xcii

Nary, Cornelius, lvii
Navigation Acts, 18, 101, 174
Nelson, Charles, xli
Newcastle, 1st Duke of. *See* Pelham-Holles, Thomas
Newfoundland, 296
Newton, Sir Isaac, 135
Nichols, John, 289, 384, 385, 453, 482
Nimrod, King of Shinar, 92
Nine Years' War, 334
Noah, 370
North America, xxiii, xxxii, xxxvii, lxii, lxiii, lxxxii, lxxxv, 93, 94, 95, 96, 102, 111, 115, 144, 179, 214, 224, 235, 237, 349–65
Nutley, Richard, li

O'Brien, George, 169
O'Brien, Gerard, xxxix, lvii
O'Brien, William, xcv
O'Carroll, Joseph, 310, 316
Ó Ciardha, Éamonn, lx, xciv, 217, 221
O'Regan, Philip, 3
Oates, Titus, 258
Oerke, Bess Viola, 82
Oldmixon, John, 102, 367
Olson, Alison Gilbert, 351
Orkney, Countess of. *See* Hamilton, Elizabeth
Orléans, Philip, Duke of, 256
Ormond, 1st and 2nd Dukes of. *See* Butler, James
Orrery, 4th Earl of. *See* Boyle, John
Orrery, 5th Earl of. *See* Boyle, John
Osborne, Sir Thomas, 1st Earl of Danby, 76
Osborough, W. N., 92
Overton, J. H., 253
Ovid, 92, 93
Oxford, 1st Earl of. *See* Harley, Robert

Palatines, 8
Pargellis, Stanley M., 357
Parker, Samuel, 250
Parliament (Acts of), lxix, lxx, 10, 19, 106, 194
Parliament (Irish), xxv, xxviii, xxxiii, xxxviii, xliii, xliv, xlv, xlvi, xlvii, xlviii, lii, lvi, lx, lxii, lxiii, lxvi, lxvii, lxix, lxxi, lxxxv, lxxxvi, xcii, xciii, xciv, xcix, ci, cii, ciii, civ, cvi, 7, 8, 9, 14, 22, 28, 29, 32, 38, 92, 106, 122, 123, 154, 165, 175, 206, 225, 229, 231, 234, 266, 271, 285, 294, 298, 306, 310, 317, 328, 331, 345, 368
Parliament (Westminster), xxxviii, lvi, lxxxi, 18, 84, 113, 122, 175, 216, 283, 298, 338, 351
Parnell, Thomas, li
Passmann, Dirk F., 156
Paterson, T. G. F., xxxii, lxxiii
Paulet (Powlett), Charles, 2nd Duke of Bolton, xlvii, lxii

INDEX

Pearce, Edward Lovett, xxx, 323
Pearce, Thomas, General, Governor of Limerick, 1
Pearce, Zachary, 195
Peirson, Samuel, 123
Pelham-Holles, Thomas, 1st Duke of Newcastle, li, liii, lvi, lix, lx, lxvii, cvi, cvii, 28, 90, 150, 154, 156, 189, 211, 297, 324, 330, 331, 371
Penn, William, 111, 360, 367
Perceval, John, 1st Earl of Egmont, xxiv, xli, xlvi, lxvi, ciii, 231
Perceval, John, 2nd Earl of Egmont, xliv, cii, ciii
Perceval, William, li
Perron, Jacques du, Cardinal, 202
Persius Flaccus, Aulus, 349
Petty, Sir William, xlii, lix, 19, 223
Philips, Ambrose, 230
Phipps, Sir Constantine, 197, 210, 250
Pilkington, Laetitia, xxxii
Pilkington, Matthew, 265, 381, 443, 465, 473
Pincus, S. C. A., 257
Pindar, 204, 396
plague (at Marseilles), 10, 46, 106, 330
   (in Denmark and Sweden), 330–1
Plato, 197, 204
Pliny (the Elder), 283
Plumb, J. H., 53
Plutarch, 53, 205, 206
Pocklington, John, 259
Poems by Eminent Ladies, 275
Poems on Affairs of State, 260
poll tax (1695), 231
Pollard, Mary, xxviii, 328, 366, 379, 380, 381
Pomfret, John E., 362
Pompeia, 53
Pompey the Great, 23
Ponsonby, Brabazon, cii
Pope, Alexander, xxvi, xxxi, xxxii, lxxvii, lxxxvii, xcv, 38, 41, 46, 49, 50, 53, 58, 63, 72, 74, 150, 186, 324, 326, 376, 377, 379, 385, 392,

399, 402, 404, 443, 444, 456, 479
The Dunciad, 50, 474
popery laws, liv
Popish Plot, 258
Popkin, R. H., 202
Porto Bello (Panama), 249
Power, T. P., lv
Powlett. *See* Paulet
Poynings' Law, xxxviii, 234, 237
Presbyterians (in south of Ireland), xc, xcix. *See also* Dissenters
Presbyterians (in Ulster), xxv, xxxi–xxxii, lxii–lxiii, lxvii, lxix, lxxv, xcix, 95, 109, 112, 113, 114–15, 144, 154, 214, 225, 235, 236, 250, 323, 337
Prescription Sacred, lxviii
Preston, 1st Viscount. *See* Graham, Richard
Preston plot (1691), 261
Pretender, the Old (James Francis Edward Stuart), xxxiv, lv, lx, xciv, 146, 154, 187, 197, 199, 208, 216, 217, 219, 222, 223, 241, 245, 248, 249, 250, 253, 256, 261, 263, 334, 335, 336, 337, 340, 341, 342, 469
Pretender, the Young (Prince Charles Edward), 256
Price, J. M., 113
Prior, Thomas, xli, xliv, xlv, xlvi, lxxv, lxxxvi, lxxxvii, ciii, 20, 25, 93, 107, 113, 129, 156, 168, 344, 345, 368
Probyn, Clive, xxvii
Psalmanazar, George, 152
Pulcher, Publius Clodius, 53
Pulteney, William, xxxiii, 209, 221, 343

Quakers (and tithe exemption), lxvi, 100
Queensberry, Duchess of. *See* Douglas, Catherine
Quin, James, 38
Quin, Mark, 38

Rabelais, François, 36, 50, 151
Radcliffe, Alexander, 251
Raleigh, Sir Walter, 38, 60
Ralph, James, lxxvii
Ram, Abel, lxxi
Ramus, Peter, 66
Rankin, Helen, xli
Rawson, Claude, liv, lviii, lxxvii, lxxix, lxxxi, lxxxii, lxxxiv, 150, 157, 158, 200, 317
Raymond, Anthony, lviii, 125
Real, Hermann J., lxxxvi, 156
Recorder (role of), 271
Rees, G. A., xlii
revenue commissioners (Ireland), 22, 25, 214, 285, 303, 345
revenue service (Ireland), 112, 164, 227, 282, 303, 368
Rhadamanthus, 92
Richard III, King of England, 127
Richardson, David, 149
Richardson, Richard, 62
Ridpath, George, 254
Robertson, John, 257
Rochfort, John and Deborah, xxxi
Rogers, Nicholas, xxxv, xciv
Rogers, Pat, 216, 261
Rogerson, Sir John, xciv
Romulus, 355
Roscommon, 4th Earl of. *See* Dillon, Wentworth
Rowley, Hercules, xl, lxvii
Royal Exchange, 8, 17, 69
Royal Exchange Assurance Company, 8
Rudé, George, 177
Russell, Thomas, 208
Ruvigny, Melville Henry de, 9th Marquis, 256
Ryder, Michael, xl, 24
Rye, George, 123

Sacheverell, Henry, li, 216
Sackville, Lionel, 1st Duke of Dorset, xlvi, lx, lxiii, xcviii, xcix, c, cii, civ, cv, 245, 282, 302, 354
Sahlins, Peter, 10
Sale, Harvey. *See* Seale

Salmon, Thomas, 261
Savoy, Charles Emanuel III, Duke of, 256
Savoy, Victor Amadeus II, Duke of, 256
Savoyard claimant (Victor Amadeus John Philip), 256
Schefferus, Johannes, 22
Scheme of the Proportions which the Protestants of Ireland May Probably Bear to the Papists; Humbly Offer'd to the Public, lix
Schultz, W. E., 49
Schwartz, S. B., 157
Schwoerer, Lois G., 298
Scipio Africanus, 60, 206
Scotch Plot (1703), 261
Scotland, xl, xli, lx, lxii, lxxix, ciii, 75, 107, 250, 262, 295, 310, 342, 359
Scott, Temple, 385
Scythians, lxxix, 19, 33, 226
Seaby, W. A., lxiii
Seale (Sale), Harvey, 162
Sekora, John, 179
Septennial Act (1716), 299
Seville, Treaty of (1729), 222
Shaftesbury, 1st and 3rd Earls of. *See* Ashley Cooper, Anthony
Shakespeare, William
    Coriolanus, 9
    Cymbeline, 250, 272
Sharp, Jane, 151
Sharp, John, 62
Sheridan, Edel, 24, 178
Sheridan, Thomas, xxviii, xxxi, xxxii, l, li, lviii, lxxix, 14, 41, 44, 82, 102, 149, 155, 207, 208, 209, 212, 214, 377, 385, 386, 392, 396, 402, 482
Sheridan, William, Bishop of Kilmore, 253
Shesgreen, Sean, 243
silk manufacture (Irish), xcv, 21, 103, 104, 105, 169, 290
Simms, J. G., xxxii, xxxviii, lvi, lxxxii, xc, 24

INDEX 543

Simnel, Lambert, 127
Singleton, Henry, xxxiii, xlviii, ci, 197, 204
Sinon, 360
Slack, Paul, lxviii, 311
Smedley, Jonathan, 385
  Gulliveriana, 385
Smithers, Peter, 71
smuggling, xxxviii, 35, 99, 169, 286
Smyrna Coffee-House, 260
Smyth, James, lxvi, lxxxvi
Smyth, Jim, lxxxi, 222
Smyth, William, xxxvii, lxvi, lxviii, lxxxvi
Sobieska, Maria Clementina, 249
Socrates, 39, 69, 205
Somers, John, 1st Lord, 62, 77, 202
Somerville (Somervell), James, xxvii, xci
South, John, 135
Southampton, 4th Earl of. *See* Wriothesley, Thomas
Southwell, Edward, liii, liv, lvi, lxvii, lxxxvi, lxxxviii, xci, xciii, 22, 114, 123, 154, 166, 182, 185, 186, 197, 200, 231, 235, 286
Spain, xxv, xxxvii, 10, 80, 103, 106, 146, 222, 249, 251, 336, 337, 359
Spanish Netherlands, 258, 259
SPCK, lix, lxx
Speck, William, xxxv
Spectator, The, xxviii, 23, 37, 41, 45, 59, 82, 149, 173, 202, 242, 267
Spenser, Edmund, lxxix, 19
St John, Henry, 1st Viscount Bolingbroke, xxvi, xxxii, xxxiii, 60, 72, 77, 164, 221, 241, 255, 298, 326, 343
St Lucia, island of, 336
St Patrick's Cathedral, Dublin, xxiii, xxx, xlvi, xciii, cii, cvi, 62, 195, 209, 211, 233, 308, 315
St Patrick's Well, 9
St Sepulchre's, Dublin, 105, 308
Stanhope–Sunderland ministry, xlvii
Stanley, Sir John, 167
Stannard, Eaton, xxxiii, lxxxviii, xci, xcvi, xcviii, ci, 161, 270, 271
Stearne, John, Bishop of Clogher, xxxi

Steele, Richard, 37, 43, 267, 342
Stephen, Leslie, lxxx
Stevenson, John, 154
Stewart, Ezekiel, 154
Stoker, Bram, lxxiv
Stopford, James, li, 209
Stoyte, Francis, 270, 271, 476
Stoyte, John, xci
Strabo, lxxix
Strafford, 1st Earl of. *See* Wentworth, Thomas
Stratford, William, 195
Strops for razors (controversy of), 37
Stuart, Henrietta, Duchess of Orleans, 256
Stubbs, W. C., 100
Suetonius, 205
Suffolk, Countess of. *See* Howard, Henrietta
Swan, Richard, 260
Sweden, 196, 285, 330
Swift, Abigail, 296
Swift, Deane, xxxi, 6, 120, 129, 161, 172, 384, 386, 388, 391, 421, 422, 427, 428, 432, 434, 435, 451, 452, 455, 463, 482, 484, 487
Swift, James, 9
Swift, Jonathan
  Correspondence of, xxxi, lxv, lxxvi, lxxxvii, xci, xcv, 9, 20, 21, 46, 49, 50, 52, 53, 55, 60, 63, 72, 80, 85, 92, 116, 127, 147, 150, 164, 186, 192, 196, 208, 209, 210, 216, 254, 255, 275, 276, 294, 296, 326, 377, 378, 379, 381, 385, 392, 399, 402, 403, 432, 434, 443, 456, 465, 479

  Works
  Advantages Proposed by Repealing the Sacramental Test, 125
  Advertisement Against Lord Allen, 158, 182–3, 453–4
  Advice to the Free-men of Dublin, lxxxviii, 280–7, 480–2

Works (cont.)
 Answer of the Right Honourable William Pulteney, Esq., to the Right Honourable Sir Robert Walpole, The, 324
 Answer to a Paper, Called A Memorial, An, xcv, 19, 27–39, 328, 330, 370, 377, 378, 399–402, 443
 Answer to Several Letters from Unknown Hands, An, 120–7, 432–3
 Answer to Several Letters from Unknown Persons, An, xliii, 87, 88, 108–18, 365, 427–31
 Answer to the Craftsman, The, lx, lxxxvi, 19, 96, 219–27, 333, 462–5
 Argument Against Abolishing Christianity, An, lxv, 85
 The Bank Thrown Down, 24
 Battle of the Books, 55, 71, 72, 204
 Causes of the Wretched Condition of Ireland, lxxxii, lxxxiv, 146
 'Character, Panegyric and Description of the Legion Club, A', xxv, lxviii, ci, cii, 29, 197, 225, 267
 'Character of Doctor Sheridan', 207
 City Cries, Instrumental and Vocal, 241, 383, 386, 468
 Concerning that Universal Hatred which Prevails against the Clergy, 32, 238
 Conduct of the Allies, The, xxiii, 35, 295
 Considerations about Maintaining the Poor, 6–11, 391
 Considerations upon Two Bills, lxv, 229, 500
 'Dialogue between Captain Tom and Sir Henry Dutton Colt, A', 261
 Directions to Servants, 44, 63, 81, 165, 205, 266

Discourse Concerning the Mechanical Operation of the Spirit, A, 149, 157
 Drapier's Letters, xxiii, xxvi, xxvii, xxxiii, 2, 19, 20, 21, 23, 24, 25, 30, 132, 148, 186, 189, 254, 363, 376, 377, 379, 383, 384, 388, 486
 Enquiry into the Behaviour of the Queen's Last Ministry, An, 60
 Epistle upon an Epistle, An, lii
 Examination of Certain Abuses, An, xxix, xxx, xxxiv, xciv, 241–63, 383, 386, 468–73
 Examiner, 102, 202, 216, 224, 258
 Fraud Detected, xxvii, 379
 'The Grand Question Debated...', 80, 213
 Gulliver's Travels, xxvi, lxxv, 36, 46, 58, 66, 75, 85, 100, 103, 146, 165, 317, 322, 360
 Hibernian Patriot, The, xxvii, 379
 'Hints for Intelligencer Papers', 321–7, 491
 'Hints of the Education of Ladies', 74
 History of the Four Last Years of the Queen, 255, 399
 History of the Second Solomon, The, 209
 'Holyhead Journal', 157
 Humble Address to Both Houses of Parliament, liv, 24, 165, 220, 304, 314
 Humble Petition of the Footmen of Dublin, The, 165, 265–8, 473–6
 Intelligencer, The, xxviii, xxix, xxxii, xxxv, lxxix, 14, 41, 42, 44, 46, 47, 49, 63, 87, 90, 102, 109, 155, 207, 225, 226, 321, 349, 350, 352, 355, 366, 377, 378, 379, 381, 382, 385, 386, 387, 393, 427, 443
 Intelligencer, no. 1, 42–6, 406–7
 Intelligencer, no. 3, 48–56, 407–9
 Intelligencer, no. 5, 57–63, 409–12
 Intelligencer, no. 7, 64–72, 412–14
 Intelligencer, no. 9, 74–85, 414–18
 Intelligencer, no. 19, 86–97, 418–21

Journal to Stella, 37, 111, 149, 215, 242, 260, 267, 296
Letter from a Member of the House of Commons in Ireland, 125
Letter from the Grand Mistress of the Female Freemasons, A, 212
Letter on M'culla's Project, lxxv, 99, 128–42, 148, 386, 421, 434–42
Letter on the Fishery, A, xxxv, 300, 483–6
Letter to the Archbishop, Concerning the Weavers, A, 99–107, 421–6
Letter to Mr. Harding, 136
Letter to . . . Mr Pope, 46
Letter to the Printer, A, 329, 491–2
Letter to . . . Viscount Molesworth, 102
Letter to the Whole People of Ireland, liv, 121, 189, 216, 297
Letter to a Young Lady, on her Marriage, A, 322
Libel on Doctor Delany, A, 186, 198
Mad Mullinix and Timothy, 197, 204, 247, 385
Maxims Controlled in Ireland, xxxix, xlii, lxxv, 23, 102, 156, 180, 207, 321, 325, 452–3
Modest Proposal, A, xxiii, xlii, xliii, xlv, lix, lx, lxxiv, lxxv, lxxvi, lxxvii, lxxviii, lxxix, lxxx, lxxxi, lxxxiv, lxxxv, lxxxvi, lxxxvii, 2, 22, 102, 136, 144–59, 179, 220, 223, 298, 325, 340, 360, 379, 383, 442–50, 452, 463, 486
Mr Collins's Discourse of Free-Thinking, 47
Observations Occasioned by the Case of the Woollen Manufacturers, 289–92, 482–3
Of the Education of Ladies, 322
On Barbarous Denominations in Ireland, 125
On the Bill for the Clergy's Residing on Their Livings, 229
'On Brotherly Love', 252, 272
On False Witness, 46, 139

On Good-Manners and Good-Breeding, 79
On Poetry, A Rhapsody, 58
On Wisdom's Defeat in a Learned Debate, 378
Poems (ed. Williams), xxxii, lxviii, xcvi, cvi, 19, 44, 45, 49, 58, 61, 66, 116, 147, 150, 157, 158, 197, 198, 200, 204, 213, 243, 244, 245, 247, 267, 272, 275, 281, 324
Polite Conversation, 44, 72, 158
Prefatory Letter to Mary Barber, 275–8, 479
Presbyterian's Plea of Merit, The, 281
Proposal for Correcting, Improving, and Ascertaining the English Tongue, A, 78, 200
Proposal for Giving Badges to the Beggars, A, lxix, lxxxii, lxxxiv, 2, 146, 306–19, 384, 388, 391, 488–91
Proposal for the Universal Use of Irish Manufacture, A, xxxix, 18, 30, 32, 92, 94, 162, 188, 486
Proposal that all the Ladies Should Appear in Irish Manufactures, A, lxxv, 34, 161–70, 450–2
Proposal to Pay Off the Debt of the Nation, A, 229–38, 303, 465–8
Reasons Against Lowering the Gold and Silver Coin, 302–4, 486–7
The Run upon the Bankers, 24
Seasonable Advice, 18, 163, 287
Sentiments of a Church of England Man, 125
Sermon on the Causes of the Wretched Condition of Ireland, 126
Short Character of Thomas Earl of Wharton, A, 202
Short View of the State of Ireland, A, xxxvii, xxxix, xli, xlii, lxxxv, 14–26, 28, 37, 41, 87, 89, 126, 156, 163, 174, 226, 297, 298, 377, 378, 386, 392–8, 399, 402, 443

Works (cont.)
  Some Arguments against Enlarging the Power of Bishops, 232
  Some Considerations in the Choice of a Recorder, xxxiii, lxvi, lxvii, 114, 123, 147, 270–3, 476–8
  Some Observations upon the Report of the Committee of . . . the Privy Council in England Relating to Woods Halfpence, 133, 157
  Some Remarks on the Barrier Treaty, 296
  Substance of What was Said by the Dean, The, 158, 185–90, 455–6
  Tale of a Tub, A, lxv, 50, 51, 156, 199, 201
  Thoughts on Various Subjects, 58, 60
  'To Charles Ford Esqr. On his Birth-day . . .', 61
  To the Whole People of Ireland, 363
  Traulus, xxxiv, xcix, 147, 158, 192, 200, 457
  Upon Giving Badges to the Poor, lxxiii, 3–4, 6, 17, 306, 377, 384, 388–90, 488
  'Verses on the Death of Dr. Swift', 45, 272
  Vindication of Lord Carteret, A, xxxiv, lii, xciv, 158, 192–217, 241, 382, 383, 456–62, 468
  Works (1735), 41, 144, 379, 383, 384, 386, 403, 405, 433, 443, 445, 457, 466, 468, 470
  'The Yahoo's Overthrow', xcvi
Swobbers, 61, 62
Sykes, Norman, 66
Synge, Edward, Archbishop of Tuam, 100, 198
Synge, Edward, Bishop of Ferns, lxvii, lxviii, 234

Tacitus, 69, 96
Talion law, 355
tanning, 32
Tantivyes, 216
Tartars, 33

Tatler, The, 9, 37, 41, 150
Tave, S. M., 49
Taylor, Stephen, lxvi, 238
Teerink–Scouten (*Bibliography*), 387, 435
teinds (tithes), 115
Teinds Act [Scot.], 115
Temple, John, 9
Temple, Sir William, 49, 50, 71
Tenison, Thomas, Archbishop of Canterbury, 61
Tennent, William, 360
Theatre Royal (Smock Alley, Dublin), 153
Themistocles, 60
Thirsk, Joan, 32
Tholsel (Dublin), 17
Thomas, Gabriel, 111
Thompson, Edward, 22, 285
Thompson, Paul V., 23, 61, 116, 188, 220
Thornton, Leicestershire, 296
Tickell, Thomas, lx, 208, 209
Tighe, Richard, xxxiv, c, 192, 197, 199, 204, 208, 254, 382, 457
  'Dick Fitzbaker', xxxiv, 197
Tillage Bill [Ire.] (1728), 331
Tisdall, William, 114, 236
tithe, xxv, lx, lxiv, lxv, lxvi, lxvii, 15, 109, 112, 114, 115, 154, 212, 224, 229, 235–6, 367, 369, 427
tithe of agistment, xxv, lxvii–lxviii, ci, 29, 225, 328
tithe-farmers, lxviii, 114, 367
tithe-jobbers, lxviii, 114, 367
To The Author of those Intelligencers, 87, 349–65, 493
Toleration Act [Ire.] (1719), lxiii
Tonge, Israel, 258
Toupees, 46, 245, 265, 266
Treadwell, Michael, 381
Treaty of the Grand Alliance (1701), 295
Treaty of Vienna (1731), 222, 337
Trenchard, John, 199
Trevor, Sir Thomas, 77

Trinity College, Dublin, xxx, xlv, xciii, 44, 82, 211
Trotter, Thomas, 318
Troy weight, 140, 151
'Trueman, Andrew', 88, 109, 365, 374, 427
Trumbach, Randolph, 55
Tupinamba (of Brazil), lxxix, 156
Twomey, Brendan, 24

Ulster Rising (1641), 175
Union of Utrecht (1579), 258
Ursa Major, 250
Utrecht, Treaty of, 259, 296, 335

vagrancy acts, lxix
Van Dam, Rip, 361
Varey, Simon, 343
Verdoen, Sir Peter, xci, 186
Vernon, James, 77
Vesey, Agmondesham, xlviii, ci
Vesey, Sir Thomas, Bishop of Ossory, lii
Victoria and Albert Museum, 17, 388, 422
Victory, Isolde, xxxix
Violante, 'Madam', alias Larini, 153, 198
Virgil, 66, 88, 226, 227, 252, 262, 349, 360
von Staden, Johann, 156

Wake, William, Archbishop of Canterbury, li, lvii, lxvi, 66, 94, 235
Wallis, John, 261
Walpole, Edward, civ
Walpole, Horace, 77
Walpole, Sir Robert, xxiv, xxv, xxvi, xxvii, xxxiii, xxxiv, xxxv, xlvi, xlvii, xlviii, li, lx, lxiii, lxvi, lxvii, xcix, ci, 35, 52, 53, 77, 90, 150, 205, 219, 221, 254, 298, 299, 333
Walsh, Patrick, xxxix, liv, lvi, xcv
Walsh, T. J., 49

Walter, Peter, 324
War of the Quadruple Alliance, 334
War of the Spanish Succession, 36, 79, 295, 296, 334
'war of the two kings', xxxvi
Ward, C. E., 260
Ward, James, 195
Ware, Sir James, 19
Waters, Edward, 18, 19, 38, 92, 121, 162, 188, 189, 486
Watson, J. R. F., 360
Watt, T. D., xcii, 242
Waugh, Evelyn, lxxiv
Wells, H. G., lxxiv
Wemyss, David, 295
Wentworth, Thomas, 1st Earl of Strafford, 60
Wesley, Samuel, 72
Whan, Robert, lxix
Wharton, Philip, 1st Duke of, 163
Wharton, Thomas, 1st Earl of, 23, 202, 283
Whisk, 61, 62
Whitehaven, Cumberland, 296
Whiteway, Martha, 384, 422, 427
Whitshed, William, Lord Chief Justice, 18, 19, 37, 38, 121, 162, 188, 189, 432
Whitwell, Sir Nathaniel, xciii
Wilkins, John, 103
William, Duke of Gloucester, 256
William III, King of England, lxxvii, 68, 71, 146, 175, 217, 251, 252, 257, 261, 285, 304, 354
Wills Coffee-House, 71
Wittkowsky, George, xlii, lxxiv
Wogan, Charles, 55, 80
Womersley, David, lxxvi
Wood, Betty, 149
Wood, Herbert, 190
Wood, William, 132, 338
Wood's Halfpence, xxiii, xxvi, xxvii, xxxv, xlii, xlvi, xlvii, xlviii, liv, lxxxvii, cvi, 132, 134, 135, 216, 302

Woodward, Donald, 32
woollen manufacture (Irish), xxxvi,
　xxxvii, xlv, xcv, xcvii, 14, 18, 31,
　99–107, 224, 289–92, 344–9
Woollen Act (1699), xxxvi, xxxviii, 18,
　31, 99, 116, 224
Woolley, David, 388, 422
Woolley, James, lxxix, 44, 56, 62, 66, 82,
　90, 91, 102, 155, 207, 349, 352,
　360, 377, 378, 379, 385, 392,
　393, 399, 403, 405
workhouse (Dublin), lxx–lxxii, lxxiv, 2,
　6, 11, 26, 267, 306, 308, 315,
　317–18
workhouses, lxix–lxxii, lxxiv, lxxvi, lxxvii,
　306

Worrall, John, 403
Worsley, Frances, 196
Worsley, Sir Robert, 196
Wriothesley, Thomas, 4th Earl of
　Southampton, 76
Wylde, Thomas, 22
Wyndham, John, 215
Wyndham, Thomas, Lord Chancellor of
　Ireland, lii, lx, xcviii, 215, 352
Wyndham, Sir William, 215
Wynn, Sir Watkin Williams, 299

Youghal, corporation of, xlix–l
Yorke, Philip, lii, lx

Zenger, John Peter, 361

Lightning Source UK Ltd.
Milton Keynes UK
UKHW022052011122
411490UK00013B/74